Lecture Notes in Computer Science   8314

Commenced Publication in 1973
Founding and Former Series Editors:
Gerhard Goos, Juris Hartmanis, and Jan van Leeuwen

Mainak Chatterjee   Jian-nong Cao
Kishore Kothapalli   Sergio Rajsbaum (Eds.)

Distributed Computing and Networking

15th International Conference, ICDCN 2014
Coimbatore, India, January 4-7, 2014
Proceedings

Springer

Volume Editors

Mainak Chatterjee
University of Central Florida
Dept. of Electrical Engineering and Computer Science
P.O. Box 162362, Orlando, FL 32816-2362, USA
E-mail: mainak@eecs.ucf.edu

Jian-nong Cao
Hong Kong Polytechnic University
Dept. of Computing
Hung Hom, Kowloon, Hong Kong
E-mail: csjcao@comp.polyu.edu.hk

Kishore Kothapalli
International Institute of Information Technology
Hyderabad 500 032, India
E-mail: kkishore@iiit.ac.in

Sergio Rajsbaum
Universidad Nacional Autonoma de Mexico (UNAM)
Instituto de Matemáticas
Ciudad Universitaria, D.F. 04510, Mexico
E-mail: sergio.rajsbaum@gmail.com

ISSN 0302-9743   e-ISSN 1611-3349
ISBN 978-3-642-45248-2   e-ISBN 978-3-642-45249-9
DOI 10.1007/978-3-642-45249-9
Springer Heidelberg New York Dordrecht London

Library of Congress Control Number: 2013954779

CR Subject Classification (1998): C.2, D.1.3, D.2.12, C.2.4, D.4, F.2, F.1.2, H.4

LNCS Sublibrary: SL 1 – Theoretical Computer Science and General Issues

Typesetting: Camera-ready by author, data conversion by Scientific Publishing Services, Chennai, India
Printed on acid-free paper
Springer is part of Springer Science+Business Media (www.springer.com)

Message from the General Chairs

Welcome to the 15th International Conference on Distributed Computing and Networking (ICDCN 2014). The conference this year was hosted by Amrita University on its scenic Coimbatore campus, following the tradition set by previous ICDCN conferences held at reputed institutions including IITs, IIITs, TIFR, and Infosys.

ICDCN started 14 years ago as an international workshop and quickly emerged as a premier conference devoted to the latest research results in distributed computing and networking. The conference today attracts high-quality submissions and top speakers from all over the world.

An excellent technical program consisting of 32 full papers and eight short papers was put together thanks to the dedicated efforts of the program chairs, Sergio Rajsbaum and Kishore Kothapalli (Distributed Computing) and Jiannong Cao and Mainak Chatterjee (Networking), and the Program Committee members. We thank all the authors who submitted papers to the conference and all the reviewers for taking the time to provide thoughtful reviews. Springer's continued support of ICDCN by publishing the main proceedings of the conference is greatly appreciated.

ICDCN 2014 featured a number of additional events, including keynote speakers, panel discussion, workshops, tutorials, industry forum, and doctoral symposium. Rupak Biswas (NASA, Ames), Prasad Jayanti (Dartmouth College), and Misha Pavel (National Science Foundation, USA) gave the keynote talks.

Thanks to the workshop chairs and their teams, four workshops on cutting-edge topics were planned:

1. ComNet-IoT: Computing and Networking for Internet of Things
2. CoNeD: Complex Network Dynamics
3. VirtCC: Virtualization and Cloud Computing
4. SPBDA: Smarter Planet and Big Data Analytics

The workshops were held on the first day of the conference and were open to all conference attendees. This year ACM In-Cooperation status was solicited for the main conference as well as for each of the workshops, and the workshop proceedings are expected to appear in the ACM digital library.

Sajal Das and Sukumar Ghosh, the Steering Commitee co-chairs, provided their guidance at every step of the planning process. Their accumulated wisdom from steering the ICDCN conferences since inception was invaluable.

Thanks to Amrita University's vice-chancellor, Dr. Venkat Rangan, for hosting the conference, and to the organizing co-chairs, Prashant Nair and K. Gangadharan, and their entire team at Amrita for excellent local arrangements. Last but not least, the generous support of the sponsors of the ICDCN conference and workshops is greatly appreciated.

On behalf of the entire ICDCN conference team, thanks to everyone who helped make ICDCN 2014 a successful and memorable event.

January 2014   Bharat Jayaraman
                                                                         Dilip Krishnaswamy

Message from the Technical Program Chairs

It gives us great pleasure to present the proceedings of the 15th International Conference on Distributed Computing and Networking (ICDCN), which was held during January 4–7, 2014, in Coimbatore, India. Over the years, ICDCN has grown as a leading forum for presenting state-of-the-art resrach in distributed computing and networking.

This year we received 110 submissions by authors from 26 countries. To review these submissions and to create the technical program, a Technical Program Committee (TPC) consisting of 57 experts in distributed computing and networking was formed. Eventually, 32 full papers and 8 short papers were selected after the review phase followed by the discussion phase. All papers were reviewed by at least three reviewers. The help of additional reviewers was sought in some cases.

Each track selected its best papers. The selection was done by an adhoc committee comprising four to five TPC members. It is our pleasure to announce that the Best Paper Award in the Distributed Computing Track was authored by Varsha Dani, Valerie King, Mahnush Movahedi, and Jared Saia for the paper titled "Quorums Quicken Queries: Efficient Asynchronous Secure Multiparty Computation." For the Networking track, the Best Paper was awarded to the paper titled "InterCloud RAIDer: A Do It Yourself Multi-cloud Private Data Backup System" authored by Chih Wei Ling and Anwitaman Datta.

Besides the technical sessions of ICDCN 2014, there were a number of other events including workshops, keynote speeches, tutorials, industry sessions, panel discussions, and a PhD forum.

We thank all authors who submitted papers to ICDCN 2014. Compared to previous years, we feel that the quality of the papers in terms of technical novelty was better. We thank the Program Committee members and external reviewers for their diligence and commitment, both during the reviewing process and during the online discussion phase. We would also like to thank the general chairs and the Organizing Committee members for their continuous support in making ICDCN 2014 a grand success.

January 2014

Mainak Chatterjee
Jiannong Cao
Kishore Kothapalli
Sergio Rajsbaum

Organization

ICDCN 2014 was organized by Amrita University, Coimbatore, India.

General Chairs

Bharat Jayaraman   State University of New York at Buffalo, USA
Dilip Krishnaswamy   IBM Research, India

Program Chairs

Distributed Computing Track

Kishore Kothapalli   IIIT Hyderabad, India
Sergio Rajsbaum   UNAM Mexico, USA

Networking Track

Jiannong Cao   Hong Kong Polytechnic University, Hong Kong,
           SAR China
Mainak Chatterjee   University of Central Florida, USA

Doctoral Forum Chairs

Maneesh Sudheer   Amrita Vishwa Vidyapeetham University, India
Santanu Sarkar   Infosys, India
Satya Peri   IIT Patna, India

Demo Chairs

Balaji Hariharan   Amrita Vishwa Vidyapeetham University, India
Senthilkumar Sundaram   Qualcomm, Bangalore, India

Tutorial Chairs

N.V. Krishna   IIT Madras, India
Shrisha Rao   IIIT Bangalore, India

Industry Track Chairs

Ankur Narang	IBM Research, India
Dilip Krishnaswamy	IBM Research, India

Workshop Chairs

Bharat Jayaraman	SUNY Buffalo, USA
Shikharesh Majumdar	Carleton University, Canada
Vijay Krishna Menon	Amrita Vishwa Vidyapeetham University, India
Nalini Venkatasubramanian	University of California, Irvine, USA

Publicity Chairs

Habib M. Ammari	University of Michigan-Dearborn, USA
Raffele Bruno	CNR-IIT, Pisa, Italy
Salil Kanhere	University of New South Wales, Australia

Advisory Board

Venkat Rangan	Amrita Vishwa Vidyapeetham University, India

Industry Track Chairs

K. Gangadharan	Amrita Vishwa Vidyapeetham University, India
Prashant R. Nair	Amrita Vishwa Vidyapeetham University, India

Organizing Secretary

Arunkumar C.	Amrita Vishwa Vidyapeetham University, India

Steering Committee Co-chairs

Sajal K. Das	Missouri University of Science and Technology, USA
Sukumar Ghosh	University of Iowa, USA

Steering Committee

Vijay Garg	University of Texas at Austin, USA
Anurag Kumar	Indian Institute of Science, India

Sanjoy Paul   Accenture, India
David Peleg   Weizmann Institute of Science, Israel
Bhabani Sinha   Indian Statistical Institute, Kolkata, India
Michel Raynal   IRISA France

Program Committee

Networking Track Program Committee

Mohammad Zubair Ahmad   Akamai, USA
Habib Ammari   University of Michigan-Dearborn, USA
Vishal Anand   SUNY Brockport, USA
Paolo Bellavista   University of Bologna, Italy
Saad Biaz   Auburn University, USA
Subir Biswas   Michigan State University, USA
Swastik Brahma   Syracuse University, USA
Woo-Yong Choi   Dong-A University, Korea
Nabanita Das   Indian Statistical Institute, Kolkata, India
Swades De   Indian Institute of Technology, Delhi, India
Niloy Ganguli   Indian Institute of Technology, Kharagpur,
                                India
Amitabha Ghosh   Utopia Compression Corporation, USA
Preetam Ghosh   Virginia Commonwealth University, USA
Yoram Haddad   Jerusalem College of Technology, Israel
Mahbub Hassan   University of New South Wales, Australia
Sanjay Jha   University of New South Wales, Australia
Charles Kamhoua   Air Force Research Lab, USA
Joy Kuri   Indian Institute of Science, India
Baochun Li   University of Toronto, Canada
Sudip Misra   Indian Institute of Technology, Kharagpur,
                                India
Asis Nasipuri   University of North Carolina at Charlotte, USA
Loreto Pescosolido   University of Rome La Sapienza, Italy
Vaskar Raychoudhury   Indian Institute of Technology, Roorkee, India
Sushmita Ruj   Indian Institute of Technology, Indore, India
Rajarshi Roy   Indian Institute of Technology, Kharagpur,
                                India
Kaushik Roychowdhury   North Eastern University, USA
Paolo Santi   IIT CNR, Italy
Krishna Sivalingam   Indian Institute of Technology, Madras, India
Arunabha Sen   Arizona State University, USA
Sayandeep Sen   Bell Labs, India
Shamik Sengupta   University of Nevada at Reno, USA
Vinod Sharma   Indian Institute of Science, India

Dan Wang   Hong Kong Polytechnic University, Hong Kong,
                                     SAR China
Nalini Venkatasubramanian   University of California, Irvine, USA
Yanyong Zhang   Rutgers University, USA
Cliff Zou   University of Central Florida, USA

Distributed Computing Track Program Committee

Dan Alistarh   Massachusetts Institute of Technology, USA
Fernandez Antonio   Institute IMDEA Networks, Spain
James Aspnes   Yale University, USA
Armando Castaneda   Technion, Israel
Rezaul Alam Chowdhury   SUNY Stonybrook, USA
Ajoy K. Datta   University of Nevada at Las Vegas, USA
Anwitaman Datta   Nanyang Technological University, Singapore
Hughues Fauconnier   LIAFA Paris 7 Denis Diderot, France
Paola Flocchini   University of Ottawa, Canada
Pierre Fraigniaud   University of Paris Diderot - Paris 7, France
Vijay Garg   University of Texas at Dallas, USA
Rachid Guerraoui   EPFL Zurich, Switzerland
Indranil Gupta   University of Illinois, Urbana-Champaign, USA
Prasad Jayanti   Dartmouth College, USA
Evangelos Kranakis   University of Carleton, Canada
Danny Krizanc   Wesleyan University, USA
Miroslaw Kutylowski   Wroclaw University of Technology, Poland
Petr Kuznetsov   TU Berlin/Deutsche Telekom Laboratories,
                                     Germany
Toshimitsu Masuzawa   Osaka University, Japan
Alessia Milani   LaBRI, University of Bordeaux 1, France
Gadi Taubenfeld   The Interdisciplinary Center, Israel
Krishnamurthy Vidyasankar   Memorial University, Canada

Additional Reviewers

David Alves   Tyler Crain   Eleni Kanellou
Bharath   Maryam Dehnavi   Marcin Kik
  Balasubramanian   Carole Delporte   Kamil Kluczniak
Dipsankar Banerjee   Stéphane Devismes   Yaron Koral
Bruhadeshwar Bezawada   Ngoc Do Minh   Anissa Lamani
Jayeta Biswas   Luca Foschini   I-Ting Lee
Michael Borokhovich   Carlo Giannelli   Erwan Le Merrer
Angelo Capossele   Zbigniew Golebiewski   Lukas Li
Giuseppe Cardone   Ofer Hadar   Xiapu Luo
Yen-Jung Chang   Sandeep Hans   Xiaoqiang Ma
Himanshu Chauhan   Wei-Lun Hung   Alex Matveev

Table of Contents

Transactional Memory

Distributed Algorithms II

P2P and Distributed Networks

Resource Sharing and Scheduling

Cellular and Cognitive Radio Networks

Backbone Networks

Short Papers

Fast Rendezvous on a Cycle by Agents with Different Speeds

Ofer Feinerman[1,*], Amos Korman[2,**], Shay Kutten[3,***], and Yoav Rodeh[4]

[1] The Shlomo and Michla Tomarin Career Development Chair,
Weizmann Institute of Science, Rehovot, Israel
[2] CNRS and University Paris Diderot, Paris, France
[3] Faculty of IR&M, Technion, Haifa 32000, Israel
[4] Jerusalem College of Engineering

Abstract. The difference between the speed of the actions of different processes is typically considered as an obstacle that makes the achievement of cooperative goals more difficult. In this work, we aim to highlight potential *benefits* of such asynchrony phenomena to tasks involving symmetry breaking. Specifically, in this paper, identical (except for their speeds) mobile agents are placed at arbitrary locations on a (continuous) cycle of length n and use their speed difference in order to rendezvous fast. We normalize the speed of the slower agent to be 1, and fix the speed of the faster agent to be some $c > 1$. (An agent does not know whether it is the slower agent or the faster one.) The straightforward *distributed-race (DR)* algorithm is the one in which both agents simply start walking until rendezvous is achieved. It is easy to show that, in the worst case, the rendezvous time of DR is $n/(c-1)$. Note that in the interesting case, where c is very close to 1 (e.g., $c = 1 + 1/n^k$), this bound becomes huge. Our first result is a lower bound showing that, up to a multiplicative factor of 2, this bound is unavoidable, even in a model that allows agents to leave arbitrary marks (the *white board* model), even assuming sense of direction, and even assuming n and c are known to agents. That is, we show that under such assumptions, the rendezvous time of any algorithm is at least $\frac{n}{2(c-1)}$ if $c \leqslant 3$ and slightly larger (specifically, $\frac{n}{c+1}$) if $c > 3$. We then manage to construct an algorithm that precisely matches the lower bound for the case $c \leqslant 2$, and almost matches it when $c > 2$. Moreover, our algorithm performs under weaker assumptions than those stated above, as it does not assume sense of direction, and it allows agents to leave only a single mark (a pebble) and only at the place where they start the execution. Finally, we investigate the setting in which no marks can be used at all, and show tight bounds for $c \leqslant 2$, and almost tight bounds for $c > 2$.

Keywords: rendezvous, asynchrony, heterogeneity, speed, cycle, pebble, white board, mobile agents.

* Supported by the Clore Foundation, the Israel Science Foundation (FIRST grant no. 1694/10) and the Minerva Foundation.
** Supported by the ANR project DISPLEXITY, and by the INRIA project GANG.
*** Supported in part by the ISF and by the Technion TASP center.

M. Chatterjee et al. (Eds.): ICDCN 2014, LNCS 8314, pp. 1–13, 2014.
© Springer-Verlag Berlin Heidelberg 2014

1   Introduction

1.1   Background and Motivation

The difference between the speed of the actions of different entities is typically considered disruptive in real computing systems. In this paper, we illustrate some advantages of such phenomena in cases where the difference remains *fixed* throughout the execution[1]. We demonstrate the *usefulness* of this manifestation of asynchrony to tasks involving symmetry breaking. More specifically, we show how two mobile agents, identical in every aspect save their speed, can lever their speed difference in order to achieve fast rendezvous.

Symmetry breaking is a major issue in distributed computing that is completely absent from traditional sequential computing. Symmetry can often prevent different processes from reaching a common goal. Well known examples include leader election [3], mutual exclusion [14], agreement [4,25] and renaming [6]. To address this issue, various differences between processes are exploited. For example, solutions for leader election often rely on unique identifiers assumed to be associated with each entity (e.g., a process) [3]. Another example of a difference is the location of the entities in a network graph. Entities located in different parts of a non-symmetric graph can use this knowledge in order to behave differently; in such a case, a leader can be elected even without using unique identifiers [26]. If no differences exist, breaking symmetry deterministically is often impossible (see, e.g., [3,27]) and one must resort to randomized algorithms, assuming that different entities can draw different random bits [19].

We consider mobile agents aiming to rendezvous. See, e.g., [7,13,22,23,24,27]. As is the case with other symmetry breaking problems, it is well known that if the agents are completely identical then rendezvous is, in some cases, impossible. In fact, a large portion of the research about rendezvous dealt with identifying the conditions under which rendezvous was possible, as a result of some asymetries. Here, the fact that agents have different speeds implies that the mere feasibility of rendezvous is trivial, and our main concern is therefore the time complexity, that is, the time to reach a rendezvous. More specifically, we study the case where the agents are identical except for the fact that they have different speeds of motion. Moreover, to isolate the issue of the speed difference, we remove other possible differences between the agents. For example, the agents, as well as the graph over which the agents walk, are assumed to be anonymous. To avoid solutions of the kind of [26], we consider a symmetric graph, that is, specifically, a cycle topology. Further symmetry is obtained by hiding the graph features. That is, an agent views the graph as a continuous cycle of length n, and cannot even distinguish between the state it is at a node and the state it is walking over an edge.

---

[1] Advantages can also be exploited in cases where the difference in speed follows some stochastic distribution, however, in this initial study, we focus on the simpler fully deterministic case. That is, we assume a speed heterogeneity that is arbitrary but fixed throughout the execution.

1.2   The Model and the Problem

The problem of rendezvous on a cycle: Consider two identical deterministic *agents* placed on a cycle of length n (in some distance units). To ease the description, we name these agents A and B but these names are not known to the agents. Each agent is initially placed in some location on the cycle by an adversary and both agents start the execution of the algorithm simultaneously. An agent can move on the cycle at any direction. Specifically, at any given point in time, an agent can decide to either start moving, continue in the same direction, stop, or change its direction. The agents' goal is to *rendezvous*, namely, to get to be co-located somewhere on the cycle[2]. We consider continuous movement, so this rendezvous can occur at any location along the cycle. An agent can detect the presence of another agent at its location and hence detect a rendezvous. When agents detect a rendezvous, the rendezvous task is considered completed.

Orientation issues: We distinguish between two models regarding orientation. The first assumes that agents have the *sense of direction* [8], that is, we assume that the agents can distinguish clockwise from the anti-clockwise. In the second model, we do not assume this orientation assumption. Instead, each agent has its own perception of which direction is clockwise and which is anti-clockwise, but there is no guarantee that these perceptions are globally consistent. (Hence, e.g., in this model, if both agents start walking in their own clockwise direction, they may happen to walk in opposite directions, i.e., towards each other).

The pebble and the white board models: Although the agents do not hold any direct means of communication, in some cases we do assume that an agent can leave marks in its current location on the cycle, to be read later by itself and by the other agent. In the *pebble* model, an agent can mark its location by dropping a pebble [10,11]. Both dropping and detecting a pebble are local acts taking place only on the location occupied by the agent. We note that in the case where pebbles can be dropped, our upper bound employs agents that drop a pebble only once and only at their initial location [1,9,24]. On the other hand, our corresponding lower bound holds for any mechanism of (local) pebble dropping. Moreover, this lower bound holds also for the seemingly stronger *'white board* model, in which an agent can change a memory associated with its current location such that it could later be read and further manipulated by itself or the other agent [20,16,17].

Speed: Each agent moves at the same fixed speed at all times; the *speed* of an agent A, denoted $s(A)$, is the inverse of the time t_α it takes agent A to

---

[2] In some sense, this rendezvous problem reminds also the *cow-path* problem, see, e.g., [5]. Here, the agents (the cow and the treasure she seeks to find) are both mobile (in the cow-path problem only one agent, namely, the cow, is mobile). It was shown in [5] that if the cow is initially located at distance D from the treasure on the infinite line then the time to find the treasure can be $9D$, and that 9 is the best multiplicative constant (up to lower order terms in D).

traverse one unit of length. For agent B, the time t_β and speed $s(B)$ are defined analogously. Without loss of generality, we assume that agent A is faster, i.e., $s(A) > s(B)$ but emphasize that this is unknown to the agents themselves. Furthermore, for simplicity of presentation, we normalize the speed of the slower agent B to one, that is, $s(B) = 1$ and denote $s(A) = c$ where $c > 1$. We stress that the more interesting cases are when c is a function of n and arbitrarily close to 1 (e.g., $c = 1 + 1/n^k$, for some constant k). We assume that each agent has a pedometer that enables it to measure the distance it travels. Specifically, a (local) *step* of an agent is a movement of one unit of distance (not necessarily all in the same direction, e.g., in one step, an agent can move half a step in one direction and the other half in the other direction). Using the pedometer, agents can count the number of steps they took (which is a real number at any given time). In some cases, agents are assumed to posses some knowledge regarding n and c; whenever used, this assumption will be mentioned explicitly.

Time complexity: The *rendezvous time* of an algorithm is defined as the worst case time bound until rendezvous, taken over all pairs of initial placements of the two agents on the cycle. Note, a lower bound for the rendezvous time that is established assuming sense of direction holds trivially for the case where no sense of direction is assumed. All our lower bounds hold assuming sense of direction.

The Distributed Race *(DR) algorithm:* Let us consider a trivial algorithm, called *Distributed Race* (DR), in which an agent starts moving in an arbitrary direction, and continues to walk in that direction until reaching rendezvous. Note that this algorithm does not assume knowledge of n and c, does not assume sense of direction and does not leave marks on the cycle. The worst case for this algorithm is that both agents happen to walk on the same direction. Without loss of generality, assume this direction is clockwise. Let d denote the the clockwise distance from the initial location of A to that of B. The rendezvous time t thus satisfies $t \cdot s(A) = t \cdot s(B) + d$. Hence, we obtain the following.

Observation 1. *The rendezvous time of DR is $d/(c-1) < n/(c-1)$.*

Note that in the cases where c is very close to 1, e.g., $c = 1 + 1/n^k$, for some constant k, the bound on the rendezvous time of DR is very large.

1.3   Our Results

Our first result is a lower bound showing that, up to a multiplicative approximation factor of 2, the bound of DR mentioned in Observation 1 is unavoidable, even in the white board model, even assuming sense of direction, and even assuming n and c are known to agents. That is, we show that under such assumptions, the rendezvous time of any algorithm is at least $\frac{n}{2(c-1)}$ if $c \leqslant 3$ and slightly larger (specifically, $\frac{n}{c+1}$) if $c > 3$. We then manage to construct an algorithm that matches the lower bound precisely for the case $c \leqslant 2$, and almost matches it when $c > 2$. Specifically, when $c \leqslant 2$, our algorithm runs in time $\frac{n}{2(c-1)}$ and when $c > 2$, the rendezvous time is n/c (yielding a $(2 - \frac{2}{c})$-approximation when

$2 < c \leqslant 3$, and a $(\frac{c+1}{c})$-approximation when $c > 3$). Moreover, our algorithm performs under weaker assumptions than those stated above, as it does not assume sense of direction, and allows agents to leave only a single mark (a pebble) and only at the place where they start the execution.

Finally, we investigate the setting in which no marks can be used at all, and show tight bounds for $c \leqslant 2$, and almost tight bounds for $c > 2$. Specifically, for this case, we establish a tight bound of $\frac{cn}{c^2-1}$ for the rendezvous time, in case agents have sense of direction. With the absence of sense of direction, the same lower bound of $\frac{cn}{c^2-1}$ holds, and we obtain an algorithm matching this bound for the case $c \leqslant 2$, and rather efficient algorithms for the case $c > 2$. Specifically, the rendezvous time for the case $c \leqslant 2$ is $\frac{cn}{c^2-1}$, for the case $2 < c \leqslant 3$, the rendezvous time is $\frac{2n}{c+1}$, and for the case $c > 3$, the rendezvous time is $\frac{n}{c-1}$.

2 Lower Bound for the White Board Model

The following lower bound implies that DR is a 2-approximation algorithm, and it becomes close to optimal when c goes to infinity.

Theorem 1. *Any rendezvous algorithm in the white board model requires at least* $\max\{\frac{n}{2(c-1)}, \frac{n}{c+1}\}$ *time, even assuming sense of direction and even assuming n and c are known to the agents.*

Proof. We assume that agents have sense of direction; hence, both agents start walking at the same direction. We first show that any algorithm in the white board model requires $\frac{n}{2(c-1)}$ time. Consider the case that the adversary locates the agents at *symmetric locations* of the cycle, i.e., they are at distance $n/2$ apart. Now consider any algorithm used by the agents. Let us fix any c' such that $1 < c' < c$, and define the (continuous) interval

$$I := \left[0, \frac{nc'}{2(c-1)}\right].$$

For every (real) $i \in I$, let us define the following (imaginary) scenario S_i. In scenario S_i, each agent executes the algorithm for i steps and terminates[3]. We claim that for every $i \in I$, the situation at the end of scenario S_i is completely symmetric: that is, the white board at symmetric locations contain the same information and the two agents are at symmetric locations. We prove this claim by induction. The basis of the induction, the case $i = 0$, is immediate. Let us assume that the claim holds for scenario S_i, for (real) $i \in I$, and consider scenario $S_{i+\epsilon}$, for any positive ϵ such that $\epsilon < \frac{n}{4}(1 - \frac{c'}{c})$. Our goal is to show that the claim holds for scenario $S_{i+\epsilon}$[4].

---

[3] We can think of this scenario as if each agent executes another algorithm B, in which it simulates precisely i steps of the original algorithm and then terminates.

[4] Note that for some $i \in I$ and some $\epsilon < \frac{n}{4}(1 - \frac{c'}{c})$, we may have that $i + \epsilon \notin I$. Our proof will show that the claim for $S_{i+\epsilon}$ holds also in such cases. However, since we wish to show that the claim holds for S_j, where $j \in I$, we are not really interested in those cases, and are concerned only with the cases where $i + \epsilon \in I$ and $i \in I$.

Consider scenario $S_{i+\epsilon}$. During the time interval $[0, \frac{i}{c})$, both agents perform the same actions as they do in the corresponding time interval in scenario S_i. Let a denote the location of agent A at time i/c. Now, during the time period $[\frac{i}{c}, \frac{i+\epsilon}{c}]$, agent A performs some movement all of which is done at distance at most ϵ from a (during this movement it may write information at various locations it visits); then, at time $\frac{i+\epsilon}{c}$, agent A terminates.

Let us focus on agent B (in scenario $S_{i+\epsilon}$) during the time period $[\frac{i}{c}, i]$. We claim that during this time period, agent B is always at distance at least ϵ from a. Indeed, as long as it is true that agent B is at distance at least ϵ from a, it performs the same actions as it does in scenario S_i (because it is unaware of any action made by agent A in scenario $S_{i+\epsilon}$, during the time period $[\frac{i}{c}, \frac{i+\epsilon}{c}]$). Therefore, if at some time $t' \in [\frac{i}{c}, i]$, agent B is (in scenario $S_{i+\epsilon}$) at distance less than ϵ from a then the same is true also for scenario S_i. However, in scenario S_i, by the induction hypothesis, agent B was at time i at $\bar{a}$, the symmetric location of a, that is, at distance $n/2$ from a. Thus, to get from a distance less than ϵ from a to $\bar{a}$, agent B needs to travel a distance of $n/2 - \epsilon$, which takes $n/2 - \epsilon$ time. This is impossible since

$$i - i/c \leqslant \frac{nc'}{2c} < \frac{n}{2} - \epsilon,$$

where the first inequality follows from the definition of I and the second follows from the definition of ϵ. It follows that during the time period from $[\frac{i}{c}, i)$, agent B behaves (in scenario $S_{i+\epsilon}$) the same as it does in the corresponding time period in scenario S_i. Therefore, according to the induction hypothesis, at the corresponding i'th steps in scenario $S_{i+\epsilon}$, agent B is at distance $n/2$ from where agent A is at its i'th step (recall, agent A is at a at its i'th step), and the cycle configuration (including the white boards) is completely symmetric. Now, since $\epsilon < n/4$, during the time period $[i, i + \epsilon]$, agent B is still at a distance more than ϵ from a and remains unaware of any action made by agent A, during the time period $[\frac{i}{c}, \frac{i+\epsilon}{c}]$. (Similarly, agent A, during the time period $[\frac{i}{c}, \frac{i+\epsilon}{c}]$, is unaware of any action made by agent B during this time period.) Hence, at each time $i' \in [i, i + \epsilon]$, agent B takes the same action as agent A in the corresponding time i'/c. This establishes the induction proof. To sum up, we have just shown that for any $i \in I$, the cycle configuration at the end of scenario S_i is completely symmetric.

Now assume by contradiction that the rendezvous time t is less than the claimed one, that is, $t < \frac{n}{2(c-1)}$. At time t, both agents meet at some location u. Since $t \in I$, the above claim holds for S_t. Hence, at time t/c, agent A is at $\bar{u}$, the symmetric location of u. Since rendezvous happened at time t, this means that agent A traveled from $\bar{u}$ to u (i.e., a distance of $n/2$) during the time period $[\frac{t}{c}, t]$. Therefore $t(1 - \frac{1}{c})c \geqslant n/2$, contradicting the assumption that $t < \frac{n}{2(c-1)}$. This establishes that any algorithm requires $\frac{n}{2(c-1)}$ time.

We now show the simpler part of the theorem, namely, that the rendezvous time of any algorithm in the white board model is at least $\frac{n}{c+1}$. Let us represent the cycle as the reals modulo n, that is, we view the cycle as the continuous collection of reals $[0,n]$, where n coincides with 0. Assume that the starting point of agent A is 0. Consider the time period $T = [0, \frac{n}{c+1} - \epsilon]$, for some small positive ϵ. In this time period, agent A moves a total length of less than $\frac{nc}{c+1}$. Let r (and ℓ, correspondingly) be the furthest point from 0 on the cycle that A reached while going clockwise (or anti-clockwise, correspondingly), during that time period. Note that there is a gap of length larger than $n - \frac{nc}{c+1} = \frac{n}{c+1}$ between ℓ and r. This gap corresponds to an arc not visited by agent A during this time period. On the other hand, agent B walks a total distance of less than $\frac{n}{c+1}$ during the time period T. Hence, the adversary can locate agent B initially at some point in the gap between r and ℓ, such that during the whole time period T, agent B remains in this gap. This establishes the $\frac{n}{c+1}$ time lower bound, and concludes the proof of the theorem.

3 Upper Bound for the Pebble Model

Note that the assumptions of the pebble model are weaker than the white board model. Hence, in view of Theorem 1, the following theorem establishes a tight bound for the case where $c \leqslant 2$, a $(2 - \frac{2}{c})$-approximation for the case $2 < c \leqslant 3$, and a $(c+1)/c$-approximation for the case $c > 3$.

Theorem 2. *There exists an algorithm that in the pebble model whose rendezvous time is* $\max\{\frac{n}{2(c-1)}, \frac{n}{c}\}$. *Moreover, this algorithm does not assume sense of direction, uses only one pebble and drops it only once: at the initial position of the agent. The algorithm assumes that agents know n and whether or not $c > 2$.*

Proof. Consider the following algorithm. Each agent (1) leaves a pebble at its initial position and then starts walking in an arbitrary direction while counting the distance travelled. If (2) an agent reaches a location with a pebble for the first time and (3) the distance it walked is strictly less than $\tau := \min\{n/2, n/c\}$, then (4) the agent turns around and walks continuously in the other direction.

First note that if both agents happen to start walking in opposite directions (due to lack of sense of direction), then they walk until they meet. In this simple case, their relative speed is $c + 1$, hence rendezvous happens in time at most $\frac{n}{c+1} < \max\{\frac{n}{2(c-1)}, \frac{n}{c}\}$. For the remaining of the proof, we consider the case that both agents start walking at the same direction, which is without loss of generality, the clockwise direction. Let d be the initial clockwise distance from A to B. Consider three cases.

1. $d = \tau$.
   Here, no agent turns around. In other words, they behave exactly as in DR. If $d = n/2$, Observation 1 implies that the rendezvous time is $\frac{n}{2(c-1)}$. Otherwise, $c > 2$ and $d = n/c$. By Observation 1, the rendezvous is reached earlier, specifically, by time $\frac{d}{c-1} = \frac{n}{c(c-1)}$.
2. $d < \tau$.
   In this case, Agent A will reach B's starting point v_B, at time d/c, before B reaches A's starting point v_A. Moreover, agent B does not turn, since its

initial distance to A's starting point is at least τ. At time d/c, agent B is at distance d/c clockwise from v_B. By the algorithm, Agent A then turns and walks anti-clockwise. The anti-clockwise distance from A to B is then $n - d/c$. Their relative speed is $c + 1$. Hence, they will rendezvous in an additional time of $\frac{n - d/c}{1+c}$, since no agent may turn around after time d/c. Hence, the total time for reaching rendezvous is at most

$$d/c + \frac{n - d/c}{1 + c} = \frac{d + n}{1 + c}.$$

This function is maximized when $d = \tau$ where it is $\frac{\tau + n}{1+c}$. Now, if $c \leqslant 2$, we have $\tau = n/2$ and the rendezvous time is therefore $\frac{3n}{2(1+c)}$. Since $c \leqslant 2$, the later bound is at most $\frac{n}{2(c-1)}$. On the other hand, if $c > 2$, we have $\tau = n/c$ and the rendezvous time is n/c.

3. $d > \tau$.

   In this case, A doesn't turn when it hits B's initial position. Consider the following sub-cases.

   (a) The agents meet before B reaches A's initial position.

   In this case, the rendezvous time (as in DR) is $d/(c-1)$. On the other hand, the rendezvous time is at most $n - d$ since B did not reach A's initial position. So $d/(c-1) \leqslant n - d$. A simple calculation now implies that the rendezvous time $d/(c-1)$ is at most n/c.

   (b) Agent B reaches A's initial position before rendezvous.

   In this case, Agent B walks for $d' = n - d$ time to first reach A's initial position. We first claim that $d' < \tau$. One case is that $c \leqslant 2$, and thus, $\tau = n/2$. Since $d > \tau$, we have $d' < n/2 = \tau$. The other case is that $c > 2$, so $\tau = n/c$. We claim that also in this case, we have $d' < \tau$. Otherwise, we would have had $d' \geqslant n/c$, which would have meant that the faster agent A would have had, at least, n/c time before B reached the initial position of A. So much time would have allowed it to cover the whole cycle. This contradicts the assumption that B reached A's initial position before rendezvous. This establishes the fact that, regardless of the value of c, we have $d' < \tau$. This fact implies that when agent B reaches A's initial position, it turns around and both agents go towards each other. By the time B turns around, A has walked a distance of cd'. Hence, at that point in time, they are $n - cd'$ apart. This implies to the following rendezvous time:

   $$d' + \frac{n - cd'}{1 + c} = \frac{2n - d}{1 + c}.$$

   Now recall that we are in the case that agent B reaches A's initial position before they rendezvous. This implies that $n - d < n/c$. Hence, the running time is at most

   $$\frac{2n - d}{1 + c} < \frac{n + \frac{n}{c}}{1 + c} = \frac{n}{c}.$$

4 Rendezvous without Communication

In this section, we consider the case that agents cannot use are marks (e.g., pebbles) to mark their location. More generally, the agents cannot communicate in any way (before rendezvous).

Theorem 3. *Consider the setting in which no communication is allowed, and assume both n and c are known to the agents.*

1. *The rendezvous time of any algorithm is, at least, $\frac{cn}{c^2-1}$, even assuming sense of direction.*
2. *Assuming sense of direction, there exists an algorithm whose rendezvous time $\frac{cn}{c^2-1}$.*
3. *Without assuming sense of direction, there exists an algorithm whose rendezvous time is:*
   - $\frac{cn}{c^2-1}$, *for $c \leqslant 2$,*
   - $\frac{2n}{c+1}$, *for $2 < c \leqslant 3$,*
   - $\frac{n}{c-1}$, *for $c > 3$.*

Proof. Let us first show the first part of the theorem, namely, the lower bound.

Proof of Part 1: Given an algorithm, let $\hat{t}$ denote the rendezvous time of the algorithm, that is, the maximum time (over all initial placements and all cycles of length n) for the agents (executing this algorithm) to reach rendezvous. Recall, in this part of the theorem, we assume that agents have sense of direction. Without loss of generality, we assume that the direction an agent starts walking is clockwise.

Consider, first, two identical cycles C_A and C_B of length n each. Let us mark a location $v \in C_A$ and a location $u \in C_B$. Let us examine the (imaginary) scenario in which agent A (respectively, B) is placed on the cycle C_A (respectively, C_B) alone, that is, the other agent is not on the cycle. Furthermore, assume that agent A is placed at v and agent B is placed at u. In this imaginary scenario, agents A and B start executing the protocol at the same time, separately, on each of the corresponding cycles. Viewing u as homologous to v, a homologous location $h(x) \in C_B$ can be defined for each location in $x \in C_A$ in a natural way (in particular, $h(v) = u$).

For each time $t \in [0, \hat{t}]$, let $d(t)$ denote the clockwise distance between the location $b_t \in C_B$ of the slower agent B at time t and the homologous location $h(a_t) \in C_B$ of the location $a_t \in C_A$ of the faster agent A at time t. Note that $d(t)$ is a real value in $[0, n)$. Initially, we assume that all reals in $[0, n)$ are colored *white*. As time passes, we *color* the corresponding distances by black, that is, at every time t, we color the distance $d(t) \in [0, n)$ by black. Note that the size of the set of black distances is monotonously non-decreasing with time.

We first claim that, by time $\hat{t}$, the whole range $[0, n)$ is colored black. To prove by contradiction, assume that there is a real $d \in [0, n)$ that remains white. Now, consider the execution on a single cycle of length n, where agent A is initially placed at anti-clockwise distance d from agent B. In such a case, rendezvous is not reached by time $\hat{t}$, contrary to the assumption that it is. This implies that the time T it takes until all reals in $[0, n)$ are colored black in the imaginary scenario, is a lower bound on the rendezvous time, that is, $T \leqslant \hat{t}$. It is left to analyze the time T.

With time, the change in the distance $d(t)$ has to follow two rules:

- **R1.** After one time unit, the distance can change by at most $1 + c$ (the sum of the agents' speeds).
- **R2.** At time x, the distance, in absolute value is, at most, $x(c - 1)$.

To see why Rule R2 holds, recall that the programs of the agents are identical. Hence, if agent A is at some point $a \in C_A$, at A's kth step, then agent B is at point $b = h(a)$ at its own kth step. This happens for agent B at time k and for agent A at time k/c. Since A's speed is c, the maximum it can get away from point a during the time period from k/c until c is $c(k - k/c) = k(c - 1)$.

Consider the path $P := d(t)$ covering the range $[0, n)$ in T time. First, note that this path P may go several times through the zero point (i.e., when $d(t) = 0$). At a given time s, we say that the path is *on the right* side, if the last time it left the zero point before time s was while going towards 1. Similarly, the path is *on the left*, if the last time it left the zero point before time s was while going towards $n - 1$. Let x denote the largest point on the range $[0, n)$ reached by the path while the path was on the right side. Let $y = n - x$. By time T, path P had to go left to distance y from the zero point. Assume, w.l.o.g. that $x < y$. (In particular, x may be zero.) The fastest way to color these two points (and all the rest of the points, since those lie between them), would be to go from zero to the right till reaching x, then return to zero and go to distance y on the left. Hence, T will be at least: $T \geqslant \frac{x}{c-1} + \frac{n}{c+1}$. Indeed, Rule R2, applied to the time of reaching distance x, implies the first term above. The second term uses Rule R1 to capture the time that starts with the distance reaching x, proceeds with the distance reaching the zero point and ends when the distance reaches y when going left. Since $c > 1$, we obtain

$$x \leqslant \left(T - \frac{n}{c+1}\right)(c - 1). \tag{1}$$

On the other hand, applying Rule R2 to the final destination y, we have $T(c - 1) \geqslant y = n - x$. This implies that:

$$x \geqslant n - T(c - 1). \tag{2}$$

Combining Equations 1 and 2, we get $T \geqslant \frac{cn}{c^2-1}$. This establishes the first part of the theorem. We now prove the second and third parts of the theorem, namely, the upper bounds.

Proof of Parts 2 and 3: Note that the DR algorithm does not assume sense of direction, and its complexity is the one required by the third part of the theorem for the case $c > 3$. We now revise DR and consider an algorithm, called

Turn(k), which consists of two stages. At the first stage, the agent walks over its own clockwise direction for k steps. Subsequently (if rendezvous hasn't occurred yet), the agent executes the second stage of the algorithm: it turns around and goes in the other direction until rendezvous.

Let us now concentrate on proving the second part of the theorem, and assume that agents have sense of direction. Here we consider Algorithm **Turn**(k), with parameter $k = \frac{cn}{c^2-1}$. Since we assume sense of direction, both agents walk initially in the same direction (clockwise). Assume by contradiction that rendezvous hasn't occurred by time k. By that time, agent B took k steps. Agent A took those k steps by time k/c. At that time, agent A turns. (However, agent B will turn only at time k). Hence, between those two turning times, there is a time duration $k(1 - \frac{1}{c})$ where the two agents walk towards each other. Hence, at each time unit they shorten the distance between them by $1 + c$. Let d' denote the maximum distance between the agents at time k/c. It follows that $d' > k(1 - \frac{1}{c})(1 + c) = n$. A contradiction. This establishes the second part of the theorem.

We now prove the third part of the theorem, which focuses on the case where no sense of direction is assumed. Let us first consider the case $c \leqslant 2$. Here we apply the same algorithm above, namely Algorithm **Turn**(k), with parameter $k = \frac{cn}{c^2-1}$. As proved before, if the two agents happen to start at the same direction then rendezvous occurs by time $\frac{cn}{c^2-1}$. Hence, let us consider the case that both agents walk initially at opposite directions. Assume by contradiction, that rendezvous hasn't occurred by time k/c. In this case, by time k/c the faster agent A walked k steps toward B, and the slower agent B walked k/c steps towards A. Hence, the initial distance between them must be greater than $k(1 + 1/c) = n/(c - 1) > n$, a contradiction. This proves the first item in Part 3 of the Theorem.

Note that Algorithm DR establishes the third item in Part 3 of the Theorem. Hence, it is left to prove the second item in Part 3, namely, the case $2 < c \leqslant 3$. For this case, we apply Algorithm **Turn**(k), with parameter $k = \frac{cn}{c+1}$. First note, if the two agents happen to start walking towards each other they continue to do that until time $k/c = \frac{n}{c+1}$, hence they would meet by this time. Therefor, we may assume that initially, both agents start in the same direction. In this case, if rendezvous haven't occurred by time k/c, then at this time agent A turns around, and both agents walk towards each other for at least $k(1 - 1/c)$ more time (the time when agent B is supposed to turn). Since $c > 2$, we have $k(1 - 1/c) > k/c$, and hence, from the time agent A turns, both agents walk towards each other for at least $\frac{k}{c} = \frac{n}{c+1}$ time, which means they must meet by this time. Altogether, the time to rendezvous is $\frac{2k}{c} = \frac{2n}{c+1}$, as desired.

5   Discussion and Future Work

We show how some form of asynchrony could be useful for solving a symmetry breaking problem efficiently. Our study could be considered as a first attempt to harness the (unknown) heterogeneity between individuals in a cooperative population towards more efficient functionality.

There are many natural ways of further exploring this idea in future work. First, we have studied the exploitation of asynchrony for a specific kind of problems. It seems that it can be useful for other symmetry breaking problems as well. Another generalization: the "level" of asynchrony considered in this paper is very limited: the ratio c between the speeds of the agents is the same throughout the execution, and is known to the agents. Exploiting a higher level of asynchrony should also be studied, for example, the case that the speed difference is stochastic and changes through time.

Our main interest was the exploitation of asymmetry, rather than the specific problem of rendezvous. Still, even for the rendezvous problem, this current study leaves many open questions. First, even for the limited case we study, not all our bounds are completely tight, and it would be interesting to close the remaining gaps between our lower and upper bounds (these gaps hold for some cases when $c > 2$). In addition, it would be interesting to study further the uniform case [21], in which n and c are not known to agents. Another direction is to generalize the study to multiple agents (more than two, see, e.g., [15,18]) and to other graph classes. This would also allow one to study interactions between various means of breaking symmetry (such as different speeds together with different locations on a graph).

References

1. Alpern, S.: Rendezvous Search: A Personal Perspective. LSE Research Report, CDAM-2000-05, London School of Economics (2000)
2. Alpern, S., Gal, S.: The Theory of Search Games and Rendezvous. Kluwer Academic Publishers (2003)
3. Angluin, D.: Local and global properties in networks of processors. In: ACM STOC 1980, pp. 82–93 (1980)
4. Attiya, H., Gorbach, A., Moran, S.: Computing in Totally Anonymous Asynchronous Shared Memory Systems. Information and Computation 173(2), 162–183 (2002)
5. Baeza-Yates, R.A., Culberson, J.C., Rawlins, G.J.E.: Searching in the plane. Inform. and Comput. 106(2), 234–252 (1993)
6. Attiya, H., Bar-Noy, A., Dolev, D., Peleg, D., Reischuk, R.: Renaming in an asynchronous environment. Journal of the ACM 37(3), 524–548 (1990)
7. Bampas, E., Czyzowicz, J., Gąsieniec, L., Ilcinkas, D., Labourel, A.: Almost Optimal Asynchronous Rendezvous in Infinite Multidimensional Grids. In: Lynch, N.A., Shvartsman, A.A. (eds.) DISC 2010. LNCS, vol. 6343, pp. 297–311. Springer, Heidelberg (2010)
8. Barriére, L., Flocchini, P., Fraigniaud, P., Santoro, N.: Rendezvous and Election of Mobile Agents: Impact of Sense of Direction. Theory Comput. Syst. 40(2), 143–162 (2007)
9. Baston, V., Gal, S.: Rendezvous search when marks are left at the starting points. Naval Research Logistics 48(8), 722–731 (2001)
10. Bender, M.A., Fernandez, A., Ron, D., Sahai, A., Vadhan, S.: The power of a pebble: Exploring and mapping directed graphs. In: Proc. 30th ACM Symp. on Theory of Computing (STOC), pp. 269–287 (1998)

11. Blum, M., Kozen, D.: On the power of the compass (or, why mazes are easier to search than graphs). In: 19th Annual Symposium on Foundations of Computer Science (FOCS 1978), October 16-18 (1978)
12. Czyzowicz, J., Dobrev, S., Krizanc, D., Kranakis, E.: The Power of Tokens: Rendezvous and Symmetry Detection for Two Mobile Agents in a Ring. In: Geffert, V., Karhumäki, J., Bertoni, A., Preneel, B., Návrat, P., Bieliková, M. (eds.) SOFSEM 2008. LNCS, vol. 4910, pp. 234–246. Springer, Heidelberg (2008)
13. Czyzowicz, J., Ilcinkas, D., Labourel, A., Pelc, A.: Asynchronous deterministic rendezvous in bounded terrains. Theor. Comput. Sci. 412(50), 6926–6937 (2011)
14. Dijkstra, E.W.: Self-stabilizing systems in spite of distributed control. Communications of the ACM 17(11), 643–644 (1974)
15. Dobrev, S., Flocchini, P., Prencipe, G., Santoro, N.: Multiple Agents RendezVous in a Ring in Spite of a Black Hole. In: Papatriantafilou, M., Hunel, P. (eds.) OPODIS 2003. LNCS, vol. 3144, pp. 34–46. Springer, Heidelberg (2004)
16. Flocchini, P., Nayak, A., Schulz, A.: Cleaning an Arbitrary Regular Network with Mobile Agents. In: Chakraborty, G. (ed.) ICDCIT 2005. LNCS, vol. 3816, pp. 132–142. Springer, Heidelberg (2005)
17. Flocchini, P., Ilcinkas, D., Santoro, N.: Ping Pong in Dangerous Graphs: Optimal Black Hole Search with Pebbles. Algorithmica 62(3-4), 1006–1033 (2012)
18. Flocchini, P., Kranakis, E., Krizanc, D., Santoro, N., Sawchuk, C.: Multiple Mobile Agent Rendezvous in a Ring. In: Farach-Colton, M. (ed.) LATIN 2004. LNCS, vol. 2976, pp. 599–608. Springer, Heidelberg (2004)
19. Itai, A., Rodeh, M.: Symmetry Breaking in Distributive Networks. In: FOCS, pp. 150–158 (1981)
20. Korach, E., Kutten, S., Moran, S.: A Modular Technique for the Design of Efficient Distributed Leader Finding Algorithms. In: ACM PODC 1985, pp. 163–174 (1985)
21. Korman, A., Sereni, J.-S., Viennot, L.: Toward More Localized Local Algorithms: Removing Assumptions Concerning Global Knowledge. In: ACM PODC 2011, pp. 49–58 (2011)
22. Kranakis, E., Krizanc, D., Markou, E.: The Mobile Agent Rendezvous Problem in the Ring. Morgan & Claypool Publishers (2010)
23. Kranakis, E., Krizanc, D., Rajsbaum, S.: Mobile Agent Rendezvous: A Survey. In: Flocchini, P., Gąsieniec, L. (eds.) SIROCCO 2006. LNCS, vol. 4056, pp. 1–9. Springer, Heidelberg (2006)
24. Kranakis, E., Santoro, N., Sawchuk, C.: Mobile Agent Rendezvous in a Ring. In: ICDCS 2003, pp. 592–599 (2003)
25. Suzuki, I., Yamashita, M.: Distributed Anonymous Mobile Robots: Formation of Geometric Patterns. SIAM J. Computing. 28(4), 1347–1363 (1999)
26. Yamashita, M., Kameda, T.: Computing on an Anonymous Network. In: ACM PODC 1988, pp. 117–130 (1988)
27. Yu, X., Yung, M.: Agent Rendezvous: A Dynamic Symmetry-Breaking Problem. In: Meyer auf der Heide, F., Monien, B. (eds.) ICALP 1996. LNCS, vol. 1099, pp. 610–621. Springer, Heidelberg (1996)

Iterative Byzantine Vector Consensus
in Incomplete Graphs

Nitin H. Vaidya

Department of Electrical and Computer Engineering,
University of Illinois at Urbana-Champaign
nhv@illinois.edu

Abstract. This work addresses *Byzantine vector consensus*, wherein the input at each process is a d-dimensional vector of reals, and each process is required to decide on a *decision vector* that is in the *convex hull* of the input vectors at the fault-free processes [9,12]. The input *vector* at each process may also be viewed as a *point* in the d-dimensional Euclidean space $\mathbf{R}^d$, where $d > 0$ is a finite integer. Recent work [9,12] has addressed Byzantine vector consensus, and presented algorithms with optimal fault tolerance in complete graphs. This paper considers Byzantine vector consensus in incomplete graphs using *a restricted class* of iterative algorithms that maintain only a small amount of memory across iterations. For such algorithms, we prove a necessary condition, and a sufficient condition, for the graphs to be able to solve the vector consensus problem iteratively. We present an iterative Byzantine vector consensus algorithm, and prove it correct under the sufficient condition. The necessary condition presented in this paper for vector consensus does not match with the sufficient condition for $d > 1$; thus, a weaker condition may potentially suffice for Byzantine vector consensus.

1   Introduction

This work addresses *Byzantine vector consensus* (BVC), wherein the input at each process is a d-dimensional vector consisting of d real numbers, and each process is required to decide on a *decision vector* that is in the *convex hull* of the input vectors at the fault-free processes [9,12]. The input *vector* at each process may also be viewed as a *point* in the d-dimensional Euclidean space $\mathbf{R}^d$, where $d > 0$ is a finite integer. Due to this correspondence, we use the terms *point* and *vector* interchangeably. Recent work [9,12] has addressed Byzantine vector consensus, and presented algorithms with optimal fault tolerance in complete graphs. The correctness conditions for Byzantine vector consensus (elaborated below) cannot be satisfied by independently performing consensus on each element of the input vectors; therefore, new algorithms are necessary [9,12].

In this paper, we consider Byzantine vector consensus in incomplete graphs using *a restricted class* of iterative algorithms that maintain only a small amount of memory across iterations. We prove a necessary condition, and a sufficient condition, for the graphs to be able to solve the vector consensus problem using

M. Chatterjee et al. (Eds.): ICDCN 2014, LNCS 8314, pp. 14–28, 2014.

such restricted algorithms. We present an iterative Byzantine vector consensus algorithm, and prove it correct under the sufficient condition; our proof of correctness follows a structure previously used in our work to prove correctness of other consensus algorithms [11,14]. The use of matrix analysis tools in our proofs is inspired by the prior work on non-fault tolerant consensus (e.g., [6]). For lack of space, the proofs of most claims in the paper are omitted here. Further details can be found in [15]. The necessary condition presented in this paper for vector consensus does not match with the sufficient condition for $d > 1$; thus, it is possible that a weaker condition may also suffice for Byzantine vector consensus.

This paper extends our past work on *scalar* consensus (i.e., consensus with scalar inputs) in incomplete graphs in presence of Byzantine faults [13], using similarly restricted iterative algorithms. The work in [13] yielded an exact characterization of graphs in which the scalar Byzantine consensus problem is solvable.

Related Work: Approximate consensus has been previously explored in synchronous as well as asynchronous systems. Dolev et al. [3] were the first to consider approximate consensus in presence of Byzantine faults in asynchronous systems. Subsequently, for complete graphs, Abraham, Amit and Dolev [1] established that approximate Byzantine consensus is possible in asynchronous systems if $n \geq 3f + 1$. Other algorithms for approximate consensus in presence of Byzantine faults have also been proposed (e.g., [4]). Scalar consensus in incomplete graphs under a *malicious* fault model in which the faulty nodes are restricted to sending identical messages to their neighbors has also been explored by other researchers (e.g., [7,8]).

The paper is organized as follows. Section 2 presents our system model. The iterative algorithm structure considered in our work is presented in Section 3. Section 4 presents a necessary condition, and Section 5 presents a sufficient condition. Section 5 also presents an iterative algorithm and proves its correctness under the sufficient condition. The paper concludes with a summary in Section 6.

2   System Model

The system is assumed to be *synchronous*.[1] The communication network is modeled as a simple *directed* graph $G(\mathcal{V}, \mathcal{E})$, where $\mathcal{V} = \{1, \ldots, n\}$ is the set of n processes, and $\mathcal{E}$ is the set of directed edges between the processes in $\mathcal{V}$. Thus, $|\mathcal{V}| = n$. We assume that $n \geq 2$, since the consensus problem for $n = 1$ is trivial. Process i can reliably transmit messages to process j, $j \neq i$, if and only if the directed edge (i, j) is in $\mathcal{E}$. Each process can send messages to itself as well, however, for convenience of presentation, we exclude self-loops from set $\mathcal{E}$. That is, $(i, i) \notin \mathcal{E}$ for $i \in \mathcal{V}$. We will use the terms *edge* and *link* interchangeably.

For each process i, let N_i^- be the set of processes from which i has incoming edges. That is, $N_i^- = \{ j \mid (j, i) \in \mathcal{E} \}$. Similarly, define N_i^+ as the set of processes to which process i has outgoing edges. That is, $N_i^+ = \{ j \mid (i, j) \in \mathcal{E} \}$. Since

---

[1] Analogous results can be similarly derived for asynchronous systems, using the asynchronous algorithm structure presented in [13] for the case of $d = 1$.

we exclude self-loops from $\mathcal{E}$, $i \notin N_i^-$ and $i \notin N_i^+$. However, we note again that each process can indeed send messages to itself.

We consider the Byzantine failure model, with up to f processes becoming faulty. A faulty process may *misbehave* arbitrarily. The faulty processes may potentially collaborate with each other. Moreover, the faulty processes are assumed to have a complete knowledge of the execution of the algorithm, including the states of all the processes, contents of messages the other processes send to each other, the algorithm specification, and the network topology.

We use the notation $|X|$ to denote the size of a set or a multiset, and the notation $\|x\|$ to denote the absolute value of a real number x.

3   Byzantine Vector Consensus and Iterative Algorithms

Byzantine vector consensus: We are interested in iterative algorithms that satisfy the following conditions in presence of up to f Byzantine faulty processes:

- *Termination*: Each fault-free process must terminate after a finite number of iterations.
- *Validity*: The state of each fault-free process at the end of *each iteration* must be in the convex hull of the d-dimensional input vectors at the fault-free processes.
- *ϵ-Agreement*: When the algorithm terminates, the l-th elements of the decision vectors at any two fault-free processes, where $1 \leq l \leq d$, must be within ϵ of each other, where $\epsilon > 0$ is a pre-defined constant.

Any information carried over by a process from iteration t to iteration $t + 1$ is considered the state of process t at the end of iteration t. The above *validity* condition forces the algorithms to maintain "minimal" state, for instance, precluding the possibility of remembering messages received in several of the past iterations, or remembering the history of detected misbehavior of the neighbors. We focus on such restricted algorithms with the iterative structure below.

Iterative structure: Each process i maintains a state variable $\mathbf{v}_i$, which is a d-dimensional vector. The initial state of process i is denoted as $\mathbf{v}_i[0]$, and it equals the *input* provided to process i. For $t \geq 1$, $\mathbf{v}_i[t]$ denotes the state of process i at the *end* of the t-th iteration of the algorithm. At the *start* of the t-th iteration ($t \geq 1$), the state of process i is $\mathbf{v}_i[t-1]$. The iterative algorithms of interest will require each process i to perform the following three steps in the t-th iteration. Each "value" referred in the algorithm below is a d-dimensional vector (or, equivalently, a point in the d-dimensional Euclidean space).

1. *Transmit step:* Transmit current state, namely $\mathbf{v}_i[t-1]$, on all outgoing edges to processes in N_i^+.
2. *Receive step:* Receive values on all incoming edges from processes in N_i^-. Denote by $r_i[t]$ the multiset[2] of values received by process i from its neighbors. The size of multiset $r_i[t]$ is $|N_i^-|$.

---

[2] The same value may occur multiple times in a multiset.

3. *Update step:* Process i updates its state using a transition function T_i as follows. T_i is a part of the specification of the algorithm, and takes as input the multiset $r_i[t]$ and state $\mathbf{v}_i[t-1]$.

$$\mathbf{v}_i[t] = T_i \left(r_i[t], \mathbf{v}_i[t-1] \right) \tag{1}$$

The decision (or output) of each process equals its state when the algorithm terminates.

We assume that each element of the input vector at each fault-free process is lower bounded by a constant μ and upper bounded by a constant U. The iterative algorithm may terminate after a number of rounds that is a function of μ and U. μ and U are assumed to be known *a priori*. This assumption holds in many practical systems, because the input vector elements represent quantities that are constrained. For instance, if the input vectors represent locations in 3-dimensional space occupied by mobile robots, then U and μ are determined by the boundary of the region in which the robots are allowed to operate [12].

In Section 4, we develop a necessary condition that the graph $G(\mathcal{V}, \mathcal{E})$ must satisfy in order for the Byzantine vector consensus algorithm to be solvable using the above iterative structure. In Section 5, we develop a sufficient condition, such that the Byzantine vector consensus algorithm is solvable using the above iterative structure in any graph that satisfies this condition. We present an iterative algorithm, and prove its correctness under the sufficient condition.

4   A Necessary Condition

Hereafter, when we say that an algorithm solves Byzantine vector consensus, we mean that the algorithm satisfies the termination, validity and ϵ-agreement conditions stated above. Thus, the state the algorithm can carry across iterations is restricted by the above validity condition. Also, hereafter when we refer to an iterative algorithm, we mean an algorithm with the structure specified in the previous section. In this section, we state a necessary condition on graph $G(\mathcal{V}, \mathcal{E})$ to be able to solve Byzantine vector consensus. First we present three definitions.

Definition 1

- *Define $\mathbf{e}_0$ to be a d-dimensional vector with all its elements equal to 0. Thus, $\mathbf{e}_0$ corresponds to the origin in the d-dimensional Euclidean space.*
- *Define $\mathbf{e}_i$, $1 \leq i \leq d$, to be a d-dimensional vector with the i-th element equal to 2ϵ, and the remaining elements equal to 0. Recall that ϵ is the parameter of the ϵ-agreement condition.*

Definition 2. *For non-empty disjoint sets of processes A and B, and a non-negative integer c,*

- *$A \xrightarrow{c} B$ if and only if there exists a process $v \in B$ that has at least $c+1$ incoming edges from processes in A, i.e., $|N_v^- \cap A| \geq c+1$.*
- *$A \xnrightarrow{c} B$ iff $A \xrightarrow{c} B$ is not true.*

Definition 3. $\mathcal{H}(X)$ *denotes the convex hull of a multiset of points* X.

Now we state the necessary condition.

Condition NC: For any partition $V_0, V_1, \cdots, V_p, C, F$ *of set* $\mathcal{V}$, *where* $1 \le p \le d$, $V_k \ne \emptyset$ *for* $0 \le k \le p$, *and* $|F| \le f$, *there exist* i, j $(0 \le i, j \le p, i \ne j)$, *such that*

$$V_i \cup C \xrightarrow{f} V_j$$

That is, there are $f + 1$ *incoming links from processes in* $V_i \cup C$ *to some process in* V_j.

The proof of the necessary condition below extends the proofs of necessary conditions in [9,12,13].

Lemma 1. *If the Byzantine vector consensus problem can be solved using an iterative algorithm in* $G(\mathcal{V}, \mathcal{E})$, *then* $G(\mathcal{V}, \mathcal{E})$ *satisfies Condition NC.*

Proof. The proof is by contradiction. Suppose that Condition NC is not true. Then there exists a certain partition $V_0, V_1, \cdots, V_p, C, F$ such that $V_k \ne \emptyset$ ($1 \le k \le p$), $|F| \le f$, and for $0 \le i, k \le p$, $V_k \cup C \xcancel{\xrightarrow{f}} V_i$.

Let the initial state of each process in V_i be $\mathbf{e}_i$ ($0 \le i \le p$). Suppose that all the processes in set F are faulty. For each link (j, k) such that $j \in F$ and $k \in V_i$ ($0 \le i \le p$), the faulty process j sends value $\mathbf{e}_i$ to process j in each iteration.

We now prove by induction that if the iterative algorithm satisfies the validity condition then the state of each fault-free process $j \in V_i$ at the start of iteration t equals $\mathbf{e}_i$, for all $t > 0$. The claim is true for $t = 1$ by assumption on the inputs at the fault-free processes. Now suppose that the claim is true through iteration t, and prove it for iteration $t + 1$. Thus, the state of each fault-free process in V_i at the start of iteration t equals $\mathbf{e}_i$, $0 \le i \le p$.

Consider any fault-free process $j \in V_i$, where $0 \le i \le p$. In iteration t, process j will receive $\mathbf{v}_g[t-1]$ from each fault-free incoming neighbor g, and receive $\mathbf{e}_i$ from each faulty incoming neighbor. These received values form the multiset $r_j[t]$. Since the condition in the lemma is assumed to be false, for any $k \ne i$, $0 \le k \le p$, we have

$$V_k \cup C \xcancel{\xrightarrow{f}} V_i.$$

Thus, at most f incoming neighbors of j belong to $V_k \cup C$, and therefore, at most f values in $r_j[t]$ equal $\mathbf{e}_k$.

Since process j does not know which of its incoming neighbors, if any, are faulty, it must allow for the possibility that any of its f incoming neighbors are faulty. Let $A_k \subseteq V_k \cup C$, $k \ne i$, be the set containing all the incoming neighbors of process j in $V_k \cup C$. Since $V_k \cup C \xcancel{\xrightarrow{f}} V_i$, $|A_k| \le f$; therefore, all the processes in A_k are *potentially* faulty. Also, by assumption, the values received from all fault-free processes equal their input, and the values received from faulty processes in F equal $\mathbf{e}_i$. Thus, due to the validity condition, process j must choose as its new state a value that is in the convex hull of the set

$$S_k = \{\mathbf{e}_m \mid m \ne k, 0 \le m \le p\}.$$

where $k \neq i$. Since this observation is true for each $k \neq i$, it follows that the new state $\mathbf{v}_j[t]$ must be a point in the convex hull of

$$\cap_{1 \leq k \leq p, \; k \neq i} \mathcal{H}(S_k).$$

It is easy to verify that the above intersection only contains the point $\mathbf{e}_i$. Therefore, $\mathbf{v}_j[t] = \mathbf{e}_i$. Thus, the state of process j at the start of iteration $t + 1$ equals $\mathbf{e}_i$. This concludes the induction.

The above result implies that the state of each fault-free process remains unchanged through the iterations. Thus, the state of any two fault-free processes differs in at least one vector element by 2ϵ, precluding ϵ-agreement. $\qquad\square$

The above lemma demonstrates the necessity of Condition NC. Necessary condition NC implies a lower bound on the number of processes $n = |\mathcal{V}|$ in $G(\mathcal{V}, \mathcal{E})$, as stated in the next lemma.

Lemma 2. *Suppose that the Byzantine vector consensus problem can be solved using an iterative algorithm in $G(\mathcal{V}, \mathcal{E})$. Then, $n \geq (d + 2)f + 1$.*

Proof. Since the Byzantine vector consensus problem can be solved using an iterative algorithm in $G(\mathcal{V}, \mathcal{E})$, by Lemma 1, graph G must satisfy Condition NC. Suppose that $2 \leq |\mathcal{V}| = n \leq (d + 2)f$. Then there exists p, $1 \leq p \leq d$, such that we can partition $\mathcal{V}$ into sets $V_0, ..., V_p, F$ such that for each V_i, $0 < |V_i| \leq f$, and $|F| \leq f$. Define $C = \emptyset$. Since $|C \cup V_i| \leq f$ for each i, it is clear that this partition of $\mathcal{V}$ cannot satisfy Condition NC. This is a contradiction. $\qquad\square$

When $d = 1$, the input at each process is a scalar. For the $d = 1$ case, our prior work [13] yielded a tight necessary and sufficient condition for Byzantine consensus to be achievable in $G(\mathcal{V}, \mathcal{E})$ using iterative algorithms. For $d = 1$, the necessary condition stated in Lemma 1 is equivalent to the necessary condition in [13]. We previously showed that, for $d = 1$, the same condition is also sufficient [13]. However, in general, for $d > 1$, Condition NC is not proved sufficient. Instead, we prove the sufficiency of another condition stated in the next section.

5   A Sufficient Condition

We now present Condition SC that is later proved to be sufficient for achieving Byzantine vector consensus in graph $G(\mathcal{V}, \mathcal{E})$ using an iterative algorithm. Condition SC is a generalization of the sufficient condition presented in [13] for $d = 1$.

Condition SC: For any partition F, L, C, R of set $\mathcal{V}$, such that L and R are both non-empty, and $|F| \leq f$, at least one of these conditions is true: $R \cup C \xrightarrow{df} L$, or $L \cup C \xrightarrow{df} R$.

Later in the paper we will present a Byzantine vector consensus algorithm named `Byz-Iter` that is proved correct in all graphs that saitsfy Condition SC. The proof makes use of Lemmas 3 and 4 presented below.

Lemma 3. For $f > 0$, if graph $G(\mathcal{V}, \mathcal{E})$ satisfies Condition SC, then in-degree of each process in $\mathcal{V}$ must be at least $(d + 1)f + 1$. That is, for each $i \in \mathcal{V}$, $|N_i^-| \geq (d + 1)f + 1$.

Proof. The proof is by contradiction. As per the assumption in the lemma, $f > 0$, and graph $G(\mathcal{V}, \mathcal{E})$ satisfies condition SC.

Suppose that some process i has in-degree at most $(d + 1)f$. Define $L = \{i\}$, and $C = \emptyset$. Partition the processes in $\mathcal{V} - \{i\}$ into sets R and F such that $|F| \leq f$, $|F \cap N_i^-| \leq f$ and $|R \cap N_i^-| \leq df$. Such sets R and F exist because in-degree of process i is at most $(d+1)f$. L, R, C, F thus defined form a partition of $\mathcal{V}$.

Now, $f > 0$ and $d \geq 1$, and $|L \cup C| = 1$. Thus, there can be at most 1 link from $L \cup C$ to any process in R, and $1 \leq df$. Therefore, $L \cup C \overset{df}{\nrightarrow} R$. Also, because $C = \emptyset$, $|(R \cup C) \cap N_i^-| = |R \cap N_i^-| \leq df$. Thus, there can be at most df links from $R \cup C$ to process i, which is the only process in $L = \{i\}$. Therefore, $R \cup C \overset{df}{\nrightarrow} L$. Thus, the above partition of $\mathcal{V}$ does not satisfy Condition SC. This is a contradiction. $\square$

Definition 4. Reduced Graph: *For a given graph $G(\mathcal{V}, \mathcal{E})$ and $\mathcal{F} \subset \mathcal{V}$ such that $|\mathcal{F}| \leq f$, a graph $H(\mathcal{V}_\mathcal{F}, \mathcal{E}_\mathcal{F})$ is said to be a reduced graph, if: (i) $\mathcal{V}_\mathcal{F} = \mathcal{V} - \mathcal{F}$, and (ii) $\mathcal{E}_\mathcal{F}$ is obtained by first removing from $\mathcal{E}$ all the links incident on the processes in $\mathcal{F}$, and then removing up to df additional incoming links at each process in $\mathcal{V}_\mathcal{F}$.*

Note that for a given $G(\mathcal{V}, \mathcal{E})$ and a given $\mathcal{F}$, multiple reduced graphs may exist (depending on the choice of the links removed at each process).

Lemma 4. *Suppose that graph $G(\mathcal{V}, \mathcal{E})$ satisfies Condition SC, and $\mathcal{F} \subset \mathcal{V}$, such that $|\mathcal{F}| \leq f$. Then, in any reduced graph $H(\mathcal{V}_\mathcal{F}, \mathcal{E}_\mathcal{F})$, there exists a process that has a directed path to all the remaining processes in $\mathcal{V}_\mathcal{F}$.*

The proof of Lemma 4 is omitted for lack of space. This proof, and the other omitted proofs in the paper, are presented in [15].

5.1   Algorithm `Byz-Iter`

We prove that, if graph $G(\mathcal{V}, \mathcal{E})$ satisfies Condition SC, then Algorithm `Byz-Iter` presented below achieves Byzantine vector consensus. Algorithm `Byz-Iter` has the three-step structure described in Section 3.

The proposed algorithm is based on the following result by Tverberg [10].

Theorem 1. (Tverberg's Theorem [10]) *For any integer $f \geq 0$, and for every multiset Y containing at least $(d + 1)f + 1$ points in $\mathbf{R}^d$, there exists a partition $Y_1, \cdots, Y_{f+1}$ of Y into $f + 1$ non-empty multisets such that $\cap_{l=1}^{f+1} \mathcal{H}(Y_l) \neq \emptyset$.*

The points in Y above need not be distinct [10]; thus, the same point may occur multiple times in Y, and also in each of its subsets (Y_l's) above. The partition in Theorem 1 is called a *Tverberg partition*, and the points in $\cap_{l=1}^{f+1} \mathcal{H}(Y_l)$ in Theorem 1 are called Tverberg points.

Algorithm. Byz-Iter

Each iteration consists of three steps: *Transmit, Receive,* and *Update*:
1. *Transmit step:* Transmit current state $\mathbf{v}_i[t-1]$ on all outgoing edges.
2. *Receive step:* Receive values on all incoming edges. These values form multiset $r_i[t]$ of size $|N_i^-|$. (If a message is not received from some incoming neighbor, then that neighbor must be faulty. In this case, the missing message value is assumed to be $\mathbf{e}_0$ by default. Recall that we assume a *synchronous* system.)
3. *Update step:* Form a multiset $Z_i[t]$ using the steps below:
   – Initialize $Z_i[t]$ as empty.
   – Add to $Z_i[t]$, any one *Tverberg point* corresponding to *each* multiset $C \subseteq r_i[t]$ such that $|C| = (d+1)f + 1$. Since $|C| = (d+1)f + 1$, by Theorem 1, such a Tverberg point exists.

   $Z_i[t]$ is a multiset; thus a single point may appear in $Z_i[t]$ more than once. Note that $|Z_i[t]| = \binom{|r_i[t]|}{(d+1)f+1} \leq \binom{n}{(d+1)f+1}$. Compute new state $\mathbf{v}_i[t]$ as:

$$\mathbf{v}_i[t] = \frac{\mathbf{v}_i[t-1] + \sum_{\mathbf{z} \in Z_i[t]} \mathbf{z}}{1 + |Z_i[t]|} \qquad (2)$$

Termination: Each fault-free process terminates after completing t_{end} iterations, where t_{end} is a constant defined later in Equation (10). The value of t_{end} depends on graph $G(\mathcal{V}, \mathcal{E})$, constants U and μ defined earlier in Section 3 and parameter ϵ of ϵ-agreement.

The proof of correctness of Algorithm Byz-Iter makes use of a matrix representation of the algorithm's behavior. Before presenting the matrix representation, we introduce some notations and definitions related to matrices.

5.2   Matrix Preliminaries

We use boldface letters to denote matrices, rows of matrices, and their elements. For instance, $\mathbf{A}$ denotes a matrix, $\mathbf{A}_i$ denotes the i-th row of matrix $\mathbf{A}$, and $\mathbf{A}_{ij}$ denotes the element at the intersection of the i-th row and the j-th column of matrix $\mathbf{A}$.

Definition 5. *A vector is said to be stochastic if all its elements are non-negative, and the elements add up to 1. A matrix is said to be row stochastic if each row of the matrix is a stochastic vector.*

For matrix products, we adopt the "backward" product convention below, where $a \leq b$,

$$\Pi_{\tau=a}^{b} \mathbf{A}[\tau] = \mathbf{A}[b] \mathbf{A}[b-1] \cdots \mathbf{A}[a] \tag{3}$$

For a row stochastic matrix $\mathbf{A}$, coefficients of ergodicity $\delta(\mathbf{A})$ and $\lambda(\mathbf{A})$ are defined as follows [17]:

$$\delta(\mathbf{A}) = \max_{j} \max_{i_1, i_2} \| \mathbf{A}_{i_1 j} - \mathbf{A}_{i_2 j} \|$$

$$\lambda(\mathbf{A}) = 1 - \min_{i_1, i_2} \sum_{j} \min(\mathbf{A}_{i_1 j}, \mathbf{A}_{i_2 j})$$

Lemma 5. *For any p square row stochastic matrices $\mathbf{A}(1), \mathbf{A}(2), \ldots, \mathbf{A}(p)$,*

$$\delta(\Pi_{\tau=1}^{p} \mathbf{A}(\tau)) \leq \Pi_{\tau=1}^{p} \lambda(\mathbf{A}(\tau)).$$

The above lemma is proved in [5]. The lemma below follows directly from the definition of $\lambda(\cdot)$.

Lemma 6. *If all the elements in any one column of matrix $\mathbf{A}$ are lower bounded by a constant γ, then $\lambda(\mathbf{A}) \leq 1 - \gamma$. That is, if $\exists g$, such that $\mathbf{A}_{ig} \geq \gamma$, $\forall i$, then $\lambda(\mathbf{A}) \leq 1 - \gamma$.*

5.3   Correctness of Algorithm `Byz-Iter`

Let $\mathcal{F}$ denote the actual set of faulty processes in a given execution of Algorithm `Byz-Iter`. Let $|\mathcal{F}| = \psi$. Thus, $0 \leq \psi \leq f$. Without loss of generality, suppose that processes 1 through $(n - \psi)$ are fault-free, and if $\psi > 0$, processes $(n - \psi + 1)$ through n are faulty.

In the analysis below, it is convenient to view the state of each process as a point in the d-dimensional Euclidean space. Denote by $\mathbf{v}[0]$ the column vector consisting of the initial states of the $(n - \psi)$ fault-free processes. The i-th element of $\mathbf{v}[0]$ is $\mathbf{v}_i[0]$, the initial state of process i. Thus, $\mathbf{v}[0]$ is a vector consisting of $(n - \psi)$ points in the d-dimensional Euclidean space. Denote by $\mathbf{v}[t]$, for $t \geq 1$, the column vector consisting of the states of the $(n - \psi)$ fault-free processes at the end of the t-th iteration. The i-th element of vector $\mathbf{v}[t]$ is state $\mathbf{v}_i[t]$.

Lemma 7 below states the key result that helps in proving the correctness of Algorithm `Byz-Iter`. In particular, Lemma 7 allows us to use results for non-homogeneous Markov chains to prove the correctness of Algorithm `Byz-Iter`.

Lemma 7. *Suppose that graph $G(\mathcal{V}, \mathcal{E})$ satisfies Condition SC. Then the state updates performed by the fault-free processes in the t-th iteration ($t \geq 1$) of Algorithm `Byz-Iter` can be expressed as*

$$\mathbf{v}[t] = \mathbf{M}[t] \, \mathbf{v}[t-1] \tag{4}$$

where $\mathbf{M}[t]$ *is a* $(n-\psi) \times (n-\psi)$ *row stochastic matrix with the following property: there exists a reduced graph* $H[t]$, *and a constant* β $(0 < \beta \leq 1)$ *that depends only on graph* $G(\mathcal{V}, \mathcal{E})$, *such that*

$$\mathbf{M}_{ij}[t] \geq \beta$$

if $j = i$ *or edge* (j, i) *is in* $H[t]$.

The proof is presented in [15].

Matrix $\mathbf{M}[t]$ above is said to be a transition matrix. As the lemma states, $\mathbf{M}[t]$ is a row stochastic matrix. The proof of Lemma 7 shows how to identify a suitable row stochastic matrix $\mathbf{M}[t]$ for each iteration t. The matrix $\mathbf{M}[t]$ depends on t, as well as the behavior of the faulty processes. $\mathbf{M}_i[t]$ is the i-th row of transition matrix $\mathbf{M}[t]$. Thus, (4) implies that

$$\mathbf{v}_i[t] = \mathbf{M}_i[t] \mathbf{v}[t-1]$$

That is, the state of any fault-free process i at the end of iteration t can be expressed as a convex combination of the state of just the fault-free processes at the end of iteration $t-1$. Recall that vector $\mathbf{v}$ only includes the state of fault-free processes.

Theorem 2. *Algorithm* Byz-Iter *satisfies the termination, validity and ϵ-agreement conditions.*

Proof. This proof follows a structure used to prove correctness of other consensus algorithms in our prior work [14,11]. Sections 5.4, 5.5 and 5.6 provide the proof that Algorithm Byz-Iter satisfies the three conditions for Byzantine vector consensus, and thus prove Theorem 2.

5.4 Algorithm Byz-Iter Satisfies the Validity Condition

Observe that $\mathbf{M}[t+1]\,(\mathbf{M}[t]\mathbf{v}[t-1]) = (\mathbf{M}[t+1]\mathbf{M}[t])\,\mathbf{v}[t-1]$. Therefore, by repeated application of (4), we obtain for $t \geq 1$,

$$\mathbf{v}[t] = \left(\Pi_{\tau=1}^{t} \mathbf{M}[\tau] \right) \mathbf{v}[0] \tag{5}$$

Since each $\mathbf{M}[\tau]$ is row stochastic, the matrix product $\Pi_{\tau=1}^{t} \mathbf{M}[\tau]$ is also a row stochastic matrix. Recall that vector $\mathbf{v}$ only includes the state of fault-free processes. Thus, (5) implies that the state of each fault-free process i at the end of iteration t can be expressed as a convex combination of the initial state of the fault-free processes. Therefore, the validity condition is satisfied.

5.5 Algorithm Byz-Iter Satisfies the Termination Condition

Algorithm Byz-Iter stops after a finite number (t_{end}) of iterations, where t_{end} is a constant that depends only on $G(\mathcal{V}, \mathcal{E})$, U, μ and ϵ. Therefore, trivially, the algorithm satisfies the termination condition. Later, using (10) we define a suitable value for t_{end}.

5.6   Algorithm Byz-Iter Satisfies the ϵ-Agreement Condition

The proof structure below is derived from our previous work [14] wherein we proved the correctness of an iterative algorithm for *scalar* Byzantine consensus (i.e., the case of $d = 1$), and its generalization to a broader class of fault sets [11].

Let R_F denote the set of all the reduced graph of $G(\mathcal{V}, \mathcal{E})$ corresponding to fault set F. Thus, $R_{\mathcal{F}}$ is the set of all the reduced graph of $G(\mathcal{V}, \mathcal{E})$ corresponding to actual fault set $\mathcal{F}$. Let

$$r = \max_{|F| \leq f} |R_F|.$$

r depends only on $G(\mathcal{V}, \mathcal{E})$ and f, and it is finite. Note that $|R_{\mathcal{F}}| \leq r$.

For each reduced graph $H \in R_{\mathcal{F}}$, define connectivity matrix $\mathbf{H}$ as follows, where $1 \leq i, j \leq n - \psi$:

- $\mathbf{H}_{ij} = 1$ if either $j = i$, or edge (j, i) exists in reduced graph H.
- $\mathbf{H}_{ij} = 0$, otherwise.

Thus, the non-zero elements of row $\mathbf{H}_i$ correspond to the incoming links at process i in the reduced graph H, and the self-loop at process i. Observe that $\mathbf{H}$ has a non-zero diagonal.

Lemma 8. *For any $H \in R_F$, and any $k \geq n - \psi$, matrix product $\mathbf{H}^k$ has at least one non-zero column (i.e., a column with all elements non-zero).*

Proof. Each reduced graph contains $n - \psi$ processes because the fault set $\mathcal{F}$ contain ψ processes. By Lemma 4, at least one process in the reduced graph, say process p, has directed paths to all the processes in the reduced graph H. Element $\mathbf{H}_{jp}^k$ of matrix product $\mathbf{H}^k$ is 1 if and only if process p has a directed path to process j containing at most k edges; each of these directed paths must contain less than $n - \psi$ edges, because the number of processes in the reduced graph is $n - \psi$. Since p has directed paths to all the processes, it follows that, when $k \geq n - \psi$, all the elements in the p-th column of $\mathbf{H}^k$ must be non-zero.

For matrices $\mathbf{A}$ and $\mathbf{B}$ of identical dimensions, we say that $\mathbf{A} \leq \mathbf{B}$ if and only if $\mathbf{A}_{ij} \leq \mathbf{B}_{ij}, \forall i, j$. Lemma 9 relates the transition matrices with the connectivity matrices. Constant β used in the lemma below was introduced in Lemma 7.

Lemma 9. *For any $t \geq 1$, there exists a reduced graph $H[t] \in R_{\mathcal{F}}$ such that $\beta \mathbf{H}[t] \leq \mathbf{M}[t]$, where $\mathbf{H}[t]$ is the connectivity matrix for $H[t]$.*

The proof is presented in [15].

Lemma 10. *At least one column in the matrix product $\Pi_{t=u}^{u+r(n-\psi)-1} \mathbf{H}[t]$ is non-zero.*

The proof is presented in [15].

Let us now define a sequence of matrices $\mathbf{Q}(i)$, $i \geq 1$, such that each of these matrices is a product of $r(n - \psi)$ of the $\mathbf{M}[t]$ matrices. Specifically,

$$\mathbf{Q}(i) = \Pi_{t=(i-1)r(n-\psi)+1}^{ir(n-\psi)} \mathbf{M}[t] \tag{6}$$

From (5) and (6) observe that

$$\mathbf{v}[kr(n - \psi)] = \left(\Pi_{i=1}^{k} \mathbf{Q}(i) \right) \mathbf{v}[0] \tag{7}$$

Lemma 11. *For $i \geq 1$, $\mathbf{Q}(i)$ is a row stochastic matrix, and*

$$\lambda(\mathbf{Q}(i)) \leq 1 - \beta^{r(n-\psi)}.$$

The proof is presented in [15].

Let us now continue with the proof of ϵ-agreement. Consider the coefficient of ergodicity $\delta(\Pi_{i=1}^{t}\mathbf{M}[i])$.

$$\delta(\Pi_{i=1}^{t}\mathbf{M}[i]) = \delta \left(\left(\Pi_{i=\lfloor \frac{t}{r(n-\psi)} \rfloor r(n-\psi)+1}^{t} \mathbf{M}[i] \right) \left(\Pi_{i=1}^{\lfloor \frac{t}{r(n-\psi)} \rfloor} \mathbf{Q}(i) \right) \right) \tag{8}$$

$$\text{by definition of } Q(i)$$

$$\leq \lambda \left(\Pi_{i=\lfloor \frac{t}{r(n-\psi)} \rfloor r(n-\psi)+1}^{t} \mathbf{M}[i] \right) \Pi_{i=1}^{\lfloor \frac{t}{r(n-\psi)} \rfloor} \lambda(\mathbf{Q}(i)) \qquad \text{by Lemma 5}$$

$$\leq \Pi_{i=1}^{\lfloor \frac{t}{r(n-\psi)} \rfloor} \lambda(\mathbf{Q}(i)) \qquad \text{because } \lambda(.) \leq 1$$

$$\leq \left(1 - \beta^{r(n-\psi)} \right)^{\lfloor \frac{t}{r(n-\psi)} \rfloor} \qquad \text{by Lemma 11}$$

$$\leq (1 - \beta^{rn})^{\lfloor \frac{t}{rn} \rfloor} \qquad \text{because } 0 < \beta \leq 1 \text{ and } 0 \leq \psi < n. \tag{9}$$

Observe that the upper bound on right side of (9) depends only on graph $G(\mathcal{V}, \mathcal{E})$ and t, and is independent of the input vectors, the fault set $\mathcal{F}$, and the behavior of the faulty processes. Also, the upper bound on the right side of (9) is a non-increasing function of t. Define t_{end} as the smallest positive integer t for which the right hand side of (9) is smaller than $\frac{\epsilon}{n \max(\|U\|, \|\mu\|)}$, where $\|x\|$ denotes the absolute value of real number x. Thus,

$$\delta(\Pi_{i=1}^{t_{end}} \mathbf{M}[i]) \leq (1 - \beta^{rn})^{\lfloor \frac{t_{end}}{rn} \rfloor} < \frac{\epsilon}{n \max(\|U\|, \|\mu\|)} \tag{10}$$

Recall that β and r depend only on $G(\mathcal{V}, \mathcal{E})$. Thus, t_{end} depends only on graph $G(\mathcal{V}, \mathcal{E})$, and constants U, μ and ϵ.

Recall that $\Pi_{i=1}^{t}\mathbf{M}[i]$ is a $(n - \psi) \times (n - \psi)$ row stochastic matrix. Let $\mathbf{M}^* = \Pi_{i=1}^{t}\mathbf{M}[i]$. From (5) we know that state $\mathbf{v}_j[t]$ of any fault-free process j is obtained as the product of the j-th row of $\Pi_{i=1}^{t} \mathbf{M}[i]$ and $\mathbf{v}[0]$. That is, $\mathbf{v}_j[t] = \mathbf{M}_j^*\mathbf{v}[0]$.

Recall that $\mathbf{v}_j[t]$ is a d-dimensional vector. Let us denote the l-th element of $\mathbf{v}_j[t]$ as $\mathbf{v}_j[t](l)$, $1 \le l \le d$. Also, by $\mathbf{v}[0](l)$, let us denote a vector consisting of the l-th elements of $\mathbf{v}_i[0], \forall i$. Then by the definitions of $\delta(.)$, U and μ, for any two fault-free processes j and k, we have

$$\|\mathbf{v}_j[t](l) - \mathbf{v}_k[t](l)\| = \|\mathbf{M}_j^* \mathbf{v}[0](l) - \mathbf{M}_k^* \mathbf{v}[0](l)\| \tag{11}$$

$$= \|\sum_{i=1}^{n-\psi} \mathbf{M}_{ji}^* \mathbf{v}_i[0](l) - \sum_{i=1}^{n-\psi} \mathbf{M}_{ki}^* \mathbf{v}_i[0](l)\| \tag{12}$$

$$= \|\sum_{i=1}^{n-\psi} \left(\mathbf{M}_{ji}^* - \mathbf{M}_{ki}^*\right) \mathbf{v}_i[0](l)\| \tag{13}$$

$$\le \sum_{i=1}^{n-\psi} \|\mathbf{M}_{ji}^* - \mathbf{M}_{ki}^*\| \|\mathbf{v}_i[0](l)\| \tag{14}$$

$$\le \sum_{i=1}^{n-\psi} \delta(\mathbf{M}^*) \|\mathbf{v}_i[0](l)\| \tag{15}$$

$$\le (n-\psi)\delta(\mathbf{M}^*) \max(\|U\|, \|\mu\|) \tag{16}$$

$$\le (n-\psi) \max(\|U\|, \|\mu\|) \, \delta(\Pi_{i=1}^t \mathbf{M}[i])$$

$$\le n \max(\|U\|, \|\mu\|) \, \delta(\Pi_{i=1}^t \mathbf{M}[i]) \text{ because } \psi \le n \tag{17}$$

Therefore, by (10) and (17),

$$\|\mathbf{v}_i[t_{end}](l) - \mathbf{v}_j[t_{end}](l)\| < \epsilon, \qquad 1 \le l \le d. \tag{18}$$

The output of a fault-free process equals its state at termination (after t_{end} iterations). Thus, (18) implies that Algorithm `Byz-Iter` satisfies the ϵ-agreement condition.

6   Summary

This paper addresses *Byzantine vector consensus* (BVC), wherein the input at each process is a d-dimensional vector of reals, and each process is expected to decide on a *decision vector* that is in the *convex hull* of the input vectors at the fault-free processes [9,12]. We address a particular class of *iterative* algorithms in *incomplete* graphs, and prove a necessary condition (NC), and a sufficient condition (SC), for the graphs to be able to solve the vector consensus problem iteratively. This paper extends our past work on *scalar* consensus (i.e., $d = 1$) in incomplete graphs in presence of Byzantine faults [13,14], which yielded an exact characterization of graphs in which the problem is solvable for $d = 1$. However, the necessary condition NC presented in the paper for *vector* consensus does not match with the sufficient condition SC. We hope that this paper will motivate further work on identifying the tight sufficient condition.

Acknowledgments. The results presented in the paper are generalizations of results in prior work [12,13,16] performed in collaboration with Vijay Garg, Guanfeng Liang and Lewis Tseng. The author has benefited from the discussions with his collaborators.

This research is supported in part by National Science Foundation award CNS-1059540 and Army Research Office grant W-911-NF-0710287. Any opinions, findings, and conclusions or recommendations expressed here are those of the authors and do not necessarily reflect the views of the funding agencies or the U.S. government.

References

1. Abraham, I., Amit, Y., Dolev, D.: Optimal resilience asynchronous approximate agreement. In: Higashino, T. (ed.) OPODIS 2004. LNCS, vol. 3544, pp. 229–239. Springer, Heidelberg (2005)
2. Dasgupta, S., Papadimitriou, C., Vazirani, U.: Algorithms. McGraw-Hill Higher Education (2006)
3. Dolev, D., Lynch, N.A., Pinter, S.S., Stark, E.W., Weihl, W.E.: Reaching approximate agreement in the presence of faults. J. ACM 33, 499–516 (1986)
4. Fekete, A.D.: Asymptotically optimal algorithms for approximate agreement. In: Proceedings of the Fifth Annual ACM Symposium on Principles of Distributed Computing, PODC 1986, pp. 73–87. ACM, New York (1986)
5. Hajnal, J.: Weak ergodicity in non-homogeneous markov chains. Proceedings of the Cambridge Philosophical Society 54, 233–246 (1958)
6. Jadbabaie, A., Lin, J., Morse, A.S.: Coordination of groups of mobile autonomous agents using nearest neighbor rules. IEEE Transactions on Automatic Control 48, 988–1001 (2003)
7. LeBlanc, H., Koutsoukos, X.: Consensus in networked multi-agent systems with adversaries. In: 14th International Conference on Hybrid Systems: Computation and Control, HSCC (2011)
8. LeBlanc, H., Koutsoukos, X.: Low complexity resilient consensus in networked multi-agent systems with adversaries. In: 15th International Conference on Hybrid Systems: Computation and Control, HSCC (2012)
9. Mendes, H., Herlihy, M.: Multidimensional approximate agreement in byzantine asynchronous systems. In: 45th ACM Symposium on the Theory of Computing, STOC (June 2013)
10. Perles, M.A., Sigron, M.: A generalization of Tverberg's theorem, CoRR (2007), http://arxiv.org/abs/0710.4668
11. Tseng, L., Vaidya, N.: Iterative approximate byzantine consensus under a generalized fault model. In: Frey, D., Raynal, M., Sarkar, S., Shyamasundar, R.K., Sinha, P. (eds.) ICDCN 2013. LNCS, vol. 7730, pp. 72–86. Springer, Heidelberg (2013)
12. Vaidya, N.H., Garg, V.K.: Byzantine vector consensus in complete graphs. In: ACM Symposium on Principles of Distributed Computing (PODC) (July 2013)
13. Vaidya, N.H., Tseng, L., Liang, G.: Iterative approximate byzantine consensus in arbitrary directed graphs. In: ACM Symposium on Principles of Distributed Computing (PODC) (July 2012)

14. Vaidya, N.H.: Matrix representation of iterative approximate byzantine consensus in directed graphs. CoRR (March 2012), http://arxiv.org/abs/1203.1888
15. Vaidya, N.H.: Iterative Byzantine vector consensus in incomplete graphs. CoRR (July 2013), http://arxiv.org/abs/1307.2483
16. Vaidya, N.H., Garg, V.: Byzantine vector consensus in complete graphs. CoRR (July 2013), http://arxiv.org/abs/1302.2543
17. Wolfowitz, J.: Products of indecomposable, aperiodic, stochastic matrices. In: Proceedings of the American Mathematical Society, pp. 733–737 (1963)

Mutual Exclusion Algorithms in the Shared Queue Model*

Junxing Wang and Zhengyu Wang

The Institute for Theoretical Computer Science (ITCS),
Institute for Interdisciplinary Information Sciences,
Tsinghua University, Beijing, China
thuwjx@andrew.cmu.edu, wangsincos@163.com

Abstract. Resource sharing for asynchronous processors with mutual exclusion property is a fundamental task in distributed computing. We investigate the problem in a natural setting: for the communications between processors, they only share several queues supporting enqueue and dequeue operations. It is well-known that there is a very simple algorithm using only one queue when the queue also supports the peek operation, but it is still open whether we could implement mutual exclusion distributed system without the peek operation. In this paper, we propose two mutual exclusion starvation-free algorithms for this more restricted setting. The first algorithm is a protocol for arbitrary number of processors which share 2 queues; the second one is a protocol for 2 processors sharing only one queue.

Keywords: Mutual Exclusion, Starvation Free, Queue, Distributed Algorithm.

1 Introduction

In a distributed system, processors often need to share a unique resource, while at the same time it is required that the processors are mutual exclusive, which means that at any time, there is at most one processor who uses the resource (i.e. enters the critical section). That fundamental problem is known as mutual exclusion problem. Dijkstra [1] gives the first formulation of the problem, and devices an algorithm with shared atomic registers for that purpose. However, the algorithm does not satisfy starvation free property, i.e., there might be some processor who wants to enter the critical section, but it never enters. Lamport [2] further proposes bakery algorithm obtaining starvation free property, and moreover, the processors share weaker registers called safe registers. There are a huge amount of literatures on the design of mutual exclusion algorithms, which can be even formed a book several decades ago [3].

---

* This work was supported in part by the National Basic Research Program of China Grant 2011CBA00300, 2011CBA00301, the National Natural Science Foundation of China Grant 61033001, 61061130540.

M. Chatterjee et al. (Eds.): ICDCN 2014, LNCS 8314, pp. 29–43, 2014.

Shared queues have been studied as objects for communication between processors. Informally, the *enqueue* operation inserts an element to the tail of the queue; the *dequeue* operation returns as well as deletes the head element of the queue; the *peek* operation returns the head element of the queue without modifying it. Specially, if there is no element in the queue, it will return a symbol indicating the queue is empty upon the *dequeue* or *peek* operation. It is well known that if the queue object supports *enqueue*, *dequeue* and *peek* operations, we can use a single queue to implement a mutual exclusion system satisfying starvation free property: initially let the queue be empty; if one processor wants to use the resource, it will enqueue its *id* to the queue and then peek the queue over and over again until it finds that the top element of the queue is the id of itself so that it could enter the critical section; after one's critical section, it removes the top element of the queue by *dequeue* and then exits. Notice that the *peek* operation is the key for obtaining mutual exclusion property, and the queue structure enables starvation free property. Since *peek* is a more advanced operation of the queue object, one interesting question is that *can we succeed without the peek operation?* We have not found the answer to the question in the literature, and we found it to be non-trivial to solve. In this paper, we give a positive answer by showing two algorithms. The first algorithm uses two queues to support arbitrary number of processors, and the second one uses one queue to support 2 processors.

In our model, we assume that the processors are failure-free, and for every processor, if it is active, it will execute a step in finite time. More formally, the problem concerned here is how to design a protocol with 1 or 2 queues without peek operation such that the distributed system satisfies the following properties.

a) Mutual exclusion property: there is no time when two processors run in the critical section.

b) No starvation (starvation-free) property: every processor that wants to enter the critical section eventually enters the critical section.

Note that the problem studied in our paper is different from consensus in that (1) In the problem setting of making consensus, one processor might crash and never recover again; while in our model, one processor never crash (or might crash, but recover in finite time and return to the state before crash); (2) The consensus problem (or calculating the consensus number) typically concerns only making one consensus, while mutual exclusion deals with many critical sections. Furthermore, in the consensus problem, we have not found the concept of starvation-free. It might be interesting to consider that property, since it is natural and fair to make every proposer having the chance of being admitted in the period of infinite times of consensus making.

We can define a concept called mutual exclusion number, denoted by MEN, which is similar to the definition of consensus number [4]. We call a system has mutual exclusion number k, if it can support starvation-free mutual exclusion requirement of k processors, while it cannot support $k + 1$ processors. If it can support arbitrary number of processors, we define that number to be ∞. For example, we have already known that MEN (n atomic registers) $\geq n - 1$ by

Bakery Algorithm. And the conclusion of our work can be written as

(1) MEN (1 queue with peek) $= \infty$;
(2) MEN (2 queues without peek operation) $= \infty$;
(3) MEN (1 queue without peek operation) ≥ 2.

The paper is organized as follows. Section 2 gives a protocol with 2 queues that supports arbitrary number of processors. In Section 3, we present a protocol with one queue that supports 2 processors. Finally we conclude and refer to further work in Section 4.

2 Algorithm with Two Queues

In this section, we present an algorithm using two queues that solves the mutual exclusion problem for arbitrary number of processors. In the first part, we exhibit some intuitions behind the design of the algorithm. Next, we give some data type notation which will be used in the algorithm. Then we show the proposed algorithm, and finally give a technical correctness justification in the last subsection.

2.1 Designing Idea

In order to satisfy mutual exclusion property, we could adopt a token-based approach: place a unique token in queues; any processor can get into critical section only if it obtains the token from queues by *dequeue*; when the processor leaves its critical section, it should return the token back to queues by *enqueue*. To satisfy no starvation property, we should design a rule to guarantee that all the processors with intent to enter critical section will get the token in a finite time. Since every active processor must *dequeue* from queues to get messages from other processors, it becomes a trouble that how to avoid the processors getting the token who are not supposed to do so. To tackle it, we could attach the token with additional information such as the processors which have the right to enter critical section, operations that each processors are executing, etc. As a result, the processor which gets the token "wrongly" can take some actions to "help" the processor which is supposed to get the token according to information attached with the token. At the same time, we should also make sure that the new processor with intent to enter critical section can notify other processors, the processors which have the ability to guide it to get the token.

2.2 Notation

Before describing the proposed algorithm, we need to define some notations that will be used in the following algorithm description and analysis. Suppose that there are n processors numbered with 1 to n, which have intent to get into critical section at any time they want (or will never have such intent). Mark two shared queues mentioned above with q_0 and q_1. To formalize the notation of operations, we use $enqueue(q_i, x)$ to represent command that inserts the element x to the tail of q_i. Also, $x \leftarrow dequeue(q_i)$ means that the processor reads the head element of q_i and save it into variable x together with removing that element form q_i.

All the elements in queues are of type *number* or of type *order*. For element x, we can acquire the type of x by referring $x.type$. For instance, x's type is *number* if and only if $x.type = number$. Specially, if we execute an operation $x \leftarrow dequeue(q_i)$ while q_i is empty, we can obtain *NULL* while referring $x.type$.

While one processor executes the operation $x \leftarrow number(i)$, it can get an element x of type *number* with an attached value i which can be referred by $x.value$, which ranges from 1 to n. We can regard type *number* as an indicator telling the processor who gets this element that processor i wants to get into critical section. Consider the case that $x.type = order$, i.e., x is of type *order*. We can refer $x.queue$ to get a sequence of numbers, which can be empty (i.e., $x.queue = \phi$). We can obtain the head number of $x.queue$ by $x.head$. If $x.queue = \phi$, mark $x.head$ to be 0. We can also refer $x.wait$ to get an n-dimension vector, ith entry of which is a 0-or-1 value, acquired by notation $x.wait[i]$. Such an element x, of type *order*, is just the token we mentioned in Subsection 2.1.

2.3   Algorithm

To begin with, let q_0 contain only one element x of type *order*, i.e., $x.type = order$, where $x.queue = \phi$ and $x.wait[i] = 0$ for all $i \in \{1, 2, \cdots, n\}$. Then, if processor i wants to get into critical section, it should run the following algorithm DQB for processor i. In this algorithm, processor i has some local memory: a 0-or-1 variable k, a queue tmp containing at most n numbers, a Boolean variable *allow* and two temporary variables x and y used to record the element dequeued from queues.

The proposed algorithm is depicted in Algorithm 1.

2.4   Properties

In this subsection, we will discuss two important properties of algorithm DQB: mutual exclusion and no starvation.

Call processor i as p_i and mark p_i's local queue as tmp_i. For convenience, we divide the whole algorithm into three parts: trying section (from Line 1 to Line 10), control section (from Line 11 to Line 25) and exit section (from Line 26 to the end). If we say trying-control section, we mean the union of trying section and control section. In the same way, we say control-exit section to express the union of control section and exit section. To claim these sections clearly, if we say that processor i enters or gets into one section, we mean that processor i has executed one command of this section. To say that processor i leaves or gets out of one section, we mean that processor i has executed the last operation-command in this section, the command that would change the memory used in the whole algorithm including shared memory and local memory, and next operation-command p_i will execute is out of this section. For instance, if processor i with local variable *allow* true has just executed the command at Line

Algorithm 1. Algorithm DQB for Processor i

1: $enqueue(q_1, number(i))$	▷ trying section
2: $k \leftarrow 0$	
3: **repeat**	
4: $tmp \leftarrow \phi$	
5: **repeat**	
6: $x \leftarrow dequeue(q_k)$	
7: **if** $x.type = number$ **then**	
8: $tmp \leftarrow (tmp, x.value)$	
9: **end if**	
10: **until** $x.type = order$	
11: $allow \leftarrow (x.head \in \{0, i\})$	▷ control section
12: $x.queue \leftarrow (x.queue, tmp)$	
13: **repeat**	
14: $y \leftarrow dequeue(q_1)$	
15: **if** $y.type = number$ **then**	
16: $x.queue \leftarrow (x.queue, y.value)$	
17: **end if**	
18: **until** $y.type = NULL$	
19: **if** $allow = false$ **then**	
20: $x.wait[i] \leftarrow 1 - k$	
21: $enqueue(q_k, x)$	
22: $k \leftarrow 1 - k$	
23: **end if**	
24: **until** $allow = true$	
25: **Critical Section**	
26: Delete number i from $x.queue$	▷ exit section
27: $x.wait[i] \leftarrow 0$	
28: **if** $x.queue = \phi$ **then**	
29: $enqueue(q_0, x)$	
30: **else**	
31: $enqueue(q_{x.wait[x.head]}, x)$	
32: **end if**	
33: **Remainder Section**	

14 and has obtained its local element y of type $NULL$, we can say that processor i leaves control section because the next several commands (at Line 15, 18, 19, 24, 25) processor i will execute make no chance on the memory used in the algorithm. If we say that processor i is running in one section, we mean that processor i has entered this section and has not left yet. For simplicity of the proof, we postulate that local queue tmp should be cleared up automatically after executing Line 12, and that local element x should be cleared up after executing $enqueue(\cdot, x)$ command. Such postulations make no chance of the function of algorithm.

Now, we will show some basic observations and lemmas. In the algorithm, a processor can get into control-exit section if and only if it acquires an element of type $order$ at Line 6 and then executes the first command at Line 11. Whatever its local variable *allow* returned by command at Line 11 is, the last command it will execute before leaving is *enqueue* command at Line 21 or 29 or 31, which is also the first command of *enqueue* operation it executes in control-exit section, i.e., an element of type *order* is enqueued back to queues if and only if this processor leaves control-exit section. These can be concluded in the observation below.

Obseravation 1. *A processor has an element of type* order *in its local memory if and only if it is running at control-exit section.*

Based on this observation, we will propose the following lemma about uniqueness of the element of type *order*, which will be used on whole analysis of this paper.

Lemma 1 (Conservation of *Order*)
There is exact one element of type order in queues and all processors' local memories.

Proof. Call the time as *free* when there is no processor in control-exit section. Oppositely, if there exists one processor in control-exit section, we mark this moment as *busy*.

Let's consider the case in *free* time first. If there is exact one element of type *order* in queues (we call this as one-element-in-queues condition), Lemma 1 can be proved because all the processors have no element of type *order* in their memories by Observation 1. We say beginning time is such a *free* time that satisfies one-element-in-queues condition.

From the beginning time on, Lemma 1 keeps correct until a processor *i* obtains an element of type *order* and will enter control-exit section later. After processor *i* gets into control-exit section, the time becomes *busy*. This time no elements of type *order* can be found in queues. Then, no processor can acquire an element of type *order* by *dequeue* unless one processor *enqueues* it. In *busy* time, the only case that the element of type *order* is *enqueued* to queues is that processor *i* executes its last command and gets out of control-exit section. Therefore, queues and all the processors except *i* can not get the element of type *order* in *busy* time. As processor *i* holds it during the whole *busy* time, Lemma 1 keeps correct.

After processor *i* leaves control-exit section, queues gains an element of type *order* again, which satisfies one-element-in-queues condition. Therefore, the case become the first one again. Lemma 1 can keep correct forever.

According to Lemma 1, if we say *order* in the following context, we refer to that unique element of type *order* placed in queues or one process's local memory. Combining Lemma 1 with Observation 1, we can directly get the following lemma.

Lemma 2. *At most one processor is running in control-exit section.*

Using the similar analysis, we can also acquire some observations as follows.

Obseravation 2 (Conservation of *Number*). *processor i is running in trying-control section if and only if exact one of following events happens.*

1. *q_1 contains number(i) exactly once;*
2. *order.queue contains i exactly once;*
3. *there exists exact one processor whose local queue contains i exactly once.*

Obseravation 3. *If order.head $\neq 0$, order is stored in $q_{order.wait[order.head]}$ or one process's local memory. Otherwise, order is stored in q_0 or one process's local memory.*

Obseravation 4. *processor i executes dequeue(q_k) (Line 6) in trying section only if order.wait[i] = k.*

Now, let's consider the property of Mutual Exclusion first.

Theorem 1. *Algorithm DQB satisfies Mutual Exclusion.*

Proof. In the algorithm, critical section is in control-exit section. Therefore, Mutual Exclusion is directed indicated by Lemma 2.

Next, let's discuss the property of No Starvation.

Lemma 3. *If one processor is running in control section, it will get out of control section in a finite time.*

Proof. If one processor stays in control section forever, it must keep repeating the commands in repeat-until paragraph from Line 13 to Line 18. Then we can only consider that processor i is running in control section before passing repeat-until paragraph. Suppose that the current time is t while there are m processors running the algorithm for them. By Observation 2, there are at most m elements of type *number* in q_1 at this time. By Lemma 2, no processor can enter exit section except p_i before p_i ends. Therefore, the *enqueue* command at Line 1 can be executed at most $n - m$ times before p_i gets out of control section, i.e., processor i can get non-empty local element y by *dequeue* operations at most $m + (n - m)$ times before it gets out of control section. Then, in a finite time, processor i will *dequeue* and obtain the element of type *NULL* stored in p_i's local memory y, and pass the until-condition at Line 18. Finally, it will get into critical section and exit section if its local variable *allow* is true, or it will return trying section in the case *allow = false*.

Here, we claim an extended version of Lemma 3, which can be directed demonstrated based on Lemma 3. It is that *if one processor is running in control-exit section, it will leave in a finite time.*

Lemma 4. *If order.head = $i \neq 0$, processor i has been in critical section or will get into critical section in a finite time.*

Proof. Because of the command at Line 26, processor i is impossible to run in exit section. Then we will discuss this lemma in two parts according to the section processor i is running in.

In first part, let's consider the case that p_i is running in control section but has not entered critical section now. processor i's local variable *allow* must be true because there is no operation in control section that can modify the head element in *order.queue*, i.e., *order.head* $= i$ or *order.head* $= 0$ (in the case that processor i inserts i into the empty *order.queue*) when p_i executed the first command (at Line 11) of control section. By Lemma 3, processor i will get out of control section in a finite time. As its local variable *allow* is true, it can pass until-condition at Line 24 and then get into critical section.

In second part, we will discuss the case that p_i is running in trying section at t_0. Let a dynamic set S_t for time t contain all the processors that will execute their next *dequeue* operation at $q_{order.wait[i]}$ (say q^* for short in following analysis). Before p_i gets into critical section, any other processor will enter control section with local variable *allow* = *false*, and will not be able to pass until-condition at Line 24. Therefore, there will be finite times for processors to *enqueue* the elements of type *number* to q^* before p_i gets into critical section. By Observation 2, there are finite elements of type *number* in q^*. According to the similar analysis in Lemma 3, it is impossible for processors to execute *dequeue*(q^*) acquiring an element of type *number* forever. By Observation 3, *order* is placed in q^*. Then, from any time $t \geq t_0$ to the moment p_i enters critical section, there will be a processor $j \in S_{t+\Delta t}$ (Δt represents a finite period of time) acquiring *order* by *dequeue* operation. If $j \neq i$, processor j enters control section with local variable *allow* = *false*. In a finite time, processor j will execute the command at Line 20, which changes *order.wait*$[j]$. Suppose that p_j reaches Line 19 at time t_- and finishes the command at Line 20 at time t_+. The dynamic set S_t updates according to $S_{t_+} \leftarrow S_{t_-} \setminus \{j\}$. As time t goes on, the elements in the dynamic set S_t will be eliminated one by one. According to Observation 4, we guarantee $i \in S_t$ at time t. Therefore, there will be a moment p_i obtains *order*. In extreme case that all the elements except i will be eliminated from S_t as time t goes on, processor i will still acquire *order* in a finite time. Now, we can only consider the case $j = i$ which will happen in a finite time. In this case, processor i will enter control section and then it will critical section in finite time by the proof in first part.

Lemma 5. *From any time on, queues will contain* order *in a finite time.*

Proof. We can only consider the case that queues do not contain *order* now. By Lemma 1, there must be a processor owning *order* in the local memory. According to 1, this processor is currently running in control-exit section. Using the extended version of Lemma 3, this processor will leaves control-exit section together with inserting *order* by *enqueue* operation in a finite time.

Lemma 6. *If* order.queue *contains* i, *processor* i *has been in critical section or will get into critical section in a finite time.*

Proof. Suppose the *order.queue* contains i currently at time t_0. Consider the first time t_1 at or after t_0, when *order* is placed in queues. By Lemma 5, t_1 is bound to be a finite number.

If number i is not in *order.queue* at time t_1, processor i must have entered critical section during the time t_0 to t_1, because the command to delete i from *order.queue* is right down the critical section in algorithm. In fact, this case happens when processor i is running in control-exit section with local variable *allow* = *true* at time t_0. Otherwise, *order.queue* contains number i. Then it will keep non-empty till processor i enters critical section, i.e., *order.head* $\neq 0$ before processor i gets into critical section. Therefore, processor j enters critical section before p_i does only if *order.head* = j. In other words, the next processor to enter critical section is processor *order.head*. By Lemma 4, processor *order.head* will get into critical section in a finite time. Then it will delete the head element of *order.queue* at Line 26. Meanwhile, the rank of number i (i.e., the number of elements prior to i) in *order.queue* will be decreased by 1. Thereby, the rank will be 0 in a finite time. At that time, processor i, the processor indicated in the head element of *order.queue*, will get into critical section finally.

Lemma 7. *If q_1 contains number(i), there is one event of the following two that will happen in a finite time.*

1. *number i is in a certain processor j's local queue tmp_j;*
2. *order.queue contains number i.*

Proof. In the algorithm, the elements of type *number* can be dequeued only at Line 6 or Line 14. If a certain processor j acquires *number* at Line 6, it will store it in its local queue tmp_j. If one processor obtains it at Line 14, it will be inserted to the tail of *order.queue*. Therefore, we should only claim that these two events will happen in a finite time.

Suppose that q_1 contains *number(i)* at time t_0. Pick the first time t_1 at or after t_0 when *order* is placed in queues. By Lemma 5, t_1 is a finite time.

Now consider the case that *number(i)* is still in q_1 at time t_1. If *order.head* = 0 at time t_1, *order* should be contained in q_0 by Observation 3. At this time, there are at least one processor including p_i trying to dequeue at q_0. Therefore, a certain processor j will obtain *order* in a finite time. (We can get this result by the similar proof in second part of Lemma 4. Then processor j will keep executing *dequeue(q_1)* until it obtains an empty reply. This procedure will be finished in a finite time by Lemma 3. Before this procedure ends, one of two events must have happened. In the other case that *order.head* = $j \neq 0$, processor j will get into critical in a finite time by Lemma 4. Before processor j enters critical section, it will get *order* and clear up q_1, before which two events mentioned in this lemma must have happened.

To prove that the algorithm has no starvation property, we should consider such a dynamic graph model. For any time t, we can construct a directed graph $G_t = (V, E_t)$ where $V = \{0, 1, \cdots, n\}$, and where an edge from i to j exists in E_t if and only if one event of the following two happens.

1. tmp_i contains j
2. $i = 0$ and *order.queue* contains j

Lemma 8. *If there is a directed path from 0 to i in G_t, processor i will get into critical section in a finite time after time t.*

Proof. In a specific dynamic graph G_t, we shall prove this lemma using mathematical induction on the length of the directed path.

Clearly, the lemma holds when the length of a directed path is 1, since if there is a directed edge from 0 to i in G_t, i.e., *order.queue* contains i at time t, processor i will enter critical section in a finite time by Lemma 6.

Suppose the lemma holds for the directed path of length k in G_t. That is, if there is a directed path of length k from 0 to i in G_t, processor i will get into critical section in a finite time after time t. Consider the case of the length of directed path being $k + 1$. For any directed path of length $k + 1$ from 0 to i in G_t, there must be an unique node j which has an out-edge pointing to node i in G_t by Observation 2. In the same time, there is a directed path of length k from 0 to j in G_t. By the induction hypothesis, processor j will enter critical section in a finite time after time t. Before that, processor j must execute the command at Line 12 before entering critical section. Therefore, i must be added to *order.queue*. By Lemma 6, processor i will enter critical section in a finite time. Hence, if lemma holds for the directed path of length k, it also holds for the directed path of length $k + 1$.

By the principle of mathematical induction, we conclude that for all natural numbers k, if there is a directed path of length k from 0 to i in G_t, processor i will get into critical section in a finite time after time t.

Lemma 9. *If one node has an in-edge in G_t, there is a directed path from 0 to it.*

Proof. At the beginning time t_0, G_{t_0} is a graph with no edge, while the lemma is apparently correct. Suppose that the lemma is correct from time t_0 to time t_1, let's consider the case in time t_2, which is the atomically-next time of t_1, i.e., there is at most one command executed from t_1 to t_2. In fact, we should only consider the commands at Line 8, 12, 16 and 26, which insert or delete edges on G_{t_1} so that new dynamic graph G_{t_2} is different from G_{t_1}. Among these, the commands at Line 8 and 16 insert in-edges to the nodes without any in-edges. The command at Line 12 connects the nodes, which already have in-edges, with some other in-edges. For the command at Line 26, it makes a node isolated by deleting its in-edge. Now, we will discuss all these commands respectively.

If processor i executes the command at Line 8 during the time t_1 to t_2, we can construct G_{t_2} by inserting an edge from node i to j on G_{t_1} where j is the number indicated in a *number* element in q_1 at time t_1 and node j is isolated node in G_{t_1}. During this time, processor i's local variable k must be 1 because elements of type *number* can only be *dequeued* in q_1. Hence we can imply that processor i obtained at least one *order* before, because only if processor i has ever acquired *order*, can it have the opportunity to make a change on its local variable

k from 0, the initial value of k, to 1. In the algorithm, processor i must clear up q_1 before it enqueues *order*. Before p_i got an empty reply while dequeuing q_1, $number(i)$ must be read by some processor and then be stored in *order.queue* or one process's local queue, i.e., node i must have an in-edge before. As the only command which can make node i connected with no in-edges is the command at Line 26 in exit section and processor i is still running at trying section, it is impossible for it to run that command. Therefore, node i still has an in-edge at G_{t_1}. By the assumption that the lemma is correct in G_{t_1}, there exists a directed path from 0 to i in G_{t_1}. Hence, there must be a directed path 0 to j in G_{t_2}, and so the lemma holds on this case.

Next, let's consider the case that processor i executes the commands at Line 12 and 16. Whatever processors do during the time t_1 to t_2, all the nodes with in-edges to be changed or added in G_{t_1} will be connected to node 0 by in-edges pointing to them from 0 in G_{t_2}. Therefore, the lemma holds on this case too.

Finally, consider the case when one processor executes the command at Line 26 which deletes number i from *order.queue*. After executing this command, a directed edge from 0 to i is deleted from G_{t_1} and node i will become the node without any in-edge in G_{t_2}. In fact, node i will be isolated in G_{t_2} because processor i must execute the command at Line 12 before entering critical section, which deleted all the out-edges from node i. Therefore, this command makes no influence on other nodes in G_{t_2}, i.e., the lemma also holds on this case.

Theorem 2. *Algorithm DQB satisfies no starvation property.*

Proof. For any processor i which wants to get into critical section, it should enqueue an element of type *number* which contains the value of i to q_1. By Lemma 7, number i will be contained either in one process's local queue or *order.queue* in a finite time. At this moment t, there is an in-edge for node i on the dynamic graph G_t. By Lemma 9, there is a directed path from 0 to i on G_t. According to Lemma 8, processor i will get into critical section in a finite time after time t. Therefore, Algorithm DQB satisfies no starvation property.

3   Algorithm with One Queue

In this section, we show a protocol which implements a mutual exclusion system for two processors with one single queue. We first specify the data format for elements in the queue, together with the initial value of the queue. Then we describe the proposed protocol in pseudo-code in Algorithm 2. Due to the length limit, we leave the correctness proof to the online version.

3.1   Data Format and Initial Value

Every element in the queue is a record with several fields. The first field is *type*, whose value is either OFFER or APPLY, identifying the type of the record.

If the type is OFFER, meaning that it is an invitation for some processor (or both) to enter the critical section, then the second field will be *name* (whose value is 1, 2 or ALL), indicating the processor to which the offer will give. The third field is *id*, which starts from 1 and goes larger, making the offer unique, (in fact, its concrete meaning in our algorithm is that after accepting that offer, it will be the *id*-th time for these two processors to use the resource), so that we can use this information to discern overdue offers. If *name* is not equal to ALL, there will be a fourth field *version* (a natural number, and in the following algorithm it will always be 1 or 2), which serves for identifying different versions of the same information (i.e. records with the same type, name and id), and in the following algorithm, you will find the use of the *version* field to convince one processor that its command (APPLY or OFFER) has been successfully received by the other, which is one crucial technique for our success.

If the type is APPLY, meaning that it is the application of a processor for using the resource (i.e., for entering the critical section), there will be two more fields, *name* (the one who applies) and *version* (the same meaning as above)

We will write the record as

$$(type, name[[, id], version]).$$

And if we *dequeue* when the queue is empty, we will get EMPTY as return.

At the beginning, the only element in the queue is (OFFER,ALL,1).

3.2   The Protocol

We give the proposed protocol in Algorithm 2. Because of the length of the protocol, we list the types and initial values of the variables used in the protocol here. Variable i is either 1 or 2, indicating the processor number. We use i' to represent $3 - i$, i.e. the other process, in a concise way. Variable j is a temporary variable for version number. Temporary variable t will be used for storing one record dequeued from the queue. The initial value of the temporary Boolean variable $flag$ is 0. It serves for deciding whether processor i should give offer to i' after finishing the critical section. Variable $m1, m2$ are also temporary ones storing version numbers, whose initial values are 2. *idmaker* is a persistent variable (its value will remain after exit), whose initial value is 0. It stores the maximum *id* value among all the offers known by processor i. *eaten* is a temporary variable for counting the number of applies of the other that are received by processor i, and its initial value is 0.

3.3   Explanations

The protocol consists of 3 parts, trying section (Line 1 to Line 16), critical section (Line 17) and exit section (Line 18 to Line 51).

a) The trying section contains two parts. In the first part (Line 1 to Line 3), processor i enqueues two coupled applies for itself (the first is of *version* 1 and the second is of *version* 2). The second part (Line 4 to Line 16) is an endless loop. It will jump out of the loop whenever it can enter critical section. For each loop, it firstly dequeues an element (Line 5), and then make decisions based on the dequeued element t.

Algorithm 2. Algorithm SQ2 for processor i ($i = 1$ or 2)

```
1:  for j = 1 to 2 do                                    ▷ trying section starts
2:      enqueue(APPLY, i, j)
3:  end for
4:  repeat
5:      t ← dequeue()                    ▷ "*" means ignoring the field when comparing
6:      if t = (APPLY, i', *) then            ▷ i' refers to 3 − i, i.e., the other processor
7:          flag = 1
8:      else if t = (APPLY, i, *) then
9:          if m1 ≠ t.version then
10:             m1 ← t.version
11:             enqueue(t)
12:         end if
13:     else if t.type = OFFER and (t.name = ALL or t.name = i) and t.id ≥ idmaker
    then
14:             break()
15:     end if
16: until false                                          ▷ trying section ends
17: Critical Section                                     ▷ critical section
18: idmaker = t.id + 1                                   ▷ exit section starts
19: if t.name = i then
20:     flag = 0
21: end if
22: repeat
23:     t = dequeue()
24:     if t = (APPLY, i', *) then
25:         flag ← 1
26:     end if
27: until t = EMPTY
28: if !flag then
29:     enqueue(OFFER, ALL, idmaker)
30: else
31:     for j = 1 to 2 do
32:         enqueue(OFFER, i', j, idmaker)
33:     end for
34:     repeat
35:         t ← dequeue()
36:         if t = (OFFER, i', *, *) then
37:             if t.version = m2 then
38:                 exit()
39:             end if
40:             m2 ← t.version
41:             enqueue(t)
42:         else if t = (OFFER, ALL, *) then
43:             enqueue(t)
44:             exit()
45:         else if t = (APPLY, i', *) and eaten < 2 then
46:             eaten ← eaten + 1
47:         else
48:             exit()
49:         end if
50:     until false
51: end if                                               ▷ exit section ends
```

Case 1 (Line 6): $t.type = $ APPLY and $t.name = i'$, meaning that this is the other's apply. The processor will simply assign $flag$ to 1 (Line 7), marking the fact that the other is also applying.

Case 2 (Line 8): $t.type = $ APPLY and $t.name = i$, meaning that this is its own apply. The processor will make decisions based on $t.version$ (Line 9). If $t.version = m1$, the processor will do nothing because in that case, it knows the same apply with a different $version$ number is received by the other processor. Otherwise, the processor updates $m1$ as $t.version$ (Line 10), and then enqueues t back (Line 11).

Case 3: $t.type = $ OFFER, meaning that this is an offer. If the offer is for processor i or both, and the offer is not overdue (Line 13), the processor will jump out of the loop (Line 14) to finish the trying section. Otherwise, it will do nothing.

Case 4: $t = EMPTY$. Do nothing.

b) After finishing trying section, The processor enters into critical section, where it will stay for finite time and then go to exit section.

c) The exit section is more complicated. It can be divided into two phases: Clear-up Phase (Line 18 to Line 27) and Release-offer Phase (Line 28 to Line 51).

i) In Clear-up Phase, the processor will clear up the queue, and update some local variables. On Line 18, processor i updates its $idmaker$ according to the offer, which will become the id number of the offer it soon releases. If the offer comes from the other, i.e., $t.name = i$, the processor will clear $flag$ (Line 19 to Line 21), because the applies sent by the other processor before in fact meaningless, since processor i' is able to give offer to processor i. Then processor i enters a loop (Line 22 to Line 27), dequeuing until it reads the EMPTY symbol. Meanwhile, it keeps track on whether there are applies from the other processor. If so, it will assign 1 to $flag$.

ii) In Release-offer Phase, the processor will release an offer whose name depends on $flag$ (Line 28), i.e., whether the other processor has been applied before. If the other has not applied, the processor simply enqueues an offer for all whose id is $idmaker$ (Line 29), and then exits. Otherwise, the processor will give offer to the other (Run Line 31 to Line 50). It will enqueue two coupled offers to processor i' (Line 31 to Line 33). From Line 34 to Line 50, processor i execute an endless loop until it can make sure that processor i' really receives the offer. For each loop, processor i will dequeue one element first (Line 35). And then its decision will depend on that element. We discuss it in several cases as follows.

Case 1 (Line 36): t is an offer for processor i'. In this case, if the version of the offer is the same with $m2$ (Line 37), then processor i will exit (Line 38) because it will be convinced that processor i' has already received the offer. Otherwise, it will update $m2$ (Line 40), and dequeue t back (Line 41).

Case 2 (Line 42): t is an offer for all. In this case, t is produced by processor i' after critical section. processor i will enqueue t back (Line 43), and exit (Line 44).

Case 3 (Line 45): t is an apply of i'. If processor i has read such apply for more than 2 times before, it will exit. Otherwise, it will increase *eaten* by 1, which is the number of times processor i has read $(APPLY, i', *)$.

Case 4: $t = EMPTY$. processor i will exit. Notice that it is impossible that $t.name = i$ in this loop.

4   Conclusion

In this paper, we investigate the classical mutual exclusion problem in a new setting, by which communication is made through shared queues. Without the *peek* operation, the protocol becomes quite hard to design since every processor has to modify the shared objects in order to make contact with others. We propose two novel algorithms for the problem. The designing ideas of both algorithms give new insights for the mutual exclusion problem, as well as the usage of the shared queue objects in the distributed computing setting. We leave the question of finding a protocol or proving impossibility results for more than 2 processors using one single shared queue as our further research work.

Acknowledgments. We would like to thank Wei Chen for telling us the open question concerned here. We also would like to thank Danny Dolev, Wei Chen and Lingqing Ai for helpful discussions.

References

1. Dijkstra, E.W.: Solution of a problem in concurrent programming control. CACM 8(9), 569 (1965)
2. Lamport, L.: A new solution of Dijkstra's concurrent programming problem. CACM 17(8), 453–455 (1974)
3. Raynal, M.: Algorithms for mutual exclusion (1986)
4. Herlihy, M.: Wait-free synchronization. ACM Transactions on Programming Languages and Systems (TOPLAS) 13(1), 124–149 (1991)

On the Signaling Problem*

Gal Amram

Ben Gurion University of the Negev, Beer-Sheva, Israel
galamra@cs.bgu.ac.il

Abstract. Aguilera et al. introduced and solved the mailbox problem in [4], and used their mailbox algorithm to provide an efficient solution to the N-buffer problem. In the same paper, they also pointed out that both the mailbox problem and the N-buffer problem are solved by means of a more general problem: the signaling problem. The authors of [4] presented a non-blocking solution to the signaling problem, and asked whether a wait-free solution to the signaling problem exists. In our paper, we provide a positive answer to this question by introducing a bounded wait-free signaling algorithm and proving its correctness. In addition, our algorithm is more efficient than the one presented in [4] since it uses flags of smaller size. Furthermore, by using our algorithm, we provide a wait-free solution to the N-buffer problem which is more efficient than the one in [4].

Keywords: distributed algorithms, shared memory, synchronization, linearizability.

1 Introduction

The signaling problem is a theoretical synchronization problem that has been introduced by Aguilera, Gafni and Lamport in [4] (see also [3]). The problem involves two processes, named p_0 and p_1, and a computable function

$$F : Vals \times Vals \longrightarrow D,$$

where $Vals$ is possibly an infinite set and D is a finite set. Occasionally, p_0 writes to register V_0 and p_1 writes to register V_1, values from the set $Vals$. In addition, from time to time, the processes are required to compute the value of $F(V_0, V_1)$. However, for the purpose of efficiency, for the computation of $F(V_0, V_1)$, the processes are allowed to access only bounded registers (that is, registers that may store a finite number of values).

Aguilera et al. motivated the signaling problem, by pointing that a wait-free solution to the signaling problem provides a wait-free solution to a natural producer/consumer problem: the N-buffer problem [4]. This producer/consumer problem consists of a producer process, p_0, which puts messages into a buffer and a consumer process, p_1, which removes these messages. We assume that the buffer can hold at most N messages where $N \geq 1$. The two processes must be synchronized so that the producer does not try to

---

* Research partially supported by the Frankel Center for Computer Science at Ben-Gurion University.

M. Chatterjee et al. (Eds.): ICDCN 2014, LNCS 8314, pp. 44–65, 2014.

put a message into a full buffer, and the consumer does not try to remove a message from an empty buffer. The problem is to provide a wait-free algorithm for the producer/consumer problem which implements three operations:

1. check, which determines whether the buffer is empty, full or neither empty nor full.
2. add a message, which is executed only on non-full buffers.
3. remove a message, which is executed only on non-empty buffers.

In addition, we require that the registers accessed by check operations are bounded.

A solution to the signaling problem provides an easy solution to this bounded buffer producer/consumer problem. V_0 records the number of messages added, and V_1 records the number of messages removed. In a check operation, the processes compute the value of the function F, defined by:

$$F(V_0, V_1) = \begin{cases} full, & \text{if } V_0 - V_1 = N \\ neither\text{-}full\text{-}nor\text{-}empty, & \text{if } 0 < V_0 - V_1 < N \\ empty, & \text{if } V_0 - V_1 = 0 \end{cases}.$$

The mailbox problem is a variant of the N-buffer problem in which $N = \infty$ (the buffer is of unbounded size), and hence only the consumer is required to perform check operations. In similar to the N-buffer problem, a solution to the signaling problem provides a solution to this problem. V_0 records the number of messages added, V_1 records the number of messages removed and in a check operation, the consumer computes the value of the function F, defined by:

$$F(V_0, V_1) = \begin{cases} not\ empty, & \text{if } 0 < V_0 - V_1 \\ empty, & \text{if } V_0 - V_1 = 0 \end{cases}.$$

In both the mailbox problem and the N-buffer problem (as described in [4]), a check operation is allowed to access only bounded registers. The authors of [4] adopted this restriction for the purpose of efficiency, as the check operations are assumed to be invoked more often. Of course, for generalizing the mailbox and the N-buffer problem (in the way described above), the signaling problem inherits this restriction and the compute operations are not allowed to access bounded registers. Furthermore, from a theoretical point of view, we find this problem fascinating. Interestingly, without this restriction the signaling problem is easily solved by using 2-reader 2-writer atomic snapshot (for examples see [2] or [5]), and when the discussed restriction is assumed, the problem is, for the least, not trivial.

Now we describe the signaling problem in a more precise manner. Assume that p_0 and p_1 are two serial processes that communicate through shared memory, and share two registers, V_0 and V_1. Each process repeatedly executes a set(v) procedure with arbitrary values $v \in Vals$, or a compute procedure which returns a value in D. While executing a set(v) procedure, a process p_i ($i \in \{0, 1\}$) sets the value of V_i to v. An invocation of a compute procedure returns the value of $F(V_0, V_1)$. The problem is to implement these two procedures, set(v) and compute, such that:

1. The procedures are wait-free. i.e. any execution of a procedure by a process p_i eventually returns, provided that p_i keep taking steps, regardless of the behavior of p_{1-i}.

2. Only read/write registers are used.
3. During an execution of a compute procedure, only bounded registers are accessed.

The safety condition is defined first for a sequential execution, that is, an execution in which two procedure executions never overlap. This sequential specification is described in Figure 1. The correctness condition is the *linearizability condition* that has been formulated by Herlihy and Wing in [6]. We say that a procedure execution A precedes a procedure execution B, if A ends before B begins, this ordering is a partial ordering. The correctness condition is the requirement that any execution is linearizable i.e. there is an extension of the precedence partial order $<$, into a linear ordering $\prec$, such that the sequential specification is satisfied.

---

1. The procedure executions are partitioned into set(v) and compute operations, and are totally ordered by $\prec$ in the order-type of the natural numbers (if the number of operations is infinite). Two initial set operations by p_0 and p_1 are assumed, which write initial values to V_0 and V_1.
2. For any compute event C, if S_0 is the $\prec$-maximal set operation executed by p_0 such that $S_0 \prec C$, and S_1 is the $\prec$-maximal set operation executed by p_1 such that $S_1 \prec C$, and if in addition S_0 is of the form set(v_0) and S_1 is of the form set(v_1), then C returns $F(v_0, v_1)$.

Fig. 1. The signaling sequential specification

The authors of [4] presented a non-blocking solution to the signaling problem and asked if a wait-free solution exists. In this paper we answer affirmatively to this question by presenting a wait-free signaling algorithm. In a joint work with Uri Abraham [1], some of the ideas behind the algorithm presented here were used to design a mailbox algorithm with flags of smaller size than the one in [4]. The code for the set procedure is based on the code of a remove procedure in [1]. On the other hand, for designing the code for the compute procedure, new ideas were needed. The main difference between these two problems, the mailbox problem and the signaling problem, is that in the first only one process (the homeowner) may call a check operation, while in the second, both processes can invoke a compute procedure. Thus, radical changes and novel ideas were needed for designing the code for a compute procedure.

The rest of the paper is organized as follows, in Section 2 we present our algorithm and provide a detailed explanation of the ideas behind the algorithm and present some examples for execution patterns. We prove the correctness of our algorithm in Section 3 and conclusions are given in Section 4.

2   The Algorithm

In this section we present our algorithm (in Figure 2). Each process p_i ($i \in \{0,1\}$) can write into its register V_i, which carries values from the set $Vals$. In addition, p_i can write into two bounded registers T_i and B_i (these are the "flag" registers of p_i). All the registers are single-writer atomic read/write registers.

- T_i is a boolean register and initially $T_i = 0$.
- B_i is a register with two fields, $B_i = (B_i.color, B_i.val)$, where $B_i.val$ carries values from D, and $B_i.color$ is a boolean field (initially, $B_i = (0, d)$, where d is some initial value from the set D). Thus, B_i carries values from the set $\{0, 1\} \times D$.

The initial values of V_0 and V_1 are v' and v'' respectively, where $F(v', v'') = d$ (d is the initial value of $B_0.val$ and $B_1.val$). The local variables of each process are t, val and b.

set(v)	set(v)
1. $V_0 := v$; 2. $t := T_1$; 3. $T_0 := t$; 4. $val := V_1$; 5. $B_0 := (t, F(v, val))$;	1. $V_1 := v$; 2. $t := T_0$; 3. $T_1 := 1 - t$; 4. $val := V_0$; 5. $B_1 := (1 - t, F(val, v))$;
compute	compute

1. $t := T_1$;
2. $b := B_1$;
3. if $(t \neq T_0) \wedge (b.color = t)$
   return $(b.val)$;
4. return $B_0.val$;
	1. $t := T_0$;
	2. $b := B_0$;
	3. if $(t = T_1) \wedge (b.color = t)$
	   return $(b.val)$;
	4. return $B_1.val$;

Fig. 2. p_0's set and compute procedures (on the left), and p_1's set and compute procedures (on the right)

In a system execution, the processes repeatedly execute compute and set(v) procedures, where v is an arbitrary value from $Vals$. Formally, a system execution is the corresponding infinite sequence of atomic actions (see [8] for futher discussion). The atomic actions (also named actions or low level events) in a system execution are totally ordered by the relation $<$, where $a < b$ means that a ends before b begins. We identify a procedure execution (also named operation or a high-level event [8]) with the corresponding set of low level events. Thus, for every action e, there is a unique operation, E, such that $e \in E$. In this case we write $E = [e]$. For two operations E_1 and E_2, we write $E_1 < E_2$ if every action in E_1 precedes every action in E_2. In the same way, we say that $E < e$ for a high level event E and a low level event e, if any action $e' \in E$ precedes e. The notation $e < E$ is defined analogously. If $\neg(E_1 < E_2)$ and $\neg(E_2 < E_1)$, then E_1 and E_2 are said to be concurrent.

If E is a compute event or a set event, executed by p_i, we may say that E is a p_i-compute event, or a p_i-set event. If S is a set event of the form set(v), we say that $val(S) = v$, and for a compute event C, we write $val(C) = d$ if the operation C returns $d \in D$. For convenience, we assume that there are initial set events I_0 and I_1, executed by p_0 and p_1 respectively. In those events, the processes write the initial values into the registers. I_0 and I_1 are concurrent and precede any other operation. In addition, $val(I_0) = v'$ and $val(I_1) = v''$, which are the initial values of V_0 and V_1 respectively.

Let $\prec$ be an extension of the relation $<$ defined on the high level events into a total order, and let C be a **compute** event. For $i \in \{0, 1\}$, we use $pre_i(C)$ to denote the maximal p_i-**set** event that precedes C in $\prec$. One can verify that if $\prec$ is an extension of $<$ into a total order, then $\prec$ has the order type of $\mathbb{N}$. Thus, since we assume initial **set** events, if C is a **compute** operation, then there is a maximal p_i-**set** event that precedes C, and hence $pre_i(C)$ is well defined.

It is obvious that the algorithm satisfies the following two conditions

1. The algorithm is bounded wait-free i.e. for some constant N, each procedure execution returns after at most N steps.
2. During an execution of a **compute** procedure, only bounded registers are accessed.

Thus, the main requirement that we need to prove is that each execution is linearizable:

3. In any system execution the precedence relation $<$ defined on the high level events can be extended into a total order $\prec$, such that the sequential specification (Figure 1) is satisfied.

We shall prove,

Theorem 1. *Any system execution is linearizable, that is, there is an extension of $<$ into a total order $\prec$, such that for any* **compute** *event C, $val(C) = F(val(pre_0(C)), val(pre_1(C)))$.*

2.1   Some of the Ideas behind the Algorithm and Examples of Executions

According to the problem's limitations, the processes are not allowed to access registers V_0 or V_1 during an execution of a **compute** procedure, because these are unbounded registers. However, a process should eventually return $F(V_0, V_1)$ at the end of a **compute** execution, which should be a value that corresponds to the sequential specification. The way we overcome this problem is by reading the values of V_0 and V_1 during a **set** event and storing the outcome in the field $B_i.val$ of register B_i (where p_i is the process that executes the **set** procedure). As the range of F is finite, B_0 and B_1 are bounded and the processes may access these registers during an execution of a **compute** procedure. Therefore, instead of reading registers V_0 and V_1, a process p_i only reads the bounded registers B_0 and B_1, and it has to decide which value is more up-to-date, the one stored in $B_i.val$ or perhaps the value found in $B_{1-i}.val$? The shared registers T_0 and T_1 in addition to the fields $B_0.color$ and $B_1.color$ are used for achieving this goal, namely for estimating which value is more up-to-date among $\{B_0.val, B_1.val\}$. In order to explain the way our algorithm achieve this we describe several examples of executions and explain the ideas behind the instructions and their ordering.

The first example we consider is one in which the procedure executions do not over-lap. This example shows that a process p_i "makes the right choice" during a compute event C, and returns the value that has been written to $B_j.val$ during the last set event that precedes C.

Example 1. Consider an execution in which high level events do not overlap. Assume that C is a p_0-compute event and the last set event that precedes C, S, is a p_j-set event. If $j = 1$, then during the execution of S, p_1 writes to T_1 the opposite value than the one it read from T_0 (lines 2 and 3), and writes the value it wrote to T_1 into $B_1.color$ (line 5). Thus, during the execution of C, p_0 finds that condition $(t \neq T_0) \wedge (b.color = t)$ holds and returns the value stored in $B_1.val$, i.e. the value that has been written to $B_1.val$ in S. Now, if S is a p_0-set event (i.e. j=i), then during the execution of S, p_0 writes to T_0 the value it read from T_1 (line 2 and 3). Therefore, in C, p_0 finds that condition $(t \neq T_0) \wedge (b.color = t)$ (line 3) does not hold and returns the value stored in $B_0.val$

Example 1 describes the importance of registers T_0 and T_1. These registers are used by the processes to estimate which value is more up-to-date among $B_0.val$ and $B_1.val$. When p_0 executes a set procedure it compares the value of T_0 to the one it reads from T_1, and when p_1 executes a set operation it reads the value stored in T_0 and writes the opposite value to T_1. Thus, if the values in T_0 and T_1 are identical, it suggests that p_0 is the more updated process, and inequality between these registers suggest the exact opposite. This simple and nice idea was used in the classical work of Tromp [9]. However, when process p_0 (for example) executes a compute event and finds that the values of T_0 and T_1 are different, it still cannot conclude that the value stored in B_1 is more up-to-date. Thus, the process performs an additional test and checks if the value stored in $B_1.color$ (line 2) is identical to the value it read from T_1 (line 3). The importance of this additional check is reflected by our next example and its illustration in Figure 3.

Example 2. Assume that process p_1 executes a set event and sets the values of T_1 and $B_1.color$ to 1. Then, p_0 executes a set operation in which it compares the values of T_0 and $B_0.color$ to the value it read from T_1 (namely, 1). Now, p_1 starts executing a set procedure, executes lines 1-4 in which it changes the value of T_1 to 0 (the opposite value than the one it read from T_0), and then stops. At this point, p_0 become active again and executes a compute operation. During the execution of this compute event, p_0 reads from register T_1 (line 2) a different value than the one stored in T_0. However, since p_1 has not completed its set event, the value of $B_1.val$ is outdated, and p_0 should not return this value. Indeed, while executing line 3, p_0 finds that the value stored in $B_1.color$ (line 1) is 1, that is, the value that has been written to $B_1.color$ in the first p_1-set event. As this value is different from the one it read from T_1 (line 2), p_0 returns the value stored in $B_0.val$ (line 4).

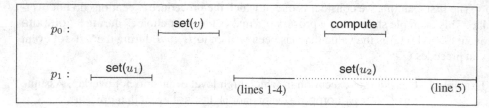

Fig. 3. Example 2

Example 2 demonstrates the purpose of the field $B_i.color$. When a process p_i executes a compute procedure and finds that the condition in line 3 holds, it concludes that p_{1-i} has succeeded to execute lines 2-5 in some recent set event, and the value that p_{1-i} wrote to $B_i.val$ is up-to-date.

The explanations given above clarify the ideas behind the code specified in Figure 2, but this intuitive explanations should not be considered as "informal" proof for correctness. Some ideas such as "if $T_0 \neq T_1$, then p_1 was the last to write to one of these registers" or "if $T_0 = B_0.color$, then p_0 has completed its last set event" may sound almost trivial at first, but unfortunately they are both false. Therefore, the rigorous proof we provide in Section 3 is crucial and the reader should not be satisfied with these explanations alone. To illustrate the evasive nature of the problem we mention that swapping lines 1 and 2 in the code of a compute event, results in an incorrect code. Example 3 and Figure 4 present an incorrect execution in case that we do the discussed change in the code (swapping lines 1 and 2 in the code for a compute procedure). The reason that this changes harm the correctness is that now, a process p_i is allowed to read values from registers T_1 and B_1, in the order opposite to the order they were written by p_{1-i}.

Example 3 Assume that p_0 executes a set(v_1) operation, p_1 executes a set(u_1) operation, and then p_0 executes a set(v_2) operation (this operations are not concurrent). Now, p_0 starts executing a compute procedure C, read the value of B_1 and stops. Now p_1 become active again and executes a set(u_2). From this point, p_0 completes the compute procedure C in a solo run. Since p_1 has updated register T_1 during its last set event, p_0 finds that the condition in line 3 holds and returns the value it read from B_1, which is $F(v_1, u_1)$. However, since the last p_0-set event that precedes C has been invoked with value v_2, this execution is not linearizable.

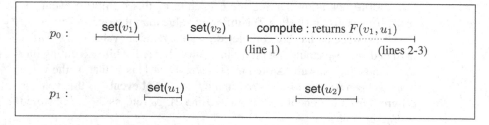

Fig. 4. Example 3

3 Correctness

In this section we prove theorem 1. We fix a system execution and we aim to prove that there is an extension of the relation $<$ which defined on the set of all high level events, into a total order $\prec$, such that the conditions of the sequential specification (Figure 1) hold. One of the standard approaches to prove linearizability is to identify a high level event with its linearization point. However, just like the queue algorithm in [6], our algorithm does not admit fixed linearization points, so it may be very difficult to prove linearizability by identifying a high level event with a specific low level events. Thus, in order prove correctness we put our efforts in extending $<$ into a linear ordering that satisfies the conditions of the sequential specification. The idea is to extend $<$ into a partial order $<^*$ in such a way, that each extension of $<^*$ into a total ordering $\prec$ satisfies the requirements of the sequential specification. For any pair of concurrent operations E, E' such that one of them is a compute event and the other is a set event, relation $<^*$ determines if $E <^* E'$ or $E' <^* E$. Moreover, $<^*$ will be a strict partial ordering, that is, an irreflexive and transitive relation. In order to achieve our goal, the following definition is important.

Definition 1. *Let C be a compute event. If C returns after executing the command in line 3, we say that C is external, and otherwise, C is said to be internal.*

If E is a p_i-operation (compute or set event), p_i performs in E several writes to the shared memory (possibly none), and several reads from the shared memory. We use the notation $write(E, r)$ to denote the write into register r in E (if such a low-level event exists), and the notation $read(E, r)$ to denote the read from register r in E (if such an event exists). For example, assume that S is a p_0-set event, then $read(S, T_1)$ is the read from the register T_1, i.e. the execution of line 2 in the procedure set(v). We may observe that in our algorithm, if r is a shared register and E an operation, then there is at most single write on r and at most single read from r in E. Thus, the terms $read(E, r)$ and $write(E, r)$ are well defined.

The value of a read/write event e, is denoted by $val(e)$. Furthermore, any read event $e = read(E, r)$ is preceded by a write event $e' = write(E', r)$, such that e' is the latest write into r that satisfies $e' < e$. Therefore, the process that executes e reads the value that has been written into r in the action e' (and hence, $val(e) = val(e')$). According to this observation, we define a function

$$\omega : \text{read actions} \longrightarrow \text{write actions},$$

by $\omega(e) = e'$.

If S is a p_i-set event that is not the initial set event, then we define:

$$\rho(S) = [\omega(read(S, V_{1-i}))].$$

That is, $\rho(S)$ is the p_{1-i}-set event in which p_{1-i} wrote to V_{1-i} the value that has been read by p_i in S (recall that for a low level event e, $[e]$ denotes the unique high level event E so that $e \in E$). In addition, for the initial set events, I_0 and I_1, we define

$$\rho(I_i) = I_{1-i}.$$

The following lemma emphasizes the importance of the function ρ for our proof.

Lemma 1. *If S is a p_0-set event, then p_0 writes in S to $B_0.val$ the value: $F(val(S),$ $val(\rho(S)))$. In addition, if S is a p_1-set event, then p_1 writes in S to $B_1.val$ the value: $F(val(\rho(S)), val(S))$*

Proof. By the symmetry of the algorithm it suffices to prove the lemma in case that S is a p_0-*set* event. If S is the initial p_0-set event I_0, then $\rho(S) = I_1$. By examining the initial values of the shared registers, we see that p_0 writes into $B_0.val$ the value $d = F(v', v'') = F(val(I_0), val(I_1)) = F(val(S), val(\rho(S)))$ as required.

It is left to deal with the case that $S \neq I_0$. In this case $\rho(S) = [\omega(read(S, V_1))] = S'$. Write $val(S) = v$ and $val(S') = v'$. Thus, $v' = val(write(S', V_1)) = val(read(S, V_1))$, i.e. v' is the value that p_0 reads from register V_1 in S. According to line 5 in the code of a set procedure, p_0 writes into $B_0.val$ the value $F(v, v') = F(val(S), val(S')) = F(val(S), val(\rho(S)))$ as required. □

Let C be a p_i-compute event. Thus, there is a last p_i-set event that precedes C. We denote this *set* event by $pre(C)$ (not to be confused with $pre_0(C)$ and $pre_1(C)$ which are defined only for an extension of $<$ into a total order).

For a compute event C, there are some set events S^0 and S^1, executed by p_0 and p_1 respectively, such that C returns $F(val(S^0), val(S^1))$. We denote these set events by $\alpha(C)$ and $\beta(C)$. The formal definition of $\alpha(C)$ and $\beta(C)$ is as follows.

Definition 2. *Let C be a p_0-compute event. If C is external, we define*

$$\beta(C) = [\omega(read(C, B_1))] \text{ and } \alpha(C) = \rho(\beta(C)),$$

and if C is internal

$$\alpha(C) = pre(C) \text{ and } \beta(C) = \rho(\alpha(C)).$$

For a p_1-compute event C, we define $\alpha(C)$ and $\beta(C)$ analogously: if C is external, then

$$\alpha(C) = [\omega(read(C, B_0))] \text{ and } \beta(C) = \rho(\alpha(C)),$$

and if C is internal

$$\beta(C) = pre(C) \text{ and } \alpha(C) = \rho(\alpha(C)).$$

Thus, α and β are functions so that

$$\alpha : \text{compute events} \longrightarrow p_0\text{-set events},$$

$$\beta : \text{compute events} \longrightarrow p_1\text{-set events}.$$

At this point we remind our strategy. We aim to extend the precedence partial order, $<$, defined on the high level events into a partial order $<^*$. We aim to do so, such that each linear extension $\prec$ of $<^*$, satisfies the requirements of theorem 1. As we shall see, it suffices to construct $<^*$ such that, if $\prec$ is a total order that extends $<^*$ and C is a compute event, then $\alpha(C) = pre_0(C)$ and $\beta(C) = pre_1(C)$. First we shall prove two simple lemmas. These lemmas are merely stating that the definitions of the functions α and β are reasonable for achieving this goal.

Lemma 2. *For any* compute *event C, C returns $F(val(\alpha(C)), val(\beta(C)))$.*

Proof. Since our algorithm is symmetric, it suffices to prove the lemma in case that C is a p_0-compute event. There are two possible cases:

Case 1. C is external. In this case C returns the value that has been written into $B_1.val$ in the event $[\omega(read(C, B_1))] = \beta(C)$. By definition, $\alpha(C) = \rho(\beta(C))$ and by lemma 1, p_1 writes to $B_1.val$ the value $F(val(\rho(\beta(C))), val(\beta(C))) = F(val(\alpha(C)), val(\beta(C)))$ as required.

Case 2. C is internal. In this case C returns the value that has been written into $B_0.val$ in the p_0-set event, $pre(C)$. By definition $pre(C) = \alpha(C)$ and $\beta(C) = \rho(\alpha(C))$. By lemma 1, p_0 writes in $\alpha(C)$ into $B_0.val$ the value $F(val(\alpha(C)), val(\rho(\alpha(C)))) = F(val(\alpha(C)), val(\beta(C)))$ as required.

$\square$

Lemma 3. *For any* compute *event C, $\neg(C < \alpha(C))$ and $\neg(C < \beta(C))$.*

Proof. We prove the lemma in case that C is a p_0-compute event, and by the symmetry of the algorithm, we conclude that the lemma holds for a p_1-compute event as well. Let C be a p_0-compute event and note that if $\alpha(C) = I_0$, then $\alpha(C) < C$ and if $\beta(C) = I_1$, then $\beta(C) < C$. Therefore, we may also assume that $\alpha(C)$ and $\beta(C)$ are not the initial *set* events. There are two possible cases:

Case 1. C is external. In this case $\beta(C) = [\omega(read(C, B_1))]$. Thus, $write(\beta(C), B_1) < read(C, B_1)$ and hence, $\neg(C < \beta(C))$. In addition, $\alpha(C) = \rho(\beta(C))$ and hence (by definition of ρ), $write(\alpha(C), V_0) < read(\beta(C), V_0)$. By the code of the algorithm (and since $\beta(C) \neq I_1$), $read(\beta(C), V_0) < write(\beta(C), B_1)$. Therefore, since $write(\beta(C), B_1) < read(C, B_1)$ and by the transitivity of $<$, we conclude that $write(\alpha(C), V_0) < read(C, B_1)$ and hence, $\neg(C < \alpha(C))$ as required.

Case 2. C is internal. In this case $\alpha(C) = pre(C)$ and hence $\alpha(C) < C$ (which implies that $\neg(C < \alpha(C))$). Furthermore, $\beta(C) = [\omega(read(\alpha(C), V_1))]$ and hence, $write(\beta(C), V_1) < read(\alpha(C), V_1)$. By transitivity of $<$ we conclude that $write(\beta(C), V_1) < C$ and hence, $\neg(C < \beta(C))$.

$\square$

Now the strategy for defining $<^*$ should be clear: for a p_0-*compute* event C and a p_1-*set* event S, we should decide that $S <^* C$ if $S \leq \beta(C)$, and otherwise we decide $C <^* S$. The definition of $<^*$ for a p_1-*compute* event, and a p_0-*set* event is similar (the formal definition will be given later). The reason to define $<^*$ in such a way is the fact mentioned earlier, i.e. that each extension of $<^*$ into a total order will satisfy the requirement of Theorem 1, namely that each compute event C returns $F(val(pre_0(C)), val(pre_1(C)))$. However, unfortunately, Lemmas 2 and 3 still do not suffice to prove Theorem 1. The reason is that although any extension of $<^*$ will satisfy the requirements, it is not clear if there are any linear extensions of $<^*$ that extend $<$ as well. To illustrate that Lemmas 2 and 3 do not suffice for proving linearizability we consider the following examples (Figure 5).

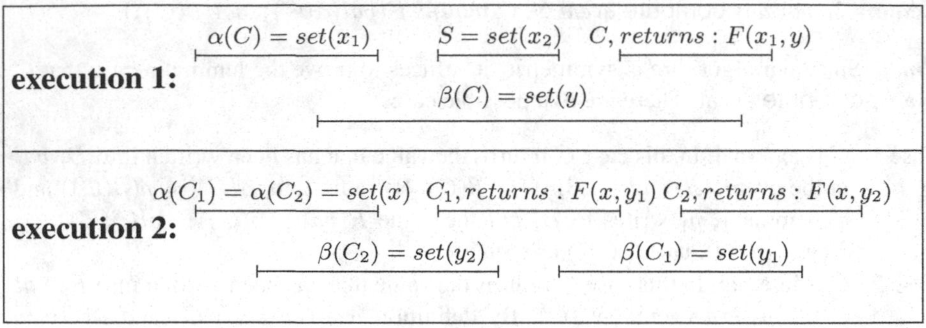

$$\alpha(C) = set(x_1) \qquad S = set(x_2) \quad C, returns : F(x_1, y)$$

execution 1:
$$\beta(C) = set(y)$$

$$\alpha(C_1) = \alpha(C_2) = set(x) \quad C_1, returns : F(x, y_1) \; C_2, returns : F(x, y_2)$$

execution 2:
$$\beta(C_2) = set(y_2) \qquad\qquad \beta(C_1) = set(y_1)$$

Fig. 5. Not linearizable executions

In execution 1, each extension $\prec$ of $<$ must satisfy $\alpha(C) \prec S \prec C$. But C returns $F(val(\alpha(C)), val(\beta(C)))$ and not $F(val(S), val(\beta(C)))$. Hence, $<$ cannot be extended to a linear order that satisfies the sequential specification in this particular example. Execution 2 is more complicated. In this execution, a linear extension $\prec$ of $<$ must satisfy $\beta(C_1) \prec C_1$ (since C_1 returns $F(x, val(\beta(C_1)))$). But then we get $\beta(C_2) \prec \beta(C_1) \prec C_1 \prec C_2$. This of course prove that $\prec$ does not satisfy the sequential specification since C_2 returns $F(val(\alpha(C_2)), val(\beta(C_2)))$.

The reader may verify that both of the executions in Figure 5 satisfy the conditions of Lemmas 2 and 3. The conclusion is that Lemmas 2 and 3 do not suffice to prove the correctness of the algorithm. Therefore, we are required to show that executions that resemble the executions in Figure 5 cannot occur. In order to do so we state two additional lemmas. The proofs of these lemmas require a technical analysis of the algorithm, and can be found in the appendix.

Lemma 4. *Let C be a* compute *event, then there is no p_0-*set *event, S^0, such that $\alpha(C) < S^0 < C$, and there is no p_1-*set *event, S^1, such that $\beta(C) < S^1 < C$.*

Lemma 5. *If C_1, C_2 are two* compute *events by the same process such that $C_1 < C_2$, then $\alpha(C_1) \le \alpha(C_2)$ and $\beta(C_1) \le \beta(C_2)$.*

Lemmas 2, 3, 4 and 5 describe important properties of the algorithm. We shall prove that Theorem 1 stems from these properties. We shall define a relation $\lhd$ on the set of all high level events and finally, $<^*$ will be defined to be the transitive closure of $< \cup \lhd$. Recall that we aim to define $<^*$ so that, any linear extension of $<^*$ satisfies the sequential specification.

The idea of the definition of $\lhd$ is simple. Since each compute event C returns $F(val(\alpha(C)), val(\beta(C)))$, we aim that in any linear extension $\prec$, of $<$, conditions $\alpha(C) = pre_0(C)$ and $\beta(C) = pre_1(C)$ hold. Thus, if S is a p_0-set event and C is a p_1-compute event, we decide that $S \lhd C$ if $S \le \alpha(C)$ and otherwise, we decide that $C \lhd S$. In the same way, for a p_1-set event S and a p_0-compute event C, we decide $S \lhd C$ if $S \le \beta(C)$, and $C \lhd S$ otherwise.

Definition 3. *We define $\lhd$ to be the union of the following sets:*

1. $\{\langle S, C\rangle : C$ *is a* p_0-compute *event,* S *is a* p_1-set *event and* $S \leq \beta(C)\}$
2. $\{\langle C, S\rangle : C$ *is a* p_0-compute *event,* S *is a* p_1-set *event and* $\beta(C) < S\}$
3. $\{\langle S, C\rangle : C$ *is a* p_1-compute *event,* S *is a* p_0-set *event and* $S \leq \alpha(C)\}$
4. $\{\langle C, S\rangle : C$ *is a* p_1-compute *event,* S *is a* p_0-set *event and* $\alpha(C) < S\}$

As we have mentioned, $<^*$ will be defined to be the transitive closure of $< \cup \lhd$. Hence, $<^*$ is a partial order iff there are no cycles in $< \cup \lhd$. The following lemmas verify this requirement.

Lemma 6. *If* $X \lhd Y$, *then* $\neg(Y < X)$.

Proof. Assume that $X \lhd Y$ and first, assume that X is a set event. Hence, Y is a compute event, and $X \leq \alpha(Y)$ or $X \leq \beta(Y)$. If $Y < X$, then $Y < X \leq \alpha(Y)$ or $Y < X \leq \beta(Y)$. Thus, $Y < \alpha(Y)$ or $Y < \beta(Y)$. This contradicts Lemma 3, and hence $\neg(Y < X)$.

Now, assume that X is a compute event and hence, Y is a set event. Y is p_0-set event and $\alpha(X) < Y$, or Y is p_1-set event and $\beta(X) < Y$. If $Y < X$, then Y is a p_0-set event and $\alpha(X) < Y < X$, or Y is a p_1-set event and $\beta(X) < Y < X$. This contradicts Lemma 4 and hence, $\neg(Y < X)$. $\qquad\square$

Corollary 1. *If* $X < Y \lhd Z$, *then* $X \neq Z$.

Lemma 7. *If* $X < Y \lhd Z < V$, *then* $X < V$.

Proof. By Lemma 6, $\neg(Z < Y)$. Therefore, for some $y \in Y$ and $z \in Z$, $y < z$. Thus, $X < y < z < V$ and hence, $X < V$. $\qquad\square$

Lemma 8. *If* $X \lhd Y \lhd Z$, *then* $X < Z$.

Proof. There are two possible cases.

Case 1. Y is a compute event. Assume w.l.o.g. that Y is a p_0-compute event. Thus, X, Z are p_1-set events and

$$X \leq \beta(Y) < Z.$$

Since X, Z are both p_1-operations, $X < Z$ or $Z < X$. If we assume that $Z < X$ we conclude that

$$X \leq \beta(Y) < Z < X.$$

This conclusion implies that $X < X$ in contradiction to the fact that $<$ is an irreflexive relation. Therefore, $X < Z$ as required.

Case 2. Y is a set event. Assume w.l.o.g. that Y is a p_0-set event. Thus, X, Z are p_1-compute events and

$$\alpha(X) < Y \leq \alpha(Z).$$

Therefore, $\alpha(X) < \alpha(Z)$. Since X, Z are both p_1-operations, either $X < Z$ or $Z < X$. By Lemma 5, if $Z < X$ we must have $\alpha(Z) \leq \alpha(X)$. Hence, since $\alpha(X) < \alpha(Z)$, necessarily $X < Z$ as required.

$\qquad\square$

Now we can prove that there are no cycles in $< \cup \lhd$, i.e. there is no finite sequence $x_1, \ldots, x_n$ such that $x_1 = x_n$, and for each $1 \le i < n$, $(x_i, x_{i+1}) \in < \cup \lhd$. A sequence $x_1, \ldots, x_n$ that satisfies these requirements ($x_1 = x_n$ and for each $1 \le i < n$, $(x_i, x_{i+1}) \in < \cup \lhd$) is said to be a cycle of length n.

Lemma 9. *There are no cycles in $< \cup \lhd$.*

Proof. Assume for a contradiction that there are cycles in $< \cup \lhd$, and let $n > 1$ be the minimal length of a cycle in $< \cup \lhd$. First, since $<$ and $\lhd$ are irreflexive, there are no cycles of length 2. Now, since $<$ is transitive, by Lemma 8, and since $n > 2$, a cycle of minimal length is of the form

$$x_1 < x_2 \lhd x_3 < x_4 \lhd \ldots < x_{n-1} \lhd x_n = x_1.$$

By Corollary 1, $n > 3$. Thus, $n \ge 4$, but then, by Lemma 7, $x_1 < x_4$ in contradiction to the minimality of n. □

Finally we define $<^*$ to be the transitive closure of $< \cup \lhd$, i.e.

Definition 4. *for two high level events E, E', we define $E <^* E'$ iff there is a path in $< \cup \lhd$ from E to E'.*

Corollary 2. *$<^*$ is a partial order on the set of all high level events.*

Now we can prove theorem 1.

Proof (Proof of Theorem 1.). Let $\prec$ be any linear extension of $<^*$ and let C be any compute event, we need to prove that C returns $F(val(pre_0(C)), val(pre_1(C)))$. By Lemma 2, C returns $F(val(\alpha(C)), val(\beta(C)))$. Hence, we need to verify that $\alpha(C) = pre_0(C)$ and $\beta(C) = pre_1(C)$. Assume w.l.o.g. that C is a p_0-compute event. Since $\alpha(C)$ is a p_0 event, either $\alpha(C) < C$ or $C < \alpha(C)$. By Lemma 3, $\neg(C < \alpha(C))$ and hence,

$$\alpha(C) < C.$$

In addition, $\beta(C)$ is a p_1-set event and according to the definition of $\lhd$,

$$\beta(C) \lhd C.$$

Now, $<^*$ extends $< \cup \lhd$ and $\prec$ extends $<^*$. Hence,

$$\alpha(C) \prec C \text{ and } \beta(C) \prec C.$$

We conclude that $\alpha(C) \preceq pre_0(C)$ and $\beta(C) \preceq pre_1(C)$. In order to prove equality, we shall prove that there is no p_0-set event S such that $\alpha(C) \prec S \prec C$, and there is no p_1-set event S' such that $\beta(C) \prec S' \prec C$. Equivalently, we shall prove: if $S \ne \alpha(C)$ is a p_0-set event, then $S \prec \alpha(C)$ or $C \prec S$, and if $S' \ne \beta(C)$ is a p_1-set event, then $S' \prec \beta(C)$ or $C \prec S'$.

First, let $S \ne \alpha(C)$ be any p_0-set event. By Lemma 4 $\neg(\alpha(C) < S < C)$. Thus, since $\alpha(C), S, C$ are all p_0 events, either $S < \alpha(C)$ or $C < S$. Since $\prec$ extends $<$, either $S \prec \alpha(C)$ or $C \prec S$ as required.

Now, let $S' \ne \beta(C)$ be any p_1-set event. Since S' and $\beta(C)$ are both p_1 events, either $S' < \beta(C)$ or $\beta(C) < S'$. If $S' < \beta(C)$, then necessarily $S' \prec \beta(C)$ since $\prec$ extends $<$. On the other hand, if $\beta(C) < S'$, by definition of $\lhd$, $C \lhd S'$. $\prec$ extends $\lhd$ and hence, in this case $C \prec S'$ as required. □

4 Conclusions

Aguilera et al. presented in [4] a non-blocking solution to the signaling problem, and asked if a wait-free algorithm that solves this problem exists. We provide a positive answer to this question by introducing a simple bounded wait-free algorithm that solves the signaling problem, and proving its correctness. Our algorithm is very short and although its correctness is not trivial, the algorithm itself is quite easy.

The bounded registers that the processes access during a compute operations named flags . By the essence of the problem, the main complexity measure we are interested in is the size of the processes flags, that is, the amount of distinct values that the flags may store. In Aguilera et al. solution [4] each process's flag is of size $7|D|$ where D is the range of F. In our solution, a process p_i uses a boolean register T_i and a $2|D|$-valued register B_i. Thus, in our algorithm the flags are of size $4|D|$. Therefore, our solution improves the one in [4] not only since it is wait-free, but also in view of the size of the flags.

As explained in the introduction, the mailbox problem can be solved by means of the signaling problem. Although the signaling algorithm presented in [4] is not wait-free, Aguilera et al. used their solution to construct a wait-free mailbox algorithm with 14-valued flags. With our signaling algorithm we are able to provide a mailbox algorithm with 8-valued flags, as the range of the corresponding function is of size 2 (as explained in the introduction). However, more efficient solution to the mailbox problem can be found in [1]. Although the solution in [1] uses flags of size 6 and 4, we do not overrule the possibility that in practice, one may prefer to use the algorithm we present here to solve the mailbox problem due to its simplicity.

We pointed out that a solution to the signaling problem also provides a solution to the N-buffer problem. Many solutions to the N-buffer problem were suggested, with flags of size at least $N+1$ (see [7], and also the Conclusion section in [4]). As far as we know, the first wait-free solution to the N-buffer problem with flags of size independent of N, was presented in [4]. In this solution the flags are of size 14^2 (by using two instances of a mailbox algorithm), regardless of the size of the buffer. However, using our algorithm, the N-buffer problem is solved with a 12-valued flags (i.e. $4 \cdot 3$, where 3 is the cardinality of $D = range(F)$, see the introduction for details).

Several questions concerning the signaling problem are open. Natural questions concerns the size of the bounded registers that are read during an execution of a compute procedure (the flags). In our algorithm, as well as in [4], only single-writer registers are employed and our solution sets an upper bound of $4|D|$ to the size of each process flag, where $|D|$ is the cardinality of the range of the function F which is a parameter of the problem (see the introduction for details).

1. Is there any wait-free solution to the signaling problem with flags of smaller size? Are there any lower bounds results?
2. We do not know if there is a wait-free solution to the signaling problem that uses multi-writer flags in which the size of the flags is smaller.
3. A natural generalization of the signaling problem involves n serial processes, $p_0, \ldots, p_{n-1}$, and an $1 < n$-variable computable function $F : Vals^n \longrightarrow D$ (the n-signaling problem). We do not know if there is a wait-free solution for the n-signaling problem where $n > 2$.

We believe that the proof that we have provided for the correctness of our algorithm, can be used to prove the correctness of other signaling algorithms as well. Although proving Lemmas 2, 3, 4 and 5 require technical analysis of our particular algorithm, the rest of the proof relies only upon the correctness of these lemmas, and does not rely on the code of the algorithm. Thus, for proving the correctness of a suggested signaling algorithm, it suffices to prove only a corresponding variant of Lemmas 2, 3, 4 and 5. In a more precise manner, one may verify that the following proposition holds:

Proposition 1. *Let $\mathcal{A}$ be an algorithm for the signaling problem, let τ be an infinite execution of $\mathcal{A}$ and let $<$ be the precedence partial order defined on the high level events in τ. Thus, there is an extension of $<$ into a total order $\prec$ that satisfies the conditions of the sequential specification, iff there are functions*

$$\alpha : \text{compute } events \longrightarrow p_0\text{-set } events,$$

$$\beta : \text{compute } events \longrightarrow p_1\text{-set } events$$

such that Lemmas 2, 3, 4 and 5 hold.

Indeed, by the proof we have provided for Theorem 1 it stems that Lemmas 2, 3, 4 and 5 imply that the system execution is linearizable (this is the "if" direction of Proposition 1). In addition, for proving the other direction we take a linear extension $\prec$, of $<$, (that satisfies the sequential specification) and we simply define $\alpha(C)$ and $\beta(C)$ to be the maximal p_0 and p_1 set events that precede C in $\prec$ respectively.

Acknowledgments. I would like to thank Uri Abraham for his valuable help and his excellent advises.

References

1. Abraham, U., Amram, G.: On the Mailbox Problem. arXiv:1307.5619 [cs.DC] (2013)
2. Afek, Y., Attiya, H., Dolev, D., Gafni, E., Merritt, M., Shavit, N.: Atomic snapshots of shared memory. Journal of the ACM 40, 873–890 (1993)
3. Aguilera, M.K., Gafni, E., Lamport, L.: The Mailbox Problem (Extended Abstract). In: Taubenfeld, G. (ed.) DISC 2008. LNCS, vol. 5218, pp. 1–15. Springer, Heidelberg (2008)
4. Aguilera, M.K., Gafni, E., Lamport, L.: The Mailbox Problem. Distributed Computing 23, 113–134 (2010)
5. Anderson, J.H.: Composite registers. Distributed Computing 6, 141–154 (1993)
6. Herlihy, M., Wing, J.: Linearizability: A correctness condition for concurrent objects. ACM Transactions on Programming Languages and Systems 12, 463–492 (1990)
7. Lamport, L.: Proving the Correctness of Multiprocess Programs. IEEE Transactions on Software Engineering 3, 125–145 (1977)
8. Lamport, L.: On Interprocess Communication, Part I: Basic formalism, Part II: Algorithms. Distributed Computing 1, 77–101 (1986)
9. Tromp, J.: How to Construct an Atomic Variable (extended abstract). In: Bermond, J.-C., Raynal, M. (eds.) WDAG 1989. LNCS, vol. 392, pp. 292–302. Springer, Heidelberg (1989)

Appendix

For proving Lemma 4, we use the following two lemmas:

Lemma 10. *Let C be a p_0-compute event and suppose that $S = pre(C)$ is a set event so that $S \neq I_0$. Say $r_1 = read(S, T_1)$, $r_2 = read(C, T_1)$ and $q = read(C, B_1)$ thus if $[\omega(r_1)] = [\omega(r_2)]$ or $[\omega(r_1)] = [\omega(q)]$, then C is internal.*

Proof. First we assume that $[\omega(r_1)] = [\omega(r_2)]$ and we need to verify that C is internal. In this case, p_0 reads the same value from register T_1 in S and in C. Let $j \in \{0, 1\}$ denotes this value (i.e. $val(r_1) = val(r_2) = j$). By the code of a set procedure, p_0 writes j into register T_0 in S (i.e. $val(write(S, T_0)) = j$). During the execution of C, p_0 reads the value j into variable t and find that $(t = T_0)$ (recall that $S = pre(C)$ and hence the value of register T_0 during the execution of C is j). Therefore, the condition $(t \neq T_0) \wedge (b.color = t[1])$ does not hold in C, and hence C is internal.

Now we assume that $[\omega(r_1)] = [\omega(q)]$. We shall conclude that also in this case, C is internal. As in the previous case, let j denotes the value that p_0 reads from register T_1 in action r_1. Write $E = [\omega(r_1)] = [\omega(q)]$ thus E is a p_1-set event and $val(write(E, T_1)) = j$. Therefore, p_1 writes into register B_1 in E the value (j, d) for some $d \in D$ and this is the value that p_0 reads in C into the local variable b. Since $val(r_1) = j$ and since $S \neq I_0$, by the code of a set procedure, p_0 writes into register T_0 in S the value j. Let k denotes the value that p_0 reads from T_1 in C into the local variable t. Since the value of T_0 during the execution of C is $val(write(S, T_0)) = j$, either $k = j$ (and then $t = T_0$) or either $k \neq j$ (and then $t \neq b.color$). Thus, in any case, the condition $(t \neq T_0) \wedge (b.color = t)$ does not hold in C and hence C is internal. $\square$

Lemma 11. *Let C be a p_0-compute event and $S = pre(C)$. Say, $r_1 = read(C, T_1)$, $r_2 = read(C, B_1)$ and $E_1 = [\omega(r_1)]$, $E_2 = [\omega(r_2)]$. If E_1, E_2 are not the initial p_1-set event I_1, and $[\omega(read(E_1, T_0))] = [\omega(read(E_2, T_0))] = S$, then C is external.*

Proof. Let j denotes the value that p_0 writes into T_0 in S (i.e. $val(write(S, T_0)) = j \in \{0, 1\}$). Since $S = pre(C)$, the value of T_0 during the execution of C is j. Since $[\omega(read(E_1, T_0))] = S$, p_1 reads in E_1 the value j from T_0 and writes into T_1, $1 - j$, this value is read by p_0 in C into the local variable t. Since $[\omega(read(E_2, T_0))] = S$, p_1 reads in E_2 the value j from T_0 and writes into B_1, $(1 - j, d)$ for some $d \in D$, this value is read by p_0 in C into the local variable b. Thus, the condition $(t \neq T_0) \wedge (b.color = t)$ holds in C, and hence C is external. $\square$

Proof (Proof of Lemma 4.). By the symmetry of the algorithm, we may assume that C is a p_0-compute event. First, we assume that C is an external event and in this case we have to prove that:

a. There is no p_0-set event, S^0, such that $\alpha(C) < S^0 < C$.
b. There is no p_1-set event, S^1, such that $\beta(C) < S^1 < C$.

We begin by proving b. Let S be any p_1-set event such that $S < C$, we need to verify that $S \leq \beta(C)$. Since $\beta(C) = [\omega(read(C, B_1))]$, there is no write action into register B_1 between the events $write(\beta(C), B_1)$ and $read(C, B_1)$. Thus,

$write(S, B_1) \leq write(\beta(C), B_1)$ and as a consequence, $S = [write(S, B_1)] \leq [write(\beta(C), B_1)] = \beta(C)$.

Now we prove a. Let S be some p_0-set event and assume for a contradiction that $\alpha(C) < S < C$, and in addition, choose S to be the latest p_0-set event with this property (hence $S = pre(C)$). Note that since $\alpha(C) < S$, $S \neq I_0$. First we shall prove that

$$write(\beta(C), T_1) < read(S, T_1). \tag{1}$$

Since C is assumed to be external, if $\beta(C) \neq I_1$, then $\omega(read(\beta(C), V_0)) = write(\alpha(C), V_0)$ and hence, since $\alpha(C) < S < C$, $read(\beta(C), V_0) < write(S, V_0)$. Thus, we conclude

$$write(\alpha(C), V_0) < read(\beta(C), V_0) < write(S, V_0) < read(S, T_1).$$

The last relation is justified by the code of a set procedure and by the fact that $S \neq I_0$. Since $write(\beta(C), T_1) < read(\beta(C), V_0)$, necessarily $write(\beta(C), T_1) < read(S, T_1)$. On the other hand, if it is the case that $\beta(C) = I_1$, then $\beta(C) < S$. Thus, in any case (1) holds.

By (1), either $\omega(read(S, T_1)) = write(\beta(C), T_1)$, or there is a p_1-set event, $S' > \beta(C)$, such that $\omega(read(S, T[1])) = write(S', T_1)$. First, assume that $\omega(read(S, T_1)) = write(\beta(C), T_1)$. Since C is external, by definition of $\beta(C)$, $\omega(read(C, B_1)) = write(\beta(C), B_1)$. Thus, $\beta(C) = [\omega(read(C, B_1))] = [\omega(read(S, T_1))]$ and since $S = pre(C)$, by Lemma 10, C is internal in contradiction to our assumption that C is an external compute event. Hence, $\omega(read(S, T_1)) \neq write(\beta(C), T_1)$ and thus

$$\omega(read(S, T_1)) = write(S', T_1)$$

for some p_1-set event $S' > \beta(C)$. According to case b, there is no p_1-set event E such that $\beta(C) < E < C$. Thus, for some action $e \in S'$, $read(C, T_1) < e$ (since $read(C, T_1)$ is the first action in C). As a consequence, $write(S', T_1) < read(S, T_1) < read(C, T_1)$ and there is no write event into T_1 that follows $write(S', T_1)$ and precedes $read(C, T_1)$. Thus,

$$\omega(read(C, T_1)) = \omega(read(S, T_1)) = write(S', T_1).$$

But then, by Lemma 10, we conclude again that C is internal in contradiction to our assumption. Thus, we see that if C is external, conditions a and b hold as required.

It is left to deal with the case that C is internal. By definition, $\alpha(C)$ is the latest p_0-set event that precedes C (i.e. $\alpha(C) = pre(C)$), and hence surely there is no p_0-set event, S, such that $\alpha(C) < S < C$. So, we only need to verify that there is no p_1-set event between $\beta(C)$ and C.

Assume for a contradiction that there is some p_1-set event S, such that $\beta(C) < S < C$. Thus, for some p_1-set event $E_1 \geq S$, $E_1 = [\omega(read(C, T_1))]$, and for some p_1-set event $E_2 \geq S$, $E_2 = [\omega(read(C, B_1))]$. Since $\beta(C) < S \leq E_1$ and $\beta(C) < S \leq E_2$, $E_1 \neq I_1$ and $E_2 \neq I_1$. In order achieve contradiction we shall use Lemma 11, and for that we need to verify that $[\omega(read(E_1, T_0))] = [\omega(read(E_2, T_0))] = \alpha(C)$. There are two cases:

Case 1. $\alpha(C) = I_0$. In this case, since $E_1 \neq I_1$ and $E_2 \neq I_1$, $\alpha(C) < E_1$ and $\alpha(C) < E_2$ and in particular

$$write(\alpha(C), T_0) < read(E_1, T_0) \text{ and } write(\alpha(C), T_0) < read(E_2, T_0).$$

Now, since $\omega(read(C, T_1)) = write(E_1, T_1)$, $write(\alpha(C), T_0) < read(E_1, T_0)$ $< write(E_1, T_1) < read(C, T_1)$ and hence, for some $e \in C$,

$$write(\alpha(C), T_0) < read(E_1, T_0) < e.$$

Thus, since $\alpha(C) = pre(C)$, there is no write action into T_0 between $write(\alpha(C), T_0)$ and e, and in particular there is no write action into T_0 between $write(\alpha(C), T_0)$ and $read(E_1, T_0)$. Hence,

$$[\omega(read(E_1, T_0))] = \alpha(C).$$

In the same way, since $\omega(read(C, B_1)) = write(E_2, B_1)$, $write(\alpha(C), T_0) < read(E_2, T_0) < write(E_2, B_1) < read(C, B_1)$ and hence, for some $e \in C$,

$$write(\alpha(C), T_0) < read(E_1, T_0) < write(E_2, B_1) < e.$$

Thus, since $\alpha(C) = pre(C)$, we conclude that there is no write action into T_0 between $write(\alpha(C), T_0)$ and e, and in particular there is no write action into T_0 between $write(\alpha(C), T_0)$ and $read(E_2, T_0)$. Hence,

$$[\omega(read(E_2, T_0))] = \alpha(C).$$

Therefore, by Lemma 11, C is an external compute event, in contradiction to our assumption that C is internal.

Case 2. $\alpha(C) \neq I_0$. In this case, since C is internal, $\omega(read(\alpha(C), V_1)) = write(\beta(C), V_1)$, and hence $write(\beta(C), V_1) < read(\alpha(C), V_1)$. Recall that $E_1 = [\omega(read(C, T_1))]$, $E_2 = [\omega(read(C, B_1))]$, $\beta(C) < E_1$ and $\beta(C) < E_2$. Since there is no write action into V_1 between $write(\beta(C), V_1)$ and $read(\alpha(C), V_1)$, we conclude:

$$read(\alpha(C), V_1) < write(E_1, V_1) \text{ and } read(\alpha(C), V_1) < write(E_2, V_1).$$

In a p_0-set event (which is not the initial set event), p_0 writes to T_0 before it reads from V_1, in addition, in a p_1-set event (which is not the initial set event), p_1 reads from T_0 after it writes to V_1. Thus, by the transitivity of $<$,

$$write(\alpha(C), T_0) < read(E_1, T_0) \text{ and } write(\alpha(C), T_0) < read(E_1, T_0).$$

Now, since $E_1 = [\omega(read(C, T_1))]$ and $E_2 = [\omega(read(C, B_1))]$, and since $read(E_1, T_0) < write(E_1, T_1)$ and $read(E_2, T_0) < write(E_2, B_1)$, for some $e, e' \in C$,

$$write(\alpha(C), T_0) < read(E_1, T_0) < e \text{ and } write(\alpha(C), T_0) < read(E_1, T_0) < e'.$$

Since $\alpha(C) = pre(C)$, we conclude that there is no write action into T_0 between $write(\alpha(C), T_0)$ and e, and that there is no write action into T_0 between $write(\alpha(C), T_0)$ and e'. In particular, we conclude that there is no write action into T_0 between $write(\alpha(C), T_0)$ and $read(E_1, T_0)$, and that there is no write action into T_0 between $write(\alpha(C), T_0)$ and $read(E_1, T_0)$. As a consequence, $[\omega(read(E_1, T_0))] = [\omega(read(E_2, T_0))] = \alpha(C)$ and again, Lemma 11 provides a contradiction to the assumption that C is internal

$\square$

For proving Lemma 5, we use the following Lemma:

Lemma 12. *Let* C_1, C_2 *be two* p_i-compute *events for some* $i \in \{0, 1\}$. *If* $pre(C_1) = pre(C_2)$, $val(read(C_1, B_{1-i})).color = val(read(C_2, B_{1-i})).color$ *and* $val(read(C_1, T_{1-i})) = val(read(C_2, T_{1-i}))$, *then* C_1 *and* C_2 *are both internal or both external.*

Proof. For any p_i-compute event C, the value of register T_i during the execution of C is the value that has been written to register T_i in the action $write(pre(C), T_i)$. Therefore, since $pre(C_1) = pre(C_2)$, the value of T_i during the executions of C_1 and C_2 is the same. Since p_i reads the same values from T_{1-i} and $B_{1-i}.color$ in C_1 and C_2, condition $(t \neq T_i) \wedge (b.color = t)$ holds in C_1 iff it holds in C_2, and condition $(t = T_i) \wedge (b.color = t)$ holds in C_1 iff it holds in C_2. Thus, C_1 is external iff C_2 is external as required. $\square$

Proof (Proof of Lemma 5.). By the symmetry of the algorithm we may assume that $C_1 < C_2$ are both p_0-compute events. We need to verify that $\alpha(C_1) \leq \alpha(C_2)$ and $\beta(C_1) \leq \beta(C_2)$. By Lemma 3, and since C_1 and $\alpha(C_1)$ are both p_0-operations, $\alpha(C_1) < C_1$ and similarly $\alpha(C_2) < C_2$. If we assume that $\alpha(C_2) < \alpha(C_1)$, then we get

$$\alpha(C_2) < \alpha(C_1) < C_1 < C_2.$$

Thus, $\alpha(C_1)$ is a p_0-set event and $\alpha(C_2) < \alpha(C_1) < C_2$ in contradiction to Lemma 4. Hence we conclude

$$\alpha(C_1) \leq \alpha(C_2) \tag{2}$$

as required.

Now, we need to verify that $\beta(C_1) \leq \beta(C_2)$. Assume for a contradiction that

$$\beta(C_2) < \beta(C_1) \tag{3}$$

and conclude that $\beta(C_1) \neq I_1$. There are two cases:

Case 1. C_1 is external. In this case, by definition of $\beta(C_1)$, $\omega(read(C_1, B_1)) = write(\beta(C_1), B_1)$, and hence $write(\beta(C_1), B_1) < read(C_1, B_1)$. Since $write(\beta(C_1), B_1)$ is the last event in $\beta(C_1)$, we conclude

$$\beta(C_1) < read(C_1, B_1). \tag{4}$$

By (3), (4), and since $C_1 < C_2$, we get

$$\beta(C_2) < \beta(C_1) < read(C_1, B_1) < C_2.$$

Thus, $\beta(C_1)$ is between $\beta(C_2)$ and C_2 in contradiction to Lemma 4, therefore C_1 cannot be external.

Case 2. C_1 is internal. In this case, by definition of $\alpha(C_1)$, $\alpha(C_1) = pre(C_1)$. Say $pre(C_1) = S$. By definition of β, $\beta(C_1) = \rho(S)$. We first observe that C_2 is not internal. To prove this observation assume on the contrary that C_2 is an internal compute event. Since $S < C_1 < C_2$, $S \le pre(C_2)$ and hence $\rho(S) \le \rho(pre(C_2))$. But $\rho(S)$ is $\beta(C_1)$ and $\rho(pre(C_2))$ is $\beta(C_2)$ (as C_2 is assumed to be internal), and so $\beta(C_1) \le \beta(C_2)$ is in contradiction to (3). So we conclude that C_2 is external and hence $\alpha(C_2) = \rho(\beta(C_2))$.

Our next goal is to verify that $\alpha(C_1) = \alpha(C_2)$. We assume for a contradiction that $\alpha(C_1) \ne \alpha(C_2)$, and hence we conclude (by (2)) that $\alpha(C_1) < \alpha(C_2)$. Now, since C_2 is external, $\alpha(C_2) = \rho(\beta(C_2))$ and hence $\neg(\beta(C_2) < \alpha(C_2))$. This observation yields that for some $e \in \alpha(C_2)$ and $e' \in \beta(C_2)$, $e < e'$. According to our assumption (3), $\beta(C_2) < \beta(C_1)$ and hence we get,

$$\alpha(C_1) < e < e' < \beta(C_1).$$

We conclude that $\alpha(C_1) < \beta(C_1)$ in contradiction to $\beta(C_1) = \rho(\alpha(C_1))$ (since C_1 is assumed to be internal in this case). Therefore

$$\alpha(C_1) = \alpha(C_2)$$

and in addition $S = \rho(\beta(C_2))$.

Now we shall prove that $\beta(C_2) \ne I_1$. Assume for a contradiction that $\beta(C_2) = I_1$. Since C_2 is external, $S = \rho(\beta(C_2)) = \rho(I_1) = I_0$. Thus, $S = \alpha(C_1) = I_0$, the initial p_0-set event. Since C_1 is assumed to be internal, $\beta(C_1) = \rho(S) = \rho(I_0) = I_1$. Thus, $\beta(C_2) = \beta(C_1) = I_1$ in contradiction to (3). Hence, we conclude that $\beta(C_2) \ne I_1$, and since $\beta(C_2) < \beta(C_1)$, $\beta(C_1) \ne I_1$ either.

We sum-up our observations in the following.

C_1 is internal, C_2 is external, $\alpha(C_1) = \alpha(C_2) = pre(C_1) = pre(C_2) = S$ and $\beta(C_2) \ne I_1$.

Now we are ready to obtain the contradiction which will prove the lemma. We will show that $read(C_1, T_1)$ returns the same value as $read(C_2, T_1)$, and likewise $read(C_1, B_1)$ obtains the same value as $read(C_2, B_1)$. Since $pre(C_1) = pre(C_2)$, by Lemma 12, it follows that C_1 and C_2 are either both internal or both external, which is in contradiction to the case with which we are dealing now, namely that C_1 is internal and C_2 external.

We claim that the following precedence relations can be established at this stage:

$$write(S, V_0) < read(\beta(C_2), V_0) < write(\beta(C_2), B_1) <$$
$$write(\beta(C_1), V_1) < read(S, V_1) < C_1 < read(C_2, B_1) < write(\beta(C_1), B_1).$$

$$(5)$$

The first relation is a consequence of $S = \rho(\beta(C_2))$. The second relation is a consequence of the algorithm (as the read of V_0 comes before the write on B_1) and since $\beta(C_2) \neq I_1$. The third relation is a consequence of $\beta(C_2) < \beta(C_1)$. The fourth is a consequence of $\beta(C_1) = \rho(S)$. The fifth is a consequence of $S = pre(C_1)$ (so that $S < C$). The sixth is a consequence of our assumption that $C_1 < C_2$. The last relation is argued as follows. If it were not the case that $read(C_2, B_1) < write(\beta(C_1), B_1)$ then we would have that $write(\beta(C_1), B_1) < read(C_2, B_1)$. But this would imply that $\beta(C_1) \leq \beta(C_2) = [\omega(read(C_2, B_1))]$, in contradiction to $\beta(C_2) < \beta(C_1)$.

We note that these relations (5) imply that there is no p_1-set event between $\beta(C_2)$ and $\beta(C_1)$. For if U is a p_1-set event such that $\beta(C_2) < U < \beta(C_1)$, then relations $write(\beta(C_1), V_1) < read(S, V_1) < C_1 < C_2$ imply that $\beta(C_2) < U < write(\beta(C_1), V_1) < C_1 < C_2$ and hence in particular $\beta(C_2) < U < C_2$, in contradiction to Lemma 4. So $\beta(C_1)$ is the immediate p_1-set successor of $\beta(C_2)$, and hence $write(\beta(C_1), B_1)$ is the immediate write event on B_1 that comes after $write(\beta(C_2), B_1)$.

These relations, and specifically $write(\beta(C_2), B_1) < read(C_1, B_1) < read(C_2, B_1) < write(\beta(C_1), B_1)$ show that the two reads, r_1 and r_2, of B_1, in C_1 and C_2, are between two successive writes on this register. Hence $\omega(read(C_1, B_1)) = \omega(read(C_2, B_1)) = write(\beta(C_2), B_1)$, and these two read events get the same value. Let $j \in \{0, 1\}$ be the value of the color field of the write $write(\beta(C_2), B_1)$, which is as we have said the color field of the value of the two reads of B_1, r_1 and r_2.

Let t_1 and t_2 be the reading events of register T_1 in C_1 and C_2 respectively. We shall prove that $val(t_1) = val(t_2) = j$, and this concludes the proof of Lemma 5. We first observe that $j = val(write(\beta(C_2), T_1))$. This observation is deduced from the fact that the code of a set procedure for p_1 determines that the color field of the write onto B_1 (which is j) is equal to the value that is written into T_1.

Now we observe that the value of t_2 is j. This follows from our conclusion that C_2 is an external p_0-compute event and hence equation $(t \neq T_0) \wedge (b.color = t)$ holds when line 3 is executed. But we know that $b.color$ is j (as the read of B_1 in C_2 obtains the value of the write into B_1 in $\beta(C_2)$) and hence t is evaluated to j.

We have proved: $pre(C_1) = pre(C_2)$, $val(read(C_1, B_1)).color = val(read(C_1, B_1)).color = j$ and $val(t_2) = j$. Thus, in order to invoke Lemma 12 we need to prove that $val(t_1) = j$ as well. First we shall prove that p_0 reads in t_1 the value that has been written to register T_1 in $\beta(C_1)$ or in $\beta(C_2)$ i.e. we shall prove that $\omega(t_1) \in \{write(\beta(C_1), T_1), write(\beta(C_2), T_1)\}$. By the relations in (5), for some $e, e' \in \beta(C_1)$, $e < C_1 < e'$ (namely, $e = write(\beta(C_1), V_1)$ and $e' = write(\beta(C_1), B_1)$). As a consequence, either $\omega(t_1) = write(\beta(C_1), T_1)$ or $\omega(t_1) = write(U, T_1)$ where U is some p_1-set event that precedes $\beta(C_1)$. However, by (5), and since $write(\beta(C_2), T_1) < write(\beta(C_2), B_1)$ we conclude that $write(\beta(C_2), T_1) < C_1$. Thus, if $\omega(t_1) =$

$write(U, T_1)$ for some p_1-set event $U < \beta(C_1)$, since $\beta(C_1)$ is the p_1-set event successor of $\beta(C_2)$, necessarily $\omega(t_1) = write(\beta(C_2), T_1)$ and hence,

$$\omega(t_1) \in \{write(\beta(C_1), T_1), write(\beta(C_2), T_1)\} \tag{6}$$

as required.

Now we can show that $val(t_1) = j$ and invoke Lemma 12 to prove Lemma 5. First, if $\omega(t_1) = write(\beta(C_2), T_1)$ then $val(t_1) = j$ since we have already concluded that $j = val(write(\beta(C_2), T_1))$. On the other hand, if $\omega(t_1) \neq write(\beta(C_2), T_1)$, then by (6), $\omega(t_1) = write(\beta(C_1), T_1)$. In this case, $write(\beta(C_1), T_1) < t_1 < t_2$. We use this observation together with the relations in (5) to conclude that

$$write(\beta(C_1), T_1) < t_1 < t_2 < read(C_2, B_1) < write(\beta(C_1), B_1).$$

Thus, necessarily $\omega(t_2) = write(\beta(C_1), T_1)$ as well. Therefore, also in this case $val(t_1) = val(t_2) = j$. So, by Lemma 12, C_1 and C_2 are both external or both internal, and this contradicts our assumption that C_1 is internal and our conclusion that C_2 is external.

$\square$

Optimization of Execution Time under Power Consumption Constraints in a Heterogeneous Parallel System with GPUs and CPUs

Paweł Czarnul and Paweł Rościszewski

Faculty of Electronics, Telecommunications and Informatics
Gdansk University of Technology, Poland
{pczarnul,pawel.rosciszewski}@eti.pg.gda.pl

Abstract. The paper proposes an approach for parallelization of computations across a collection of clusters with heterogeneous nodes with both GPUs and CPUs. The proposed system partitions input data into chunks and assigns to particular devices for processing using OpenCL kernels defined by the user. The system is able to minimize the execution time of the application while maintaining the power consumption of the utilized GPUs and CPUs below a given threshold. We present real measurements regarding performance and power consumption of various GPUs and CPUs used in a modern parallel system. Furthermore we show, for a parallel application for breaking MD5 passwords, how the execution time of the real application changes with various upper bounds on the power consumption.

Keywords: parallel computing, GPGPU, OpenCL, heterogeneous environments, performance, power consumption.

1 Introduction

Traditionally, high performance computing (HPC) was performed on supercomputers and clusters composed of multiple CPU nodes with distributed memory. Message Passing Interface (MPI) has become a standard API for this type of processing. In recent years, several hardware developments have made it possible to extend the levels of parallelization. This includes:

1. multiple core technology within CPUs which makes it possible to use multiple threads for HPC,
2. developments of GPUs that allows launching thousands of lightweight threads for parallel computing.

However, high performance of modern devices comes at the cost of significant power consumption. What is more, various devices often show different performance and power characteristics. This paper addresses trade–offs between performance and power limits for parallelization of a real application in a real parallel environment. A solution is presented that is able to select compute devices such as CPUs and GPUs out of those available in the network so that the execution time of an application is minimized while the power consumption of the devices used does not exceed the given threshold.

M. Chatterjee et al. (Eds.): ICDCN 2014, LNCS 8314, pp. 66–80, 2014.

The outline of the paper is as follows. Section 2 presents related work while Section 3 justifies motivations for taking up this work. The problem is stated in Section 4. The proposed solution is presented in Section 5 with the architecture of the system shown in Section 5.1 and the proposed optimization algorithm in Section 5.2. Section 6 presents experiments with the testbed application and the environment described in Sections 6.1 and 6.2 respectively. Measurements of device performance and power consumption are shown in Section 6.2. Optimization of input data partitioning is shown in Section 6.3 while the obtained results in Section 6.4. Finally, Section 7 summarizes and presents future work.

2   Related Work

Nowadays, parallel computing can be performed at various levels, either specifically designed or adapted to the given environments:

- shared memory systems:
    - multiprocessor SMP systems with technologies such as OpenMP, Pthreads, Java Threads for multithreaded programming [1];
    - General Purpose GPU (GPGPU) programming with NVIDIA CUDA and Open-CL [2,3]. Recently OpenACC was proposed as an easy–to–use alternative for extension of sequential programs for parallel computing on GPU enabled devices, similarly to OpenMP for SMP systems;
    - multithreaded programming for hybrid multicore CPU and GPU systems by using OpenCL and particular implementations;
- distributed memory systems:
    - dedicated High Performance Computing (HPC) systems: PVM [4], MPI [5] often for demanding applications using the geometric parallelism [6] [7] pattern;
    - metaclusters composed of distributed HPC systems: MPICH-G2 [8], PACX-MPI [9], BC-MPI [10] for programming using the multi–process MPI paradigm;
    - grid computing for controlled resource sharing among Virtual Organizations. Virtual Organizations may expose services through so-called grid middlewares such as Globus Toolkit [11], Unicore, Gridbus with scheduling and management of resources [12,13]. Subsequently, the services may be integrated into service based workflow applications built on top of grid systems [14];
    - volunteer-based systems in which independent volunteers contribute to parallel execution of predefined projects by allowing client code to run on their computers. The code downloads portions of input data from a server, processes on the client side and sends the result back to the server. This type of processing is best suited for embarrassingly parallel applications [5]. Redundancy is used to provide correctness of results. Exemplary implementations of this kind of systems are BOINC [15] or COMCUTE[1] [7];
    - approaches for distributed computations using GPUs such as Many GPUs Package (MGP) [16], rCUDA[2], CUDA on Hadoop [17].

---

[1] http://comcute.eti.pg.gda.pl
[2] http://www.rcuda.net

Power-aware computing considers not only performance optimization but trade-offs between performance and power consumption and optimizes performance under power consumption constraints [18], [19]. The idea behind this approach is as follows: it might be more preferable to take into account the cost of energy used by computing devices and the cooling system and still obtain performance close to optimal.

The approaches in this area focus at different levels. For example, in [20] the authors incorporate hardware-related solutions (Dynamic Voltage and Frequency Scaling, Dynamic Concurrency Throttling) into a hybrid MPI/OpenMP computing system. In [21] the authors propose a methodology for estimating power consumption of certain devices, based on important characteristics, accessible through an available API. In contrast to these works, we consider power efficiency of a distributed system by incorporation of the power consumption of compute devices into the scheduling process.

At this level, scheduling policies were proposed in [22], particularly one based on predictive online-simulation. The Heterogeneity Aware Meta-scheduling Algorithm [23] aims to schedule more important tasks on more power-efficient devices. This solution needs to be integrated and tested within existing meta-scheduler implementations. In our paper, using a greedy approach to the knapsack problem, we propose a way to deploy such ideas in a real system.

3 Motivations

In spite of established programming APIs such as MPI, OpenMP, OpenCL or Open-ACC that aim at exposing a well defined abstraction as functions and hide low–level details, parallel computing is still possible on various levels and often requires use of several tools to make the most of a heterogeneous system. In modern parallel computing systems, integration of GPUs and CPUs has become the way to build state–of–the–art clusters which is demonstrated by the top computers on the TOP500[3] list.

The two issues that need to be addressed in parallel and distributed computing systems today are:

1. increasing heterogeneity – integration of CPUs, GPUs including multiple GPUs per node, distributed clusters, grids, clouds is not easy and straightforward for a programmer. It requires knowledge of multiple software packages and advanced programming skills;
2. incorporation of not only performance and minimization of execution time which have been the primary goals for HPC system historically. Other important factors in today's systems include reliability and power consumption. The latter appears in several practical scenarios such as:
   (a) various prices of electrical energy during day and nighttime. In such cases, it might be even desirable to migrate computations across continents,
   (b) changing power requirements of e.g. other devices in the office. For instance, in case of very high temperatures, power consumption of air conditioning systems both for computers and the office space may be increased which might pose a temporary limit on computers.

---

[3] http://top500.org

This leads to the need for multi–criteria optimization and proper measurement and optimization techniques.

From this perspective, the motivations for this work are as follows:

1. integrate distributed CPUs and GPUs in possibly various computing nodes into a system that would allow parallelization of computations across these computing devices,
2. incorporation optimization of execution time under power consumption constraints in this real system and demonstration using a testbed example.

4 Problem Formulation

Firstly, we distinguish a collection of nodes (computers) $N = \{N_1, N_2, \ldots, N_{|N|}\}$ available for computations. Secondly, computing devices D_j such as CPUs and GPUs are known, each of which is installed in exactly one node. However, there can be several computing devices in a single node. The following parameters are distinguished:

$pow_{D_j}(A)$ – average power consumption of compute device D_j when executing application A,

$perf_{D_j}(A)$ – the performance of device D_j for application A,

I – size of input data that is partitioned into K data packets of size d_k for the k-th packet to be distributed from a data server among the compute devices as shown in Figure 1. Let d_k^{out} denote the size of output for d_k and $a(k)$ denote the index of the device to which the k-th data packet is assigned.

$comp_A(d)$ – function that expresses the processing time spend by application A on data of size d; for various applications $comp$ may have various complexities,

$t_{exec\ D_j}(A)$ – the execution time of A on D_j. This execution time can be modeled as:

$$t_{exec\ D_j}(A) = \sum_{k:a(k)=j} (\alpha \frac{comp_A(d_k)}{perf_{D_j}(A)} + t_{startup} + \frac{d_k}{B} + t_{startup} + \frac{d_k^{out}}{B}) \quad (1)$$

where α is a constant for modeling computations, $t_{startup}$ is the startup time for communication and B denotes bandwidth of the network. Note that $t_{exec\ D_j}(A) = 0$ for D_j with no data packets assigned.

If we assume that each data packet is of equal size d along with its output, Equation 1 becomes:

$$t_{exec\ D_j}(A) = \sum_{k:a(k)=j} (\alpha \frac{comp_A(d)}{perf_{D_j}(A)} + 2t_{startup} + \frac{2d}{B}) \quad (2)$$

Now, given application A, input data of size I and an available system, the optimization goal can be stated as follows:

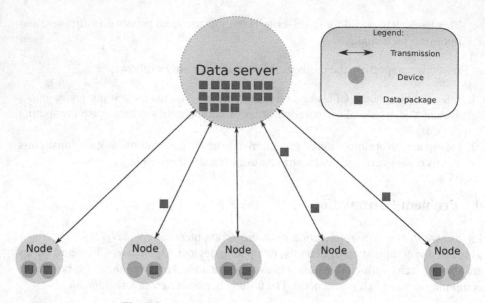

Fig. 1. Distribution of data among compute devices

Find a set of computing devices for execution $D_{exec} \in D$ and assign input data to devices in D_{exec} i.e. define function $a(k)$ such that the total execution time is minimized across the devices (to which data packets were assigned):

$$\text{minimize } max_{D_j}\{t_{exec\ D_j}(A)\} \tag{3}$$

i.e.

$$\text{minimize } max_{D_j}\{ \sum_{k:a(k)=j} (\alpha\frac{comp_A(d)}{perf_{D_j}(A)} + 2t_{startup} + \frac{2d}{B})\} \tag{4}$$

while the total power consumption is below the given threshold P_{max}:

$$\sum_{i:D_i \in D_{exec}} pow_{D_i}(A) \leq P_{max} \tag{5}$$

5 Proposed Solution

5.1 Architecture

A heterogeneous environment employing as many different models of devices as possible is crucial for this study and it also corresponds to many real systems. In order to be able to parallelize computations in such an environment, we developed a flexible system using OpenCL at the lowest level. The application is implemented as OpenCL kernels that are distributed by the layered framework of components shown in Figure 2. This requires the OpenCL way of environment initialization at the computing device level.

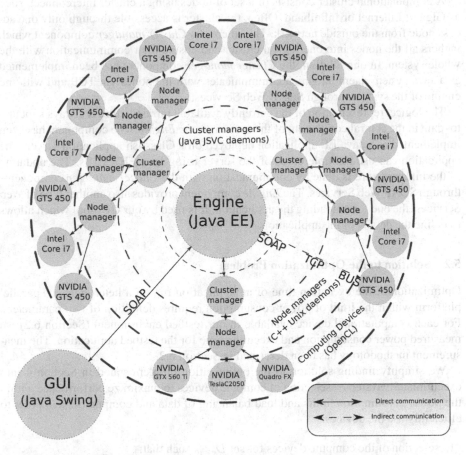

Fig. 2. Architecture of the parallel system implementation used for the experiment

Depending on the number of available devices we can specify the number of packets into which the input data is divided. We calculate this number by multiplying the number of devices by a data packet multiplier. The latter is an important parameter as it can improve granularity and thus improve the ability of the system to balance computations across heterogeneous computing devices such as CPUs and GPUs.

In modern computers, we will often find multiple computational devices within one machine, both CPUs and GPUs. In order to manage them, we developed the *Node manager* component which runs on every node as a Unix daemon and connects to the higher system layer via TCP. It provides the system with full information about the machines' capabilities and then waits for jobs to run. Given a job to run, the *Node manager* component runs the relevant pre–defined binary, providing it with the input data which consists of the computational kernel, as well as input data for it.

A computational cluster consists of a set of nodes using a cluster interconnect, such as Gigabit Ethernet or Infiniband. Often, the cluster is accessible through only one access node from the outside network. Thus there is a *Cluster manager* component which gathers all the nodes into one logical cluster and ensure their communication with the whole system. In our solution, the *Cluster manager* component has been implemented as a Java system daemon, which communicates with the nodes via TCP and with the engine of the system through SOAP Web Services.

The logical representation of the currently available infrastructure is always kept up–to–date in the central component of the system — *the Engine*. The component has been implemented as a Java EE application deployed on a Glassfish application server. The application can use multiple cores of the server using Java EE's EJBs. The updating of the infrastructure is done by communication with the *Cluster manager* components through SOAP Web Services. The *Engine* component provides also another type of Web Services: the one for uploading the application. It is used by our GUI tool which allows to define the details of the application.

5.2   Solution to the Optimization Problem

Optimization of the execution time of an application run on a heterogeneous parallel platform within the limit of power consumption requires definition of two parameters. For each computational device available in our testbed environment (Section 6.2) we measured power consumption and execution time for the testbed application. The measurement methodology has been described in Section 6.2.

We simplify finding solution to the optimization problem stated in Section 4 into execution of two steps – selection of compute devices to maximize performance within the power consumption limits and load balancing of data and computations in order to efficiently use the devices:

1. selection of the compute devices for set D_{exec} such that:

$$\max \sum_{j:D_j \in D_{exec}} perf_{D_j}(A) \tag{6}$$

with bound

$$\sum_{i:D_i \in D_{exec}} pow_{D_i}(A) \leq P_{max} \tag{7}$$

This problem can be generalized to the 0/1 knapsack problem [24]. Although the 0/1 knapsack problem is NP–Hard, a variety of approximation algorithms could be used for the optimization. For the tests a greedy approximation algorithm was chosen for choosing successive elements for packing. The algorithm has been implemented in Java as part of the execution engine of the parallel system. The source code is as follows:

```
public boolean[] solve(List<IKnapsackItem> items,int capacity) {

        boolean[] ret = new boolean[items.size()];

        Collections.sort(items);

        int usedWeight = 0;
        for(int i = 0; i != items.size(); i++) {
                if(usedWeight + items.get(i).getWeight() <=
                    capacity) {
                        usedWeight += items.get(i).getWeight();
                        ret[i] = true;
                }
        }

        return ret;
}
```

The capacity parameter of the above method is the parameter of each test case while the first argument is a list of objects implementing the following Java interface:

```
public interface IKnapsackItem extends Comparable<IKnapsackItem>
    {
    public int getWeight();
    public int getValue();
}
```

The proposed interface requires from the implementing class to define its weight, value and a way of comparing two such items. In case of computational devices modeled in the execution engine by the Device class, the weight corresponds to power consumption and the value stands for the inverse of the execution time. For following tests, we implemented comparing two devices in such a way that out of two devices the one with a higher ratio of computational power to power consumption is preferred.

It should be noted that the complexity of the heuristic algorithm used is $O(nlogn)$ where n is the number of compute devices available. It is determined by the sorting phase of the algorithm. Thus, in practice the algorithm is very fast and adds only marginally to the total execution time of the application.

This process allows selection of devices for set D_{exec}.

2. optimization of data partitioning and communication along with assignment of data packets to devices (function $a(k)$) – given the input data I and devices D_js with possibly various relative $perf_{D_j}(A)$, we partition the data into a certain number of equal data packets so that the load can be balanced well in this heterogeneous environment with CPUs and GPUs. Too few data packets would results in big differences between execution times on the devices, on the other hand too many packets would result in too much overhead due to startup times. The process of data partitioning is described in detail in Section 6.3. A special simulator simulates runtime

distribution and assignment of data packets to particular devices. This way it gives us $a(k)$. This process considers communication overheads present in Equation 4.

6   Experiments

6.1   Testbed Application

For the tests, we have chosen a parallel MD5 password breaking application with brute–force and its parallel implementation using OpenCL kernels to be executed on either CPUs or GPUs. This application with a high ratio of computation time/communication time was chosen intentionally to verify the scalability potential of our distributed solution given various power bounds.

The input data for this application is defined as a range of passwords for which hashes need to be calculated and compared with a given pattern. The set of possible passwords is determined by a predefined alphabet. Every password on this alphabet is assigned an integer number. When sending a password list we use a range of integers.

Irrespective of the given hash pattern, the application calculates and compares every hash from the given range. This allows to control the expected length of the application execution by specifying the number of hashes to compute. For the following experiments, the input data for the application specifies the range of over 1679 billions of passwords. The execution times measured for this application on different devices are given in Table 1.

6.2   Testbed Environment and Measurements of Parameters

For subsequent tests we used a parallel cluster with several nodes with the following specifications:

Desstd – 8 GB RAM, Intel(R) Core(TM) i7-2600K CPU @ 3.40GHz for 8 logical cores, NVIDIA GTS 450 running SUSE Linux version 3.1.10-1.16,

Des03 – 8 GB RAM, Intel(R) Core(TM) i7-2600K CPU @ 3.40GHz for 8 logical cores, NVIDIA GTX 480 running SUSE Linux version 3.1.10-1.16,

Cuda1 – 12 GB RAM, Intel(R) Xeon(R) CPUs W3540 @ 2.93GHz with 8 computational units, NVIDIA 560Ti, NVIDIA Tesla 2050, NVIDIA Quadro FX 3800 running Debian Linux version 2.6.32-5.

Let us define the following parameters that were measured directly:

$pow_{N_i}^{idle}$ – average power consumption of N_i in the idle state i.e. not running any applications,

$pow_{N_i+D_j}(A)$ – average power consumption of N_i running application A on D_j,

$t_{exec\ D_j}(A)$ – the execution time of application A on compute device D_j.

Power consumption was measured using a hardware power meter. The compute devices were not used by other users when running simulations. The processors used the maximum possible frequency when computing and ran at full speed without dynamic frequency scaling. When performing computations, measurements indicated constant power consumption of compute devices. Based on these values we calculated $pow_{D_j}(A)$ using the following formula: $pow_{D_j}(A) = pow_{N_i+D_j}(A) - pow_{N_i}^{idle}$ which gives the power required by compute device D_j. Table 1 lists the various devices used in our laboratory along with the measured and computed values for the application. It should be noted that an application may be running on more devices on a single node at the same time e.g. a CPU and a GPU or a CPU and more than one GPU. In that case, the total power consumption is estimated as a sum of particular $pow_{D_j}(A)$s for various js. It should be noted that when running an application on a GPU, the CPU on the same node also takes part in control of the simulation by being a proxy in uploading input data to the global memory of the GPU and downloading results back to the RAM. However, this job is already considered in $pow_{N_i+D_j}(A)$ for power consumption and $t_{exec\ D_j}(A)$ for execution time for a compute device being a GPU.

We also checked the sum of $pow_{N_i}^{idle} + pow_{DCPU_i}(A) + pow_{DGPU_i^j}(A)$ against $pow_{N_i+DCPU_i+DGPU_i^j}(A)$ where $DCPU_i$ denotes the CPU of N_i and $DGPU_i^j$ denotes the j-th GPU of N_i and $pow_{N_i+DCPU_i+DGPU_i^j}(A)$ the power consumption of N_i when running application A on $DCPU_i$ and $DGPU_i^j$ at the same time. The verification for the nodes that we had at our disposal showed matching results with differences up to a few percent that justified the approach for our environment. Table 1 presents power consumption and execution time of the given application on different computational devices as well as the performance approximations and the performance to power consumption ratios. Before simulations, we chose best OpenCL NDRange and work group configurations for the testbed application.

Table 1. Measurements of execution time and power consumption

Node	Compute Device	Ptotal [W]	Pdevice $pow_{D_j}(A)$	Execution Time [s] $t_{exec\ D_j}(A)$	$\frac{\alpha}{t_{exec\ D_j}(A)}$	$\frac{\alpha}{t_{exec\ D_j}(A)} \cdot \frac{1}{pow_{D_j}(A)}$
Desstd	idle	50	—	—	—	—
Desstd	Core i7	125	75	216028	4.629	0.062
Desstd	GTS450	150	100	5140	194.552	1.946
Des03	idle	75	—	—	—	—
Des03	Core i7	150	75	216028	4.629	0.062
Des03	GTX480	250	175	4097	244.081	1.395
Cuda1	idle	230	—	—	—	—
Cuda1	GTX560Ti	395	165	8194	122.040	0.740
Cuda1	Tesla	380	150	8194	90.098	0.601
Cuda1	Quadro	290	60	36680	27.263	0.454

6.3 Data Partitioning

For each configuration composed of a certain number of nodes and thus particular computing devices as well as a given power consumption limit, a certain number of data packets should be generated. A small number of packets each of which requires reasonably long computations would not be enough to balance load across a large number of compute devices that differ in parameters as shown in Table 1. On the other hand, too many small packets would increase communication overhead and thus decrease speed-up.

For our testbed application and each tested power consumption limit, we used an in-house developed simulator to plot predicted execution time against various values of data packet multiplier m.

The execution simulator works on a model of our real infrastructure. For each available device the model defines a parameter that denotes the time necessary to compute a single data package on this device. Additionally, it stores a variable of time spent on the currently assigned package. This variable is consequently increased by the simulator and compared with the necessary time parameter.

The main simulating loop attempts to schedule a task on one of the devices as long as there are data packages left. For the next loop cycle, the simulator always chooses a moment in time when the next scheduling is possible and increases the time counter by the appropriate value. It means, that the time counter is increased by the smallest of the values needed by the devices to finish their tasks.

Additionally, in order to account for the communication time, the job completion times are always increased by a certain constant. Thus, communication overheads are introduced to the simulation.

For a given m, the number of data packets equal to mn was used where n is the number of devices used. As an example, Figure 3 shows simulated execution times for $P_{max} = 1500W$. In this case, m close to 34 is preferable and was used in real tests. For specific numbers of data packets, if a slow device (such as a CPU in our case) gets a packet, other faster devices (GPUs) will need to wait for its completion. This results in steps in the chart.

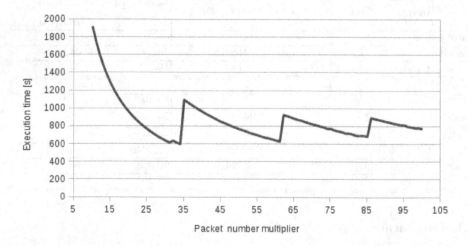

Fig. 3. Simulated execution time vs data packet multiplier for $P_{max} = 1500W$

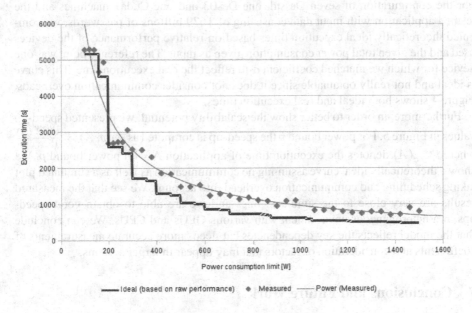

Fig. 4. Measured execution time compared to ideal values

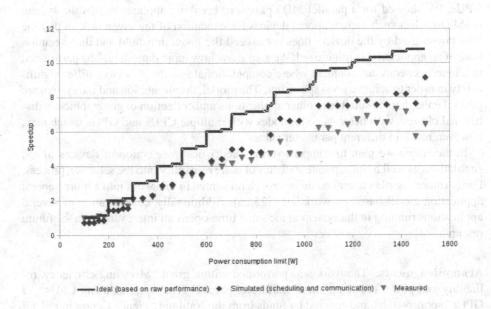

Fig. 5. Measured speed-up compared to simulated values

6.4 Results of Experiments

For the configuration of seven Desstd, one Des03 and one Cuda1 machines and the testbed application with input data consisting of 1679 billions of passwords, we computed theoretically ideal execution times based on relative performance of the devices used and the given total power consumption given as input. The reference point was one device for which we matched coefficient α to reflect the real execution time. This curve is ideal and not really obtainable since it does not consider communication overheads. Figure 4 shows both ideal and real execution times.

Furthermore, in order to better show the scalability potential, we presented speed-up values in Figure 5. For power bound p the speed-up is computed as $sp(p, A) = \frac{t_{exec}^{100W}(A)}{t_{exec}^{p}(A)}$ where $t_{exec}^{p}(A)$ denotes the execution time of application A with power bound p. We show a theoretically ideal curve assuming no communication as well as a simulated plot taking scheduling and communication overhead into account. We see that the measured results are very close to the simulated ones and we are able to obtain good speed-ups in a heterogeneous environment with various GPUs and CPUs. We can conclude that the model reflects the key dependencies but needs more accurate measurements of coefficients and consideration of factors that may appear in larger systems.

7 Conclusions and Future Work

In the paper we presented an approach for multi–level parallelization of computations among several clusters each of which may be equipped with a number of CPUs and GPUs. We showed for a parallel MD5 password breaking application that the system is able to select such computational devices for execution of the given task so that the total power used by the devices does not exceed the given threshold and the execution time of an application is minimized. We also show how input data should be partitioned in a heterogeneous environment where computational speeds of devices differ significantly in order to achieve good speed-ups. The model, the simulation and the system are general enough to be suitable to other applications and collection of geographically distributed clusters with heterogeneous nodes with multiple CPUs and GPUs which may, however, result in different parameter values.

In the future we plan to compare various heuristics in selection of devices to run simulations as well as incorporate statistics of node reliability into the selection process. Furthermore, we plan to embed the approach presented in this work into a more general application model based on workflows [25,26]. Additionally, consideration of several applications running in the system at the same time opens an interesting area for future research.

Acknowledgments. The work was performed within grant "Modeling efficiency, reliability and power consumption of multilevel parallel HPC systems using CPUs and GPUs" sponsored by and covered by funds from the National Science Center in Poland based on decision no DEC-2012/07/B/ST6/01516.

References

1. Buyya, R. (ed.): High Performance Cluster Computing, Programming and Applications. Prentice Hall (1999)
2. Kirk, D.B., Hwu, W.-M.W.: Programming Massively Parallel Processors: A Hands-on Approach 2nd edn. Morgan Kaufmann (2012) ISBN-13: 978-0124159921
3. Sanders, J., Kandrot, E.: CUDA by Example: An Introduction to General-Purpose GPU Programming. Addison-Wesley Professional (2010) ISBN-13: 978-0131387683
4. Geist, A., Beguelin, A., Dongarra, J., Jiang, W., Mancheck, R., Sunderam, V.: PVM Parallel Virtual Machine. In: A Users Guide and Tutorial for Networked Parallel Computing. MIT Press, Cambridge (1994), http://www.epm.ornl.gov/pvm/
5. Wilkinson, B., Allen, M.: Parallel Programming: Techniques and Applications Using Networked Workstations and Parallel Computers. Prentice Hall (1999)
6. Czarnul, P., Grzeda, K.: Parallel simulations of electrophysiological phenomena in myocardium on large 32 and 64-bit linux clusters. In: Kranzlmüller, D., Kacsuk, P., Dongarra, J. (eds.) EuroPVM/MPI 2004. LNCS, vol. 3241, pp. 234–241. Springer, Heidelberg (2004)
7. Balicki, J., Krawczyk, H., Nawarecki, E. (eds.): Grid and Volunteer Computing. Gdansk University of Technology, Faculty of Electronics Telecommunication and Informatics Press, Gdansk (2012) ISBN: 978-83-60779-17-0
8. Karonis, N.T., Toonen, B., Foster, I.: Mpich-g2: A grid-enabled implementation of the message passing interface. Journal of Parallel and Distributed Computing 63, 551–563 (2003); Special Issue on Computational Grids
9. Keller, R., Müller, M.: The Grid-Computing library PACX-MPI: Extending MPI for Computational Grids, http://www.hlrs.de/organization/amt/projects/pacx-mpi/
10. Czarnul, P.: BC-MPI: Running an MPI application on multiple clusters with beesyCluster connectivity. In: Wyrzykowski, R., Dongarra, J., Karczewski, K., Wasniewski, J. (eds.) PPAM 2007. LNCS, vol. 4967, pp. 271–280. Springer, Heidelberg (2008)
11. Sotomayor, B.: The globus toolkit 4 programmer's tutorial (2005), http://www.casa-sotomayor.net/gt4-tutorial/
12. Garg, S.K., Buyya, R., Siegel, H.J.: Time and cost trade-off management for scheduling parallel applications on utility grids. Future Gen. Comp. Systems 26, 1344–1355 (2010)
13. Chin, S.H., Suh, T., Yu, H.C.: Adaptive service scheduling for workflow applications in service-oriented grid. J. Supercomput. 52, 253–283 (2010)
14. Yu, J., Buyya, R.: A taxonomy of workflow management systems for grid computing. Journal of Grid Computing 3, 171–200 (2005)
15. Anderson, D.P.: Boinc: A system for public-resource computing and storage. In: Proceedings of 5th IEEE/ACM International Workshop on Grid Computing, Pittsburgh, USA (2004)
16. Barak, A., Ben-nun, T., Levy, E., Shiloh, A.: A package for opencl based heterogeneous computing on clusters with many gpu devices. In: Proc. of Int. Conf. on Cluster Computing, pp. 1–7 (2011)
17. He, C., Du, P.: Cuda performance study on hadoop mapreduce clusters. Univ. of Nebraska-Lincoln (2010), http://cse.unl.edu/~che/slides/cuda.pdf
18. Stan, M.R., Skadron, K.: Guest editors' introduction: Power-aware computing. IEEE Computer 36, 35–38 (2003)
19. Cameron, K.W., Ge, R., Feng, X.: High-performance, power-aware distributed computing for scientific applications. Computer 38, 40–47 (2005)
20. Li, D., De Supinski, B., Schulz, M., Cameron, K., Nikolopoulos, D.: Hybrid mpi/openmp power-aware computing. In: 2010 IEEE International Symposium on Parallel Distributed Processing (IPDPS), pp. 1–12 (2010)

21. Kasichayanula, K., Terpstra, D., Luszczek, P., Tomov, S., Moore, S., Peterson, G.D.: Power aware computing on gpus. In: Symposium on Application Accelerators in High-Performance Computing, pp. 64–73 (2012)
22. Lawson, B., Smirni, E.: Power-aware resource allocation in high-end systems via online simulation. In: Arvind, Rudolph, L. (ed.) ICS, pp. 229–238. ACM (2005)
23. Garg, S., Buyya, R.: Exploiting heterogeneity in grid computing for energy-efficient resource allocation. In: Proceedings of the 17th International Conference on Advanced Computing and Communications (ADCOM 2009), Bengaluru, India (2009)
24. Cormen, T.H., Leiserson, C.E., Rivest, R.L.: Introduction to Algorithms. The Massachusetts Institute of Technology (1994)
25. Czarnul, P.: Integration of compute-intensive tasks into scientific workflows in beesyCluster. In: Alexandrov, V.N., van Albada, G.D., Sloot, P.M.A., Dongarra, J. (eds.) ICCS 2006. LNCS, vol. 3993, pp. 944–947. Springer, Heidelberg (2006)
26. Czarnul, P.: A model, design, and implementation of an efficient multithreaded workflow execution engine with data streaming, caching, and storage constraints. Journal of Supercomputing 63, 919–945 (2013)

Multicore Parallelization of the PTAS Dynamic Program for the Bin-Packing Problem

Anirudh Chakravorty[1], Thomas George[2], and Yogish Sabharwal[2]

[1] Indraprastha Institute of Information Technology, Delhi
anirudh10014@iiitd.ac.in
[2] IBM Research – India
{thomasgeorge,ysabharwal}@in.ibm.com

Abstract. Dynamic Programming (DP) is an efficient technique to solve combinatorial search and optimization problems. There have been many research efforts towards parallelizing dynamic programs. In this paper, we study the parallelization of the Polynomial Time Approximation Scheme (PTAS) DP for the classical bin-packing problem. This problem is challenging due to the fact that the number of dimensions of the DP table is not known a priori and is dependent on the input and the accuracy desired by the user. We present optimization techniques for parallelizing the DP for this problem, which include diagonalization, blocking and optimizing dependency lookups. We perform a comprehensive evaluation of our parallel DP on a multicore platform and show that the parallel DP scales well and that our proposed optimizations lead to further substantial improvement in performance.

1 Introduction

Dynamic programming (DP) is a classical technique used to solve a large variety of combinatorial optimization problems in the areas of scheduling, inventory management, VLSI design, bioinformatics, etc [9,14]. The main idea behind dynamic programming is to solve complex problems by breaking them into simpler subproblems. It is applicable to problems exhibiting the *optimal substructure* and *overlapping subproblems* properties:

- *Optimal substructure* implies that the solution to a given optimization problem can be obtained by combining optimal solutions to its subproblems.
- *Overlapping subproblems* means that the space of subproblems must be small. While a recursive algorithm solving the problem would solve the same subproblems over and over again, a dynamic program solves each subproblem only once and stores the solution to be reused thereafter.

Dynamic Programming can also be applied to obtain approximation algorithms for many problems, e.g. 0-1 knapsack, bin-packing and minimum makespan scheduling[17,18]. As a matter of fact, *Polynomial Time Approximation Schemes (PTAS)* can be designed for many of these problems based on dynamic programming, wherein, we can obtain a solution having cost within a

M. Chatterjee et al. (Eds.): ICDCN 2014, LNCS 8314, pp. 81–95, 2014.

factor of $1 + \epsilon$ of the optimal solution for any ϵ provided by the user. Thus, a DP can be designed to produce a solution S, such that

$$Cost(S) \leq (1 + \epsilon) \cdot Cost(Opt)$$

where Opt is an optimal solution to the problem. While such accuracy is desirable in many applications, the running time of such dynamic programs can be prohibitively large, typically exponential in $1/\epsilon$. The storage requirements can also be very high. This makes parallel processing an attractive approach to implement such dynamic programs.

Many parallel applications of dynamic programming have been described in research literature; they have been generally designed for very specific problems and only run on special parallel architectures (torus, hypercube, etc.) [10,7,19,4,8,3,12,13,11,5]. Most of these problems deal with dynamic programs having fixed (generally 2) number of dimensions.

In this paper, we study the parallelization of the PTAS dynamic program for the classical bin-packing problem. The bin-packing problem is a fundamental problem in combinatorial optimization that is used as a kernel for many other optimization problems, such as minimum makespan scheduling on parallel machines. What makes this problem more challenging is the fact that the number of dimensions of the dynamic programming table is variable – it is dependent on the characteristics (*weights*) of the the input set of items to be packed and also on the desired accuracy (ϵ parameter specified by the user). Thus, computation of an entry of the DP table is dependent on a variable number of entries (not known a priori). These distinguishing characteristics make the problem more challenging and it is unclear if known and tried optimizations apply to this problem or not. In this paper, we make the following contributions:

(1) We show that the approach of filling the DP table by traversing the entries along the diagonals is well suited for parallelism. We also show that the degree of parallelism increases with increasing number of dimensions.
(2) We next show that the blocking (tiling) approach also works well in our scenario. The main reason is that due to the particular structure of the dependencies in the bin-packing problem, while filling an entry of the DP table, we require to look up a lot of entries that are packed close together. Therefore, blocking (tiling) improves cache-efficiency due to data-locality.
(3) Lastly, we propose an optimization for the bin-packing problem that takes advantage of the relationship amongst the dependencies in order to avoid some of the dependency lookups. For this, we partition the dependencies into two sets, called the *primary dependencies* and the *secondary dependencies*. While filling an entry of the DP table, we first process the primary dependencies and if all the primary dependencies are valid, we do not need to process the secondary dependencies. This reduces the random memory accesses thereby improving the running-time. We show that this can lead to up to 20% improvement in performance.
(4) We do a comprehensive study of the parallelization of the bin-packing dynamic program and report our observations.

2   Related Work

Parallel processing is an efficient approach for solving large-scale DP problems and is the subject of extensive research. Grama et. al.[9] presented a classification of dynamic programming formulations in order to characterize the kind of parallel programming techniques that can be applied in each case. Specifically, they categorize dynamic programs along two directions: (a) the first based on the proximity of dependent sub-problems that make up the overall multistage problem , (b) the second based on the multiplicity of terms in the recurrence that determines the solution to the optimization problem. A dynamic program is considered *serial* if the subproblems at all levels depend only on the results of the immediately preceding levels and *non-serial* otherwise. It is considered *monadic* if the recurrence relation contains a single recursive term and *polyadic* otherwise. Based on this classification, one can define four classes of DP formulations: serial monadic (e.g., single source shortest path problem, 0/1 knapsack problem), serial polyadic (e.g., Floyd all pairs shortest paths algorithm), nonserial monadic (e.g., longest common subsequence problem, Smith-Waterman algorithm) and nonserial polyadic (e.g., optimal matrix parenthesization problem and Zuker algorithm). Note that not all DP problems can be categorized into the above classes. The classical bin-packing problem is one such problem that does not fall into any of the above classifications discussed by Grama et. al.[9]. It is closest to the nonserial polyadic class. However, the fact that the number of terms in the recurrence is not determined a priori and is dependent on the input makes the problem stand apart from other DP problems and also makes the parallelization a challenge.

In the past, there has been some work on parallelization of nonserial polyadic and related DP programs. However, most of the existing work generally pertains to very specific problems and is applicable to special parallel architectures (torus, hypercube, etc.) [10,7,19,4,8,3,12,13,11]. In particular, Tan and Gao[15,16] study the parallel performance of nonserial polyadic DP algorithms in the context of the RNA secondary structure prediction problem on a specific multi-core architecture. They propose parallel processing of independent triangular tiles that lie along the diagonal. Elkihel and Baz[2,6] presented parallel algorithms for the closely related 0-1 knapsack problem using a novel load-balancing strategy for distributing the workload. Alves et. al.[1] presented parallel dynamic programming algorithms for the string editing problem based on dynamic scheduling of blocks to the processors. They recursively divide the blocks into smaller blocks that are then scheduled for processing.

An important aspect that makes our problem very different from previously studied parallel dynamic programs is the number of dimensions of the dynamic programming table – while previous literature deals with two dimensional dynamic programs, the number of dimensions in our problem can be very large depending on the number of distinct item weights and the desired accuracy parameter. While our approach to parallelization via diagonalization and blocking is similar to those proposed in the past[15,16,1], we study these approaches for multi-dimensional dynamic programs for the first time. Another distinguishing factor in our problem is the large number of terms that appear in the DP recurrence. This calls for different kind of optimizations than previously known in the research literature.

3   The Bin-Packing Problem

In the bin-packing problem, we are given a set $\mathcal{A} = \{a_1, a_2, \ldots, a_n\}$ of n items where each item, a_i, has a weight $0 < w(a_i) \leq 1$ associated with it. The goal is to find the minimum number of bins, each of unit capacity, required to store the items so that the total weight of the items stored in any bin does not exceed its capacity, 1. This problem is known to be NP-hard[1].

We now discuss the dynamic programming based PTAS for the Bin-packing problem[17,18]. This algorithm reduces the bin-packing problem to a special instance wherein there are only a constant number of item weights. In this specialization, called the *restricted bin-packing* problem, the weights of all the items are sampled from a fixed set $\mathcal{W} = \{w_1, w_2, \ldots, w_k\}$ of k weights, where k is a constant. That is $w(a_i) \in \mathcal{W}$ for all $a_i \in \mathcal{A}$. This special version can be solved optimally in polynomial time using dynamic programing (c.f. Section 3.1).

The pseudocode for the PTAS is presented in Figure 1. The algorithm can be divided into three phases. In the first phase we reduce the bin-packing problem to an instance of the restricted bin-packing problem after removing some items and rounding the weights of the remaining items. In the second phase, we solve the restricted bin-packing problem optimally using a dynamic program. Finally in the third phase, we augment the solution of the restricted bin-packing problem with the earlier removed items to form a feasible solution to the original bin-packing instance.

First Phase: We first remove all the items having weight less than ϵ. Let $\mathcal{A}_\epsilon$ be the set of removed items and $\mathcal{A}'$ be the resulting set of items. We partition the set $\mathcal{A}'$ into $r = \lceil log_{(1+\epsilon)} \frac{1}{\epsilon} \rceil$ groups $A_1, A_2, \ldots, A_r$ where for $1 \leq i \leq r$, A_i is the set of all the items having weight in the range $[\epsilon(1 + \epsilon)^{i-1}, \epsilon(1 + \epsilon)^i)$. Next, for each $1 \leq i \leq r$, we round down the weight of all the items in the group A_i to $\epsilon(1 + \epsilon)^{i-1}$. Note that the instance determined by the items $\mathcal{A}'$ with the modified weights is an instance of the restricted bin packing problem with at most r different weights.

Second Phase: In this phase we solve the restricted bin-packing problem optimally on the instance $\mathcal{A}'$ with the modified weights. The dynamic program for achieving this is formally described in Section 3.1. Let the solution thus obtained be S', i.e., S' is a partition of the items of $\mathcal{A}'$ into sets $R_1, R_2, \ldots, R_t$ where R_j specifies the set of items packed into bin j.

Third Phase: In the third phase we augment the solution returned by the restricted bin-packing problem to a solution for the original instance of the bin-packing problem. This is achieved by introducing back the items removed in phase 1 using the *first-fit* algorithm. For this, we consider the items of $\mathcal{A}_\epsilon$ in an

---

[1]   The Bin-packing problem is weakly NP-hard; it is solvable in polynomial time when the input is in unary.

Input: Item Set, $\mathcal{A}$; weight function, w; and approximation parameter, ϵ

Phase 1:
Let $\mathcal{A}_\epsilon$ be the set of items having weight $< \epsilon$, i.e., $\mathcal{A}_\epsilon = \{a \in \mathcal{A} : w(a) < \epsilon\}$
Let $\mathcal{A}'$ be the remaining set of items, i.e., $\mathcal{A}' = \mathcal{A} \setminus \mathcal{A}_\epsilon$
For $i = 1$ to $\lceil log_{(1+\epsilon)} \frac{1}{\epsilon} \rceil$
    Let $A_i = \{a \in \mathcal{A}' : \epsilon(1 + \epsilon)^{i-1} \leq w(a) < \epsilon(1 + \epsilon)^i\}$
    For all $a \in A_i$, define $w'(a) = \epsilon(1 + \epsilon)^{i-1}$

Phase 2:
Let $S' = \{R_1, R_2, \ldots, R_t\}$ be the solution obtained on invoking
    Restricted-Bin-Packing($\mathcal{A}'$, w', k)

Phase 3:
Initialize $S = S'$
For each $a \in \mathcal{A}_\epsilon$
    If $\exists R \in S$, such that $\sum_{a' \in R} w(a') + w(a) \leq 1$
        add a to R
    else
        create a new bin $R_{|S|+1}$ and add a to $R_{|S|+1}$

Return S

Fig. 1. PTAS for the bin-packing problem

arbitrary order. For each item, we find the first bin in which it fits using the original weights. If we find such a bin, the item is added to that bin. If no such bin exists, we create a new bin and add the item to this new bin.

3.1   Restricted Bin-Packing Problem

We now discuss a dynamic program that solves the restricted bin-packing problem optimally in polynomial time. Let $\mathcal{A}'$ be the set of all the items. We fix an ordering on the item weights say $w'_1, w'_2, \ldots w'_k$. Let n_i be the number of items of weight w'_i for $1 \leq i \leq k$. Note that an instance, I, of the packing problem can be defined by a k-tuple $(p_1, p_2, \ldots, p_k)$ specifying the number of items for each weight. We set up a k-dimensional table $BINS$ of size $(n_1+1, n_2+1, \ldots, n_k+1)$. $BINS(p_1, p_2, \ldots, p_k)$ denotes the minimum number of bins required to pack the items of $I = (p_1, p_2, \ldots, p_k)$, i.e., p_1 items of weight w'_1, p_2 items of weight w'_2, ..., p_k items of weight w'_k. Note that the total weight for an instance, $I = (p_1, p_2, \ldots, p_k)$, is given by $\sum_{i=1}^{k} p_i \cdot w'_i$. We first compute the set Q of all instances for which the total weight is at most 1 – clearly only one bin is required to fit these items. Thus

Input: Item Set, $\mathcal{A}'$; weight function, w'; number of distinct item weights, k

For $i = 1$ to k
    Let $A_i' = \{a \in \mathcal{A}' : w(a) = w_i'\}$
    Let $n_i = |A_i'|$

Let $\mathcal{U} = \{(p_1, \ldots, p_k) : 0 \le p_i \le n_i \; \forall \; 1 \le i \le k\}$ be the set of all valid k-tuples
Let $\mathcal{Q} = \{(p_1, \ldots, p_k) : 0 \le p_i \le n_i \; \forall \; 1 \le i \le k \text{ and } \sum_{i=1}^{k} p_i \cdot w_i \le 1\}$

For all $(q_1, q_2, \ldots, q_k) \in \mathcal{Q}$
    set $\mathcal{BINS}(q_1, q_2, \ldots, q_k) = 1$
    set $\mathcal{Q}_{BINS}(q_1, q_2, \ldots, q_k) = (q_1, q_2, \ldots, q_k)$

For all $(p_1, p_2, \ldots, p_k) \in \mathcal{U} \setminus \mathcal{Q}$
    Let $(\hat{q}_1, \hat{q}_2, \ldots, \hat{q}_k) =$
                $argmin_{(q_1, q_2, \ldots, q_k) \in \mathcal{Q} : q_i \le p_i \forall i} \mathcal{BINS}(p_1 - q_1, p_2 - q_2, \ldots, p_k - q_k)$
    set $\mathcal{BINS}(p_1, p_2, \ldots, p_k) = 1 + \mathcal{BINS}(\hat{q}_1, \hat{q}_2, \ldots, \hat{q}_k)$
    set $\mathcal{Q}_{BINS}(p_1, p_2, \ldots, p_k) = (\hat{q}_1, \hat{q}_2, \ldots, \hat{q}_k)$

Initialize solution $S' = \phi$.
Let $(p_1, p_2, \ldots, p_k) = (n_1, n_2, \ldots, n_k)$
While $(p_1, p_2, \ldots, p_k) \ne (0, 0, \ldots, 0)$
    Let $(\hat{q}_1, \hat{q}_2, \ldots, \hat{q}_k) = \mathcal{Q}_{BINS}(p_1, p_2, \ldots, p_k)$
    Let R be a subset of $\mathcal{A}'$ such that $R \cap A_i' = \hat{q}_i \; \forall 1 \le i \le k$
    Add R to S' and update $\mathcal{A}' = \mathcal{A}' \setminus R$
    Update $(p_1, p_2, \ldots, p_k) = (p_1 - \hat{q}_1, p_2 - \hat{q}_2, \ldots, p_k - \hat{q}_k)$

Return S'

Fig. 2. Restricted bin-packing problem

$$Q = \{(p_1, p_2, \ldots, p_k) : 0 \le p_i \le n_i \; \forall \; 1 \le i \le k \text{ and } \sum_{i=1}^{k} p_i \cdot w_i' \le 1\}$$

For all instances $(q_1, q_2, \ldots, q_k) \in Q$, we initialize $BINS(q_1, q_2, \ldots, q_k) = 1$.

Now we can use the following recurrence for computing the remaining entries:

$$BINS(p_1, p_2, \ldots, p_k) = 1 + \min_{\substack{(q_1, q_2, \ldots, q_k) \in Q: \\ q_i \le p_i \; \forall i}} BINS(p_1 - q_1, p_2 - q_2, \ldots, p_k - q_k)$$

In order to trace back the optimal solution, we maintain another k-dimensional table Q_{BINS} of size $(n_1 + 1, n_2 + 1, \ldots, n_k + 1)$. For an entry $BINS(p_1, p_2, \ldots, p_k)$, we store in $Q_{BINS}(p_1, p_2, \ldots, p_k)$ the corresponding entry of Q that yields the optimal solution for this entry of $BINS$.

Once the DP table is completely filled, we can trace back and retrieve the optimal solution as follows. The entry $BINS(n_1, n_2, \ldots, n_k)$ tells us the optimal number of bins required. The entry $Q_{BINS}(n_1, n_2, \ldots, n_k)$ tells us the contents of one bin of this optimal solution, i.e., the number of items of each weight that fit in one bin in the optimal solution. Let $Q_{BINS}(n_1, n_2, \ldots, n_k)$ be $(\hat{q}_1, \hat{q}_2, \ldots, \hat{q}_k)$. Thus we can now create one bin of the optimal solution by selecting any $\hat{q}_1$ items of weight w'_1, $\hat{q}_2$ items of weight w'_2, $\ldots$, $\hat{q}_k$ items of weight w'_k from $\mathcal{A}'$. We add this bin to the solution and then remove these items from $\mathcal{A}'$ so that they are not considered for any further bins. We then process $BINS(n_1 - \hat{q}_1, n_2 - \hat{q}_2, \ldots, n_k - \hat{q}_k)$ in a similar manner. We proceed recursively like this, adding bins to the solution until no more items remain.

To analyze the complexity of the dynamic program, we see that computing each entry takes $O(n^k)$ time. Thus, the entire table can be computed in $O(n^{2k})$ time as Q is of size $O(n^k)$. The final solution is obtained in the entry $BINS(n_1, n_2, \ldots, n_k)$.

4   Multicore Parallelization and Optimization

In this section, we discuss our strategies for parallelizing the dynamic program for the bin-packing problem efficiently on multicore platforms.

4.1   Parallelization via Diagonalization

The maximum time in the dynamic program is spent in computing the entries of the k-dimensional table $BINS$. Recall that the dynamic program recurrence is given by

$$BINS(p_1, p_2, \ldots, p_k) = 1 + \min_{\substack{(q_1, q_2, \ldots, q_k) \in Q: \\ q_i \leq p_i \ \forall i}} BINS(p_1 - q_1, p_2 - q_2, \ldots, p_k - q_k)$$

We note that we cannot parallelize the computation of any two entries that lie along the same dimension, this is because the entries of Q may have 0's in some of their entries implying that the entries of $BINS$ lying along the same dimension may be dependent on each other.

Consider the sum function, $\mathcal{Z}$, that maps the k-tuple index of each entry of the $BINS$ array to the sum of the indices in the k-tuple, i.e., for any index $(p_1, p_2, \ldots, p_k)$ of the $BINS$ array, $\mathcal{Z}((p_1, p_2, \ldots, p_k)) = \sum_{i=1}^{k} p_i$. An important observation from the recurrence above is that the set of entries that a particular entry of $BINS$ depends on, all have a smaller value of $\mathcal{Z}$ associated with them; this is because $\mathcal{Z}((q_1, q_2, \ldots, q_k)) > 0$ for all entries $(q_1, q_2, \ldots, q_k) \in Q$. This suggests that we can process the entries of the table $BINS$ in increasing order of their $\mathcal{Z}$ values. That allows us to process all the entries of $BINS$ that have the same $\mathcal{Z}$ value in parallel. Thus we process the entries of $BINS =$ in $n_1 + n_2 + \ldots + n_k$ iterations; in iteration i, we process all the entries for which the associated $\mathcal{Z}$ value is i. This is the same as processing the entries of $BINS$ diagonally as the sum of the indices of all the entries lying along the same diagonal is the same. (see Figure 5 (a) for an illustration in 2 dimensions).

For $i = 1$ to $n_1 + n_2 + \ldots + n_k$

 # pragma omp parallel for ...
For $j = 1$ to $size(\mathcal{Z}ptrlist[i])$
      Retrieve index of $BINS$ entry pointed to by $\mathcal{Z}ptrlist[i][j]$
      Compute DP entry for this index using the DP recurrence

Fig. 3. OpenMP parallelization using diagonalization

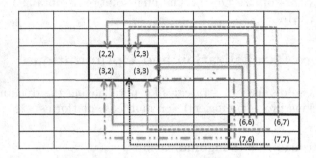

Fig. 4. Dependencies of entries within blocks

Before getting into the dynamic program, we preprocess and create some additional data structures to allow diagonal parallelization of the dynamic program. We create $n_1 + n_2 + \ldots + n_k$ lists (arrays), $\mathcal{Z}ptrlist[i]$, one for each possible value that the function $\mathcal{Z}$ can take. In list i, we store pointers to all the entries of $BINS$ for which $\mathcal{Z}(\cdot) = i$. The DP can now be updated using two loops; the outer loop runs over all the possible values that $\mathcal{Z}$ can take in increasing order and the inner loop runs over all the entries of $BINS$ having the corresponding $\mathcal{Z}$ value and process them as specified by the DP. The inner loop can now be parallelized using OpenMP (See Figure 3).

4.2 Block Decomposition for Cache Efficiency

Blocking is a well-known technique that has been used in optimization of numerical linear algebra implementations on high performance computing platforms. Instead of operating on entire rows or columns of a matrix, blocked algorithms operate on submatrices (called blocks). Operating on blocks leads to improved data locality as the blocks loaded into the faster levels of memory hierarchy result in better data reuse in comparison to the data loaded in case of operations performed on entire rows or columns.

In this section, we present a blocking optimization for our dynamic program and illustrate how it can benefit the performance of the DP. Consider the

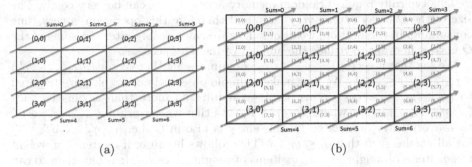

Fig. 5. Processing of (a) *entries* and (b) *blocks* having same sum of indices in parallel

restricted bin-packing problem with 2 weights. Thus, the $BINS$ array in this case is a 2-dimensional array. Suppose that the Q array contains the entries $(4, 4)$, $(4, 3)$, $(3, 4)$ and $(3, 3)$. Now consider the dependencies for entries $(6, 6)$, $(6, 7)$, $(7, 6)$ and $(7, 7)$. These are illustrated in Figure 4. Entry $(6, 6)$ depends on all the four entries $(2, 2)$, $(2, 3)$,$(3, 2)$ and $(3, 3)$; entry $(6, 7)$ depends on the entries $(2, 3)$ and $(3, 3)$; entry $(7, 6)$ depends on the entries $(3, 2)$ and $(3, 3)$; entry $(7, 7)$ depends on the entry $(3, 3)$. Thus if we create blocks of 2×2 in this example, we see that we can benefit from data locality of the entries of $BINS$ that are fetched; this is because the Q array has entries that are packed close together. More precisely, whenever $(q_1, q_2, \ldots, q_k) \in Q$, then all the entries dominated by this entry also belong to Q. For instance in 2 dimensions, if $(4, 4) \in Q$, then $(4, 3), (3, 4), (3, 3) \in Q$ as well.

We next discuss how blocks can be used in conjunction with the diagonalization optimization discussed in the previous section. Consider the case of $BINS$ array being 2-dimensional. Figure 5 (b) illustrates the $BINS$ array divided into blocks of size 2×2. We can number the blocks in 2-dimensions as illustrated in the figure. We note that the entries for which the indices of the block numbers are the same are independent of each other. Thus, we can process all the blocks having the same sum of indices in parallel. This is the same as before, except that the sum of indices is now computed over the blocks instead of the elements. However, note that the entries within a block are not independent. Therefore, we need to process them in increasing order of the sum of indices as before.

Note that since in the bin-packing problem the DP can have large number of dimensions, the blocks are themselves multi-dimensional and hence large. For instance, even with a modest value of $k = 6$ (unique item weights), a block size of $2 \times \ldots \times 2$ has $2^6 = 64$ elements. Thus we shall use small block sizes for our DP so that the blocks fit in the L1 cache.

4.3   Optimizing Dependency Lookups

Recall that the dynamic program recurrence is given by

$$BINS(p_1, p_2, \ldots, p_k) = 1 + \min_{\substack{(q_1, q_2, \ldots, q_k) \in Q: \\ q_i \leq p_i \ \forall i}} BINS(p_1 - q_1, p_2 - q_2, \ldots, p_k - q_k)$$

This typically requires random memory accesses that can be very costly. The size of the Q array can be very large and therefore this operation is very time consuming. In this section, we discuss how we can possibly filter out some of the Q entries in order to reduce the number of memory accesses.

We say that a vector $(p_1, p_2, \ldots, p_k)$ dominates another vector $(p'_1, p'_2, \ldots, p'_k)$ if $p'_i \leq p_i \, \forall \, 1 \leq i \leq k$. We first make a simple observation: if x bins are required to pack $(p_1, p_2, \ldots, p_k)$ items, then we require no more than x bins to pack $(p'_1, p'_2, \ldots, p'_k)$ items, where $p'_i \leq p_i \, \forall \, i$. Note that whenever $(q_1, q_2, \ldots, q_k) \in Q$, then every entry dominated by this entry is also in Q, i.e. $(q'_1, q'_2, \ldots, q'_k) \in Q$ for all entries such that $q'_i \leq q_i \, \forall \, i$. This follows because, if q_1 items of weight w_1, q_2 items of weight w_2, ..., q_k items of weight w_k can fit in a bin, then so can any subset of these items. Now, if while computing an entry $(p_1, p_2, \ldots, p_k)$ of $BINS$, the entry $(p_1 - q_1, p_2 - q_2, \ldots, p_k - q_k)$ is valid, i.e., $p_i - q_i \geq 0 \, \forall 1 \leq i \leq k$, then we do not need to lookup the entries $(p_1 - q'_1, p_2 - q'_2, \ldots, p_k - q'_k)$, where $(q'_1, q'_2, \ldots, q'_k) \in Q$ is dominated by $(q_1, q_2, \ldots, q_k)$. This is because the number of bins required to pack $(p_1 - q'_1, p_2 - q'_2, \ldots, p_k - q'_k)$ items cannot be anymore than required to pack $(p_1 - q_1, p_2 - q_2, \ldots, p_k - q_k)$ items. Thus, while updating an entry of $BINS$, if the lookup for some entry of Q results in a valid entry of $BINS$, then we do not need to perform lookup for the entries of Q that are dominated by this entry (however, we cannot throw away all the dominated entries as lookups for the dominating entry may be an invalid entry of $BINS$).

In order to address this problem, we divide the entries of Q into two parts, called the *primary* and the *secondary* entries of Q. The primary entries correspond to entries that are not dominated by any other entry of Q. The secondary entries correspond to entires of Q that are dominated by some entry of Q. We can now filter the entries of Q as follows. We first determine the minimum by looking up all the primary entries of Q. In case any of these is invalid, then we also lookup the minimum using the secondary entries of Q. If all the primary entries of Q are valid, then there is no need to lookup any secondary entry of Q. The pseudocode for this procedure is illustrated in Figure 6. Note that it may seem that we can design more optimal algorithms for optimizing on all the dependencies amongst the Q entries; however, we emphasize here that what we are trying to save by avoiding one lookup is a single memory access – a more complicated scheme will require maintaining additional information that will also need to be looked up from the memory and result in additional memory accesses. Therefore, we choose to implement a simple strategy that does not require any additional data structures to be maintained.

5   Experimental Evaluation

In this section, we describe experimental evaluation of the proposed parallelization and optimization strategies.

5.1   Experimental Setup

Data. The characteristics of a restricted bin packing problem instance are largely controlled by three properties: (a) number of distinct weights, (b) item-weight

Let $numP$ = number of primary entries of Q
Let $numS$ = number of secondary entries of Q

For $i = 1$ to $numP$
 Let $(q_1, q_2, \ldots, q_k)$ be the ith primary entry of Q
 If $(p_1 - q_1, p_2 - q_2, \ldots, p_k - q_k) \geq (0, 0, \ldots, 0)$
  Increment $numAccessed$
  Let $\mathcal{X} = BINS(p_1 - q_1, p_2 - q_2, \ldots, p_k - q_k) + 1$
  If $\mathcal{X} < BINS(p_1, p_2, \ldots, p_k)$
   $BINS(p_1, p_2, \ldots, p_k) = \mathcal{X}$

If ($numAccessed \neq numP$)
 For $i = 1$ to $numS$
  Let $(q_1, q_2, \ldots, q_k)$ be the ith secondary entry of Q
  If $(p_1 - q_1, p_2 - q_2, \ldots, p_k - q_k) \geq (0, 0, \ldots, 0)$
   Let $\mathcal{X} = BINS(p_1 - q_1, p_2 - q_2, \ldots, p_k - q_k) + 1$
   If $\mathcal{X} < BINS(p_1, p_2, \ldots, p_k)$
    $BINS(p_1, p_2, \ldots, p_k) = \mathcal{X}$

Fig. 6. Dependency lookup optimization of the Q array in the DP

generating distribution, (c) number of items. For the current study, we evaluated the different DP variants on synthetic problem instances with varying number of distinct weights $(2, 3, 4, 5, 6, 7, 8)$ and varying number of items $(50, 100, 200, 300)$. We also considered two different distributions (uniform and Zipf) for generating item weights. The weights were chosen to be contiguous.

Hardware Configuration. The experiments were performed on a Dell Precision T7600 system with a 8 core Intel Xeon processor running 64 bit Ubuntu 12.04 LTS. This machine has 20MB cache for all the 2GHz processor cores, supports hyper-threading, and has 256 GB DDR3 RAM. The bin packing code was compiled using GNU gcc compiler with -O3 optimization and openMP was used for shared memory parallelization. To study the benefits of parallelization, each problem instance was solved using varying number of parallel threads $(1, 2, 4, 8, 16)$.

5.2   Results and Discussion

Parallel Speedup with Increasing Number of Distinct Weights. Figure 7 shows the speedup relative to the single thread implementation for problem instances with a fixed ($=100$) number of items and varying number of distinct weights $(4, 6, 8)$ for both uniform and Zipf distributions. The performance times in this case correspond to the parallelization without any optimizations. The range for the number of distinct weights was chosen so that the problem sizes are large enough to benefit from parallelization. We observe that a larger number of

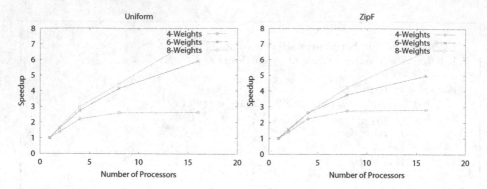

Fig. 7. Speedup with increasing number of distinct weights for a fixed(=100) number of items

distinct weights results in higher speedups for both the distributions. In particular, for the case of 8 distinct weights with uniform distribution, we obtain speedups of around 7.5× with 16 threads. This increased speed-up is to be expected as the problem size becomes exponentially large as we go to higher number of distinct weights. Specifically, when k is the number of distinct weights, the size of parallelizable work, (i.e., the number of blocks in the intersection of the "diagonal" hyperplane of the form $p_1 + \cdots + p_k = r$ and the k-dimensional cuboid to be explored) increases exponentially with k allowing more opportunity for parallelization.

Parallel Speedup with Increasing Number of Items. Figure 8 shows the speedup relative to the sequential case for a fixed (=5) number of distinct weights with varying number of items $(100, 200, 300)$ and two distributions (uniform and Zipf). As in the previous case, the performance times correspond to parallelization without additional optimizations. We observe that relative to the previous case with varying number of distinct weights, there is only a modest increase in speedup with increasing number of items. For instance, in case of uniform distribution, with 16 threads and 5 distinct weights , there is a jump in speedup from 4.2× to 4.8× when the number of items goes from 100 to 200. On the other hand as we observed in Figure 7, with 16 threads and 100 items generated using uniform distribution, there is a jump in speedup from 5.8× to nearly 7.8× when the number of distinct weights goes from 6 to 8. The increase in speedup is also much more pronounced in case of uniform distribution than Zipf distribution. This behavior can be explained by the fact that the size of parallelizable work (i.e., the number of blocks in the intersection of the "diagonal" hyperplanes and the k-dimensional cuboid to be explored) increases polynomially with the number of items n in case of uniform distribution. However, in case of Zipf distribution, the cuboid is very skewed in a few dimensions so that the size of the intersection with the diagonal hyperplanes is much smaller as a result of which there is barely any increase in the speedup.

Effect of Optimizations: Next, we study the effect of the proposed optimizations on the performance of the parallel DP. We consider four different variants of the code:

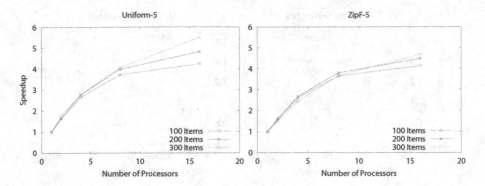

Fig. 8. Speedup with increasing number of items for a fixed(=5) number of distinct weights

(i) `NOOPT`: This is the base code without any optimizations, i.e., the block sizes are $1 \times \ldots \times 1$ and all the dependencies from the Q array are looked up;

(ii) `BLK2`: This is the code with the blocking optimization wherein the block sizes are $2 \times \ldots \times 2$ and all the dependencies from the Q array are looked up;

(iii) `DEP`: This is the code with the optimization wherein the dependencies are split into primary and secondary and the block sizes are $1 \times \ldots \times 1$;

(iv) `DEP-BLK2`: This is the code with both the optimizations, i.e., block sizes are $2 \times \ldots \times 2$ and the dependencies are split into primary and secondary.

Figure 9 shows the performance improvement of the optimized versions relative to `NOOPT` with varying number of threads and a fixed (=100) number of items. The different plots correspond to two different choices $(6, 8)$ for the number of distinct weights and two different (uniform and Zipf) item-weight generating distributions.

In all the four cases, we observe that for a fixed block size, splitting up dependencies into primary and secondary results in a performance improvement, i.e., `DEP-BLK2` is superior to `BLK2` and `DEP` is superior to `NOOPT`. For uniform distribution and 6 distinct weights, `DEP` and `DEP-BLK2` provide roughly $10 - 20\%$ improvement over `NOOPT` and `BLK2` respectively. The relative improvement seems to be similar for both uniform and Zipf distribution.

From the plots, we also observe the blocking optimization is beneficial to some extent in all the four cases. However, the relative improvement depends on the problem size and the number of parallel threads and even the choice of the distribution. On an average, there is substantial increase in the improvement as the number of distinct weights goes up. For instance, with uniform distribution and 16 threads, we observe a 10% improvement with 6 distinct weights, but nearly 30% improvement with 8 distinct weights. In case of Zipf distribution, the improvements for equivalent scenarios are much smaller, but the trend holds. For a fixed choice of distribution and problem size, we also notice a decrease in improvement due to larger block size as the number of threads increase. This behavior can be readily explained by the fact that larger block sizes result in fewer

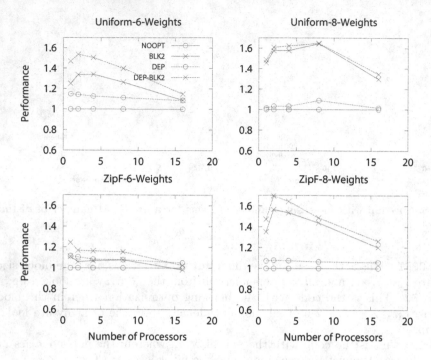

Fig. 9. Performance improvement with the proposed optimizations – blocking and secondary Q array

opportunities for parallelization resulting in poorer performance with increasing number of threads.

Overall, we notice that combining the blocking optimization and dependency partitioning can result in a substantial improvement. For instance, in case of uniform distribution with 8 distinct weights, we observe that DEP–BLK2 provides up to 65% improvement over NOOPT algorithm.

6   Conclusions

We presented a study on shared-memory parallelization of the PTAS dynamic program for the classical bin-packing problem, one of the fundamental problems in combinatorial optimization. Parallelizing multi-dimensional DP where each entry in the DP table depends on variable and potentially large number of other entries is highly challenging. To the best of our knowledge, this paper is the first work that attempts to address this problem for the scenario where the number of dimensions is greater than two. We demonstrated that certain tried and tested techniques such as diagonal traversal and blocking (tiling) perform well. We also propose a novel technique to optimize dependency lookups that arise in the bin-packing problem by partitioning them into two categories- primary and secondary, with the latter ones required only when at least one of the primary lookups is not valid. Experimental evaluation on synthetic data indicates significant performance gains due to the proposed optimizations (up to 65 % in certain cases). There is scope for much more improvement in optimizing these dependency lookups especially in case of distributed memory systems.

References

1. Alves, C.E.R., Cáceres, E., Dehne, F.K.H.A.: Parallel dynamic programming for solving the string editing problem on a cgm/bsp. In: SPAA, pp. 275–281 (2002)
2. El Baz, D., Elkihel, M.: Load balancing methods and parallel dynamic programming algorithm using dominance technique applied to the 0-1 knapsack problem. J. Parallel Distrib. Comput. 65(1), 74–84 (2005)
3. Bradford, P.G.: Efficient parallel dynamic programming (1994)
4. Calvet, J.-L., Viargues, G.: Parallelism in dynamic programming: an issue to feedback control. In: First IEEE Conference on Control Applications, vol. 2, pp. 1063–1064 (1992)
5. Chowdhury, R.A., Ramachandran, V.: Cache-efficient dynamic programming algorithms for multicores. In: SPAA, pp. 207–216. ACM (2008)
6. Elkihel, M., El Baz, D.: Load balancing in a parallel dynamic programming multi-method applied to the 0-1 knapsack problem. In: PDP, pp. 127–132. IEEE Computer Society (2006)
7. Huang, S.H.S., Liu, H., Viswanathan, V.: Parallel dynamic programming. IEEE Trans. Parallel Distrib. Syst. 5(3), 326–328 (1994)
8. Karypis, G., Kumar, V.: Efficient parallel mappings of a dynamic programming algorithm: A summary of results. In: IPPS, pp. 563–568 (1993)
9. Kumar, V., Grama, A., Gupta, A., Karypis, G.: Introduction to Parallel Computing. Benjamin/Cummings (1994)
10. Larson, R.E., Tse, E.: Parallel processing algorithms for optimal control of nonlinear dynamic systems. IEEE Trans. Comput. 22(8), 777–786 (1973)
11. Lau, K.K., Kumar, M.J.: Parallel implementation of the unit commitment problem on nows. In: High Performance Computing on the Information Superhighway, HPC Asia 1997, pp. 128–133 (1997)
12. Lewandowski, G., Condon, A., Bach, E.: Asynchronous analysis of parallel dynamic programming. In: SIGMETRICS, pp. 268–269 (1993)
13. Rodríguez, C., Roda, J.L., García, F., Almeida, F., González, D.: Paradigms for parallel dynamic programming. In: EUROMICRO, p. 553. IEEE Computer Society (1996)
14. Smith, T.F., Waterman, M.S.: Identification of common molecular subsequences. Journal of Molecular Biology 147(1), 195–197 (1981)
15. Tan, G., Feng, S., Sun, N.: Biology - locality and parallelism optimization for dynamic programming algorithm in bioinformatics. In: SC, p. 78. ACM Press (2006)
16. Tan, G., Sun, N., Gao, G.R.: A parallel dynamic programming algorithm on multi-core architecture. In: SPAA, pp. 135–144. ACM (2007)
17. Vazirani, V.V.: Approximation algorithms. Springer (2001)
18. Williamson, D.P., Shmoys, D.B.: The Design of Approximation Algorithms. Cambridge University Press (2011)
19. Xu, H.H., Hanson, F.B., Chung, S.L.: Optimal data parallel methods for stochastic dynamical programming. In: ICPP (3), pp. 142–146 (1991)

Energy Accounting and Control with SLURM Resource and Job Management System

Yiannis Georgiou[1], Thomas Cadeau[1], David Glesser[1],
Danny Auble[2], Morris Jette[2], and Matthieu Hautreux[3]

[1] BULL S.A.S
{Yiannis.Georgiou,Thomas.Cadeau,David.Glesser}@bull.net
[2] SchedMD
{da,jette}@schedmd.com
[3] CEA DAM
Matthieu.Hautreux@cea.fr

Abstract. Energy consumption has gradually become a very important parameter in High Performance Computing platforms. The Resource and Job Management System (RJMS) is the HPC middleware that is responsible for distributing computing power to applications and has knowledge of both the underlying resources and jobs needs. Therefore it is the best candidate for monitoring and controlling the energy consumption of the computations according to the job specifications. The integration of energy measurment mechanisms on RJMS and the consideration of energy consumption as a new characteristic in accounting seemed primordial at this time when energy has become a bottleneck to scalability. Since Power-Meters would be too expensive, other existing measurement models such as IPMI and RAPL can be exploited by the RJMS in order to track energy consumption and enhance the monitoring of the executions with energy considerations.

In this paper we present the design and implementation of a new framework, developed upon SLURM Resource and Job Management System, which allows energy accounting per job with power profiling capabilities along with parameters for energy control features based on static frequency scaling of the CPUs. Since the goal of this work is the deployment of the framework on large petaflopic clusters such as CURIE, its cost and reliability are important issues. We evaluate the overhead of the design choices and the precision of the monitoring modes using different HPC benchmarks (Linpack, IMB, Stream) on a real-scale platform with integrated Power-meters. Our experiments show that the overhead is less than 0.6% in energy consumption and less than 0.2% in execution time while the error deviation compared to Power-meters less than 2% in most cases.

1 Introduction

Energy Consumption is playing a very significant role in the evolution of High Performance Computing Platforms. The increase in computation performance of Supercomputers has come with an even greater increase in energy consumption, turning energy an undisputed barrier towards the exascale. Research efforts upon all different abstraction layers of computer science, from hardware, to middleware upto applications, strive to

M. Chatterjee et al. (Eds.): ICDCN 2014, LNCS 8314, pp. 96–118, 2014.

improve energy conservations. The advances on hardware layer need to be followed by evolutions on systems software and middleware in order to achieve important results.

As far as the systems middleware concerns, the Resource and Job Management System (RJMS) can play an important role since it has both knowledge of the hardware components along with information upon the users workloads and the executed applications. Energy consumption is the result of application computation hence it should be treated as a job characteristic. This would enable administrators to profile workloads and users to be more energy aware. Furthermore power consumption analysis with timestamps would enable users to profile their applications and perform optimizations in their code. Hence the first step that needs to be made is to measure power and energy through the RJMS and map them to jobs. Introducing Power-Meters on Supercomputers would be too expensive in terms of money and additional energy hence using the already available interfaces seemed the most viable approach.

This paper presents the design and evaluation of energy accounting and control mechanisms implemented upon the SLURM Resource and Job Management System. SLURM [1] is an open-source RJMS specifically designed for the scalability requirements of state-of-the-art supercomputers. In Junes' 2013 Top 500 list [2] SLURM was the default RJMS of 5 supercomputers in the top 10. The new framework allows power and energy consumption monitoring per node and accounting per job based on IPMI and RAPL measuring interfaces. The new monitoring modes are enhanced with mechanisms to control energy consumption based on static frequency scaling of the CPUs, allowing users to experiment on the trade-offs between energy consumption and performance. The new features presented in this paper are currently in the latest 2.6 version of SLURM released on July 2013.

Having as goal the deployment of the framework on large petaflopic clusters such as the French PRACE Tier0 system *CURIE* [1], its cost and reliability are important issues. We perform experimentations of the new framework upon a real-scale platform with integrated Power-Meters and we evaluate the overhead of the monitoring modes and the precision of the power and energy data during the executions of different HPC applications (Linpack, IMB, Stream).

The remainder of this article is presented as follows: The next section provides the Background and Related Work upon power and energy monitoring and power management for RJMS. Section 3 describes the new framework. In Section 4 we present and discuss our evaluation results upon the overhead and precision of the new energy monitoring framework. Finally, the last section presents the conclusions along with current future directions.

2   Background and Related Work

The best approach to accurately track power and energy consumption data in HPC platforms would be to use dedicated devices such as power-meters [3] for the collection of the power of the whole node or devices like PowerInsight [4] and PowerPack [5] for power consumption of node's individual components. In more detail the PowerPack framework

---

[1] http://www.prace-ri.eu/CURIE-Grand-Opening-on-
  March-1st-2012?lang=en

[5] consists of hardware sensors for power data collection and software components to use those data for controlling power profiling and code synchronization. Nevertheless, the usage of additional hardware on large HPC clusters would be too expensive therefore the alternative to exploit built-in interfaces seemed more viable for now.

The Intelligent Platform Management Interface [6] is a message-based, hardware-level interface specification concieved to operate even independently of the operating system in an out-of-band function. It is used by system administrators mainly to perform recovery procedures or monitor platform status (such as temperatures, voltages, fans, power consumption,etc) The main intelligence of IPMI is hidden on the baseboard management controller (BMC) which is a specialized microcontroller embedded on the motherboard of a computer which collects the data from various sensors such as the power sensors. The advantage of IPMI is that it can be found in nearly all current Intel architectures and if power senosrs are supported it can provide a very cheap built-in way for power collection. Various opensource software[2,3] exist for in-band and out-of-band collection of IPMI sensors data. Hackenberg et al. in [7] show that the power data collected from IPMI are sufficiently accurate but the calculation of energy consumption might not be precise for jobs with small duration. In the evaluation section we argue that this might not be the case with newer architectures and BMC. Collectl[4] is a system monitoring tool that tracks various sensors, amongst which the power, through in-band IPMI using ipmitool[1]. The data are stored in a compressed format per node basis.

The Running Average Power Limit (RAPL) interface has been introduced with the Intel Sandy Bridge processors [8] and exists on all later Intel models. It provides an operating system access to energy consumption information based on a software model driven by hardware counters. One of the specificities of the model is that it tracks the energy consumption of sockets and DRAM but not that of the actually memory of the machine. Various articles have been published that use RAPL to measure energy consumption within systems [9],[10] and they have all reported reliable results. PAPI [11] performance profiling tool provides the support of monitoring energy consumption through RAPL interfaces.

Unfortunately RAPL model reports energy on the level of socket and not on the level of core. However, model-based power estimates [12] have shown to be fairly precise, opening the way for near future support of core based power consumption on hardware and software.

High resolution power profiling would allow application performance tools to correlate them with MPI traces, hardware performance counters and other performance metrics. Hence having this data in OTF2 format [13] would allow a scenario like this. Nevertheless in the context of real-time power profiling through a Resource and Job Management system high resolution might increase the overhead which will have a direct interference to the application execution. In this context usage of binary files such as the Hierarchical Data Format v5 (HDF5) [14],[15] would provide a more viable approach.

Various Resource and Job Management Systems such as MOAB, PBSPro and Condor advertise Power Management techniques especially based on exploitation of idle

---

[2] http://ipmitool.sourceforge.net/
[3] http://www.gnu.org/software/freeipmi/
[4] http://collectl.sourceforge.net/

resources. LoadLeveler which is a proprietary software seems to be one of the first to provide power and energy monitoring [5] along with energy aware scheduling based on automatic CPU Frequency setting by the system according to a prediction model. LoadLeveler with those energy aware features is used on SuperMUC supercomputer in LRZ. Hennecke et al. present the retrieval of power consumption data from IBM Blue Gene/P supercomputer [16] through a particular LoadLeveler tool called LLview. In addition, LLview has the capability to provide power consumption data per job basis in high precision with about 4 samples per second. Nevertheless, this tool is closed source and specifically developed for BlueGene/P platforms.

One common mechanism on newer microprocessors is the mechanism of on the fly frequency and voltage selection, often called DVFS. Reducing CPU frequency may lead in energy reductions. Various strategies, using DVFS technique, have been widely studied to improve the energy consumptions of MPI applications [17],[18]. Other studies have shown that adaptive usage of frequency scaling may result in important energy benefits for small performance losses [19]. The control of energy consumption through CPU Frequency scaling as a user feature was initially studied and implemented on OAR [20] which is another flexible RJMS for HPC clusters.

3 Integrating Power/Energy Consumption Retreival and Control on SLURM

SLURM has a particular plugin dedicated on gathering information about the usage of various resources per node during job executions. This plugin, which is called *jobacct_gather*, collects information such as CPU and Memory utilization of all tasks on each node and then aggregates them internally across all nodes and returns single maximum and average values per job basis.

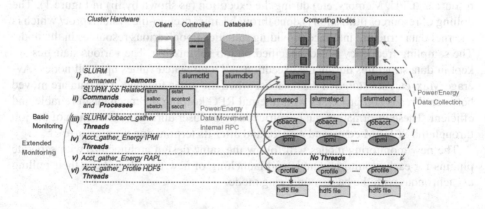

Fig. 1. SLURM Monitoring Framework Architecture with the different monitoring modes

---

[5] http://spscicomp.org/wordpress/pages/
   energy-aware-scheduling-for-large-clusters/

Resource utilization collection was already supported in SLURM. The goal of our new developments was to extend this mechanism to gather power and energy consumption as new characteristics per job. Of course, as we will see in this section, only per job energy consumption is stored in the SLURM database. Instant power consumption needs to be stored in relation with timestamps and thus a different model is used. This section is composed by 5 parts. Initially we describe the whole framework design of the new monitoring modes, then RAPL dedicated mode is presented, followed by the subsection for IPMI mode. Subsection 3.4 describes how power profiling with HDF5 is implemented and finally the last part describes the function of setting the CPU Frequency for controlling the energy consumption.

3.1   SLURM Monitoring Framework Architecture

We will begin by delving a bit more into the details of SLURM's architecture of the monitoring mechanisms. Figure 1 shows an overview of SLURM's deamons, processes and child threads as they are deployed upon the different components of the cluster. In the figure the real names of deamons, processes and plugins have been used (as named in the code) in order to make the direct mapping with the code. In SLURM architecture, a job may be composed by multiple parallel sub-jobs which are called steps. A job is typically submitted through the `sbatch` command with the form of a bash script. This script may contain multiple invocations of SLURM's `srun` command to launch applications (sub-jobs) in parts or the entire job allocation as specified by `sbatch`. To simplify the explanation let us consider the simpler case of job with one step. When this job is launched, the `srun` command will be invoked on the first node of job allocation and the slurmd deamons will launch a slurmstepd process on each node which will be following the execution of the whole step (shown by latin number ii) in figure 1).

If the basic monitoring mode is activated the *jobacct_gather* plugin is invoked and the slurmstepd process will launch a thread upon each node that will monitor various resources (CPU, Memory, etc) during the execution (as shown by iii) in Figure 1). The polling of resources utilization is done through Linux pseudo-file system /proc/ which is a kernel data structure interface providing statistics upon various resources in the node. The sampling frequency is user specified on job submission. The various statistics are kept in data structures during the execution and aggregated values upon all nodes (Average,Max, etc) are stored in the database when the job is finished. The data are moved between threads and processes with internal RPC keeping the mechanism reliable and efficient. These information can be retrieved by the user during the execution of the job through the SLURM command `sstat` and after its termination through `sacct`.

The new monitoring modes will follow the same design architecture with seperate plugins for each monitoring mode and launching of new threads to keep their polling asynchronous with the basic monitoring mode.

3.2   Power Data Collection through IPMI Interface

There are various opensource software to support the IPMI protocol and enable the retrieval of power data from the BMC: Ipmitool[6], OpenIPMI,etc. Our choice was to

---

[6] http://ipmitool.sourceforge.net/

select freeipmi[7] for various reasons, it is dedicated to HPC, it does not need kernel modules and it provides an easily integrated API. One important difference between IPMI and RAPL retrieval is the duration of the call. The call would usually take from 4ms up to 80ms but sometimes the call could take more than 2 or 3 sec. Hence we needed to turn the collection asynchronous to the tracking of the rest of the resources and the job control of execution. So a seperate thread was required to deal with the IPMI call. Furthermore we wanted to communicate to this thread not only from the jobacct thread during the execution of the job but also from the slurmd in order to get information about the power consumption of the node for system information.

Hence the choice was to launch the IPMI polling thread from slurmd as we can see on figure 1 with the latin number iii) the IPMI threads have the same color as the slurmd processes. An important issue here is that IPMI collects power in watts and we are interested to calculate the energy consumption of the job. Hence a particular algorithm needs to be used initially to calculate energy consumption per node and then aggregate that for all the allocated nodes to obtain the energy consumption per job. The sampling frequency is fixed with a particular option defined by the administrator for each node. A sleep function inside the thread allows to add energy depending on this frequency dt. Let's consider t_n a polling time, then the next polling time would be $t_{n+1} = t_n + dt$. We need to note that times are computed using the C function "time(NULL)", which is in seconds. thus the difference $t_{n+1} - t_n$ which will take values in $dt - 1, dt, dt + 1$ would always be in seconds. Considering that the corresponding power values for the above times would be w_n and w_{n+1}, the energy consumption dE_n between t_n and t_{n+1} is computed from the following equation upon each node:

$$dE_n = (t_{n+1} - t_n) \times \frac{w_n + w_{n+1}}{2} \tag{1}$$

This formula is used to add the energy consumption dE_n to the total energy EN used since the node has started.

To deduce the energy consumption for the job per node we take the difference between the consumed energy of the node on the start of the job and the respective energy at the time the job has terminated $EN_{job} = EN(start) - EN(stop)$ Finally the sum of the energies on each node as calculated from the above equation would give us the energy consumption of the job.

$$E_{job} = \sum_{k=0}^{K} EN_{job}(k) \tag{2}$$

The energy data are communicated between the IPMI thread towards jobacct thread and slurmd using internal Remote Procedure Calls. The instant power data are communicated with another RPC towards the profile thread if profiling is activated, as show us the red arrows in Fig.1.

3.3 Energy Data Collection from RAPL Model

As we show in section 2 RAPL model returns energy consumption value representing the energy consumed since the boot of the machine. Having energy data directly

---

[7] http://www.gnu.org/software/freeipmi/

simplifies the procedure for the calculation of the energy consumption of the whole job but complexifies the power consumption profiling. The collection of energy data is made through the particular Linux MSR driver following the technique described here. The actual call for data retrieval is really fast about $17\mu s$. In addition, the collection of only 2 energy data per node are sufficient for the calculation of the energy consumption of the entire job (one in the beginning and on in the end of the job). The final energy consumption of the job on one node will be the difference of the energy in the end and that in the start. Finally, adding the energies calculated on each node will give us the energy consumption of the entire job.

Based on the fact that the actual call to RAPL is fast and the fact that we do not need seperate sampling there is no need to have a particular thread responsible for collecting the energy data on each node (as shown on Fig.1 with latin number v)). Hence the dedicated functions of the *acct_gather_energy* RAPL plugin collect data from the RAPL model whenever they are asked and transfer those data through internal RPC (red arrows in Fig.1) towards the demanding threads or processes.

The calculation of instant power consumption per node can be calculated by collecting 2 samples of energy and dividing their difference by the frequency of the sampling. Hence a parameter has been defined to allow the adiministrator to provide this frequency in order to be able to extract power consumption through the RAPL energy data. Currently the choice has been to set this frequency no less than 1sec. However, as explained by Hackenberg et al. in [7], the precision of the power data is directly dependent on the actual sampling of RAPL internally which is about 10ms. We believe that allowing lower sampling might increase the overhead and we wanted to make evaluations before allowing something like that. Hence, initially our choice was to loose a little bit in precision but gain in terms of overhead.

3.4   Power Data Profiling with hdf5 File Format

Energy consumption is a global value for a job so it is obvious that it can be stored in the database as a new job characteristic. However, power consumption is instantaneous and since we are interested to store power consumption for application profiling purposes; a highly scalable model should be used. Furthermore since the application profiling will also contain profiling statistics collected from various resources (like network, filesystem, etc), a mechanism with extensible format would be ideal to cover our needs.

Hence a new plugin has been created called *acct_gather_profile*, presented by latin number vi) in Fig.1. This plugin is responsible for the profiling of various resources. Apart energy profiling, network, filesystem and tasks profiling is supported but the analysis of these types goes beyond the purposes of this paper. As we can see in the graphic representation of Fig.1 the profile thread is launched from slurmstepd (same color) and it collects the power and energy consumption data from IPMI thread or RAPL functions through internal RPC. The collected data are logged on hdf5 files per node. Ideally the storage of these files should be made upon a shared filesystem in order to facilitate the merging of files after the end of the job. The profiling information cannot be retrieved by the user during the execution of the job and this is because the hdf5 files are binaries which are readable only after the job termination.

The sampling frequency is an important parameter of profiling and the choice of implementation was to allow users to provide the particular frequency they need for each different type of profiling. Currently the lowest possible sampling frequency is 1 second, which according to other studies is long for the RAPL case, where the sampling frequency should be around 1ms in order to obtain the highest precision possible. Nevertheless we argue that having a thread polling 1000 samples per second would probably introduce a large overhead and we wanted to be sure about the overall overhead and precision with 1 sample per second before we try to optimize the measurements.

So during the execution of the job, each profile thread creates one hdf5 file per node and at the end of the job a merging phase takes place where all hdf5 files are merged into one binary file, decreasing the actual profile size per job. The profiling takes place only while the job is running, which is a big advantage opposed to other profiling techniques such as collectl where the profiling is continuous resulting in enormous volume of data that is not even correlated to jobs.

3.5 Control Static CPU Frequency Scaling

Giving the possibility to users to account power and energy consumption per job is an interesting feature but it would be limited if they don't have a way to control it. One method that is used a lot to control energy consumption, both in modeled and practical studies, is the CPU Frequency Scaling. Based on particular Linux kernels features we have provided the support of static CPU Frequency Scaling through a newly introduced parameter in srun command. The implementation passes from cgroups or cpusets in order to track the exact cores that the application is being executed and the actual setting of CPU Frequency is made with manipulation of cpufreq/scaling_cur_freq under /sys/ along with particuler governor drivers. The mechanism sets the demanded frequency on the allocated CPUs when the job is started and set them back to their initial value after the job is finished. Dynamic Frequency Scaling would be equally interesting to implement because of the needs of particular applications for finer grained energy profiling. The problem is that we are still limited of the latency for the frequency change. Newer architectures seem to have lower latencies so perhaps this would be an interesting feature to implement when the technology would allow it.

4 Evaluations and Comparisons

In this section we present and discuss real scale performance evaluations of the new SLURM power management implementations. The section is composed of four different parts. The first part presents the experimental platform along with various configuration details. The second part studies the overhead of the new monitoring features measured upon a cluster during MPI executions and provides a comparison between the different monitoring modes in terms of overhead. The third part analyzes the precision of the energy measurements in comparison with real wattmeters. Finally in the last part we provide a study of the fluctuations in energy consumption and execution times of three different benchmarks through static CPU frequency scaling.

4.1   Experimental Testbed

The experiments have been performed upon resources of Grid5000 platform [21] which is collection of a number of clusters with various hardware characteristics, geographically distributed across different sites in France, Luxembourg and Brazil. The purpose of Grid'5000 is to serve as an experimental testbed for research in High Performance Computing, Grid and Cloud Computing. It's advantage is that it provides a deep reconfiguration mechanism allowing researchers to deploy, install, boot and run their specific software environments, possibly including all the layers of the software stack. Furthermore we have particularly chosen the resources of Lyon, France, clusters which provide integrated power-meters for each node. This enables the comparison of the precision of the internal monitoring mechanisms with external power meters which have been proven to be reliable and have been used in various other studies.

Our experimental platform consisted of 17 nodes Dell PowerEdge R720 with Intel Xeon E5-2630 2.3GHz (6x256 KB (L2) + 15 MB (L3) / 7.2 GT/s QPI) processors with 2 CPUs per node and 6 cores per CPU, 32 GB of Memory and 10 Gigabit Ethernet Network. 3 of the above 17 nodes have also Nvidia Tesla M2075 GPU. In our software stack, we deployed the latest SLURM version as released on July 2013 (v2.6.0) which includes the new energy consumption monitoring and control features. From those 17 nodes, 1 was used only as the SLURM controller (slurmctld) and 16 were the computing nodes (slurmd) of our experimental cluster.

As far as the power-meters concern, they are customized hardware: Omegawatt box [8] produced by Omegawatt to measure the consumption of several nodes at the same time. These systems are able to take a precise measurement per computing node every second. The power measurements are logged on RRD databases through a dedicated library that captures and handles the data with sampling period of 1 second. A particular web interface is used for retrieval of the power and energy data by setting the list of nodes with start and end time.

In the experiments that follow the internal sampling periods of IPMI and RAPL monitoring modes were set to 1 second, which is the minimum value that can be currently configured by SLURM and represents the worst case scenario in terms of overhead. We argue that this might not be the best in terms of precision especially since both IPMI and RAPL have internal sampling frequencies lower than 1 second, but since in resource management the important is to allow applications to use efficiently the resources we wanted to be certain that the overhead of the framework will be as low as possible.

4.2   Overhead Evaluation

In this section we evaluate the overhead of the monitoring modes described in section 3. The Resource and Job Management is mainly responsible for providing the means for efficient execution of jobs upon the resources. Hence it needs to make sure that all internal functions are as lightweight as possible. Our goal is to compare the different depths of energy monitoring in SLURM and see if and how they influence the actual execution of jobs. We consider the following monitoring modes which can be configured through manipulation of particular parameters in the slurm configuration files:

---

[8] http://www.omegawatt.fr/gb/2_materiel.html

1. **NO_JOBACCT** : No resources monitoring whatsoever on computing nodes
2. **JOBACCT_0_RAPL** : Monitoring with Jobacct plugin for tasks and RAPL plugin for energy but only at the beginning and at the end of the job. No way to track the usage of resources during the execution of the job
3. **JOBACCT_RAPL** : Monitoring with Jobacct plugin for tasks with 10s sampling and RAPL plugin for energy during the execution of the job.
4. **JOBACCT_RAPL_PROFILE** : Monitoring with Jobacct plugin for tasks with 10s sampling, RAPL plugin for energy and profiling energy activated with 1s sampling during the execution of the job.
5. **JOBACCT_0_IPMI** : Monitoring with Jobacct plugin for tasks and IPMI plugin for energy but only at the beginning and at the end of the job. No way to track the usage of resources during the execution of the job
6. **JOBACCT_IPMI** : Monitoring with Jobacct plugin for tasks with 10s sampling and IPMI plugin for energy with 1s sampling during the execution of the job.
7. **JOBACCT_IPMI_PROFILE** : Monitoring with Jobacct plugin for tasks with 10s sampling, IPMI plugin for energy with 1s sampling and profiling energy activated with 1s sampling during the execution of the job.

We organize our experiments considering the following details:

– We execute the same job with each different monitoring mode for energy consumption and compare the different scenario
– The deployed jobs execute HPL Linpack benchmark that makes a quite high utilization of hardware resources (CPU and Memory)
– We profile the usage of CPU by enabling the cgroups kernel mechanism and in particular the cpuacct subsystem to track the CPU usage per process
– We profile the usage of memory by following the per process usage of RSS through the Linux ps command

Table 1. Monitoring Modes Comparisons in terms of Execution Times and Energy Consumption for Linpack deployment upon 16 nodes

Monitoring Modes	Execution Time (s)	Energy Consumption (J)	Time Overhead Percentage	Energy Overhead Percentage
NO_JOBACCT	2657	12623276.73	-	-
JOBACCT_0_RAPL	2658	12634455.87	0.04%	0.09%
JOBACCT_RAPL	2658	12645455.87	0.04%	0.18%
JOBACCT_RAPL_PROFILE	2658	12656320.47	0.04%	0.26%
JOBACCT_0_IPMI	2658	12649197.41	0.04%	0.2%
JOBACCT_IPMI	2659	12674820.52	0.07%	0.41%
JOBACCT_IPMI_PROFILE	2661	12692382.01	0.15 %	0.54%

The configuration of the Linpack executions was made in order to take about 80% of the memory per node and it take about 44 minutes to execute upon this platform which is a sufficient time to see how the different SLURM processes may influence its execution. We have launched different executions for each monitoring mode and figure 2 presents our observations concerning CPU and Memory usage on the first computing node of the computation. We have performed 5 repetitions for each monitoring mode and the results presented on figure 2 had less than 1% differences.

At first sight we see that each monitoring mode involves different overheads. As expected the IPMI modes have bigger overheads than the RAPL ones. The worst case

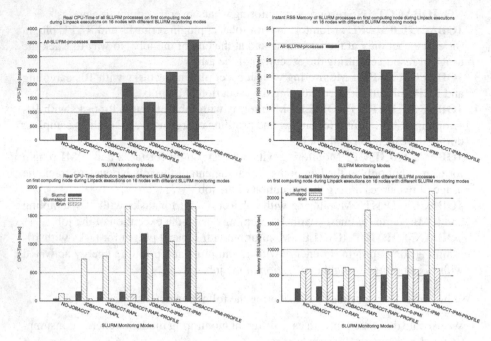

Fig. 2. CPU and Memory usage, tracked on first computing node, for all SLURM processes (top) and per different SLURM process (bottom) for Linpack executions upon 16 computing nodes with different SLURM Montitoring Modes

overhead is 3.5 sec for CPU-Time and 34MB for RSS in the case of IPMI plugin with profiling. We have tracked the CPU and Memory usage of the MPI processes as well but due to the big difference with SLURM processes in the order of magnitudes (around 30K sec for CPU time and 27GB for RSS) we do not display them on the same graphics. There is indeed an important difference in overhead with monitoring disabled and the various monitoring modes but if we compare it with the actual MPI CPU-Time even the worst case of 3.5 sec and 34MB of RSS seems benign.

It is interesting to see how the CPU-Time and Memory usage is distributed between the different SLURM processes. The bottom graphics in figure 2 confirm our expectations during the design of the features as described in section 3. As far as the CPU overhead concern we observe that slurmstepd usage increases significantly when monitoring is activated no matter if it is RAPL or IPMI. This is because of the polling thread launched from slurmstepd on job submission which is responsible for monitoring the various resources. We can also see how slurmstepd usage increases more when profiling is activated. This is due to the new thread which is launched within slurmstepd and that is responsible for the logging of energy consumption data on the hdf5 files. There is an important difference between the slurmd CPU usage when having IPMI instead of RAPL plugin activated. As explained in section 3, this is due to the fact that, for the IPMI plugin, a thread is launched within slurmd to poll data from the BMC asynchronously. It caches that information in order to avoid potential delays during further retrievals because of the freeipmi protocol overhead or the BMC itself. The CPU usage is also influenced by the sampling of energy polling and profiling. Lower frequency sampling would result in higher CPU-Time Usage. In our case we have set the sampling for the IPMI logic on the slurmd thread to 1 sec and the profiling also to 1 sec which are the lowest values that can currently be configured. The communications between threads take place through RPC calls and since there are more info to exchange between the processes as we go towards more detailed monitoring, the slurmd usage increases gradually

Concerning the memory usage of slurmd, the new IPMI thread is responsible for the memory consumption increase. The significant increase in memory usage on the slurmstepd side when having profiling activated, is explained by the memory reserved for hdf5 internals. As a matter of fact, even if the RSS value for memory consumption remains stable during the execution, it is interesting to note that in the case of profiling, the RSS starts with a high value that gradually increases during the computation. The value ploted in the graphics is the maximum RSS usage which was observed just before the end of the job.

We have observed the actual overheads in terms of CPU and Memory upon each computing node during job execution. We then need to evaluate their effects on the actual computations. Our concern is not only that it uses the same resources as the actual execution, but that the interference of the slurm processes may destabilize the execution of each MPI process or influence their interactions. This would have effect in either the execution time or the energy consumption. Table 1 show the differences in terms of these characteristics. The results on table 1 do not actually describe the general case but rather a tendency. In particular the results in figure 2 are true on every repetitions but the results on table 1 represent the median of the 5 repetitions per monitoring mode. There were runs where the actual overhead changed slightly, modifying the order between the monitoring modes, but their overhead percentages never increased more than 0.2% for execution time and 0.6% for energy consumption. This detail further confirms that the execution and energy consumption are not influenced by the monitoring mode.

In this study we do not profile the Network usage to see if SLURM exchanges influences the MPI communications. One of the reasons is that in real production systems SLURM communications and applications communications go through different networks.

4.3   Measurements Precision Evaluation

SLURM has been extended to provide the overall energy consumption of an execution and to provide a mean to profile the instant power consumption per job on each node. The overall energy consumption of a particular job is added to the Slurm accounting DB as a new step characteristic. The instant power consumption of a job is profiled specifically on each node and logged upon hdf5 files. Each plugin, IPMI or RAPL, has these two different ways of logging energy and instant power.

In this section we evaluate the accuracy of both logging mechanisms for IPMI and RAPL plugins. The acquired measurements are compared to the measurements reported from the Power-meters . As the power-meters report instant power consumptions per node, we can directly compare them with the acquired values for instant power.

However, IPMI is the only plugin that measures at the same level as the Power-meters, RAPL plugin only reporting at the level of sockets, thus limiting the comparisons to the sensibility and tendency of power consumptions and not the exact values.

The comparisons are presented through two different forms : either graphs to compare the instant power consumption per node or per job and tables to compare the overall energy consumption per job. The data used for the plotted graphics representing the instant power consumption evaluations are collected externally from the Watt-meters and from the hdf5 files that are constructed internally on each node by the SLURM monitoring mechanisms. The data used for the tables representing the energy consumption comparisons are produced from calculations of energy per job using the Watt-meter values and for the SLURM case they are retrieved by the SLURM accounting database after the end of the job.

In order to cover different job categories we conducted experiments with 3 different benchmarks for different durations and stressing of different kind of resources Hence the following benchmarks are used:

- long running jobs with Linpack benchmark which consumes mainly CPU and Memory and runs more then 40 minutes for each case
- medium running jobs with IMB benchmark which stresses the network and runs about 15 minutes
- short running jobs with Stream benchmark which stresses mainly the memory and runs for about 2 minutes

Long Running Jobs: The 2 top graphics of figure 3 show us results with executions of the Linpack benchmark and the RAPL monitoring mode. The top left graphic refers to the instant power consumption of one node and the top right graphic shows the aggregated power consumption for all 16 nodes that participated in the computation. The red line represents measurements for the whole node (left) and all the whole nodes (right). The black line gives the power consumption of the 2 sockets and the associated memory banks of one node (left) and the aggregation of the same value for all the nodes (right). It is interesting to see how the RAPL graph follows exactly the Wattmeter graph which means that power consumption of the whole node is mainly defined by the CPU and memory plus a certain stable value which would reflect the other components of the system. Furthermore we realize that RAPL plugin is equally sensitive as a wattmeter in terms of power fluctuations.

These graphs show us that RAPL plugin with profiling activated can be used for energy profiling of the application with a very high sensitivity.

The 2 bottom graphics of figure 3 represent the comparison of Wattmeter and SLURM IPMI monitoring mode collections. We can see that IPMI values do not have the same sensitivity as Wattmeters or the one we can see with the RAPL plugins. Nevertheless, the black line of SLURM IPMI monitoring follows an average value along the fluctuations that the Wattmeters may have. Hence in the end the final energy consumptions as calculated by producing the surfaces of the graphs have a fairly good precision that has less than 2% of error deviation.

Table 2 shows the precision of the internal algorithm used in SLURM IPMI monitoring mode to compute the overall energy consumption of the job. All computations

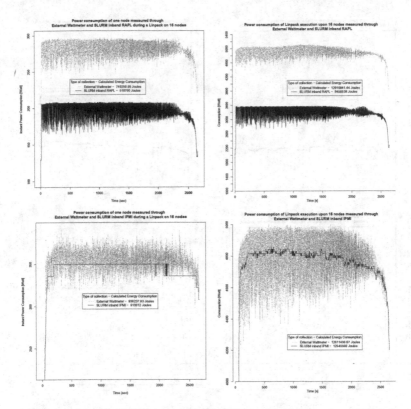

Fig. 3. Precision for RAPL (top) and IPMI (bottom) with Linpack executions)

use the Linpack benchmark based on the same configuration with only differences in the value of the CPU Frequency on all the computing nodes. It is interesting to see that the error deviation for those long running jobs is even less than 1% except for 2 cases where it increases up to 1.51%.

Table 2. SLURM IPMI precision in Accounting for Linpack executions

Monitoring Modes / CPU-Frequencies	2.301	2.3	2.2	2.1	2.0	1.9	1.8	1.7	1.6	1.5	1.4	1.3	1.2
External Wattmeter Postreatment Value	12754247.9	12234773.92	12106046.58	12022993.23	12034150.98	12089444.89	12086545.51	12227059.66	12401076.21	12660924.25	12989792.06	13401105.05	13932355.15
SLURM IPMI Reported Accounting Value	12708696	12251694	12116440	11994794	11998483	12187105	12093060	12136194	12518793	12512486	13107353	13197422	14015043
Error Deviation	0.35%	0.13%	0.08%	0.23%	0.29%	0.8%	0.05%	0.74%	0.94%	1.17%	0.89%	1.51%	0.58%

Medium Running Jobs: Figure 4 show the results observed with the execution of medium sized jobs (around 15min) using the IMB benchmark. Similar to the previous figure, the graphics on top show comparisons of Wattmeter and RAPL while in the bottom we have Wattmeter with IPMI.

The RAPL plugin graphics show once more that those measurements follow closely the ones of Wattmeters. On the other hand, IPMI plugin shows some shifting to the right compared to the Wattmeters trace. The explanation of this delay is further discussed

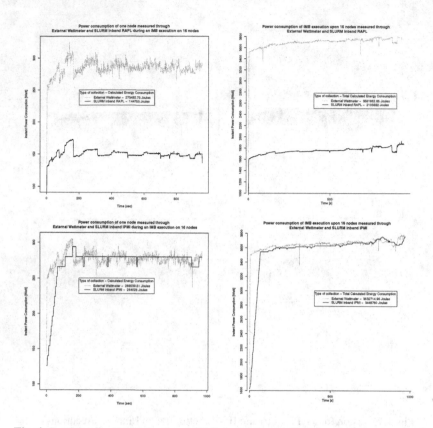

Fig. 4. Precision for RAPL (top) and IPMI (bottom) with IMB benchmark executions)

later on. We can see the black line following a slow fluctuation within average values of the Wattmeter values.

In terms of energy consumption calculation we can see that the error deviations remain on acceptable rates mainly lower than 2% except for 3 cases with error deviations higher than 1.7%. For jobs with a smaller duration, the IPMI plugin lost accuracy for both instant power and energy consumption calculation.

Table 3. SLURM IPMI precision in Accounting for IMB benchmark executions

Monitoring Modes / CPU-Frequencies	2.301	2.3	2.2	2.1	2.0	1.9	1.8	1.7	1.6	1.5	1.4	1.3	1.2
External Wattmeter Postreatment Value	3495186.61	3378778.52	3142598.78	2919285.68	2951550.69	2807384.15	2884394.56	2714138.65	2754539.52	2646738.25	2695689.76	2629889.08	2623654.43
SLURM IPMI Reported Accounting Value	3468024	3358145	3142223	2893499	2950052	2789780	2855237	2728572	2705661	2626645	2705367	2574712	2577540
Error Deviation	0.77%	0.61%	0.01%	0.88%	0.05%	0.62%	1.01%	0.52%	1.77%	0.75%	0.35%	2.09%	1.75%

Short Running Jobs: In figure 5 we present the measurements obtained with short sized jobs (no more than 2.5min per execution) with Stream benchmark. Similarly with the previous figure the graphics on the top show comparisons of Wattmeter and RAPL while in the bottom we have Wattmeter with IPMI.

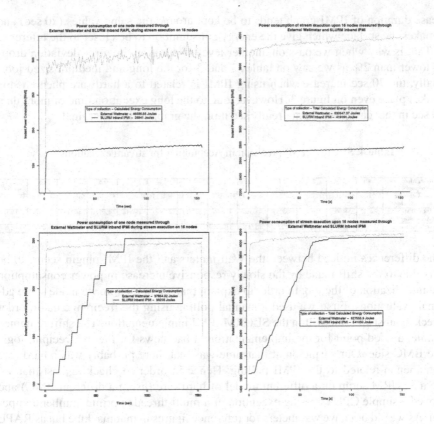

Fig. 5. Precision for RAPL (top) and IPMI (bottom) with stream benchmark executions)

The Stream benchmark is mainly a memory bound application and based on that we can deduce that the small fluctuations of the Watt-meters (red line) are produced by memory usage. The RAPL plugin graphics shows a smaller sensitivity in comparison with the Wattmeter and this is because the actual memory is not measured through RAPL. Nevertheless the RAPL model provides a reliable copy of what happens in reality and proves that even for small jobs it is interesting to use this plugin for profiling. IPMI plugin gives a different view where the shift we observed in the medium running jobs and didn't even exist in long running jobs, is here relatively important. We see that the IPMI black line grows slowly during about 70 seconds until it reaches the reference value of the Watt-meters. In figure 5 the growth had nearly the same duration. We can also observe the same tendency in the right graph for all the nodes that participated in the computation.

Similarly with instant power consumption the calculation of energy consumption presents an important error deviation between Wattmeter values and IPMI ones, that goes even beyond 10% (table 4). It is interesting to observe how the error deviation drops while we decrease the CPU Frequency. This is because higher frequencies tend to finish faster and lower frequencies induce longer execution times. This means that the increase duration of IPMI graph tends to be kept around the same values (70 sec) and this makes the surface which give the energy consumption to be closer to the reference one. That is why when we pass on another level of duration the error deviation drops even lower than 2% as we saw on tables 2 and 3 for the long and medium sized jobs. Actually, the 70 sec increase when using IPMI is related to a hardware phenomenon and takes place even on figure 3. However, due to the long execution time of more than 2600 sec in that case, we can not really see it on the graph as it is marginal.

Table 4. SLURM IPMI precision in Accounting for stream executions

Monitoring Modes / CPU-Frequencies	2.301	2.3	2.2	2.1	2.0	1.9	1.8	1.7	1.6	1.5	1.4	1.3	1.2
External Wattmeter Postreatment Value	627555.9	583841.11	567502.72	556249.55	540666.46	528064.44	518834.96	510849.85	505922.15	503095.21	504505.76	513403.46	529519.07
SLURM IPMI Reported Accounting Value	544740	510902	500283	488257	482566	467600	467719	460810	454118	459774	460005	468846	497637
Error Deviation	13.19%	12.49%	11.84%	12.22%	10.74%	11.45%	9.85%	9.79%	10.23%	8.61%	8.82%	8.67%	6.02 %

The differences noticed between the Watt-meters and the IPMI plugin seems to be mostly due to the shift made by the slowly responsive increase in power consumption at the initialization of the job. In order to explain that phenomenon, we made some additional evaluations. First, we used a manual polling using the freeipmi calls in order to check against an issue within the SLURM IPMI implementation. The shift remained the same, a good point for the implementation, a bad news for the the freeipmi logic or the BMC side. Our suspicion at that time was that there probably was a hardware pheonomenon related to the IPMI polling. Hence in order to check against that we made a SLURM setup on a different model of hardware (using a different BMC) and deployed a simple CPU stressing execution of a multi-threaded prime number computation. As we did not have wattmeters for reference figures in that machine but as RAPL was proved to follow closely the Wattmeter tendency, we took that latter as a reference instead. Figure 6 shows the execution of a simple CPU bound application with SLURM -IPMI and SLURM - RAPL plugins on two different machines: One with the DELL-Poweredge R720 that we used in all our previous experiments and one with a BULL B710 node. We can see that the delayed increase we observed on our previous experiments is confirmed one more time on the orignial machine with this application (left graph). However we observe that there is practically no delay at all on the other technology of machines (right graph). It is worthy to note that we do not see any improvement on the sensitivity of the actual values in comparison with the reference ones.

Hence we can deduce that the problematic increase and shift of measurements depends firmly on the BMC type and can change depending on the architecture or the firmware of the BMC. So the precision of the power consumption and energy consumption calculations depend on the actual hardware and while the technology gets better we expect that the precision of our measurements will be improved. Unfortunately we did not have tha ability to provide complete executions with newer machines hardware to see how exactly the error deviation is diminished, but initial observations on figure 6 show us promising results. Furthermore, since the overhead of the monitoring modes was low as seen in the previous section, future works may allow the usage of internal sampling frequency lower than 1 second which can further improve the precision of power and energy data.

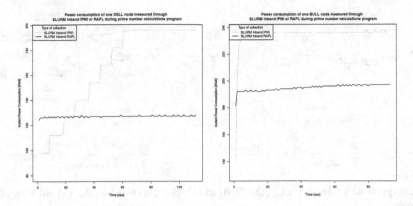

Fig. 6. RAPL and IPMI precision upon different nodes with different versions of BMC

4.4 Performance-Energy Trade-Offs

In this section we are interested in the observation of performance-energy trade-offs with particular applications. This kind of tests is common for dedicated profiling programs like PAPI but the interesting part now is that a Resource and Job Management System such as SLURM has been extended to have the same capabilities configurable at run time. The tracking of performance and energy consumption can be made either during the execution with particular commands (sstat or scontrol show node) or at the end of the job with results directly stored in the SLURM database or on hdf5 files dedicated for profiling. Furthermore this tracking is not passing from the overhead of the integration of a dedicated profiling program but rather through a direct integration of sensor polling inside the core of SLURM code. Hence this section shows the type of research that can be possible using the extensions on SLURM for monitoring and control of energy consumption and how these features can be helpful in order to make the right choice of CPU Frequency for the best performance-energy trade-off. We make use of three different benchmarks (Linpack, IMB and stream) and make various runs by changing the CPU Frequency and compare the overall energy consumption of the whole job. For this we use the setting of CPU Frequency through the particular parameter of (cpufreq) on the job submission. Concerning the measurements we compare the IPMI and RAPL monitoring modes with the reference one using Wattmeters.

The figures that follow show the performance-energy tradeoffs with different CPU Frequencies. Figure 7 shows us the runs for Linpack (left graphic) and IMB benchmark (right) and figure 8 shows us the runs for Stream benchmark.

Linpack benchmark shows that the turbo mode using a frequency of 2.301GHz gives the fastsest run but is fairly higher in terms of energy consumption. The lowest energy consumption is reached using 2.1GHz and in fact this is the best tradeoff between energy and performance. We can also observe that while the energy consumption is droping until this frequency it kind of stabilizes then with higher executions times until 1.7 GHz but increases after that. It is intersting to see that dropping the frequency lower than 1.4 has no benefit at all because we lose both in energy and performance in comparison with the turbo mode. Between IPMI and Wattmeter graphs there are

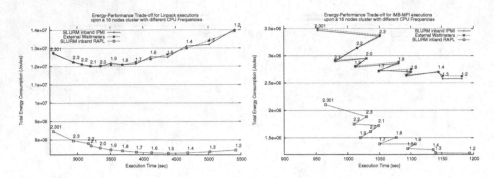

Fig. 7. Energy-Time Tradeoffs for Linpack (left) and IMB (right) benchmarks and different CPU frequencies

some small differences but in general the IPMI follows closely the same tendencies of Wattmeters which proves that we can trust this kind of monitoring for this type of energy-performance profiling too. If we do not specify a particular frequency, Linux kernel decides which frequency the run will be made according to particular settings on the CPU scaling modules. The most common is the on-demand where the run will be made on the higher frequency that exists. RAPL graph for the Linpack benchmark (left) shows us a kind of different behaviour with best tradeoff performance-energy between the frequencies 1.6 and 1.5. In addition we do not see the same tendency like the Wattmeter or IPMI graphs. This is related to the fact that RAPL only monitors a partial view of the active elements of the node, elements for which the energy consumption is mostly related to the frequency (and thus voltage) of the cores. The static consumption of the nodes, including the disks, network cards, motherboard chipsets and every others electrical components or fans are not took into account in RAPL. Increasing the computation time of an application involves increasing the share of the energy usage of all these second tier elements up to counter-balancing the benefits of running at a lower frequency. If the node was only made of sockets, RAPL shows that the best frequency to save energy would be lower than 1.5GHz.

IMB benchmark on the right has a different appearance than Linpack. For example frequency of 2.1 has better energy consumption and performance than 2.2 or 2.3 and then again 1.9 is better in both in comparison with 2.0. The best trade-off between energy and performance would probably be either 2.1 , 1.9 or 1.7. If we consider the RAPL graph 1.9 would be probably the best choice. IMB benchamark mainly stresses the Network and that is why small changes in CPU frequency have different kind of effects on performance and energy that is why the graph has nothing to do with linear or logarithmic evolution.

Finally on figure 8 we can see graphically the error deviation of IPMI vs Wattmeters that we observed on table 4. We can observe that the best tradeoff is performed with Frequencies 1.6 or 1.5 . It is interesting to see how this graph has an obvious logarithmic design with stability on execution times and changes on energy from 2.301GHz until 1.6 and stability on energy consumption and changes on execution times from 1.6 until 1.2. This makes it easier to find the best choice of CPU-Frequency for performance-energy

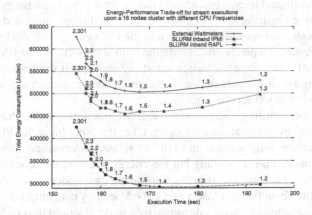

Fig. 8. Energy Time tradeoffs for Stream benchmark and different CPU frequencies

tradeoffs. We can also observe how the difference of IPMI values with Wattmeters which are due to the BMC delays as we have explained in the previous section tend to become smaller as the time of execution grows.

Overall, it is interesting to see how each application has different tradeoffs. That is the reason why particular profiling is needed for every application to find exactly the best way to execute it in terms of both energy and performance. The outcome of these evaluations is to raise the importance of energy profiling to improve the behaviour of the applications in terms of performance and energy and show how the new extensions in SLURM can be used to help the user for this task and find the best tradeoffs in energy and performance. Furthermore the comparison of monitoring modes with Wattmeters proves that SLURM internal monitoring modes provide a reliable way to monitor the overall energy consumption and that controlling the CPU Frequency is made correctly with real changes on performance and energy. We argue that most real life applications have execution times far bigger than our long running jobs here (Linpack) so the energy performance tradeoffs will definitely be more important than reported in this paper.

5   Conclusions and Future Works

This paper presents the architecture of a new energy accounting and control framework integrated upon SLURM Resource and Job Management System. The framework is composed of mechanisms to collect power and energy measurements from node level built-in interfaces such as IPMI and RAPL. The collected measurements can be used for job energy accounting by calculating the associated consumed energy and for application power profiling by logging power with timestamps in HDF5 files. Furthermore, it allows users to control the energy consumption by selecting the CPU Frequency used for their executions.

We evaluated the overhead of the framework by executing the Linpack benchmark and our study showed that the cost of using the framework is limited; less than 0.6% in energy consumption and less than 0.2% in execution time. In addition, we evaluated the precision of the collected measurements and the internal power-to-energy calculations and vice versa by comparing them to measures collected from integrated Wattmeters. Our experiments showed very good precision in the job's energy calculation with IPMI and even if we observed a precision degradation with short jobs, newer BMC hardware showed significant improvements. Hence our study shows that the framework may be safely used in large scale clusters such as Curie and no power-meters are needed to add energy consumption in job accounting.

In terms of power profiling with timestamps, IPMI monitoring modes had poor sensitivity but the actual average values were correct. On the other hand, RAPL monitoring modes, which capture only sockets and DRAM related informations, had very good sensitivity in terms of power profiling but the energy consumption could not be compared with the energy calculation from the Wattmeters data. Indeed, the RAPL provides interesting insights about the processors and DRAM energy consumptions but does not represent the real amount of energy consumed by a node. It would thus be interesting to use both the IPMI and the RAPL logics at the same time in further studies. This would help to identify the evolution of the consumption of the other active parts of the node over time. Having a similar ability to monitor and control these active parts, like hard-disk drives and interconnect adapters, could help to go further in the description and the adaptation of the power consumption of the nodes according to applications needs. This particular field of interest is getting an increasing attention, as witnessed by the ISC'13 Gauss Award winner publication [22] concerning the interest of having the capability to differentiate the IT usage effectiveness of nodes to get more relevant energy indicators. Enhanced and fine-grained energy monitoring and stearing of more node components would really help to make an other step forward in energy efficient computations.

Treating energy as a new job characteristic opens new doors to treat is as a new resource. The next phase of this project will be to charge users for power consumption as a means of aligning the user's interest with that of the organization providing the compute resources. In this sense, energy fairsharing should be implemented to keep the fairness of energy distribution amongst users. Any resource for which there is no charge will likely be treated by users as a resource of no value, which is clearly far from being the case when it comes to power consumption.

Longer term plans call for leveraging the infrastructure described in this paper to optimize computer throughput with respect to energy availability. Specifically the optimization of system throughput within a dynamic power cap reflecting the evolutions of the amount of available power over time seems necessary. It could help to make a larger use of less expensive energy at night for CPU intensive tasks while remaining at a lower threshold of energy consumption during global demand peaks, executing memory or network intensive applications.

Continuing research in the area of energy consumption is mandatory for the next decades. Having in mind the impact of the power consumption on the environment, even a major break in computation technology enabling more efficient execution would not change that fact. The HPC ecosystem needs to minimize its impact for long term sustainability and managing power efficiently is a key part in that direction.

Acknowledgements. The authors would like to thank Francis Belot from CEA-DAM for his advices on the energy accounting design and his comments on the article. Experiments presented in this paper were carried out using the Grid'5000 experimental testbed, being developed under the INRIA ALADDIN development action with support from CNRS, RENATER and several Universities as well as other funding bodies (see https://www.grid5000.fr).

References

1. Yoo, A.B., Jette, M.A., Grondona, M.: SLURM: Simple Linux utility for resource management. In: Feitelson, D.G., Rudolph, L., Schwiegelshohn, U. (eds.) JSSPP 2003. LNCS, vol. 2862, pp. 44–60. Springer, Heidelberg (2003)
2. Top500 supercomputer sites, http://www.top500.org/
3. Assunão, M., Gelas, J.P., Lefèvre, L., Orgerie, A.C.: The green grid'5000: Instrumenting and using a grid with energy sensors. In: Remote Instrumentation for eScience and Related Aspects, pp. 25–42. Springer, New York (2012)
4. James, L., David, D., Phi, P.: Powerinsight - a commodity power measurement capability. In: The Third International Workshop on Power Measurement and Profiling (2013)
5. Ge, R., Feng, X., Song, S., Chang, H.C., Li, D., Cameron, K.: Powerpack: Energy profiling and analysis of high-performance systems and applications. IEEE Transactions on Parallel and Distributed Systems 21(5), 658–671 (2010)
6. Intel: (intelligent platform management interface specification v2.0)
7. Hackenberg, D., Ilsche, T., Schone, R., Molka, D., Schmidt, M., Nagel, W.E.: Power measurement techniques on standard compute nodes: A quantitative comparison. In: 2013 IEEE International Symposium on Performance Analysis of Systems and Software (ISPASS), pp. 194–204 (2013)
8. Rotem, E., Naveh, A., Ananthakrishnan, A., Weissmann, E., Rajwan, D.: Power-management architecture of the intel microarchitecture code-named sandy bridge. IEEE Micro 32(2), 20–27 (2012)
9. Dongarra, J., Ltaief, H., Luszczek, P., Weaver, V.: Energy footprint of advanced dense numerical linear algebra using tile algorithms on multicore architectures. In: 2012 Second International Conference on Cloud and Green Computing (CGC), pp. 274–281 (2012)
10. Hähnel, M., Döbel, B., Völp, M., Härtig, H.: Measuring energy consumption for short code paths using rapl. SIGMETRICS Perform. Eval. Rev. 40(3), 13–17 (2012)
11. Weaver, V.M., Johnson, M., Kasichayanula, K., Ralph, J., Luszczek, P., Terpstra, D., Moore, S.: Measuring energy and power with papi. In: ICPP Workshops, pp. 262–268 (2012)
12. Goel, B., McKee, S., Gioiosa, R., Singh, K., Bhadauria, M., Cesati, M.: Portable, scalable, per-core power estimation for intelligent resource management. In: 2010 International Green Computing Conference, pp. 135–146 (2010)
13. Eschweiler, D., Wagner, M., Geimer, M., Knüpfer, A., Nagel, W.E., Wolf, F.: Open trace format 2: The next generation of scalable trace formats and support libraries. In: Bosschere, K.D., D'Hollander, E.H., Joubert, G.R., Padua, D.A., Peters, F.J., Sawyer, M. (eds.) PARCO. Advances in Parallel Computing, vol. 22, pp. 481–490. IOS Press (2011)
14. Folk, M., Cheng, A., Yates, K.: HDF5: A file format and i/o library for high performance computing applications. In: Proceedings of Supercomputing 1999 (CD-ROM), Portland, OR. ACM SIGARCH and IEEE (1999)
15. Biddiscombe, J., Soumagne, J., Oger, G., Guibert, D., Piccinali, J.G.: Parallel computational steering for HPC applications using HDF5 files in distributed shared memory. IEEE Transactions on Visualization and Computer Graphics 18(6), 852–864 (2012)

16. Hennecke, M., Frings, W., Homberg, W., Zitz, A., Knobloch, M., Böttiger, H.: Measuring power consumption on ibm blue gene/p. Computer Science - Research and Development 27(4), 329–336 (2012)
17. Rountree, B., Lownenthal, D.K., de Supinski, B.R., Schulz, M., Freeh, V.W., Bletsch, T.: Adagio: making dvs practical for complex hpc applications. In: ICS 2009: Proceedings of the 23rd International Conference on Supercomputing, pp. 460–469. ACM, New York (2009)
18. Huang, S., Feng, W.: Energy-efficient cluster computing via accurate workload characterization. In: CCGRID 2009: Proceedings of the 2009 9th IEEE/ACM International Symposium on Cluster Computing and the Grid, pp. 68–75. IEEE Computer Society, Washington, DC (2009)
19. Lim, M.Y., Freeh, V.W., Lowenthal, D.K.: Adaptive, transparent frequency and voltage scaling of communication phases in mpi programs. In: SC 2006: Proceedings of the 2006 ACM/IEEE Conference on Supercomputing, p. 107. ACM, New York (2006)
20. Costa, G.D., de Assunção, M.D., Gelas, J.P., Georgiou, Y., Lefèvre, L., Orgerie, A.C., Pierson, J.M., Richard, O., Sayah, A.: Multi-facet approach to reduce energy consumption in clouds and grids: the green-net framework. In: e-Energy, pp. 95–104 (2010)
21. Bolze, R., Cappello, F., Caron, E., Daydé, M., Desprez, F., Jeannot, E., Jégou, Y., Lantéri, S., Leduc, J., Melab, N., Mornet, G., Namyst, R., Primet, P., Quetier, B., Richard, O., Talbi, I.G., Iréa, T.: Grid'5000: a large scale and highly reconfigurable experimental grid testbed. Int. Journal of High Performance Computing Applications 20(4), 481–494 (2006)
22. Patterson, M.K., Poole, S.W., Hsu, C.-H., Maxwell, D., Tschudi, W., Coles, H., Martinez, D.J., Bates, N.: TUE, a new energy-efficiency metric applied at ORNL's jaguar. In: Kunkel, J.M., Ludwig, T., Meuer, H.W. (eds.) ISC 2013. LNCS, vol. 7905, pp. 372–382. Springer, Heidelberg (2013)

Asynchronous Reconfiguration
for Paxos State Machines

Leander Jehl and Hein Meling

Department of Electrical Engineering and Computer Science
University of Stavanger, Norway

Abstract. This paper addresses reconfiguration of a Replicated State
Machine (RSM) in an asynchronous system. It is well known that consensus cannot be solved in an asynchronous system. Therefore an RSM providing strong consistency, cannot guarantee progress in an asynchronous
system. However, we show that reconfiguring the RSM is possible in a
purely asynchronous system. This differs from all existing reconfiguration
methods which rely on consensus to choose a new configuration. Since a
reconfiguration to a new set of machines or even a different datacenter
can serve to restore synchrony between replicas, asynchronous reconfiguration can also serve to increase the availability of an RSM.

1 Introduction

State machine replication [1] is a common approach for building fault-tolerant
services. In this approach, all service replicas of the state machine execute the
same requests. To ensure that replicas remain consistent after multiple updates,
the order of requests has to be synchronized across replicas. Typically this is accomplished using a consensus protocol, such as Paxos [2, 3], which is an essential
component in a Replicated State Machine (RSM). Paxos helps to prevent the
replicas from entering an inconsistent state, despite any number of replica failures. Moreover, the RSM can continue to process new requests, as long as *more
than half of the replicas* remain operational. If this bound is violated, however,
the current RSM is forced to stop making progress indefinitely. Therefore real
systems need to be able to react to failures and include new replicas, before this
bound is exceeded. Additionally, in todays cloud computing infrastructures, a
fault tolerant, replicated service should be able to add, or move replicas based on
the systems load and redistribute the replicas to new physical locations. Therefore real systems should include a reconfiguration method, ensuring a continuous
correct service while enabling the changes above.

The initial descriptions of the state machine approach [1] and Paxos [2, 3] described a reconfiguration method. This method lets the RSM reconfigure itself
by executing a special command, which specifies the new configuration. It was
refined and implemented, e.g. for the Zookeeper service [4], enabling reconfiguration for a replicated system in production.

To use this method however, the old configuration (being changed) must be
operational to complete the reconfiguration command. Thus the old configuration needs to have a single leader and a majority of correct servers, to use

M. Chatterjee et al. (Eds.): ICDCN 2014, LNCS 8314, pp. 119–133, 2014.
© Springer-Verlag Berlin Heidelberg 2014

reconfiguration. Vertical Paxos [5] developed a different reconfiguration method, showing that reconfiguration is possible with only a minority of correct replicas, if it is coordinated by an abstract, fault tolerant configuration manager. In Vertical Paxos, synchrony is needed to guarantee a working configuration manager.

In this paper we target the synchrony assumption of traditional reconfiguration. We present ARec, an asynchronous reconfiguration protocol, showing that reconfiguration is possible in an asynchronous system. This means that, agreeing on a single leader is not necessary to change to a new set of replicas. Reconfiguring an RSM can therefore take place during a period of asynchrony, e.g. when clocks are not synchronized and the network introduces unpredictable delays. This is an important result, because it means that replicas could be moved to a set of machines or a datacenter where synchrony assumptions hold.

1.1   ARec: Reconfiguration without Consensus

A *configuration* is a set of replicas running on different machines. To change the set of replicas, a reconfiguration simply proposes a new configuration. We assume that any two configurations are disjoint. Thus every replica belongs to exactly one configuration. However we do not require replicas of different configurations to run on different machines. Thus reconfiguration also enables operations like adding or removing one replica. For example, to add a replica to the configuration $\{r_1, r_2, r_3\}$, running on machines m_1, m_2, and m_3, one simply proposes a new configuration $\{r_1', r_2', r_3', r_4\}$ on machines m_1, m_2, m_3, and m_4. Thus our reconfiguration allows all possible changes both in number and placement of replicas.

The main challenges in reconfiguration are to ensure that when stopping the old configuration, exactly one new configuration starts and that all requests that have been committed by the old, stay committed in the new configuration. Assume for example two new configurations C_1 and C_2 are proposed, while an initial configuration C_0 is running the RSM. Classical reconfiguration uses consensus in one configuration to choose the next configuration. Thus replicas in C_0 would choose whether to change to C_1 or C_2. Thus, the new configuration that is chosen can then simply copy the state from C_0.

Since consensus is impossible in an asynchronous system [6], ARec uses eventual consistency to determine the next configuration. For this, we assume that new configurations are issued together with a unique timestamp. If several configurations are proposed concurrently, we let the one with the highest timestamp be the next configuration. Thus, if the replicas eventually become aware of all configurations, they will agree on which configuration should take over.

However this complicates state transfer, since it is difficult to determine which configuration can transfer a correct state to the new configuration. Assume for example C_1 and C_2 have timestamps 1 and 2. In this case, we can ignore C_1 and C_2 can receive the state from C_0. However if C_2 is only proposed after C_1 received the state from C_0 and started the RSM, C_2 has to copy its state from C_1. This problem is solved in Section 4.

Another problem in asynchronous reconfiguration is to find a correct state for the new configuration to start. In classical reconfiguration, the old configuration again uses consensus to decide on the last request. Any replica can then tell this decision to the new configuration, which can choose new requests. In an asynchronous system, the old configuration cannot decide on a final request. Thus, some requests might be committed in the old configuration but remain unknown to some replicas. ARec therefore collects the state of a majority of a configuration's replicas, to determine the new configuration's state. Luckily leader change in Paxos already includes a mechanism to find any value, that might be committed. We reuse this mechanism in ARec.

2   Paxos

In this section we briefly present Paxos [2, 3] and how replicas agree on a single request. We then elaborate on how this is used to implement an RSM.

2.1   Paxos

Paxos is a consensus algorithm used by several participants (our replicas) to decide on exactly one value (our request). To get chosen, a value has to be proposed by a leader and accepted by a majority of the replicas. Only one value may be chosen and every correct replica should be able to learn what was decided on. Paxos assumes a partially synchronous network, tolerating asynchrony, but relying on eventual synchrony to guarantee progress. That means that single messages can be lost or arbitrarily delayed (asynchrony). However, eventually all messages between correct processes arrive within some fixed delay (synchrony). Since an initial leader might fail and a single leader cannot be chosen during periods of asynchrony, multiple leaders can try concurrently to get their values decided. To coordinate concurrent proposals, leaders use preassigned round numbers for their proposals. Replicas cooperate only with the leader using the highest round. However, after leader failure it might be necessary for replicas to cooperate with several leaders. Paxos solves this problem by enforcing that, once a value has been decided, leaders of higher rounds will also propose this locked-in value. Therefore in the first phase of a round, the leader determines if it is safe to propose any value or if there is another value that was already voted for. In the second phase, the leader then tries to get a safe value accepted. If not interrupted a round proceeds as follows:

PREPARE (1a) The leader sends a PREPARE message to all replicas, starting a new round.

PROMISE (1b) Replicas return a PROMISE not to vote in lower rounds, and include their last vote.

ACCEPT (2a) After receiving a quorum of PROMISE messages, the leader determines a safe value and proposes it to all replicas in an ACCEPT message.

LEARN (2b) Replicas vote for the proposal, by sending the value and round number in a LEARN message to all other replicas, if no higher round was started in the meantime.

DECIDE Receiving a quorum of LEARNs for one value and round, a replica decides on that value.

A *quorum* is a majority of the replicas and a *quorum of messages* is a set of messages of the same type, sent by a quorum in the same round. A value v is *chosen* if a quorum of LEARN messages with value v was sent. The DECIDE step above ensures that only chosen values get learned.The above can be repeated in new rounds, until all replicas have learned the value. From a quorum of PROMISE messages, *safe* values can be determined following these rules:

- If no replica reports a vote, all values are safe.
- If some replica reports a vote in round r for value v and no replica reports a vote in a round higher than r, then v is safe.

These rules ensure, that once a value is chosen, only this value is safe in higher rounds. Thus all replicas learn the same value, even if they learn it in different rounds. We call this property *safety*. Clearly to be able to report their votes in a later PROMISE message, replicas have to store their last vote (round and value) in variables $vrnd$ and $vval$. For a replica to be able to promise not to vote in lower rounds, it must also store the last round it participated in. We refer to this as rnd. These variables are all that is needed to ensure *safety*. We call them the Paxos State of a replica. We also write Φ for the tuple $(rnd, vrnd, vval)$.

We say that an execution of Paxos is *live* if a value can get learned. For Paxos to be live, a leader has to finish a round, communicating with a quorum of correct replicas, while no other leader starts a higher round.

2.2 The Paxos State Machine

A state machine is an application that, given a state and a request, deterministically computes a new state and possibly a reply to the request. When this state machine is replicated for fault tolerance, it is important that the replicas execute the same requests to maintain a consistent state among themselves. Since several requests might interfere with each other, it is also important that replicas execute requests in the same order.

The replicas in a Paxos State Machine achieve this by using Paxos to choose requests. For every new request, a new Paxos instance is started. Its messages are tagged with a request number i, saying that this instance is choosing the ith request. A replica only executes the ith request, if it has executed request $i - 1$ and has learned the request chosen for the ith instance via the Paxos protocol. Thus, as long as Paxos is live, new request can be processed. These will eventually be learned and executed by all correct replicas.

Though execution has to be done in correct order, the Paxos instances can be performed concurrently. Thus it is possible to propose and choose a request in instance $i + 1$, without waiting for the ith request to be learned.

Note that, if concurrent Paxos instance have the same leader, round change can be common for all instances. Thus, PREPARE and PROMISE messages for concurrent Paxos instances can be sent in the same message. [3] explains how this is done, even for all future instances.

3   Liveness for a Dynamic RSM

In this section, we define the problem of asynchronous reconfiguration. That is, we both define the interface used to issue reconfigurations and specify the liveness conditions for a Dynamic RSM and ARec.

A reconfiguration is initialized by sending $\langle \text{RECONF}, C_i, i, C_l \rangle$ to the new configuration C_i. Here, i is the unique timestamp of the new configuration and C_l is some old configuration. The old configuration is needed, since the new configuration needs to contact the service to take over. We require configurations to be disjoint. Thus a replica only belongs to a single configuration. However replicas from different configurations can easily be placed on the same machine. Note that a RECONF request will typically be sent by a replica in configuration C_l that wants to move the service, e.g. in response to asynchrony or crashes. It can also be sent by an external configuration manager.

We say a configuration is *available*, if a majority of the configuration's replicas are correct. A static Paxos state machine is guaranteed to process incoming requests, if the initial configuration is available and eventually a single leader is elected. In a dynamic system, this condition becomes more complicated. While a reconfiguration might require several old and new configurations to be available, a dynamic system should not require an old configuration to remain available after a new configuration has taken over and copied all relevant state. We say that a replica in a new configuration is *stateful*, if it has copied a correct system state from a previous configuration. Note that this system state might differ from the individual states of single replicas in the old configuration. We define a configuration to be *stateful*, when a majority of the replicas in this configuration are stateful. Thus, if a configuration is stateful and available, there exists a correct and stateful replica that can disseminate a correct system state to the other correct replicas. Clearly, a Dynamic RSM always needs at least one available stateful configuration. Also, new configurations must stay available during reconfiguration. We therefore define that a Dynamic RSM, at any time in an execution, *depends on* the stateful configuration with highest timestamp, C_{max}, and all configurations with higher timestamps. We can now define liveness of reconfiguration as the following:

Definition 1 (ARec Liveness). *For any execution, if*
(a) at all times the configurations that the system depends on are available, and
(b) $\langle \text{RECONF}, C_i, i, C_l \rangle$ is sent by a correct client for a stateful configuration C_l,
then the system will eventually no longer depend on C_l.

Note that ARec Liveness does not guarantee that the state machine actually makes progress. That is because this always requires some synchrony assumption.

Similar, ARec Liveness does not guarantee, that $\langle \text{RECONF}, C_i, i, C_l \rangle$ actually results in C_i running Paxos. That makes sense, since in the case of concurrent reconfigurations, we don't want several configurations to start. However it guarantees that C_l will stop running Paxos, and replicas in C_l need not stay available. Clearly implementing ARec Liveness makes sense only if also the state machine is live, under reasonable assumptions. We therefore define the following:

Definition 2 (Dynamic RSM Liveness). *For any execution, if*
(a) at all times the configurations that the system depends on are available,
(b) only finitely many configurations are initialized, and
(c) eventually a single leader is elected in C_{max},
then requests submitted to this leader will be processed.

Note that synchrony between processes in C_{max} is needed to guarantee *(c)*. *(b)* says that eventually no more reconfigurations are issued. This guarantees that eventually, one configuration will be C_{max} forever. This configuration can run Paxos without being interrupted by reconfigurations. Since it is impossible to agree on group membership in an asynchronous system [7], it can be theoretically challenging to guarantee condition *(b)*. For example, if reconfiguration is used to replace faulty replicas with new ones, false detections might cause infinitely many reconfigurations, even with only finitely many crashes. This is because in an asynchronous system, a failure detector might falsely detect a crash, causing a reconfiguration, in which a correct replica is replaced by a new one. In practice however, the number of reconfigurations are typically bounded because of their cost. That is, reconfiguration usually requires new machines, possibly transferring large amounts of state between replicas, and may also disrupt service delivery.

4 Asynchronous Reconfiguration

We now explain our reconfiguration protocol ARec and argue for its correctness using examples. See Algorithm 1 on Page 125 for details. We assume reliable communication but specify later how to reduce retransmissions. Proof of correctness is given in the following sections. We first assume that only a single instance of Paxos is reconfigured and later explain how this can be extended to an RSM. ARec maintains *safety* of Paxos by ensuring that at any time, at most one configuration is running Paxos, and that this configuration copies the Paxos State from a previous configuration, upon start-up. To achieve this, the Paxos messages are tagged with the senders configuration, and a receiver only delivers Paxos messages from its own configuration. We write C_i for the configuration with timestamp i. We define a quorum of messages from C_j as a set of messages from a majority of the replicas in configuration C_j.

A Single Reconfiguration: As specified before, a new configuration C_i is initialized by sending $\langle \text{RECONF}, C_i, i, C_l \rangle$, where C_l is some earlier configuration. The new replicas broadcast this message to their configuration to make sure

---

Algorithm 1. Asynchronous Reconfiguration

1: **State:**
2:   MyC {This replica's configuration}
3:   $MyC.ts$ {My configuration's timestamp}
4:   $Older$ {Older configurations}
5:   $Newer$ {Newer configurations}
6:   $P := \emptyset$ {Promises}
7:   $\Phi := \perp$ {Paxos State: $(rnd, vrnd, vval)$}
8:   $stateful :=$ FALSE $\{stateful =$ TRUE $\Leftrightarrow \Phi \neq \perp\}$
9:   $valid :=$ TRUE $\{valid =$ TRUE $\Leftrightarrow Newer = \emptyset\}$

10: **upon** $\langle$RECONF$, C_i, i, C_l\rangle$ **with** $l < i$ **and** C_l *stateful*   {On all replicas in C_i}
11:   $MyC := C_i$ {Start this replica in C_i}
12:   $MyC.ts := i$
13:   **send** $\langle$RECONF$, C_i, i, C_l\rangle$ to MyC {Make sure all received RECONF }
14:   $Older := \{C_l\}$
15:   **send** $\langle$NEWCONF$, C_i\rangle$ to C_l

16: **upon** $\langle$NEWCONF$, C_j\rangle$ **with** $j > MyC.ts$ {A newer configuration exists}
17:   **if** *valid* **and** *stateful* **then**
18:     **stop Paxos**
19:     $\Phi := (rnd, vrnd, vval)$ {Get state from Paxos}
20:     $valid :=$ FALSE
21:     $Newer := Newer \cup \{C_j\}$
22:     **send** $\langle$CPROMISE$, \Phi, Newer, MyC\rangle$ to C_j

23: **upon** $\langle$CPROMISE$, \Phi', Confs, ID, C\rangle$ **when not** *stateful*
24:   $P := P \cup \{\Phi', Confs, ID, C\}$
25:   $oldC := \{C_j \in Confs | j < MyC.ts\}$
26: • $newC := \{C_j \in Confs | j > MyC.ts\}$
27:   **if** $newC \not\subset Newer$ **then** $\{newC$ already known?$\}$
28:     $Newer := Newer \cup newC$
29:     $valid :=$ FALSE
30:   **if** $\exists Q \subset P; Q$ is stateful valid Quorum **then**   {See Definition 3}
31:     $\Phi := \text{findState}(Q)$ {See Algorithm 3}
32:     $stateful :=$ TRUE
33:     **send** $\langle$ACTIVATION$, \Phi, Newer\rangle$ to MyC {Optimization: See Algorithm 2}
34:     **if** *valid* **then**
35:       **start Paxos** with Φ in MyC
36:     **else**
37:       **send** $\langle$CPROMISE$, \Phi, Newer, MyC\rangle$ to $C_t \in newC$
38:   **else if** $\Phi' \neq \perp$ **and** $oldC \not\subset Older$ **then**   {CPromise stateful and not valid?}
39:     $Older := Older \cup oldC$
40:     **send** $\langle$NEWCONF$, MyC\rangle$ to $oldC$ {Ask other configurations}

---

that all correct replicas in C_i receive it. (See Lines 10 and 13 in Algorithm 1.) A replica from C_i then informs the replicas in C_l about the reconfiguration, sending $\langle$NEWCONF$, C_i\rangle$ (Line 15). Upon receiving this message, replicas in C_l stop running Paxos, retrieve their local Paxos State Φ and send it in a

---

Algorithm 2. Asynchronous Reconfiguration (Continued)

40:	**upon** ⟨ACTIVATION, Φ', *Confs*⟩ **when not** *stateful* {From replica in MyC}
41:	$\Phi := \Phi'$
42:	*stateful* := TRUE
43:	*Newer* := *Newer* ∪ *Confs*
44:	**send** ⟨ACTIVATION, Φ, *Newer*⟩ to MyC {Activate other replicas in MyC}
45:	**if** *Newer* = ∅ **then** {I'm the newest conf.}
46:	**start Paxos** with Φ in MyC
47:	**else** {There's a newer conf.}
48:	*valid* := FALSE
49:	**send** ⟨CPROMISE, Φ, *Newer*, MyC⟩ to *Newer*

Configuration-Promise ⟨CPROMISE, Φ, *Confs*, C_l⟩ to the replicas in C_i, including all known configurations with timestamp larger than l in *Confs* (Lines 18-22). The replicas in C_l store the new configuration C_i in the set *Newer* and include it in all future CPROMISEs (Line 21).

Upon receiving a quorum Q of CPROMISEs from C_l with empty *Confs* fields, the replicas in C_i can determine a Paxos State as explained in Algorithm 3. This corresponds to the processing of PROMISE messages in Paxos. *rnd* is set to a higher value than any one reported in Q, *vrnd* is set to the highest value reported in Q and *vval* to the value, reported in *vrnd*. Paxos is then started with a new round, where the leader sends out PREPARE messages. We say that a replica is *stateful*, after it has determined a Paxos State (*rnd*, *vrnd*, *vval*) (See Lines 31,32). This matches the notion of statefulness, introduced in Section 3.

Concurrent Reconfigurations: When several configurations are initialized concurrently, we have to ensure that exactly one of them starts running Paxos. To do this, a replica keeps track of the new configurations it has seen, using the set *Newer*, and includes it in CPROMISEs (Lines 21, 22). Thus, for any two concurrent reconfigurations, at least one will know about the other. To prevent several new configurations from starting Paxos simultaneously, a new replica remembers the configurations included in CPROMISEs (Lines 28, 39). If a replica knows about a configuration with higher timestamp, it will consider itself *not valid* (Lines 9, 29), and therefore will not start running Paxos (Lines 34, 35). Further, if a new replica receives a CPROMISE, informing it about another configuration with lower timestamp, it will also ask this configuration for CPROMISEs (Lines 25 and 38-40). To make sure a new replica receives its state from the latest stateful configuration, we require a stateful valid quorum to determine a correct state (Lines 30-31). A stateful valid quorum is defined as follows:

Definition 3. *A set Q of CPROMISEs sent from a majority of the replicas in C_i to a replica in C_j, is a stateful valid quorum from C_i, if*

(1) all messages contain a Paxos State, that is $\Phi \neq \bot$,
(2) and if for any configuration C_t, included in the Confs field of a CPROMISE in Q, $t \geq j$ holds.

Algorithm 3. Procedure to find the highest Paxos state in Q

1: **Input:**
2: $MyC.ts$ {This configurations timestamp}
3: $Q = \{(\Phi, Confs, ID, C), \ldots\}$ {CPROMISES with $\Phi = (rnd, vrnd, vval)$}
                                                      {and $\forall C_i \in Confs : i \geq MyC.ts$}

4: **procedure** findState(Q)
5:    $rnd := \max rnd \in Q + 1$ {Highest rnd from Paxos states, Φ, in Q}
6:    $vrnd := \max vrnd \in Q$ {Highest $vrnd$ from Paxos states, Φ, in Q}
7:    $vval := vval(vrnd)$ {$vval$ reported with $vrnd$}
8:    **return** $(rnd, vrnd, vval)$

Note that a CPROMISE is stateful, if and only if it was sent by a stateful replica. The following example shows how our algorithm ensures that only one of two configurations starts running Paxos.

Example 1. Assume an initial stateful configuration C_0 with replicas x, y, and z. Assume two new configurations C_1 and C_2 are initialized. If C_2 receives a stateful valid quorum of CPROMISES from x and y, and starts Paxos, then x and y received the NEWCONF message from C_2 before the one from C_1. They will include C_2 in their CPROMISES to C_1. C_1 will therefore never start running Paxos.

This next example shows, how stateful valid quorums guarantee that a new configuration gets its Paxos State from the last stateful configuration.

Example 2. Assume as above an initial configuration C_0 and concurrently initialized configurations C_1 and C_2. Assume C_1 received an stateful valid quorum of CPROMISES from C_0 and started running Paxos.

Thus, the replicas in C_0 will inform C_2 about C_1 in there CPROMISES, and because of condition (2), the CPROMISES from C_0 to C_2 will not make a stateful valid quorum. Therefore C_2 will ask C_1 for CPROMISES. The replicas in C_1 will either directly reply to C_2 with a statefulCPROMISE, or send it, after they determined a Paxos State (Lines 22, 37 and 49).

Optimizations: Algorithm 1 assumes that all replicas in a new configuration are initialized with a RECONF message. And all send NEWCONF messages and receive CPROMISES. However, if one replica has determined a Paxos State, the others can simply copy it, instead of waiting for a quorum of CPROMISES. Thus, after a replica has determined a correct Paxos State using Algorithm 3, it sends this state to all replicas in its configuration, using an ACTIVATION message (Line 33). Other replicas can just copy this state, instead of waiting for a quorum of CPROMISES as explained in Algorithm 2. To reduce the message load, processes in the new configuration can further run a weak leader election algorithm and only the leader would send NEWCONF messages and receive CPROMISES. The other replicas can then be started by an ACTIVATION message. Note that we do not require a single leader to emerge. It is only needed that eventually one or several correct leaders are elected. [1] Finally, since we assume reliable communication, messages have to be resent until an acknowledgement is received. In an asynchronous system, this means that messages to faulty processes have to be sent infinitely often. However, NEWCONF and CPROMISE messages must only be resent until the new configuration is stateful. The rest can be done by ACTIVATION messages.

4.1   The ARec State Machine

Just as PREPARE and PROMISE messages in Paxos, we can send NEWCONF and CPROMISE messages for infinitely many instances of Paxos at the same time, since the Paxos State will be the initial state ($\Phi = (0, 0, \text{nil})$), for all except finitely many instances. However it is unpractical to replay all requests of an execution history on the new configuration. A more practical solution is to provide a snapshot of the replicated application to the new replicas when invoking RECONF. If this snapshot incorporates all requests chosen in the first k Paxos instances, it is enough to exchange NEWCONF and CPROMISE messages for the Paxos instances starting with $k + 1$.

While in undecided instances a new configuration needs to receive a quorum of Paxos States, in a decided instance, it would suffice to receive the decided value from one replica. This can be used to further reduce the size of CPROMISE messages in an implementation.

5   Safety of the RSM

We now prove that RSM *safety* cannot be compromised by ARec. That is, only a single value can get chosen in a Paxos instance, even if the instance runs over several configurations. Proving *safety* for Paxos usually relies on the condition that any two quorums intersect [3]. However, this condition does not hold in a dynamic system. We derive a substitute for this condition in Corollary 1.

Recall that a replica is *stateful* if it has Paxos State and *valid* if it does not know of any configuration higher than its own (Lines 8 and 9). A message is stateful or valid *iff* its sender is.

According to Algorithm 1, a replica only starts Paxos when it is stateful and valid (Lines 32-35 and 42-46), and stops Paxos when it becomes invalid (Lines 16-18). A stateful replica always stays stateful. Thus, the sender of a Paxos message is always stateful and valid. We can therefore define all quorums of PROMISE or LEARN messages to be stateful valid quorums, analogue to Definition 3.

Since two quorums do not necessarily intersect, we define the following property to describe that one quorum knows about another quorum.

---

[1] This leader election is strictly weaker than the one required for Paxos [8]. In this case, a failure detector suspecting everybody forever, and therefore electing all replicas as leaders gives an inefficient but correct solution.

Definition 4. *For two stateful valid quorums of messages, Q and Q', we say that Q' knows Q, writing $Q \mapsto Q'$, if*

(1) Q is a quorum of Paxos messages, and some replica first sent a message in Q and then a message in Q', or
(2) Q is a stateful valid quorum of CPROMISES and the Paxos State of some replica, sending a message in Q' was derived using Algorithm 3 on Q.

We say that Q' knows about Q, writing $Q \dashrightarrow Q'$, if there exist k stateful valid quorums $Q_1, \ldots, Q_k$, such that $Q \mapsto Q_1 \mapsto \ldots \mapsto Q_k \mapsto Q'$.

Note that, condition (2) applies both, if a replica in Q' called findState(Q), or if it received an ACTIVATION message including $\Phi = $ findState(Q).

In Lemma 1 we show how this notion is related to Paxos variables rnd and $vrnd$. We therefore first define the rnd and $vrnd$ of a stateful valid quorum. Note that a stateful valid quorum from C_i, can either be a quorum of LEARN or PROMISE messages sent in the same round, or a quorum of stateful CPROMISES from C_i.

Definition 5. *For a stateful valid quorum of messages Q we define:*

$$rnd(Q) = \begin{cases} rnd \text{ msgs were send} & \text{for LEARNs and PROMISEs} \\ \text{maxrnd} & \text{for CPROMISEs} \end{cases}$$

$$vrnd(Q) = \begin{cases} rnd \text{ msgs were send} & \text{for LEARNs} \\ \text{maxvrnd} & \text{for PROMISEs} \\ \text{maxvrnd} & \text{for CPROMISEs} \end{cases}$$

Where maxrnd and maxvrnd refer to the highest rnd and vrnd reported in the messages.

Lemma 1. *Let Q and Q' be stateful valid quorums from C_i and C_j.*
(1) If $Q \mapsto Q'$ and $i = j$, then $rnd(Q) \leq rnd(Q')$.
(2) If $Q \mapsto Q'$ and $i < j$, then $rnd(Q) < rnd(Q')$ and $vrnd(Q) \leq vrnd(Q')$.
(3) If $Q \mapsto Q'$, and Q are LEARNs, then $vrnd(Q) \leq vrnd(Q')$ holds.

Proof. Using the following facts, all cases easily follow from the definitions. In cases (1) and (3) of the Lemma, $Q \mapsto Q'$ is caused by case (1) in Definition 4. The claims easily follow, since Q and Q' have a sender in common. In case (2) of the Lemma, Q is a quorum of CPROMISES and case (2) of the Definition 4 holds. The claim follows, since $(rnd, vrnd, vval) = $ findState(Q) implies $rnd = rnd(Q) + 1$ and $vrnd = vrnd(Q)$. (Compare Algorithm 3 and Definition 5.)   □

Lemma 2. *For two quorums of Paxos messages Q in C_i and Q' in C_j, if $i < j$ then $Q \dashrightarrow Q'$. Further, we can choose all quorums $Q_1, \ldots, Q_k$ to be quorums of CPROMISES and $Q \mapsto Q_1 \mapsto \ldots \mapsto Q_k \mapsto Q'$ still holds.*

Proof. Clearly there exist sequences $Q_0 \mapsto Q_1 \mapsto \ldots \mapsto Q$ and $Q'_0 \mapsto Q'_1 \mapsto \ldots \mapsto Q'$ with Q_0 and Q'_0 in the initial configuration C_0. We want to show, that there exists a Q_i' in C_i. Choose maximal t and t', s.t. Q_t and $Q_{t'}'$ are in the same configuration C_u. It follows that $u \leq i$, and Q_t and $Q_{t'}'$ have at least one sender in common. For $u < i$ maximality implies that both Q_t and $Q_{t'}'$ are CPROMISES.

Assume first $Q_t \mapsto Q_{t'}'$ and $u < i$. Let messages in Q_t be sent to C_v. Thus C_v will be included in at least one CPROMISE from $Q_{t'}'$. Since $Q_{t'}'$ is a stateful valid quorum it follows from Definition 3, that $Q_{t'}'$ was sent to a configuration $C_{v'}$ with $u < v' \leq v$. Maximality of u implies that $v' < v$. It follows similar, that all quorums $Q_{t''}'$ for $t'' > t'$ are stateful valid quorums of CPROMISES send to configurations $C_{v''}$ with $v'' < v$. This contradicts that Q' is a valid quorum of Paxos messages.

If we assume that $Q_{t'}' \mapsto Q_t$ and $u < i$, we similarly reach a contradiction, to the fact that Q is a quorum of Paxos messages. It therefore follows, that $u = i$ and $Q_{t'}'$ is from C_i. Since $Q_{t'}'$ is still a quorum of CPROMISES and no replica sends a Paxos message, after sending a CPROMISE, it follows that $Q \mapsto Q_{t'}'$. This proofs the Lemma. $\square$

Corollary 1. *For two quorums of Paxos messages, Q and P, either $Q \dashrightarrow P$ or $P \dashrightarrow Q$ holds.*

Proof. This follows from Lemma 2 if Q and P do not happen in the same configuration. Otherwise, it is clear since two quorums of messages in one configuration have at least one sender in common. $\square$

The following corollary and theorem show that ARec preserves safety:

Corollary 2. *Only a single value can be chosen in one round.*

Proof. It is clear that only one value can be chosen in round r in configuration C_i. Assume another value was chosen in round s in configuration C_j, $j \neq i$. Let Q_r be the quorum of LEARNs in round r in C_i and Q_s the quorum of LEARNs in round s in C_j. From Corollary 1 it follows that $Q_s \dashrightarrow Q_r$ or vice versa. Since $j \neq i$, $Q_s \mapsto Q_1 \mapsto \ldots \mapsto Q_k \mapsto Q_r$ with $k > 0$ and at least one quorum of CPROMISES. From Lemma 1 part (1) and (2) it follows that $rnd(Q_s) < rnd(Q_r)$ or vice versa. Therefore $s \neq r$.

Theorem 1. *If a value is safe in round r, no other value was chosen in a lower round.*

Proof. We prove this by induction over r. If $r = 0$, there is nothing to show. Assume $r > 0$ and that the Theorem holds for all rounds smaller than r. If some value v is safe in round r, then a quorum P of PROMISES showing this was send in round r. Therefore v was also safe in round $vrnd(P)$. Assume some value v' was chosen in round $s < r$, then a quorum Q of LEARNs was send in round s. From Corollary 1 and Lemma 1 part (1) it follows that $Q \dashrightarrow P$. If we show that $vrnd(P) > s$, we can apply the induction hypothesis on $vrnd(P) < r$, and see that $v' = v$. If $vrnd(P) = s$, we can apply Corollary 2 and get that $v = v'$.

Since $Q \dashrightarrow P$ there exist quorums $Q_1, \ldots, Q_k$, such that $Q \mapsto Q_1 \mapsto \ldots \mapsto Q_k \mapsto P$. According to Lemma 2 we can choose all Q_i to be quorums of CPROMISES. Now $s = vrnd(Q) \leq vrnd(Q_1)$ follows from Lemma 1, part (3). And $vrnd(Q_1) \leq \ldots \leq vrnd(P)$ follows from Lemma 1, part (2). Thus $s = vrnd(Q) \leq vrnd(P)$ □

6   Liveness for Reconfiguration

We now proof that ARec is live, that is that ARec Liveness and Dynamic RSM Liveness define in Section 3 hold. We assume throughout this section, that at any point during an execution, all configurations our system depends on are available. Proofs of both liveness properties rely on the following Lemma:

Lemma 3. *If configuration C_i is stateful and some correct replica in C_i knows about a configuration C_j, $j > i$, then the system will eventually no longer depend on C_i.*

Proof. Assume the system depends on C_i. According to the definition in of the depends on relation, the system also depends on all configurations with higher timestamp than i. It is enough, to show that one of these configurations will eventually become stateful. Assume therefore, that C_j is not stateful. Let $c \in C_i$ be a replica that knows about configuration C_j. c learned about C_j, either by receiving a NEWCONF message from C_j (See Line 16 in Algorithm 1), or by receiving a CPROMISE or ACTIVATION message including C_j (Lines 23,40). In the later cases, c will itself send a CPROMISE to C_j (Lines 37,49). Since the system depends on C_j, it is available, and will send NEWCONF messages to C_i either upon initialization (Line 15), or on receiving the CPROMISE from c (Line 40). Thus eventually the majority of correct replicas in C_i will send CPROMISEs to C_j. If these build an stateful valid quorum, C_j will become stateful and the system will no longer depend on C_i. If the CPROMISEs are no stateful valid quourum, one of the senders knows about a configuration C_k with $i < k < j$. We can now repeat the above arguement with C_k instead of C_j. Clearly we will eventually arrive at a configuration C_l, such that no configuration with timestamp between i and l exists. This configuration will become stateful and the system will no longer depend on C_i.   □

Theorem 2. *ARec implements ARec Liveness.*

Proof. Assume there is a stateful configuration C_l and some correct client initialized a reconfiguration $\langle \text{RECONF}, C_i, i, C_l \rangle$. If the system does not depend on C_l, there is nothing to show. Otherwise, both C_l and C_i are available. Since the client is correct, eventually a correct replica in C_i will receive the RECONF message and send a NEWCONF message. On recieving this message, some correct replica in C_l will know about C_i. Lemma 3 says, that the system will eventually no longer depend on C_l.   □

Theorem 3. *ARec, together with the Paxos implement Dynamic RSM Liveness.*

Proof. If, in an execution only finitely many configurations are initialized, eventually one configuration will forever be the stateful configuration with highest timestamp C_{max} and the system will depend on this configuration forever. Thus Lemma 3 implies, that no correct replica in C_{max} knows about a configuration with higher timestamp. Thus all corret replicas in C_{max} are valid (Line 9). Since at least one correct replica in C_{max} is stateful, it will send ACTIVATION messages, until all correct replicas in C_{max} are stateful. Since C_{max} is available by assumption (a) from Dynamic RSM Liveness, it eventually holds a majority of correct, stateful and valid replicas that will run Paxos. If additionally a single replica is elected as a leader, Liveness of Paxos implies that submitted requests can get learned and executed. □

7   Related Work

As mentioned in the introduction, the classical method to reconfigure an RSM was already explained in [1] and [2, 3]. Variations of this method where presented in [9] and it was refined and implemented in works like [10] and [4]. All these works use consensus to decide on the next configuration, resulting in a unique sequence of configurations, where each reconfiguration only involves one old and one new configuration. For this, a configuration must be available and have a single correct leader before it can be changed by reconfiguration.

The work most closely related to ARec is Vertical Paxos [5]. Vertical Paxos also changes configuration between rounds rather than between instances, and uses Paxos' first phase to deduce a starting state for the new configuration, similar to ARec. Also similar to ARec, a new configuration C_i knows about one past configuration C_l that is stateful and must receive a quorum from all configurations with sequence numbers between l and i. Different from ARec however, Vertical Paxos assumes that upon receiving a reconfiguration request, configuration C_i knows about all configurations C_j with $l \leq j < i$. Finally, Vertical Paxos relies on an abstract, fault tolerant configuration manager to order new configurations. Instead of relying on synchrony in the old configuration, Vertical Paxos relies on synchrony in the configuration manager, which must be implemented by another RSM to be fault tolerant. Note also that the configuration manager RSM cannot use Vertical Paxos to reconfigure itself, but has to rely on classical reconfiguration. ARec does not rely on a separate configuration manager.

That asynchronous reconfiguration is possible has previously only been proven for atomic R/W registers [11]. In their protocol, DynaStore, a reconfiguration does not specify a new configuration as a set of replicas, but as a set of operations, each adding or removing one replica. When several reconfigurations are issued concurrently, DynaStore takes the union of these reconfigurations as the configuration that the replicas eventually agree upon. If reconfigurations are issued by several parties, this interface has some disadvantages. For example, if several parties try to reduce the number of replicas, but disagree on the replica to be removed, they could by accident remove all replicas. Thus it is possible to violate DynaStore's Liveness property by issuing an "unlucky" reconfiguration. This is not possible with ARec.

As described in [9], a Dynamic RSM has similarities to group communication systems that provide totally ordered message delivery [12]. However, while view synchronous communication requires that a message received by one process in view v is received by all processes in view v, therefore consensus is required to end a view. A Dynamic RSM ensures that requests learned by one replica in a configuration, are learned by all replicas in some future configuration. Therefore ARec only requires consensus in some future configuration.

8   Conclusion

We have presented ARec a reconfiguration protocol for a Paxos State Machine that enables reconfiguration in a completely asynchronous system. To our knowledge this is the first protocol for asynchronous reconfiguration of an RSM. We have precisely specified the liveness conditions for asynchronous reconfiguration, improving on previous specifications, which allow unlucky reconfigurations to break liveness. Using ARec, availability of RSM based systems can be improved, since reconfiguration can be used to restore synchrony, and thus enable the RSM to make progress. However, since our work mainly focused on proving the possibility of asynchronous reconfiguration, we expect that ARec can be significantly optimized when adjusting it to a specific system.

References

[1] Schneider, F.B.: Implementing fault-tolerant services using the state machine approach: a tutorial. ACM Comput. Surv. 22(4), 299–319 (1990)
[2] Lamport, L.: The part-time parliament. ACM Trans. Comput. Syst. 16(2), 133–169 (1998)
[3] Lamport, L.: Paxos made simple. ACM SIGACT News (December 2001)
[4] Shraer, A., Reed, B., Malkhi, D., Junqueira, F.: Dynamic reconfiguration of primary/backup clusters. USENIX ATC (2011)
[5] Lamport, L., Malkhi, D., Zhou, L.: Vertical paxos and primary-backup replication. In: PODC (2009)
[6] Fischer, M.J., Lynch, N.A., Paterson, M.S.: Impossibility of distributed consensus with one faulty process. J. ACM 32(2), 374–382 (1985)
[7] Chandra, T.D., Hadzilacos, V., Toueg, S., Charron-Bost, B.: On the impossibility of group membership. In: PODC (1996)
[8] Chandra, T.D., Toueg, S.: Unreliable failure detectors for reliable distributed systems. J. ACM 43, 225–267 (1996)
[9] Lamport, L., Malkhi, D., Zhou, L.: Reconfiguring a state machine. SIGACT News 41(1), 63–73 (2010)
[10] Lorch, J.R., Adya, A., Bolosky, W.J., Chaiken, R., Douceur, J.R., Howell, J.: The smart way to migrate replicated stateful services. In: EuroSys (2006)
[11] Aguilera, M.K., Keidar, I., Malkhi, D., Shraer, A.: Dynamic atomic storage without consensus. J. ACM 58(2), 7 (2011)
[12] Chockler, G.V., Keidar, I., Vitenberg, R.: Group communication specifications: a comprehensive study. ACM Comput. Surv. 33(4), 427–469 (2001)

A Causal Checkpointing Algorithm for Mobile Computing Environments

Astrid Kiehn, Pranav Raj, and Pushpendra Singh

Indraprastha Institute of Information Technology,
New Delhi, India
{astrid,pranav09032,psingh}@iiitd.ac.in
http://www.iiitd.ac.in

Abstract. Checkpointing algorithms suitable for mobile computing environments should be economical in terms of storage and energy consumption, and they should be able to handle that at starting time not all processes are known which are to be involved in the checkpointing. We propose such an algorithm by generalizing Chandy/Lamport's snapshot algorithm [4] in two ways: processes are given a certain autonomy when to take their local checkpoints, and processes send checkpoint requests only to processes they knowingly depend on. As [4], our algorithm comprises the so-called phase 1 of coordinated checkpointing, only, which - under reasonable progress assumptions - ensures that all the local checkpoints will be taken. We present the algorithm in terms of its operational semantics over which we prove the consistency of the calculated snapshot.

Keywords: Coordinated Checkpointing, Consistency, Distributed Systems.

1 Introduction

High mobility, frequent disconnections, and lack of vital resources such as memory and computing power, are the characteristics of mobile computing environments. This makes applications susceptible to faults. With more and more applications becoming available on mobile platforms, it is necessary to provide good fault-tolerant mechanisms to ensure reliable working of distributed mobile applications.

Coordinated Checkpointing is a major technique to provide fault-tolerance to distributed applications. In coordinated checkpointing, processes may take multiple checkpoints coordinated by request and confirm messages, but the last set of checkpoints taken form a consistent snapshot of the entire computation ([8], [5]). A checkpointing algorithm suitable for mobile computing environments should be minimally affected by the following issues:

Limited Resources. The amount of storage and energy of the underlying mobile devices is limited.

Dynamic Dependencies. Not all processes participating in the checkpointing are known at checkpoint initiation time.

M. Chatterjee et al. (Eds.): ICDCN 2014, LNCS 8314, pp. 134–148, 2014.
© Springer-Verlag Berlin Heidelberg 2014

Unreliable Network. Processes might frequently get disconnected, and messages exchanged might get reordered during transmission time.

Various coordinated checkpointing algorithms for mobile computing environments have been proposed in the literature (see [3] for a good overview, [7], [15], [11] and most relevant to our work [2], [3], [13], and [14]). Roughly, these algorithms try to minimise the use of resources while dealing with dynamic dependencies. They differ in when a local process takes a checkpoint, when a checkpoint is made permanent or discarded and for what reason, and whether a process gets blocked.

The coordinated checkpointing algorithm proposed in this paper, similarly, assumes dynamic dependencies and aims at a minimal use of resources. It contributes to power reduction by minimizing the number of coordination messages and the checkpoints to be taken. It further gives to processes a certain autonomy over when to take their checkpoints. This allows them to complete a computationally expensive local subtask avoiding the entire recalculation at recovery time. Moreover, if the subtask is non-interruptible the checkpointing request does not need to be rejected but can be postponed. A process takes at most one checkpoint without being blocked and will eventually take it without this having to be triggered, externally.

The algorithm can be seen as an adaption of Chandy/Lamport's algorithm [4] for mobile computing environments. It is closely related to the work of Cao/Singhal [3] and Singh/Cabillic [13]. However, both their algorithms are based on two interrelated phases while our algorithm like Chandy/Lamport's has an independent first phase as far as the checkpointing is concerned. We only model and prove this first phase, the second phase could be implemented along standard lines, see [13].

The algorithm is informally introduced in Section 2 and formally in Section 3. It is given by its operational semantics, and over this semantics we prove correctness in Section 4: we show reachability of the calculated snapshot which implies consistency and the absence of orphans (any message reported as received must have been sent, also). Our proof is based on forward reasoning rather than by contradiction - the method employed in most of the papers cited earlier - and we see it as a major contribution of the paper. In Section 5 we briefly discuss the impact of an unreliable network on our algorithm. A final resumé is given in the conclusions of Section 6.

2 The Checkpointing Algorithm

Briefly, the algorithm can be described as follows. The initiating process – always assumed to be P_1 – requests the processes it depends on to take a checkpoint. A process receiving such a request will set its checkpoint alert and propagate the request to the so far uninformed processes it itself depends on. It continues with its local computations taking the checkpoint at any time but before receiving a new message. Having taken the checkpoint, all outgoing messages will have a flag

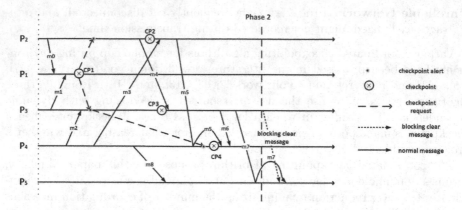

Fig. 1. P_1 initiates the checkpointing and sends checkpoint requests to its depending processes P_2 and P_3. Messages m_0, m_1, m_2 and m_3 are consumed directly when received. Message m_5 would become an orphan message if consumed immediately. It is therefore delayed and consumed only after CP4 has been taken. Message m_6 is received after CP4 as it cannot become an orphan. P_5 does not take part in the checkpointing process but receives message m_7 sent after CP4. This message will be consumed by P_5 only after it receives the *blocking clear message* sent by P_3 during phase 2.

(blockbit set) indicating that the checkpoint had been taken. A process receiving a flagged message will not process it until it has taken its own checkpoint or - if not involved in the checkpointing - until it receives a blocking clear message from the same process. The latter is part of phase two not modelled in this paper.[1]

In Chandy/Lamport's algorithm a process after having taking its checkpoint sends out a checkpoint request to all other processes from which it hadn't received a request itself. In our algorithm aiming at calculating a partial snapshot only, processes proceed just like that but since dependencies can arise dynamically it may not know all the processes which need to be informed. For that reason it is indispensable to attach a flag bit to messages sent out after the checkpointing which guarantee that all processes are aware of the checkpoint taken. The second main difference wrt Chandy/Lamport's algorithm is that a process has a certain freedom when to take its checkpoint. Having received a request it may complete some of its local computations (which may include the sending of messages) according to its own judgements.

More details on our algorithm are given next. Rule numbers in brackets refer to corresponding operational semantic rules given in the next section.

---

[1] Phase two would deal with declaring that the snapshot taking is complete and over. For our algorithm that would imply that all participating processes would report back to the initiator that they have taken their checkpoint. In turn, they would be informed about the completion of the checkpointing and having received this information they would forward it to the processes to whom they had sent a message with blockbit 1. The latter then could clear their blocking queues.

1. In our model there are n processes $P_1, P_2, \ldots, P_n$ and processes are connected via FIFO channels C_{ij}. As part of their computations processes send messages to each other which come attached with a blockbit (Rules 1.1. and 1.2). If the blockbit is set, this indicates that the sending process has already taken its checkpoint. Such messages are called blocking as they might lead to blocking a blocking queue.

2. Every process maintains a dependency vector which provides all the processes it depends on. A process P_i depends on process P_j if P_i has received a message from P_j. This is a dynamic notion of dependency as at the time of initiating the checkpointing all dependencies may not be known. The checkpointing will involve all processes which are dependent in a transitive way. In Figure 1 at the time of initiating, the checkpointing process P_1 depends on P_2 and P_3. However, P_4 needs to be included in the checkpointing as P_3 depends on it.

3. Every process maintains a set of blocking queues BQ_{ij}, one for each incoming channel. Blocking queues are required to model *receiving a message without processing it*. The interplay between channel and blocking queue is depicted in Figure 2. Conceptually, one can see C_{ij} and BQ_{ij} as one FIFO queue $C_{ij} \circ BQ_{ij}$ where messages cannot be removed from the channel if the blocking queue is nonempty. In such a case reading from the channel amounts to inspecting the message, only, and pushing it into the blocking queue (Rule 2.4). Inspection, however, is only possible if the latter is blocked.

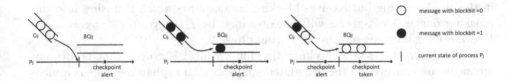

Fig. 2. Channels and Blocking Queues

4. The initiator takes its checkpoint and sends the checkpoint request to the processes it depends on using its dependency vector. It attaches the dependency vector to its request (Rule 3).

5. When a process P_i receives a checkpoint request (with attached dependency vector) for the first time, it prepares to take the checkpoint in near future which is modelled by setting the checkpoint alert (Rule 4.1), and it propagates the request to all processes on which it depends and which have not been informed yet according to the received dependency vector. It does not immediately take the checkpoint but continuing with its own computation may delay it to any time before receiving another message (Rule 5, there is no rule which allows a process under alert to receive a message before the checkpoint has been taken).

If it was not the first request then the alert had already been set and the new request will simply be removed from the channel (Rule 4.2).

6. If a process P_i removes a message (with attached blockbit) from a channel then either of the following will happen:

   - If P_i has not yet received any checkpoint request and the blockbit of the message is 1 then it pushes the message into its respective blocking queue (Rules 2.3 and 2.4).
   - If P_i has not yet received any checkpoint request and the blockbit is 0 then it processes the message. It recognizes the sending process as one of the processes it depends on and updates its dependency vector if necessary. (Rule 2.1)
   - If P_i has received a checkpoint request but not taken the checkpoint yet then it pushes the message (with any blockbit) into its respective blocking queue. (Rule 2.2 - 2.4)
   - If P_i has already taken the checkpoint then it processes the message irrespective of its blockbit (Rule 2.5) provided it has emptied the respective blocking queue (Rule 6).

Figure 1 can now be explained in terms of the internals of the algorithm. Process P_1 initiates the checkpointing and sends checkpoint requests to P_2 and P_3 (because of the dependency arising from m_0 and m_1). Messages m_0, m_1, m_2 and m_3 are non-blocking messages and will be consumed directly when received. Message m_5 is a blocking message and will be pushed into blocking queue BQ_{24} to be consumed only after CP4. Message m_6 is a blocking message, but it is received after CP4 and will be consumed directly. Process P_5 does not take part in the checkpointing but receives blocking message m_7 which it pushes into the blocking queue. Message m_7 will be consumed by P_5 only after it receives the *blocking clear message* sent by P_3 during phase 2.

For the correctness of a checkpointing algorithm it is crucial that no orphan messages are captured in the calculated snapshot. An orphan message is a message which is recorded as received but not as sent. Intuitively, our algorithm is correct in this sense, as messages received by P_i before the checkpoint of P_i has been taken have either been sent before the sender has taken its checkpoint or their consumption is delayed by storing them in the respective blocking queue. In our proof, however, we show more than this. We prove reachability of the snapshot obtained from taking the local checkpoints and the local states of the non-participating processes. This implies the absence of orphans and consistency of the snapshot. The proof is based on the operational semantics of the algorithm given in the next section.

3   Operational Semantics of the Algorithm

We describe the algorithm formally by its operational semantics. It is given by a set of rules which state the preconditions (above the line) under which an event (below the line) may happen:

<u>preconditions</u>
event and system's change

An event executed by a process changes the global state of the system. We write $S \xrightarrow{e} T$ if at state S event e leads to state T. At state S, any event that is permitted by the rules may happen. The algorithm is thus nondeterministic, as any process at any time can send a message, and a process may locally choose between sending and receiving a message.

A process P_i is defined via the three components

1. the history p_i (a list of events)
2. the dependency array dep_i (a binary vector)
3. the blocking queues BQ_{ji} (a list of messages removed from channel C_{ji})

Processes are connected via channels C_{ij} leading from P_i to P_j.

List of events and messages:

cp_alert_i	process P_i sets up the checkpoint alert
cp_taken_i	P_i takes the checkpoint
$send_{ij}$	P_i adds a message to channel C_{ij}
$receive_{ij}$	P_j removes and processes a message from channel C_{ij}
$inspect_{ij}$	P_j removes a message from C_{ij} and
	pushes it into blocking queue BQ_{ij}
$consume_{ij}$	P_{ij} removes and processes a message from blocking queue BQ_{ij}
$\langle cpa_i, dep \rangle$	the message that P_i has set up the checkpoint alert with attached
	dependency vector
$\langle msg, bb \rangle$	a message (always assumed to be new when sent out first) and
	attached blockbit

We use *Events* for the set of events listed in the upper part of the table and *MSG* for the messages in the lower part of the table. Blocking queues and channels are FIFO queues modelled as words (strings) over MSG^*. The first element of a queue is at the rightmost position and provided by *first*. So if the channel contents of C_{ij} at state S is $(msg_3, 1).(msg_2, 0).(cpa_1, dep_1).(msg_1, 0)$ then $first(C_{ij}^S) = (msg_1, 0)$ and $rem(C_{ij}^S) = (msg_3, 1).(msg_2, 0).(cpa_1, dep_1)$ provides the remainder of the queues. We use the simple dot to separate letters in a word. For the concatenation of words, however, for emphasis we use ∘.

A global state S of a system with checkpointing is of the form:

$$S = ((p_1, dep_1, BQ_1), \ldots, (p_n, dep_n, BQ_n), Chan)$$

where

$$Chan : \{C_{ij} \mid i, j \leq n, i \neq j\} \to MSG^*,$$
$$BQ_i \ : \{C_{ji} \mid j \leq n, i \neq j\} \to MSG^*, \quad 1 \leq i \leq n$$

and $p_i \in Events^*$. To ease readability we attach S as a superscript to its components and abbreviate $Chan(C_{ij})^S$ by C_{ij}^S and $BQ_i^S(C_{ji})$ by BQ_{ji}^S. In the initial state S_0 by definition $p_i^{S_0} = \varepsilon$, $dep_i^{S_0}(j) = \begin{cases} 1 \text{ if } i = j \\ 0 \text{ otherwise} \end{cases}$, $BQ_{ij}^{S_0} = C_{ij}^{S_0} = \varepsilon$ for all i, j. If an event occurs in the history of a process at state S then we state this as a predicate $event_i^S$. For example, $\neg cp\_taken_i^S$ stands for that cp_taken_i does not occur in the history p_i^S. It represents that P_i has not taken its checkpoint at state S.

Rules are grouped according to their functionality.

Rules for Sending Messages. A message can be sent out at any time and the attached blockbit shows whether this happened before or after the checkpoint was taken.

Rule 1.1

$$\frac{\neg cp\_taken_i^S}{S \overset{send_{ij}(\langle msg,0 \rangle)}{\longrightarrow} T} \quad \text{where } T \text{ differs from } S \text{ in } \begin{array}{l} (1) \ p_i^T = p_i^S.send_{ij}(\langle msg, 0 \rangle) \\ (2) \ C_{ij}^T = \langle msg, 0 \rangle.C_{ij}^S \end{array}$$
only.

Rule 1.2

$$\frac{cp\_taken_i^S}{S \overset{send_{ij}(\langle msg,1 \rangle)}{\longrightarrow} T} \quad \text{where } T \text{ differs from } S \text{ in } \begin{array}{l} (1) \ p_i^T = p_i^S.send_{ij}(\langle msg, 1 \rangle) \\ (2) \ C_{ij}^T = \langle msg, 1 \rangle.C_{ij}^S \end{array}$$
only.

Rules for Removing Messages from Channels. A message removed from a channel will be processed immediately only if the attached blockbit is 0 and the removal happens before the checkpoint alert, or the message has been removed after the checkpoint was taken and the blocking queue is empty. In all other cases the message will be added to the blocking queue. Note, that with Rule 2.1 a new dependency may arise.

Rule 2.1

$$\frac{first(C_{ij}^S) = \langle msg,0 \rangle, \ BQ_{ij}^S = \varepsilon \text{ and } \neg cp\_alert_j^S}{S \overset{receive_{ij}(\langle msg,0 \rangle)}{\longrightarrow} T} \quad \text{where } T \text{ differs from } S \text{ in } \begin{array}{l} (1) \ p_j^T = p_j^S.receive_{ij}(\langle msg, 0 \rangle) \\ (2) \ C_{ij}^T = rem(C_{ij}^S) \\ (3) \ dep_j^T(i) = 1 \end{array}$$
at most.

Rule 2.2

$$\frac{first(C_{ij}^S) = \langle msg, 0\rangle, \; BQ_{ij}^S = \varepsilon \;, \; cp\_alert_j^S \text{ and } \neg cp\_taken_j^S}{S \xrightarrow{inspect_{ij}(\langle msg, 0\rangle)} T}$$

where T differs from S in (1) $p_j^T = p_j^S.inspect_{ij}(\langle msg, 0\rangle)$
(2) $C_{ij}^T = rem(C_{ij}^S)$
(3) $BQ_{ij}^T = \langle msg, 0\rangle$

only.

Rule 2.3

$$\frac{first(C_{ij}^S) = \langle msg, 1\rangle, \; BQ_{ij}^S = \varepsilon \text{ and } \neg cp\_taken_j^S}{S \xrightarrow{inspect_{ij}(\langle msg, 1\rangle)} T}$$

where T differs from S in (1) $p_j^T = p_j^S.inspect_{ij}(\langle msg, 1\rangle)$
(2) $C_{ij}^T = rem(C_{ij}^S)$
(3) $BQ_{ij}^T = \langle msg, 1\rangle$

only.

Rule 2.4

$$\frac{first(C_{ij}^S) = \langle msg, bb\rangle, \; BQ_{ij}^S \neq \varepsilon \text{ and } \neg cp\_taken_i^S}{S \xrightarrow{inspect_{ij}(\langle msg, bb\rangle)} T}$$

where T differs from S in (1) $p_j^T = p_j^S.inspect_{ij}(\langle msg, bb\rangle)$
(2) $C_{ij}^T = rem(C_{ij}^S)$
(3) $BQ_{ij}^T = \langle msg, bb\rangle.BQ_{ij}^S$

only.

Rule 2.5

$$\frac{first(C_{ij}^S) = \langle msg, bb\rangle, \; BQ_{ij}^S = \varepsilon \text{ and } cp\_taken_j^S}{S \xrightarrow{receive_{ij}(\langle msg, bb\rangle)} T}$$

where T differs from S in (1) $p_j^T = p_j^S.receive_{ij}(\langle msg, bb\rangle)$
(2) $C_{ij}^T = rem(C_{ij}^S)$

only.

Rule for Initiating the Checkpointing. We assume that this will be done by P_1. It sends the checkpoint alert to all the processes it depends on and immediately takes the checkpoint.

Rule 3

$$\frac{\neg cp\_taken_1^S}{S \xrightarrow{cp\_taken_1} T}$$

where T differs from S in (1) $p_1^T = p_1^S.cp\_alert_1.cp\_taken_1$
(2) $C_{1k}^T = \langle cpa_1, dep_1^S\rangle.C_{1k}^S$
for all $k > 1$ with $dep_1^S(k) = 1$

only.

Rules for Receiving and Setting an Alert. Receiving, setting and propagating an alert is modelled as one atomic event. This event comprises removing the alert from the channel, setting the alert and propagating the alert and causal dependencies to the concerned processes. These are the processes on which the alerting process depends but which are not listed in the dependency array received with the incoming alert.

Rule 4.1

$$\frac{first(C^S_{ij}) = \langle cpa_i, dep \rangle \text{ and } \neg cp\_alert^S_j}{S \xrightarrow{cp\_alert_j} T}$$

where T differs from S in (1) $p^T_j = p^S_j.receive\langle cpa_i, dep \rangle.cp\_alert_j$
(2) $C^T_{ij} = rem(C^S_{ij})$
(3) $C^T_{jk} = \langle cpa_j, dep \lor dep^S_j \rangle.C^S_{jk}$ for
all k with $dep(k) = 0,\ dep^S_j(k) = 1$

only.

Rule 4.2

$$\frac{first(C^S_{ij}) = \langle cpa_i, dep \rangle \text{ and } cp\_alert^S_j}{S \xrightarrow{receive\langle cpa_i, dep \rangle} T}$$

where T differs from S in (1) $p^T_j = p^S_j.receive\langle cpa_i, dep \rangle$
(2) $C^T_{ij} = rem(C^S_{ij})$

only.

Rule for Taking the Checkpoint

Rule 5

$$\frac{cp\_alert^S_i \text{ and } \neg cp\_taken^S_i}{S \xrightarrow{cp\_taken_i} T}$$

where T differs from S in (1) $p^T_i = p^S_i.cp\_taken_i$
only.

Rule for Emptying the Blocking Queue. As these rules only cover phase 1 there is no rule for processes not participating in the checkpointing to clear their blocking queues.

Rule 6

$$\frac{first(BQ^S_{ij}) = \langle msg, bb \rangle \text{ and } cp\_taken^S_j}{S \xrightarrow{consume_{ij}(\langle msg, bb \rangle)} T}$$

where T differs from S in (1) $p^T_j = p^S_j.consume_{ij}(\langle msg, bb \rangle)$
(2) $BQ^T_{ij} = rem(BQ^S_{ij})$

only.

The rules are adjusted for non-checkpointing global states by removing everything concerning checkpointing.

4   Correctness Proof

In a distributed system by definition a snapshot is a consistent global state. Consistency (cf. [8]) involves local states and messages sent: a message sent should either be in a channel or have been received (C1) and a message not sent should neither be in a channel nor have been received (C2). In our formalism this amounts to

C1 $send_{ij}^S(msg)$ implies $msg \in C_{ij}^S$ or $receive_{ij}^S(msg)$ but not both,

C2 $\neg send_{ij}^S(msg)$ implies $msg \notin C_{ij}^S$ and $\neg receive_{ij}^S(msg)$.

In the framework of mobile computing the focus lies on local states while the contents of channels or what is on the way somewhere in the net is less important when resetting a system. Correctness proofs for checkpointing algorithms, therefore, essentially prove the absence of so-called orphans. An orphan is a message which has been received but never sent. Their absence can be expressed as

C3 $receive_{ij}^S(msg)$ implies $send_{ij}^S(msg)$.

which is a direct consequence of **C2**.

As Chandy/Lamport in [4] we take a finer view and show reachability of the partial snapshot computed with our algorithm. As a corollary we obtain consistency and the absence of orphans.

In the proof we will make use of projections of various form:

$|_{bb=0}$ This projection is applied to strings of messages, only. It removes from the string all cpa-messages and messages with attached blockbit 1. For example, if $w = \langle msg_1, 1 \rangle.\langle cpa_7, dep \rangle.\langle msg_2, 0 \rangle.\langle msg_3, 0 \rangle$ then $w|_{bb=0} = \langle msg_2, 0 \rangle.\langle msg_3, 0 \rangle$.

$\downarrow_{cp\_taken_j}$ It is applied to the local history of P_j and yields the string of receive and send events of messages occurring before cp_taken_j in their respective order.

Eg, for $p_4 = receive_{24}(\langle msg_1, 0 \rangle).send_{47}(\langle msg_2, 0 \rangle).receive_{24}(\langle cpa_1, dep \rangle).$ $cp\_alert_4.inspect_{24}(\langle msg_3, 0 \rangle).cp\_taken_4.consume_{24}(\langle msg_3, 0 \rangle)$ the projection $p_4 \downarrow_{cp\_taken_4} = receive_{24}(\langle msg_1, 0 \rangle).send_{47}(\langle msg_2, 0 \rangle).$

$p_j \downarrow_{cp\_taken_j} = (p_j.cp\_taken_j) \downarrow_{cp\_taken_j}$ if cp_taken_j does not occur in p_j.

$\uparrow_{cp\_taken_j}^i$ It is applied to the local history of P_j and yields the string of messages occurring in $receive_{ij}$- and $consume_{ij}$-events after cp_taken_j in their respective order.

Eg, for $p_1 = cp\_alert_1.cp\_taken_1.consume_{71}(\langle msg_1, 0 \rangle).consume_{21}(\langle msg_2, 1 \rangle).$ $receive_{21}(\langle msg_3, 0 \rangle)$ the projection $p_1 \uparrow_{cp\_taken_1}^2 = \langle msg_2, 1 \rangle.\langle msg_3, 0 \rangle$.

If cp_taken_j does not occur in the history then $p_j \uparrow_{cp\_taken_j}^i = \varepsilon$.

The proof is based on the idea to simultaneously compute the snapshot on course of a computation. From a state S a *potential snapshot* $psn(S)$ is extracted. It is a state of the system without checkpointing. The local states are those where the checkpoint has been taken (if that had happened by then) otherwise the local state is as in S. On the course of computation whenever a checkpoint is taken in S, in $psn(S)$ the respective process is frozen to this state while other processes may continue in their computation. The contents of the channel is given by the actual contents of C_{ij} and BQ_{ij} at S and what has been recorded in the history.

$$psn(S) := (p_1 \downarrow_{cp\_taken_1}, \ldots, p_n \downarrow_{cp\_taken_n}, Chan')$$

where

$$Chan'(C_{ij}) = C_{ij}^S|_{bb=0} \circ BQ_{ij}^S|_{bb=0} \circ rec_{ij}^S|_{bb=0} \qquad \text{for all } C_{ij}, i \neq j$$

$$rec_{ij} = reverse(p_j^S \uparrow^i_{cp\_taken_j}).$$

Proposition 1. *Let $P_1, \ldots, P_n$ be a concurrent system communicating via FIFO channels C_{ij} with initial state S_0. For each state S reachable from S_0 the potential snapshot $psn(S)$ is reachable in the respective system without checkpointing.*

Proof by induction on the number of events leading to state S, where the last step was $S' \xrightarrow{e} S$ we show that

1. $psn(S)$ is reachable,
2. (a) event e can be performed at state $psn(S')$, that is $psn(S') \xrightarrow{e} X$ and X is identical to $psn(S)$ or
   (b) $psn(S) = psn(S')$.

The proof is a routine check of each of the cases.

The previous proposition shows that each potential snapshot is reachable and thus consistent. However, it does not imply that the snapshotting does come to an end in the sense that all processes causally linked to the initiating process take their checkpoint. To ensure this, progress assumptions have to be imposed which we formulate using linear time logic operators $\Box$ (always) and $\diamond$ (eventually).

P1. Every process continues to receive, inspect or consume messages of each other process as far as possible (that is if the link is not blocked).
   (1) $\Box(cp\_taken_j \wedge (C_{ij} \circ BQ_{ij} \neq \varepsilon) \rightarrow \diamond(consume_{ij} \vee receive_{ij}))$
   (2) $\Box(\neg cp\_taken_j \wedge (C_{ij} \neq \varepsilon \wedge BQ_{ij} = \varepsilon) \rightarrow \diamond(receive_{ij} \vee inspect_{ij}))$

P2. Every process that set the checkpoint alert will eventually take the checkpoint. $\Box(cp\_alert_j \rightarrow \diamond cp\_taken_j)$

Note, that it is already guaranteed with the operational semantics that no channel looses messages or allows the order of messages to be changed.

Proposition 2. *Under assumptions **P1** and **P2** each snapshot computation contains a state S from which onwards*

1. *no more local checkpoints will be taken,*
2. *all processes causally linked to the initiating process have taken their checkpoint and*
3. *all reachable states T satisfy*

$$C_{ij}^{psn(T)} = \begin{cases} rec_{ij}^T|_{bb=0} & \text{if } cp\_taken_i^S \wedge cp\_taken_j^S \\ \varepsilon & \text{if } cp\_taken_i^S \wedge \neg cp\_taken_j^S \\ C_{ij}^T \circ rec_{ij}^T & \text{if } \neg cp\_taken_i^S \wedge cp\_taken_j^S \\ C_{ij}^T & \text{if } \neg cp\_taken_i^S \wedge \neg cp\_taken_j^S \end{cases}$$

Proof. It is easy to see that with **P1** and **P2** all processes causally linked to the initiator will eventually take their checkpoint: if a process P_i receives a cpa-message then it sets the cp_alert_i and propagates the request since all this is part and parcel of one atomic action (rule 4.1). **P2** implies that the checkpoint will be taken by P_i as this can be done unconditionally (rule 5). The cpa_i-messages propagated are added to the channels of processes on which P_i depends but which have not been informed according to the dependency vector received. Consider one such C_{ij}-channel where P_j has not taken the cp_alert_j, yet. All messages before cpa_i in the queue will have blockbit 0 (as $\neg cp\_taken_i$). Thus, provided that no other cpa-request is received by P_j from some other channel, by **P1** the cpa_i-message will eventually be received. If, however, some other cpa-request is received by P_j before the cpa_i-message is received then this ensures that P_j will take its checkpoint. The cpa_i request will be later received but not processed (rule 4.2). As there is a finite number of processes, only, and each process takes at most one checkpoint (1) and (2) are proved.

To verify (3) recall that

$$C_{ij}^{psn(T)} = C_{ij}^T|_{bb=0} \circ BQ_{ij}^T|_{bb=0} \circ rec_{ij}^T|_{bb=0} \ .$$

Case: $cp\_taken_i^S \wedge cp\_taken_j^S$. If P_i has taken a checkpoint then eventually all messages in C_{ij} will have blockbit 1. After P_j has taken its checkpoint it will empty BQ_{ij} and finally no message with blockbit 0 will be left in $C_{ij} \circ BQ_{ij}$.

Case: $cp\_taken_i^S \wedge \neg cp\_taken_j^S$. If P_j has not taken a checkpoint it will have received all messages with blockbit 0 (by **P1**). The messages left in $C_{ij} \circ BQ_{ij}$ will all have blockbit 1.

Case: $\neg cp\_taken_i^S \wedge cp\_taken_j^S$. If P_i has not taken a checkpoint by S then it will only send out messages with blockbit 0. If P_j has taken its checkpoint then after that it will clear the blocking queue (by **P1**). There will be no further blocking, hence, the blocking queue will remain empty (rule 2.4 does not apply).

Case: $\neg cp\_taken_i^S \wedge \neg cp\_taken_j^S$. In case that P_j had not taken a checkpoint rec_{ij}^T will be empty. All messages with blockbit 0 will eventually be removed from $C_{ij} \circ BQ_{ij}$ (by **P1**).

5 Lossy Channels with Reorderings

Problems often encountered in mobile computing are the loss of messages and that the ordering in which messages are received differs from the ordering in which these messages had been sent. We discuss next how these issues affect our algorithm.

Loss of Messages. If a computation message (i.e. not a *cp_alert*) is lost then this does not affect the correctness of the algorithm as, clearly, such a message cannot become an orphan. The operational semantics can easily be adapted by adding the rule

$$\frac{first(C_{ij}^S) = \langle msg, bb\rangle}{S \xrightarrow{\tau} T} \quad \text{where } T \text{ differs from } S \text{ in (1) } C_{ij}^T = rem(C_{ij}^S)$$
$$\text{only.}$$

where τ is an internal transition. The correctness proof remains valid with the new rule to be inspected in the case analysis.

If a *cp_alert* message gets lost then the process which was to receive it may never get to know that it should take a checkpoint. So phase 2 (not described in this paper) would not terminate successfully, at least with no further adaptations of the algorithm.

Reordering of Messages in Channels. Our algorithm is robust wrt reordering of messages in channels. Consider a message that is put into C_{ij} by P_i after it had taken its checkpoint. Due to some reordering in the channel the message is received by P_j before the reception of P_i's *cp_alert*. As the message had been sent after *cp_taken* of P_i the blockbit will be 1 and such messages will always be blocked. So the message cannot become an orphan as blocking queues will only be emptied after the checkpoint has been taken. Intuitively, this is the only case that raises concern.

In the formal setup, one would have to model the channels as sets of messages, rather than strings of messages. With the required changes, the invariant and the case analysis are straight forward. However, an additional progress assumption is necessary to show termination of phase 1.

P3. Every *cp_alert* that is put into a channel will eventually be removed from the channel: $\square(send_{ij}(\langle cp\_alert_i, dep\rangle)) \rightarrow \diamond\, receive_{ij}(\langle cp\_alert_i, dep\rangle)$,

It turns out that in dealing with channels where reordering of messages is possible, our algorithm has similarities to Lai/Yang's adaption [10] of Chandy/Lamport's algorithm for this scenario.

6   Conclusion

Mobile Computing environment has features like high mobility and frequent disconnections, which makes applications running in such environments more susceptible to failure. Coordinated checkpointing is a major technique to confine faults and restart applications faster.

In this paper, we have presented a coordinated checkpointing algorithm for non-deterministic applications. Our algorithm requires only a minimum number of processes to take a checkpoint. We use a delayed checkpointing approach, along with partial channel blocking to achieve the consistent snapshot. Previous related algorithms are Cao/Singhal [3] and Singh/Cabillic [13]. The Cao/Singhal algorithm takes multiple temporary checkpoints to avoid any possible orphan message. Though some of the temporary checkpoints are made permanent and form a part of the consistent state, others are rejected. The taking and rejecting of checkpoints will lead to increased energy consumption not suitable for mobile environment. Singh/Cabillic suggest an improvement over Cao/Singhal in this respect, however they also take extra checkpoints; moreover they do not provide any proof of correctness. Both of the algorithms, proposed by Cao/Singhal and Singh/Cabillic, require a process to either take a checkpoint immediately or reject the request which will eventually lead to the whole checkpointing process being canceled. A process may send a reject if it is engaged in a computation that cannot be interrupted. We consider this a limitation for mobile computing environment and in our proposed algorithm, we do not force a process to take a checkpoint immediately after receiving a checkpoint request but provide it with a certain autonomy over when to take it. This may allow processes to be more prudent with rejecting a request, which will eventually increase the possibility of the whole checkpointing process to succeed. We have provided a formal proof of correctness for our algorithm under progress assumptions which are not too restrictive and satisfy the real-world requirements. We also argue that our approach will have less energy consumption, since we do not take any unnecessary checkpoints, and that it can be extended to non-FIFO channels.

On a critical note, our algorithm may lead to temporary blocking of some channels of processes which do not participate in the checkpointing. A totally non-blocking checkpointing algorithm is impossible if - as in our set-up - the number of checkpoints to be taken is minimal (see [2]). Still, another trade-off between minimal number of checkpoints and no blocking might be desirable. It is subject of future work to find improvements in this respect, as well as how to deal with lossy channels and multiple checkpointing.

Checkpointing remains an active area of research with new applications emerging in the areas of mobile code offloading [9] and in High Performance Computing [5], [6]. We believe that our work can be used in these emerging areas.

References

1. Acharya, A., Badrinath, B.R.: Checkpointing distributed applications on mobile computers. In: Proceedings of the 3rd International Conference on Parallel and Distributed Information Systems. IEEE (1994)
2. Cao, G., Singhal, M.: On coordinated checkpointing in distributed systems. IEEE Transactions on Parallel and Distributed Systems 9(12) (1998)
3. Cao, G., Singhal, M.: Mutable checkpoints: a new checkpointing approach for mobile computing systems. IEEE Transactions on Parallel and Distributed Systems 12(2) (2001)
4. Chandy, K.M., Lamport, L.: Distributed snapshots: determining global states of distributed systems. ACM Transactions on Computer Systems (TOCS) 3(1) (1985)
5. Egwutuoha, I.P., Levy, D., Selic, B., Chen, S.: A survey of fault tolerance mechanisms and checkpoint/restart implementations for high performance computing systems. The Journal of Supercomputing (2013)

6. Elliott, J., Kharbas, K., Fiala, D., Mueller, F., Ferreira, K., Engelmann, C.: Combining partial redundancy and checkpointing for HPC. In: 2012 IEEE 32nd International Conference on Distributed Computing Systems (ICDCS), pp. 615–626. IEEE (2012)
7. Koo, R., Toueg, S.: Checkpointing and rollback-recovery for distributed systems. IEEE Transactions on Software Engineering (1987)
8. Kshemkalyani, A.D., Singhal, M.: Distributed Computing. Cambridge University Press (2010)
9. Kwon, Y.-W., Tilevich, E.: Energy-efficient and fault-tolerant distributed mobile execution. In: IEEE 32nd International Conference on Distributed Computing Systems (ICDCS), pp. 586–595. IEEE (2012)
10. Lai, T.H., Yang, T.H.: On distributed snapshots. Information Processing Letters 25 (1987)
11. Manivannan, D., Singhal, M.: A low-overhead recovery technique using quasi-synchronous checkpointing. In: Proceedings of the 16th International Conference on Distributed Computing Systems, pp. 100–107. IEEE (1996)
12. Netzer, R.H.B., Xu, J.: Necessary and sufficient conditions for consistent global snapshots. IEEE Transactions on Parallel and Distributed Systems 6(2) (1995)
13. Singh, P., Cabillic, G.: Successive checkpointing approach for mobile computing environments. In: 2003 International Conference on Wireless Networks (2003)
14. Singh, P., Cabillic, G.: A checkpointing algorithm for mobile computing environment. In: Conti, M., Giordano, S., Gregori, E., Olariu, S. (eds.) PWC 2003. LNCS, vol. 2775, pp. 65–74. Springer, Heidelberg (2003)
15. Wang, Y.-M., Kent Fuchs, W.: Lazy checkpoint coordination for bounding rollback propagation. In: Proceedings of the 12th Symposium on Reliable Distributed Systems, pp. 78–85. IEEE (1993)
16. Wang, Y.-M., Huang, Y., Vo, K.-P., Chung, P.-Y., Kintala, C.: Checkpointing and its applications. In: Twenty-Fifth International Symposium on Fault-Tolerant Computing, FTCS-25. Digest of Papers, pp. 22–31. IEEE (1995)

Gathering and Exclusive Searching on Rings under Minimal Assumptions*

Gianlorenzo D'Angelo[1], Alfredo Navarra[1], and Nicolas Nisse[2]

[1] Dipartimento di Matematica e Informatica, Università degli Studi di Perugia, Italy
gianlorenzo.dangelo@dmi.unipg.it, alfredo.navarra@unipg.it
[2] Inria and Univ. Nice Sophia Antipolis, CNRS, I3S, UMR 7271, France
nicolas.nisse@inria.fr

Abstract. Consider a set of mobile robots with minimal capabilities placed over distinct nodes of a discrete anonymous ring. Asynchronously, each robot takes a snapshot of the ring, determining which nodes are either occupied by robots or empty. Based on the observed configuration, it decides whether to move to one of its adjacent nodes or not. In the first case, it performs the computed move, eventually. The computation also depends on the required task. In this paper, we solve both the well-known *Gathering* and *Exclusive Searching* tasks. In the former problem, all robots must simultaneously occupy the same node, eventually. In the latter problem, the aim is to clear all edges of the graph. An edge is cleared if it is traversed by a robot or if both its endpoints are occupied. We consider the *exclusive* searching where it must be ensured that two robots never occupy the same node. Moreover, since the robots are oblivious, the clearing is *perpetual*, i.e., the ring is cleared infinitely often. In the literature, most contributions are restricted to a subset of initial configurations. Here, we design two different algorithms and provide a characterization of the initial configurations that permit the resolution of the problems under minimal assumptions.

1 Introduction

In the field of robot-based computing systems, the study of the minimal settings required to accomplish specific tasks represents a challenging issue. We consider k robots initially placed on distinct nodes of a discrete ring of n nodes, and we investigate two fundamental problems requiring complex coordination: *Gathering* (see, e.g., [5,10,13,26]) and *Exclusive Searching* (see, e.g., [2,19,20]).

We assume minimal abilities for the robots. They are oblivious (without memory of the past), uniform (running the same deterministic algorithm), autonomous (without a common coordinate system, identities or chirality), asynchronous (without central coordination), without the capability to communicate. Neither nodes nor edges are labeled and no local memory is available on nodes. Robots are equipped with visibility sensors and motion actuators, and operate

---

* This work has been partially supported by the Research Grant 2010N5K7EB 'PRIN 2010' ARS TechnoMedia (Algoritmica per le Reti Sociali Tecno-mediate) from the Italian Ministry of University and Research.

M. Chatterjee et al. (Eds.): ICDCN 2014, LNCS 8314, pp. 149–164, 2014.

in *Look-Compute-Move* cycles in order to achieve a common task (see [17]). The Look-Compute-Move model considers that in each cycle a robot takes a snapshot of the current global configuration (Look), then, based on the perceived configuration, takes a decision to stay idle or to move to one of its adjacent nodes (Compute), and in the latter case it moves to this node (Move). In other words, each robot executes an algorithm that takes as input a snapshot or *configuration*, i.e., the graph topology and the set of nodes occupied by the robots, and computes the *move* of the robot. Cycles are performed asynchronously, i.e., the time between Look, Compute, and Move operations is finite but unbounded, and it is decided by an adversary for each robot. Hence, robots that cannot communicate may move based on outdated perceptions. The adversary (scheduler) is assumed to be fair: each robot performs its cycle within finite time and infinitely often.

The asynchronous Look-Compute-Move model, also called *CORDA*, has first been defined in continuous environment [18,27]. The inaccuracy of the sensors used by robots to scan the surrounding environment motivates its discretization. Robots can also model software agents moving on a computer network. Many robots coordination problems have been considered in discrete environments. Exploration with stop has been studied in paths [16], trees [15], rings [14] and general graphs [6]. More recently, the gathering problem (a.k.a. Rendez-vous) has been considered in rings [9,11,25] and grids [1,7]. Exclusive perpetual exploration has been studied in rings [3] and grids [4]. The *exclusivity property* states that any node must be occupied by at most one robot. Very recently, exclusive perpetual searching has been defined and studied in trees [2] and rings [11]. In all previous works as well as in this paper, initial *configurations* are assumed to be *exclusive*, that is, any node is occupied by at most one robot.

In this paper, we focus on the ring topology. The relevance of the ring topology is motivated by its completely symmetric structure. It means that algorithms for rings are more difficult to devise as they cannot exploit any topological structure, assuming that all nodes look the same. In fact, our algorithms are only based on robots' disposal and not on topology. On rings, different types of exclusive configurations may require different approaches. In particular, periodicity and symmetry arguments must be carefully handled. An exclusive configuration is called *periodic* if it is invariable under non-complete rotations. It is called *symmetric* if the ring has an *axis of symmetry* that reflects single robots into single robots, and empty nodes into empty nodes. It is called *rigid* if it is aperiodic and asymmetric. We consider the following two problems.

Gathering: The gathering problem consists in moving all the robots towards the same node and remain there. On rings, under the Look-Compute-Move model, the gathering is unsolvable if the robots are not empowered by the so-called *multiplicity detection* capability [25], either in its *global* or *local* version. In the former type, a robot is able to perceive whether any node of the graph is occupied by a single robot or more than one (i.e., a *multiplicity* occurs) without perceiving the exact number. In the latter (and weaker) type, a robot is able to perceive the multiplicity only if it is part of it. Using the global multiplicity detection capability, in [25] some impossibility results have been proven. Then, several algorithms have been proposed for different kinds of exclusive initial configurations in [8,24,25]. These papers left open some cases which have been closed in [9] where a unified strategy has been provided. With local multiplicity detection capability, an algorithm starting from rigid configurations where the number of robots k is strictly smaller than $\lfloor \frac{n}{2} \rfloor$ has been designed in [21]. In [22], the case where k is odd and strictly smaller than $n - 3$ has been solved. In [23], the authors provide an algorithm for the case where n is odd, k is even, and $10 \leq k \leq n - 5$. Recently, the case of rigid configurations has been solved in [11]. The remaining cases are left open and the design of a unified algorithm for all the cases is still unknown.

Exclusive Searching: Graph searching has been widely studied in centralized and distributed settings (e.g., [19,20]). The aim is to make the robots clear all the edges of a contaminated graph. An edge is cleared if it is traversed by a robot or if both its endpoints are occupied. However, a cleared edge is recontaminated if there is a path without robots from a contaminated edge to it. A graph is *searched* if there exists a time when all its edges are simultaneously cleared. For instance, in a centralized setting, two robots are sufficient to clear a ring, starting from a node and moving in opposite directions. In a distributed setting, the task is much harder due to symmetries and asynchronicity. Following [2,11], we also consider an additional constraint: the so called *exclusivity property*, that is, no two robots can be concurrently on the same node or cross the same edge. Moreover, as the robots are oblivious, they cannot recognize which edges are already cleared, therefore they must repeatedly perform the task. The searching is called *perpetual* if it is accomplished infinitely many times. The study of perpetual exclusive searching in the discrete model has been introduced in [2] for tree topologies. Concerning rings, in [11] the case of initial rigid configurations has been tackled.

Contribution: We consider the gathering with local multiplicity detection and the perpetual exclusive searching problems for k robots in an n-nodes ring.

For any $k < n - 4$, $k \neq 4$, we fully characterize the exclusive configurations from which the gathering problem is feasible. In particular, we design an algorithm that solves the problem starting from any exclusive configuration with $k < n - 4$, $k \neq 4$, robots empowered by the local multiplicity detection, but for the unsolvable configurations that will be specified later. Similarly to the case of $k = 4$ in [9] and $(n, k) = (7, 6)$ in [8], the cases left out from our characterization ($k = 4$ and $k \geq n - 4$), if gatherable, would require specific algorithms difficult to generalize.

We then provide a characterization of any aperiodic exclusive configuration with $k \neq 4$, and $(n, k) \notin \{(10, 5), (10, 6)\}$ from which exclusive searching is solvable. That is, we design an algorithm that solves the problem starting from any such aperiodic exclusive configurations but for the unsolvable ones. For periodic configurations, we provide some impossibility results. Designing a unified algorithm for all (periodic or not) configurations seems challenging.

The algorithms for gathering and exclusive searching (given in Sections 4 and 5, resp.) exploit a common technique (provided in Section 3) that allows to achieve some special configurations suitable for the subsequent phases.

This result mainly relies on a non-trivial characterization of aperiodic configurations in a ring that could be used for further problems. Due to space constraints, most of the proofs and the pseudo-codes of the algorithms are reported in [12].

2   Notation and Preliminary

In this paper, we consider a ring with $n \geq 3$ nodes $\{v_0, \cdots, v_{n-1}\}$, where v_i is connected to $v_{i+1 \bmod n}$ for any $0 \leq i < n$. Moreover, let $k \geq 1$ robots occupy k distinct nodes of the ring. A *configuration* $\mathcal{C}$ is defined by the k nodes occupied by robots. In what follows, any configuration is seen as a binary sequences where "0" represents an occupied node while "1" stands for an empty node. More formally, given a configuration $\mathcal{C}$, and for any $i \leq n$, let $\mathcal{S}_i = (r_0^i, \cdots, r_{n-1}^i) \in \{0,1\}^n$ be the sequence such that $r_j^i = 0$ if $v_{i+j \bmod n}$ is occupied in $\mathcal{C}$ and $r_j^i = 1$ otherwise, $1 \leq j \leq n$. Intuitively, $\mathcal{S}_i$ represents the positions of robots, starting at v_i. For any $X = (x_0, \cdots, x_r)$, let us denote $\overline{X} = (x_r, \cdots, x_0)$ and $X_i = (x_{i \bmod r}, \ldots, x_{r+i \bmod r})$. A *representation* of $\mathcal{C}$ is any sequence in $\mathcal{S}_{\mathcal{C}} = \{\mathcal{S}_i, \overline{(\mathcal{S}_i)}\}_{i<n}$. Abusing the notation, we say $\mathcal{C} = S$ for any $S \in \mathcal{S}_{\mathcal{C}}$. Note that, for any exclusive configuration $S = (s_0, \cdots, s_{n-1}) \in \mathcal{S}_{\mathcal{C}}$, $\sum_{i<n} s_i = n - k$. A *supermin* of $\mathcal{C}$ is any representation of $\mathcal{C}$ that is minimum in the lexicographical order. We denote the supermin of $\mathcal{C}$ as $\mathcal{C}^{\min}$. In any supermin $(s_0, \cdots, s_{n-1})$, if $k < n$ then $s_{n-1} = 1$.

We denote by x^h a sequence of $h \geq 0$ consecutive x, $x \in \{0,1\}$. We say that a sequence X is *palindrome* if $X = \overline{X}$, it is *symmetric* if X_i is palindrome or $X_i = \overline{(X_{i+1})}$ for some i, and it is *periodic* if $X = X_i$, for some $0 < i < |X| - 1$. A configuration is symmetric (periodic, respectively) if at least one of its representations is symmetric (periodic, respectively). It is known that an aperiodic configuration admits at most one axis of symmetry [9]. Moreover, an aperiodic configuration has either a unique supermin representation or two symmetrical supermins [9].

Allowed Configurations: Let us summarize the known feasible and unfeasible exclusive configurations for both gathering and graph searching. In [25], it is shown that gathering is not solvable for $k = 2$, for any periodic initial configuration, and for any initial configuration with an axis of symmetry passing through two edges. In [11], it is shown that, for any exclusive configuration, it is not possible to search a ring using k robots if $n \leq 9$ or $k \leq 3$, or $k \geq n - 2$. Here, we prove that exclusive searching is not feasible for any k even starting from any configuration with an axis of symmetry passing through an empty node.

In what follows, an exclusive configuration is *allowed* for problem P if it is not periodic, if it does not admit an axis of symmetry (as described above) for which P is unsolvable, and if the number of robots does not fall in the above defined impossibility ranges. In particular, all rigid configurations with a number of robots out of the defined ranges are allowed. For gathering, the symmetric allowed configurations are all aperiodic ones with the axis of symmetry not passing through two edges and $3 \leq k < n - 4$, $k \neq 4$. For exclusive searching, the symmetric allowed configurations are all aperiodic ones with k odd and those with k even where the axis does not pass through an empty node, provided that $3 < k < n - 2$ and $n > 9$.

Dealing with Symmetry: The core of the technique in [11] for solving the problems from asymmetric exclusive configurations is Algorithm ASYM. This allows to achieve a particular configuration called $\mathcal{C}^a = (0^{k-1}, 1, 0, 1^{n-k-1})$ made of $k - 1$ consecutive robots, one empty node and one robot.

Lemma 1 ([11]). *Let $3 \leq k < n - 2$ robots standing in an n-node ring and forming a rigid exclusive configuration, Algorithm ASYM eventually terminates achieving configuration $\mathcal{C}^a$ and all intermediate configurations obtained are exclusive and rigid.*

Basically, Algorithm ASYM ensures that, from any rigid exclusive configuration, one robot, that can be uniquely distinguished, moves to an unoccupied neighbor, achieving another rigid configuration while strictly decreasing the supermin. Here, our main contribution is Algorithm ALIGN that generalizes ASYM by handling all allowed configurations (not only rigid). Difficulties are multiple.

First, in allowed symmetric configurations, we cannot ensure that a unique robot will move. In such a case, the algorithm may allow a robot r to move, while r is reflected by the axis of symmetry to another robot r'. Since r and r' are indistinguishable and execute the same algorithm, r' should perform the same (symmetric) move. However, due to asynchronicity, r may move while the corresponding move of r' is postponed (i.e. r' has performed the Look phase but not yet the Move phase). The configuration reached after the move of r has a potential so-called *pending* move (the one of r' that will be executed eventually). To deal with this problem, our algorithm ensures that reached configurations that might have a pending move are asymmetric, distinguishable and the pending move is unique. Therefore, in such a case, our algorithm forces the pending move. That is, contrary to [11] where Algorithm ASYM ensures to only go through rigid configurations, the subtlety here consists in possibly going from an asymmetric configuration to a symmetric one. To distinguish such configurations, we define the notion of adjacent configurations. An asymmetric configuration $\mathcal{C}$ is *adjacent* to a symmetric configuration $\mathcal{C}'$ with respect to a procedure M allowed by the algorithm if $\mathcal{C}$ can be obtained from $\mathcal{C}'$ by applying M to only one of the robots permitted to move by M. In other words, if $\mathcal{C}$ is adjacent to $\mathcal{C}'$ with respect to M, there might exist a pending move permitted by M in $\mathcal{C}$. Another difficulty is to ensure that all met configurations are allowed for the considered problem P.

Overview of Algorithm ALIGN: Our contribution mainly relies on Algorithm ALIGN, described in Section 3. Such an algorithm starts from any configuration that is allowed either for the gathering or the exclusive searching problems and aims at reaching one of the configurations $\mathcal{C}^a$, $\mathcal{C}^b$, or $\mathcal{C}^c$ having supermin $(0^{k-1}, 1, 0, 1^{n-k-1})$, $(0^k, 1^{n-k})$, or, $(0^{\frac{k}{2}}, 1^j, 0^{\frac{k}{2}}, 1^{n-k-j})$ for k even and $j < \frac{n-k}{2}$, respectively. From such configurations, we will show how to solve the gathering and the exclusive searching problems. Here, we describe the main principles of Algorithm ALIGN. Let $3 \leq k < n - 2$, $k \neq 4$, and let us consider any allowed configuration $\mathcal{C}$ for Problem P. Algorithm ALIGN proceeds as follows:

– If no two robots occupy two adjacent nodes in $\mathcal{C}$, we prove that only two cases are possible. If $\mathcal{C}$ is symmetric, then Algorithm ALIGN-ONE is executed by two symmetric robots. In this case, if only one of them actually moves, then the obtained configuration is asymmetric and adjacent only to $\mathcal{C}$. Then, the possible pending move is forced. Otherwise, if $\mathcal{C}$ is asymmetric and not adjacent to a symmetric configuration, Algorithm ASYM can be executed without ambiguity.

– If two robots occupy two adjacent nodes in $\mathcal{C}$ (i.e., the supermin representation of $\mathcal{C}$ starts by 0^2) and $\mathcal{C}$ is symmetric, then moving only one robot can lead to a configuration which is symmetric or adjacent to a different symmetric configuration. One of our main results is the characterization of the symmetric configurations that may lead to these cases. Therefore, the procedures performed by Algorithm ALIGN in case of symmetric configurations are designed in a way that it is possible to univocally determine the possible pending move in the case that only one of two symmetric robots actually moves (Algorithm ALIGN-TWO-SYM). If $\mathcal{C}$ is asymmetric, there are two cases: either $\mathcal{C}$ is not adjacent to any symmetric configuration and Algorithm ASYM is executed or we force to perform the unique possible pending move (Algorithm ALIGN-TWO-ASYM).

In detail, if the initial allowed configuration is symmetric and k is even, ALIGN achieves either configuration $\mathcal{C}^b$ or $\mathcal{C}^c$, and the original type of symmetry is preserved, hence the obtained configuration is still allowed. If the configuration is asymmetric and k is even, then any of $\mathcal{C}^a$, $\mathcal{C}^b$, and $\mathcal{C}^c$ can be achieved, if they are allowed. If k is odd, then the configuration achieved is either $\mathcal{C}^a$ or $\mathcal{C}^b$, if this latter is allowed. The general strategy of the algorithm is the following.

– If the configuration is symmetric, then ALIGN preserves the symmetry by performing a procedure that moves two symmetric robots in a way that, if only one of such robots actually moves, then the obtained configuration is guaranteed to be asymmetric and not adjacent to another symmetric configuration with respect to any other procedure that can be possibly performed by ALIGN. When k is odd, the symmetry is preserved until it can be safely broken by moving in an arbitrary direction the unique robot lying on the axis of symmetry.

– If the configuration is asymmetric, then always only one robot is permitted to move by ALIGN. First, the algorithm checks whether the asymmetric configuration is adjacent to some allowed symmetric configuration with respect to some procedure possibly performed by ALIGN. In this case, ALIGN forces the only possible pending move. We recall that the procedures performed on a symmetric configuration are designed in a way that the configuration obtained is not adjacent to any other symmetric configuration different from the correct one. Therefore, from an asymmetric configuration adjacent to an allowed symmetric one with respect to the procedures of ALIGN, the robot that has to move can be univocally determined and the original symmetry preserved. Note that, such behavior is performed even if the initial configuration is asymmetric. In this case, the configuration obtained after the move

is symmetric and allowed, and the algorithm proceeds like in the case that the initial configuration was symmetric. In fact, as the robots are oblivious, they cannot distinguish the two cases.
- If an asymmetric configuration is not adjacent to any symmetric configuration with respect to any procedure of ALIGN, then the algorithm in [11] is performed. Such algorithm, ensures that only one move is performed and the obtained configuration is always rigid, thus it is allowed.

We prove that ALIGN always reduce the supermin and that only allowed configuration are reached.

3   ALIGN Algorithm

In this section, we devise algorithm ALIGN that, starting from any allowed configuration, reaches one of the exclusive configurations $\mathcal{C}^a$, $\mathcal{C}^b$, and $\mathcal{C}^c$ previously defined. Algorithm ALIGN is based on four procedures described below. Let $\mathcal{C}$ be any allowed configuration and let $\mathcal{C}^{\min} = (v_0, v_1, \ldots, v_{n-1})$ be its supermin.[1] Let ℓ_1 be the smallest integer such that $\ell_1 > 0$, $v_{\ell_1} = 0$ and $v_{\ell_1-1} = 1$; let ℓ_2 be the smallest integer such that $\ell_2 > \ell_1$, $v_{\ell_2} = 0$ and $v_{\ell_2-1} = 1$; let ℓ_{-1} be the largest integer such that $\ell_{-1} < n$ and $v_{\ell_{-1}} = 0$. The four procedures permitted by ALIGN are the following:

- **REDUCE$_0$**($\mathcal{C}$): The robot at node v_0 moves to node v_1;
- **REDUCE$_1$**($\mathcal{C}$): The robot at node v_{ℓ_1} moves to node v_{ℓ_1-1};
- **REDUCE$_2$**($\mathcal{C}$): The robot at node v_{ℓ_2} moves to node v_{ℓ_2-1};
- **REDUCE$_{-1}$**($\mathcal{C}$): The robot at node $v_{\ell_{-1}}$ moves to node $v_{\ell_{-1}+1}$.

Note that in some configurations ℓ_1 and ℓ_2 might be not defined. However, we will show that in these cases our algorithm does not perform procedures REDUCE$_1$ and REDUCE$_2$, respectively.

Algorithm ALIGN works in two phases: the first phase (Algorithm ALIGN-ONE) copes with configurations without any consecutive occupied nodes (i.e. $v_1 = 1$) while the second phase copes with configurations having at least two consecutive occupied nodes (Algorithm ALIGN-TWO-SYM, if the configuration is symmetric, and ALIGN-TWO-ASYM otherwise).

Algorithm ALIGN-ONE. If $v_1 = 1$ and the configuration $\mathcal{C}$ is symmetric, the general strategy is to reduce the supermin by performing REDUCE$_0$. If the two symmetric robots that should move perform their Look-Compute-Move cycles synchronously, then the obtained configuration $\mathcal{C}'$ is symmetric where the supermin is reduced and the axis of symmetry of $\mathcal{C}$ is preserved. Hence, $\mathcal{C}'$ is allowed.

If only one of the two symmetric robots that should move actually performs the move (due to the asynchronous execution of their respective Look-Compute-Move cycles), then the following lemma ensures that the configuration $\mathcal{C}'$ obtained is asymmetric and not adjacent to any symmetric configuration with respect to any possible procedure that allows at most two robots to move.

---

[1] By v_i we denote both the i-th node and the i-th value of sequence $\mathcal{C}^{\min}$.

Lemma 2 ([9]). *Let C be an allowed configuration and let C' be the one obtained from C after a REDUCE$_0$ performed by a single robot. Then, C' is asymmetric and at least two robots have to move to obtain C' from an aperiodic symmetric configuration different from C.*

It follows that robots can recognize whether C' has been obtained by performing REDUCE$_0$ from C. In the affirmative case, ALIGN forces to perform the possible pending move.

However, it is not always possible to perform REDUCE$_0$ on a symmetric configuration C. Indeed, in case that $C^{\min} = (0, 1, 0, R)$, for some $R = \overline{R}$, then performing REDUCE$_0$ would imply that two robots occupy the same node (a multiplicity occurs but we want to avoid it in this phase). In fact, note that in this case the node symmetric to v_0 is v_2 and performing REDUCE$_0$ consists in moving both robots from v_0 and v_2 to v_1. In this case, we perform REDUCE$_{-1}$. In [12] (Lemma 5 for $j = 1$), we show that such a procedure performed by only one robot from a configuration C such that $C^{\min} = (0, 1, 0, R)$, with $R = \overline{R}$, does not create a symmetric configuration and the configuration obtained is not adjacent with respect to any possible procedures performed by ALIGN.[2] Therefore, we can again preserve the symmetry by forcing to perform the symmetric move. Note that also in this case, performing REDUCE$_{-1}$ results in reducing the supermin.

If the configuration is asymmetric and it cannot be obtained by performing REDUCE$_0$ or REDUCE$_{-1}$ from any possible allowed symmetric configuration, then we execute the algorithm in [11] (Algorithm ASYM). Lemma 1 ensures that such algorithm always leads to rigid configurations.

Algorithm ASYM ensures that each procedure permits only one robot to change its position, and then no pending moves are possible. If by applying ASYM, we produce an asymmetric configuration which is adjacent to a symmetric configuration with respect to some of the procedures permitted by ALIGN, then we force to perform the possible pending move.

Note that, in some symmetric configurations there exists a robot r that occupies a node lying on the axis of symmetry. In these cases, REDUCE$_0$ or REDUCE$_{-1}$ may consists in moving r (in any arbitrary direction). The obtained configuration is asymmetric and not adjacent to any other symmetric configuration with respect to the procedures of ALIGN. Then, we can safely perform ASYM as there are no pending moves.

It follows that ALIGN-ONE leads to a configuration with two consecutive occupied nodes. In detail, we can obtain: (i) an asymmetric configuration with two consecutive occupied nodes which is not adjacent to any symmetric configuration with respect to a procedure permitted by ALIGN-ONE; (ii) an asymmetric configuration with two consecutive occupied nodes which is adjacent to a symmetric configuration with respect to some procedure permitted by ALIGN-ONE; (iii) a symmetric configuration with two or three consecutive occupied nodes with the axis of symmetry passing in their middle; (iv) a symmetric configuration with two symmetric pairs of consecutive occupied nodes.

---

[2] Configuration $C = (0, 1, 0, 1, 1, 0, 1, 1)$ is the only exception, see [12].

Algorithm ALIGN-TWO-SYM. Once a configuration with two consecutive occupied nodes is achieved, the second phase of Algorithm ALIGN starts. Now it is not possible to perform REDUCE$_0$ as it would cause a multiplicity. Hence, one procedure among REDUCE$_1$, REDUCE$_2$ or REDUCE$_{-1}$ is performed.

In symmetric configurations, we perform REDUCE$_1$ every time it is possible. This occurs when the asynchronous execution of the two symmetric robots that should perform the procedure cannot generate a symmetric configuration with a different axis of symmetry or a configuration which is adjacent to a different symmetric configuration with respect to any procedure permitted by ALIGN.

If it is not possible to perform REDUCE$_1$, we perform REDUCE$_2$. It can be proven that asynchronous executions cannot generate other symmetries or configurations adjacent to symmetric ones potentially reachable.

There are cases when we cannot perform REDUCE$_1$ and REDUCE$_2$. For instance this can happen if $\mathcal{C}^{\min} = (0^i, 1^j, 0^i, R)$, with $R = \overline{R}$. In fact, in this case, $\mathcal{C}^{\min} = \overline{(\mathcal{C}^{\min}_{2i+j})}$ and performing REDUCE$_1$ corresponds to move the robot at v_{i+j} which is symmetric to that at v_{i-1}. Similar instances where it is not possible to perform REDUCE$_2$ can occur. In such cases, we perform REDUCE$_{-1}$ and show that this cannot create any different symmetry or configuration adjacent to symmetric ones with respect to any procedure permitted by ALIGN.

To give more detail on the behavior of the algorithm in the case of symmetric configurations, we define the following three sets. Let S_1 be the set of symmetric configurations with supermin $(0^i, 1, R)$, where $i \geq 2$ and R contains a sequence 0^i. Let S_2 be the set of configurations $\mathcal{C} \in S_1$ such that $\mathcal{C}^{\min} = (0^i, 1^j, 0^i, Z)$ for some $Z = \overline{Z}$ and $j \geq 1$. Finally, let S_3 be the set of configurations $\mathcal{C} \in S_1$ such that $\mathcal{C}^{\min} = (0^i, 1^{j'}, 0^x, 1^j, 0^x, 1^{j'}, 0^i, Z)$ for some $Z = \overline{Z}$, $j, j' > 0$ and $1 \leq x \leq i$ or configurations $\mathcal{C} \in S_1$ such that $\mathcal{C}^{\min} = (0^i, 1^j, 0^{i-1}, 1, 0, R, 1)$, $R = \overline{R}$, $j > 0$.

The sets S_2 and S_3 contain the configurations where it is not possible to perform REDUCE$_1$ or REDUCE$_2$, respectively. In Lemmata 6-10 of [12], we identify the procedures that can be safely performed on the configurations in such sets. Based on these results, Algorithm ALIGN-TWO-SYM works as follows. If $\mathcal{C}$ is in S_2, then REDUCE$_1$ cannot be performed. However, we can safely perform REDUCE$_{-1}$. If $\mathcal{C} \notin S_2$, then ALIGN-TWO-SYM first computes the configuration $\mathcal{C}'$ that would be obtained from $\mathcal{C}$ by applying REDUCE$_1$ on only one robot. If $\mathcal{C}'$ is symmetric, then we know that $\mathcal{C} \in S_1 \setminus S_3$, $\mathcal{C}^{\min} = (0^i, 1, 0, 0, 1, 0^i, (1, 0, 1, 0^i)^\ell, 1, 0, 1)$, or $\mathcal{C}^{\min} = (0^i, 1, 0^i, 1, 0^i, 1, 0^i, (1, 0^{i-1}, 1, 0^i, 1, 0^i)^\ell, 1, 0^{i-1}, 1)$, for some $\ell > 0$. In the former case, we can safely perform REDUCE$_2$ as the obtained configuration is neither symmetric nor adjacent to any other symmetric configuration. In the latter two cases, we cannot perform REDUCE$_2$ but we can safely perform REDUCE$_{-1}$.

If $\mathcal{C}'$ is asymmetric, then ALIGN-TWO-SYM checks whether it can be obtained by applying REDUCE$_1$ from a symmetric configuration $\mathcal{C}''$ different from $\mathcal{C}$. To this aim, it computes all the configurations that can possibly generate $\mathcal{C}'$. As REDUCE$_1$ reduces the supermin, then by performing it, the starting node of the supermin in the obtained configuration is either the same of the previous one or it is one of the endpoints of a sequence of consecutive occupied nodes which is generated by the procedure itself. It follows that $\mathcal{C}''$ can be computed by increasing the supermin of $\mathcal{C}'$ by moving one of the robots in the endpoints of the sequence of consecutive occupied nodes at the beginning of the supermin sequence or the possible robot in position v_{ℓ_1}. In other words, if $\mathcal{C}' = (0^i, 1^j, 0, R, 1)$ for $i \geq 2$ and $j \geq 1$, then $\mathcal{C}''$ can be only one of the following configurations: $\mathcal{C}^\alpha := (0^{i-1}, 1, 0, 1^{j-1}, R, 1)$, $\mathcal{C}^\beta := (0^{i-1}, 1^j, R, 0, 1)$, and, if $R = (1, R')$, $\mathcal{C}^\gamma := (0^i, 1^{j+1}, 0, R', 1)$. If at least two among $\mathcal{C}^\alpha$, $\mathcal{C}^\beta$, and $\mathcal{C}^\gamma$ are symmetric and the procedure from both of them to $\mathcal{C}'$ corresponds to REDUCE$_1$ (i.e. two symmetric configurations are adjacent to $\mathcal{C}'$ with respect to REDUCE$_1$), then at least one of them must belong to $S_1 \setminus S_3$. Therefore, we can safely perform REDUCE$_2$ on such configuration and REDUCE$_1$ on the other one.

In any other symmetric configuration, ALIGN-TWO-SYM applies REDUCE$_1$.[3]

Algorithm ALIGN-TWO-ASYM. This algorithm works similarly to ALIGN-ONE when the configuration is asymmetric. First, it checks whether the given configuration $\mathcal{C}$ has been obtained from a symmetric and allowed configuration $\mathcal{C}'$ by performing only one of the two symmetric moves. In the affirmative case, it performs the possible pending move, otherwise it performs Algorithm ASYM. Given the procedures performed by ALIGN-ONE and ALIGN-TWO-SYM, a configuration $\mathcal{C}$ with $\mathcal{C}^{\min} = (0^i, 1^j, 0^x, 1^{j'}, R, 1)$, $j \geq 1$, $x \geq 1$, and $j' \geq 0$ can be adjacent to a symmetric configuration $\mathcal{C}'$ with respect to one of such procedures only if $\mathcal{C}'$ is one of the following configurations: $\mathcal{C}^\alpha := (0^{i-1}, 1, 0, 1^{j-1}, 0^x, 1^{j'}, R, 1)$, $\mathcal{C}^\beta := (0^{i-1}, 1^j, 0^x, 1^{j'}, R, 0, 1)$, if $j' > 0$, $\mathcal{C}^\gamma := (0^i, 1^j, 0^{x-1}, 1, 0, 1^{j'-1}, R, 1)$, or, if $R = (0, 1, R')$, $\mathcal{C}^\delta := (0^i, 1^j, 0^x, 1^{j'+1}, 0, R', 1)$. Note that, at most one of the above configurations can be symmetric. Let $\mathcal{C}^i$ be such a configuration, if by applying ALIGN-TWO-SYM (or ALIGN-ONE if $\mathcal{C}^i$ has no consecutive occupied nodes) on a single robot of $\mathcal{C}^i$ we obtain $\mathcal{C}$, then $\mathcal{C}$ has been possibly obtained from $\mathcal{C}^i$ and then ALIGN-TWO-ASYM performs the possible pending move. If none of $\mathcal{C}^i$, $i \in \{\alpha, \beta, \gamma, \delta\}$, is symmetric, then $\mathcal{C}$ has not been obtained from any symmetric configurations and then ALIGN-TWO-ASYM performs ASYM. As in the case of ALIGN-ONE, if the robot leading from $\mathcal{C}^i$ to $\mathcal{C}$ is that on the axis of symmetry of $\mathcal{C}^i$, then Algorithm ASYM is performed. The next theorem shows the correctness of ALIGN.

Theorem 1. *Let $3 \leq k < n - 2$, $k \neq 4$, robots standing in an n-node ring forming an exclusive allowed configuration, Algorithm ALIGN eventually terminates achieving one exclusive allowed configuration among $\mathcal{C}^a$, $\mathcal{C}^b$, or $\mathcal{C}^c$.*

Proof. We model all the possible executions of ALIGN as a directed graph where each configuration is represented as a node and there exists an arc (u, v) if there exist a procedure and a time schedule of the algorithm that starting from the configuration represented by u lead to that represented by v, even with possible pending moves. An execution of ALIGN is represented by a path in this graph. In what follows, we show that such paths are acyclic, are made of nodes representing allowed configurations, and they always lead to a node representing one of the configurations $\mathcal{C}^a$, $\mathcal{C}^b$, or $\mathcal{C}^c$.

---

[3] With the exception of configurations $\mathcal{C}^{s_1} = (0^{i_1}, 1, 0, 1, 0^x, 1, 0, 1)$ and $\mathcal{C}^{s_2} = (0^{i_2}, 1, 1, 0^y, 1, 1)$ with $x < i_1$ and $y < i_2$, see [12].

We can partition the nodes into three sets representing: the symmetric configurations; the asymmetric configurations which are adjacent to some symmetric configurations with respect to one of the procedures permitted by ALIGN; and the remaining asymmetric configurations. We denote such sets as S, $AS1$ and $AS2$, respectively. Lemmata 1, 2 and 5-10 in [12] imply the following properties.

- A node in S representing a configuration C has either one or two outgoing arcs. If it has exactly two outgoing arcs, then one of them is directed to the node v' representing the configuration C' obtained if both the symmetric robots permitted to move by ALIGN perform their moves synchronously. The other arc is directed to the node v'' representing the configuration C'' obtained if only one of the two symmetric robots permitted to move by ALIGN actually moves. In other words, the former arc models the case where both the two symmetric robots permitted to move perform the entire cycle Look-Compute-Move, while the latter arc models the case where only one of them performs entirely such cycle. Note that, v' belongs to S, while v'' belongs to $AS1$. Moreover, if C is allowed, then also C' is. If the node has exactly one outgoing arc then the robot r moved by ALIGN lies on the axis of symmetry. In this case, any procedure performed by ALIGN moves r in an arbitrary direction. Then, the arc is directed to a node in $AS1$.
- A node in $AS1$ representing a configuration C'' has exactly one incoming arc from a node in S, it can have some incoming arcs from nodes in $AS2$, and it has exactly one outgoing arc, directed to a node in S or in $AS2$. If the outgoing arc is directed to a node in S, then one of the incoming arcs comes from a node u in S and models the case when only one of the two symmetric robots permitted to move by ALIGN from the configuration C represented by u actually moves. From [12] (Lemmata 5-10), there exists only one of such nodes. The outgoing arc leads to the node in S representing configuration C' which can be obtained by moving synchronously both the symmetric robots permitted to move by ALIGN from C. Note that both C and C'' are allowed configurations. If the outgoing arc is directed to a node in $AS2$, then C'' has been obtained from a configuration, corresponding to a node in S, such that the robot moved by ALIGN lies on the axis of symmetry. In this case, ALIGN performs ASYM from C'' obtaining a configuration in $AS2$.
- A node in $AS2$ has exactly one outgoing arc, directed either to another node in $AS2$ or to a node in $AS1$ but it cannot be directed to a node in S (by Lemma 1). It can have some arcs coming from nodes in $AS1$ or $AS2$.

It follows that any execution path performed by the algorithm is made of nodes representing allowed configurations. Moreover, each allowed configuration has an outgoing arc that is traversed by the execution path of the algorithm. Moreover, any procedure performed by the algorithm reduces the supermin of a configuration. This implies that the graph is acyclic, as we can define a topological ordering of the nodes on the basis of the ordering given by the supermin of the corresponding configurations. The statement is then proven by observing that configurations in $\mathcal{C}^a$, $\mathcal{C}^b$, or $\mathcal{C}^c$ are those with the minimum possible super-min and hence are the only possible sinks of the graph. $\square$

4   Gathering in a Ring

In this section, we provide the full strategy for achieving the gathering. We make use of procedure ALIGN to reach one of the following configurations: $\mathcal{C}^a = (0^{k-1}, 1, 0, 1^{n-k-1})$, $\mathcal{C}^b = (0^k, 1^{n-k})$, with k or n odd, $\mathcal{C}^c = (0^{\frac{k}{2}}, 1^j, 0^{\frac{k}{2}}, 1^{n-k-j})$, with k even and j or n odd.

Algorithm ALIGN terminates when either the obtained configuration is one of the three above, or it is one of the configurations generated by Algorithm GATHERING below.

If the initial configuration has both k and n even, then ALIGN either reaches configuration $\mathcal{C}^a$ or $\mathcal{C}^c$ with j odd. In the former case, GATHERING leads to $\mathcal{C}^d = (0^{k-1}, 1, 1, 0, 1^{n-k-2})$. As $k < n - 4$, then $\mathcal{C}^d$ is asymmetric and it is not adjacent to any possible symmetric configuration with respect to any procedure of GATHERING. From $\mathcal{C}^d$, GATHERING performs REDUCE$_0$, hence creating a multiplicity, and still obtaining configuration $\mathcal{C}^d$. This process is repeated until only two nodes remain occupied. At this point, only one of the two occupied nodes contains a multiplicity, while the other contains one single robot. The single robot will be the only one permitted to move towards the other occupied node until the gathering is accomplished. In the latter case, that is, from $\mathcal{C}^c$ with j odd, GATHERING leads to configuration $\mathcal{C}^c$ with $j = 1$. This is achieved by iterating procedure COMPACT$_0$ as defined below. Let $\mathcal{C} = (v_0, v_1, \ldots, v_n)$ be a configuration of type $(0^{\frac{k}{2}-i}, 1, 0^i, 1^j, 0^i, 1, 0^{\frac{k}{2}-i}, 1^{n-k-j-2})$ where $1 \leq i \leq \frac{k}{2}$ and $j < \frac{n-k-2}{2}$. Note that for $i = \frac{k}{2}$, $\mathcal{C} = \mathcal{C}^c$. Procedure COMPACT$_0$ moves the robot at $v_{\frac{k}{2}-i-1}$ towards $v_{\frac{k}{2}-i}$. As $\mathcal{C}$ is symmetric, COMPACT$_0$ permits two robots to move. If both move synchronously, the resulting configuration $\mathcal{C}'$ is similar to $\mathcal{C}$ but with i increased by one. If only one robot moves, the obtained configuration $(0^{\frac{k}{2}-i-1}, 1, 0^{i+1}, 1^j, 0^i, 1, 0^{\frac{k}{2}-i}, 1^{n-k-j-2})$ is asymmetric and not adjacent to any other symmetric configuration, and hence $\mathcal{C}'$ can be easily obtained. Once $\mathcal{C}^c$ with $j = 1$ is reached, again COMPACT$_0$ is applied. If both the permitted robots move, a symmetric configuration $\mathcal{C}'' = (0^{\frac{k}{2}-1}, 1, 0, 1, 0^{\frac{k}{2}-1}, 1^{n-k-1})$, with $v_{\frac{k}{2}}$ being a multiplicity, is reached. This equals to the case of symmetric configurations with k odd that will be discussed later. If only one robot moves, configuration $(0^{\frac{k}{2}-1}, 1, 0^{\frac{k}{2}+1}, 1^{n-k-1})$ is reached. As k is even, then $4 < k < n - 4$ and hence, such a configuration is asymmetric and not adjacent to any other symmetric configuration. Then, $\mathcal{C}''$ can be easily obtained.

If k is even and n is odd, then ALIGN either reaches configuration $\mathcal{C}^b$ or $\mathcal{C}^c$ with either j or $n-k-j$ odd. In this case, GATHERING behaves as above but creating the multiplicity at the central node of the only odd sequence of consecutive empty nodes among j and $n - k - j$. Eventually, GATHERING achieves configuration $\mathcal{C}''$. Again, this equals to the case of symmetric configurations with k odd. Note that, this case is similar to the technique presented in [23] where the solved configurations are only those with k even and n odd.

If k is odd, then ALIGN always reaches configuration $\mathcal{C}^b$. In this case, the used technique is similar to that presented in [22] where the solved configurations are only those with k odd. From $\mathcal{C}^b$, GATHERING permits robots at $v_{\frac{k-1}{2}-1}$ and $v_{\frac{k-1}{2}+1}$ to move towards $v_{\frac{k-1}{2}}$. If only one robot actually moves, configuration $(0^{\frac{k'}{2}-1}, 1, 0^{\frac{k'}{2}+1}, 1^{n-k'-1})$ is achieved with $k' = k - 1$. By the parity of k', configuration $\mathcal{C}''$ is achieved subsequently. If both robots move synchronously, again configuration $\mathcal{C}''$ is reached. From here, GATHERING performs procedure COMPACT$_1$ defined as follows. Let $\mathcal{C} = (v_0, v_1, \ldots, v_n)$ be a configuration of type $(0^{\frac{k-i}{2}}, 1, 0^i, 1, 0^{\frac{k-i}{2}}, 1^{n-k-2})$ where $1 \leq i \leq k$, then COMPACT$_1$ moves the robot at $v_{\frac{k-i}{2}-1}$ towards $v_{\frac{k-i}{2}}$. As $\mathcal{C}$ is symmetric, COMPACT$_1$ permits two robots to move. If both move synchronously, the resulting configuration $\mathcal{C}'$ is similar to $\mathcal{C}$ but with i increased by two. If only one robot moves, as before, the obtained configuration is asymmetric and not adjacent to any other symmetric configuration, and $\mathcal{C}'$ can be easily obtained. By iterating this process, GATHERING achieves configuration $\mathcal{C}^b$ with the number of occupied nodes decreased by two. Eventually, this process terminates with only one occupied node.

Theorem 2. *Let $3 \leq k < n - 4$, $k \neq 4$ robots, forming an allowed configuration in an n-node ring, Algorithm GATHERING achieves the gathering.*

5 Exclusive Searching in a Ring

In this section, we present an algorithm that allows a team of robots to exclusively search a ring.

If k is even and there exists an axis of symmetry passing through an empty node, the searching is clearly unsolvable because a synchronous execution of any algorithm either cause a multiplicity in the node lying on the axis or does not allow to search the edges incident to such a node. Moreover, we prove that graph searching is impossible starting from any periodic configuration with one or two empty nodes per period.

In [11], an algorithm is designed allowing $5 \leq k \leq n - 3$ robots to search exclusively a ring with $n \geq 10$ nodes (but for $(k, n) = (5, 10)$), for rigid initial configurations. Here, we improve over this algorithm by addressing also aperiodic symmetric configurations. We use two sub-procedures: Algorithm COMPACT-ALIGN is used after ALIGN to achieve configuration $\mathcal{C}^b$, when ALIGN reaches configuration $\mathcal{C}^c$, and Algorithm BREAK-SYMMETRY is used to achieve $\mathcal{C}^a$ in the case that k is odd.

Algorithm SEARCH-RING. The algorithm first checks whether $k = n - 3$ or if n is odd and k is even. In the affirmative case, any allowed configuration must be asymmetric, and therefore the algorithm of [11] can be applied and the ring is searched. If k is odd, we first use Algorithm BREAK-SYMMETRY to break the potential symmetry and then use the algorithm of [11]. Each of these configurations used during the searching phase of the algorithm of [11] are asymmetric and are not adjacent to any symmetric configuration reached by Algorithm BREAK-SYMMETRY. Therefore, there is no ambiguity (no pending move) when a robot recognizes such a configuration.

If n and k are even, we may be in allowed symmetric configurations and therefore the SEARCH-RING proceeds in two phases. Algorithm COMPACT-ALIGN is first applied until one of the configurations in $\mathcal{A}$ (described in [12]) is achieved. This is guaranteed by the fact that both $\mathcal{C}^a$ and $\mathcal{C}^b$ belong to $\mathcal{A}$. Then, the algorithm proceeds to Phase 2 which actually performs the searching.

The intuitive explication of the Searching algorithm (Phase 2) is as follows. All robots are aligned on consecutive nodes. Then, both robots r and r' at the ends of this segment move (one clockwise and the other anti-clockwise) to reach the two adjacent nodes opposite to the occupied segment. Then, the two robots q and q' occupying the ends of the "long" occupied segment move to their empty neighbors. These moves indicate to r and r' that it is time to go back toward the "long" segment, and that is what happens. Finally, when r is adjacent to q and r' is adjacent to q', then q and q' move to their empty neighbors in order to re-build the original segment. Then, the process is repeated perpetually. Such a sequence of performed moves actually searches the ring. Moreover, by definition of the configurations met during the process (configurations in $\mathcal{A}$), there is no ambiguity in the choice of the robot(s) that must move. Finally, there are no conflicts between the different phases of our procedure because any configuration in $\mathcal{A}$ is not adjacent to any symmetric configuration not in $\mathcal{A}$. We then get:

Theorem 3. *Let* $4 < k \leq n - 3$ *robots, forming an allowed configuration in an n-node ring, Algorithm* SEARCH-RING *perpetually searches the ring, but for* $n = 10$ *and* $k = 5$, *and for symmetric configurations with* $n = 10$ *and* $k = 6$.

References

1. Bampas, E., Czyzowicz, J., Gąsieniec, L., Ilcinkas, D., Labourel, A.: Almost optimal asynchronous rendezvous in infinite multidimensional grids. In: Lynch, N.A., Shvartsman, A.A. (eds.) DISC 2010. LNCS, vol. 6343, pp. 297–311. Springer, Heidelberg (2010)
2. Blin, L., Burman, J., Nisse, N.: Brief announcement: Distributed exclusive and perpetual tree searching. In: Aguilera, M.K. (ed.) DISC 2012. LNCS, vol. 7611, pp. 403–404. Springer, Heidelberg (2012)
3. Blin, L., Milani, A., Potop-Butucaru, M., Tixeuil, S.: Exclusive perpetual ring exploration without chirality. In: Lynch, N.A., Shvartsman, A.A. (eds.) DISC 2010. LNCS, vol. 6343, pp. 312–327. Springer, Heidelberg (2010)
4. Bonnet, F., Milani, A., Potop-Butucaru, M., Tixeuil, S.: Asynchronous exclusive perpetual grid exploration without sense of direction. In: Fernàndez Anta, A., Lipari, G., Roy, M. (eds.) OPODIS 2011. LNCS, vol. 7109, pp. 251–265. Springer, Heidelberg (2011)
5. Chalopin, J., Das, S.: Rendezvous of mobile agents without agreement on local orientation. In: Abramsky, S., Gavoille, C., Kirchner, C., Meyer auf der Heide, F., Spirakis, P.G. (eds.) ICALP 2010. LNCS, vol. 6199, pp. 515–526. Springer, Heidelberg (2010)

6. Chalopin, J., Flocchini, P., Mans, B., Santoro, N.: Network exploration by silent and oblivious robots. In: Thilikos, D.M. (ed.) WG 2010. LNCS, vol. 6410, pp. 208–219. Springer, Heidelberg (2010)

7. D'Angelo, G., Di Stefano, G., Klasing, R., Navarra, A.: Gathering of robots on anonymous grids without multiplicity detection. In: Even, G., Halldórsson, M.M. (eds.) SIROCCO 2012. LNCS, vol. 7355, pp. 327–338. Springer, Heidelberg (2012)

8. D'Angelo, G., Di Stefano, G., Navarra, A.: Gathering of six robots on anonymous symmetric rings. In: Kosowski, A., Yamashita, M. (eds.) SIROCCO 2011. LNCS, vol. 6796, pp. 174–185. Springer, Heidelberg (2011)

9. D'Angelo, G., Di Stefano, G., Navarra, A.: How to gather asynchronous oblivious robots on anonymous rings. In: Aguilera, M.K. (ed.) DISC 2012. LNCS, vol. 7611, pp. 326–340. Springer, Heidelberg (2012)

10. D'Angelo, G., Di Stefano, G., Navarra, A.: Gathering asynchronous and oblivious robots on basic graph topologies under the look-compute-move model. In: Alpern, S., Fokkink, R., Gąsieniec, L., Lindelauf, R., Subrahmanian, V. (eds.) Search Theory: A Game Theoretic Perspective, pp. 197–222. Springer (2013)

11. D'Angelo, G., Di Stefano, G., Navarra, A., Nisse, N., Suchan, K.: A unified approach for different tasks on rings in robot-based computing systems. In: Proc. of 15th IEEE IPDPS APDCM (to appear, 2013)

12. D'Angelo, G., Navarra, A., Nisse, N.: Robot Searching and Gathering on Rings under Minimal Assumptions, Tech. Rep. RR-8250, Inria (2013)

13. Dieudonne, Y., Pelc, A., Peleg, D.: Gathering despite mischief. In: Proc. of 23rd SODA, pp. 527–540 (2012)

14. Flocchini, P., Ilcinkas, D., Pelc, A., Santoro, N.: Computing without communicating: Ring exploration by asynchronous oblivious robots. In: Tovar, E., Tsigas, P., Fouchal, H. (eds.) OPODIS 2007. LNCS, vol. 4878, pp. 105–118. Springer, Heidelberg (2007)

15. Flocchini, P., Ilcinkas, D., Pelc, A., Santoro, N.: Remembering without memory: Tree exploration by asynchronous oblivious robots. Theor. Comput. Sci. 411(14-15), 1583–1598 (2010)

16. Flocchini, P., Ilcinkas, D., Pelc, A., Santoro, N.: How many oblivious robots can explore a line. Inf. Process. Lett. 111(20), 1027–1031 (2011)

17. Flocchini, P., Prencipe, G., Santoro, N.: Distributed Computing by oblivious mobile robots. Morgan and Claypool (2012)

18. Flocchini, P., Prencipe, G., Santoro, N., Widmayer, P.: Hard tasks for weak robots: The role of common knowledge in pattern formation by autonomous mobile robots. In: Aggarwal, A.K., Pandu Rangan, C. (eds.) ISAAC 1999. LNCS, vol. 1741, pp. 93–102. Springer, Heidelberg (1999)

19. Fomin, F.V., Thilikos, D.M.: An annotated bibliography on guaranteed graph searching. Theor. Comput. Sci. 399(3), 236–245 (2008)

20. Ilcinkas, D., Nisse, N., Soguet, D.: The cost of monotonicity in distributed graph searching. Distributed Computing 22(2), 117–127 (2009)

21. Izumi, T., Izumi, T., Kamei, S., Ooshita, F.: Mobile robots gathering algorithm with local weak multiplicity in rings. In: Patt-Shamir, B., Ekim, T. (eds.) SIROCCO 2010. LNCS, vol. 6058, pp. 101–113. Springer, Heidelberg (2010)

22. Kamei, S., Lamani, A., Ooshita, F., Tixeuil, S.: Asynchronous mobile robot gathering from symmetric configurations without global multiplicity detection. In: Kosowski, A., Yamashita, M. (eds.) SIROCCO 2011. LNCS, vol. 6796, pp. 150–161. Springer, Heidelberg (2011)

23. Kamei, S., Lamani, A., Ooshita, F., Tixeuil, S.: Gathering an even number of robots in an odd ring without global multiplicity detection. In: Rovan, B., Sassone, V., Widmayer, P. (eds.) MFCS 2012. LNCS, vol. 7464, pp. 542–553. Springer, Heidelberg (2012)

24. Klasing, R., Kosowski, A., Navarra, A.: Taking advantage of symmetries: Gathering of many asynchronous oblivious robots on a ring. Theor. Comput. Sci. 411, 3235–3246 (2010)

25. Klasing, R., Markou, E., Pelc, A.: Gathering asynchronous oblivious mobile robots in a ring. Theor. Comput. Sci. 390, 27–39 (2008)

26. Kranakis, E., Krizanc, D., Markou, E.: The Mobile Agent Rendezvous Problem in the Ring. Morgan & Claypool (2010)

27. Prencipe, G.: *Instantaneous actions* vs. *full asynchronicity*: Controlling and coordinating a set of autonomous mobile robots. In: Restivo, A., Ronchi Della Rocca, S., Roversi, L. (eds.) ICTCS 2001. LNCS, vol. 2202, pp. 154–171. Springer, Heidelberg (2001)

Online Algorithms to Generate Slices for Regular Temporal Logic Predicates

Aravind Natarajan[1], Neeraj Mittal[1,*], and Vijay K. Garg[2,**]

[1] The University of Texas at Dallas, Richardson, TX 75080, USA
{aravindn,neerajm}@utdallas.edu
[2] The University of Texas at Austin, Austin, TX 78712, USA
garg@ece.utexas.edu

Abstract. Predicate detection, which involves determining if a distributed computation satisfies a given predicate, may require searching a state space that is exponential in the number of processes. To ameliorate this problem of *state explosion*, the notion of a computation slice was introduced. A computation slice is a concise representation of the consistent cuts of a computation that satisfy a given predicate. It suffices to search the state-space of the slice to detect a predicate, which is generally much smaller than the original computation. Traditionally, algorithms for computation slicing have been offline in nature, where the entire set of events is known apriori. Online algorithms are useful in applications where detecting a fault as soon as it arises is critical. To be practical, online algorithms must only perform incremental updates to the slice, and not recompute it from scratch. In this paper, we present online algorithms to generate the slice with respect to temporal logic (or path based) predicates $AG(B)$, $EG(B)$ and $EF(B)$, when B is a *regular* state-based predicate. To our knowledge, these are the first online algorithms that compute slices for path-based predicates. Our algorithms are efficient, with an amortized time complexity of $O(n^2)$, where n is the number of processes.

1 Introduction

Writing correct distributed programs is a non-trivial task. Not surprisingly, distributed systems are particularly vulnerable to software faults. Testing and debugging is an effective way of improving the dependability of a software prior to its deployment. However, software bugs that do persist after extensive testing and debugging have to be tolerated at runtime to ensure that the system continues to operate properly. *Predicate detection* is a technique used to verify the execution trace of a program with respect to a property (or predicate) [1–4]. The predicate detection problem involves determining if there exists a consistent cut (or global state) of a distributed computation (trace of a distributed program) that satisfies a given predicate.

For a distributed computation with n processes, where each process executes a maximum of k events, the number of consistent cuts (or global states) can be as large as $O(k^n)$. Detecting a predicate may, therefore, require looking at a large number of

* Neeraj Mittal is supported in part by NSF Grant CNS-1115733.
** Vijay. K. Garg is supported in part by NSF Grants CNS-1346245, CNS-1115808 and the Cullen Trust for Higher Education.

M. Chatterjee et al. (Eds.): ICDCN 2014, LNCS 8314, pp. 165–180, 2014.
© Springer-Verlag Berlin Heidelberg 2014

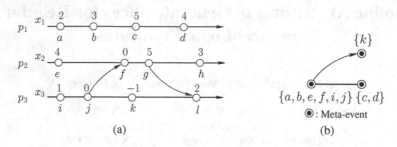

(a)   (b)

Fig. 1. (a) A computation, and (b) its slice with respect to $(3 \leqslant x_1 \leqslant 4) \wedge (x_2 < 3)$

consistent cuts. This exponential growth of search space is referred to as the *state explosion problem* [5]. *Computation slicing* [6], is a technique that helps reduce the size of the state-space for predicate detection. Intuitively, a slice is a concise representation of consistent cuts satisfying a certain condition. The slice of a computation with respect to a predicate is a sub-computation such that (a) it contains all consistent cuts of the computation for which the predicate evaluates to true, and (b) among all the sub-computations that satisfy condition (a), it has the least number of consistent cuts. If the number of consistent cuts of the slice is much smaller than those of the computation, then it is more effective to search the state-space of the slice, instead of the computation, to detect a fault. We illustrate this with the help of a simple example.

Consider the computation shown in figure 1(a). There are three processes, p_1, p_2 and p_3 hosting integer variables x_1, x_2 and x_3 respectively. Each event is labeled with the value of the variable immediately after the event is executed. For example, the value of x_1 immediately after executing event b is 3. The first event on each process (namely a on p_1, e on p_2 and i on p_3) 'initializes' the variables on the process, and every consistent cut of the computation contains these initial events. Suppose we are interested in detecting the predicate $(3 \leqslant x_1 \leqslant 4) \wedge (x_2 < 3) \wedge (x_1 + x_2 * x_3 \geqslant 4)$. Without computation slicing, we are forced to examine all consistent cuts of this computation, which are more than 30 in total. Alternatively, we can first compute the slice of the computation with respect to the predicate $(3 \leqslant x_1 \leqslant 4) \wedge (x_2 < 3)$ as follows. Initially, the value of x_1 is 2, which does not satisfy the predicate. Any cut that contains only a but not b does not satisfy the predicate, and can be ignored. Similarly, any consistent cut of the computation that contains e but not f does not satisfy the predicate and can be ignored. The slice, shown in figure 1(b), is modeled by a partial order on a set of *meta-events*. A consistent cut, either contains all events in a meta-event, or none of them. Additionally, a meta-event belongs to a consistent cut only if all of its incoming neighbors are also contained in that cut. Hence, the number of cuts of the original computation to be searched are restricted to the following four cuts: $\{a, b, e, f, i, j\}$, $\{a, b, e, f, i, j, k\}$, $\{a, b, c, d, e, f, i, j\}$, and $\{a, b, c, d, e, f, i, j, k\}$. In many cases, the number of cuts in the slice is exponentially smaller than in the computation, resulting in substantial savings.

Model checking is a formal verification technique for ascertaining that a program meets its specification [7]. In computation slicing, on the other hand, we only analyze a *single trace* of a (distributed) program. Analyzing a single trace of a program is typically much faster than analyzing the entire program. Computation slicing, in fact, can be viewed as an abstraction technique to reduce the state space for model checking a single program trace [6]. Additionally, approaches for state space exploration (e.g. [2, 3, 8, 9]) are orthogonal to slicing, and can be used in conjunction with slicing to explore the state space of a slice in a more efficient manner [10].

Computation slicing is related to runtime verification (cf. [11]), which involves analyzing a run of a program to detect violations of a given correctness property. The input program is instrumented and the trace resulting from its execution is examined by a monitor that verifies its correctness. Some examples of runtime verification tools are Temporal Rover [12], Java-MaC [13], JPaX [14], JMPaX [15], and jPredictor [16]. Chen et al. [17] note that computation slicing is orthogonal to runtime verification, and can be used to make tools like jPredictor more efficient.

Many algorithms have been proposed to detect certain types of predicates in distributed systems in an online manner (e.g., stable, termination and conjunctive predicates) [18]. Our work is different from online predicate detection in many ways. First, we consider temporal logic predicates, which are path based, whereas the focus of online predicate detection is on state-based predicates. Second, computation slicing is a more general approach and can be used to speed up detection of a broad class of predicates, which are otherwise known to be intractable to detect. As an example, suppose we want to detect whether a predicate B holds in a distributed computation. Let B be such that it can be expressed as a conjunction of B_1 and B_2, where B_1 is a regular temporal logical predicate and B_2 is an arbitrary predicate. We can first compute the slice of the computation with respect to B_1. We can then analyze the state space of the resulting slice, which is typically much smaller than that of the computation, to determine if B holds in the computation.

Offline algorithms that generate the slice of a computation with respect to temporal logic predicates have been proposed [19], where the entire set of events is known apriori. For applications such as software fault tolerance, it is beneficial to identify errors as they arise. Online slicing algorithms, where the slice is updated incrementally with the arrival of every new event, are ideal in such cases. However, online algorithms for slice generation have been developed only for non-temporal (or state based) predicates [10].

Contributions: In this paper, we present efficient online algorithms to generate slices with respect to temporal logic predicates $AG(B)$, $EG(B)$ and $EF(B)$, when B is a regular state-based predicate. To our knowledge these are the first online algorithms that compute slices for temporal logic predicates. Our work builds upon the offline algorithms proposed in [19]. In [19] the slice is built from scratch after the last event arrives, and this takes $O(n^2|E|)$ time, where n is the number of processes and $|E|$ is the size of (number of events in) the computation. In our algorithm the slice updated upon the arrival of each event in $O(n^2)$ time. Thus, once the last event arrives, the slice is updated to only reflect this event, and is available much more quickly than in the case of the offline algorithm.

Roadmap: The rest of this paper is organized as follows. We describe our system model in section 2 and the background necessary to understand the paper in section 3. We present our three online algorithms in section 4 and our conclusions in section 5.

2   Model and Notation

We assume a loosely coupled asynchronous message passing system, consisting of n reliable processes (that do not fail), denoted by $\{p_1, p_2 \ldots p_n\}$, and without any shared memory or global clock. Channels in our system are reliable and do not lose messages.

2.1   Directed Graphs and Consistent Cuts

Traditionally, a distributed computation is modeled as an irreflexive partial order on a set of events [20]. In this paper, we use directed graphs to model distributed computations as well as their slices. This allows us to handle both of them in a *uniform* and convenient manner. The set of vertices in the directed graph includes the set of events, while the edges are derived from the traditional model. However, we allow strongly connected components in our model, which are not possible in the traditional model.

Given a directed graph G, let $\mathsf{V}(G)$ and $\mathsf{E}(G)$ denote the set of its vertices and edges, respectively. A subset of vertices of a directed graph forms a *consistent cut*, if the subset contains a vertex only if it also contains all its incoming neighbors. Formally:

$$C \text{ is a consistent cut of } G \ \triangleq \ \langle \forall e, f \in \mathsf{V}(G) : (e, f) \in \mathsf{E}(G) : f \in C \implies e \in C \rangle$$

We denote the set of consistent cuts of directed graph G by $\mathcal{C}(G)$. Note that a consistent cut either contains all vertices in a strongly connected component or none of them. We say that a consistent cut D is a *successor* [19] of a consistent cut C (denoted as $C \triangleright D$) if $D = C \cup s$, where s is the set of events in some strongly connected component in G and $s \not\subseteq C$. A *consistent cut sequence* is a sequence of consistent cuts $C_0, C_1, \ldots C_k$, where $\forall i : 0 \leqslant i < k : C_i \triangleright C_{i+1}$. A consistent cut D is *reachable* from a consistent cut C if $C \subseteq D$.

2.2   Distributed Computations as Directed Graphs

Processes change their states by executing events. Events on the same process are totally ordered, while those on different processes are only partially ordered. An event executed by a process is either a *send* event, a *receive* event, or an *internal* event. A send event causes a message to be sent, and a receive event causes a message to be received. Let $proc(e)$ denote the process on which event e occurs. The predecessor and successor events of e on $proc(e)$ are denoted by $pred(e)$ and $succ(e)$, respectively, if they exist.

We assume the presence of *fictitious* initial and final events on each process. The initial event on process p_i, denoted by $\perp_i$, occurs before any other event on p_i. Likewise, the final event on process p_i, denoted by $\top_i$, occurs after all other events on p_i. We use final events only to ease the exposition of the slicing algorithms given in this paper. It *does not imply* that processes have to synchronize with each other at the end of the computation. For convenience, let $\perp$ and $\top$ denote the set of all initial events and final events, respectively. We assume that all initial and final events belong to the same strongly connected component. Any consistent cut that contains all $\perp$ events and none of the $\top$ events is termed as a *non-trivial consistent cut*. Only non-trivial consistent cuts are of interest to us. We define the *greatest cut*, $\widehat{E}$, as the final non-trivial consistent cut

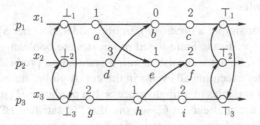

Fig. 2. A distributed computation in our model

of the computation, equal to $E - \{\top\}$. We refer to the trivial consistent cut containing the $\top$ events as the *default* cut.

In our model, a distributed computation (or simply a *computation*) is a directed graph represented by the tuple $\langle E, \mapsto \rangle$, where E is the set of events (including trivial events), and edges are given by the precedence relation $\mapsto$. The precedence relation on the set of non-fictitious events is defined by Lamport's *happened-before* relation [20], which is the smallest transitive relation satisfying the following properties: (1) if events e and f occur on the same process, and e occurred before f in real time then e happened-before f, and (2) if events e and f correspond to send and receive events, respectively, of the same message then e happened-before f. In other words, for two non-fictitious events e and f, $e \mapsto f$ only if e happened-before f. All events in $\bot$ preceed all other events in the distributed computation. All non-fictitious events preceed all events in $\top$.

As mentioned earlier, we allow strongly connected components in our model. However, in a computation, they consist entirely of fictitious events. Directed graphs are used to model computation slices, in addition to distributed computations. A strongly connected component in a computation slice can contain non-fictitious events. A strongly connected component in the slice of a computation that contains two non-fictitious events e and f implies that both events must be present in a consistent cut of the computation for that cut to satisfy the predicate. We define a *non-trivial strongly connected component* as a strongly connected component that contains (a) at least two non-fictitious events, and (b) none of the $\top$ events.

The *frontier* of a consistent cut C, denoted by $frontier(C)$, is defined as the set of those events in C whose successors are not in C. Formally,

$$frontier(C) \triangleq \{ e \in C \mid e \notin \top \Rightarrow succ(e) \notin C \}$$

Example: Consider the computation shown in Fig. 2. It has three processes p_1, p_2, and p_3. The events $\bot_1$, $\bot_2$, and $\bot_3$ are the initial events, and the events $\top_1$, $\top_2$, and $\top_3$ are the final events of the computation. The cut $X = \{\bot_1, a, b, \bot_2, d, e, f, \bot_3, g\}$ is inconsistent as $h \mapsto f$ and $f \in X$, but $h \notin X$. The cut $Y = \{\bot_1, a, b, \bot_2, d, e, f, \bot_3, g, h\}$ is a consistent cut and is represented by $frontier(Y) = \{b, f, h\}$. Consistent cut Z, where $frontier(Z) = \{c, f, h\}$, is the successor of Y. The greatest consistent cut of this computation $\widehat{E}$, where $frontier(\widehat{E}) = \{c, f, i\}$, is the successor of Z. $\widehat{E}$ is reachable from both Y and Z, while Z is only reachable from Y. The sequence of consistent cuts $Y, Z, \widehat{E}$ forms a consistent cut sequence.

2.3   Global Predicates

A *global predicate* (or simply a *predicate*), in our model, is either a *state-based* predicate or a *path-based* predicate. State-based predicates are boolean-valued function on variables of processes. Given a consistent cut, a state-based predicate is evaluated on the state resulting after executing all events in the cut. A global state-based predicate is *local* if it depends on variables of a single process. If a predicate B (state or path based) evaluates to true for a consistent cut C, we say that "C satisfies B" and denote it by $C \models B$. We leave the predicate undefined for the trivial consistent cuts. In Fig. 2, processes p_1, p_2, and p_3 host integer variables x_1, x_2, and x_3, respectively. The consistent cut C, where $frontier(C) = \{c, f, h\}$, satisfies the predicate $x_1 + x_2 \geqslant x_3$, whereas the consistent cut D, represented by $frontier(D) = \{b, e, g\}$, does not.

A path-based or temporal logic predicate is one that includes temporal operators such as **AG**, **EG** and **EF**. For a consistent cut C, the temporal operators are defined as follows [19]:

- $C \models AG(B)$, iff for *all* consistent cut sequences $C_0, \ldots, C_k$ such that (i) $C_0 = C$, and (ii) $C_k = \widehat{E}$, we have $C_i \models B$ for *all* $0 \leqslant i \leqslant k$.
- $C \models EG(B)$, iff for *some* consistent cut sequence $C_0, \ldots, C_k$ such that (i) $C_0 = C$, and (ii) $C_k = \widehat{E}$, we have $C_i \models B$ for *all* $0 \leqslant i \leqslant k$.
- $C \models EF(B)$, iff for *some* consistent cut sequence $C_0, \ldots, C_k$ such that (i) $C_0 = C$, and (ii) $C_k = \widehat{E}$, we have $C_i \models B$ for *some* $0 \leqslant i \leqslant k$.

Example: Consider a system of two processes p_1 and p_2 trying to execute a critical section in a mutually exclusive manner. Let B_1 and B_2 be the predicates that p_1 and p_2 are, respectively, in the critical section. A safe state, from which the system will never violate mutual exclusion, can be determined by detecting the predicate $EF(B_1 \wedge B_2)$. If the predicate evaluates to false at the current state, then there is no future state where both p_1 and p_2 are in the critical section simultaneously, indicating a safe state. Otherwise, the current state is unsafe.

Mittal et al. [6] defined a class of predicates termed *regular predicates* that satisfy the following property: Given two consistent cuts C and D that satisfy the predicate, the consistent cuts given by $(C \cap D)$ and $(C \cup D)$ also satisfy the predicate. Formally, predicate B is regular if for all consistent cuts C and D,

$$(C \models B) \wedge (D \models B) \implies ((C \cap D) \models B) \wedge ((C \cup D) \models B)$$

Examples of regular predicates include local predicates, conjunction of local predicates and monotonic channel predicates such as "there are at most k messages in transit from p_i to p_j" [18]. It was shown in [19] that when predicate B is regular, temporal predicates $AG(B)$, $EG(B)$ and $EF(B)$ are also regular predicates.

3   Background

In this section, we formally define the different concepts that are necessary in order to describe our online algorithms. For a detailed description of slices and efficient offline slice generation algorithms, please refer to [6].

3.1 Computation Slice

A computation slice is a concise representation of all the consistent cuts of a computation that satisfy a predicate. For a computation $\langle E, \mapsto \rangle$ and a predicate B, we use $\mathcal{C}_B(E)$ to denote the subset of those consistent cuts of $\mathcal{C}(E)$ that satisfy B. Let $\mathcal{I}_B(E)$ denote the set of all graphs on vertices E such that for every graph $G \in \mathcal{I}_B(E)$, $\mathcal{C}_B(E) \subseteq \mathcal{C}(G) \subseteq \mathcal{C}(E)$.

Definition 1 (Slice [6]). *A slice of a distributed computation with respect to a predicate B is a directed graph that contains the fewest consistent cuts, such that every consistent cut of the computation that satisfies B is contained in it. Formally, given a computation $\langle E, \mapsto \rangle$ and a predicate B,*

$$S \text{ is a slice of } \langle E, \mapsto \rangle \text{ for } B \triangleq S \in \mathcal{I}_B(E) \wedge \langle \forall G : G \in \mathcal{I}_B(E) : |\mathcal{C}(S)| \leqslant |\mathcal{C}(G)| \rangle$$

We denote the slice of computation $\langle E, \mapsto \rangle$ with respect to predicate B by $\langle E, \mapsto \rangle_B$. A slice is *empty* if it does not contain any non-trivial consistent cuts. We use a directed graph to represent the slice of a computation. In general, there can be multiple directed graphs on the same set of consistent cuts [10]. As a result, more than one graph may constitute a valid representation of a given slice. It was shown in [6] that all such graphs have the same transitive closure of edges.

Intuitively, the slice of a computation is derived from the computation, by adding edges between events to eliminate consistent cuts. In order to generate slice of computation $\langle E, \mapsto \rangle$ with respect to a predicate B, we compute $J_B(e)$, for every event e, which is defined as the least non-trivial consistent cut of the computation that contains e and satisfies B. If no such cut of the computation exists, then $J_B(e)$ is set to the default cut. *Note that e does not have to be the maximal event in $J_B(e)$.*

The slice $\langle E, \mapsto \rangle_B$ contains the set of events E as the set of vertices and has the following edges [6]:

1. $\forall e : e \notin \top$, there is an edge from e to $succ(e)$.
2. for each event e there is an edge from every event $f \in frontier(J_B(e))$ to e.

The slice of a computation with respect to a predicate, therefore, contains two types of edges: (i) those that were present in the original computation, and (ii) those added to the computation to eliminate consistent cuts that do not satisfy the predicate.

3.2 Online Algorithm for Slicing a Regular State-Based Predicate

The slicing algorithms proposed in [6] are offline in nature, where all the events in the computation are known apriori. An online algorithm to generate the slice for a regular *non-temporal* predicate B was proposed in [10], that we refer to henceforth as *online-MSG_B*. Algorithm *online-MSG_B* consists of several rounds or *iterations*. In each iteration, a new event is incorporated into the computation and the slice is updated to reflect this event.

At a high level, algorithm *online-MSG_B* works by computing J_B for the events in an online manner. Every process p_i maintains a variable $recompute_i$, which denotes the earliest event on p_i for which J_B evaluates to the trivial consistent cut. In each iteration, starting at $recompute_i$, J_B is updated. The order preserving nature of J_B [6], which is stated formally as:

$$e \mapsto f \implies J_B(e) \subseteq J_B(f) \tag{1}$$

significantly reduces the amount of work performed in each iteration. In order to compute $J_B(succ(e))$ algorithm $online\text{-}MSG_B$ starts from $J_B(e)$, instead of starting from the initial cut. If an event e is encountered on p_i such that $J_B(e)$ evaluates to the trivial consistent cut (or default cut), from equation 1 we have that for every event on p_i that happened after e, J_B also evaluates to the default cut. The variable $recompute_i$ is then set to e. After J_B has been computed for the events, edges are added to the slice. Note that upon arrival of a new event, some of these edges may be removed and new edges may be added. It was shown in [10] that the amortized time complexity of updating the slice using $online\text{-}MSG_B$ is $O(n^2)$.

We now describe our online algorithms that generate slices with respect to temporal logic predicates $AG(B)$, $EG(B)$ and $EF(B)$. Our online algorithms use algorithm $online\text{-}MSG_B$ as a sub-routine, while building the slice.

4   Online Slicing Algorithms for Temporal Logic Predicates

Temporal logic predicates differ from state based predicates in that they depend on a sequence of states (i.e. consistent cuts) rather than a single state. For a regular state-based predicate B, the result of evaluating the predicate on a consistent cut remains unchanged, even if new events are added to the computation. In other words, if the slice of the computation with respect to B contains a cut C, this cut will continue to remain in the slice after new events have been added. This is not true in the case of temporal logic predicates $AG(B)$ and $EG(B)$, however. A cut that satisfies $AG(B)$ in the current computation may not satisfy it when new events arrive. We illustrate this using the following example.

Consider the computation shown in Fig. 3 involving two processes p_1 and p_2. Let x_1 and x_2 be the boolean variables on processes p_1 and p_2 respectively. Consider a predicate $B_1 = (x_1 \leqslant 4) \wedge (x_2 \leqslant 3)$. Observe that B_1 is a regular state-based predicate as it is a conjunction of local predicates on processes p_1 and p_2. Events a, b, d, e and f satisfy the local predicate on their process. The consistent cuts, in figure 3(a) that satisfy B_1 (represented by their frontiers) are:$\{a, d\}$, $\{a, e\}$, $\{a, f\}$, $\{b, d\}$, $\{b, e\}$ and $\{b, f\}$. The greatest cut of the computation, $\{b, f\}$, satisfies B_1, and is reachable from all the mentioned cuts. All these cuts satisfy $AG(B_1)$, and belong to the slice for $AG(B_1)$. The slice for B_1 still contains these cuts even after event c arrives on p_1. However, now the greatest cut $\{c, f\}$ does not satisfy B_1. All cuts of the computation can reach this cut and, therefore, the slice of the computation shown in figure 3(b) with respect to $AG(B_1)$ is empty. Note that consistent cut $\{a, d\}$ still satisfies B_1, but no longer satisfies $AG(B_1)$. Finally, when event g arrives, as shown in figure 3(c), the cut D, given by $frontier(D) = \{g, f\}$, satisfies B_1. The slice of the new computation with respect to $AG(B_1)$ is now non-empty and contains the following consistent cuts (represented by their frontiers): $\{g, e\}$ and $\{g, f\}$.

Therefore, the slice of a computation with respect to temporal logic predicates $AG(B)$ and $EG(B)$, where B is a regular state-based predicate, can *shrink* or *grow*

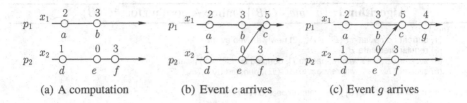

(a) A computation   (b) Event c arrives   (c) Event g arrives

Fig. 3. Illustration of growing and shrinking of slices

with the arrival of each new event, unlike the slice with respect to a state-based predicate, which can only grow. By shrinking, we mean that the number of consistent cuts in the slice decreases upon the arrival of a new event. A slice grows when the number of consistent cuts increases. If the greatest cut of a computation does not satisfy predicate B, then no cut in the computation satisfies $AG(B)$ or $EG(B)$, and both slices are empty. Upon the arrival of an event, however, the slices may again become non-empty.

Another interesting property of the slices with respect to $AG(B)$, $EG(B)$ and $EF(B)$ is that when non-empty, they can be completely represented by a single consistent cut that we refer to as the *fundamental cut*. For the slice of a computation with respect to $AG(B)$, this cut is the earliest consistent cut of the computation such that B is invariant after it. In the case of $EG(B)$, the fundamental cut is the earliest cut in the slice for B, that contains every non-trivial strongly connected component in the slice. The slice of a computation with respect to $EF(B)$ is the dual of $AG(B)$. The fundamental cut of the slice with respect to $EF(B)$ is the largest cut of the computation that satisfies B. All consistent cuts of the computation that can reach this cut satisfy $EF(B)$, and are included in the slice. Note that the fundamental cut is well defined as B is a regular predicate.

We now present our online algorithms to compute the slice with respect to $AG(B)$, $EG(B)$ and $EF(B)$ one-by-one. Due to space contraints, the proof of correctness of the three algorithms has been omitted and can be found elsewhere [21].

4.1   Online Algorithm to Generate Slice for AG(B)

A consistent cut C of computation satisfies $AG(B)$, where B is a regular state-based predicate, if B is satisfied at every consistent cut reachable from C. To generate the slice with respect to $AG(B)$, we exclude all cuts of the computation that can reach a consistent cut D, which does not satisfy B. Note that D does not belong to slice with respect to B. The slice with respect to $AG(B)$ can, therefore, be represented by the *least consistent cut* of the computation such that B is invariant after it, if such a cut exists. Otherwise, it is empty.

An offline algorithm to compute the slice with respect to $AG(B)$ was given by Sen and Garg in [19]. Given a computation $G = \langle E, \mapsto \rangle$ and its slice with respect to B, $\langle E, \mapsto \rangle_B$, every pair of events (g, h) in G are compared, and an edge from g to the initial event on its process is added in $\langle E, \mapsto \rangle_B$, if both of the following conditions hold: (a) $g \in J_B(h)$, and (b) $(g \not\mapsto h)$ in $\langle E, \mapsto \rangle$. Intuitively, if the pair (g, h) satisfies the conditions, then the computation contains a consistent cut Y, such that $h \in Y$ but

---

Algorithm 1: $\{online\text{-}AG(B)\}$ Online Algorithm for $AG(B)$

Input :
(1) current computation $\langle E, \mapsto \rangle$, (2) newly arrived event e,
(3) regular predicate B,
(4) slice of $\langle E, \mapsto \rangle$ with respect to B, denoted by $\langle E, \mapsto \rangle_B$, and
(5) slice of $\langle E, \mapsto \rangle$ with respect to $AG(B)$, denoted by $\langle flag, \mathcal{F}, \mathcal{P} \rangle$

Output: slice of $\langle E \cup \{e\}, \mapsto \rangle$ with respect to $AG(B)$

1   update slice $\langle E, \to \rangle_B$ to incorporate the newly arrived event e using the online algorithm for B;
    // the online algorithm will update $J_B(f)$ for every event f in $\widehat{E} \cup \{e\}$

2   **if** $\widehat{E} \cup \{e\}$ *satisfies* B **then**
     // the new slice with respect to $AG(B)$ will be non-empty
3   **if** $flag$ **then**
       // the current slice with respect to $AG(B)$ is non-empty
       // $J_B(e)$ is guaranteed to be a non-trivial consistent cut
4   advance-ag$(e, \mathcal{F})$;
5   **return** $\langle true, \mathcal{F}, \mathcal{P} \cup \{e\} \rangle$;
6   **else**
       // the current slice with respect to $AG(B)$ is empty
       // $J_B(f)$ is guaranteed to be a non-trivial consistent cut for all non-final events in the computation
       // execute advance-ag procedure for all non-final events except for those in $\mathcal{P}$
       // advance-ag procedure has already been executed for all events in $\mathcal{P}$
7   **foreach** $f \in (\widehat{E} \cup \{e\}) \setminus \mathcal{P}$ **do**
8   advance-ag$(f, \mathcal{F})$;
9   **return** $\langle true, \mathcal{F}, \widehat{E} \cup \{e\} \rangle$;
10 **else**
     // the new slice with respect to $AG(B)$ will be empty
11   **return** $\langle false, \mathcal{F}, \mathcal{P} \rangle$;

12 **Procedure** advance-ag(x, C) **begin**
13   **foreach** $y \in frontier(J_B(x))$ **do**
14   **if** $y \not\mapsto x$ **then**
       // advance C to include y and (all events that precede y in computation $\langle E, \mapsto \rangle$)
       // In practice, consistent cuts are represented using their frontiers. The union of two cuts corresponds to taking the component-wise maximum of their frontiers.
15        $C := C \cup J(y)$

$g \notin Y$. Note that the cut Y does not satisfy B, and all consistent cuts of the computation that can reach Y do not satisfy $AG(B)$. These cuts are eliminated from slice $\langle E, \mapsto \rangle_B$ by adding an edge from g to the initial event on its process.

A trivial online algorithm to compute the slice of a computation with respect to $AG(B)$ would be to directly apply the offline algorithm to the computation every time a new event arrives. However, this approach is extremely expensive as it requires comparing every pair of events each time the slice is updated. Instead, in our algorithm, we maintain the fundamental cut, $\mathcal{F}$, of the slice and update it incrementally, when each new event arrives. At a high level, our algorithm works as follows: Consider a computation $G = \langle E, \mapsto \rangle$, and let its slice with respect to predicates B and $AG(B)$ be denoted by S_B and $S_{AG(B)}$, respectively. Upon the arrival of an event e, let the new computation be denoted by $G' = \langle E \cup \{e\}, \mapsto \rangle$, and the slices be S'_B and $S'_{AG(B)}$, respectively. We assume that the slice with respect to B is updated using algorithm *online-MSG$_B$* [10].

As described in section 4 the slice with respect to $AG(B)$ may shrink or grow with the arrival of each new event. Therefore, the following four cases are possible:

1. $S_{AG(B)}$ is non-empty and $S'_{AG(B)}$ is empty. In this case, the emptiness of $S'_{AG(B)}$ is indicated by setting a boolean $flag$ variable to false. No other action is performed and $\mathcal{F}$ is not modified. Therefore, if the slice is empty, the fundamental cut is same as that in the last iteration the slice was non-empty.

2. $S_{AG(B)}$ is empty and $S'_{AG(B)}$ is empty. As in the previous case, no action is performed. $\mathcal{F}$ remains unchanged and the $flag$ is still set to false.

3. $S_{AG(B)}$ is non-empty and $S'_{AG(B)}$ is non-empty. In this case, the fundamental cut might need to be updated to include the newly arrived event e. Here, every pair of events (e, x), where $x \in frontier(J_B(e))$, are compared and $\mathcal{F}$ is expanded to include event x, if $x \not\mapsto e$ in G'. Note that this would require $\mathcal{F}$ to include all events that happened-before x in G', which is denoted by the set $J(x)$. We refer to this as *advancing* the fundamental cut. It must be pointed out here that the fundamental cut may remain unchanged after e has been examined. The $flag$ variable remains set to true, in this case.

4. $S_{AG(B)}$ is empty and $S'_{AG(B)}$ is non-empty. Note that $\mathcal{F}$ is not updated when the slice becomes or remains empty. Hence all events that have arrived since the slice last became empty need to be examined to determine if the fundamental cut must be advanced. Finally, $flag$ is set to true to indicate a non-empty slice.

Note that checking whether $S'_{AG(B)}$ is empty can be done easily by determining if the greatest cut of G', $\widehat{E} \cup \{e\}$ satisfies B. If $\widehat{E} \cup \{e\}$ does not satisfy B, then $S'_{AG(B)}$ is empty as all cuts of the computation can reach this cut. Otherwise, $S'_{AG(B)}$ is not empty.

The pseudocode for algorithm *online-AG(B)* is shown in Algorithm 1. The slice with respect to $AG(B)$ is represented by the triple $\langle flag, \mathcal{F}, \mathcal{P} \rangle$. The first entry $flag$, is a boolean value, when set to false indicates an empty slice. The second entry $\mathcal{F}$, is the fundamental cut. If $flag$ is false, then $\mathcal{F}$ is the fundamental cut when the slice was last non-empty. Otherwise, it is the fundamental cut of the current slice. The last entry, $\mathcal{P}$, is the set of *processed events*, containing all events which have been examined while advancing the fundamental cut. These are the events on which the advance-ag procedure has been evaluated.

The advance-ag procedure is described as follows: For every event x that has arrived since the slice was last non-empty, we check for all events $y \in frontier(J_B(x))$ whether $y \not\mapsto x$ in the computation. If $y \not\mapsto x$, the consistent cut D of the computation that contains x but not y needs to be removed from the slice for $AG(B)$ as D does not satisfy b. All cuts that can reach D do not satisfy $AG(B)$ and are eliminated by advancing $\mathcal{F}$ to include y (and all the events that precede y in the computation). Initially, $flag$ is set to false, $\mathcal{I}$ consists of only the set $\bot$ and $\mathcal{P}$ is the empty set. When an event arrives, the slice with respect to B is updated in an online manner, after which the slice with respect to $AG(B)$ is updated.

Let the current computation be denoted by $\langle E, \mapsto \rangle$, and its greatest cut by $\widehat{E}$. Also, let the current slice with respect to $AG(B)$, $S_{AG(B)}$, be $\langle flag, \mathcal{F}, \mathcal{P} \rangle$. When the new event e arrives, the resulting computation and its slice with respect to B are denoted by $\langle E \cup \{e\}, \mapsto \rangle$ and $S'_B = \langle E \cup \{e\}, \mapsto \rangle_B$ respectively. Next, the slice of $\langle E \cup \{e\}, \mapsto \rangle$ with respect to $AG(B)$, $S'_{AG(B)}$, is updated. Observe that $e \in frontier(\widehat{E} \cup \{e\})$. The following cases are possible:

- **Case 1 ($\widehat{E} \cup \{e\}$ satisfies B):** In this case, $S'_{AG(B)}$ is non-empty. There are two subcases.
  - **Subcase a ($\widehat{E}$ satisfies B):** Here, slice $S_{AG(B)}$ is non-empty. The **advance-ag** method is evaluated only on the newly arrived event e to update $\mathcal{I}$, and e is added to $\mathcal{P}$. Note that $flag$ remains set to true, indicating a non-empty slice.
  - **Subcase b ($\widehat{E}$ does not satisfy B):** Here, slice $S_{AG(B)}$ is empty. In this case, $\mathcal{F}$ contains the fundamental cut when the slice was last non-empty. The **advance-ag** procedure is evaluated on every non-fictitious event not present in $\mathcal{P}$, and $\mathcal{I}$ is updated. $\mathcal{P}$ is updated to $\widehat{E} \cup \{e\}$, and $flag$ is changed to true.
- **Case 2 ($\widehat{E} \cup \{e\}$ does not satisfy B):** Here, the greatest cut of computation $\langle E \cup \{e\}, \mapsto \rangle$ does not satisfy B. $S'_{AG(B)}$ is empty and is denoted by setting $flag$ to false.

Example: We now present a sample execution of algorithm *online-AG(B)*. Consider the computation as shown in 3(a), and let its slice with respect to predicate $AG(B_1)$, where $B_1 = (x_1 \leqslant 4) \wedge (x_2 \leqslant 3)$, be represented by $\langle \text{true}, \{a, d\}, \{b, f\} \rangle$. Note that all events in 3(a) satisfy the local predicate on their process, and the greatest cut of the computation $\{b, f\}$ satisfies predicate B_1. Hence, the slice of this computation with respect to $AG(B_1)$ is non-empty. When event c arrives, as shown in 3(b), first the slice of the resulting computation with respect to B_1 is updated. The greatest cut of this computation $\{c, f\}$ does not satisfy B_1. Therefore, from case 2, we have that the slice with respect to $AG(B_1)$ is empty, and is updated to $\langle \text{false}, \{a, d\}, \{b, f\} \rangle$.

Finally, when event g arrives, the slice with respect to $AG(B_1)$ is non-empty, as the greatest cut $\{g, f\}$ satisfies b. Here, case 1 subcase b applies, and the **advance-ag** procedure is evaluated on events c and g. The slice with respect to $AG(B_1)$ is then updated to $\langle \text{true}, \{g, e\}, \{g, f\} \rangle$.

Complexity Analysis: We first analyze the time complexity of executing **advance-ag** procedure in Algorithm 1 once.

Lemma 1. *The time complexity of executing **advance-ag** procedure in Algorithm 1 once is $O(n^2)$.*

Proof. The for loop in the **advance-ag** procedure iterates over n events. The if condition in the **advance-ag** procedure can be evaluated in $O(1)$ time. Finally, the assignment statement in the **advance-ag** procedure can be executed in $O(n)$ time.

The next lemma clearly follows from the way Algorithm 1 works:

Lemma 2. *The **advance-ag** procedure in Algorithm 1 is executed at most once for any event in the computation.*

Finally, we have:

Theorem 1. *The amortized time complexity of algorithm* online-AG(B) *is $O(n^2)$ per event.*

Algorithm 2: Procedure advance-eg

---

1 **Procedure** advance-eg(x, C) **begin**
2   **foreach** $y \in frontier(J_B(x))$ **do**
3   **if** $x \in J_B(y)$ **then**
            // x and y are in the same strongly connected component in $\langle E, \mapsto \rangle_B$
4   **if** $y \not\to x$ **then**
                // advance C to include y and (all events that precede y in slice $\langle E, \mapsto \rangle_B$)
5                  $C := C \cup J_B(y)$

Proof. The online algorithm for incrementally updating the slice with respect to B has $O(n^2)$ amortized time complexity. On arrival of a new event, if the slice with respect to $AG(B)$ is non-empty, then Algorithm 1 basically ensures that the **advance-ag** procedure is executed at least once for every non-fictitious event in the computation. This has amortized time complexity of $O(n^2)$ per event.

4.2   Online Algorithm to Generate Slice for EG(B)

A consistent cut C, of computation $G = \langle E, \mapsto \rangle$, satisfies $EG(B)$ if there is some consistent cut sequence $C \dots \widehat{E}$, such that B is satisfied at every consistent cut. Our online algorithm to compute the slice of a computation G with respect to $EG(B)$, where B is a regular state-based predicate, is similar to algorithm *online-AG(B)*. The fundamental cut in algorithm *online-AG(B)* is the least consistent cut of slice $\langle E, \mapsto \rangle_B$, such that B is invariant after it. In algorithm *online-EG(B)*, however, the fundamental cut is the least consistent cut of the computation that contains every non-trivial strongly connected component in slice $\langle E, \mapsto \rangle_B$. Recall that a non-trivial strongly connected component contains at least two non-fictitious events, and none of the $\top$ events. The slice for $EG(B)$ can then be obtained by collapsing all events before the fundamental cut in slice $\langle E, \mapsto \rangle_B$. As in algorithm *online-AG(B)*, the slice generated by algorithm *online-EG(B)* is represented by a triple $\langle flag, \mathcal{F}, \mathcal{P} \rangle$. Initially, *flag* is set to false, $\mathcal{F}$ is initialized to the set $\perp$ and $\mathcal{P}$ is empty.

Consider a computation $G = \langle E, \mapsto \rangle$, and let its slice with respect to predicate B be $\langle E, \mapsto \rangle_B$. Let the current slice with respect to $EG(B)$ be represented by $S = \langle flag, \mathcal{F}, \mathcal{P} \rangle$. Note that S may be empty. Let a new event e arrive and be incorporated into the computation. The resulting computation and slice with respect to b are denoted by $G' = \langle E \cup \{e\}, \mapsto \rangle$ and $\langle E \cup \{e\}, \mapsto \rangle_B$ respectively.

The first step in algorithm *online-EG(B)* is determining if the slice of computation G' with respect to $EG(B)$ is empty. This is done by checking if the greatest cut of G', $\widehat{E} \cup \{e\}$, satisfies B. If $\widehat{E} \cup \{e\}$ does not satisfy B, then the slice with respect to $EG(B)$ is empty and is updated to $\langle false, \mathcal{F}, \mathcal{P} \rangle$. No other action is performed. Observe that if the slice with respect to $EG(B)$ is empty, then $\mathcal{F}$ contains the fundamental cut when the slice was last non-empty, if it exists. On the other hand, if $\widehat{E} \cup \{e\}$ satisfies B, then the slice with respect to $EG(B)$ is not empty and needs to be updated. $\mathcal{F}$ is advanced by calling the **advance-eg** procedure, which is described as follows: For every event x that has arrived since the slice was last non-empty, we first check for every event $y \in frontier(J_B(x))$, whether x and y belong to the same non-trivial strongly connected component in $\langle E \cup \{e\}, \mapsto \rangle_B$. If they do, we advance $\mathcal{F}$ to include $J_B(y)$ if

---

Algorithm 3: {*online-EF(B)*} Online Algorithm for $EF(B)$

Input :
(1) current computation $\langle E, \mapsto \rangle$,
(2) newly arrived event e, (3) regular predicate B,
(4) slice of $\langle E, \mapsto \rangle$ with respect to B, denoted by $\langle E, \mapsto \rangle_B$

Output: slice of $\langle E \cup \{e\}, \mapsto \rangle$ with respect to $EF(B)$

1 update slice $\langle E, \rightarrow \rangle_B$ to incorporate the newly arrived event e using the online algorithm for B;
   // the online algorithm maintains a vector $recompute$, where $recompute_i$ stores the *earliest* event f on
   process p_i for which $J_B(f)$ is the default cut
2 compute the cut $\mathcal{M}$ such that, for each process p_i, the last event on p_i in $\mathcal{M}$ is either the predecessor of
   $recompute_i$, if it exists, and $\perp_i$ otherwise ;
3 **return** $\mathcal{M}$;

$y \not\mapsto x$ in G'. Note that this will include all events that precede y in slice $\langle E, \mapsto \rangle_B$. After the **advance-eg** procedure has been executed for all events in $(\widehat{E} \cup \{e\}) \setminus \mathcal{P}$, $\mathcal{P}$ is updated to $\widehat{E} \cup \{e\}$. The slice is then updated to $\langle true, \mathcal{F}, \mathcal{P} \rangle$. The pseudocode for algorithm *online-EG(B)* is similar to algorithm *online-AG(B)*, and we only show procedure **advance-eg** in Algorithm 2.

Complexity Analysis: The analysis of the time complexity of *online-EG(B)* is similar to that of *online-AG(B)* (both algorithms have amortized time complexity of $O(n^2)$ per event) and has been omitted.

4.3   Online Algorithm to Generate Slice for EF(B)

For a consistent cut C to satisfy $EF(B)$, some cut reachable from C in the computation, must satisfy B. Hence, to generate the slice of computation $\langle E, \mapsto \rangle$ with respect to $EF(B)$, we find the *maximal cut* $\mathcal{M}$ of $\langle E, \mapsto \rangle_B$ and eliminate all cuts of the computation after that cut. Since B is a regular predicate, $\mathcal{M}$ is well defined.

The slice of a computation with respect to $EF(B)$ is the dual of the slice with respect to $AG(B)$. In algorithm *online-AG(B)*, the $fundamental cut$ was the earliest consistent cut such that B was invariant after it, whereas the slice generated by algorithm *online-EF(B)* is represented by its *maximal cut*, $\mathcal{M}$, such that B never becomes true after it. Essentially, every iteration of algorithm *online-EF(B)* consists of finding $\mathcal{M}$, and the slice is obtained by collapsing all events in the computation after $\mathcal{M}$ into the strongly connected component containing the final events. Every consistent cut of the original computation that can reach $\mathcal{M}$ satisfies $EF(B)$ and is, therefore, present in the slice with respect to $EF(B)$. Note that if the greatest cut of the computation satisfies B, then every consistent cut of the computation satisfies $EF(B)$.

The pseudocode for algorithm *online-EF(B)* is shown in algorithm 3. Upon the arrival of the new event e, the slice of the computation $\langle E \cup \{e\}, \mapsto \rangle$ with respect to B is updated using the algorithm *online-MSG$_B$*. Recall that a vector $recompute$ is maintained by algorithm *online-MSG$_B$*, which keeps track of the earliest event on every process for which J_B evaluates to the default cut. This vector is updated in every iteration. After the slice for B has been updated, the maximal cut $\mathcal{M}$ of $\langle E \cup \{e\}, \mapsto \rangle_B$ can be determined by including, on every process p_i, every event before $recompute_i$.

Complexity Analysis: We now analyze the time complexity of *online-EF(B)*.

Theorem 2. *The amortized time complexity of algorithm* online-EF(B) *is* $O(n^2)$ *per event.*

Proof. The online algorithm for incrementally updating the slice of with respect to B has $O(n^2)$ amortized time complexity. On arrival of a new event, Algorithm 3 basically constructs a cut by using a certain event on every process, which requires $O(n)$ time.

5 Conclusion

Computation slices are useful in reducing the size of the state-space for predicate detection. In this paper we have described three efficient online algorithms to generate the slice with respect to regular temporal logic predicates $AG(B)$, $EG(B)$ and $EF(B)$, when B is a regular state-based predicate. As future work, we intend on extending them to handle a wider class of temporal logic predicates.

References

1. Chandy, K.M., Lamport, L.: Distributed Snapshots: Determining Global States of Distributed Systems. ACM Transactions on Computer Systems 3(1), 63–75 (1985)
2. Cooper, R., Marzullo, K.: Consistent Detection of Global Predicates. In: Proceedings of the ACM/ONR Workshop on Parallel and Distributed Debugging, pp. 163–173 (1991)
3. Alagar, S., Venkatesan, S.: Techniques to Tackle State Explosion in Global Predicate Detection. IEEE Transactions on Software Engineering (TSE) 27(8), 704–714 (2001)
4. Stoller, S.D., Schneider, F.: Faster Possibility Detection by Combining Two Approaches. In: Helary, J.-M., Raynal, M. (eds.) WDAG 1995. LNCS, vol. 972, pp. 318–332. Springer, Heidelberg (1995)
5. Clarke, E.M., Grumberg, O.: Avoiding the state explosion problem in temporal logic model checking. In: Proceedings of the 6th ACM Symposium on Principles of Distributed Computing (PODC), pp. 294–303 (1987)
6. Mittal, N., Garg, V.K.: Techniques and applications of computation slicing. Distributed Computing 17, 251–277 (2005)
7. Clarke, E.M., Grumberg, O., Peled, D.A.: Model Checking. MIT Press (December 1999)
8. Godefroid, P.: Partial-Order Methods for the Verification of Concurrent Systems. LNCS, vol. 1032. Springer, Heidelberg (1996)
9. Stoller, S.D., Unnikrishnan, L., Liu, Y.A.: Efficient Detection of Global Properties in Distributed Systems Using Partial-Order Methods. In: Emerson, E.A., Sistla, A.P. (eds.) CAV 2000. LNCS, vol. 1855, pp. 264–279. Springer, Heidelberg (2000)
10. Mittal, N., Sen, A., Garg, V.K.: Solving Computation Slicing Using Predicate Detection. IEEE Transactions on Parallel and Distributed Systems (TPDS) 18(12), 1700–1713 (2007)
11. Leucker, M., Schallhart, C.: A Brief Account of Runtime Verification. The Journal of Logic and Algebraic Programming 78(5), 293–303 (2009)
12. Drusinsky, D.: The Temporal Rover and the ATG Rover. In: Havelund, K., Penix, J., Visser, W. (eds.) SPIN 2000. LNCS, vol. 1885, pp. 323–330. Springer, Heidelberg (2000)
13. Kim, M., Kannan, S., Lee, I., Sokolsky, O., Viswanathan, M.: Java-MaC: A Run-time Assurance Tool for Java Programs. Electronic Notes in Theoretical Computer Science 55(2), 218–235 (2001)

14. Havelund, K., Roşu, G.: Monitoring Java Programs with Java PathExplorer. Electronic Notes in Theoretical Computer Science 55(2), 200–217 (2001)
15. Sen, K., Roşu, G., Agha, G.: Detecting Errors in Multithreaded Programs by Generalized Predictive Analysis of Executions. In: Steffen, M., Zavattaro, G. (eds.) FMOODS 2005. LNCS, vol. 3535, pp. 211–226. Springer, Heidelberg (2005)
16. Chen, F., Şerbănuţă, T.F., Roşu, G.: jPredictor: A Predictive Runtime Analysis Tool for Java. In: Proceedings of the International Conference on Software Engineering, ICSE (2008)
17. Chen, F., Roşu, G.: Parametric and Sliced Causality. In: Damm, W., Hermanns, H. (eds.) CAV 2007. LNCS, vol. 4590, pp. 240–253. Springer, Heidelberg (2007)
18. Garg, V.K.: Elements of distributed computing. John Wiley & Sons, Inc. (2002)
19. Sen, A., Garg, V.K.: Detecting Temporal Logic Predicates in Distributed Programs Using Computation Slicing. In: Papatriantafilou, M., Hunel, P. (eds.) OPODIS 2003. LNCS, vol. 3144, pp. 171–183. Springer, Heidelberg (2004)
20. Lamport, L.: Time, Clocks, and the Ordering of Events in a Distributed System. Communications of the ACM (CACM) 21(7), 558–565 (1978)
21. Natarajan, A., Mittal, N., Garg, V.K.: Online Algorithms to Generate Slices for Regular Temporal Logic Predicates. Technical Report UTDCS-11-12, Department of Computer Science, The University of Texas at Dallas (2012)

HiperTM: High Performance, Fault-Tolerant Transactional Memory

Sachin Hirve, Roberto Palmieri, and Binoy Ravindran

Virginia Tech, Blacksburg VA 24060, USA
{hsachin,robertop,binoy}@vt.edu

Abstract. We present HiperTM, a high performance active replication protocol for fault-tolerant distributed transactional memory. The active replication paradigm allows transactions to execute locally, costing them only a single network communication step during transaction execution. Shared objects are replicated across all sites, avoiding remote object accesses. Replica consistency is ensured by a) OS-Paxos, an optimistic atomic broadcast layer that total-orders transactional requests, and b) SCC, a local multi-version concurrency control protocol that enforces a commit order equivalent to transactions' delivery order. SCC executes write transactions serially without incurring any synchronization overhead, and runs read-only transactions in parallel (to write transactions) with non-blocking execution and abort-freedom. Our implementation reveals that HiperTM guarantees 0% of out-of-order optimistic deliveries and performance up to 1.2× better than atomic broadcast-based competitor (PaxosSTM).

1 Introduction

Software transactional memory (STM) [30] is a promising programming model for managing concurrency of transactional requests. STM libraries offer APIs to programmers for reading and writing shared objects, ensuring atomicity, isolation, and consistency in a completely transparent manner. STM transactions are characterized by only in-memory operations. Thus, their performance is orders of magnitude better than that of non in-memory processing systems (e.g., database settings), where interactions with a stable storage often significantly degrade performance.

Besides performance, transactional applications usually require strong dependability properties that centralized, in-memory processing systems cannot guarantee. Fault-tolerant mechanisms often involve expensive synchronization with remote nodes. As a result, directly incorporating them into in-memory transactional applications (distributed software transactional memory or DTM) will reduce the performance advantage (of in-memory operations) due to network costs. For example, the *partial replication* paradigm allows transaction processing in the presence of node failures, but the overhead paid by transactions for looking-up latest object copies at encounter time limits performance. Current partial replication protocols [25,27] report performance in the range of hundreds to tens of thousands transactions committed per second, while centralized STM systems have throughput in the range of tens of millions [8,9]. *Full replication* is a way to annul network interactions while reading/writing objects. In this

M. Chatterjee et al. (Eds.): ICDCN 2014, LNCS 8314, pp. 181–196, 2014.
© Springer-Verlag Berlin Heidelberg 2014

model, application's entire shared data-set is replicated across all nodes. However, to ensure replica consistency, a common serialization order (CSO) must be ensured.

State-machine replication (or active replication) [28] is a paradigm that exploits full replication to avoid service interruption in case of node failures. In this approach, whenever the application executes a transaction T, it is not directly processed in the same application thread. Instead, a group communication system (GCS), which is responsible for ensuring the CSO, creates a transaction request from T and issues it to all the nodes in the system. The CSO defines a total order among all transactional requests. Therefore, when a sequence of messages is delivered by the GCS to one node, it guarantees that other nodes also receive the same sequence, ensuring replica consistency.

A CSO can be determined using a solution to the *consensus* (or atomic broadcast [7]) problem: i.e., how a group of processes can agree on a value in the presence of faults in partially synchronous systems. Paxos [18] is one of the most widely studied consensus algorithms. Though Paxos's initial design was expensive (e.g., it required three communication steps), significant research efforts have focused on alternative designs for enhancing performance. A recent example is *JPaxos* [17,26], built on top of MultiPaxos [18], which extends Paxos to allow processes to agree on a sequence of values, instead of a single value. JPaxos incorporates optimizations such as batching and pipelining, which significantly boost message throughput [26]. *S-Paxos* [3] further improves JPaxos by balancing the load of the network protocol over all the nodes, instead of concentrating that on the leader.

A deterministic concurrency control protocol is needed for processing transactions according to the CSO. When transactions are delivered by the GCS, their commit order must coincide with the CSO; otherwise replicas will end up in different states. With deterministic concurrency control, each replica is aware of the existence of a new transaction to execute only after its delivery, significantly increasing transaction execution time. An optimistic solution to this problem has been proposed in [15], where an additional delivery, called *optimistic delivery*, is sent by the GCS to the replicas prior to the final CSO. This new delivery is used to start transaction execution speculatively, while guessing the final commit order. If the guessed order matches the CSO, the transaction is totally (or partially) executed and committed [19,20]. However, guessing alternative serialization orders has non-trivial overheads, which, sometimes, do not pay off.

In this paper, we present HiperTM, a high performance active replication protocol. HiperTM is based on an extension of S-Paxos, called *OS-Paxos* that we propose. OS-Paxos optimizes the S-Paxos architecture for efficiently supporting optimistic deliveries, in order to minimize the likelihood of mismatches between the optimistic order and the final delivery order. The protocol wraps transactions in transactional request messages and executes them on all the replicas in the same order. HiperTM uses a novel, speculative concurrency control protocol called SCC, which processes write transactions serially, minimizing code instrumentation (i.e., locks or CAS operations). When a transaction is optimistically delivered by OS-Paxos, its execution speculatively starts, assuming the optimistic order as the processing order. Avoiding atomic operations allows transactions to reach maximum performance in the time available between the optimistic and the corresponding final delivery. Conflict detection and any other more complex mechanisms hamper the protocol's ability to completely execute a sequence of transactions within their final notifications – so those are avoided.

For each shared object, the SCC protocol stores a list of committed versions, which is exploited by read-only transactions to execute in parallel to write transactions. As a consequence, write transactions are broadcast using OS-Paxos. Read-only transactions are directly delivered to one replica, without a CSO, because each replica has the same state, and are processed locally.

We implemented HiperTM and conducted experimental studies using benchmarks including TPC-C [5]. Our results reveal three important trends. (A) OS-Paxos provides a very limited number of out-of-order optimistic deliveries (<1% when no failures happen and <5% in case of failures), allowing transactions processed – according to the optimistic order – to more likely commit. (B) Serially processing optimistically delivered transactions guarantees a throughput (transactions per second) that is higher than atomic broadcast service's throughput (messages per second), confirming optimistic delivery's effectiveness for concurrency control in actively replicated transactional systems. Additionally, the reduced number of CAS operations allows greater concurrency, which is exploited by read-only transactions for executing faster. (C) HiperTM's transactional throughput is up to $1.2\times$ better than state-of-the-art atomic broadcast-based competitor PaxosSTM [16], and up to $10\times$ better than SCORe [25].

With HiperTM, we highlight the importance of making the right design choices for fault-tolerant DTM systems. To the best of our knowledge, HiperTM is the first fully implemented transaction processing system based on speculative processing, built in the context of active replication. The complete implementation of HiperTM, source codes, test-scripts, etc., is publicly available at https://bitbucket.org/hsachin/hipertm/.

2   System Model

We consider a classical distributed system model [12] consisting of a set of processes $\Pi = \{p_1, \ldots, p_n\}$ that communicate via message passing. Process may fail according to the fail-stop (crash) model. A non-faulty process is called correct. We assume a partially synchronous system [18], where $2f + 1$ nodes are correct and at most f nodes are simultaneously faulty. We consider only non-byzantine faults.

We consider a full replication model, where the application's entire shared data-set is replicated across all nodes. Transactions are not executed on application threads. Instead, application threads, referred to as *clients*, inject transactional requests into the replicated system. Each request is composed of a key, identifying the transaction to execute, and the values of all the parameters needed for running the transaction's logic (if any). Threads submit the transaction request to a node, and wait until the node successfully commits that transaction.

OS-Paxos is the network service responsible for defining a total order among transactional requests. The requests are considered as network messages by OS-Paxos; it is not aware of the messages' content, it only provides ordering. After the message is delivered to a replica, the transactional request is extracted and processed as a transaction.

OS-Paxos delivers each message twice. The first is called *optimistic-delivery* (or opt-del) and the second is called *final-delivery* (or final-del). Opt-del notifies replicas that a new message is currently involved in the agreement process, and therefore opt-del's order cannot be considered reliable for committing transactions. On the other hand, final-del is responsible for delivering the message along with its order such that all replicas receive that message in the same order (i.e., total order). The final-del order corresponds to the transactions' commit order.

We use a multi-versioned memory model, wherein an object version has two fields: *timestamp*, which defines the time when the transaction that wrote the version committed; and *value*, which is the value of the object (either primitive value or set of fields). Each shared object is composed of: the last committed version, the last written version (not yet committed), and a list of previously committed versions. The last written version is the version generated by an opt-del transaction that is still waiting for commit. As a consequence, its timestamp is not specified. The timestamp is a monotonically increasing integer, which is incremented when a transaction commits. Our concurrency control ensures that only one writer can update the timestamp at a time. This is because, transactions are processed serially. Thus, there are no transactions validating and committing concurrently (Section 3.3 describes the concurrency control mechanism).

We assume that the transaction logic is *snapshot-deterministic* [20], i.e., the sequence of operations executed depends on the return value of previous read operations.

3   HiperTM

3.1   Optimistic S-Paxos

Optimistic S-Paxos (or OS-Paxos) is an implementation of optimistic atomic broadcast [23] built on top of S-Paxos [3]. S-Paxos, as its predecessor JPaxos [17,26], can be defined in terms of two primitives (compliant with the atomic broadcast specification): $ABcast(m)$: used by clients to broadcast a message m to all the nodes; $Adeliver(m)$: event notified to each replica for delivering message m.

These primitives satisfy the following properties: *Validity*, if a correct process $ABcast$ a message m, then it eventually $Adeliver$ m; *Uniform agreement*, if a process $Adeliver$s a message m, then all correct processes eventually $Adeliver$ m; *Uniform integrity*, for any message m, every process $Adeliver$s m at most once, and only if m was previously $ABcast$ed; *Total order*, if some process $Adeliver$s m before m', then every process $Adeliver$s m and m' in the same order.

OS-Paxos provides an additional primitive, called $Odeliver(m)$, which is used for early delivering a previously broadcast message m before the $Adeliver$ for m is issued. OS-Paxos ensures that: 1) If a process $Odeliver(m)$, then every correct process eventually $Odeliver(m)$; 2) If a correct process $Odeliver(m)$, then it eventually $Adeliver(m)$; 3) A process $Adeliver(m)$ only after $Odeliver(m)$;
OS-Paxos's properties and primitives are compliant with the definition of optimistic atomic broadcast [23]. The sequence of $Odeliver$ notifications defines the so called *optimistic order* (or *opt-order*). The sequence of $Adeliver$ defines the so called *final order*. We now describe the architecture of S-Paxos to elaborate the design choices we made for implementing $Odeliver$ and $Adeliver$.

S-Paxos improves upon JPaxos with optimizations such as distributing the leader's load across all replicas. Unlike JPaxos, where clients only connect to the leader, in S-Paxos each replica accepts client requests and sends replies to connected clients after the execution of the requests. S-Paxos extensively uses the batching technique [26] for increasing throughput. A replica creates a batch of client requests and distributes it to other replicas. The receiver replicas store the batch of requests and send an *ack* to all other replicas. When the replicas observe a majority of *ack*s for a batch, it is considered as stable. The leader then *proposes* an order (containing only batch IDs) for non-proposed stable batches, for which, the other replicas reply with their agreement i.e., *accept* messages. When a majority of agreement for a proposed order is reached (i.e., a consensus instance), each replica considers it as *decided*.

S-Paxos is based on the MultiPaxos protocol where, if the leader remains stable (i.e., does not crash), its proposed order is likely to be accepted by the other replicas. Also, there exists a non-negligible delay between the time when an order is proposed and its consensus is reached. As the number of replicas taking part in the consensus agreement increases, the time required to reach consensus becomes substantial. Since the likelihood of a proposed order to get accepted is high with a stable leader, we exploit the time to reach consensus and execute client requests speculatively without commit. When the leader sends the proposed order for a batch, replicas use it for triggering *Odeliver*. On reaching consensus agreement, replicas fire the *Adeliver* event, which commits all speculatively executed transactions corresponding to the agreed consensus.

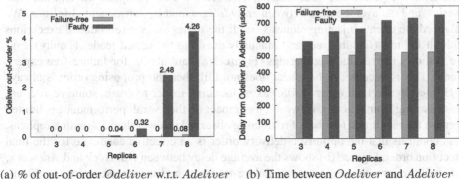

(a) % of out-of-order *Odeliver* w.r.t. *Adeliver*   (b) Time between *Odeliver* and *Adeliver*

Fig. 1. OS-Paxos performance

Network non-determinism presents some challenges for the implementation of *Odeliver* and *Adeliver* in S-Paxos. First, S-Paxos can be configured to run multiple consensus instances (i.e., pipelining) to increase throughput. This can cause out-of-order consensus agreement e.g., though an instance a precedes instance b, b may be agreed before a. Second, the client's request batch is distributed by the replicas before the leader could propose the order for them. However, a replica may receive a request batch after the delivery of a proposal that contains it (due to network non-determinism). Lastly, a proposal message may be delivered after the instance is decided.

We made the following design choices to overcome these challenges. We trigger an *Odeliver* event for a proposal only when the following conditions are met: 1) the replica receives a propose message; 2) all request batches of the propose message have been received; and 3) *Odeliver* for all previous instances have been triggered i.e., there is no "gap" for *Odeliver*ed instances. A proposal can be *Odeliver*ed either when a missing batch from another replica is received for a previously proposed instance, or when a proposal is received for the previously received batches. We delay the *Odeliver* until we receive the proposal for previously received batches to avoid out-of-order speculative execution and to minimize the cost of aborts and retries.

The triggering of the *Adeliver* event also depends on the arrival of request batches and the majority of accept messages from other replicas. An instance may be decided either after the receipt of all request batches or before the receipt of a delayed batch corresponding to the instance. It is also possible that the arrival of the propose message and reaching consensus is the same event (e.g., for a system of 2 replicas). In such cases, *Adeliver* events immediately follow *Odeliver*. Due to these possibilities, we fire the *Adeliver* event when 1) consensus is reached for a proposed message, and 2) a missing request batch for a decided instance is received. If there is any out-of-order instance agreement, *Adeliver* is delayed until all previous instances are *Adeliver*ed.

In order to assess the effectiveness of our design choices, we conducted experiments measuring the percentage of reordering between OS-Paxos's optimistic and final deliveries, and the average time between an *Odeliver* and its subsequent *Adeliver*. We balanced the clients injecting requests on all the nodes and we reproduced executions without failures (Failure-free) and manually crashing the actual leader (Faulty). Figure 1 shows the results. Reorderings (Figure 1(a)) are absent for failure-free experiments. This is because, if the leader does not fail, then the proposing order is always confirmed by the final order in OS-Paxos. Inducing leader to crash, some reorder appears starting from 6 nodes. However, the impact on the overall performance is limited because the maximum number of reordering observed is lower than 5% with 8 replicas. This confirms that the optimistic delivery order is an effective candidate for the final execution order. Figure 1(b) shows the average delay between *Odeliver* and *Adeliver*. It is ≈ 500 microseconds in case of failure-free runs and it increases up to ≈ 750 microseconds when leader crashes. The reason is related to the possibility that the process of sending the proposal message is interrupted by a fault, forcing the next elected leader to start a new agreement on previous messages.

The results highlight the trade-off between a more reliable optimistic delivery order and the time available for speculation. On one hand, anticipating the optimistic delivery results in additional time available for speculative processing transactions, at the cost of having an optimistic delivery less reliable. On the other hand, postponing the optimistic delivery brings an optimistic order that likely matches the final order, restricting the time for processing. In HiperTM we preferred this last configuration and we designed a lightweight protocol for maximizing the exploitation of this time.

3.2   The Protocol

Application threads (clients), after invoking a transaction using the *invoke* API, wait until the transaction is successfully processed by the replicated system and its outcome becomes available. Each client has a reference replica for issuing requests. When that replica becomes unreachable or a timeout expires after the request's submission, the reference replica is changed and the request is submitted to another replica.

Replicas know about the existence of a new transaction to process only after the transaction's *Odeliver*. The opt-order represents a possible, non definitive, serialization order for transactions. Only the series of *Adelivers* determines the final commit order. HiperTM overlaps the execution of optimistically delivered transactions with their co-ordination phase (i.e., defining the total order among all replicas) to avoid processing those transactions from scratch after their *Adeliver*. Clearly, the effectiveness of this approach depends on the likelihood that the opt-order is consistent with the final order. In the positive case, transactions are probably executed and there is no need for further execution. Conversely, if the final order contradicts the optimistic one, then the executed transactions can be in one of two scenarios: *i)* their serialization order is "equivalent" to the serialization order defined by the final order, or *ii)* the two serialization orders are not "equivalent". The notion of equivalence here is related to transactional conflicts: when two transactions are non-conflicting, their processing order is equivalent.

Consider four transactions. Suppose $\{T_1, T_2, T_3, T_4\}$ is their opt-order and $\{T_1, T_4, T_3, T_2\}$ is their final order. Assume that the transactions are completely executed when the respective *Adelivers* are issued. When $Adeliver(T_4)$ is triggered, T_4's optimistic order is different from its final order. However, if T_4 does not conflict with T_3 and T_2, then its serialization order, realized during execution, is equivalent to the final order, and the transaction can be committed without re-execution (case *i)*). On the contrary, if T_4 conflicts with T_3 and/or T_2, then T_4 must be aborted and restarted in order to ensure replica consistency (case *ii)*). If conflicting transactions are not committed in the same order on all replicas, then replicas could end up with different states of the shared data-set.

We use the speculative processing technique for executing optimistically (but not yet finally) delivered transactions. This approach has been proposed in [15] in the context of traditional DBMS. In addition to [15], we do not limit the number of speculative transactions executed in parallel with their coordination phase, and we do not assume a-priori knowledge on transactions' access patterns. Write transactions are processed serially, without parallel activation (see Section 3.3 for complete discussion). Even though this approach appears inconsistent with the nature of speculative processing, it has several benefits for in-order processing, which increase the likelihood that a transaction will reach its final stage before its *Adeliver* is issued.

In order to allow next conflicting transaction to process speculatively, we define a *complete buffer* for each shared object. In addition to the last committed version, shared objects also maintain a single memory slot (i.e., the complete buffer), which stores the version of the object written by the last completely executed optimistic transaction. We do not store multiple completed versions because, executing transactions serially needs only one uncommitted version per object. When an *Odelivered* transaction performs a read operation, it checks the complete buffer for the presence of a version. If the buffer is empty, the last committed version is considered; otherwise, the version in the complete buffer is accessed. When a write operation is executed, the complete buffer is immediately overwritten with the new version. This early publication of written data in memory is safe because of serial execution. In fact, there are no other write transactions that can access this version before the transaction's completion.

After executing all its operations, an optimistically delivered transaction waits until $Adeliver$ is received. In the meanwhile, the next $Odeliver$ed transaction starts to execute. When an $Adeliver$ is notified by OS-Paxos, a handler is executed by the same thread that is responsible for speculatively processing transactions. This approach avoids interleaving with transaction execution (which causes additional synchronization overhead). When a transaction is $Adeliver$ed, if it is completely executed, then it is validated for detecting the equivalence between its actual serialization order and the final order. The validation consists of comparing the versions read during the execution. If they correspond with the actual committed version of the objects accessed, then the transaction is valid, certifying that the serialization order is equivalent to the final order. If the versions do not match, the transaction is aborted and restarted. A transaction $Adeliver$ed and aborted during its validation can re-execute and commit without validation due to the advantage of having only one thread executing write transactions.

The commit of write transactions involves moving the written objects from transaction local buffer to the objects' last committed version. Although complete buffers can be managed without synchronization because only one writing transaction is active at a time, installing a new version as committed requires synchronization. Therefore, each object maintains also a list of previously committed versions. This is exploited by read-only transactions to execute independently from the write transactions.

Read-only transactions are marked by programmers and are not broadcast using OS-Paxos, because they do not need to be totally ordered. When a client invokes a read-only transaction, it is locally delivered and executed in parallel to write transactions by a separate pool of threads. In order to support this parallel processing, we define a timestamp for each replica, called *replica-timestamp*, which represents a monotonically increasing integer, incremented each time a write transaction commits. When a write transaction enters its commit phase, it assigns the replica-timestamp to a local variable, called *c-timestamp*, representing the committing timestamp, increases the c-timestamp, and tags the newly committed versions with this number. Finally, it updates the replica-timestamp with the c-timestamp.

When a read-only transaction performs its first operation, the replica-timestamp becomes the transaction's timestamp (or *r-timestamp*). Subsequent operations are processed according to the r-timestamp: when an object is accessed, its list of committed versions is traversed in order to find the most recent version with a timestamp lower or equal to the r-timestamp. After completing execution, a read-only transaction is committed without validation. The rationale for doing so is as follows. Suppose T_R is the committing read-only transaction and T_W is the parallel write transaction. T_R's r-timestamp allows T_R to be serialized a) after all the write transactions with a c-timestamp lower or equal to T_R's r-timestamp and b) before T_W's c-timestamp and all the write transactions committed after T_W. T_R's operations access versions consistent with T_R's r-timestamp. This subset of versions cannot change during T_R's execution, and therefore T_R can commit safely without validation.

Whenever a transaction commits, the thread managing the commit wakes-up the client that previously submitted the request and provides the appropriate response.

3.3 Speculative Concurrency Control

In HiperTM, each replica is equipped with a local speculative concurrency control, called SCC, for executing and committing transactions enforcing the order notified by OS-Paxos. In order to overlap the transaction coordination phase with transaction execution, write transactions are processed speculatively as soon as they are optimistically delivered. The main purpose of the SCC is to completely execute a transaction, according to the opt-order, before its $Adeliver$ is issued. As shown in Figure 1(b), the time available for this execution is limited.

Motivated by this observation, we designed SCC. SCC exploits multi-versioned memory for activating read-only transactions in parallel to write transactions that are, on the contrary, executed on a single thread. The reason for single-thread processing is to avoid the overhead for detecting and resolving conflicts according to the opt-order while transactions are executing. SCC is able to process $\approx$95K write transactions per second, in-order, while $\approx$250K read-only transactions are executing in parallel on different cores (Bank benchmark on experimental test-bed). This throughput is higher than HiperTM's total number of optimistically delivered transactions speculatively processed per second, illustrating the effectiveness of single-thread processing.

Single-thread processing ensures that when a transaction completes its execution, all the previous transactions are executed in a known order. Additionally, no atomic operations are needed for managing locks or critical sections. As a result, write transactions are processed faster and read-only transactions (executed in parallel) do not suffer from otherwise overloaded hardware bus (due to CAS operations and cache invalidations caused by spinning on locks).

Transactions log the return values of their read operations and written versions in private read- and write-set, respectively. The write-set is used when a transaction is $Adeliver$ed for committing its written versions in memory. However, for each object, there is only one uncommitted version available in memory at a time, and it corresponds to the version written by the last optimistically delivered and executed transaction. If more than one speculative transaction wrote to the same object, both are logged in their write-sets, but only the last one is stored in memory in the object's complete buffer. We do not need to record a list of speculative versions, because transactions are processed serially and only the last can be accessed by the current executing transaction.

The read-set is used for validation. Validation is performed by simply verifying that all the objects accessed correspond to the last committed versions in memory. When the optimistic order matches the final order, validation is redundant, because serially executing write transactions ensures that all the objects accessed are the last committed versions in memory. Conversely, if an out-of-order occurs, validation detects the wrong speculative serialization order.

Consider three transactions, and let $\{T_1, T_2, T_3\}$ be their opt-order and $\{T_2, T_1, T_3\}$ be their final order. Let T_1 and T_2 write a new version of object X and let T_3 reads

```
upon Read(Transaction Ti, Object X) do          upon Write(Transaction Ti, Object X, Value v) do
  if (Ti.readOnly == FALSE)                        Version Vx = createNewVersion(X,v);
    if (∃ version ∈ X.completeBuffer                X.completeBuffer = Vx;
      Ti.ReadSet.add(X.completeBuffer);             Ti.WriteSet.add(Vx);
      return X.completeBuffer.value;              upon Commit(Transaction Ti) do
    else                                            if (Validation(Ti) == FALSE)
      Ti.ReadSet.add(X.lastCommittedVersion);         return Ti.abort&restart();
      return X.lastCommittedVersion.value;          c-timesamp = replica-timestamp;
  else                                              c-timesamp++;
    if (r-timestamp == 0)                           ∀ Vx ∈ Ti.WriteSet do
      r-timestamp = X.lastCommittedVersion.timestamp;   Vx.timestamp = c-timestamp;
      return X.lastCommittedVersion.value;            X.lastCommittedVersion = Vx;
    P= {all versions V ∈ X.committedVersions s.t.    replica-timestamp = c-timesamp;
      V.timestamp ≤ r-timestamp}                   boolean Validation(Transaction Ti)
    if (∃ version Vcx ∈ P)                           ∀ Vx ∈ Ti.ReadSet do
      Vcx = maximum-timestamp(P)                       if (Vx ≠ X.lastCommittedVersion)
      return Vcx.value;                                  return FALSE;
    else                                              return TRUE;
      return X.lastCommittedVersion.value;
```

Fig. 2. SCC's pseudo code

X. When T_3 is speculatively executed, it accesses the version generated by T_2. But this version does not correspond to the last committed version of X when T_3 is *Adelivered*. Even though T_3's optimistic and final orders are the same, it must be validated to detect the wrong read version. When a transaction T_A is aborted, we do not abort transactions that read from T_A (cascading abort), because doing so will entail tracking transaction dependencies, which has a non-trivial overhead. Moreover, a restarted transaction is still executed on the same processing thread. That is equivalent to SCC's behavior, which aborts and restarts a transaction when its commit validation fails.

A task queue is responsible for scheduling jobs executed by the main thread (processing write transactions). Whenever an event such as *Odeliver* or *Adeliver* occurs, a new task is appended to the queue and is executed by the thread after the completion of the previous tasks. This allows the events' handlers to execute in parallel without slowing down the executor thread, which is the SCC's performance-critical path.

As mentioned, read-only transactions are processed in parallel to write transactions, exploiting the list of committed versions available for each object to build a consistent serialization order. The growing core count of current and emerging multicore architectures allows such transactions to execute on different cores, without interfering with the write transactions. One synchronization point is present between write and read transactions, i.e., the list of committed versions is updated when a transaction commits. In order to minimize its impact on performance, we use a concurrent sorted Skip-List for storing the committed versions.

The pseudo code of SCC is shown in Figure 2. We show the core steps of the concurrency control protocol such as reading/writing a shared object and validating/committing a write transaction.

3.4 Properties

HiperTM ensures 1-copy serializability, opacity, lock-freedom and abort-freedom for read-only transactions. We avoid formal proofs due to space constraints, but sketch the basic arguments as follows:

Opacity [11]. A protocol ensures opacity if it guarantees three properties: (Op.1) committed transactions appear as if they are executed serially, in an order equivalent to their real-time order; (Op.2) no transaction accesses a snapshot generated by a live (i.e., still executing) or aborted transaction; and (Op.3) all live and aborted transactions observe a consistent system state.

HiperTM ensures opacity for each replica. It satisfies (Op.1) because each write transaction is validated before commit, in order to certify that its serialization order is equivalent to the optimistic atomic broadcast order, which reflects the order of the client's requests. Read-only transactions perform their operations according to the r-timestamp recorded from the replica-timestamp before their first read. They access only the committed versions written by transactions with the highest c-timestamp lower or equal to the r-timestamp. Read-only transactions with the same r-timestamp have the same serialization order with respect to write transactions. Conversely, if they have different r-timestamps, then they access only objects committed by transactions serialized before. (Op.2) is guaranteed for write transactions because they are executed serially in the same thread. Therefore, a transaction cannot start if the previous one has not completed, preventing it from accessing modifications made by non-completed transactions. Under SCC, optimistically delivered transactions can access objects written by previous optimistically (and not yet finally) delivered transactions. However, due to serial execution, transactions cannot access objects written by non-completed transactions. (Op.2) is also ensured for read-only transactions because they only access committed versions. (Op.3) is guaranteed by serial execution, which prevents concurrent accesses to same objects. When a transaction is aborted, it is only because its serialization order is not equivalent to the final delivery order (due to network reordering). However, that serialization order has been realized by a serial execution. Therefore, the transaction's observed state of objects is always consistent.

1-Copy Serializability [2]. 1-copy serializability is guaranteed because each replica commits the same set of write transactions in the same order notified by the optimistic atomic broadcast layer. Read-only transactions activated on different nodes cannot observe any two write transactions that are serialized differently on those nodes.

Lock-freedom [10]. Lock-freedom guarantees that there always exists at least one thread that makes progress, which rules out deadlocks and livelocks. In HiperTM, this is a direct consequence of the fact that transactions aborted due to unsuccessful validation and already *Adelivered* can restart their execution and cannot be aborted anymore due to serial execution and its highest priority for subsequent commit.

Abort-freedom of Read-Only Transactions. Before issuing the first operation, read-only transactions save the replica-timestamp in their local r-timestamp and use it for selecting the proper committed versions to read. The subset of all the versions that read-only transactions can access during their execution is fixed when the transactions define their r-timestamp. Only one write transaction is executing when a read-only transaction acquires the r-timestamp. If this write transaction updates the replica-timestamp before the other acquires the r-timestamp, the read-only transaction is serialized after the write transaction, but before the next write transaction eventually commits. On the contrary, if the replica-timestamp's update happens after, the read-only transaction is serialized before the write transaction and cannot access the write transaction's just committed objects. In both cases, the subset of versions that the read-only transaction can access is defined and cannot change due to future commits. For this reason, when a read-only transaction completes its execution, it returns the values to its client without validation.

4   Implementation and Evaluation

HiperTM's architecture consists of two layers: network layer (OS-Paxos) and replica concurrency control (SCC). We implemented both in Java: OS-Paxos as an extension of S-Paxos, and SCC from scratch. To evaluate performance, we used two benchmarks: Bank and TPC-C. Bank emulates a bank application and is typically used in TM works for benchmarking performance [16,25,6]. TPC-C [5] is a well known benchmark that is representative of on-line transaction processing workloads.

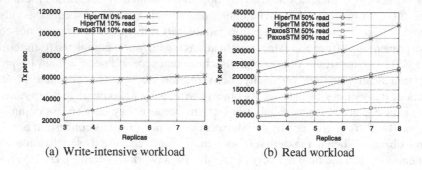

(a) Write-intensive workload   (b) Read workload

Fig. 3. Performance of HiperTM and PaxosSTM for the Bank benchmark

We used PaxosSTM [16] and SCORe [25] as competitors. PaxosSTM implements the deferred update replication scheme and relies on a non-blocking transaction certification protocol, which is based on atomic broadcast (provided by JPaxos). SCORe is a partial replication-based DTM protocol (in contrast to HiperTMs state machine-based replication, which yields full failure-masking). SCORe is designed to scale up to hundred nodes with a replication degree of two. Both represent state-of-the-art DTM.

Our test-bed consists of 8 nodes interconnected using a 1Gb/s switched network. Four of the nodes are 64-core AMD Opteron machines (128GB RAM, 2.3 GHz), while the other four are 48-core AMD Opteron (32GB RAM, 1.7 GHz). For each benchmark, we varied the percentage of read-only transactions to cover all configuration settings. Clients are balanced on all the replicas. They inject transactions for the benchmark and wait for the reply. A pool of 20 threads are deployed for serving read-only transactions. Data points plotted are the average of 10 repeated experiments.

Figure 4 shows the throughput of the Bank benchmark[1]. Figure 3(a) shows results for 0% read and 10% read, and Figure 3(b) shows results for read-intensive workloads (50% and 90% read). HiperTM OS-Paxos sustains its throughput in all configurations, achieving almost constant throughput for write-only transactions with increasing replica

---

[1] Results of PaxosSTM that we used are also available in [16].

count. Interestingly, with 3 replicas, HiperTM's write-only transaction throughput out-performs PaxosSTM's throughput for 10% of read-only transactions. This speed-up is directly due to HiperTM's speculative processing of write transactions, which allows SCC to commit most of the transactions when they are *Adeliver*ed.

Performance as well as system scalability significantly increases when read-only transactions are varied from 10% to 90%. This is mainly because, read-only transactions can execute locally without involving OS-Paxos and other nodes for computation. The maximum throughput observed is ≈400K transactions processed per second in the entire system, with a maximum speed-up of ≈1.2× over PaxosSTM.

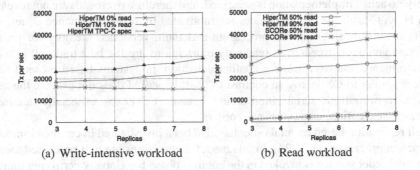

(a) Write-intensive workload   (b) Read workload

Fig. 4. Performance of HiperTM and SCORe for the TPC-C benchmark

Figure 4 compares HiperTM's performance with SCORe [25][2]. In these experiments, we ran TPC-C with the same configuration as Bank, and also with the configuration suggested by the TPC-C specification (SCORe's results are not available for all configurations). TPC-C's average transaction execution time is much higher than Bank's, due to the nature of its transactions, impacting overall throughput. However, HiperTM is still able to overlap transaction execution with coordination for committing a transaction when its *Adeliver* arrives. HiperTM outperforms SCORe with 8 replicas by up to 10×. Its effectiveness is particularly evident here, as SCORe pays the cost for looking-up remotely accessed objects, unlike HiperTM, which executes locally.

We also measured the impact of the leader's failure on transactional throughput with the TPC-C benchmark. Due to space constraints, we skip plots, but summarize the key trend: we observed a maximum degradation of ≈30% after the crash. This is because, clients directly connected to the leader's replica need time to detect the failure and reroute their connections (for write and read transactions) to other replicas. After this time window, the performance returns to a stable state.

5 Related Work

Replication in transactional systems has been widely explored in the context of DBMS, including protocol specifications [14] and infrastructural solutions [29,21,22].

---

[2] SCORe's results are available in [25].

In [1,13], two active replication techniques are presented. Both rely on atomic broadcast for ordering transaction requests, and execute them only when the final order is notified. In contrast HiperTM, based on optimistic atomic broadcast, begins to process transactions before their final delivery, i.e., when they are optimistically delivered.

Speculative processing of transactions has been originally presented in [15] and further investigated in [19,20]. [19] presents AGGRO, a speculative concurrency control protocol, which processes transactions in-order, in actively replicated transactional systems. In AGGRO, for each read operation, the transaction identifies the following transactions according to the opt-order, and for each one, it traverses the transactions' write-set to retrieve the correct version to read. The authors only present the protocol in [19]; no actual implementation is presented, and therefore overheads are not revealed.

In HiperTM, all the design choices are motivated by real performance issues. Our results show how single-thread processing and multi-versioned memory for parallel activation and abort-freedom of read-only transactions are the best trade-off in terms of performance and overhead for conflict detection, in systems based on total order services similar to OS-Paxos. In contrast to [20], HiperTM does not execute the same transaction in multiple serialization orders, because OS-Paxos, especially in case of failure-free execution, guarantees no-reorders.

Full replication based on total order has also been investigated in certification-based transaction processing [16,4,24]. In this model, transactions are first processed locally, and a total order service is invoked in the commit phase for globally certifying transaction execution (by broadcasting their read and write-sets). [4] is based on OAB and [24] is based on AB. Both suffer from (O)AB's scalability bottleneck when message size increases. In HiperTM, the length of messages does not depend on transaction operations; it is only limited by the signature of invoked transactions along with their parameters.

Granola [6] is a replication protocol based on a single round of communication. Granola's concurrency control technique uses single-thread processing for avoiding synchronization overhead, and has a structure for scheduling jobs similar to SCC.

6   Conclusions

At its core, our work shows that optimism pays off: speculative transaction execution, started as soon as transactions are optimistically delivered, allows hiding the total ordering latency, and yields performance gain. Single-communication step is mandatory for fine-grain transactions. Complex concurrency control algorithms are sometimes not feasible when the available processing time is limited.

Implementation matters. Avoiding atomic operations, batching messages, and optimizations to counter network non-determinism are important for high performance.

Acknowledgement. The authors would like to thank the authors of S-Paxos [3], PaxosSTM [16], and SCORe [25] for their willingness to share source codes.

This work is supported in part by US National Science Foundation under grants CNS 0915895, CNS 1116190, CNS 1130180, and CNS 1217385.

References

1. Agrawal, D., Alonso, G., Abbadi, A.E., Stanoi, I.: Exploiting atomic broadcast in replicated databases (extended abstract). In: Lengauer, C., Griebl, M., Gorlatch, S. (eds.) Euro-Par 1997. LNCS, vol. 1300, pp. 496–503. Springer, Heidelberg (1997)
2. Bernstein, P.A., Hadzilacos, V., Goodman, N.: Concurrency Control and Recovery in Database Systems. Addison-Wesley (1987)
3. Biely, M., Milosevic, Z., Santos, N., Schiper, A.: S-Paxos: Offloading the Leader for High Throughput State Machine Replication. In: SRDS (2012)
4. Carvalho, N., Romano, P., Rodrigues, L.: Scert: Speculative certification in replicated software transactional memories. In: SYSTOR (2011)
5. T. Council. TPC-C benchmark (2010)
6. Cowling, J., Liskov, B.: Granola: Low-overhead distributed transaction coordination. In: USENIX Annual Technical Conference (2012)
7. Defago, X., Schiper, A., Urban, P.: Total order broadcast and multicast algorithms: Taxonomy and survey. ACM Computing Surveys 36(4) (2004)
8. Dice, D., Shalev, O., Shavit, N.: Transactional locking II. In: Dolev, S. (ed.) DISC 2006. LNCS, vol. 4167, pp. 194–208. Springer, Heidelberg (2006)
9. Dragojevic, A., Guerraoui, R., Kapalka, M.: Stretching transactional memory. In: PLDI (2009)
10. Fraser, K.: Practical lock freedom. PhD thesis. Cambridge Univ. Computer Laboratory (2003)
11. Guerraoui, R., Kapalka, M.: On the correctness of transactional memory. In: PPOPP (2008)
12. Guerraoui, R., Rodrigues, L.: Introduction to Reliable Distributed Programming (2006)
13. Jiménez-Peris, R., Patiño-Martínez, M., Arévalo, S.: Deterministic scheduling for transactional multithreaded replicas. In: SRDS (2000)
14. Kemme, B., Alonso, G.: Don't be lazy, be consistent: Postgres-R, a new way to implement database replication. In: VLDB (2000)
15. Kemme, B., Pedone, F., Alonso, G., Schiper, A., Wiesmann, M.: Using optimistic atomic broadcast in transaction processing systems. IEEE TKDE 15(4) (2003)
16. Kobus, T., Kokocinski, T., Wojciechowski, P.: Practical considerations of distributed STM systems development (abstract). In: WDTM (2012)
17. Kończak, J., Santos, N., Żurkowski, T., Wojciechowski, P.T., Schiper, A.: JPaxos: State machine replication based on the Paxos protocol. Technical report, EPFL (2011)
18. Lamport, L.: The part-time parliament. ACM Trans. Comput. Syst., 133–169 (1998)
19. Palmieri, R., Quaglia, F., Romano, P.: AGGRO: Boosting STM replication via aggressively optimistic transaction processing. In: NCA (2010)
20. Palmieri, R., Quaglia, F., Romano, P.: OSARE: Opportunistic speculation in actively replicated transactional systems. In: SRDS (2011)
21. Patino-Martinez, M., Jiménez-Peris, R., Kemme, B., Alonso, G.: MIDDLE-R: Consistent database replication at the middleware level. ACM Trans. Comput. Syst. 23(4) (2005)
22. Pedone, F., Frølund, S.: Pronto: High availability for standard off-the-shelf databases. J. Parallel Distrib. Comput. 68(2) (2008)
23. Pedone, F., Schiper, A.: Optimistic atomic broadcast. In: Kutten, S. (ed.) DISC 1998. LNCS, vol. 1499, pp. 318–332. Springer, Heidelberg (1998)
24. Peluso, S., Fernandes, J., Romano, P., Quaglia, F., Rodrigues, L.: SPECULA: Speculative replication of software transactional memory. In: SRDS (2012)
25. Peluso, S., Romano, P., Quaglia, F.: SCORe: A scalable one-copy serializable partial replication protocol. In: Narasimhan, P., Triantafillou, P. (eds.) Middleware 2012. LNCS, vol. 7662, pp. 456–475. Springer, Heidelberg (2012)

26. Santos, N., Schiper, A.: Tuning paxos for high-throughput with batching and pipelining. In: Bononi, L., Datta, A.K., Devismes, S., Misra, A. (eds.) ICDCN 2012. LNCS, vol. 7129, pp. 153–167. Springer, Heidelberg (2012)
27. Schiper, N., Sutra, P., Pedone, F.: P-store:genuine partial replication in WAN. In: SRDS (2010)
28. Schneider, F.B.: Replication management using the state-machine approach. ACM Press/Addison-Wesley Publishing Co. (1993)
29. Peluso, S., Palmieri, R., Quaglia, F., Ravindran, B.: On the viability of speculative transactional replication in database systems: a case study with PostgreSQL. In: NCA (2013)
30. Shavit, N., Touitou, D.: Software transactional memory. In: PODC (1995)

Non-interference and Local Correctness in Transactional Memory

Petr Kuznetsov[1] and Sathya Peri[2]

[1] Télécom ParisTech
petr.kuznetsov@telecom-paristech.fr
[2] IIT Patna
sathya@iitp.ac.in

Abstract. Transactional memory promises to make concurrent programming tractable and efficient by allowing the user to assemble sequences of actions in atomic *transactions* with all-or-nothing semantics. It is believed that, by its very virtue, transactional memory must ensure that all *committed* transactions constitute a serial execution respecting the real-time order. In contrast, aborted or incomplete transactions should not "take effect." But what does "not taking effect" mean exactly?

It seems natural to expect that aborted or incomplete transactions do not appear in the global serial execution, and, thus, no committed transaction can be affected by them. We investigate another, less obvious, feature of "not taking effect" called *non-interference*: aborted or incomplete transactions should not force any other transaction to abort. In the strongest form of non-interference that we explore in this paper, by removing a subset of aborted or incomplete transactions from the history, we should not be able to turn an aborted transaction into a committed one without violating the correctness criterion.

We show that non-interference is, in a strict sense, not *implementable* with respect to the popular criterion of opacity that requires *all* transactions (be they committed, aborted or incomplete) to witness the same global serial execution. In contrast, when we only require *local* correctness, non-interference is implementable. Informally, a correctness criterion is local if it only requires that every transaction can be serialized along with (a subset of) the transactions committed before its last event (aborted or incomplete transactions ignored). We give a few examples of local correctness properties, including the recently proposed criterion of virtual world consistency, and present a simple though efficient implementation that satisfies non-interference and *local opacity*.

1 Introduction

Transactional memory (TM) promises to make concurrent programming efficient and tractable. The programmer simply represents a sequence of instructions that should appear atomic as a speculative *transaction* that may either *commit* or *abort*. It is usually expected that a TM *serializes* all committed transactions, i.e., makes them appear as in some sequential execution. An implication of this requirement is that no committed transaction can read values written by a transaction that is aborted or might abort in the future. Intuitively, this is a desirable

M. Chatterjee et al. (Eds.): ICDCN 2014, LNCS 8314, pp. 197–211, 2014.

property because it does not allow a write performed within a transaction to get "visible" as long as there is a chance for the transaction to abort.

But is this all we can do if we do not want aborted or incomplete transactions to "take effect"? We observe that there is a more subtle side of the "taking effect" phenomenon that is usually not taken into consideration. An incomplete or aborted transaction may cause another transaction to abort. Suppose we have an execution in which an aborted transaction T cannot be committed without violating correctness of the execution, but if we remove some incomplete or aborted transactions, then T can be committed. This property, originally highlighted in [15, 16], is called *non-interference*.

Thus, ideally, a TM must "insulate" transactions that are aborted or might abort in the future from producing any effect, either by affecting reads of other transactions or by provoking forceful aborts.

Defining non-interference. Consider non-interference as a characteristics of an *implementation*. A TM implementation M is non-interfering if removing an aborted or incomplete *not concurrently committing* transaction from a *history* (a sequence of events on the TM interface) of M would still result in a history in M. We observe that many existing TM implementations that employ *commit-time* lock acquisition or version update (e.g., RingSTM [17], NOrec [3]) are non-interfering in this sense. In contrast, some *encounter-time* implementations, such as TinySTM [5], are not non-interfering.

This paper rather focuses on non-interference as a characteristics of a *correctness criterion*, which results in a much stronger restriction on implementations. We intend to understand whether this strong notion of non-interference is achievable and at what cost, which we believe is a challenging theoretical question. For a given correctness criterion C, a TM implementation M is C-non-interfering if removing an aborted or incomplete transaction from any history of M does not allow committing another aborted transaction while still preserving C. We observe that C-non-interference produces a subset of *permissive* [6] with respect to C histories. This is not difficult to see if we recall that in a permissive (with respect to C) history, no aborted transaction can be turned into a committed one while still satisfying C.

In particular, when we focus on *opaque* histories [7, 8], we observe that non-interference gives a *strict* subset of permissive opaque histories. Opacity requires that all transactions (be they committed, aborted, or incomplete) constitute a consistent sequential execution in which every read returns the latest committed written value. This is a strong requirement, because it expects every transaction (even aborted or incomplete) to witness the same sequential execution. Indeed, there exist permissive opaque histories that do not provide non-interference: some aborted transactions force other transactions to abort.

For example, consider the history in Figure 1. Here the very fact that the incomplete operation T_2 read the "new" (written by T_3) value in object x and the "old" (initial) value in object y prevents an updating transaction T_1 from committing. Suppose that T_1 commits. Then T_2 can only be *serialized* (put in the global sequential order) after T_3 and before T_1, while T_1 can only be serialized

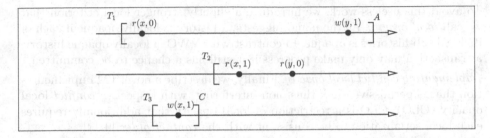

Fig. 1. An opaque-permissive opaque but not opaque-non-interfering history: T_2 forces T_1 to abort

before T_3. Thus, we obtain a cycle which prevents any serialization. Therefore, the history does not provide opaque-non-interference: by removing T_2 we can commit T_1 by still allowing a correct serialization T_1, T_3. But the history is permissive with respect to opacity: no transaction aborts without a reason!

This example can be used to show that opaque-non-interference is, in a strict sense, *non-implementable*. Every opaque permissive implementation that guarantees that every transactional operation (*read*, *write*, *tryCommit* or *tryAbort*) completes if it runs in the absence of concurrency (note that it can complete with an *abort* response), may be brought to the scenario above, where the only option for T_1 in its last event is *abort*.

Local correctness. But are there relaxed definitions of TM correctness that allow for non-interfering implementations? Intuitively, the problem with the history in Figure 1 is that T_2 should be consistent with a global order of *all* transactions. But what if we only expect every transaction T to be consistent *locally*, i.e., to fit to *some* serialization composed of the transactions that committed before T terminates? This way a transaction does not have to account for transactions that are aborted or incomplete at the moment it completes and local serializations for different transactions do not have to be mutually consistent.

For example, the history in Figure 1, assuming that T_1 commits, is still *locally* opaque: the local serialization of T_2 would simply be $T_3 \cdot T_2$, while T_1 (assuming it commits) and T_3 would both be consistent with the serialization $T_1 \cdot T_3$.

In this paper, we introduce the notion of *local correctness*. A history satisfies a local correctness property C if and only if all its "local sub-histories" satisfy C. Here a local sub-history corresponding to T_i consists of the events from all transactions that committed before the last event of T_i (transactions that are incomplete or aborted at that moment are ignored) and: (1) if T_i is committed then all its events; (2) if T_i is aborted then all its read operations. We show that every implementation that is permissive with respect to a local correctness criterion C is also C-non-interfering.

Virtual world consistency [10], that expects the history to be strictly serializable and every transaction to be consistent with its causal past, is one example of a local correctness property. We observe, however, that virtual world consistency may allow a transaction to proceed even if it has no chances to commit.

To avoid this useless work, we introduce a slightly stronger local criterion that we call *local opacity*. As the name suggests, a history is locally opaque if each of its local sub-histories is opaque. In contrast with VWC, a locally opaque history, a transaction may only make progress if it still has a chance to be committed.

Implementing conflict local opacity. Finally, we describe a novel TM implementation that is permissive (and, thus, non-interfering) with respect to *conflict* local opacity (CLO). CLO is a restriction of local opacity that additionally requires each local serialization to be consistent with the *conflict order* [9, 14].

Our implementation is interesting in its own right for the following reasons. First, it ensures non-interference, i.e., no transaction has any effect on other transactions before committing. Second, it only requires polynomial (in the number of concurrent transactions) local computation for each transaction. Indeed, there are indications that, in general, building a permissive strictly serializable TM may incur non-polynomial time [14].

The full paper is available as a technical report [12]. Future work includes focusing on an arguably more practical notion of non-interference as an implementation property, in particular, on the inherent costs of implementing non-interference.

Roadmap. The paper is organized as follows. We describe our system model in Section 2. In Section 3 we formally define the notion of C-non-interference, recall the definition of permissiveness, and relate the two. In Section 4, we introduce the notion of local correctness, show that any permissive implementation of a local correctness criterion is also permissive, and define the criterion of conflict local opacity (CLO). In Section 5 present our CLO-non-interfering implementation. Section 6 concludes the paper with remarks on the related work and open questions.

2   Preliminaries

We assume a system of n processes, $p_1, \ldots, p_n$ that access a collection of *objects* via atomic *transactions*. The processes are provided with four *transactional operations*: the *write*(x, v) operation that updates object x with value v, the *read*(x) operation that returns a value read in x, *tryC*$()$ that tries to commit the transaction and returns *commit* (c for short) or *abort* (a for short), and *tryA*$()$ that aborts the transaction and returns A. The objects accessed by the read and write operations are called as t-objects. For the sake of presentation simplicity, we assume that the values written by all the transactions are unique.

Operations *write*, *read* and *tryC*$()$ may return a, in which case we say that the operations *forcefully abort*. Otherwise, we say that the operation has *successfully* executed. Each operation specifies a unique transaction identifier. A transaction T_i starts with the first operation and completes when any of its operations returns a or c. Abort and commit operations are called *terminal operations*. For a transaction T_k, we denote all its read operations as $Rset(T_k)$ and write operations $Wset(T_k)$. Collectively, we denote all the operations of a transaction T_i as $evts(T_k)$.

Histories. A *history* is a sequence of *events*, i.e., a sequence of invocation-response pairs of transactional operations. The collection of events is denoted as $evts(H)$. For simplicity, we only consider *sequential* histories here: the invocation of each transactional operation is immediately followed by a matching response. Therefore, we treat each transactional operation as one atomic event, and let $<_H$ denote the total order on the transactional operations incurred by H. With this assumption the only relevant events of a transaction T_k are of the types: $r_k(x,v)$, $r_k(x,A)$, $w_k(x,v)$, $w_k(x,v,A)$, $tryC_k(C)$ (or c_k for short), $tryC_k(A)$, $tryA_k(A)$ (or a_k for short). We identify a history H as tuple $\langle evts(H), <_H \rangle$.

Let $H|T$ denote the history consisting of events of T in H, and $H|p_i$ denote the history consisting of events of p_i in H. We only consider *well-formed* histories here, i.e., (1) each $H|T$ consists of a read-only prefix (consisting of read operations only), followed by a write-only part (consisting of write operations only), possibly *completed* with a $tryC$ or $tryA$ operation[1], and (2) each $H|p_i$ consists of a sequence of transactions, where no new transaction begins before the last transaction completes (commits or aborts).

We assume that every history has an initial committed transaction T_0 that initializes all the data-objects with 0. The set of transactions that appear in H is denoted by $txns(H)$. The set of committed (resp., aborted) transactions in H is denoted by $committed(H)$ (resp., $aborted(H)$). The set of *incomplete* transactions in H is denoted by $incomplete(H)$ ($incomplete(H) = txns(H) - committed(H) - aborted(H)$).

For a history H, we construct the *completion* of H, denoted $\overline{H}$, by inserting a_k immediately after the last event of every transaction $T_k \in incomplete(H)$.

Transaction orders. For two transactions $T_k, T_m \in txns(H)$, we say that T_k *precedes* T_m in the *real-time order* of H, denote $T_k \prec_H^{RT} T_m$, if T_k is complete in H and the last event of T_k precedes the first event of T_m in H. If neither $T_k \prec_H^{RT} T_m$ nor $T_m \prec_H^{RT} T_k$, then T_k and T_m *overlap* in H. A history H is *t-sequential* if there are no overlapping transactions in H, i.e., every two transactions are related by the real-time order.

Sub-histories. A *sub-history*, SH of a history H denoted as the tuple $\langle evts(SH),$ $<_{SH} \rangle$ and is defined as: (1) $<_{SH} \subseteq <_H$; (2) $evts(SH) \subseteq evts(H)$; (3) If an event of a transaction $T_k \in txns(H)$ is in SH then all the events of T_k in H should also be in SH. (Recall that $<_H$ denotes the total order of events in H.) For a history H, let R be a subset of $txns(H)$, the transactions in H. Then $H.subhist(R)$ denotes the sub-history of H that is formed from the operations in R.

Valid and legal histories. Let H be a history and $r_k(x,v)$ be a read operation in H. A successful read $r_k(x,v)$ (i.e., $v \neq A$), is said to be *valid* if there is a transaction T_j in H that commits before r_K and $w_j(x,v)$ is in $evts(T_j)$. Formally, $\langle r_k(x,v)$ is valid $\Rightarrow \exists T_j : (c_j <_H r_k(x,v)) \wedge (w_j(x,v) \in evts(T_j)) \wedge (v \neq A) \rangle$. The history H is valid if all its successful read operations are valid.

We define $r_k(x,v)$'s *lastWrite* to be the latest commit event c_i such that c_i precedes $r_k(x,v)$ in H and $x \in Wset(T_i)$ (T_i can also be T_0). A successful

---

[1] This restriction brings no loss of generality [13].

read operation $r_k(x, v)$ (i.e., $v \neq A$), is said to be *legal* if transaction T_i (which contains r_k's lastWrite) also writes v onto x. Formally, $\langle r_k(x, v)$ is legal $\Rightarrow (v \neq A) \wedge (H.lastWrite(r_k(x, v)) = c_i) \wedge (w_i(x, v) \in evts(T_i))\rangle$. The history H is legal if all its successful read operations are legal. Thus from the definitions we get that if H is legal then it is also valid.

Strict Serializability and Opacity. We say that two histories H and H' are *equivalent* if they have the same set of events. Now a history H is said to be *opaque* [7,8] if H is valid and there exists a t-sequential legal history S such that (1) S is equivalent to $\overline{H}$ and (2) S respects $\prec_H^{RT}$, i.e., $\prec_H^{RT} \subset \prec_S^{RT}$. By requiring S being equivalent to $\overline{H}$, opacity treats all the incomplete transactions as aborted.

Along the same lines, a valid history H is said to be *strictly serializable* if $H.subhist(committed(H))$ is opaque. Thus, unlike opacity, strict serializability does not include aborted transactions in the global serialization order.

3 P-Non-interference

A *correctness criterion* is a set of histories. In this section, we recall the notion of permisiveness [6] and then we formally define non-interference. First, we define a few auxiliary notions.

For a transaction T_i in H, *applicable* events of T_i or $applicable(T_i)$ denotes: (1) all the events of T_i, if it is committed; (2) if T_i is aborted then all the read operations of T_i. Thus, if T_i is an aborted transaction ending with $tryC_i(A)$ (and not $r_i(x, A)$ for some x), then the final $tryC_i(A)$ is not included in $applicable(T_i)$.

We denote, H^{T_i} as the shortest prefix of H containing all the events of T_i in H. Now for $T_i \in aborted(H)$, let $\mathcal{H}^{T_i, C}$ denote the set of histories constructed from H^{T_i}, where the last operation of T_i in H is replaced with (1) $r_i(x, v)$ for some value non-abort value v, if the last operation is $r_i(x, A)$, (2) $w_i(x, v, A)$, if the last operation is $w_i(x, v, A)$, (3) $tryC_i(C)$, if the last operation is $tryC_i(A)$.

If R is a subset of transactions of $txns(H)$, then H_{-R} denotes the sub-history obtained after removing all the events of R from H. Respectively, $\mathcal{H}^{T_i, C}_{-R}$ denotes the set of histories in $\mathcal{H}^{T_i, C}$ with all the events of transaction in R removed.

Definition 1. *Given a correctness criterion P, we say that a history H is P-permissive, and we write $H \in Perm(P)$ if:*

(1) $H \in P$;
(2) $\forall T \in aborted(H), \forall H' \in \mathcal{H}^{T,C}: H' \notin P$.

From this definition we can see that a history H is permissive w.r.t. P, if no aborted transaction in H can be turned into committed, while preserving P.

The notion of non-interference or $NI(P)$ is defined in a similar manner as a set of histories parameterized by a property P. For a transaction T in $txns(H)$, $IncAbort(T, H)$ denotes the set of transactions that have (1) either aborted before T's terminal operation or (2) are incomplete when T aborted. Hence, for any T, $IncAbort(T, H)$ is a subset of $aborted(H) \cup incomplete(H)$.

Definition 2. *Given a correctness criterion P, we say that a history H is P-non-interfering, and we write $H \in NI(P)$ if:*

(1) $H \in P$;
(2) $\forall T \in aborted(H)$, $R \subseteq IncAbort(T, H)$, $\forall H' \in \mathcal{H}_{-R}^{T,C} : H' \notin P$.

Informally, non-interference states that none of transactions that aborted prior to or are live at the moment when T aborts caused T to abort: removing any subset of these transactions from the history does not help t to commit. By considering the special case $R = \emptyset$ in Definition 2, we obtain Definition 1, and, thus:

Observation 1. *For every correctness criterion P, $NI(P) \subseteq Perm(P)$.*

The example in Figure 1 (Section 1) shows that $NI(opacity) \neq Perm(opacity)$ and, thus, no implementation of opacity can satisfy non-interference. This motivated us to define a new correctness criterion, a relaxation of opacity, which satisfies non-interference.

4   Local Correctness and Non-interference

Intuitively, a correctness criterion is local if is enough to ensure that, for every transaction, the corresponding *local sub-history* is correct. One feature of any local property P is that any P-permissive implementation is also P-non-interfering.

Formally, for T_i in $txns(H)$, let $subC(H, T_i)$ denote

$$H^{T_i}.subhist(committed(H^{T_i}) \cup \{applicable(T_i)\}),$$

i.e., the sub-history of H^{T_i} consisting of the events of all committed transactions in H^{T_i} and all the applicable events of T_i. We call it local sub-history of T_i in H. Note that here we are considering applicable events of T_i. So if T_i is committed, all its events are considered. But if T_i is an aborted transaction ending with $tryC(A)$ (or $r_i(x, A)$), then only its read operations are considered.

Definition 3. *A correctness criterion P is local if for all histories H:*

$H \in P$ *if and only if , for all $T_i \in txns(H)$, $subC(H, T_i) \in P$.*

As we show in this section, one example of a local property is virtual world consistency [10]. Then we will introduce another local property that we call conflict local opacity (*CLO*), in the next section and describe a simple permissive *CLO* implementation.

Theorem 2. *For every local correctness property P, $Perm(P) \subseteq NI(P)$.*

As we observed earlier, for any correctness criterion P, $NI(P) \subseteq Perm(P)$. Hence, Theorem 2 implies that for any local correctness criterion P $NI(P) = Perm(P)$.

4.1 Virtual World Consistency

The correctness criterion of *virtual world consistency* (VWC) [10] relaxes opacity by allowing aborted transactions to be only consistent with its local *causal* past. More precisely, we say that T_i *causally precedes* T_j in a history H, and we write $T_i \prec_H^{CP} T_j$ if one of the following conditions hold (1) T_i and T_j are executed by the same process and $T_i \prec_H^{RT} T_j$, (2) T_i commits and T_j reads the value written by T_i to some object $x \in Wset(T_i) \cap Rset(T_j)$ (recall that we assumed for simplicity that all written values are unique), or (3) there exists T_k, such that $T_i \prec_H^{CP} T_k$ and $T_k \prec_H^{CP} T_j$. The set of transactions T_i such that $T_i \prec_H^{CP} T_j$ and T_j itself is called the *causal past* of T_j, denoted $CP(T_j)$.

Now H is in VWC if (1) $H.subhist(committed)$ is opaque and (2) for every $T_i \in txns(H)$, $H.subhist(CP(T_i))$ is opaque. Informally, H must be strictly serializable and the causal past of every transaction in H must constitute an opaque history.

It is easy to see that $H \in VWC$ if and only if for all $subC(H, T_i) \in VWC$. By Theorem 2, any VWC-permissive implementation is also VWC-non-interfering.

4.2 Conflict Local Opacity

As shown in [10], the VWC criterion may allow a transaction to proceed if it is "doomed" to abort: as long as the transaction's causal past can be properly serialized, the transaction may continue if it is no more consistent with the global serial order and, thus, will have to eventually abort. We propose below a stronger local property that, intuitively, aborts a transaction as soon as it cannot be put in a global serialization order.

Definition 4. *A history H is said to be* locally opaque *or* LO, *if for each transaction T_i in H: $subC(H, T_i)$ is opaque.*

It is immediate from the definition that a locally opaque history is strictly serializable: simply take T_i above to be the last transaction to commit in H. The resulting $subC(H, T_i)$ is going to be $H.subhist(committed(H))$, the sub-history consisting of all committed transactions in H. Also, one can easily see that local opacity is indeed a local property.

Every opaque history is also locally opaque, but not vice versa. To see this, consider the history H in Figure 2 which is like the history in Figure 1, except that transaction T_1 is now committed. Notice that the history is not opaque anymore: T_1, T_2 and T_3 form a cycle that prevents any legal serialization. But it is *locally* opaque: each transaction witnesses a state which is consistent with some legal total order on transactions committed so far: $subC(H, T_1)$ is equivalent to T_3T_1, $subC(H, T_2)$ is equivalent to T_3T_2, $subC(H, T_3)$ is equivalent to T_3.

We denote the set of locally opaque histories by LO. Finally, we propose a restriction of local opacity that ensures that every local serialization respects the *conflict order* [18, Chap. 3]. For two transactions T_k and T_m in $txns(H)$,

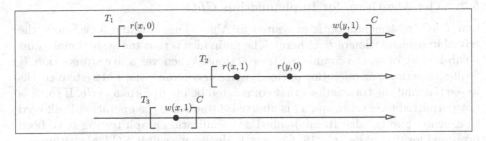

Fig. 2. A locally opaque, but not opaque history (the initial value for each object is 0)

we say that T_k *precedes* T_m *in conflict order*, denoted $T_k \prec_H^{CO} T_m$, if (w-w order) $tryC_k(C) <_H tryC_m(C)$ and $Wset(T_k) \cap Wset(T_m) \neq \emptyset$, (w-r order) $tryC_k(C) <_H r_m(x, v)$, $x \in Wset(T_k)$ and $v \neq A$, or (r-w order) $r_k(x, v) <_H tryC_m(C)$, $x \in Wset(T_m)$ and $v \neq A$. Thus, it can be seen that the conflict order is defined only on operations that have successfully executed. Using conflict order, we define a subclass of opacity, conflict opacity (co-opacity).

Definition 5. *A history H is said to be* conflict opaque *or* co-opaque *if H is valid and there exists a t-sequential legal history S such that (1) S is equivalent to $\overline{H}$ and (2) S respects $\prec_H^{RT}$ and $\prec_H^{CO}$.*

Now we define a "conflict" restriction of local opacity, *conflict local opacity (CLO)* by replacing opacity with co-opacity in Definition 4. Immediately, we derive that co-opacity is a subset of opacity and *CLO* is a subset of *LO*.

5   Implementing Local Opacity

In this section, we present our permissive implementation of *CLO*. By Theorem 2 it is also *CLO*-non-interfering. Our implementation is based on conflict-graph construction of co-opacity, a popular technique borrowed from databases (cf. [18, Chap. 3]). We then describe a simple garbage-collection optimization that prevents the memory used by the algorithm from growing without bound.

5.1   Graph Characterization of co-opacity

Given a history H, we construct a *conflict graph*, $CG(H) = (V, E)$ as follows: (1) $V = txns(H)$, the set of transactions in H (2) an edge (T_i, T_j) is added to E whenever $T_i \prec_H^{RT} T_j$ or $T_i \prec_H^{CO} T_j$, i.e., whenever T_i precedes T_j in the real-time or conflict order.

From this characterization, we get the following theorem

Theorem 3. *A legal history H is co-opaque iff $CG(H)$ is acyclic.*

5.2   The Algorithm for Implementing CLO

Our CLO implementation is presented in Algorithms 1, 2 and 3 (we omit the trivial implementation of $tryA$ here). The main idea is that the system maintains a sub-history of all the committed transactions. Whenever a live transaction T_i wishes to perform an operation o_i (read, write or commit), the TM system checks to see if o_i and the transactions that committed before it, form a cycle. If so, o_i is not permitted to execute and T_i is aborted. Otherwise, the operation is allowed to execute. Similar algorithm(s) called as serialization graph testing have been proposed for databases (cf. [18, Chap. 4]). Hence, we call it SGT algorithm.

Algorithm 1. Read of a t-object x by a transaction T_i

1: **procedure** $read_i(x)$
2:     // read *gComHist*
3:     $tHist_i = gComHist$; // create a local copy of *gComHist*
4:     // create v, to store a the value of x
5:     $v =$ the latest value written to x in $tHist_i$;
6:     // create $lseq_i$, the local copy of $gseqn$
7:     $lseq_i =$ the value of largest seq. no. of a transaction in $lComHist_i$;
8:     create the $readVar\ rop_i(x, v, lseq_i)$;
9:     // update $lComHist_i$
10:     $lComHist_i =$ merge $lComHist_i$ and $tHist_i$; append $rop_i(x, v, lseq_i)$ to $lComHist_i$;

11:     // check for consistency of the read operation
12:     **if** $(CG(lComHist_i)$ is cyclic) **then**
13:         replace $rop_i(x, v, lseq_i)$ with $(rop_i(x, A, lseq_i)$ in $lComHist_i)$;
14:         return **abort**;
15:     **end if**
16:     // current read is consistent; hence store it in the read set and return v
17:     return v;
18: **end procedure**

Algorithm 2. Write of a t-object x with value v by a transaction T_i

---

1: **procedure** $write_i(x, v)$
2:     **if** $write_i(x, v)$ is the first operation in T_i **then**
3:         // read *gComHist*
4:         $lComHist_i = gComHist$;
5:         $lseq_i =$ the value of largest seq. no. of a transaction in $lComHist_i$;
6:     **end if**
7:     create the $writeVar\ wop_i(x, v, lseq_i)$;
8:     append $wop_i(x, v, lseq_i)$ to $lComHist_i$;
9:     return ok;
10: **end procedure**

Algorithm 3. TryCommit operation by a transaction T_i

```
1: procedure tryC_i
2:     lock gLock;
3:     // create the next version of gseqn for the current T_i
4:     lseq_i = gSeqNum + 1;
5:     tHist_i = gComHist; // create a local copy of gComHist
6:     lComHist_i = merge lComHist_i and tHist_i; // update lComHist_i
7:     // create the commit operation with lseq_i
8:     create the comVar cop_i(lseq_i);
9:     append cop_i(lseq_i) to lComHist_i;
10:    if (CG(lComHist_i) is cyclic) then
11:        Replace cop_i(lseq_i) with a_i in lComHist_i;
12:        Release the lock on gLock;
13:        return abort;
14:    end if
15:    gComHist = lComHist_i;
16:    gSeqNum = lseq_i;
17:    Release the lock on gLock;
18:    return commit;
19: end procedure
```

Our SGT algorithm maintains several variables. Some of them are global to all transactions which are prefixed with the letter 'g'. The remaining variables are local. The variables are:

- $gSeqNum$, initialized to 0 in the start of the system: global variable that counts the number of transactions committed so far.
- $lseq_i$: a transaction-specific variable that contains the number of transactions currently observed committed by T_i. When a transaction T_i commits, the current value of $gSeqNum$ is incremented and assigned to $lseq_i$.
- $readVar$: captures a read operation r_i performed by a transaction T_i. It stores the variable x, the value v returned by r_i and the *sequence number* s of r_i, computed as the sequence number of the committed transaction r_i reads from. We use the notation $rop_i(x, v, s)$ to denote the read operation in the local or global history.
- $writeVar$: captures a write operation $w_i(x, v)$ performed by a transaction T_i. It stores the variable x, the value written by the write operation v and the sequence number s of w_i, computed as the sequence number of the previous op in T_i or the sequence number of the last committed transaction preceding T_i if w_i is the first operation in T_i. We use the notation $wop_i(x, v, s)$ to denote the *writeVar* operation.
- $comVar$: captures a commit operation of a transaction T_i. It stores the $lseq_i$ of the transaction. We use the notation $cop_i(s)$ to denote the *comVar* operation where s is the $lseq_i$ of the transaction.
- $gComHist$: captures the history of events of committed transactions. It is a list of *readVar*, *writeVar*, *comVar* variables ordered by real-time execution.

We assume that $gComHist$ also contains initial values for all t-variables (later updates of these initial values will be used for garbage collection).

- $gLock$: This is a global lock variable. The TM system locks this variable whenever it wishes to read and write to any global variable.

The implementations of T_i's operations, denoted by $read_i(x)$, $write_i(x, v)$ and $tryC_i()$ are described below. We assume here that if any of these is the first operation performed by T_i, it is preceded with the initialization all T_i's local variables.

We also assume that all the t-objects accessed by the STM system are initialized with 0 (which simulates the effect of having the initializing transaction T_0).

$read_i(x)$: Every transaction T_i maintains $lComHist_i$ which is a local copy $gComHist$ combined with events of T_i taken place so far, put at the right places in $gComHist$, based on their sequence numbers. From $lComHist_i$ the values v and $lseq_i$ are computed. If there are no committed writes operation on x preceding $read_i(x)$ in $lComHist_i$, then v is assumed to be the initial value 0. Then, a $readVar$ rop_i is created for the current read operation using the latest value of x, v and the current value of $gSeqNum$, $lseq_i$. Then rop_i is inserted into $lComHist_i$. A conflict graph is constructed from the resulting $lComHist_i$ and checked for acyclicity. If the graph is cyclic then A is inserted into rop_i of $lComHist_i$ and then **abort** is returned. Otherwise, the value v is returned.

$write_i(x, v)$: adds a $writeVar$ containing x and v and $lseq_i$ is inserted to $lComHist_i$. (If the write is the first operation of T_i, then $lComHist_i$ and $lseq_i$ are computed based on the current state of $gComHist_i$.)

$tryC_i(x)$: The main idea for this procedure is similar to $read_i$, except that the TM system first obtains the lock on $gLock$. Then it makes local copies of $gSeqNum$, $gComHist$ which are $lseq_i$, $tHist_i$, and $lComHist_i$. The value $lseq_i$ is incremented, and the $cop_i(lseq_i)$ item is appended to $lComHist_i$. Then a conflict graph is constructed for the resulting $lComHist_i$ and checked for acyclicity. If the graph is cyclic then $cop_i(seq_i)$ is replaced with a_i in $lComHist_i$, the lock is released and **abort** is returned. Otherwise, $lseq_i$, $lComHist_i$, are copied back into $gSeqNum$, $gComHist$, the lock is released and ok is returned.

Theorem 4. *Let H_g be a history generated by SGT algorithm. Then H_g is in Perm(CLO).*

Now Theorem 2 implies that our SGT implementation is CLO-non-interfering.

Theorem 5. *Assuming that no transaction fails while executing the tryC operation and gLock is starvation-free, every operation of SGT eventually returns.*

5.3   Garbage Collection

Over time, the history of committed transactions maintained by our SGT algorithm in the global variable $gComHist$ grows without bound. We now describe a simple garbage-collection scheme that allows to keep the size of *gComHist* proportional to the current contention, i.e, to the number of concurrently live transactions. The idea is to periodically remove from *gComHist* the sub-histories corresponding to committed transactions that become *obsolete*, i.e., the effect of them can be reduced to the updates of t-objects.

More precisely, a transaction T_i's *liveSet* is the set of the transactions that were incomplete when T_i terminated. A t-complete transaction T_i is said to be obsolete (in a history H) if all the transactions in its liveSet have terminated (in H).

To make sure that obsolete transactions can be correctly identified based on the global history *gComHist*, we update our algorithm as follows. When a transaction performs its first operation, it grabs the lock on *gComHist* and inserts the operation in it. Now when a transaction commits it takes care of all committed transactions in *gComHist* which have become obsolete. All read operations preceding the last event of an obsolete transaction are removed, In case there are multiple obsolete transactions writing to the same t-object, only the writes of the last such obsolete transaction to commit are kept in the history. If an obsolete transaction is not the latest to commit an update on any t-object, all events of this transactions are removed.

In other words, H_{im} defined as the local history *lComHist$_i$* computed by SGT within the last complete memory operation of T_i in the updated algorithm (which corresponds to line 10 of Algorithm 1 and line 9 of Algorithm 3) preserves write and commit events of the latest obsolete transaction to commit a value for every t-object. All other events of other obsolete transactions are removed. The computed history H_{im} is written back to *gComHist* in line 15 of Algorithm 1.

Let this *gComHist* be used by a transaction T_i in checking the correctness of the current local history (line 12 of Algorithm 1 or line 10 of Algorithm 3). Recall that H_{ig} denotes the corresponding local history of T_i. Let T_ℓ be any obsolete transaction in H_{ig}. Note that all transactions that committed before T_ℓ in H_{ig} are also obsolete in H_{ig}, and let U denote the set of all these obsolete transactions, including T_ℓ. Respectively, let $obs(H_{ig}, U)$ be a prefix of H_{ig} in which all transactions in $liveSet(T_\ell)$ are complete. Also, let $trim(H_{ig}, U)$ be the "trimmed" local history of T_i where all transactions in U are removed or replaced with committed updates, as described above. We can show that H_{ig} is in CLO if and only if $obs(H_{ig}, U)$ and $trim(H_{ig}, U)$ are in CLO.

Iteratively, for each T_i, all our earlier claims on the relation between the actual local history H_{ig} and the locally constructed history H_{im} hold now for the "trimmed" history $trim(H_{ig}, U)$ and H_{im}. Therefore, H_{im} is in CLO if and only if H_{ig} is in CLO. Hence, every history H_g generated by the updated algorithm with garbage collection is CLO-permissive (and, thus, CLO-non-interfering).

Note that removing obsolete transactions from *gComHist* essentially boils down to dropping a prefix of it that is not concurrent to any live transactions. As a result, the length of *gComHist* is $O(M + C)$, where M is the number of t-objects and C is the upper bound on the number of concurrent transactions. A complete correctness proof for the optimized algorithm is given in [12].

6   Concluding Remarks

In this paper, we explored the notion of non-interference in transactional memory, originally highlighted in [15, 16]. We focused on P-non-interference that grasps the intuition that no transaction aborts because of aborted or incomplete transactions in the sense that by removing some of aborted or incomplete transactions we cannot turn a previously aborted transaction into a committed one without violating the given correctness criterion P. We showed that no TM implementation can provide opacity-non-interference. However, we observed that any permissive implementation of a local correctness criterion is also non-interfering. Informally, showing that a history is locally correct is equivalent to showing that every its local sub-history is correct. We discussed two local criteria: virtual-world consistency (VWC) [10] and the (novel) local opacity (LO). Unlike VWC, LO does not allow a transaction that is doomed to abort to waste system resources. TMS1 [4] was recently proposed as a candidate for the "weakest reasonable" TM correctness criterion. Interestingly, at least for the case of atomic transactional operations, LO seems to coincide with TMS1.

We then considered CLO, a restriction of LO that, in addition, requires every local serialization to respect the conflict order [9, 14] of the original sub-history. We presented a permissive, and thus non-interfering, CLO implementation. This appears to be the only non-trivial permissive implementation known so far (the VWC implementation in [2] is only probabilistically permissive).

Our definitions and our implementation intend to build a "proof of concept" for non-interference and are, by intention, as simple as possible (but not simpler). Of course, interesting directions are to consider a more realistic notion of non-interference as a characteristics of an implementation, to extend our definitions to non-sequential histories, and to relax the strong ordering requirements in our correctness criteria. Indeed, the use of the conflict order allowed us to efficiently relate correctness of a given history to the absence of cycles in its graph characterization. Respecting conflict order makes a lot of sense if we aim at permissiveness, as efficient verification of strict serializability or opacity appear elusive [14]. But it may be too strong as a requirement for less demanding implementations.

Also, our implementation is quite simplistic in the sense that it uses one global lock to protect the history of committed transactions and, thus, it is not disjoint-access-parallel (DAP) [1, 11]. An interesting challenge is to check if it is possible to construct a permissive DAP CLO implementation with invisible reads.

References

1. Attiya, H., Hillel, E., Milani, A.: Inherent limitations on disjoint-access parallel implementations of transactional memory. In: Proceedings of the Twenty-First Annual Symposium on Parallelism in Algorithms and Architectures, SPAA 2009, pp. 69–78. ACM, New York (2009)

2. Crain, T., Imbs, D., Raynal, M.: Read invisibility, virtual world consistency and probabilistic permissiveness are compatible. In: Xiang, Y., Cuzzocrea, A., Hobbs, M., Zhou, W. (eds.) ICA3PP 2011, Part I. LNCS, vol. 7016, pp. 244–257. Springer, Heidelberg (2011)
3. Dalessandro, L., Spear, M.F., Scott, M.L.: Norec: streamlining stm by abolishing ownership records. In: PPOPP, pp. 67–78 (2010)
4. Doherty, S., Groves, L., Luchangco, V., Moir, M.: Towards formally specifying and verifying transactional memory. Formal Asp. Comput. 25(5), 769–799 (2013)
5. Felber, P., Fetzer, C., Marlier, P., Riegel, T.: Time-based software transactional memory. IEEE Trans. Parallel Distrib. Syst. 21(12), 1793–1807 (2010)
6. Guerraoui, R., Henzinger, T.A., Singh, V.: Permissiveness in transactional memories. In: Taubenfeld, G. (ed.) DISC 2008. LNCS, vol. 5218, pp. 305–319. Springer, Heidelberg (2008)
7. Guerraoui, R., Kapalka, M.: On the correctness of transactional memory. In: PPoPP 2008: Proceedings of the 13th ACM SIGPLAN Symposium on Principles and Practice of Parallel Programming, pp. 175–184. ACM, New York (2008)
8. Guerraoui, R., Kapalka, M.: Principles of Transactional Memory. Synthesis Lectures on Distributed Computing Theory. Morgan and Claypool (2010)
9. Hadzilacos, V.: A theory of reliability in database systems. J. ACM 35(1), 121–145 (1988)
10. Imbs, D., Raynal, M.: A versatile STM protocol with invisible read operations that satisfies the virtual world consistency condition. In: Kutten, S., Žerovnik, J. (eds.) SIROCCO 2009. LNCS, vol. 5869, pp. 266–280. Springer, Heidelberg (2010)
11. Israeli, A., Rappoport, L.: Disjoint-access-parallel implementations of strong shared memory primitives. In: Proceedings of the Thirteenth Annual ACM Symposium on Principles of Distributed Computing, PODC 1994, pp. 151–160. ACM, New York (1994)
12. Kuznetsov, P., Peri, S.: Non-interference and local correctness in transactional memory. CoRR, abs/1211.6315 (2013)
13. Kuznetsov, P., Ravi, S.: On the cost of concurrency in transactional memory. In: Fernàndez Anta, A., Lipari, G., Roy, M. (eds.) OPODIS 2011. LNCS, vol. 7109, pp. 112–127. Springer, Heidelberg (2011)
14. Papadimitriou, C.H.: The serializability of concurrent database updates. J. ACM 26(4), 631–653 (1979)
15. Peri, S., Vidyasankar, K.: Correctness of concurrent executions of closed nested transactions in transactional memory systems. In: Aguilera, M.K., Yu, H., Vaidya, N.H., Srinivasan, V., Choudhury, R.R. (eds.) ICDCN 2011. LNCS, vol. 6522, pp. 95–106. Springer, Heidelberg (2011)
16. Peri, S., Vidyasankar, K.: An efficient scheduler for closed nested transactions that satisfies all-reads-consistency and non-interference. In: Bononi, L., Datta, A.K., Devismes, S., Misra, A. (eds.) ICDCN 2012. LNCS, vol. 7129, pp. 409–423. Springer, Heidelberg (2012)
17. Spear, M.F., Michael, M.M., von Praun, C.: Ringstm: scalable transactions with a single atomic instruction. In: Proceedings of the Twentieth Annual Symposium on Parallelism in Algorithms and Architectures, SPAA 2008, pp. 275–284 (2008)
18. Weikum, G., Vossen, G.: Transactional Information Systems: Theory, Algorithms, and the Practice of Concurrency Control and Recovery. Morgan Kaufmann (2002)

A TimeStamp Based Multi-version STM Algorithm

Priyanka Kumar[1,*], Sathya Peri[1], and K. Vidyasankar[2]

[1] CSE Dept, Indian Institute of Technology Patna, India
{priyanka,sathya}@iitp.ac.in
[2] CS Dept, Memorial University, St John's, Canada
vidya@mun.ca

Abstract. Software Transactional Memory Systems (STM) are a promising alternative for concurrency control in shared memory systems. Multiversion STM systems maintain multiple versions for each t-object. The advantage of storing multiple versions is that it facilitates successful execution of higher number of read operations than otherwise. Multi-Version permissiveness (mv-permissiveness) is a progress condition for multi-version STMs that states that a read-only transaction never aborts. Recently a STM system was proposed that maintains only a single version but is mv-permissive. This raises a natural question: how much concurrency can be achieved by multi-version STM. We show that fewer transactions are aborted in multi-version STMs than single-version systems. We also show that any STM system that is permissive w.r.t opacity must maintain at least as many versions as the number of live transactions. A direct implication of this result is that no single-version STM can be permissive w.r.t opacity.

In this paper we present a time-stamp based multiversion STM system that satisfies opacity and is easy to implement. We formally prove the correctness of the proposed STM system. Although many multi-version STM systems have been proposed in literature that satisfy opacity, to the best of our knowledge none of them has been formally proved to be opaque. We also present garbage collection procedure which deletes unwanted versions of the transaction objects. We show that with garbage collection the number of versions maintained is bounded by number of live transactions.

1 Introduction

In recent years, Software Transactional Memory systems (STMs) [10, 21] have garnered significant interest as an elegant alternative for addressing concurrency issues in memory. STM systems take optimistic approach. Multiple transactions are allowed to execute concurrently. On completion, each transaction is validated and if any inconsistency is observed it is *aborted*. Otherwise it is allowed to *commit*.

An important requirement of STM systems is to precisely identify the criterion as to when a transaction should be aborted/committed. A commonly accepted correctness-criterion for STM systems is *opacity* proposed by Guerraoui, and Kapalka [8]. Opacity requires all the transactions including aborted one to appear to execute sequentially

---

* The author was awarded most promising researcher at the Ph.D forum of ICDCN-13 where a premiminary version of this work was presented.

M. Chatterjee et al. (Eds.): ICDCN 2014, LNCS 8314, pp. 212–226, 2014.

in an order that agrees with the order of non-overlapping transactions. Opacity unlike traditional serializability [16] ensures that even aborted transactions read consistent values.

Another important requirement of STM system is to ensure that transactions do not abort unnecessarily. This referred to as the *progress* condition. It would be ideal to abort a transaction only when it does not violate correctness requirement (such as opacity). However it was observed in [1] that many STM systems developed so far spuriously abort transactions even when not required. A *permissive* STM [7] does not abort a transaction unless committing it violates the correctness-criterion.

With increase in concurrency, more transactions may conflict and abort, especially in presence of many long-running transactions. This can have a very bad impact on performance [2]. Perelman et al [18] observe that read-only transactions play a significant role in various types of applications. But long read-only transactions could be aborted multiple times in many of the current STM systems [11, 5]. In fact Perelman et al [18] show that many STM systems waste 80% their time in aborts due to read-only transactions.

It was observed that by storing multiple versions of each object, multi-version STMs can ensure that more read operations do not abort than otherwise. History $H1$ illustrates this idea. $H1 : r_1(x, 0)w_2(x, 10)w_2(y, 10)c_2r_1(y, 0)c_1$. In this history the read on y by T_1 returns 0 but not the previous closest write of 10 by T_2. This is possible by storing multiple versions for y. As a result, this history is opaque with the equivalent correct execution being T_1T_2. Had there not been multiple versions, $r_2(y)$ would have been forced to read the only available version which is 10. This value would make the read $r_2(y)$ to not be consistent (opaque) and hence abort.

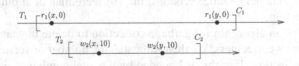

Fig. 1. Pictorial representation of a History $H1$

Maintaining multiple versions was first successfully employed in databases. Since then, many STM systems have been developed that store multiple version of objects [4, 6, 15, 18, 19, 20]. The progress condition relating to multi-version STMs is *multi-version permissiveness* or *mv-permissiveness* [19]. A mv-permissive STM system never aborts a read-only transaction; it aborts an update transaction (i.e transaction that also writes) when it conflicts with other update transactions. Unlike permissiveness, mv-permissiveness is not defined w.r.t any correctness-criterion.

Interestingly, Attiya and Hillel [1] proposed a single-version STM system that is mv-permissive. This raises an interesting question: what is the the advantage of having multiple versions if mv-permissiveness can be achieved by single vesion STMs. In this paper, we address this issue by formally proving that by storing multiple versions greater concurrency can be obtained. We then show that any STM system that is permissive w.r.t opacity must maintain at least L versions where L is the maximum number of live transactions in the system. The number of live transactions represents the concurrency in a STM system and hence can be unbounded. Thus, an implication of this result is that no single-version or for that matter any bounded-version STM can be permissive w.r.t opacity.

We then propose a multi-version STM system based on timestamp ordering called as *multi-version timestamp ordering* algorithm or *MVTO*. We formally prove that our algorithm satisfies opacity. In order to prove correctness we use a graph characterization of opacity for sequential histories which is based on the characterization developed by Guerraoui and Kapalka [9]. We believe that our algorithm is very intuitive and easy to implement. By storing multiple versions, the algorithms ensures that no read-only transaction aborts.

Although many multi-version STM systems have been proposed in literature that satisfy opacity, none of them have been formally proved. To the best of our knowledge, this is the first work that formally proves a multi-version STM to be opaque.

Another nice feature of MVTO algorithm proposed is that it does not require transactions to be annotated as read-only before the start of their execution unlike for instance in [15]. This can be very useful for transactions that have multiple control paths, where some of the paths are read-only whereas the others are not and it is not known in advance which path might be chosen.

An important issue that arises with multi-version STMs is that over time, some versions will no longer be required. So multi-version STMs must have mechanisms of deleting unwanted versions. It is necessary to regularly delete unused versions which otherwise could use a lot of memory. Some multi-version STMs solve this issue by having only fixed number of versions. Other systems have garbage collection procedures running alongside that delete older versions. In [19], Perelman et al outline principles for garbage collection.

Finally, we give an algorithm for garbage collection to delete unwanted versions in MVTO and prove its correctness. We then show that the number of versions maintained by the garbage collection algorithm is bounded by the total number of live transactions in the system.

Roadmap. The paper is organized as follows. We describe our system model in Section 2. In Section 3, we formally show that higher concurrency can be achieved by storing multiple versions. In Section 4 we formally define the graph characterization for implementing opacity. In Section 5, we describe the working principle of MVTO protocol and its algorithm. In Section 6 we are give the outline of the garbage collection algorithm. Finally we conclude in Section 7. Due to space constraints, we have only outlined the main idea. The full details can be found in [12].

2   System Model and Preliminaries

The notions and definitions described in this section follow the definitions of [13]. We assume a system of n processes, $p_1, \ldots, p_n$ that access a collection of *objects* via atomic *transactions*. The processes are provided with four *transactional operations*: the $write(x, v)$ operation that updates object x with value v, the $read(x)$ operation that returns a value read in x, $tryC()$ that tries to commit the transaction and returns *commit*

($\mathcal{C}$ for short) or *abort* ($\mathcal{A}$ for short), and *tryA()* that aborts the transaction and returns $\mathcal{A}$. Some STM systems also provide for a begin transaction function. The objects accessed by the read and write operations are called as t-objects. For the sake of simplicity, we assume that the values written by all the transactions are unique.

Operations *write*, *read* and *tryC()* may return $\mathcal{A}$, in which case we say that the operations *forcefully abort*. Otherwise, we say that the operation has *successfully* executed. Each operation is equipped with a unique transaction identifier. A transaction T_i starts with the first operation and completes when any of its operations returns a or c. Abort and commit operations are called *terminal operations*.

For a transaction T_k, we denote all its read operations as $Rset(T_k)$ and write operations $Wset(T_k)$. Collectively, we denote all the operations of a transaction T_i as $evts(T_k)$.

Histories. A *history* is a sequence of *events*, i.e., a sequence of invocations and responses of transactional operations. The collection of events is denoted as $evts(H)$. For simplicity, we only consider *sequential* histories here: the invocation of each transactional operation is immediately followed by a matching response. Therefore, we treat each transactional operation as one atomic event, and let $<_H$ denote the total order on the transactional operations incurred by H. With this assumption the only relevant events of a transaction T_k are of the types: $r_k(x, v)$, $r_k(x, \mathcal{A})$, $w_k(x, v)$, $w_k(x, v, \mathcal{A})$, $tryC_k(C)$ (or c_k for short), $tryC_k(\mathcal{A})$, $tryA_k(\mathcal{A})$ (or a_k for short). We identify a history H as tuple $\langle evts(H), <_H \rangle$.

Let $H|T$ denote the history consisting of events of T in H, and $H|p_i$ denote the history consisting of events of p_i in H. We only consider *well-formed* histories here, i.e., (1) each $H|T$ consists of a read-only prefix (consisting of read operations only), followed by a write-only part (consisting of write operations only), possibly *completed* with a *tryC* or *tryA* operation[1], and (2) each $H|p_i$ consists of a sequence of transactions, where no new transaction begins before the last transaction completes (commits or a aborts).

We assume that every history has an initial committed transaction T_0 that initializes all the data-objects with 0. The set of transactions that appear in H is denoted by $txns(H)$. The set of committed (resp., aborted) transactions in H is denoted by *committed(H)* (resp., *aborted(H)*). The set of *live* (or *incomplete*) transactions in H is denoted by $live(H)$ ($live(H) = txns(H) - committed(H) - aborted(H)$). For a history H, we construct the *completion* of H, denoted $\overline{H}$, by inserting a_k immediately after the last event of every transaction $T_k \in live(H)$.

Transaction orders. For two transactions $T_k, T_m \in txns(H)$, we say that T_k *precedes* T_m in the *real-time order* of H, denote $T_k \prec_H^{RT} T_m$, if T_k is complete in H and the last event of T_k precedes the first event of T_m in H. If neither $T_k \prec_H^{RT} T_m$ nor $T_m \prec_H^{RT} T_k$, then T_k and T_m *overlap* in H. A history H is *t-sequential* if there are no overlapping transactions in H, i.e., every two transactions are related by the real-time order.

Valid and legal Histories. Let H be a history and $r_k(x, v)$ be a successful read operation (i.e $v \neq \mathcal{A}$) in H. Then $r_k(x, v)$, is said to be *valid* if there is a transaction T_j in H that commits before r_K and $w_j(x, v)$ is in $evts(T_j)$ (T_j can also be T_0). Formally, $\langle r_k(x, v)$

---

[1] This restriction brings no loss of generality [14].

is valid $\Rightarrow \exists T_j : (c_j <_H r_k(x,v)) \wedge (w_j(x,v) \in evts(T_j)) \wedge (v \neq \mathcal{A})\rangle$. Since we assume that all the writes are unique there exists only one transaction T_j that writes of v to x. We say that the commit operation c_j is r_k's *valWrite* and formally denote it as $H.valWrite(r_k)$. The history H is valid if all its successful read operations are valid.

We define $r_k(x,v)$'s *lastWrite* as the latest commit event c_j such that c_j precedes $r_k(x,v)$ in H and $x \in Wset(T_i)$. Formally, we denote it as $H.lastWrite(r_k)$. A successful read operation $r_k(x,v)$ (i.e $v \neq \mathcal{A}$), is said to be *legal* if transaction T_j (which contains r_k's lastWrite) also writes v onto x. Formally, $\langle r_k(x,v)$ is legal $\Rightarrow (v \neq \mathcal{A}) \wedge (H.lastWrite(r_k(x,v)) = c_i) \wedge (w_i(x,v) \in evts(T_i))\rangle$. The history H is legal if all its successful read operations are legal. Thus from the definitions we get that if H is legal then it is also valid.

It can be seen that in $H1$, $c_0 = H1.valWrite(r_1(x,0)) = H1.lastWrite(r_1(x,0))$. Hence, $r_1(x,0)$ is legal. But $c_0 = H1.valWrite(r_1(y,0)) \neq c_1 = H1.lastWrite(r_1(y,0))$. Thus, $r_1(y,0)$ is valid but not legal.

Correctness Criteria and Opacity. A correctness-criterion is a set of histories. We say that two histories H and H' are *equivalent* if they have the same set of events.

A history H is said to be *opaque* [8, 9] if H is valid and there exists a t-sequential legal history S such that (1) S is equivalent to $\overline{H}$ and (2) S respects $\prec_H^{RT}$, i.e $\prec_H^{RT} \subseteq \prec_S^{RT}$. We denote the set of all opaque histories as *opacity*. Thus, opacity is a correctness-criterion. By requiring S being equivalent to $\overline{H}$, opacity treats all the live transactions as aborted.

Implementations and Linearizations. A STM *implementation* provides the processes with functions for implementing read, write, tryC (and possibly tryA) functions. We denote the set of histories *generated* by a STM implementation I as $gen(I)$. We say that an implementation I is correct w.r.t to a correctness-criterion C if all the histories generated by I are in P i.e. $gen(I) \subseteq P$.

The histories generated by an STM implementations are normally not sequential, i.e., they may have overlapping transactional operations. Since our correctness definitions are proposed for sequential histories, to reason about correctness of an implementation, we order the events in a non-sequential history to obtain an equivalent sequential history. The implementation that we propose has enough information about ordering of the overlapping operations. We denote this total ordering on the events as *linearization*.

Progress Conditions. Let C be a correctness-criterion with H in it. Let T_a be an aborted transaction in H. We say that a history H is permissive w.r.t C if committing T_a, by replacing the abort value returned by an operation in T_a with some non-abort value, would cause H to violate C. In other words, if T_a is committed then H will no longer be in C. We denote the set of histories permissive w.r.t C as $Perm(C)$. We say that STM implementation I is permissive [7] w.r.t some correctness-criterion C (such as opacity) if every history H generated by I is permissive w.r.t C, i.e., $gen(I) \subseteq Perm(C)$.

A STM implementation is *mv-permissive* if it forcibly aborts an update transaction that conflicts with another update transaction. A mv-permissive STM implementation does not abort read-only transactions.

3   Concurrency Provided by Multi-version Systems

It has been observed that by storing multiple versions, more concurrency can be gained. History $H1$ is an example of this. Normally, multi-version STM systems, help read operations to read consistent values. By allowing the read operation to read the appropriate version (if one exists), they ensure that read operations do not read inconsistent values and abort. To capture this notion precisely, Perelman et al [19] defined the notion of mv-permissiveness which (among other things) says that a read operations always succeed.

Although Perelman et al defined mv-permissiveness in the context of multi-version STMs, recently Attiya and Hillel [1] proposed a single-version STM system that is mv-permissive. In their implementation, Attiya and Hillel maintain only a single-version for each t-object, but ensure that no read-only transaction aborts. As a result, their implementation achieves mv-permissiveness. Thus, if single-version STMs can achieve mv-permissiveness, a natural question that arises is how much extra concurrency can be achieved by multi-version STMs?

To address this question, we were inspired by the theory developed for multi-versions in databases by Kanellakis and Papadimitriou [17]. They showed that the concurrency achievable by multi-version databases schedulers is greater than single-version schedulers. More specifically they showed that the greater the number of versions stored, the higher the concurrency. For showing this, they used *view-serializability (vsr)*, the correctness-criterion for databases. They defined a classes of histories: 1-vsr, 2-vsr, ... n-vsr, etc., where k-vsr is the class of histories that maintain k versions and are serializable. They showed that 1-vsr $\subset$ 2-vsr $\subset$ ... $\subset$ n-vsr.

We extend their idea to STMs by generalizing the concept of legality. Consider a read $r_i(x, v)$ in a history H. Let r_i's valWrite be c_j. Let $n - 1$ other transactions commit between c_j and r_i that have also written to x in H, i.e., $c_j <_H c_{k1} <_H c_{k2} <_H \cdots <_H c_{(n-1)} <_H r_i$. Thus, n versions have been created before r_i. Suppose r_i reads from the version created by c_j. Then, we say that r_i is *n-legal*. Kanellakis and Papadimitriou [17] denote n as *width* of x. Extending this idea further, we say that a history H is *m-legal* if each of its read operation is *n-legal* for some $n \leq m$. Thus by this definition, if a history is *n-legal* then it is also *m-legal* for $n \leq m$ but not he vice-versa. If the history H is *1-legal*, we denote it as *single-versioned*.

Extending this idea of legality to opacity, we say that a history H is *m-opaque* if H is *n-legal* and opaque, where $n \leq m$. Thus, if a history is *n-opaque* then it is also *m-opaque* for $n \leq m$. We denote the set of histories that are *m-opaque* as *m-opacity*. Clearly, $opacity = \bigcup_{m \geq 1} m\text{-}opacity$. From this, we get the following theorem.

Theorem 1. *For any $k > 0$, k-opacity $\subset (k + 1)$-opacity.*

This theorem shows that there exists an infinite hierarchy of classes of opacity. This further shows that even though single-version STMs can achieve mv-permissiveness, these systems by definition can only satisfy *1-opacity*. On the other hand, multi-version STMs storing k version (for $k > 1$) are a subset of *k-opacity*. Hence, higher concurrency can be achieved by these systems.

Next, we show that any multi-version STM must store as many versions as maximum possible live transactions for each t-object for achieving mv-permissiveness. For showing this, we define the notion of *maxLiveSet* for a history H as is the maximum number of live transactions present in any prefix of H. Formally, $maxLiveSet(H) = (\max\limits_{H' \in prefixSet(H)} \{|live(H')|\})$ where $prefixSet(H)$ is the set of all prefixes of H. We say that an implementation I *maintains* k versions if during its execution, it creates k versions. We now have the following theorem,

Theorem 2. *Consider a multi-version implementation I that is permissive w.r.t opacity and let H be a history generated by it. Then, I must maintain at least $maxLiveSet(H)$ versions.*

Although, we have assumed sequential histories in our model, these results also generalize to non-sequential histories as well since sequential histories can be viewed as a restriction over non-sequential histories. The number of live transactions represents the concurrency in a STM system and hence can be unbounded. Thus, an implication of Theorem 2 is that no single-version or any fixed-version STM can be permissive w.r.t opacity.

Having proved a few theoretical properties of multi-version STMs, in the following sections we give an implementation of a multi-version STM and we prove it to be opaque. Motivated by Theorem 1 and Theorem 2, the proposed multi-version STM does not keep any bound on the number of versions to maximize concurrency but uses garbage collection to delete unwanted versions. In the following sections, we only consider opacity and not k-opacity any more.

4   Graph Characterization of Opacity

To prove that a STM system satisfies opacity, it is useful to consider graph characterization of histories. In this section, we describe the graph characterisation of Guerraoui and Kapalka [9] modified for sequential histories. It is similar to the characterization by Bernstein and Goodman [3] which is also for sequential histories but developed for databases transactions.

Consider a history H which consists of multiple version for each t-object. The graph characterisation uses the notion of *version order*. Given H and a t-object x, we define a version order for x as any (non-reflexive) total order on all the versions of x ever created by committed transactions in H. It must be noted that the version order may or may not be the same as the actual order in which the version of x are generated in H. A version order of H, denoted as $\ll_H$ is the union of the version orders of all the t-objects in H.

Consider the history $H4 : r_1(x, 0)r_2(x, 0)r_1(y, 0)r_3(z, 0)w_1(x, 5)w_3(y, 15)$ $w_2(y, 10)w_1(z, 10)c_1c_2r_4(x, 5)r_4(y, 10)w_3(z, 15)c_3r_4(z, 10)$. Using the notation that a committed transaction T_i writing to x creates a version x_i, a possible version order for $H4 \ll_{H4}$ is: $\langle x_0 \ll x_1 \rangle, \langle y_0 \ll y_2 \ll y_3 \rangle, \langle z_0 \ll z_1 \ll z_3 \rangle$.

We define the graph characterisation based on a given version order. Consider a history H and a version order $\ll$. We then define a graph (called opacity graph) on H using $\ll$, denoted as $OPG(H, \ll) = (V, E)$. The vertex set V consists of a vertex for each transaction T_i in $\overline{H}$. The edges of the graph are of three kinds and are defined as follows:

1. *rt*(real-time) edges: If T_i commits before T_j starts in H, then there is an edge from v_i to v_j. This set of edges are referred to as $rt(H)$.
2. *rf*(reads-from) edges: If T_j reads x from T_i in H, then there is an edge from v_i to v_j. Note that in order for this to happen, T_i must have committed before T_j and $c_i <_H r_j(x)$. This set of edges are referred to as $rf(H)$.
3. *mv*(multiversion) edges: The mv edges capture the multiversion relations and is based on the version order. Consider a successful read operation $r_k(x, v)$ and the write operation $w_j(x, v)$ belonging to transaction T_j such that $r_k(x, v)$ reads x from $w_j(x, v)$ (it must be noted T_j is a committed transaction and $c_j <_H r_k$). Consider a committed transaction T_i which writes to x, $w_i(x, u)$ where $u \neq v$. Thus the versions created x_i, x_j are related by $\ll$. Then, if $x_i \ll x_j$ we add an edge from v_i to v_j. Otherwise ($x_j \ll x_i$), we add an edge from v_k to v_i. This set of edges are referred to as $mv(H, \ll)$.

We now show that if a version order $\ll$ exists for a history H such that it is acyclic, then H is opaque.

Theorem 3. *A valid history H is opaque iff there exists a version order $\ll_H$ such that $OPG(H, \ll_H)$ is acyclic.*

5 Multiversion Timestamp Ordering (MVTO) Algorithm

We describe a timestamp based algorithm for multi-version STM systems, multiversion timestamp ordering (MVTO) algorithm. We then prove that our algorithm satisfies opacity [9, 8] using the graph characterization developed in the previous section.

5.1 The Working Principle

In our algorithm, each transaction, T_i is assigned a unique timestamp, i, when it is initially invoked by a thread. We denote i to be the id as well as the timestamp of the transaction T_i. Intuitively, the timestamp tells the "time" at which the transaction began. It is a monotonically increasing number assigned to each transaction and is numerically greater than the timestamps of all the transactions invoked so far. All read and write operations carry the timestamp of the transaction that issued it. When an update transaction T_i commits, the algorithm creates new version of all the t-objects it writes to. All these versions have the timestamp i.

Now we describe the main idea behind read, write and tryC operations executed by a transaction T_i. These ideas are based on the read and write steps for timestamp algorithm developed for databases by Bernstein and Goodman [3]:

1. **read rule:** T_i on invoking $r_i(x)$ reads the value v, where v is the value written by a transaction T_j that commits before $r_i(x)$ and j is the largest timestamp $\leq i$.
2. **write rule:** T_i writes into local memory.

3. **commit rule:** T_i on invoking tryC operation checks for each t-object x, in its $Wset$:
   (a) If a transaction T_k has read x from T_j, i.e. $r_k(x, v) \in evts(T_k)$ and $w_j(x, v) \in evts(T_j)$ and $j < i < k$, then $tryC_i$ returns abort,
   (b) otherwise, the transaction is allowed to commit.

5.2   Data Structures and Pseudocode

The algorithm maintains the following data structures. For each transaction T_i:

- $T_i.RS$(read set): It is a list of data tuples (d_tuples) of the form $\langle x, v \rangle$, where x is the t-object and v is the value read from the transaction T_i.
- $T_i.WS$(write set): It is a list of (d_tuples) of the form $\langle x, v \rangle$, where x is the t-object to which transaction T_i writes the value v.

For each transaction object (t_object) x:

- $x.vl$(version list): It is a list consisting of version tuples (v_tuple) of the form $\langle ts, v, rl \rangle$ where ts is the timestamp of the committed transaction that writes the value v to x. The list rl is the read list consisting of a set of transactions that have read the value v (described below). Informally the version list consists of all the committed transaction that have ever written to this t-object and the set of corresponding transactions that have read each of those values.
- rl(read list): This list contains all the read transaction tuples (rt_tuples) of the form $\langle j \rangle$, where j is the timestamp of the reading transaction. The read list rl is stored in each tuple of the version list described above.

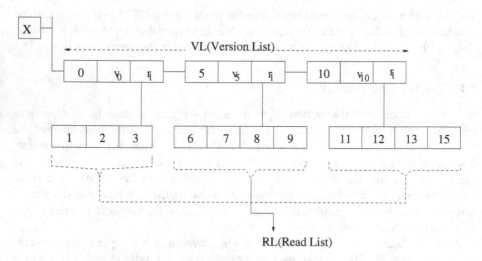

Fig. 2. Data Structures for Maintaining Versions

Figure 2 illustrates how the version list and read list are managed. In addition, the algorithm maintains two global data-structures:

- tCounter: This counter is used to generate the ids/timestamp for a newly invoked transaction. This is incremented everytime a new transaction is invoked.
- liveList: This list keeps track of all the transactions that are currently incomplete or live. When a transaction begins, its id is added to this list. When it terminates (by abort or commit), the id is deleted from this list.

The STM system consists of the following operations/functions. These are executed whenever a transaction begins, reads, write or tries to commit:

$initialize()$: This operation initializes the STM system. It is assumed that the STM system knows all the t-objects ever accessed. All these t-objects are initialized with value 0 by the initial transaction T_0 in this operation. A version tuple $\langle 0, 0, nil \rangle$ is inserted into all the version list of all the t-objects.

$begin\_tran()$: A thread invokes a transaction by executing this operation. It returns an unique transaction identifier which is also its timestamp. The id is used in all other operations exported by the STM system. The id is further stored in the $liveList$.

$read_i(x)$: This operation is invoked when transaction T_i wants to read a t-object x. First, the t-object x is locked. Then the version list of x is searched to identify the correct $version\_tuple$ (i.e the version created by a writing transaction). The tuple with the largest timestamp less than i, say $\langle j, v \rangle$ is identified from the version-list. Then, i is added to the read list of j's version tuple. Finally, the value v written by transaction j, is returned.

$find\_lts(i, x)$: This function is invoked by $read_i(x)$ and finds the tuple $\langle j, v, rl \rangle$ having the largest timestamp value j smaller than i (denoted as lts).

$write_i(x, v)$: Here write is performed onto the local memory by transaction T_i. This operation appends the data tuple $\langle x, v \rangle$ into the WS of transaction T_i.

$tryC_i()$: This operation is invoked when a transaction T_i has completed all its operations and wants to commit. This operation first checks whether T_i is read-only transaction or not. If it is read-only then it returns commit. Otherwise, for each t-object x (accessed in a predefined order) in T_i's write set, the following check is performed: if timestamp of T_i, i, lies between the timestamps of the T_j and T_k, where transaction T_k reads x from transaction T_j, i.e $j < i < k$, then the transaction T_i is aborted.

If this check succeeds for all the t-objects written by T_i, then the version tuples are appended to the version lists and the transaction T_i is committed. Before returning either commit or abort, the transaction id i is removed from liveList.

The system orders all the t-objects ever accessed as $x_1, x_2, ..., x_n$ by any transaction (assuming that the system accesses a total of n t-objects). In this operation, each transaction locks and access t-objects in this increasing order which ensures that the system does not deadlock.

$check\_versions(i, x)$: This function checks the version list of x. For all version tuples $\langle j, v, rl \rangle$ in $x.vl$ and for all transactions T_k in rl, it checks if the timestamp of T_i is between the timestamp of the T_j and T_k, i.e $j < i < k$. If so, it returns false else true.

Theorem 4. *The history generated by MVTO algorithm is opaque.*

Theorem 5. *Assuming that no transaction fails and all the locks are starvation-free, every operation of MVTO algorithm eventually returns.*

Algorithm 1. STM $initialize()$: Invoked at the start of the STM system. Initializes all the t-objects used by the STM System

1: **for all** x used by the STM System **do**
2:     /* T_0 is initializing x */
3:         add $\langle 0, 0, nil \rangle$ to $x.vl$;
4: **end for**;

Algorithm 2. STM $begin\_tran()$: Invoked by a thread to being a new transaction T_i

1: lock $liveList$;
2: // Store the latest value of $tCounter$ in i.
3: $i = tCounter$;
4: $tCounter = tCounter + 1$;
5: add i to $liveList$;
6: unlock $liveList$;
7: return i;

Algorithm 3. STM $read_i(x)$: A Transaction T_i reads t-object x

1: lock x;
2: // From $x.vls$, identify the right $version\_tuple$.
3: $\langle j, v, rl \rangle = find\_lts(i, x)$;
4: Append i into rl; // Add i into j's rl.
5: $unlock\ x$;
6: return (v); // v is the value returned

Algorithm 4. $find\_lts(i, x)$: Finds the tuple $\langle j, v, rl \rangle$ created by the transaction T_j with the largest timestamp smaller than i

1: // Initialize $closest\_tuple$
2: $closest\_tuple = \langle 0, 0, nil \rangle$;
3: **for all** $\langle k, v, rl \rangle \in x.vl$ **do**
4:     **if** $(k < i)$ and $(closest\_tuple.ts < k)$ **then**
5:         $closest\_tuple = \langle k, v, rl \rangle$;
6:     **end if**;
7: **end for**;
8: return $(closest\_tuple)$;

Algorithm 5. STM $write_i(x, v)$: A Transaction T_i writes into local memory

1: Append the $d\_tuple\langle x, v \rangle$ to $T_i.WS$.
2: return ok;

Algorithm 6. STM $tryC()$: Returns ok on commit else return Abort

1: **if** $(T_i.WS == NULL)$ **then**
2:     $removeId(i)$;
3:     return ok; // A read-only transaction.
4: **end if**;
5: **for all** $d\_tuple(x, v)$ in $T_i \cdot WS$ **do**
6:     /* Lock the t-objects in a predefined order to avoid deadlocks */
7:     Lock x;
8:     **if** $(check\_versions(i, x) == false)$ **then**
9:        $removeId(i)$;
10:       unlock all the variables locked so far;
11:       return $Abort$;
12:     **end if**;
13: **end for**;
14: /* Successfully checked for all the write variables and not yet aborted. So the new write versions can be inserted. */
15: **for all** $d\_tuples\langle x, v\rangle$ in $T_i.WS$ **do**
16:     insert $v\_tuple\langle i, v, nil\rangle$ into $x.vl$ in the increasing order;
17: **end for**;
18: $removeId(i)$;
19: unlock all the variables;
20: return ok;

Algorithm 7. $check\_versions(i, x)$:Checks the version list; it returns True or false

1: **for all** $v\_tuples\langle j, v, rl\rangle$ in $x \cdot vl$ **do**
2:     **for all** T_k in rl **do**
3:       /* T_k has already read the version created by T_j */
4:       **if** $(j < i < k)$ **then**
5:         return $false$;
6:       **end if**;
7:     **end for**;
8: **end for**;
9: return $true$;

Algorithm 8. $removeId(i)$:Removes transaction id i from the $liveList$

1: lock $liveList$;
2: remove i from $liveList$;
3: unlock $liveList$;

On mv-permissiveness of MVTO: It can be seen that MVTO algorithm does not abort read-only transactions. It also has the nice property that it does not require transactions to be annotated as read-only before execution. Interestingly this implementation satisfies the definition of mv-permissiveness as defined by Perelman et al [19]: an update transaction aborts only when it conflicts with another update transaction.

But intuitively by mv-permissiveness, Perelman et al meant "read-only transactions do not cause update transactions to abort" as stated by them in [19, section 4]. But this property is not true for MVTO. For instance, consider the following history generated by the MVTO algorithm: $H5 : w_1(x, 1)w_1(y, 1)c_1r_4(x, 1)w_2(x, 2)w_1(y, 2)a_2$. Here, when T_2 tries to commit after writing to x, the MVTO algorithm will abort it. Thus, it can be argued that the read-only transaction T_4 has caused the update transaction T_2 to abort.

6   Garbage Collection

As one can see with multi-version STMs, multiple versions are created. But storing multiple versions can unnecessarily waste memory. Hence, it is important to perform garbage collection by deleting unwanted versions of t-objects. Some of the earlier STM systems solve this problem by maintaining a fixed number of versions for each t-object. We on the other hand, do not restrict the number of versions. The STM system will detect versions that will never again be used (i.e. have become garbage) and delete them. The garbage collection routine will be invoked from the tryC function whenever the number of versions of a t-object has become greater than a predefined threshold. If required, the threshold can be decided dynamically by the application invoking the STM system based on the current memory requirements. If the threshold is set to 0, then the garbage collection routine will be invoked every time an update transaction invokes tryC and commits.

The STM system will delete a version of a t-object x created by transaction T_i when the following conditions are satisfied: (1) At least one another version of x has been created by T_k and $i < k$; (2) Let T_k be the transaction that has the smallest timestamp larger than i and has created a version of x. Then for every j such that $i < j < k$, T_j has terminated (either committed or aborted).

The reason for having condition 1 is to ensure that there exists at least one version in every state. This rule also ensures that the version created by the transaction with the largest timestamp is never deleted. Now in condition 2, if all the transactions between T_i and T_k have committed then no other transaction will ever read from T_i. Hence, the version of T_i can be deleted.

The complete details of the algorithm is mentioned in [12]. The garbage collection algorithm maintains the read and write rules (described in SubSection 5.1). Hence, its correctness is preserved and the histories generated are opaque. Further, it can be shown that the garbage collection algorithm has the nice property that the number of versions maintained by MVTO is bounded by the total number of live transactions.

7 Discussion and Conclusion

There are many applications that require long running read-only transactions. Many STM systems can cause such transactions to abort. Multi-version STM system ensure that a read-only transactions does not need to abort by maintaining sufficient versions. To capture this notion precisely, Perelman et al [19] defined the notion of mv-permissiveness which (among other things) says that read operations always succeed.

Recently Attiya and Hillel [1] proposed a single-version STM system that is mv-permissive. Thus, if single-version STMs can achieve mv-permissiveness, a natural question that arises is how much extra concurrency can be achieved by multi-version STMs. To address this issue, we have formally shown that with multiple versions, higher concurrency can possibly be achieved. We then show that any STM system that is permissive w.r.t opacity must maintain at least L versions where L is the maximum number of live transactions in the system. The number of live transactions represents the concurrency in a STM system and hence can be unbounded. Thus, an implication of this result is that no single-version or any bounded-version STM can be permissive w.r.t opacity.

We then presented a timestamp based multiversion STM system (MVTO) that satisfies opacity and ensures that no read-only transaction aborts. We believe that the proposed algorithm is very intuitive and easy to implement. Our algorithm is similar in spirit to Lu and Scott's multiversion STM system [15]. Like their algorithm, even our algorithm uses timestamps to decide which version to read from. But unlike their algorithm, it does not need transactions to be annotated as read-only prior to the start of the execution. We also presented an algorithm for garbage collection that deletes version that will never be used. The garbage collection algorithm ensures that on being invoked, reduces the number of versions to less than or equal to the number of live transactions in the history (if number of live transactions is greater than 0).

Although several multi-version STM systems have been proposed that are opaque, to the best of our knowledge none of them have formally been proved to be opaque. In fact, Perelman et al [19] formally prove that their algorithm satisfies strict-serializability. Even though they claim that their algorithm can be easily proved to satisfy opacity, it is not clear how.

As a part of future work, we would like to modify our algorithm to ensure that it satisfies mv-permissiveness. We also plan to implement this algorithm and test its performance on various benchmarks. As a part of the implementation, we would like to compare the performance of our algorithm with Attiya and Hillel's algorithm. We would to see how much benefit do multiple versions offer in practice and the cost required to achieve this.

References

[1] Attiya, H., Hillel, E.: A Single-Version STM that is Multi-Versioned Permissive. Theory Comput. Syst. 51(4), 425–446 (2012)

[2] Aydonat, U., Abdelrahman, T.: Serializability of Transactions in Software Transactional Memory. In: TRANSACT 2008: 3rd Workshop on Transactional Computing (February 2008)

[3] Bernstein, P.A., Goodman, N.: Multiversion Concurrency Control: Theory and Algorithms. ACM Trans. Database Syst. 8(4), 465–483 (1983)

[4] Cachopo, J., Rito-Silva, A.: Versioned Boxes as the basis for Memory Transactions. Science of Computer Programming 63(2), 172–185 (2006)

[5] Dice, D., Shalev, O., Shavit, N.: Transactional locking II. In: Dolev, S. (ed.) DISC 2006. LNCS, vol. 4167, pp. 194–208. Springer, Heidelberg (2006)

[6] Fernandes, S.M., Cachopo, J.: Lock-free and Scalable Multi-version Software Transactional Memory. In: Proceedings of the 16th ACM Symposium on Principles and Practice of Parallel Programming, PPoPP 2011, pp. 179–188. ACM, New York (2011)

[7] Guerraoui, R., Henzinger, T.A., Singh, V.: Permissiveness in Transactional Memories. In: Taubenfeld, G. (ed.) DISC 2008. LNCS, vol. 5218, pp. 305–319. Springer, Heidelberg (2008)

[8] Guerraoui, R., Kapalka, M.: On the Correctness of Transactional Memory. In: PPoPP 2008: Proceedings of the 13th ACM SIGPLAN Symposium on Principles and Practice of Parallel Programming, pp. 175–184. ACM, New York (2008)

[9] Guerraoui, R., Kapalka, M.: Principles of Transactional Memory, Synthesis Lectures on Distributed Computing Theory. Morgan and Claypool (2010)

[10] Herlihy, M., Moss, J.E.B.: Transactional memory: Architectural Support for Lock-Free Data Structures. SIGARCH Comput. Archit. News 21(2), 289–300 (1993)

[11] Herlihy, M., Luchangco, V., Moir, M., Scherer III, W.N.: Software transactional memory for dynamic-sized data structures. In: PODC 2003: Proc. 22nd ACM Symposium on Principles of Distributed Computing, pp. 92–101 (July 2003)

[12] Kumar, P., Peri, S.: A timestamp based multi-version stm protocol that satisfies opacity. CoRR, abs/1305.6624 (2013)

[13] Kuznetsov, P., Peri, S.: On non-interference of transactions. CoRR, abs/1211.6315 (2012)

[14] Kuznetsov, P., Ravi, S.: On the cost of concurrency in transactional memory. In: Fernàndez Anta, A., Lipari, G., Roy, M. (eds.) OPODIS 2011. LNCS, vol. 7109, pp. 112–127. Springer, Heidelberg (2011)

[15] Lu, L., Scott, M.L.: Unmanaged Multiversion STM. Transact (2012)

[16] Papadimitriou, C.H.: The serializability of concurrent database updates. J. ACM 26(4), 631–653 (1979)

[17] Papadimitriou, C.H., Kanellakis, P.C.: On Concurrency Control by Multiple Versions. ACM Trans. Database Syst. 9(1), 89–99 (1984)

[18] Perelman, D., Byshevsky, A., Litmanovich, O., Keidar, I.: SMV: Selective Multi-Versioning STM. In: Peleg, D. (ed.) Distributed Computing. LNCS, vol. 6950, pp. 125–140. Springer, Heidelberg (2011)

[19] Perelman, D., Fan, R., Keidar, I.: On Maintaining Multiple Versions in STM. In: PODC, pp. 16–25 (2010)

[20] Riegel, T., Felber, P., Fetzer, C.: A Lazy Snapshot Algorithm with Eager Validation. In: Dolev, S. (ed.) DISC 2006. LNCS, vol. 4167, pp. 284–298. Springer, Heidelberg (2006)

[21] Shavit, N., Touitou, D.: Software Transactional Memory. In: PODC 1995: Proceedings of the Fourteenth Annual ACM Symposium on Principles of Distributed Computing, pp. 204–213. ACM, New York (1995)

Optimized OR-Sets without Ordering Constraints

Madhavan Mukund*, Gautham Shenoy R.**, and S.P. Suresh

Chennai Mathematical Institute, India
{madhavan,gautshen,spsuresh}@cmi.ac.in

Abstract. Eventual consistency is a relaxation of strong consistency that guarantees that if no new updates are made to a replicated data object, then all replicas will converge. The *conflict free replicated datatypes (CRDTs)* of Shapiro et al. are data structures whose inherent mathematical structure guarantees eventual consistency. We investigate a fundamental CRDT called *Observed-Remove Set (OR-Set)* that robustly implements sets with distributed add and delete operations. Existing CRDT implementations of OR-Sets either require maintaining a permanent set of "tombstones" for deleted elements, or imposing strong constraints such as causal order on message delivery. We formalize a concurrent specification for OR-Sets without ordering constraints and propose a generalized implementation of OR-sets without tombstones that provably satisfies strong eventual consistency. We introduce *Interval Version Vectors* to succinctly keep track of distributed time-stamps in systems that allow out-of-order delivery of messages. The space complexity of our generalized implementation is competitive with respect to earlier solutions with causal ordering. We also formulate *k-causal delivery*, a generalization of causal delivery, that provides better complexity bounds.

1 Introduction

The Internet hosts many services that maintain replicated copies of data across distributed servers with support for local updates and queries. An early example is the Domain Name Service (DNS) that maintains a distributed mapping of Internet domain names to numeric IP addresses. More recently, the virtual shopping carts of online merchants such as Amazon also follow this paradigm.

The users of these services demand high availability. On the other hand, the underlying network is inherently prone to local failures, so the systems hosting these replicated data objects must be partition tolerant. By Brewer's CAP theorem, one has to then forego strong consistency, where local queries about distributed objects return answers consistent with the most recent update [1].

Eventual consistency is a popular relaxation of consistency for distributed systems that require high availability alongside partition tolerance [2–4]. In such

---

* Partially supported by Indo-French CNRS LIA Informel.
** Supported by TCS Research Scholarship.

M. Chatterjee et al. (Eds.): ICDCN 2014, LNCS 8314, pp. 227–241, 2014.

systems, the local states of nodes are allowed to diverge for finite, not necessarily bounded, durations. Assuming that all update messages are reliably delivered, eventual consistency guarantees that the states of all the replicas will converge if there is a sufficiently long period of quiescence [2]. However, convergence involves detecting and resolving conflicts, which can be problematic.

Conflict free replicated datatypes (CRDTs) are a class of data structures that satisfy strong eventual consistency by construction [5]. This class includes widely used datatypes such as replicated counters, sets, and certain kinds of graphs.

Sets are basic mathematical structures that underlie many other datatypes such as containers, maps and graphs. To ensure conflict-freeness, a robust distributed implementation of sets must resolve the inherent non-serializability of add and delete operations of the same element in a set. One such variant is known as an *Observed-Remove Set (OR-Set)*, in which adds have priority over deletes of the same element, when applied concurrently.

The naïve implementation of OR-sets maintains all elements that have ever been deleted as a set of *tombstones* [5]. Consider a sequence of add and delete operations in a system with N replicas, in which t elements are added to the set, but only p are still present at the end of the sequence because of intervening deletes. The space complexity of the naïve implementation is $O(t \log t)$, which is clearly not ideal. If we enforce causal ordering on the delivery of updates, then the space complexity can be reduced to $O((p + N) \log t)$ [6].

On the other hand, causal ordering imposes unnecessary constraints: even independent actions involving separate elements are forced to occur in the same order on all replicas. Unfortunately, there appears to be no obvious relaxation of causal ordering that retains enough structure to permit the simplified algorithm of [6]. Instead, we propose a generalized implementation that does not make any assumptions about message ordering but reduces to the algorithm of [6] in the presence of causal ordering. We also describe a weakening of causal ordering that allows efficient special cases of our implementation.

The main contributions of this paper are as follows:

- We identify some gaps in the existing concurrent specification of OR-Sets [6], which assumes causal delivery of updates. We propose a new concurrent specification for the general case without assumptions on message ordering.
- We present a generalized implementation of OR-sets whose worst-case space complexity is $O((p+Nm) \log t)$, where m is the maximum number of updates at any one replica. We introduce *Interval Version Vectors* to succinctly keep track of distributed-time stamps in the presence of out-of-order messages.
- We formally prove the correctness of our generalized solution, from which the correctness of all earlier implementations follows.
- We introduce k-*causal delivery*, a delivery constraint that generalizes causal delivery. When updates are delivered in k-causal order, the worst-case space complexity of our generalized implementation is $O((p + Nk) \log t)$. Since 1-causal delivery is the same as causal delivery, the solution presented in [6] is a special case of our generalized solution.

The paper is organized as follows. In Section 2, we give a brief overview of *strong eventual consistency* and *conflict free replicated datatypes (CRDTs)*. In the next section, we describe the naïve implementation of OR-Sets and the existing concurrent specification that assumes causal delivery. In Section 4, we propose a generalized specification of OR-sets along with an optimized implementation, neither of which require any assumption about delivery constraints. In the next section, we introduce k-causal delivery and analyze the space-complexity of the generalized algorithm. In Section 6, we provide a proof of correctness for the generalized solution. We conclude with a discussion about future work.

2 Strong Eventual Consistency and CRDTs

We restrict ourselves to distributed systems with a fixed number of nodes (or replicas). We allow both nodes and network connections to fail and recover infinitely often, but we do not consider Byzantine faults. We assume that when a node recovers, it starts from the state in which it crashed.

In general, concurrent updates to replicas may conflict with each other. The replicas need to detect and resolve these conflicts to maintain eventual consistency. For instance, consider two replicas r_1 and r_2 of an integer with value 1. Suppose r_1 receives an update *multiply*(3) concurrently with an update *add*(2) at r_2. If each replica processes its local update before the update passed on by the other replica, the copies at r_1 and r_2 would have values 5 and 9, respectively.

Conflict resolution requires the replicas to agree on the order in which to apply the set of updates received from the clients. In general, it is impossible to solve the consensus problem in the presence of failures [7]. However, there are several eventually consistent data structures whose design ensures that they are conflict free. To characterize their behaviour, a slightly stronger notion of eventual consistency called *strong eventual consistency (SEC)* has been proposed [8].

Strong eventual consistency is characterized by the following principles

- **Eventual delivery:** An update delivered at some correct replica will eventually be delivered to all correct replicas.
- **Termination:** All delivered methods are eventually enabled (their preconditions are satisfied) and method executions terminate.
- **Strong Convergence:** Correct replicas that have been delivered the same updates have equivalent state.

Strong convergence ensures that systems are spared the task of performing conflict-detection and resolution. Datatypes that satisfy strong eventual consistency are called *conflict-free replicated datatypes (CRDTs)*.

Conflict-free Replicated DataTypes (CRDTs)

In a replicated datatype, a client can send an update operation to any replica. The replica that receives the update request from the client is called the *source replica* for that update. The source replica typically applies the update locally and·then propagates information about the update to all the other replicas. On receiving this update, each of these replicas applies it in its current state.

Replicated datatypes come in two flavours, based on how replicas exchange information about updates. In a *state-based replicated data object*, the source replica propagates its entire updated state to the other replicas. State-based replicated objects need to specify a *merge* operation to combine the current local state of a replica with an updated state received from another replica to compute an updated local state. Formally, a state-based replicated datatype is a tuple $O = (\mathcal{S}, S_\perp, Q, U, m)$ where $\mathcal{S}$ is the set of all possible states of the replicated object, $S_\perp$ is the initial state, Q is the set of all side-effect free query operations, U is the set of all update-operations that source replicas apply locally, and $m : \mathcal{S} \times \mathcal{S} \to \mathcal{S}$ is the merge function.

Propagating states may not be practical—for instance, the payload may be prohibitively large. In such cases replicas can, instead, propagate update operations. These are called *operation based (op-based) replicated datatypes*. When a source replica receives an update request, it first computes the arguments required to perform the actual update and sends a confirmation to the client. This is called the *update-prepare* phase and is free of side-effects. It then sends the arguments prepared in the update-prepare phase to all other replicas, including itself, to perform the actual update. This phase modifies the local state of each replica and is called the *update-downstream phase*. At the source replica, the prepare and downstream phases are applied *atomically*. Formally, an op-based replicated datatype is a tuple $O = (\mathcal{S}, S_\perp, Q, V, P)$ where $\mathcal{S}$, $S_\perp$, and Q are as in state-based replicated datatypes, V is the set of updates of the form (p, u) where p is the side-effect free update-prepare method and u is the update-downstream method, and P is a set of delivery preconditions that control when an update-downstream message can be delivered at a particular replica.

We denote the kth operation at a replica r of a state-based or object-based datatype by f_r^k and the state of replica r after applying the kth operation by S_r^k. Note that for all replicas r, $S_r^0 = S_\perp$. The notation $S \circ f$ is used to denote the result of applying operation f on state S. The notation $S \xrightarrow{f} S'$ is used to denote that $S' = S \circ f$. The argument of the operation f is denoted $\arg(f)$.

A reachable state of a replica is obtained by a sequence of operations $S_r^0 \xrightarrow{f_r^1} S_r^1 \xrightarrow{f_r^2} \cdots \xrightarrow{f_r^k} S_r^k$. The *causal history* of a reachable state S_r^k, denoted by $\mathcal{H}(S_r^k)$, is the set of updates (for state-based objects) or update-downstream operations (for op-based objects) received so far. This is defined inductively as follows:

- $\mathcal{H}(S_r^0) = \emptyset$.
- $\mathcal{H}(S_r^k) = \mathcal{H}(S_r^{k-1})$ if f_r^k is a query operation or an update-prepare method.
- $\mathcal{H}(S_r^k) = \mathcal{H}(S_r^{k-1}) \cup \{f_r^k\}$ if f_r^k is an update or update-downstream operation.
- $\mathcal{H}(S_r^k) = \mathcal{H}(S_r^{k-1}) \cup \mathcal{H}(S_{r'}^\ell)$ if f_r^k is a merge operation and $\arg(f_r^k) = (S_r^{k-1}, S_{r'}^\ell)$.

An update (p, u) at source replica r is said to have *happened before* an update (p', u') at source replica r' if $\exists k : p' = f_{r'}^k \wedge u \in \mathcal{H}(S_{r'}^{k-1})$. We denote this by

$(p, u) \xrightarrow{hb} (p', u')$ or simply $u \xrightarrow{hb} u'$. Any pair of updates that are not comparable through this relation are said to be *concurrent updates*. A pair of states S and S' are said to be *query-equivalent*, or simply *equivalent*, if for all query operations $q \in Q$, the result of applying q at S and S' is the same. A collection of updates is said to be *commutative* if at any state $S \in \mathcal{S}$, applying any permutation of these updates leads to equivalent states. We say that the delivery subsystem satisfies *causal delivery* if for any two update operations (p, u) and (p', u'),

$$(p, u) \xrightarrow{hb} (p', u') \implies \forall r, k : (u' \in \mathcal{H}(S_r^k) \implies u \in \mathcal{H}(S_r^{k-1})).$$

That is, whenever (p, u) has happened before (p', u'), at all other replicas, the downstream method u is delivered before u'.

A state-based replicated object that satisfies strong eventual consistency is called a *Convergent Replicated DataType (CvRDT)*. A sufficient condition for this is that there exists a partial order $\leq$ on its set of states $\mathcal{S}$ such that: i) $(\mathcal{S}, \leq)$ forms a join-semilattice, ii) whenever $S \xrightarrow{u} S'$ for an update u, $S \leq S'$, and iii) all merges compute least upper bounds [8].

Assuming termination and causal delivery of updates, a sufficient condition for an op-based replicated datatype to satisfy strong eventual consistency is that concurrent updates should commute and all delivery preconditions are compatible with causal delivery. Such a replicated datatype is called a *Commutative Replicated DataType (CmRDT)* [8].

In this paper we look at a conflict-free *Set* datatype that supports features of both state-based and op-based datatypes.

3   Observed-Remove Sets

Consider a replicated set of elements over a universe $\mathcal{U}$ across N replicas $Reps = [0..N-1]$. Clients interact with the set through a query method *contains* and two update methods *add* and *delete*. The set also provides an internal method *compare* that induces a partial order on the states of the replicas and a method *merge* to combine the local state of a replica with the state of another replica. Let i be the source replica for one of these methods op. Let S_i and S'_i be the states at i before and after applying the operation op, respectively. The sequential specification of the set is the natural one:

- $S_i \circ contains(e)$ returns true iff $e \in S_i$.
- $S_i \xrightarrow{contains(e)} S'_i$ iff $S'_i = S_i$.
- $S_i \xrightarrow{add(e)} S'_i \implies S'_i = S_i \cup \{e\}$.
- $S_i \xrightarrow{delete(e)} S'_i \implies S'_i = S_i \setminus \{e\}$.

Thus, in the sequential specification, two states S, S' are query-equivalent if for every element $e \in \mathcal{U}$, $S \circ contains(e)$ returns true iff $S' \circ contains(e)$. Notice that the state of a replica gets updated not only when it acts as a source replica for some update operation, but also when it applies updates, possibly concurrent ones, propagated by other replicas, either through downstream operations or through a *merge* request.

Defining a concurrent specification for sets is a challenge because *add(e)* and *delete(e)*, for the same element e, do not commute. If these updates are concurrent, the order in which they are applied determines the final state.

An *Observed-Remove Set* (OR-Set) is a replicated set where the conflict between concurrent *add(e)* and *delete(e)* operations is resolved by giving precedence to the *add(e)* operation so that e is eventually present in all the replicas [5]. An OR-Set implements the operations *add*, *delete*, *adddown*, *deldown*, *merge*, and *compare*, where *adddown* and *deldown* are the downstream operations corresponding to the *add* and *delete* operations, respectively.

A concurrent specification for OR-sets is provided in [6]. Let S be the abstract state of an OR-set, $e \in \mathcal{U}$ and $u_1 \parallel u_2 \parallel \cdots \parallel u_n$ be a set of concurrent update operations. Then, the following conditions express the fact that if even a single update adds e, e must be present after the concurrent updates.

- $(\exists i : u_i = delete(e) \land \forall i : u_i \neq add(e)) \implies e \notin S$ after $u_1 \parallel u_2 \parallel \cdots \parallel u_n$
- $(\exists i : u_i = add(e)) \implies e \in S$ after $u_1 \parallel u_2 \parallel \cdots \parallel u_n$

As we shall see, this concurrent specification is incomplete unless we assume causal delivery of updates.

Naïve Implementation. Algorithm 1 is a variant of the naïve implementation of this specification given in [5]. Let $\mathcal{M} = \mathcal{U} \times \mathbb{N} \times [0 \ldots N-1]$. For a triple $m = (e, c, r)$ in $\mathcal{M}$, we say $data(m) = e$ (the data or payload), $ts(m) = c$ (the timestamp), and $rep(m) = r$ (the source replica). Each replica maintains a local set $E \subseteq \mathcal{M}$. When replica r receives an $add(e)$ operation, it tags e with a unique identifier (c, r) (line 8), where this $add(e)$ operation is the cth *add* operation overall at r, and propagates (e, c, r) downstream to be added to E. Symmetrically, deleting an element e involves removing every triple m from E with $data(m) = e$. In this case, the source replica propagates the set $M \subseteq E$ of elements matching e downstream to be deleted at all replicas (lines 16–17).

For an add operation, each replica downstream should add the triple m

```
A Naïve OR-set implementation for replica r
 1   E ⊆ M, T ⊆ M, c ∈ ℕ: initially ∅, ∅, 0.
 2
 3   Boolean CONTAINS(e ∈ 𝒰):
 4       return (∃m : m ∈ E ∧ data(m) = e)
 5
 6   ADD(e ∈ 𝒰):
 7       ADD.PREPARE(e ∈ 𝒰):
 8           Broadcast downstream((e, c, r))
 9       ADD.DOWNSTREAM(m ∈ 𝓜):
10           E := (E ∪ {m}) \ T
11           if (rep(m) = r)
12               c = ts(m) + 1
13
14   DELETE(e ∈ 𝒰):
15       DELETE.PREPARE(e ∈ 𝒰):
16           Let M := {m ∈ E | data(m) = e}
17           Broadcast downstream(M)
18       DELETE.DOWNSTREAM(M ⊆ 𝓜):
19           E := E \ M
20           T := T ∪ M
21
22   Boolean COMPARE(S′, S″ ∈ 𝒮):
23       Assume that S′ = (E′, T′, c′)
24       Assume that S″ = (E″, T″, c″)
25       Let b_seen := (E′ ∪ T′) ⊆ (E″ ∪ T″)
26       Let b_deletes := T′ ⊆ T″
27       return b_seen ∧ b_deletes
28
29   MERGE(S′ ∈ 𝒮):
30       Assume that S′ = (E′, T′, c′)
31       E := (E \ T′) ∪ (E′ \ T)
32       T := T ∪ T′
```

Algorithm 1. Naïve implementation

to its local copy of E. However, with no constraints on the delivery of messages, a *delete* operation involving m may overtake an *add* update for m. For example in Figure 1, replica r'' receives $deldown(\{(e, c+1, r)\})$ before it receives $adddown(e, c+1, r)$. Alternatively, after applying a *delete*, a replica may merge its state with another replica that has not performed this *delete*, but has performed the corresponding *add*. For instance, in Figure 1, replica r'' merges its state with replica r when r'' has applied $deldown(\{(e, c+1, r)\})$ but r has not. To ensure that m is not accidentally added back in E in such cases, each replica maintains a set T of *tombstones*, containing every triple m ever deleted (lines 19–20). Before adding m to E, a replica first checks that it is not in T (line 10).

State S of replica r is more up-to-date than state S' of replica r' if r has seen all the triples present in S' (either through an add or a delete) and r has deleted all the triples that r' has deleted. This is checked by *compare* (lines 22–27). Finally, the *merge* function of states S and S' retains only those triples from $S.E \cup S'.E$ that have not been deleted in either S or S' (line 31). The *merge* function also combines the triples that have been deleted in S and S' (line 32).

Eliminating Tombstones [6]. Since T is never purged, $E \cup T$ contains every element that was ever added to the set. To avoid keeping an unbounded set of tombstones, a solution is proposed in [6] that requires all updates to be delivered in causal order. The solution uses a version vector [9] at each replica to keep track of the latest add operation that it has received from every other replica.

Causal delivery imposes unnecessary restrictions on the delivery of independent updates. For example, updates at a source replica of the form $add(e)$ and $delete(f)$, for distinct elements e and f, need not be delivered downstream in the same order to all other replicas. For the concurrent specification presented earlier to be valid, it is sufficient to have causal delivery of updates involving the same element e. While this is weaker than causal delivery across all updates, it puts an additional burden on the underlying delivery subsystem to keep track of the partial order of updates separately for each element in the universe. A weaker delivery constraint is FIFO, which delivers updates originating at the same source replica in the order seen by the source. However, this is no better than out-of-order delivery since causally related operations on the same element that originate at different sources can still be delivered out-of-order.

On the other hand, the naïve implementation works even when updates are delivered out-of-order. However, reasoning about the state of the replicas is nontrivial in the absence of any delivery guarantees. We illustrate the challenges posed by out-of-order delivery before formalizing a concurrent specification for OR-Sets that is independent of delivery guarantees.

Life without Causal Delivery: Challenges

If we assume causal delivery of updates, then it is easy to see that all replicas apply non-concurrent operations in the same order. Hence it is sufficient for the specification to only talk about concurrent operations. However, without causal

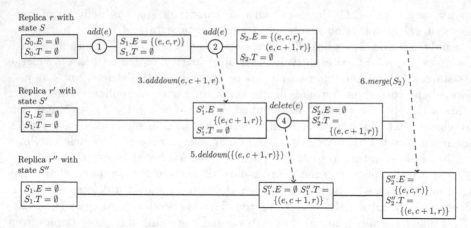

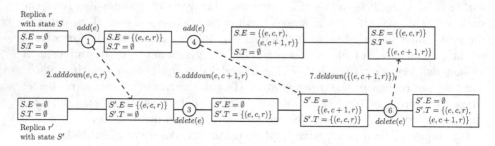

Fig. 1. Non-transitivity of the happened-before relation

delivery, even non-concurrent operations can exhibit counter-intuitive behaviours. We identify a couple of them in Examples 1 and 2.

Example 1. *In the absence of causal delivery, the happened-before relation need not be transitive. For instance, in Figure 1, if we denote the add operations at 1 and 2 as $\text{add}_1(e)$ and $\text{add}_2(e)$, respectively, then we can observe that $\text{add}_1(e) \xrightarrow{hb} \text{add}_2(e)$ and $\text{add}_2(e) \xrightarrow{hb} \text{delete}(e)$. However, it is not the case that $\text{add}_1(e) \xrightarrow{hb} \text{delete}(e)$ since the source replica of delete(e), which is r', has not processed the downstream of $\text{add}_1(e)$ before processing the prepare method of delete(e).*

Fig. 2. Non-intuitive behaviour of *deletes* in the absence of causal delivery

Example 2. *In the absence of causal delivery, a delete-downstream(e) may not remove all copies of e from the set—even copies corresponding to add(e) operations that happened before. Say (e, c, r) is added at r, propagated to r', and subsequently deleted at r'. Suppose $(e, c + 1, r)$ is later added at r, propagated to r', and subsequently deleted at r'. If the second delete is propagated from r' to r before the first one, r removes only $(e, c + 1, r)$ while retaining (e, c, r), as illustrated in Figure 2.*

To address these issues, we present a more precise formulation of the concurrent specification that captures the intent of [5] and allows us to uniformly reason about the states of the replicas of OR-Sets independent of the order of delivery of updates.

4   Optimized OR-Sets

Revised Specification. For an $add(e)$ operation op, the set of *nearest delete* operations, $NearestDel(op)$, is defined to be the following set:

$$\{op' \mid op' = delete(e) \wedge op \xrightarrow{hb} op' \wedge \neg(\exists op''.op'' = delete(e) \wedge op \xrightarrow{hb} op'' \xrightarrow{hb} op')\}$$

If u is the downstream operation of op and u' is the downstream operation of $op' \in NearestDel(op)$ then we extend this notation to write $u' \in NearestDel(u)$. Our new concurrent specification for OR-Sets is as follows.

> For any reachable state S and element e, $e \in S$ iff $\mathcal{H}(S)$ contains a downstream operation u of an $add(e)$ operation such that $NearestDel(u) \cap \mathcal{H}(S) = \emptyset$.

The specification ensures that a delete operation at a replica removes only those elements whose add operations the replica has *observed*. Thus, whenever a replica encounters concurrent add and delete operations with the same argument, the add wins, since the delete has not seen the element added by that particular add. The specification also ensures that any two states that have the same causal history are query-equivalent. Hence the order in which the update operations in the causal history were applied to arrive at these two states is not relevant. Since there are no delivery preconditions in the specification, any implementation of this specification is a *CmRDT*, as all the operations commute.

The revised specification generalizes the concurrent OR-set specification from [6]. Suppose $u_1 \parallel u_2 \parallel \cdots \parallel u_n$ is performed at a replica with state S. Let $S' = S \circ (u_1 \parallel u_2 \parallel \cdots \parallel u_n)$. If one of the u_i's is $add(e)$, it is clear that $NearestDel(u_i) \cap \mathcal{H}(S') = \emptyset$. Thus, $e \in S'$. On the other hand, if at least one of the u_i's is $del(e)$ and none of the u_i's is an $add(e)$, then, *assuming causal delivery*, for every u_i of the form $delete(e)$, if $e \in S$, there is an $add(e)$ operation $u \in \mathcal{H}(S)$ such that $u_i \in NearestDel(u)$. Thus $e \notin S'$, as expected.

The new specification also explains Examples 1 and 2. In Example 1, the $add(e)$ operation at 1 does not have a nearest delete in $\mathcal{H}(S_2'')$, which explains why $e \in S_2''$. Similarly in the other example, the $add(e)$ operation at 1 does not have a nearest delete in the history of replica r, but it has a nearest delete (operation 3) in the history of replica r'. This explains why e is in the final state of r but does not belong to the final state of r'.

Generalized Implementation. Algorithm 2 describes our optimized implementation of OR-sets that does not require causal ordering and yet uses space comparable to the solution provided in [6]. Our main observation is that tomb-stones are only required to track $delete(e)$ operations that overtake $add(e)$ operations from the same replica. Since a source replica attaches a timestamp (c, r) with each $add(e)$ operation, all we need is a succinct way to keep track of those timestamps that are "already known".

For a pair of integers $s \leq \ell$, $[s, \ell]$ denotes the *interval* consisting of all integers from s to ℓ. A finite set of intervals $\{[s_1, \ell_1], \ldots, [s_n, \ell_n]\}$ is *nonoverlapping* if for all distinct $i, j \leq n$, either $s_i > \ell_j$ or $s_j > \ell_i$. An *interval sequence* is a finite set of nonoverlapping intervals. We denote by $\mathcal{I}$ the set of all interval sequences.

The basic operations on interval sequences are given below. The function PACK(N) collapses a set of numbers N into an interval sequence. The function UNPACK(A) expands an interval sequence to the corresponding set of integers. Fundamental set operations can be performed on interval sequences by first unpacking and then packing. For $N \subseteq \mathbb{N}$, $A, B \in \mathcal{I}$, and $n \in \mathbb{N}$:

- PACK$(N) = \{[i, j] \mid \{i, i+1, \ldots, j\} \subseteq N, i - 1 \notin N, j + 1 \notin N\}$.
- UNPACK$(A) = \{n \mid \exists [n_1, n_2] \in A \wedge n_1 \leq n \leq n_2\}$.
- $n \in A$ iff $n \in$ UNPACK(A).
- **add**$(A, N) =$ PACK$($UNPACK$(A) \cup N)$.
- **delete**$(A, N) =$ PACK$($UNPACK$(A) \setminus N)$.
- **max**$(A) =$ max$($UNPACK$(A))$.
- $A \cup B =$ PACK$($UNPACK$(A) \cup$ UNPACK$(B))$.
- $A \cap B =$ PACK$($UNPACK$(A) \cap$ UNPACK$(B))$.
- $A \subseteq B$ iff UNPACK$(A) \subseteq$ UNPACK(B).

As in the algorithm of [6], when replica r receives an $add(e)$ operation, it tags e with a unique identifier (c, r) and propagates (e, c, r) downstream to be added to E. In addition, each replica r maintains the set of all timestamps c received from every other replica r' as an interval sequence $V[r']$. The vector V of interval sequences is called an *Interval Version Vector*. Since all the downstream operations with source replica r are applied at r in causal order, $V[r]$ contains a single interval $[1, c_r]$ where c_r is the index of the latest add operation received by r from a client. Notice that if $delete(e)$ at a source replica r' is a *nearest delete* for an $add(e)$ operation, then the unique identifier $(ts(m), rep(m))$ of the triple m generated by the add operation will be included in the interval version vector propagated downstream by the $delete$ operation. When this vector arrives at a replica r downstream, r updates the interval sequence $V[rep(m)]$ to record the missing add operation (lines 25–26) so that, when m eventually arrives to be added through the add-downstream operation, it can be ignored (lines 10–12).

Thus, we avoid maintaining tombstones altogether. The price we pay is maintaining a collection of interval sequences, but these interval sequences will eventually get merged once the replica receives all the pending updates, collapsing the representation to contain at most one interval per replica.

In [6], the authors suggest a solution in the absence of causal delivery using *version vectors with exceptions (VVwE)*, proposed in [10]. A VVwE is an array each of whose entries is a pair consisting of a timestamp and an *exception set*, and is

Optimized OR-set implementation for the replica r

```
1   E ⊆ M, V : Reps → I, c ∈ N: initially ∅, [∅, ..., ∅], 0
2
3   Boolean CONTAINS(e ∈ U):
4       return (∃m : m ∈ E ∧ data(m) = e)
5
6   ADD(e ∈ U):
7       ADD.PREPARE(e ∈ U):
8           Broadcast downstream((e, c, r))
9       ADD.DOWNSTREAM(m ∈ M):
10          if (ts(m) ∉ V[rep(m)])
11              E := E ∪ {m}
12              V[rep(m)] :=
                    add(V[rep(m)], {ts(m)})
13          if (rep(m) = r)
14              c = ts(m) + 1
15
16  DELETE(e ∈ U):
17      DELETE.PREPARE(e ∈ U):
18          Let V' : Reps → I = [0, ..., 0]
19          for m ∈ E with data(m) = e
20              add(V'[rep(m)], {ts(m)})
21          Broadcast downstream(V')
22      DELETE.DOWNSTREAM(V' : Reps → I):
23          Let M = {m ∈ E |
                    ts(m) ∈ V'[rep(m)]}
24          E := E \ M
25          for i ∈ Reps
26              V[i] := V[i] ∪ V'[i]
27
```

```
28  Boolean COMPARE(S', S'' ∈ S):
29      Assume that S' = (E', V')
30      Assume that S'' = (E'', V'')
31      b_seen := ∀i(V'[i] ⊆ V''[i])
32      b_deletes := ∀m ∈ E'' \ E'
                    (ts(m) ∉ V'[rep(m)])
33      // If m is deleted from E' then
34      // it is also deleted in E''.
35      // So anything in E'' \ E'
36      // is not even visible in S'.
37      return b_seen ∧ b_deletes
38
39  MERGE(S' ∈ S):
40      Assume that S' = (E', V')
41      E := {m ∈ E ∪ E' |
                m ∈ E ∩ E' ∨
                ts(m) ∉ V[rep(m)] ∩ V'[rep(m)]}
42      // You retain m if it is either
43      // in the intersection, or if it is fresh
44      // (so one of the states has not seen it).
45      ∀i.(V[i] := V[i] ∪ V'[i])
```

Algorithm 2. An optimized OR-Set implementation

used to handle out-of-order message delivery. For instance, if replica r sees operations of r' with timestamps $1, 2$, and 10, then it will store $(10, \{3, 4, 5, 6, 7, 8, 9\})$, signifying that 10 is the latest timestamp of an r'-operation seen by r, and that $\{3, 4, \ldots, 9\}$ is the set of operations that are yet to be seen. The same set of timestamps would be represented by the interval sequence $\{[1, 2], [10, 10]\}$. In general, it is easy to see that interval sequences are a more succinct way of representing timestamps in systems that allow out-of-order delivery.

5 k-Causal Delivery, Add-Coalescing and Space Complexity

Let S_r denote the state of a replica $r \in [0 \ldots N-1]$. Let n_ℓ be the number of *adddown* operations whose source is ℓ. The space required to store S_r in the naïve implementation is bounded by $O(n_t \log(n_t))$, where $n_t = \sum_{\ell=0}^{N-1} n_\ell$.

Let n_p denote the number all *adddown* operations $u \in \mathcal{H}(S_r)$ such that $NearestDel(u) \cap \mathcal{H}(S_r) = \emptyset$. Clearly $n_p \leq n_t$. Let $n_m = \max(n_0, \ldots, n_{N-1})$ and let n_{int} denote the maximum number of intervals across any index r' in $V_r[r']$. In our optimized implementation, the space required to store $S_r.V$ is bounded by $Nn_{int} \log(n_t)$ and the space required to store $S_r.E$ is bounded by $n_p \log(n_t)$. The space required to store S_r is thus bounded by $O((n_p + Nn_{int}) \log(n_t))$.

In the worst case, n_{int} is bounded by $n_m/2$, which happens when r sees only the alternate elements generated by any replica. Thus the worst case complexity is $O((n_p + N n_m) \log(n_t))$. Note that the factor that is responsible for increasing the space complexity is the number of intervals n_{int}. We propose a reasonable way of bounding this value below.

Let (p, u) be an update operation whose source is replica r. For a given $k \geq 1$, we say that the delivery of updates satisfies k-causal delivery iff

$$\forall r, r' : (p = f_r^j \wedge u = f_{r'}^{j'}) \implies \forall u' \in \mathcal{H}(S_r^{j-k}), u' \in \mathcal{H}(S_{r'}^{j'-1}).$$

Intuitively it means that when a replica r' sees the jth add operation originating at replica r, it should have already seen all the operations from r with index smaller than $j - k$. Note that when $k = 1$, k-causal delivery is the same as causal delivery. Thus k-causal delivery ensures that the out of order delivery of updates is restricted to a bounded suffix of the sequence of operations submitted to the replicated datatype.

In particular, if the latest add-downstream operation u received by a replica r from a replica r' corresponds to the cth add operation at r', then k-causal delivery ensures that r would have received all the add-downstream operations from r' whose index is less than or equal to $(c-k)$. Thus, the number of intervals in $S_r.V[r']$ is bounded by k and hence n_{int} is bounded by $O(k)$.

With k-causal delivery, we can also coalesce the adds of the same elements that originate from the same replica. This is discussed in detail in the full version of the paper [11]. The key idea is that whenever a replica r sees a triple (e, c, r') , it can evict all the triples of the form (e, c', r') with $c' \leq c - k$. Thus each replica keeps at most k triples corresponding to each visible element originating from a replica. If there are n_a visible elements, then n_p is bounded by $O(n_a N k)$. With add-coalescing and k-causal delivery, the total space complexity at a replica is is $O((n_a + 1) N k \log(n_t))$. Furthermore, the message complexity of a *deldown* operation with this optimization would be bounded by $O(N k \log(n_t))$. If we assume causal delivery of updates ($k = 1$), the space complexity is bounded by $O((n_a + 1) N \log(n_t))$ and the message complexity of *deldown* is $O(N \log(n_t))$ which matches the complexity measures in [6]. If the delivery guarantee is FIFO delivery, then with add-coalescing, n_p can be bounded by $O(n_a N K)$. However, there is no natural way of bounding the number of intervals n_{int} with FIFO order, and hence the space complexity with FIFO ordering would be $O((n_a k + n_{int}) N \log(n_t))$ as discussed in [11].

6   Correctness of the Optimized Implementation

In this section we list down the main lemmas and theorems, with proof sketches, to show the correctness of our optimized solution. The complete proofs can be found in [11]. Our aim is show that the solution satisfies the specification of OR-Sets and is a CvRDT as well as a CmRDT. For a detailed proof of the equivalence between the naïve implementation and our optimized implementation, the reader is encouraged to refer to [11].

Recall that $\mathcal{U}$ is the universe from which elements are added to the OR-Set and $Reps = [0 \ldots N-1]$ is the set of replicas. We let $\mathcal{M} = \mathcal{U} \times \mathbb{N} \times Reps$ denote the set of *labelled elements*. We use r to denote replicas, e to denote elements of $\mathcal{U}$, and m to denote elements of $\mathcal{M}$, with superscripts and subscripts as needed. For $m = (e, c, r) \in \mathcal{M}$, we set $data(m) = e$ (the data or payload), $ts(m) = c$ (the timestamp), and $rep(m) = r$ (the source replica).

A set of labelled elements $M \subseteq \mathcal{M}$ is said to be *valid* if it does not contain distinct items from the same replica with the same timestamp. Formally,

$$\forall m, m' \in M : (ts(m) = ts(m') \land rep(m) = rep(m')) \implies m = m'$$

A downstream operation u is said to be an e-add-downstream operation (respectively, e-delete-downstream operation) if it is a downstream operation of an $add(e)$ (respectively, $delete(e)$) operation. If $\mathcal{O}$ is a collection of commutative update operations then for any state S, $S \circ \mathcal{O}$ denotes the state obtained by applying these operations to S in any order.

We say that two states S and S' are *equivalent* and write $S \equiv S'$ iff $S.E = S'.E$ and $S.V = S'.V$. It is easy to see that if S and S' are equivalent then they are also query-equivalent.

Lemma 1. *Let S be some reachable state of the* OR-Set, $\mathcal{O} = \{u_1, u_2, \ldots u_n\}$ *be a set of downstream operations and π_1 and π_2 are any two permutations of $[1 \cdots n]$. If $S_1 = S \circ u_{\pi_1(1)} \circ u_{\pi_1(2)} \cdots u_{\pi_1(n)}$ and $S_2 = S \circ u_{\pi_2(1)} \circ u_{\pi_2(3)} \cdots u_{\pi_2(n)}$ then $S_1 = S_2$.*

Proof Sketch: If u is any downstream update and S is any state it can be easily shown that $S \circ u = S \circ merge(S_\perp \circ u)$ Now for any three states S_1, S_2, S_3, it can be seen that $(S_1 \circ merge(S_2)) \circ merge(S_3) = (S_1 \circ merge(S_3)) \circ merge(S_2)$, thereby proving commutativity of merges. Using these two results, it follows that any collection of update operations commute. $\square$

Using the lemma above, one can conclude the following, by induction over $|\mathcal{H}(S)|$.

Lemma 2. *Let S be any reachable state, with $\mathcal{H}(S) = \{u_1, u_2, \ldots u_n\}$. Then $S = S_\perp \circ \mathcal{H}(S)$.*

Lemma 3. *Let S be any state and u be an e-add downstream operation such that $u \notin \mathcal{H}(S)$ and $arg(u) = m$, and let $S' = S \circ u$. Then $m \in S'.E$ iff $NearestDel(u) \cap \mathcal{H}(S) = \emptyset$.*

Proof Sketch: If $NearestDel(u) \cap \mathcal{H}(S) = \emptyset$ then $ts(m) \notin S.V[rep(m)]$ and, from the code of *adddown*, it follows that $m \in S'.E$. Conversely suppose $u' \in NearestDel(u) \cap \mathcal{H}(S)$. Since downstream operations commute (and prepare and query operations do not change state), we can assume that there is a state S'' such that $S = S'' \circ u'$. One can then show (by examining the code for the *add* and *delete* methods) that $S'' \circ u' \circ u = S'' \circ u'$. Thus $S = S'$. Since $u \notin \mathcal{H}(S)$, we have that $m \notin S.E$. Hence $m \notin S'.E$ $\square$

Theorem 1. *The optimized OR-set implementation satisfies the specification of OR-Sets.*

Proof Sketch: Given a state S and an element e, let $\mathcal{O}_{add}$ be the set of all e-add-downstream operations u in $\mathcal{H}(S)$ such that $NearestDel(u) \cap \mathcal{H}(S) = \emptyset$. If $\mathcal{O}_{others} = \mathcal{H}(S) \setminus \mathcal{O}_{add}$ then, $S = S_\perp \circ \mathcal{O}_{others} \circ \mathcal{O}_{add}$ (since the downstream operations commute). Using Lemma 3 we can show that $e \notin S_\perp \circ \mathcal{O}_{others}$. Again from Lemma 3, $e \in S$ iff $\mathcal{O}_{add}$ is non-empty iff there exists an e-add-downstream operation u such that $NearestDel(u) \cap \mathcal{H}(S) = \emptyset$.   □

Given a reachable state S we define the set of timestamps of all the elements added and deleted, $Seen(S)$, as $\{(c, r) \mid c \in S.V[r]\}$, and the set of timestamps of elements deleted in S, $Deletes(S)$, as $Seen(S) \setminus \{(ts(m), rep(m)) \mid m \in S.E\}$. For states S, S' we say $S \leq_{compare} S'$ to mean that $compare(S, S')$ returns true.

Lemma 4. *For states S_1, S_2 and S_3 ,*

1. $S_1 \leq_{compare} S_2$ *iff* $Seen(S_1) \subseteq Seen(S_2)$ *and* $Deletes(S_1) \subseteq Deletes(S_2)$. *Therefore $\leq_{compare}$ defines a partial order on S.*
2. $S_3 = S_1 \circ merge(S_2)$ *iff* $Seen(S_3) = Seen(S_1) \cup Seen(S_2)$ *and* $Deletes(S_3) = Deletes(S_1) \cup Deletes(S_2)$ *iff S_3 is the least upper bound of S_1 and S_2 in the partial order defined by $\leq_{compare}$.*

Proof Sketch:

1. Follows from the definitions of *Seen, Deletes* and the code of *compare* in the optimized solution.
2. The first equivalence follows from the code of *merge*, and the definitions of *Seen, Deletes*. The second equivalence follows from the first part, and the fact that $A \cup B$ is the least upper bound of sets A and B over the partial order defined by $\subseteq$.

□

From Lemma 1 and Lemma 4, we have the following.

Theorem 2. *The optimized OR-Set implementation is a CmRDT and CvRDT.*

7   Conclusion and Future Work

In this paper, we have presented an optimized OR-Set implementation that does not depend on the order in which updates are delivered. The worst-case space complexity is comparable to the naïve implementation [5] and the best-case complexity is the same as that of the solution proposed in [6].

The solution in [6] requires causal ordering over all updates. As we have argued, this is an unreasonably strong requirement. On the other hand, there seems to be no simple relaxation of causal ordering that retains the structure required by the simpler algorithm of [6]. Our new generalized algorithm can accommodate any specific ordering constraint that is guaranteed by the delivery subsystem. Moreover, our solution has led us to identify k-causal ordering as a natural generalization of causal ordering, where the parameter k directly captures the impact of out-of-order delivery on the space requirement for bookkeeping.

Our optimized algorithm uses interval version vectors to keep track of the elements that have already been seen. It is known that regular version vectors have a bounded representation when the replicas communicate using pairwise synchronization [9]. An alternative proof of this in [12] is based on the solution to the *gossip problem* for synchronous communication [13], which has also been generalized to message-passing systems [14]. It would be interesting to see if these ideas can be used to maintain interval version vectors using a bounded representation. This is not obvious because intervals rely on the linear order between timestamps and reusing timestamps typically disrupts this linear order.

Another direction to be explored is to characterize the class of datatypes with noncommutative operations for which a CRDT implementation can be obtained using interval version vectors.

References

1. Gilbert, S., Lynch, N.A.: Brewer's conjecture and the feasibility of consistent, available, partition-tolerant web services. SIGACT News 33(2), 51–59 (2002)
2. Shapiro, M., Kemme, B.: Eventual consistency. In: Encyclopedia of Database Systems, pp. 1071–1072 (2009)
3. Saito, Y., Shapiro, M.: Optimistic replication. ACM Comput. Surv. 37(1), 42–81 (2005)
4. Vogels, W.: Eventually consistent. ACM Queue 6(6), 14–19 (2008)
5. Shapiro, M., Preguiça, N., Baquero, C., Zawirski, M.: A comprehensive study of Convergent and Commutative Replicated Data Types. Rapport de recherche RR-7506. INRIA (January 2011),
   http://hal.inria.fr/inria-00555588/PDF/techreport.pdf
6. Bieniusa, A., Zawirski, M., Preguiça, N.M., Shapiro, M., Baquero, C., Balegas, V., Duarte, S.: An optimized conflict-free replicated set. CoRR abs/1210.3368 (2012)
7. Fischer, M.J., Lynch, N.A., Paterson, M.: Impossibility of distributed consensus with one faulty process. J. ACM 32(2), 374–382 (1985)
8. Shapiro, M., Preguiça, N., Baquero, C., Zawirski, M.: Conflict-free replicated data types. In: Défago, X., Petit, F., Villain, V. (eds.) SSS 2011. LNCS, vol. 6976, pp. 386–400. Springer, Heidelberg (2011)
9. Almeida, J.B., Almeida, P.S., Baquero, C.: Bounded version vectors. In: Guerraoui, R. (ed.) DISC 2004. LNCS, vol. 3274, pp. 102–116. Springer, Heidelberg (2004)
10. Malkhi, D., Terry, D.B.: Concise version vectors in WinFS. Distributed Computing 20(3), 209–219 (2007)
11. Mukund, M., Shenoy, G.R., Suresh, S.P.: Optimized or-sets without ordering constraints. Technical report, Chennai Mathematical Institute (2013),
    http://www.cmi.ac.in/~madhavan/papers/pdf/mss-tr-2013.pdf
12. Mukund, M., Shenoy, G.R., Suresh, S.P.: On bounded version vectors. Technical report, Chennai Mathematical Institute (2012),
    http://www.cmi.ac.in/~gautshen/pubs/BVV/on_bounded_version_vectors.pdf
13. Mukund, M., Sohoni, M.A.: Keeping track of the latest gossip in a distributed system. Distributed Computing 10(3), 137–148 (1997)
14. Mukund, M., Narayan Kumar, K., Sohoni, M.A.: Bounded time-stamping in message-passing systems. Theor. Comput. Sci. 290(1), 221–239 (2003)

Quorums Quicken Queries: Efficient Asynchronous Secure Multiparty Computation*

Varsha Dani[1], Valerie King[2], Mahnush Movahedi[1], and Jared Saia[1,**]

[1] University of New Mexico
[2] University of Victoria

Abstract. We describe an asynchronous algorithm to solve secure multiparty computation (MPC) over n players, when strictly less than a $\frac{1}{8}$ fraction of the players are controlled by a static adversary. For any function f over a field that can be computed by a circuit with m gates, our algorithm requires each player to send a number of field elements and perform an amount of computation that is $\tilde{O}(\frac{m}{n} + \sqrt{n})$. This significantly improves over traditional algorithms, which require each player to both send a number of messages and perform computation that is $\Omega(nm)$.

Additionaly, we define the *threshold counting problem* and present a distributed algorithm to solve it in the asynchronous communication model. Our algorithm is load balanced, with computation, communication and latency complexity of $O(\log n)$, and may be of independent interest to other applications with a load balancing goal in mind.

1 Introduction

Recent years have seen a renaissance in secure multiparty computation (MPC), but unfortunately, the distributed computing community is in danger of missing out. In particular, while new MPC algorithms boast dramatic improvements in latency and communication costs, none of these algorithms offer significant improvements in the highly *distributed* case, where the number of players is large.

This is unfortunate, since MPC holds the promise of addressing many important problems in distributed computing. How can peers in Bittorrent auction off resources without hiring an auctioneer? How can we design a decentralized Twitter that enables provably anonymous broadcast of messages. How can we create deep learning algorithms over data spread among large clusters of machines?

In this paper, we take a first step towards solving MPC for large distributed systems. We describe algorithms that require each player to send a number of messages and perform an amount of computation that is $\tilde{O}(\frac{m}{n} + \sqrt{n})$, where n is the number of players and m is the number of gates in the circuit to be computed. This significantly improves over current algorithms, which require each player to both send a number of messages and perform computation that is $\Omega(nm)$. We now describe our model and problem.

---

* Full version of this paper is available at http://cs.unm.edu/~movahedi/mpc.pdf.
** Partially supported by NSF CAREER Award 0644058 and NSF CCR-0313160.

M. Chatterjee et al. (Eds.): ICDCN 2014, LNCS 8314, pp. 242–256, 2014.

Model: There are n players, with a private and authenticated channel between every pair of players. Communication is via asynchronous message passing, so that sent messages may be arbitrarily and adversarially delayed. Latency in this model is defined as the maximum length of any chain of messages (see [11,3]).

We assume a Byzantine adversary controls an unknown subset of up to t of the players. These players are *bad* (*i.e.* Byzantine) and the remaining players are *good*. The good players run our algorithm, but the bad players may deviate in an arbitrary manner. Our adversary is *static, i.e.* it must select the set of bad players at the start of our algorithm. The adversary is computationally unbounded. Thus, we make no cryptographic hardness assumptions.

MPC Problem: Each player, p_i, has a private input x_i. All players know a n-ary function f. We want to ensure that: 1) all players learn the value of f on the inputs; and 2) the inputs remain as private as possible: each player p_i learns nothing about the private inputs other than what is revealed by the output of f and the player's private value x_i.

In the asynchronous setting, the problem is challenging even with a trusted third party. In particular, the trusted party can not determine the difference between a message never being sent and a message being arbitrarily delayed, and so the t bad players can always refrain from sending any messages to the trusted party. Thus, the trusted party must wait to receive $n - t$ inputs. Then it must compute the function f using default values for the missing inputs, and send the output back to the players as well as the number of received inputs.[1] The goal of an asynchronous MPC protocol is to simulate the above scenario, without the trusted third party.

The function to be computed is presented as a circuit C with m gates. For convenience of presentation, we assume each gate has fan-in two and fan-out at most two. For any two gates x and y in C, if the output of x is input to y, we say that x is a *child* of y and that y is a *parent* of x. We also assume that all computations in the circuit occur over a finite field $\mathbb{F}$; The size of $\mathbb{F}$ depends on the specific function to be computed but must always be $\Omega(\log n)$. All the inputs, outputs and messages sent during the protocol are elements of $\mathbb{F}$, and consequently, messages will be of size $\log |\mathbb{F}|$.

Our MPC result requires solutions to the following two problems, which may be of independent interest.

Threshold Counting: There are n good players each with a bit initially set to 0. At least τ of the players will eventually set their bits to 1. The goal is for all the players to learn when the number of bits with values 1 is at least τ.

Quorum Formation: There are n players, up to t of whom may be bad. A *quorum* is a set of $c \log n$ players for some constant c. A quorum is called *good* if the fraction of bad players in it is at most $t/n + \delta$ for a fixed positive δ. We want all n players to agree on a set of n good quorums, and we want the quorums to be load-balanced: each player is mapped to $O(\log n)$ quorums.

---

[1] We send back only the number of inputs used, not the set of players whose inputs are used. This is required to ensure scalability; see Section 6.

1.1   Our Results

The main result of this paper is summarized by the following theorem.

Theorem 1. *Assume there are n players, less than a $\frac{1}{8} - \epsilon$ fraction of which are bad for some fixed $\epsilon > 0$, and an n-ary function, f that can be computed by a circuit of depth d with m gates. If all good players follow Algorithm 1, then with high probability (w.h.p.), they will solve MPC, while ensuring:*

1. *Each player sends at most $\tilde{O}(\frac{m}{n} + \sqrt{n})$ field elements,*
2. *Each player performs $\tilde{O}(\frac{m}{n} + \sqrt{n})$ computations, and*
3. *Expected total latency is $\tilde{O}(d \operatorname{polylog}(n))$.*

Our additional results are given by the following two theorems.

Theorem 2. *Assume n good players follow Algorithm τ-COUNTER. Then w.h.p., the algorithm solves the threshold counting problem, while ensuring:*

1. *Each player sends at most $O(\log n)$ messages of constant size,*
2. *Each player receives at most $O(\log n)$ messages,*
3. *Each player performs $O(\log n)$ computations,*
4. *Total latency is $O(\log n)$.*

Theorem 3. *Assume n players, up to $t < (\frac{1}{4} - \epsilon)n$ of whom are bad, for fixed $\epsilon > 0$. If all good players follow the CREATE-QUORUM protocol, the following are ensured w.h.p.:*

1. *The players agree on n good quorums,*
2. *Each player sends at most $\tilde{O}(\sqrt{n})$ bits,*
3. *Each player performs $\tilde{O}(\sqrt{n})$ computations,*
4. *Total latency is $O(\operatorname{polylog}(n))$.*

In the rest of the paper we discuss the algorithms and ideas involved in obtaining these results. Detailed proofs are deferred to the full version [16].

2   Related Work

The study of secure computation started in 1982 with the seminal work of Yao [27]. Later Goldrich, Micali, and Wigderson [20] proposed the first generic scheme for solving a cryptographic notion of MPC. This work was followed by some unconditionally-secure schemes in late 1980s [6,10,26,5,21,22,4]. Unfortunately, these methods all have poor communication scalability that prevents their wide-spread use. In particular, if there are n players involved in the computation and the function f is represented by a circuit with m gates, then these algorithms require each player to send a number of messages and perform a number of computations that is $\Omega(mn)$ (see [18,19,17]).

Recent years have seen exciting improvements in the cost of MPC when m is much larger than n [12,14,13]. For example, the computation and communication cost for the algorithm described by Damgård *et al.* in [13] is $\tilde{O}(m)$ plus a polynomial in n. However, the additive polynomial in n is large (e.g. $\Omega(n^6)$) and so these new algorithms are only efficient for relatively small n. Thus, there is still a need for MPC algorithms that are efficient in both n and m.

We first introduced the notion of using quorums for local communication to decrease the message cost in a brief announcement [15]. In that paper, we described a synchronous protocol with bit complexity of $\tilde{O}(\frac{m}{n} + \sqrt{n})$ per player that can tolerate a computationally unbounded adversary who controls up to $(\frac{1}{4} - \epsilon)$ fraction of the players for any fixed positive ϵ. This paper improves our previous result by handling asynchronous communication. One important challenge in the asynchronous communication model is to ensure that at least $n - t$ inputs are committed to, before the circuit evaluation. To address this issue we introduce and solve the *threshold counting problem*.

Boyle, Goldwasser, and Tessaro [8] describe a synchronous cryptographic protocol to solve MPC problem that is also based on quorums. Their algorithm uses a fully homomorphic encryption (FHE) scheme and thus, tolerates a computationally-bounded adversary that can take control of up to $(\frac{1}{3} - \epsilon)$ fraction of players for any fixed positive ϵ. Their protocol requires each player to send polylog(n) messages of size $\tilde{O}(n)$ bits and requires polylog(n) rounds. Interestingly the cost of the protocol is independent of the circuit size.

Counting Networks: Threshold counting can be solved in a load-balanced way using *counting networks*, which were first introduced by Aspnes, Herlihy, and Shavit [2]. Counting networks are constructed from simple two-input two-output computing elements called *balancers* connected to one another by wires. A counting network can count any number of inputs even if they arrive at arbitrary times, are distributed unevenly among the input wires, and propagate through the network asynchronously. Aspnes, Herlihy, and Shavit [2] establish an $O(\log^2 n)$ upper bound on the depth complexity of counting networks. Since the latency of counting is dependent to the depth of the network, minimizing the network's depth is a goal for papers in this area. A simple explicit construction of an $O(\log n c^{\log^* n})$-depth counting network, and a randomized construction of an $O(\log n)$-depth counting networkwhich works with high probability is described in [24,25]. These constructions use the AKS sorting network [1] as a building block. While the AKS sorting network and the resulting counting networks have $O(\log n)$ depth, large hidden constants render them impractical. We note that the threshold counting problem is simpler than general counting.

3   Preliminaries

We say an event occurs *with high probability (w.h.p)*, if it occurs with probability at least $1 - 1/n^c$, for some $c > 0$ and sufficiently large n. We assume all computations occur over a finite field $\mathbb{F}$. Every time we use a mask during the protocol, we assume the mask is a value chosen uniformly at random from $\mathbb{F}$.

We now describe protocols that we use as building blocks in this paper.

Secret Sharing In secret sharing, a player, called the dealer, wants to distribute a secret amongst a group of participants, each of whom is allocated a share of the secret. The secret can be reconstructed only when a sufficient number of shares are combined together and each of the shares reveals nothing to the player possessing it. If a method is used to ensure the dealer sends shares of a real secret and not just some random numbers, then the new scheme is called Verifiable Secret Sharing (VSS). As our model is asynchronous, we use the asynchronous VSS (or AVSS) scheme described by Benor, Canneti and Goldreich in [5]. We denote the sharing phase by AVSS-SHARE and the reconstruction phase by AVSS-REC. The protocol of [5] works correctly even if up to $\frac{1}{4}$ of the players are bad. The latency of the protocols is $O(1)$ and the communication cost is poly(q), where q is the number of players participating in the protocol. In this paper, we will use the protocols only among small sets of players (quorums) of logarithmic size, so q will be $O(\log n)$ and the communication cost per invocation will be polylog(n).

Heavy-Weight MPC: We use a heavy-weight asynchronous algorithm for MPC donated by HW-MPC. This algorithm, due to Ben-Or et al. [5], is an errorless MPC protocol that tolerates up to $\frac{1}{4}$ bad players. Let q be the number of players who run a HW-MPC to compute a circuit with $O(q)$ gates. The expected latency of HW-MPC is $O(q)$ and the number of messages sent poly(q). In this paper, we will use HW-MPC only for logarithmic number of players and gates, *i.e.*, $q = O(\log n)$ and the communication cost per invocation is polylog(n).[2]

Asynchronous Byzantine Agreement: In the Byzantine agreement problem, each player is initially given an input bit. All good players want to agree on a bit which coincides with at least one of their input bits. Every time a broadcast is required in our protocol, we use an asynchronous Byzantine agreement algorithm from [9], which we call ASYNCH-BA.

4   Technical Overview

We briefly sketch the ideas behind our three results.

Quorum-Based Gate Evaluation: The main idea for reducing the amount of communication required in evaluating the circuit is quorum-based gate evaluation. Unfortunately, if each player participates in the computation of the whole circuit, it must communicate with all other players. Instead, in quorum-based gate evaluation, each gate of the circuit is computed by a *gate gadget*. A gate gadget consists of three quorums: two *input quorums* and one *output quorum*. Input quorums are associated with the gate's children which serve inputs to the

---

[2] To make sure our algorithm has the expected total latency equal to $O(d \, \text{polylog}(n))$, every time we need to run the HW-MPC algorithm, we run $O(\log n)$ same copy of it each for $O(\text{polylog}(n))$ steps.

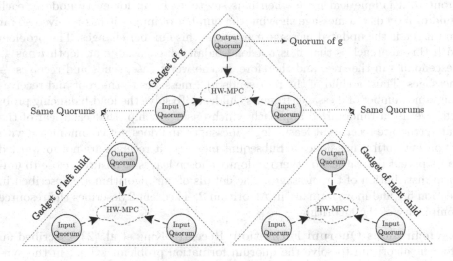

Fig. 1. The gate gadgets for gate g and its left and right children

gate. Output quorum is associated with the gate itself and is responsible to create a shared random mask and maintain the output of the quorum for later use in the circuit. As depicted in Figure 1, these gate gadgets connect to form the entire circuit. In particular, for any gate g, the output quorum of g's gadget is the input quorum of the gate gadget for all of g's parents (if any).

The players in each gate gadget run Hw-MPC among themselves to perform the gate operation. To make sure the computation is correct and secure, each gate gadget maintains the invariant that the value computed by the gadget is the value that the corresponding gate in the original circuit would compute, masked by a uniformly random element of the field. This random number is not known to any individual player. Instead, shares of it are held by the members of the output quorum. Thus, the output quorum can participate as an input quorum for the evaluation of any parent gate and provide the masked version of the inputs and shares of the mask.

This gate gadget computation is continued in the same way for all gates of the circuit until the final output of whole circuit is evaluated. This technique for evaluating a gate of the circuit using quorums, is illustrated in Figure 5.2 and the details are described in Section 5.1.

Threshold Counting: Our interest in threshold counting for this paper is to ensure that at least $n-t$ inputs are committed to, before the circuit evaluation occurs. To solve the threshold counting problem, we design a new distributed data structure and algorithm called τ-COUNTER. The τ-COUNTER enables threshold counting with asynchronous communication, and may be of use for other problems beyond MPC.

To give intuition, we first consider a naive approach for counting in asynchronous model. Assume a complete binary tree where each player sends its input to a unique leaf node when it is set to 1. Then, for every node v, each child of v sends v a message showing the number of inputs it has received so far and it sends the updated message every time this number changes. The problem with this approach is that it is not load-balanced: each node at depth i has $\frac{n}{2^i}$ descendants in the tree, and therefore, in the worst case, sends and receives $\frac{n}{2^i}$ messages. Thus, a child of the root sends $n/2$ messages to the root and receives the same number of messages from its children. To solve the load-balancing problem, we use a randomized approach which ensures w.h.p. that each leaf of the data structure receives at least $7 \log n$ messages and does not communicate with its parent until it has done so. Subsequnt messages it receives are not forwarded to its parent but rather to other randomly chosen leaves to ensure a close to uniform distribution of the messages. The details of our algorithm are described in Section 5.1 and more formally in Algorithm 2. Theorem 2 describes the resource complexity of the algorithm.

Asynchronous Quorum Formation: Recently, King et al. [23] described an efficient algorithm to solve the quorum formation problem, w.h.p., in the synchronous model with full information. Our new algorithm, CREATE-QUORUM, builds on the result of [23] to solve the quorum formation problem in the asynchronous model, with private channels. The properties of CREATE-QUORUM, are described by Theorem 3. The algorithm and the proof are deferred to the full version [16] due to space restrictions.

5   Our Algorithm

Our algorithm makes use of a *circuit graph*, G, which is based on the circuit C that computes f. We assume the gates of the circuit C are numbered $1, 2, \ldots, m$, where the gate numbered 1 is the output gate. The circuit graph is a directed acyclic graph over $m + n$ nodes. There are n of these nodes, one per player, that we call *input nodes*. There are m remaining nodes, one per gate, that we call *gate nodes*. For every pair of gate nodes x and y, there is an edge from x to y iff the output of the gate represented by node x is an input to the gate represented by node y. Also, for any input node z and gate node y, there is an edge from z to y if the player represented by gate node z has an input that feeds into the gate represented by node y. Similar to our definition in C, for any two nodes x and y in G, if x has an edge to y, we say that x is a *child* of y and that y is a *parent* of x. Also, for a given node v, we will say the *height* of v is the number of edges on the longest path from v to any input node in G. For each node in G, we define the following variables. Q_v is the quorum associated with node v. y_v is the output of the gate corresponding to v. Finally, r_v is a random mask and $\hat{y}_v$ is the masked output associated with node v, i.e. $\hat{y}_v = y_v + r_v$.

We number the nodes of G canonically in such a way that the input node numbered i corresponds to player p_i. We refer to the node corresponding to the output gate as the *output node*.

Algorithm 1 consists of four parts. The first part is to run CREATE-QUORUM in order to agree on n good quorums. The second part of the algorithm is

INPUT-COMMITMENT in which, quorums form the count tree. Then, each player p_i *commits* its input values to quorum i at the leaf nodes of the count tree and finally the players in that quorum decide whether these values are part of the computation or not. The details of this part of the algorithm is described in Section 5.1. The third part of the algorithm is evaluation of the circuit, described in detail in Section 5.2). Finally, the output from the circuit evaluation is sent back to all the players by quorums arranged in a complete binary tree.

Algorithm 1. Main Algorithm

---

1. All players run CREATE-QUORUM,
2. All players run INPUT-COMMITMENT,
3. All players run CIRCUIT-EVAL,
4. Propagate the output by quorums arranged in a complete binary tree.

5.1   Input-Commitment

In this section we describe a Monte Carlo algorithm, called τ-COUNTER that performs threshold counting for a threshold $\tau \geq n/2$.

The algorithm consists of up and down stages. For the up stage the players are arranged in a (pre-determined) tree data structure consisting of a root node with $O(\log n)$ children, each of which is itself the root of a complete binary tree; these subtrees have varying depths. The players in the trees count the number of 1-inputs, *i.e.* the number of players' inputs that are set to 1. As a result, the root can decide when the threshold is reached. In the down stage, the root notifies all the players of this event via a complete binary tree of depth $\log n$. Note that the trees used in the up and down stages have the same root. In what follows, unless otherwise specified, "tree" will refer to the tree data structure used for the up stage.

Let $D = \lceil \log \frac{\tau}{14 \log n} \rceil$. Note that $D = O(\log n)$. The root of our tree has degree D. Each of the D children of the root is itself the root of a complete binary subtree, which we will call a *collection subtree*. For $1 \leq j \leq D$, the jth collection subtree has depth $D + 1 - j$. Player 1 is assigned to the root and players 2 to $D + 1$, are assigned to its children, *i.e.* the roots of the collection subtrees, with player $j + 1$ being assigned to the jth child. The remaining nodes of the collection trees are assigned players in order, starting with $D + 2$, left to right and top to bottom. One can easily see that the entire data structure has fewer than n nodes, (in fact it has fewer than $\frac{\tau}{3 \log n}$ nodes) so some players will not be assigned to any node.

The leaves of each collection subtree are *collection nodes* while the internal nodes of each collection tree are *adding nodes*.

When a player's input is set to 1, it sends a $\langle \mathsf{Flag} \rangle$ message, which we will sometimes simply refer to as a flag, to a uniformly random collection node from the first collection subtree. Intuitively, we want the flags to be distributed close to evenly among the collection nodes. The parameters of the algorithm are set up so that w.h.p. each collection node receives at least $7 \log n$ $\langle \mathsf{Flag} \rangle$ messages.

Each collection node in the jth collection tree waits until it has received $7 \log n$ flags. It then sends its parent a $\langle \text{Count} \rangle$ message. For each additional flag received, up to $14 \log n$, it chooses a uniformly random collection node in the $(j + 1)$st collection subtree and forwards a flag to it. If $j = D$ then it forwards these $14 \log n$ flags directly to the root. Subsequent flags are ignored. Again, we use the randomness to ensure a close to even distribution of flags w.h.p.

Each adding node waits until it has received a $\langle \text{Count} \rangle$ message from each of its children. Then it sends a $\langle \text{Count} \rangle$ message to its parent. We note that each adding node sends exactly one message during the algorithm. The parameters of the algorithm are arranged so that all the $\langle \text{Count} \rangle$ messages that are sent in the the jth collection subtree together account for $\tau/2^j$ of the 1-inputs. Thus all the $\langle \text{Count} \rangle$ messages in all the collection subtrees together account for $\tau \left(1 - \frac{1}{2^D}\right)$ of the 1-inputs. At least $\frac{\tau}{2^D}$ 1-inputs remain unaccounted for. These and upto $O(\log n)$ more are collected as flags at the root.

Algorithm 2. τ-COUNTER

n is the number of players, τ is the threshold. $D = \lceil \log(\frac{\tau}{14 \log n}) \rceil$

1. Setup (no messages sent here):
   (a) Build the data structure:
       − Player 1 is the root.
       − For $1 \leq j \leq D$, player $j + 1$ is a child of the root and the root of the jth collection subtree, which has depth $D + 1 - j$.
       − The remainder of the nodes in the collection subtrees are assigned to players left to right and top to bottom, starting with player $D + 2$.
   (b) Let $sum = 0$ for the root.
2. Up stage
   (a) Individual Players: upon input change to **1** choose a uniformly random collection node v from collection subtree 1 and send a $\langle \text{Flag} \rangle$ to v.
   (b) Collection nodes in collection subtree j:
       − Upon receiving $7 \log n$ $\langle \text{Flag} \rangle$s from collection subtree $j - 1$, if $j > 1$, or from individual players if $j = 1$, send parent a $\langle \text{Count} \rangle$ message.
       − Upon subsequently receiving a $\langle \text{Flag} \rangle$, send it to a uniformly random collection node in collection subtree $j + 1$, if $j < D$. If $j = D$ then send these directly to the root. Do this for up to $14 \log n$ flags. Then ignore all subsequent $\langle \text{Flag} \rangle$ messagess.
   (c) Adding nodes: Upon receiving $\langle \text{Count} \rangle$ messages from both children, send parent a $\langle \text{Count} \rangle$ message.
   (d) Root: While $sum < \tau$
       − Upon receiving a $\langle \text{Count} \rangle$ message from the root of collection subtree j, increment sum by $\tau/2^j$
       − Upon receiving a $\langle \text{Flag} \rangle$ message, add one to sum.
3. Down stage (now $sum \geq \tau$)
   (a) Player 1 (the root): Send $\langle \text{Done} \rangle$ to Players 2 and 3, then terminate.
   (b) Player j for $j > 1$: Upon receiving $\langle \text{Done} \rangle$ from Player $\lfloor j/2 \rfloor$, forward it to Players $2j$ and $2j + 1$ (if they exist) and then terminate.

When player 1, at the root, has accounted for at least τ 1-inputs, it starts the down stage by sending the $\langle$Done$\rangle$ message to players 2 and 3. For $j > 1$, when player j receives the $\langle$Done$\rangle$ message, it forwards to players $2j$ and $2j + 1$. Thus, eventually the $\langle$Done$\rangle$ message reaches all the players, who then know that the threshold has been met. The formal algorithm is shown in Algorithm 2.

The algorithm INPUT-COMMITMENT is based on τ-COUNTER assuming that the nodes in the data structure are assigned quorums. We assume that the quorums have a canonical numbering $Q_1, Q_2, \ldots Q_n$ and the role of "player" i in τ-COUNTER is played by quorum Q_i. When we say quorum A sends a message M to quorum B, we mean that every (good) player in quorum A sends M to every player in quorum B. A player in quorum B is said to have received M from A if it receives M from at least 7/8 of the players in A.

Algorithm 3. INPUT-COMMITMENT
___
Run the following algorithms in parallel:

1. Algorithm IC-PLAYER.
2. Algorithm IC-INPUT.
3. Algorithm τ-COUNTER with $\tau = n - t$ and with quorums as participants.

Algorithm 4. IC-PLAYER
___
Run by player p_i with input x_i

1. $Q_v \leftarrow$ the quorum at the leaf node v associated with input of player p_i
2. Sample a uniformly random value from $\mathbb{F}$ and set r_v to this value.
3. $\hat{y}_v \leftarrow x_i + r_v$
4. Send $\hat{y}_v$ to all the players in Q_v
5. Run AVSS-SHARE to commit the secret value r_v to the players in Q_v.

Algorithm 5. IC-INPUT
___
Run by player p_j in Quorum Q_v associated with node v responsible for the input of p_i

1. After receiving $\hat{y}_v$ and a share of r_v, participate in the AVSS-SHARE verification protocol and agreement protocol to determine whether consistent shares for r_v and the same $\hat{y}_v$ are sent to everyone.
2. If the AVSS-SHARE verification protocol and the agreement protocol end and it is agreed that $\hat{y}_v$ was the same for all and shares of r_v are valid and consistent, set $b_{i,j} \leftarrow 1$ and you are ready to start the τ-COUNTER algorithm with $\langle$Flag$\rangle$ message.
3. Upon receiving $\langle$Done$\rangle$ from your parent quorum, participate in 5/8-MAJORITY using $b_{i,j}$ as your input. If it returns FALSE, reset $\hat{y}_v$ to the default value and your share of r_v to 0.

The τ-COUNTER is used for input commitment in the following way. Let v denote the input node associated with player p_i who holds input x_i. Quorum Q_i is assigned to this node. Player p_i samples r_v uniformly at random from $\mathbb{F}$, sets $\hat{y}_v$ to $x_i + r_v$ and sends $\hat{y}_v$ to all players in Q_i. Next, player p_i uses AVSS-SHARE to commit to the secret value r_v to all players in Q_i. Once player p_i has verifiably completed this process for the values x_i and r_{v_i}, we say that player p_i has *committed* its masked value to Q_i, and each player p_j in Q_i then sets a bit $b_{i,j}$ to 1. If player p_i's shares *fail* the verification process, then the $b_{i,j}$'s are set to 0, which is also the default value. Note that the quorum Q_i's input for τ-COUNTER will be 1 if 5/8 of the $b_{i,j}$ are 1. The quorums acting as nodes in the τ-COUNTER data structure, run Algorithm 2 with threshold of $n - t$ to determine when at least $n - t$ inputs have been committed. Note that when a quorum has to select a random quorum to communicate with, they must agree on the quorum via a multiparty computation.

Based on the down stage in τ-COUNTER, when at least $n - t$ inputs have been detected at the root node, it sends a ⟨Done⟩ message to all the quorums via a complete binary tree. When a player p_j who is a member of quorum Q_i receives the ⟨Done⟩ message, p_j participates in a HW-MPC with other members of Q_i, using $b_{i,j}$ as its input. This HW-MPC determines if at least 5/8 of the bits are set to 1. If they are, then the quorum determines that the i-th input (x_i) is part of the computation and uses the received value of $\hat{y}_v$ and shares of r_v as their input into GATE-EVAL. Otherwise, they set $\hat{y}_v$ to the default input and the shares of r_v to 0. We call this the 5/8-MAJORITY step.

5.2   Evaluating the Circuit

We assign nodes of G to quorums in the following way. The output node of G is assigned to quorum 1; then every node in G numbered i (other than the output node) is assigned to quorum number j, where $j = (i \mod n)$. Assume player p is in quorum Q_v at the leaf node v of count tree, which is the same quorum assigned to input node v in G. The circuit evaluation phase of the protocol for player p starts after the completion of the 5/8-MAJORITY step for node v in INPUT-COMMITMENT. After this step, for each input node v, players in Q_v know the masked input $\hat{y}_v$ and each has a share of the random element r_v, although the actual input and mask are unknown to any single player. The first step is to generate shares of uniformly random field elements for all gate nodes. If player p is in a quorum at gate node v, he generates shares of r_v, a uniformly random field element, by participating in the MASK-GENERATION algorithm. These shares are needed as inputs to the subsequent run of HW-MPC.

Next, players form the gadget for each gate node v with children left(v) and right(v) to evaluate the gate associated with v using GATE-EVAL as depicted in Figure 2. The values $y_{\text{left}(v)}$ and $y_{\text{right}(v)}$ are the inputs to the gate associated with v, and y_v is the output of v as it would be computed by a trusted party. First section of figure describes the initial conditions of the gate quorum and two input quorums before participating in HW-MPC. Each player in gate quorum Q_v has a share of the random element r_v (via MASK-GENERATION). Every player in the left input quorum $Q_{\text{left}(v)}$ has the masked value $\hat{y}_{\text{left}(v)} = y_{\text{left}(v)} + r_{\text{left}(v)}$ and a share of $r_{\text{left}(v)}$ (resp. for the right input quorum). In the second section, all the players of the three quorums run HW-MPC, using their inputs, in order to

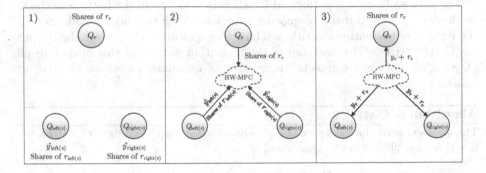

Fig. 2. Example Computation of a Gate associate with node v

Algorithm 6. CIRCUIT-EVAL

Run by each player p in a quorum associated with each node $v \in G$

1. For each input node v, after finishing INPUT-COMMITMENT with $\hat{y}_v$ and a share of r_v as output, p uses these as inputs to GATE-EVAL on each parent node of v.
2. For each gate node v:
   (a) p runs MASK-GENERATION on v and gets a share of r_v as output
   (b) p runs GATE-EVAL on v with its share of r_v as the input and gets $\hat{y}_v$ as output
   (c) p runs GATE-EVAL on each parent node of v with input $\hat{y}_v$ and p's share of r_v
3. After finishing computation of the gate represented by the output node, the players at the output node run OUTPUT-REC to reconstruct the output.

Algorithm 7. MASK-GENERATION

This protocol is run by each player p in a quorum associated with each gate node $v \in G$ to generate r_v.

1. Choose uniformly at random an element $r_{p,v} \in \mathbb{F}$ (this must be done independently each time this algorithm is run and independently of all other randomness used to generate shares of inputs etc.)
2. Run AVSS-SHARE to create verifiable secret shares of $r_{p,v}$ for each player in the quorum associated with v and deal these shares to all the players in the quorum associated with v including itself.
3. Participate in the AVSS-SHARE verification protocol for each received share. If the verification fails, set the particular share value to zero.
4. Add together all the shares (including the one dealt by yourself). This sum will be player p's share of the value r_v.

---

compute $\hat{y}_v$, which is equal to $y_v + r_v$. Third section shows the output of the gate evaluation after participating in HW-MPC. Each player in Q_v now knows 1) the output of the gate plus the value of r_v; and 2) shares of r_v. Thus, players in Q_v now have the input to perform the computation associated with the parents of v (if any). Note that both y_v and r_v themselves are unknown to any individual.

The gate evaluation is performed for all gate nodes from the bottom of the G to the top. The output of the quorum associated with the output node in G is the output of the entire algorithm. Thus, this quorum will unmask the output via OUTPUT-REC. The last step of the algorithm is to send this output to all players. We do via a complete binary tree of quorums, rooted at the output quorum.

Algorithm 8. GATE-EVAL

This protocol is run for each gate node v with children $\mathsf{left}(v)$ and $\mathsf{right}(v)$, the participants are the players in Q_v, $Q_{\mathsf{left}(v)}$ and $Q_{\mathsf{right}(v)}$.

1. If you are a player in $Q_{\mathsf{left}(v)}$, (resp. $Q_{\mathsf{right}(v)}$) use $(\hat{y}_{\mathsf{left}(v)},$ share of $r_{\mathsf{left}(v)})$ (resp. $(\hat{y}_{\mathsf{right}(v)},$ share of $r_{\mathsf{right}(v)}))$ as your input to HW-MPC. If you are a player in Q_v, use share of r_v as your input to HW-MPC.
2. Participate in HW-MPC.
3. $\hat{y}_v \leftarrow$ value returned by HW-MPC.

Algorithm 9. OUTPUT-REC

This protocol is run by all players in $Q_{\mathsf{output\text{-}node}}$.

1. Reconstruct $r_{\mathsf{output\text{-}node}}$ from its shares using AVSS-REC.
2. Set the circuit output message: $\langle O \rangle \leftarrow \hat{y}_{\mathsf{output\text{-}node}} - r_{\mathsf{output\text{-}node}}$.
3. Send $\langle O \rangle$ to all players in the quorums numbered 2 and 3.

---

6   Some Remarks

As described in the introduction, the goal of MPC is to simulate a trusted third party in computation of the circuit and then send back the computation result to the players. Let S denote the set of players from whom input is received by the (simulated) trusted party. Recall that $|S| \geq n - t$.[3] Thus, for an arbitrary S a description of S requires $\Omega(n)$ bits, and cannot be sent back to the players using only a scalable amount of communication. Therefore, we relax the standard requirement that S be sent back to the players. Instead, we require that at the end of the protocol each good player learns the output of f; whether or not their own input was included in S; and the *size* of S.

Also note that although we have not explicitly included this in INPUT-COMMITMENT, it is very easy for the players to compute the size of the computation set S. Once each input quorum Q_i has performed the 5/8-MAJORITY step and agreed on the bit $b_i = \mathbf{1}_{i \in S}$ they can simply use an addition circuit to add these bits together and then disperse the result. This is an MPC, all of whose inputs are held by good players, since each input bit b_i is jointly held

---

[3] We allow $|S| > n - t$ because the adversary is not limited to delivering one message at a time; two or more messages may be received simultaneously.

by the entire quorum Q_i and all the quorums are good. Thus the computation can afford to wait for all n inputs and computes the correct sum.

In the protocol proposed in this paper, it may be the case that a player p participates more than one time in the quorums performing a single instance of Hw-MPC. In such a case, we allow p to play the role of more than one different players in the MPC, one for each quorum to which p belongs. This ensures that the fraction of bad players in any instance of Hw-MPC is always less than $1/4$. Hw-MPC maintains privacy guarantees even in the face of gossiping coalitions of constant size. Thus, player p will learn no information beyond the output and its own inputs after running this protocol.

7 Conclusion

We have described a Monte Carlo algorithm to perform asynchronous secure multiparty computation in an scalable manner. Our algorithms are scalable in the sense that they require each player to send $\tilde{O}(\frac{m}{n} + \sqrt{n})$ messages and perform $\tilde{O}(\frac{m}{n} + \sqrt{n})$ computations. They tolerate a static adversary that controls up to a $\frac{1}{8} - \epsilon$ fraction of the players, for ϵ any positive constant.

Many problems remain open including the following. Can we prove lower bounds for the communication and computation costs for Monte Carlo MPC? Can we implement and adapt our algorithm to make it practical for a MPC problem such as the beet auction problem described in [7]. Finally, can we prove upper and lower bounds for resource costs to solve MPC in the case where the adversary is *dynamic*, able to take over players at any point during the algorithm?

Acknowledgments. This work was supported by the NSF under grants CCR-0313160 and CAREER Award 0644058. We are grateful to Tom Hayes, Mahdi Zamani and the anonymous reviewers for useful suggestions and comments.

References

1. Ajtai, M., Komlós, J., Szemerédi, E.: An 0(n log n) sorting network. In: Proceedings of STOC 1983, pp. 1–9. ACM, New York (1983)
2. Aspnes, J., Herlihy, M., Shavit, N.: Counting networks and multi-processor coordination. In: Proceedings of STOC 1991, pp. 348–358. ACM (1991)
3. Attiya, H., Welch, J.: Distributed Computing: Fundamentals, Simulations and Advanced Topics, 2nd edn., p. 14. John Wiley Interscience (March 2004)
4. Beerliová-Trubíniová, Z., Hirt, M.: Efficient multi-party computation with dispute control. In: Halevi, S., Rabin, T. (eds.) TCC 2006. LNCS, vol. 3876, pp. 305–328. Springer, Heidelberg (2006)
5. Ben-Or, M., Canetti, R., Goldreich, O.: Asynchronous secure computation. In: Proceedings of STOC 1993 (1993)
6. Ben-Or, M., Goldwasser, S., Wigderson, A.: Completeness theorems for non-cryptographic fault-tolerant distributed computing. In: Proceedings of STOC 1988, pp. 1–10 (1988)

7. Bogetoft, P., et al.: Secure multiparty computation goes live. In: Dingledine, R., Golle, P. (eds.) FC 2009. LNCS, vol. 5628, pp. 325–343. Springer, Heidelberg (2009)
8. Boyle, E., Goldwasser, S., Tessaro, S.: Communication locality in secure multiparty computation: how to run sublinear algorithms in a distributed setting. In: Sahai, A. (ed.) TCC 2013. LNCS, vol. 7785, pp. 356–376. Springer, Heidelberg (2013)
9. Canetti, R., Rabin, T.: Fast asynchronous byzantine agreement with optimal resilience. In: Proceeding of STOC 1993, pp. 42–51 (1993)
10. Chaum, D., Crépeau, C., Damgård, I.: Multiparty unconditionally secure protocols. In: Proceedings of STOC 1988, pp. 11–19 (1988)
11. Chor, B., Dwork, C.: Randomization in Byzantine agreement. Advances in Computing Research 5, 443–498 (1989)
12. Damgård, I., Ishai, Y.: Scalable secure multiparty computation. In: Dwork, C. (ed.) CRYPTO 2006. LNCS, vol. 4117, pp. 501–520. Springer, Heidelberg (2006)
13. Damgård, I., Ishai, Y., Krøigaard, M., Nielsen, J.B., Smith, A.: Scalable multiparty computation with nearly optimal work and resilience. In: Wagner, D. (ed.) CRYPTO 2008. LNCS, vol. 5157, pp. 241–261. Springer, Heidelberg (2008)
14. Damgård, I., Nielsen, J.B.: Scalable and unconditionally secure multiparty computation. In: Menezes, A. (ed.) CRYPTO 2007. LNCS, vol. 4622, pp. 572–590. Springer, Heidelberg (2007)
15. Dani, V., King, V., Movahedi, M., Saia, J.: Breaking the o(nm) bit barrier: Secure multiparty computation with a static adversary. In: Proceedings of PODC 2012 (2012)
16. Dani, V., King, V., Movahedi, M., Saia, J.: Quorums quicken queries: Efficient asynchronous secure multiparty computation. Manuscript (2013)
17. Du, W., Atallah, M.: Secure multi-party computation problems and their applications: a review and open problems. In: Proceedings of the 2001 Workshop on New Security Paradigms, pp. 13–22. ACM (2001)
18. Frikken, K.: Secure multiparty computation. In: Algorithms and Theory of Computation Handbook, p. 14. Chapman & Hall/CRC (2010)
19. Goldreich, O.: Secure multi-party computation. Manuscript (1998)
20. Goldreich, O., Micali, S., Wigderson, A.: How to play any mental game. In: Proceedings of STOC 1987, pp. 218–229. ACM (1987)
21. Hirt, M., Maurer, U.: Robustness for free in unconditional multi-party computation. In: Kilian, J. (ed.) CRYPTO 2001. LNCS, vol. 2139, pp. 101–118. Springer, Heidelberg (2001)
22. Hirt, M., Nielsen, J.B.: Upper bounds on the communication complexity of optimally resilient cryptographic multiparty computation. In: Roy, B. (ed.) ASIACRYPT 2005. LNCS, vol. 3788, pp. 79–99. Springer, Heidelberg (2005)
23. King, V., Lonargan, S., Saia, J., Trehan, A.: Load balanced scalable byzantine agreement through quorum building, with full information. In: Aguilera, M.K., Yu, H., Vaidya, N.H., Srinivasan, V., Choudhury, R.R. (eds.) ICDCN 2011. LNCS, vol. 6522, pp. 203–214. Springer, Heidelberg (2011)
24. Klugerman, M., Plaxton, C.G.: Small-depth counting networks. In: Proceedings of STOC 1992, pp. 417–428 (1992)
25. Klugerman, M.R.: Small-depth counting networks and related topics (1994)
26. Rabin, T., Ben-Or, M.: Verifiable secret sharing and multiparty protocols with honest majority. In: Proceedings of STOC 1989, pp. 73–85. ACM (1989)
27. Yao, A.: Protocols for secure computations. In: Proceedings of FOCS 1982, pp. 160–164 (1982)

Conscious and Unconscious Counting
on Anonymous Dynamic Networks

Giuseppe Antonio Di Luna[1], Roberto Baldoni[1],
Silvia Bonomi[1], and Ioannis Chatzigiannakis[2]

[1] Cyber Intelligence and Information Security Research Center and
Dipartimento di Ingegneria Informatica, Automatica e Gestionale Antonio Ruberti
Universitá degli Studi di Roma La Sapienza, Roma, Italy
{baldoni,bonomi,diluna}@dis.uniroma1.it
[2] Computer Technology Institute & Press "Diophantus" (CTI)
Patras, Greece
ichatz@cti.gr

Abstract. This paper addresses the problem of counting the size of a network
where (i) processes have the same identifiers (anonymous nodes) and (ii) the network topology constantly changes (dynamic network). Changes are driven by a
powerful adversary that can look at internal process states and add and remove
edges in order to contrast the convergence of the algorithm to the correct count.
The paper proposes two leader-based counting algorithms. Such algorithms are
based on a technique that mimics an energy-transfer between network nodes.

The first algorithm assumes that the adversary cannot generate either disconnected network graphs or network graphs where nodes have degree greater than
D. In such algorithm, the leader can count the size of the network and detect
the counting termination in a finite time (i.e., *conscious* counting algorithm). The
second algorithm assumes that the adversary only keeps the network graph connected at any time and we prove that the leader can still converge to a correct
count in a finite number of rounds, but it is not conscious when this convergence
happens.

Keywords: Anonymous Networks, Dynamic Networks, Counting Algorithms,
Dynamic Graph Adversary.

1 Introduction

Computing global properties of a distributed system based on a static topology (i.e.
counting the nodes belonging to the system) is of primary importance to build applications that take decisions locally at each node, based on global information. As an
example, making a distributed near-optimal load balancing among the nodes of the system cannot be computed without knowing the network size. Additionally, knowing the
size of the network is needed to ensure distributed termination of algorithms (e.g, terminating broadcast). Recently, dynamic distributed systems have attracted a lot of interest
[5,8], due to the fact that static ones do not capture anymore the new kind of software
applications designed to run on top of emerging environment like mobile and sensors
networks. In this environment, the topology of the network connecting the distributed

M. Chatterjee et al. (Eds.): ICDCN 2014, LNCS 8314, pp. 257–271, 2014.
© Springer-Verlag Berlin Heidelberg 2014

system participants constantly changes. The high dynamicity of the topological connections between processors brings new challenges for solving problems that were already solved on the top of static distributed systems. Moreover, privacy concerns are becoming more and more important and they could be addressed considering models where processors does not have unique IDs [18]. In this paper we consider the problem of counting the size of *anonymous dynamic network*. More specifically, we study round-based computations under worst-case dynamicity as originally introduced by [17] and then refined in [14]. We consider that the network graph is controlled by a *dynamic graph adversary* that, at each round, may introduce or remove any number of edges, still ensuring the graph remains connected. Communication along edges is assumed to be bidirectional and nodes are not aware of which edges are made available by the adversary at each round. Messages are then delivered to current sender's neighbors, as chosen by the adversary; nodes change their states, and the next round begins. Each node runs a deterministic algorithm that generates messages based on processes internal state that the adversary is able to read. Counting on anonymous *static* networks with broadcast has been proved to be non-solvable when there is no leader available [16]. The authors also conjectured that counting in networks under *dynamic graph adversary* without having knowledge (or estimation) of some network characteristics is impossible. In this work, we introduce a technique for computing the size of an anonymous network that is resilient to a dynamic graph adversary. The technique mimics an *energy-transfer* and it is embedded in a leader-based algorithm to circumvent the impossibility result. Informally the technique works as follows: each node v_i is assigned with a fixed energy charge, stored in the variable e_{v_i}, and during each round it discharges itself by disseminating energy around to its neighbors i.e., e_{v_i} decreases of a value $k \leq e_{v_i}/2$, then this quantity k is equally split among the neighbors of v_i and this value is added to v_i's neighbors variable. The leader acts as a sink collecting energy (i.e., energy is not transferred by the leader to neighbors). Our technique enforces, at each round, a global invariant on the sum of energy among networks' nodes (i.e., $\sum_{v_i} e_{v_i} = \#nodes$), that resorts to the fact that energy is not created or destroyed in the anonymous dynamic distributed system (energy conservation property). Considering the behavior of the nodes, the energy is eventually transferred to the leader and stored there. The leader measures the energy received to count the size of the network. In particular, we present a leader-based algorithm that employs the *energy-transfer technique* and is tolerant to the dynamic graph adversary additionally constrained by the fact that it cannot generate graphs including nodes with a degree over a certain bound. *At the best of our knowledge, the algorithm proposed in this work is the first algorithm that provides, in a finite time, an exact count on an anonymous dynamic network with broadcast.* In the worst-case, the algorithm requires exponential time to complete and the leader is always able to detect when the counting is over (*conscious counting*). As second result, we show that the conjecture presented in [16] is not valid when considering counting algorithms that are not able to detect the time at which the convergence happens (*unconscious counting*). To this aim, we present an unconscious leader-based algorithm exploiting the energy transfer technique that is able to reach the correct count being resilient to the dynamic graph adversary. The rest of the paper is organized as follows: Section 2 presents relevant previous work, and in Section 3 we formally define both the anonymous network model, the dynamic graph adversary and the counting problem specifying the properties of convergence and consciousness. Using the energy transfer technique, in Section 4 we present a counting algorithm, namely $\mathcal{A}_D$, resilient to a dynamic graph adversary with bounded degree. Finally, Section 5 shows a counting algorithm $\mathcal{A}_{NoK}$, that is able to count the size of the network under dynamic graph adversary, however such algorithm does not verify the consciousness property. Section 6 concludes the paper.

2 Related Work

To the best of our knowledge, the only other work that discusses the problem of counting and naming in an anonymous network with worst-case adversary is [16]. However, the authors just provided an algorithm that knowing an upper bound on the maximum degree of graphs generated by the adversary, makes possible to each node to compute an upper bound on the size of the network. This algorithm is used as basic building block in our counting algorithm as shown in Section 4. In the rest of the section we consider other works done in the contexts of anonymous static networks, fully identifiable dynamic networks and adversary models that are related to our problem.

Static Anonymous Networks. The question concerning which problems can be solved on top of an anonymous network, where all nodes have the same identifier, has been pioneered by Angluin in [2]. Yamashita and Kameda [18] proposed several characterizations for problems that are solvable under certain topological constraints when considering known the size of the network. Further investigation led to the classification of computable functions [4,18]. The work presented in [7] has been the first one that removed the assumption of knowing the network size n and provided characterizations of the relations that can be computed with arbitrary knowledge.

Fraigniaud *et al.* [11] assumed a unique leader in order to break symmetry and assign short labels as fast as possible. To circumvent the further symmetry introduced by broadcast message transmissions they also studied other natural message transmission models as sending only one message to a single neighbor. Recently, Chalopin *et al.* [9] have studied the problem of naming static anonymous networks in the context of snapshot computation; such work uses the notion of *"graph covering"* [4,18], that is usable only on static topologies and is not defined for highly dynamic system like the one studied in our work.

Finally, Aspnes *et al.* [3] studied the relative power of reliable anonymous distributed systems with different communication mechanisms: anonymous broadcast, read-write registers, or read-write registers plus additional shared-memory objects.

Dynamic Distributed Systems Where All Processes Have Distinct Identifiers. Distributed systems with worst-case dynamicity were first studied in [17] by introducing the 1-interval connectivity model. They studied flooding and routing problems in asynchronous communication and allowed nodes to detect local neighborhood changes. Under the same model, [14] studied the problem of counting in networks where nodes have unique IDs and provided an algorithm that requires $O(n^2)$ rounds using $O(\log n)$ bits per message.

Adversarial vs Random Dynamic Graph. The gossiping model [12,13] can be seen as a dynamic graph where, at each round, each node randomly selects some neighbors to execute the view exchange. The adversarial model considered in this paper differs from random dynamic graph since in our case the adversary is able to read the state of nodes and compute the set of best edges to add/remove in order to break the correctness of the counting while the gossip adversary simply selects nodes randomly without any strategy.

3   System Model and Problem Specification

We consider a distributed system composed by a finite set of processes V (also called *nodes*). Nodes in V are *anonymous*, i.e., they initially have no identifier and execute a deterministic *round-based* computation. We assume the set V remains the same throughout the computation. To ease of presentation, in the following we sometimes refer to processes using names as v_i but such names cannot be used by processes themselves in the algorithms.

Every round is divided in three phases: (i) *send* where processes send all the messages for the current round, (ii) *receive* where processes receive all the messages sent at the beginning of the current round and (iii) *computation* where nodes process received messages and prepare those that will be sent in the next round. Rounds are *synchronous* and they are controlled by a fictional global clock accessible to all the nodes. Thus, all nodes have access to the current round number via a local variable that we usually denote by r. Processes have a local view of the network, i.e. they know a subset of processes called *neighbors*. Processes are arranged in a communication network and they can communicate only by exchanging messages trough an *anonymous broadcast* primitive. Such primitive ensures that a message m sent by node v_i at the beginning of a certain round r will be delivered to all its neighbors during round r.

Dynamic Network and the Dynamic Graph Adversary. The communication network is *dynamic*, i.e. its topology changes along time due to possible nodes or communication links failures. A *dynamic network* is modeled by a *dynamic graph* $G(r) = (V, E(r))$, where V is the set of nodes (or processors) and $E : \mathbb{N} \to \mathcal{P}(E')$, where $E' = \{\{u, v\} : u, v \in V\}$, is a function mapping a round number $r \in \mathbb{N}$ to a set $E(r)$ of bidirectional links drawn from E' [14]. The neighborhood of a node v_i at round r is denoted by $N_{v_i}(r) = \{u : \{u, v\} \in E(r)\}$.

Intuitively, a dynamic graph $G(r)$ is an infinite sequence $G(1), G(2), \ldots$ of *instantaneous graphs*, whose edge sets are subsets of E' chosen by an *adversary*. If there are no topology properties imposed on the graphs generated by the adversary (e.g., upper/lower bound on the degree of a node, bound on the diameter of the network), the adversary can generate any graph ranging from a fully connected one to a graph composed by all singleton nodes.

In the paper, we assume that the dynamic graph/network $G(r) = (V, E(r))$ is 1-*interval connected* as defined in [14]. A network is 1-*interval connected* if for all $r \in \mathbb{N}$, the static graph $G(r)$ is connected. Thus, the adversary can change arbitrarily the graphs in the sequence (by adding and removing edges) while ensuring that each graph $G(r)$ in the sequence is connected. Additionally, the adversary is able to read each process state building thus a sequence of graphs that could prevent an algorithm to be correct. We call such adversary, *dynamic graph adversary*. In addition, we also consider a less powerful adversary that generates only instances $G(r) = (V, E(r))$ where the number of neighbors that each node v_i may have is always bounded by a constant upper bound D (i.e. $\forall v_i \in V, \forall r \in \mathbb{N}, |N_{v_i}(r)| \leq D$). We call this adversary *dynamic graph adversary with bounded degree*. For the easy of presentation and whenever it does not generate confusion, in the remaining of the paper we will use the term adversary and dynamic graph adversary interchangeably.

The Counting Problem. The counting problem can be formalized by the following properties:
Let g be a variable representing a guess on the size of the network at a process v.

- **Convergence:** There exists a round r after which at least one process p has permanently a correct guess on the size of the network, i.e., $g = |V|$.
- **Consciousness:** If a node v has a correct guess g on $|V|$, then there exists a round r' (with $r' \geq r$) such that v is aware about the correctness of the guess.

In the following, given a counting algorithm $\mathcal{A}$, we will say that it is *conscious* if it is able to satisfy both the properties; on the contrary, if it satisfies only the convergence property we will say that it is *unconscious*.

4   Conscious Counting Algorithm Resilient to a Dynamic Graph Adversary with Bounded Degree

This section presents a distributed algorithm, denoted as $\mathcal{A}_D$, that assumes (i) the existence of a leader node starting from a different initial state and (ii) all other nodes execute identical programs. In addition, $\mathcal{A}_D$ assumes that the bound on nodes degree D (which limits the powerfulness of the adversary) is known by all processes.

$\mathcal{A}_D$ is composed by a sequence of iterations $i = 0 \ldots \ell$ run by the leader and each iteration takes several rounds. Each iteration i starts considering two parameters: (i) the upper bound on nodes degree D and (ii) an upper bound K_i on the network size; then, the algorithm computes a guess for the network size. If the guess matches the current considered bound K_i, then the algorithm terminates and K_i corresponds to the size of the network $|V|$. Otherwise iteration $i + 1$ is started taking D and $K_{i+1} = K_i - 1$ as inputs.

Let us notice that, starting from the upper bound D on nodes degree, an upper bound K_0, to be used in the first algorithm iteration, can be easily computed (e.g. by using the algorithm shown in [16]). Thus, the hard part of $\mathcal{A}_D$ is to compute the guess on the network size at the end of each iteration. To this aim, $\mathcal{A}_D$ employs the idea of *energy-transfer* and exploits the invariant on the energy globally stored in network: the sum of the energy stored by each node at the end of each round remains constant during the algorithm execution. Note that the energy we are considering is not the real energy that nodes may have but it is rather an abstraction used to explain the details of the algorithm.

At the beginning of each iteration i (with $i \geq 0$), every node is assigned with a fixed energy charge, and during each round r it discharges itself by disseminating the energy

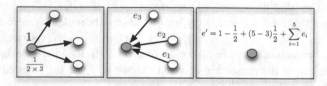

Fig. 1. Send, Receive and Update of energy for a non leader node

to its neighbors. The leader acts as a sink collecting energy (i.e., it does not transfer energy to its neighbors).

Considering the behavior of the nodes, the energy is eventually transferred to the leader. The leader measures the level of energy received to verify if the energy level matches the bound K_i considered in the current iteration i. More specifically, the leader starts iteration i of $\mathcal{A}_D$ algorithm by assuming that the network has size K_i and computes the first round r_final_i where, in the worst case, it should have received strictly more than $K_i - 1$ energy by all the others (see Lemmas 2,3). If at round r_final_i, the leader has received such amount of energy then it outputs $|V| = K_i$. Otherwise the algorithm starts iteration $i + 1$ with $K_{i+1} = K_i - 1$.

Algorithm $\mathcal{A}_D$ – *Conscious Counting Algorithm resilient to a Dynamic Graph Adversary with Bounded Degree.*

(Step 1) The algorithm starts taking as input D and computes an upper bound K on the network size by running an estimation algorithm as the one shown in [16];

(Step 2) The leader and the anonymous nodes start the step 2 at round r_start;

leader : The leader v_l maintains the following local variables: $e_{v_l} \leftarrow 1$ representing the initial energy charge, $rcv_{v_l} \leftarrow \emptyset$ is a set variable where v_l stores all the messages received during each round, $i \leftarrow 0$ is the iteration number, $K_i \leftarrow K$ is the upper bound on the network size at iteration i, $r\_init_i \leftarrow r\_start$ is the starting round of iteration i, r_final_i is the termination round of iteration i when the leader will be able to either validate the guess (i.e., $|V| = K_i$) or not (i.e., $|V| < K_i$) - see Lemmas 2, 3.

start iteration i at round r_init$_1$: take D and K_i as inputs

The leader computes the minimum $R \in \mathbb{N}^+$ such that R satisfies $K_i - (1 - (\frac{B-1}{B})^R)K_i < 1$, where $B = (2D)^K$ and sets $r\_final_i \leftarrow r\_init_i + RK_i$.

for each round r:

- **Send phase of round r:** at the beginning of each round, v_l broadcasts a ENERGY_RELEASE(0) message releasing no energy.
- **Receive and Computation phases of round r:** ENERGY_RELEASE(e') messages are stored in the rcv_{v_l} variable. At the end of the round, when all the messages have been received, v_l updates, its local energy charge as follows:

$$e_{v_l} \leftarrow e_{v_l} + received$$

  where *received* is the sum of all the charges received by neighbors (i.e., $\sum_{e' \in rcv_{v_l}} e'$).

- **When $(r = r\_final_i)$ % Terminating Condition %**
  if $(K_i - e_{v_l} < 1)$
  then v_l terminates and broadcasts for K_i rounds STOP(K_i) message to other nodes and then it outputs $count \leftarrow K_i$;
  else v_l sends a message RE-START($r\_final_i + K_i$) to other nodes declaring that it will start a new iteration. This message is broadcast for K_i rounds and then v_l starts iteration $i + 1$ considering the new bound $K_{i+1} = K_i - 1$ and $r\_init_{i+1} = (r\_final_i + |K_i|)$.

anonymous node: Each non leader node v_i maintains the following local variables: $e_{v_i} \leftarrow 1$ representing the initial energy charge of v_i, $rcv_{v_i} \leftarrow \emptyset$ is a set variable where v_i stores all the messages received during each round.

for each round r:

- **Send phase of round** r: at the beginning of each round, v_i broadcasts a ENERGY_RELEASE($\frac{e_{v_i}}{2D}$) message, releasing at most half of its energy to its neighbors (at most D).
- **Receive and Computation phases of round** r:
  switch
    case $(\exists\, m =\text{STOP}(count) \in rcv_{v_i})$
       v_i broadcasts STOP($count$) for $count$ rounds, then v_i stops to execute the algorithm and outputs the value $count$.
    case $(\exists\, m =\text{RE-START}(r') \in rcv_{v_i})$
       v_i broadcasts RE-START(r') until the current round is r' and then v_i initializes all local variables.
    default   %$\mathbf{rcv_{v_i}}$ **contains only** ENERGY_RELEASE(e') **messages** %
       v_i updates its local energy charge as follows:

$$e_{v_i} \leftarrow e_{v_i} - released + recharged + received =$$

where the energy *released* is given by the the quantity of energy sent to its current neighbors (i.e. ($D \times \frac{e_{v_i}}{2D}$)), the energy *recharged* is the amount of energy not effectively released due a possible neighborhood over estimation (that, in the current round, is smaller than D) and computed by considering the difference between the estimated number of neighbors D and the effective ones $|rcv_i|$ (i.e. $(D - |rcv_{v_i}|) \times \frac{e_{v_i}}{2D}$). Thus,

$$e_{v_i} \leftarrow e_{v_i} - \left(D \times \frac{e_{v_i}}{2D}\right) + (D - |rcv_{v_i}|) \times \frac{e_{v_i}}{2D} + \sum_{e' \in rcv_{v_i}} e'$$

Figure 1 shows the execution of a generic round r at node v_i with initial energy 1 where $D = 5$ and the number of v_i neighbors is 3.

Correctness Proofs. In the following, we will prove that protocol $\mathcal{A}_D$ is correct. We first prove in Lemma 1 the existence of the following invariant: the global energy stored in the system is preserved (i.e. the sum of all the energy variables e_{v_i} at each $v_i \in V$ remain constant). Note that, this is a fundamental property to ensure the correctness of the guess computed and returned by the leader. Then, in Lemma 2, we derive a lower bound on the energy that the leader will receive during the computation. Finally, in Lemma 3, we prove the terminating condition that the leader has to verify in order to check if the bound matches the network size. From these results Theorem 1 naturally follows. In the following, we use the notation $e_{v_i}^r$ to indicates the quantity of energy stored at round r in $v_i \in V$.

Lemma 1. *(Invariant - Energy Conservation) At the end of each round, the sum of the energy over all the nodes of the anonymous dynamic network is an invariant and it is equal to the total energy present in the system at the beginning of the computation.*

Proof. Let us notice that energy is created only during the initialization phase and then it is only transferred. Thus, in the following, we will prove that energy is never lost. For ease of presentation, in the prove we refer only to the energy $e_{v_i}^r$ stored at non-leader nodes (i.e. $v \in V \setminus \{v_l\}$) as v_l does not send energy. At the beginning of each round r, every v_i sends $\frac{e_{v_i}^r}{2D}$ energy to the set of its neighbors (i.e. the released energy is $D \times \frac{e_{v_i}^r}{2D}$). However, v_i does not know the exact number of current neighbors $N_{v_i}(r)$ but it just know an upper bound on them. Thus, while sending the energy, due to a possible over estimation of its neighborhood, v_i may transfer more energy that the one will never received by other processes (loss of energy of $(D - |N_{v_i}(r)|) \times \frac{e_{v_i}^r}{2D}$). However, v_i will

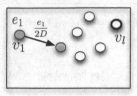 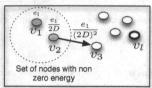 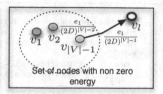

Fig. 2. Lower bound on the energy received by the leader from a single node

know the exact number of neighbors by counting the number of received messages in the current round ($|N_{v_i}(r)| = |rcv_{v_i}|$) and it will compensate the extra energy released.

Thus, v_i will have a remaining energy of $\frac{e^r_{v_i}}{2} + e^r_v \frac{D-|N_{v_i}(r)|}{2D}$. The energy initially possessed by v_i was $e^r_{v_i}$, at the end of r the sum of energy over nodes in $N_{v_i}(r) \cup \{v_i\}$ is $e^r_{v_i}$. Iterating this reasoning over all nodes we have that the conservation of energy is not violated.

$\square$ *Lemma 1*

Lemma 2. *Let $G(r) = (V, E(r))$ be a dynamic anonymous graph, let K be an upper bound on the network size and let $R \in \mathbb{N}^+$. Given the algorithm $\mathcal{A}_D$, at the end of round r_{RK}, the energy stored at the leader is at least $e^{RK}_{v_l} \geq (1 - (\frac{B-1}{B})^R)|V|$, where $B = (2D)^K$.*

Proof. Let us first compute the energy that a single node v_i provides to the leader v_l when it is the only one releasing energy (i.e. v_i has an energy charge of $e_{v_i} = 1$ while all the other non-leader nodes v_j has no energy and $e_{v_i} = 0$).

At round 0, v_i transfers $e = \frac{1}{2D}$ to each of its neighbors. Due to 1-interval connectivity, v_i has at least one neighbor v_j that will receive such energy charge and will update its residual energy to $e^0_{v_j} \geq \frac{1}{2D}$. As a consequence, an additional node (i.e. v_j) will have a quantity of energy greater than 0, no matter of the adversary move.

At round 1, due to the adversary action, v_i and v_j may change their neighbors and a node v_k, with no energy, may become neighbor of v_j. Due to the rules of the algorithm, v_j will transfer to v_k a quantity of energy at least $e_j \geq \frac{e}{(2D)} \geq \frac{1}{(2D)^2}$. Let us notice that the such quantity is a lower bound on the energy that an empty node may receive after 2 rounds.

Iterating the reasoning, it is possible to define the lower bound on the energy that the leader v_l received from v_i after $|V| - 1$ rounds in case v_i is the only one releasing energy, i.e. $e^{|V|-1}_{v_l} \geq \frac{1}{(2D)^{|V|}}$. Considering the individual contribution of each node in V, we obtain $e^{|V|-1}_{v_l} \geq \frac{|V|}{(2D)^{|V|}}$. However, node contributions interfere and the real quantity of energy that each of them transfers to the leader at each round is greater than the computed one; thus the formula above represents a lower bound on the energy transferred from all nodes to the leader after $|V| - 1$ rounds.

Due to Lemma 1, $e^{|V|-1}_{v_l} + \sum_{v_i \in V \setminus \{v_l\}} e^{|V|-1}_{v_i} = |V|$, this implies that after $|V| - 1$ rounds, the energy not stored at the leader is, at most, $|V| - e^{|V|-1}_{v_l}$.

Using the same argument, after $2(|V| - 1)$ rounds the lower bound on the energy that the leader stores is $e_{v_l}^{2(|V|-1)} \geq \frac{|V|-e_{v_l}^{|V|-1}}{(2D)^{|V|}} + e_{v_l}^{|V|-1}$. We can use the same argument even if the distribution of energy at round $r = |V|$ is different from the uniform initial distribution, the basic idea is to consider the contribution that each node has to send to the leader independently, then summing up these contribution we will end up with the same bound. After $R(|V| - 1)$ rounds, the energy at the leader is at least $e_{v_l}^{R(|V|-1)} \geq \frac{|V|-e_{v_l}^{(R-1)(|V|-1)}}{(2D)^{|V|}} + e_{v_l}^{(R-1)(|V|-1)}$ that is a recurrence equation with boundary condition $e_{v_l}^0 = 0$.

Solving the equation we obtain: $e_{v_l}^{R(|V|-1)} \geq |V| \times (1 - (\frac{b-1}{b})^R)$ where $b = (2D)^{|V|}$, that is a lower bound on the energy of the leader after $R \times (|V| - 1)$ rounds. Let us recall that $K \geq |V|$, thus we can compute a lower bound for the energy in the leader after RK rounds on a network of size $|V|$, with $B = (2D)^K$ since $\frac{|a|}{b} \geq \frac{|a|}{B}$ the following inequality holds:

$$e_{v_l}^{RK} \geq |V| \times \left(1 - \left(\frac{B-1}{B}\right)^R\right)$$

$\square_{Lemma\ 2}$

Lemma 3. *Let $G(r) = (V, E(r))$ be a dynamic anonymous graph, let K_i be an upper bound on the network size. Given the algorithm $\mathcal{A}_D$, at the end of each iteration i, the leader can either accept or reject the hypothesis $|V| = K_i$.*

Proof. Let us note that the algorithm outputs the exact count when the upper bound K_i is equal to the real network size $|V|$. Initially, K_i is set by running the algorithm in [16] that has been proved to provide an upper bound on the network size (i.e. $K_0 \geq |V|$). The leader can compute the difference Δ_r as follows

$$\Delta_r = K_i - e_{v_l}^r \geq K_i - \left(1 - \left(\frac{B-1}{B}\right)^R\right) K_i$$

that is the difference, at round $r = RK_i$, between the total energy stored in a network of size $|V| = K_i$ and the lower bound on the minimum amount of energy that the leader has to receive after r rounds if $|V| = K_i$ (as computed in Lemma 2).

According to the algorithm, the leader computes the minimum $R' \in \mathbb{N}^+$ such that $r\_final_i = R'K_i$ satisfies $\Delta_{r\_final_i} < 1$. At round r_final_i two cases are possible:

1. The energy accumulated in the leader $e_{v_l}^{r\_final_i}$ is less or equal than $K_i - 1$: in this case, we have necessary that $|V| < K_i$. By construction, in fact, R' is selected in such a way that the quantity $\Delta_{r\_final_i} < 1$; thus, if the real network size is K_i, the leader must collect $e_{v_l}^{r\_final_i} > K_i - 1$. On the contrary, the only possibility is that $|V| < K_i$ since in this case the quantity of energy in V will not allow the leader to reach a value $e_{v_l}^{r\_final_i} = K_i - 1 + \epsilon$ with $\epsilon > 0$.
2. The energy accumulated in the leader $e_{v_l}^{r\_final_i} = K_i - 1 + \epsilon$ (with $\epsilon > 0$): this implies that there are at least K_i nodes in V. Considering that K_i is an upper bound we have that necessary $|V| = K_i$.

$\square_{Lemma\ 3}$

Theorem 1. *Let $G(r) = (V, E(r))$ be a dynamic anonymous graph and let K_0 be an upper bound on the network size. If the adversary is a dynamic graph adversary with bounded degree and any process $v_i \in V$ knows the upper bound D on the number of neighbors, then the algorithm $\mathcal{A}_D$ satisfies the **consciousness** and **convergence** properties*

Proof. Let us first prove the **convergence** property. $\mathcal{A}_D$, during the Step 1, computes an upper bound K_0 on the size of the network (i.e. $K_0 \geq |V|$) and then it moves to Step 2 starting a sequence of iteration $I = \{i_0, ..., i_{final}\}$, each one taking as input an upper bound K_{i_x}. According to Lemma 3, at the end of an iteration i_x, the leader checks the terminating condition, evaluates the hypothesis $K_{i_x} = |V|$ and in case of rejection, it decreases by one the upper bound considered in the following iteration. Considering that (i) K_0 is an upper bound on the real network size and (ii) every iteration i_{x+1} starts with a new upper bound $K_{i_{x+1}} = K_{i_x} - 1$ it follows that, in a finite number of iterations, $\mathcal{A}_D$ will evaluate the real size of the network accepting the hypothesis $K_i = |V|$.

The **consciousness** is also ensured by Lemma 3, considering that when the leader accepts the hypothesis $K_i = |V|$ starts to disseminate a STOP message letting the algorithm terminate at each node.

$\square_{Theorem\ 1}$

4.1 Complexity and Discussion

Theorem 2. *Let $G(r) = (V, E(r))$ be a dynamic anonymous graph and let K_0 be an upper bound on the network size. If the adversary is a dynamic graph adversary with bounded degree and any process $v_i \in V$ knows the upper bound D on the number of neighbors, then the algorithm $\mathcal{A}_D$ outputs the correct size of the network after at most $O(e^{K_0^2} K_0^2(K_0 - 1))$ rounds.*

Proof. The claim follows from Lemma 2 and Lemma 3 by considering that each iteration i of the algorithm lasts $\Delta_R(K_i) \times K_i$, where $\Delta_R(K_i)$ is the number of $K_i - 1$ rounds that the algorithm has to execute in order to check the hypothesis $|V| = K_i$ (cfr. Lemma 3). Moreover, we have that the maximum number of iterations is K_0 (i.e., the worst case obtained starting from evaluating the hypothesis on the size $|V| = K_0$ when the real size is $|V| = 1$). $\Delta_R(K_i)$ can be computed by solving $\Delta_{r\_final_i} < 1$ inequality obtaining:

$$\Delta_R(K_i) \geq \left\lceil \frac{\log(\frac{1}{K_i})}{\log(\frac{B-1}{B})} \right\rceil + 1$$

where $B = (2D)^{K_i}$.

Let us notice that, in the worst case, $D = K_i$, so we have $\Delta_R(K_i) = \Theta\left(\frac{\log(\frac{1}{K_i})}{\log(1 - K_i^{-K_i})}\right)$.

Since the limit $\lim_{K_i \to +\infty}\left(\frac{\Delta_R(K_i)}{e^{K_i^2}}\right) = 0$ we have that the number of rounds for each iteration is $O\left(e^{K_i^2}(K_i - 1)\right)$ this seamlessly leads to the theorem.

$\square_{Theorem\ 2}$

The complexity aforementioned is a direct consequence of the energy release mechanism where each non leader node transfers half of its energy at each round. Let us suppose to modify the algorithm in such a way that each node sends the whole energy to its neighbors. In this case the problem became equivalent to token circulation, the trivial example is a chain $\{v_1, v_2, ..., v_n\}$, that is transformed at odd rounds in $v_2, v_1, ..., v_n$ and in even rounds as $v_1, v_2, ..., v_n$, this dynamic adversary will prevent the initial energy present in v_1 to reach other nodes apart v_2. On the contrary halving the energy allow us to obtain the bound on energy dissemination (See Lemma 2). Let us remark that changing the quantity of energy sent by nodes (i.e. sending a fraction different from $\frac{1}{2}$) does not change the complexity from being exponential since the termination round is only influenced by a multiplicative factor.

5 Unconscious Counting Resilient to a Dynamic Graph Adversary

This section shows that the impossibility of designing a counting algorithm without any network knowledge assumption (i.e., impossibility of designing a counting resilient to a dynamic graph adversary) presented in [16] does not hold if if we consider unconscious counting algorithms. To prove such claim, we will propose an algorithm, namely $\mathcal{A}_{NoK}$, that is able to eventually count the number of processes in the dynamic anonymous network without having any assumption on the network. $\mathcal{A}_{NoK}$ is actually a modification of the algorithm presented in Section 4 where nodes have to cope with the uncertainty about the number of neighbors (and thus, with the uncertainty about the energy they have to release in each round).

$\mathcal{A}_{NoK}$ works in the following way: each non-leader node v_i starts, at round r_0, with energy quantity $e_{v_i} \leftarrow 1$ and it transfers half of its current energy to the neighbors. However, v_i has no knowledge about the network and thus it cannot know the exact number of neighbors at round r before receiving messages, but it can only guess such number. Thus, v_i supposes to have D_{max} neighbors and it broadcasts a quantity of energy $\frac{1}{2D_{max}}$ (as if there are really D_{max} neighbors). Then v_i starts to collect messages transmitted by its neighbors at the beginning of the round and it stores such messages in a local variable rcv_{v_i}. At the end of the round, v_i updates its energy, as in the previous algorithm, to preserve the quantity of energy over all the network.

Notice that, if the real number of neighbors at round r is lower than the estimation (i.e., $|rcv_{v_i}| \leq D_{max}$) then the global energy conserved among all the processes is still constant (this is due to the compensation done by v_i at the end of the round, based on the effective number of received messages). On the contrary, if the number of neighbors is greater than the estimation (i.e., $|rcv_{v_i}| > D_{max}$) then, there is the release of a *local surplus* of energy. As an example, consider the case where v_i has energy e_{v_i} the estimation of neighbors is $D_{max} = 2$ and the real number of neighbors is $|rcv_{v_i}| = 8$. When v_i sends $\frac{e_{v_i}}{4}$ to each neighbors, the total amount of energy transferred is twice the energy stored by v_i (i.e., the energy transferred is $8 \times \frac{e_{v_i}}{4} = 2e_{v_i}$ while node v_i had only e_{v_i} residual energy). However, since v_i adjusts its local residual energy considering the number of received messages $|rcv_{v_i}|$, it follows that its residual energy will become negative and globally the energy is still preserved. Considering the previous example at the end of the round v_i stores a residual energy $-e_{v_i}$.

Unfortunately, the local surplus of positive/negative energy could create, in the leader, a temporary value of energy e_{v_l} that is greater than $|V|$ or negative. Moreover, the adversary could change, at each round, the degree of nodes in order to avoid the convergence of the leader. To overcome these issues each processes stores locally the highest number of neighbors it has ever seen and it uses the double of such number as D_{max}. In this way, the surplus of local negative/positive energy that the adversary can create is upper bounded by a function $f(|V|)$: each node v_i can increase D_{max} at most $log(|V|)$ times, from 1 to $|V|$. This implies that the worst case adversary cannot create an infinite surplus of local energy. Thus, the adversary could delay the convergence of the count only a finite number of rounds.

Algorithm $\mathcal{A}_{NoK}$ – Unconscious Counting resilient to a Dynamic Graph Adversary.

leader : The leader v_l maintains the following local variables: (i) $e_{v_l} \leftarrow 1$ representing the initial energy charge and (ii) $rcv_{v_l} \leftarrow \emptyset$ is a set variable where v_l stores all the messages received during each round. (iii) $count_{v_l} \leftarrow 0$ this variable is used to keep trace of the latest estimated count.
for each round r:

- **Send phase of round** r: at the beginning of each round, v_l broadcasts a ENERGY_RELEASE(0) message releasing no energy.
  v_l broadcasts COUNT($\lceil e_{v_l} \rceil, r$).
- **Receive and Computation phases of round** r: ENERGY_RELEASE(e') messages are stored in the rcv_{v_l} variable. At the end of the round, when all the messages have been received, v_l updates, its local energy charge as follows:

$$e_{v_l} \leftarrow e_{v_l} + \sum_{e' \in rcv_{v_l}} e'$$

  v_l sets $count_{v_l} \leftarrow \lceil e_{v_l} \rceil$

anonymous node: Each non leader node v_i maintains the following local variables: (i) $e_{v_i} \leftarrow 1$ representing the initial energy charge of v_i, (ii) $rcv_{v_i} \leftarrow \emptyset$ is a set variable where v_i stores all the messages received during each round and (iii) $D_{max} \leftarrow 1$ is an integer variable storing the maximum number of neighbor v_i has ever had (initially set to 1 as it has no knowledge about the network). (iv) $count_{v_i} \leftarrow 0$ this variable is used to keep trace of the latest count estimate seen by the node (v) $r\_count_{v_i} \leftarrow 0$ is the round number associated with the latest count accepted.
for each round r:

- **Send phase of round** r: at the beginning of each round, v_i broadcasts a ENERGY_RELEASE($\frac{e_{v_i}}{2D_{max}}$) message, releasing at most half of its energy to its neighbors.
- **Receive and Computation phases of round** r:
  for each message $m \in rcv_{v_i}$ such that m is an ENERGY_RELEASE message, v_i updates its local energy charge as in the previous algorithm:

$$e_{v_i} \leftarrow e_{v_i} - \left(D_{max} \times \frac{e_{v_i}}{2D_{max}}\right) + \left((D_{max} - |rcv_{v_i}|) \times \frac{e_{v_i}}{2D_{max}} + \sum_{e' \in rcv_{v_i}} e'\right)$$

  In addition, if $|rcv_{v_i}| > D_{max}$, v_i also updates the maximum number of neighbors it has ever saw by setting $D_{max} \leftarrow 2|rcv_{v_i}|$.
  for each message $m \in rcv_{v_i}$ such that m is an COUNT message, if the round number in m is greater than $r\_count_{v_i}$ updates $count_{v_i}$ and $r\_count_{v_i}$ with the content of m.

Correctness Proofs. In the following, we will prove that protocol $\mathcal{A}_{NoK}$ converges to the exact count in a finite number of rounds. We first prove that the quantitive of negative energy that the dynamic adversary is able to create is bounded by a function of the network size $|V|$ (Lemma 4). From this result, we prove that the leader will obtain the correct count in a finite but unknown number of rounds (Lemma 6), so we will prove that $\mathcal{A}_{NoK}$ respects the **convergence** property, but not the **consciousness**. Let us notice that since the energy transfer mechanism is the same of $\mathcal{A}_D$ the global invariant on energy still holds, so Lemma 1 keeps holding for $\mathcal{A}_{NoK}$ too. Moreover, it is clear that for each round r the leader will receive energy from its neighbors. So, even if it is not possible to have a bound like the one obtained in Lemma 2, it is straightforward to see that the absolute value of the sum of energy that the leader receives is a monotonically increasing function.

Lemma 4. *Let $G(r) = (V, E(r))$ be a dynamic anonymous graph. During any execution of $\mathcal{A}_{NoK}$, the amount of negative energy that can be generated is finite. Moreover, during any round r a single node $v_i \in V$ with energy $e^r_{v_i}$ can create at most $(|V|-2)e^r_{v_i}$ negative energy.*

Proof. Let us focus on the negative energy that can be generated during the execution of the algorithm by a generic node $v_i \in V$. Let $E_n : \{r_{i,1}, r_{i,2}, ..., r_{i,t}\}$ be the set of rounds (not necessarily consecutive) in which v_i creates negative energy; we will show that the number t is finite. For the generic round $r_{i,j} \in E_n$ we must have that $|rcv_i| > 2D_{max}$; this follows by imposing $\frac{e}{2} + (|rcv_{v_i}| - D_{max})\frac{e}{2} < 0$. This means that we have at least $|rcv_i| \geq 2D_{max} + 1$, and at the end of round $r_{i,j}$ the number D_{max} will be doubled. Since $|rcv_i| \leq |V|$ and $D_{max} \geq 1$, we have that the condition $|rcv_i| > 2D_{max}$ could happen at most $log(|V|)$ times. So, $t \leq O(log(|V|))$. Moreover, the negative energy created by a node v_i with energy e during a single round is at most $(|rcv_{v_i}| - 2D_{max})e$ that is maximized when $|rcv_{v_i}| = |V|$ and $D_{max} = 1$. $\square_{Lemma\ 4}$

Lemma 5. *Let $G(r) = (V, E(r))$ be a dynamic anonymous graph. During any execution of $\mathcal{A}_{NoK}$, for any $\epsilon \in \mathbb{R}^+$ there exists a round $r_{|V,\epsilon|}$ after which the amount of negative energy that could be transferred to the leader in the following rounds is less than ϵ.*

Proof. Due to the invariant on energy (Lemma 1), we have that the negative energy that each node could create is related to the energy that the nodes already possess (since the sum of negative and positive energy has to be equal zero). In addition, for Lemma 1 and for the monotonically increasing energy received by the leader, we have that, if no negative energy is created, the absolute value of energy in $V \setminus \{v_l\}$ is a monotonically decreasing function of r. The maximum amount of negative energy that can be created starting from round r is bounded (see lemma 4) and from the previous consideration it is a monotonic function f of $\sum_{\forall v \in V \setminus \{v_l\}} |e^r_v|$. From Lemma 2 we have that $\forall \epsilon_1 \in \mathbb{R}^+$ $\exists r_{\epsilon_1} \in \mathbb{N}^+ |$ $\sum_{\forall v \in V \setminus \{v_l\}} |e^{r_{\epsilon_1}}_v| \leq \epsilon_1$, since f is monotonic exists ϵ_1 such that $f(\epsilon_1) \leq \epsilon$. $\square_{Lemma\ 5}$

Lemma 6. *Let $G(r) = (V, E(r))$ be a dynamic anonymous graph and let us consider an execution of $\mathcal{A}_{NoK}$. Then, $\forall v_i \lim_{r \to \infty} count_{v_i} = |V|$. So $\mathcal{A}_{NoK}$ is a counting algorithm that respects the* **convergence** *property.*

Proof. Lemma 5 shows that there exists a round $r_{|V,\epsilon|}$ after which the maximal amount of negative energy that can be created in the network is bounded by a quantity ϵ that can be made arbitrarily small. For energy conservation Lemma, this means that the total amount of negative and positive energy in $V \setminus \{v_l\}$ is bounded at each round by a monotonically decreasing function of the round number. So $\lim_{r \to \infty}(|V| - e^r_{v_l}) = 0$, this means that there exists a round r such that $\forall r' \geq r$ holds $|V| - e_{v_l}^{r'} < 1$. So the variable $count_{v_l}$ will be equals to $|V|$ $\forall r' \geq r$. This means that $\mathcal{A}_{NoK}$ respects the *convergence* property.

$$\square_{Lemma\ 6}$$

The previous Lemma has an interesting implication: there exists a round r such that $\forall r' \geq r$ holds $|V| - e_{v_l}^{r'} < 1$. However, this condition is not detectable by any node in the network. As a consequence, $\mathcal{A}_{NoK}$ respects **convergence** property but not **conscious** property. Unconscious algorithms can be used in any practical context where the safety of the application does not depend by a correct count and where liveness and/or fairness need just an eventually correct count (e.g. fair load balancing). In a companion paper [15], we show a performance evaluation of $\mathcal{A}_{NoK}$ and we propose an heuristics to let $\mathcal{A}_{NoK}$ terminate together with the comparison between the basic $\mathcal{A}_{NoK}$ and the heuristic-based one.

Energy vs. Mass Conservation. Our idea of *energy transfer* and the principle of *energy conservation* is similar to the one used in [13] where a global invariant called *conservation of mass* is used and a push-only mechanism is employed to implement a gossip-based protocol for aggregation. Despite the similarities in the principle, the underling graph considered in [13] is obtained trough a sampling function while our model is governed by a worst case adversary (as discussed in Section 2). Moreover, Kempe et Al. assume that each node knows in advance the number of neighbors for the message-exchange while in our model this is not possible. As a consequence, they obtain probabilistic bounds on the convergence time and each node of the system converges to the average of the inputs value while in our algorithm the leader always absorbs energy converging to the correct count and the other nodes converge to zero.

6   Conclusion

We presented a distributed (deterministic) algorithm that assumes the existence of a unique leader node in order to precisely count the number of nodes of the network. The leader node executes a different code from the rest of the nodes and acts as a sink for the energy transfer. This algorithm is resilient to an adversary that can change the communication graph at any round with the constraint of not creating disconnected graphs or graphs including nodes with a degree that exceed a given bound.

Secondly, we have shown that the conjecture presented in [16] stating that "in dynamic networks ensuring 1-interval connectivity we cannot count even with a leader" is still valid but only if the count is conscious. We have indeed presented an algorithm that is able to unconsciously count the size of the network. Thus the conjecture can be reworded as follows "in dynamic networks ensuring 1-interval connectivity we cannot count consciously even with a leader". This leaves open an interesting problem concerning the existence of a conscious counting algorithm resilient to a dynamic graph adversary only constrained to ensure 1-interval connectivity.

Let us finally remark that our algorithms work in a ever changing dynamic graph. This continuous dynamic behavior is similar to the churn analyzed in [6] for building regular registers. We believe that these forms of dynamic behaviors are the natural way to think about dynamic distributed systems with respect to distributed systems whose form of dynamic behavior eventually stabilizes such as [1,10].

Acknowledgments. This work has been partially supported by the TENACE project (MIUR-PRIN 20103P34XC) and by the EU-FP7 IP project PANOPTESEC and "Foundations of Dynamic Distributed Computing Systems" (FOCUS) which is implemented under the "ARISTEIA" Action of the Operational Programme "Education and Lifelong Learning" and is co-funded by the European Union (European Social Fund) and Greek National Resources.

References

1. Aguilera, M.K., Keidar, I., Malkhi, D., Shraer, A.: Dynamic atomic storage without consensus. J. ACM 58(2), 7 (2011)
2. Angluin, D.: Local and global properties in networks of processors (extended abstract). In: STOC, pp. 82–93. ACM (1980)
3. Aspnes, J., Fich, F.E., Ruppert, E.: Relationships between broadcast and shared memory in reliable anonymous distributed systems. Distrib. Comput. 18(3), 209–219 (2006)
4. Attiya, H., Snir, M., Warmuth, M.K.: Computing on an anonymous ring. J. ACM 35(4), 845–875 (1988)
5. Baldoni, R., Bertier, M., Raynal, M., Tucci-Piergiovanni, S.: Looking for a definition of dynamic distributed systems. In: Malyshkin, V.E. (ed.) PaCT 2007. LNCS, vol. 4671, pp. 1–14. Springer, Heidelberg (2007)
6. Baldoni, R., Bonomi, S., Raynal, M.: Implementing a Regular Register in an Eventually Synchronous Distributed System Prone to Continuous Churn. IEEE Transaction on Parallel Distributed Systems 23(1), 102–109 (2012)
7. Boldi, P., Vigna, S.: Computing anonymously with arbitrary knowledge. In: PODC, pp. 181–188. ACM (1999)
8. Casteigts, A., Flocchini, P., Quattrociocchi, W., Santoro, N.: Time-varying graphs and dynamic networks. CoRR, abs/1012.0009 (2010)
9. Chalopin, J., Métivier, Y., Morsellino, T.: On snapshots and stable properties detection in anonymous fully distributed systems (Extended abstract). In: Even, G., Halldórsson, M.M. (eds.) SIROCCO 2012. LNCS, vol. 7355, pp. 207–218. Springer, Heidelberg (2012)
10. Chockler, G., Gilbert, S., Gramoli, V., Musial, P.M., Shvartsman, A.A.: Reconfigurable distributed storage for dynamic networks. J. Parallel Distrib. Comput. 69(1), 100–116 (2009)
11. Fraigniaud, P., Pelc, A., Peleg, D., Pérennes, S.: Assigning labels in unknown anonymous networks. In: PODC, pp. 101–111. ACM (2000)
12. Jelasity, M., Montresor, A., Babaoglu, Ö.: Gossip-based aggregation in large dynamic networks. ACM Trans. Comput. Syst. 23(3), 219–252 (2005)
13. Kempe, D., Dobra, A., Gehrke, J.: Gossip-based computation of aggregate information. In: FOCS, pp. 482–491 (2003)
14. Kuhn, F., Lynch, N., Oshman, R.: Distributed computation in dynamic networks. In: STOC, pp. 513–522. ACM, New York (2010)
15. Di Luna, G., Bonomi, S., Chatzigiannakis, I., Baldoni, R.: Counting in Anonymous Dynamic Networks: An Experimental Perspective. In: ALGOSENSORS 2013 (to appear), http://www.dis.uniroma1.it/~midlab/articoli/main_2.pdf
16. Michail, O., Chatzigiannakis, I., Spirakis, P.G.: Naming and counting in anonymous unknown dynamic networks. In: Higashino, T., Katayama, Y., Masuzawa, T., Potop-Butucaru, M., Yamashita, M. (eds.) SSS 2013. LNCS, vol. 8255, pp. 281–295. Springer, Heidelberg (2013)
17. O'Dell, R., Wattenhofer, R.: Information dissemination in highly dynamic graphs. In: DIALM-POMC, pp. 104–110. ACM, New York (2005)
18. Yamashita, M., Kameda, T.: Computing on an anonymous network. In: PODC, pp. 117–130. ACM, New York (1988)

On Probabilistic Snap-Stabilization

Karine Altisen and Stéphane Devismes

VERIMAG UMR 5104, Université de Grenoble
{Karine.Altisen,Stephane.Devismes}@imag.fr
http://www-verimag.imag.fr

Abstract. In this paper, we introduce *probabilistic snap-stabilization*. We relax the definition of deterministic snap-stabilization without compromising its safety guarantees. In an unsafe environment, a probabilistically snap-stabilizing algorithm satisfies its safety property *immediately* after the last fault; whereas its liveness property is only ensured with probability 1.

We show that probabilistic snap-stabilization is more expressive than its deterministic counterpart. Indeed, we propose two probabilistic snap-stabilizing algorithms for a problem having no deterministic snap- or self-stabilizing solution: *guaranteed service leader election* in arbitrary anonymous networks. This problem consists in computing a correct answer to each process that initiates the question "Am I the leader of the network?", *i.e.*, (1) processes always computed the same answer to that question and (2) exactly one process computes the answer *true*.

Our solutions being probabilistically snap-stabilizing, the answers are only delivered within an almost surely finite time; however any delivered answer is correct, regardless the arbitrary initial configuration and provided the question has been properly started.

Keywords: Snap-stabilization, probabilistic algorithms, leader election.

1 Introduction

Self-stabilization [14] is a versatile technique to withstand *any* transient fault in a distributed system: a self-stabilizing algorithm is able to recover, *i.e.*, reach a legitimate configuration, in finite time, regardless the *arbitrary* initial configuration of the system, and therefore also after the occurrence of transient faults. Thus, self-stabilization makes no hypotheses on the nature or extent of transient faults that could hit the system, and recovers from the effects of those faults in a unified manner. Such versatility comes at a price. After transient faults, there is a finite period of time, called the *stabilization phase*, before the system returns to a legitimate configuration. During this phase, there is no safety guarantee at all. In addition, a process cannot locally detect whether the system is actually in a legitimate configuration. Moreover, self-stabilizing algorithms may require a large amount of resources, *e.g.*, extra memory is usually required to crosscheck inconsistencies. Finally, symmetries occurring in the initial configuration could cause a problem to be impossible to solve, *e.g.*, leader election [27] and token passing [21] have no deterministic self-stabilizing solutions in anonymous networks. To cope with those

M. Chatterjee et al. (Eds.): ICDCN 2014, LNCS 8314, pp. 272–286, 2014.
© Springer-Verlag Berlin Heidelberg 2014

issues, two categories of variants of self-stabilization have been introduced: *weakened* and *strengthened* forms of self-stabilization.

Related Work. *Weakened forms* of self-stabilization have been introduced to cope with impossibility results, reduce the stabilization time, or limit the resource consumption. *Weak stabilization* [20] stipulates that starting from *any* initial configuration, *there exists* a run that eventually reaches a legitimate configuration. Unlike for self-stabilization, token passing and leader election have weak stabilizing solutions in anonymous networks [13]. *k-stabilization* [3] prohibits some of the configurations from being initial, as an initial configuration may only be the result of at most k faults. There are k-stabilizing token passing algorithms that guarantee small convergence time depending only on k [3]. *Probabilistic self-stabilization* [22] weakens the convergence property: starting from any initial configuration, the system converges to a legitimate configuration with probability 1. Problems such as token passing and leader election in anonymous networks have probabilistic self-stabilizing solutions [22,15].

Strengthened forms of self-stabilization have been mainly introduced to offer stringent safety guarantees. A *fault containing* self-stabilizing algorithm [19] ensures that when few faults hits the system, the faults are both spatially and temporally contained. "Spatially" means that if only few faults occur, those faults cannot be propagated further than a preset radius around the corrupted nodes. "Temporally" means quick stabilization when few faults occur. A *superstabilizing algorithm* [16] is self-stabilizing and has two additional properties. In presence of single topological change, it recovers fast, and a safety predicate, called a *passage* predicate, should be satisfied along the stabilization. Finally, *(deterministic) snap-stabilization* [8] offers strong safety guarantees: regardless of the configuration to which transient failures drive the system, after the failures stop, a snap-stabilizing system immediately resumes correct behavior. Precisely, a snap-stabilizing algorithm guarantees that any computation started after the faults will operate correctly. However, we have no guarantees for those executed all or a part during faults. Actually, snap-stabilization is often used to offer *user-centric* guarantees: the problems considered consist of executing finite tasks called *services*: a service is started by some initiating process and terminates by providing a result to that initiator. The goal is to ensure that, starting from any configuration, a service eventually starts if requested by some process; and every started service is computed correctly. We call those problems *guaranteed service problems*.

Contribution. We introduce a new property called *probabilistic snap-stabilization*, a probabilistic variant of (deterministic) snap-stabilization. Just as for the probabilistic extension of self-stabilization, we choose to adopt a "Las Vegas" approach and relax the definition of snap-stabilization without altering its safety guarantees. Considering a specification as the conjunction of safety and liveness properties, a probabilistically snap-stabilizing algorithm immediately satisfies the safety property at the end of the faults, whereas the liveness property is ensured with probability 1.

We show that probabilistic snap-stabilization is strictly more expressive than its deterministic counterpart, as we give two probabilistic snap-stabilizing algorithms for a problem having no deterministic self- or snap-stabilizing solution: *guaranteed service leader election* in anonymous networks. This problem consists in computing a correct answer to each process that initiates the question "Am I the leader of the network ?", *i.e.*, (1) processes always computed the same answer to that question and (2) exactly one process computes the answer *true*. Our solutions being probabilistically snap-stabilizing, the answers are delivered within an almost surely finite time; however, any delivered answer is correct, regardless the arbitrary initial configuration and provided that the question has been properly started.

Our two algorithms work in the locally shared memory model. The first solution, $S_{\mathcal{GSLE}}$, assumes a synchronous daemon. The second, $A_{\mathcal{GSLE}}$, assumes an unfair (distributed) daemon, the most general daemon of the model. Both algorithms need an additional assumption:[1] the knowledge of a bound B such that $B < n \leq 2B$, where n is the number of processes. The memory requirement of both algorithms is in $O(\log n)$ bits per process. The expected delay, response, and service times of $S_{\mathcal{GSLE}}$ are each $O(n)$ rounds, while these times are $O(n^2)$ rounds for $A_{\mathcal{GSLE}}$. If we add the assumption that processes know an upper bound, D, on the diameter of the network, the expected time complexity of $A_{\mathcal{GSLE}}$ can be made $O(D.n)$ rounds.

Roadmap. In the next section we define the computational model. In Section 3, we introduce *probabilistic snap-stabilization*. In the same section, we formally define the guaranteed service problem, and give one example, namely guaranteed service leader election. In Section 4, we propose our two probabilistic snap-stabilizing algorithms. We conclude in Section 5.

2   Preliminaries

Below, we define a general model to handle probabilistic algorithms in anonymous networks. It settles the formal context in which probabilistic snap-stabilization is defined.

Distributed Systems. We consider distributed systems of $n \geq 2$ *anonymous* processes, *i.e.*, they all have the same program, and have no parameter (such as an identity) permitting them to be differentiated. Each process p can directly communicate with a subset of other processes, called its *neighbors*. Communication is *bidirectional*. We model a distributed system as a simple undirected connected graph $G = (V, E)$, where V is the set of processes and E is a set of edges representing (direct) communication relations. Every processor p can distinguish its neighbors using a local labeling. All labels of p's neighbors are stored into the set $\mathcal{N}_p$. Moreover, we assume that each process p can identify its local label in the set $\mathcal{N}_q$ of each neighbor q. By an abuse of notation, we use p to designate both the process p itself, and also its local labels.

Computational Model. We assume the *locally shared memory model* [14], where each process communicates with its neighbors using a finite set of locally shared registers, henceforth called simply *variables*. A process can read its own variables and those of its neighbors, but can write only to its own variables. Each process operates according to its *program*. A *(distributed) algorithm* $\mathcal{A}$ is defined to be a collection of n *programs*, each operating on a single process. The program of each process consists of a finite set of actions of the form: $\langle guard \rangle \longrightarrow \langle statement \rangle$. The *guard* of an action in the program of a process p is a Boolean expression involving the variables of p and its neighbors; the *statement* updates some variables of p. An action can be executed only

---

[1] We otherwise prove that our problem is probabilistically unsolvable.

if its guard evaluates to *true*. The *state* of a process p is the vector consisting of the values of all its variables. The set of all variables of p is noted Var_p, and for a variable $v \in \text{Var}_p$, $\text{Dom}_p(v)$ denotes the set of all possible values of v. A variable v in Var_p can be either a *discrete* variable, which ranges over a discrete (but possibly infinite) set of values (namely, $\text{Dom}_p(v)$ is a countable set) or v is a real variable for which $\text{Dom}_p(v)$ is a given interval of reals.[2] The set S_p of all possible states of process p, is defined to be the Cartesian product of the sets $\text{Dom}_p(v)$, over all $v \in \text{Var}_p$.

A *configuration*, γ, consists of one state, $\gamma(p) \in S_p$ for each process p, *i.e.*, $\gamma \in C \overset{\text{def}}{=} \prod_{p \in V} S_p$, the set of all possible configurations. We denote by $\gamma(p).x$ the value of the variable x of process p in γ.

An action in the program of a process p is said to be *enabled in* γ if and only if its guard is true in γ, and we say p is enabled in γ if and only if some action in the program of p is enabled in γ. Let $Enabled(\gamma)$ be the set of processes which are enabled in γ.

When the system is in configuration γ, a *daemon* selects a subset ϕ of $Enabled(\gamma)$ to execute an *(atomic) step*: every process of ϕ atomically executes one of its enabled actions, leading to a configuration γ'. So, a daemon is a function $d : C^+ \to 2^V$: Considering the finite sequence of configurations $\rho = (\gamma_0, ..., \gamma_k)$ through which the system has evolved, the daemon gives the next chosen subset $d(\rho) \subseteq Enabled(\gamma_k)$ of enabled processes that will execute in the next step. Let $\mathcal{D}_{all}$ be the set of all possible daemons.

Deterministic Algorithms. We model a distributed *deterministic* algorithm $\mathcal{A}$ as a function $F_{\mathcal{A}} : C \times 2^V \to C$, *i.e.*, the next configuration is only determined by the current configuration and the set of processes that will execute the next step. A *run* of a deterministic algorithm $\mathcal{A}$ under the daemon d is an infinite sequence $r = (\gamma_i)_{i \geq 0} \in C^{\omega}$ inductively defined as follows: $\gamma_0 \in C$ and $\forall i \geq 0$, $\gamma_{i+1} = F_{\mathcal{A}}(\gamma_i, d(\gamma_0, \ldots, \gamma_i))$, *i.e.*, γ_{i+1} is obtained from γ_i by an atomic step of all processes in $d(\gamma_0, \ldots, \gamma_i)$.[3]

Probabilistic Algorithms. The modeling of probabilistic distributed algorithms is a bit more intricate since it has to handle the interactions between probabilities and non-determinism, like in Markov Decision Process [25]. In our case, probabilities come from the use of random functions in process programs, while non-determinism is due to asynchrony. Below, we provide a concise model and semantics using infinite Markov chains; alternative models can be found in [4,17].

Following the literature [18], for every process p and for every variable $v \in \text{Var}_p$, we define $\sigma_{p,v}$, the *sigma-field* (informally, the set of possible events on the value of v) associated with v:

- If v is discrete, then $\sigma_{p,v}$ is the *discrete sigma-field* on $\text{Dom}_p(v)$ formed by the power-set of $\text{Dom}_p(v)$.
- If v is real, then $\sigma_{p,v}$ is the *Borel sigma-field* of $\text{Dom}_p(v)$.

The *sigma-field over* C, denoted by Σ_C, is the *minimal sigma-field* of C, generated by the subsets of the form $\prod_{p \in V} \prod_{v \in \text{Var}_p} s_{p,v}$, where $s_{p,v} \in \sigma_{p,v}$.

We model a distributed *probabilistic* algorithm $\mathcal{A}$ as a family of probability kernels $\mu_d : C^+ \times \Sigma_C \to [0, 1]$ indexed on any possible daemon $d \in \mathcal{D}_{all}$. Namely, for any fixed $s \in \Sigma_C$, the function $x \to \mu_d(x, s)$ is Σ_{C^+}-measurable, and for any prefix $p \in C^+$,

---

[2] Our algorithms only deal with finite-state variables, whereas our model is more general.

[3] Note that $F_{\mathcal{A}}(\gamma_i, \emptyset) = \gamma_i$.

the function $x \to \mu_d(p, x)$ is a probability measure. Considering the finite sequence of configurations $\rho = (\gamma_0, ..., \gamma_k)$ through which the system has evolved using the daemon d, $x \to \mu_d(\rho, x)$ describes the probability law for the next configuration. In particular, $\mu_d(\rho, \{\gamma_{k+1}\})$ is the probability of reaching configuration γ_{k+1} after prefix ρ. The sequence $r = (\gamma_i)_{i \geq 0} \in \mathcal{C}^\omega$ is a *run* of $\mathcal{A}$ under the daemon d if and only if there exists a sequence of choices of d, $(\phi_i)_{i \geq 0} \in (2^V)^\omega$, such that $\forall i \geq 0$, $\phi_i = d(\gamma_0, ..., \gamma_i)$ and there exists $s \in \Sigma_{\mathcal{C}}$ such that $\gamma_{i+1} \in s$ and $\mu_d(\gamma_0, ..., \gamma_i, s) > 0$.

Given a daemon d and a probabilistic algorithm $\mathcal{A}$, let R_n be a random variable over $\mathcal{C}^n$, representing a prefix of size $n \in \mathbb{N}$ of a run: $R_n = \Gamma_0 \cdots \Gamma_n$, where each Γ_{i+1} is obtained from Γ_i after one more step of $\mathcal{A}$. Note that the sequence $(R_n)_{n \in \mathbb{N}}$ is a Markov chain, since the possible values for R_{n+1} on $R_0, ..., R_{n-1}, R_n$ only depends on R_n. The probability space for the model is naturally derived from the usual Markov chain theory. Let R be a random variable on $\mathcal{C}^\omega$ and $\mathcal{R} \subseteq \mathcal{C}^\omega$ be a measurable set of runs of $\mathcal{A}$. Let $\gamma_0 \in \mathcal{C}$. We denote by $\mathsf{Pr}_{\mathcal{A}}^{d, \gamma_0}(\mathcal{R})$ the probability that a run of $\mathcal{R}$ occurs on $R_0 = \gamma_0$.[4]

Daemon Families. We only consider here daemons that are *proper*, namely for every run $(\gamma_i)_{i \geq 0}$ of a distributed algorithm $\mathcal{A}$, under a proper daemon d, for every $i \geq 0$, $Enabled(\gamma_i) \neq \emptyset \Rightarrow d(\gamma_0, ..., \gamma_i) \neq \emptyset$. Daemons are usually classified into *families* according to their fairness property. The family of *unfair (distributed) daemons*, noted $\mathcal{D}_U$, is the set of all proper daemons. A daemon d is said to be *synchronous* if and only if for every run $(\gamma_i)_{i \geq 0}$ under d, for every $i \geq 0$, $d(\gamma_0, ..., \gamma_i) = Enabled(\gamma_i)$. We denote by $\mathcal{D}_S$ the set of all synchronous daemons. We denote by $\mathcal{R}_{\mathcal{A}}^{\mathcal{D}}$ the set of all possible runs of $\mathcal{A}$ using a daemon of family $\mathcal{D}$. We denote by $\mathcal{R}_{\mathcal{A}}^{\mathcal{D}, \gamma_0}$ the subset of runs of $\mathcal{R}_{\mathcal{A}}^{\mathcal{D}}$ starting from configuration γ_0.

Rounds. In some run $r = (\gamma_i)_{i \geq 0}$ of an algorithm $\mathcal{A}$ under a daemon d, we say that a process p is *neutralized* in the step γ_i, γ_{i+1} if p is enabled in γ_i and not enabled in γ_{i+1}, but does not execute any action between these two configurations.

We use the notion of *round* to evaluate the time complexity of $\mathcal{A}$. This notion captures the execution rate of the slowest processor in every run. The first *round* of r, noted r', is the minimal prefix of r in which every process that are enabled in γ_0 either execute an action or become neutralized. Let r'' be the suffix of r starting from the last configuration of r'. The second round of r is the first round of r'', and so forth. Notice that, by definition, under a synchronous daemon, each round lasts exactly one step.

3   Snap-Stabilization and Guaranteed Service Problems

In this section, we first recall the definition of deterministic snap-stabilization. Then, we introduce the probabilistic snap-stabilization. Finally, we define the guaranteed service problems, and we instantiate this notion to define guaranteed service leader election.

Following [1], we express the *specification* SP of an algorithm as a set of runs, or equivalently as a predicate that any run should satisfy: $SP \subseteq \mathcal{C}^\omega$. We use the usual result [1,23] that a specification can always be expressed as the conjunction of a safety property and a liveness property: $SP = Safe \cap Live$.

---

[4] We fix γ_0, since we do not assume any distribution on the initial configurations.

In (self- or snap-) stabilization, we consider the system right after the occurrence of the last fault, *i.e.*, we study the system starting from an arbitrary configuration reached due to the occurrence of transient faults, but from which no additional fault will ever occur. By abuse of language, this *arbitrary* configuration is referred to as *initial* configuration of the system. Deterministic snap-stabilization has been defined as follows:

Definition 1 (Deterministic Snap-Stabilization [8]). *An algorithm $\mathcal{A}$ is* snap-stabilizing *w.r.t. a specification $SP = Safe \cap Live$ and a family of daemons $\mathcal{D}$ iff(def) $\forall r \in \mathcal{R}_{\mathcal{A}}^{\mathcal{D}}, r \in SP$ (i.e., $r \in Safe$ and $r \in Live$).*

The idea behind *probabilistic snap-stabilization* is to weaken deterministic snap-stabilization without compromising its strong safety guarantees. The safety part remains unchanged, but, we allow the algorithm to compute for a possibly long, yet almost surely finite, time.

Definition 2 (Probabilistic Snap-Stabilization). *An algorithm $\mathcal{A}$ is* probabilistically snap-stabilizing *w.r.t. a specification $SP = Safe \cap Live$ and a family of daemons $\mathcal{D}$ iff(def)*
Strong Safety: $\forall r \in \mathcal{R}_{\mathcal{A}}^{\mathcal{D}}, r \in Safe$, *and*
Almost Surely Liveness: $\forall \gamma_0 \in \mathcal{C}, \forall d \in \mathcal{D}, \Pr_{\mathcal{A}}^{d,\gamma_0}(Live) = 1$.

Almost all snap-stabilizing solutions proposed so far solve *guaranteed service* problems, *i.e.*, problems consisting in executing finite tasks upon the request at some process. Propagation of Information with Feedback [10] is an example of such a problem: when an application at a given process p needs to broadcast some data, the service consists in ensuring that all processes eventually acknowledge the receipt of the data and that p eventually receives acknowledgment from all processes. Generally, a guaranteed service problem consists in ensuring three properties:

1. If an application at some process continuously requires the execution of the service, then the process — called *the initiator* — eventually starts a computation of the service (involving the whole or a part of the network).
2. Every started service eventually ends by a decision at its initiator, allowing it to get back a *result*.
3. Every result obtained from any started service is correct *w.r.t.* the service.

To formalize these properties, we use the following predicates, where $p \in V, s, s' \in S_p$, and $\gamma_0 \dots \gamma_t \in \mathcal{C}^+$:
- *Request(s)* means that the state s indicates to p that some application needs an execution of the service.
- *Start(s, s')* means that p starts a computation of the service by switching its state from s to s'.
- *Result(s, s')* means that p executes the decision event to get back the result of a computation by switching its state from s to s'.
- *Correct-Result($\gamma_0 \dots \gamma_t, p$)* means that the computed result is correct *w.r.t.* the service.

Definition 3 (Specification for Guaranteed Service). *A guaranteed service specification is a specification $\mathcal{S}_{gs} = Safe_{gs} \cap Live_{gs}$ where $Safe_{gs}$ and $Live_{gs}$ are defined as follows: let $r = (\gamma_i)_{i \geq 0}$,*

(a) $r \in Safe_{gs}$ if and only if $\forall k \geq 0, \forall p \in V, (Result(\gamma_k(p), \gamma_{k+1}(p)) \wedge \exists l <$
k, $Start(\gamma_l(p), \gamma_{l+1}(p))) \Rightarrow Correct\text{-}Result(\gamma_0 \ldots \gamma_k, p))$.
(b) $r \in Live_{gs}$ if and only if the following two conditions hold:
(1) $\forall k \geq 0, \forall p \in V, \exists l \geq k, (Request(\gamma_l(p)) \Rightarrow Start(\gamma_l(p), \gamma_{l+1}(p)))$.
(2) $\forall k \geq 0, \forall p \in V, (Start(\gamma_k(p), \gamma_{k+1}(p)) \Rightarrow (\exists l > k, Result(\gamma_l(p), \gamma_{l+1}(p))))$.

The safety condition *(a)* means that when a result is delivered, it is *correct*, provided that the task that computed the result was started. The liveness condition *(b)* means that *(1)* it cannot happen that an application continuously requests the service without being served and *(2)* any started computation eventually delivers a result.

When a guaranteed service solution is snap-stabilizing, this implies that whatever the initial configuration is, every started service delivers within a finite time a correct result to its initiator. Considering probabilistic snap-stabilization, when a result is delivered, it is *correct*, provided that the service corresponding to this result has been properly started (similar to the deterministic case), but the time elapsed between the starting and the corresponding result is only *almost surely finite*.

The classical definition of *leader election* requires that there should be always at most one leader, and if a process is designated as leader it remains leader forever (safety), and that eventually there should exist a leader (liveness). This specification can be turned into a guaranteed service specification. Every process may initiate a computation (*i.e.*, a question) to know whether it is the leader. The results should be consistent, *i.e*, the result from any initiated leader-computation by some process p is a *constant* truth value, and exactly one process always obtains the result *true* to its initiated leader-computations.

In the following definition, we use the predicate $Unique(\gamma, p)$, which is true if and only if there is exactly one process p that designates itself as *leader* in configuration γ.

Definition 4 (Guaranteed Service Leader Election Specification). *The* guaranteed service leader election specification $S_{gs,leader}$ *is given using Definition 3 of guaranteed service, where the predicate Correct-Result is instantiated as follows.*

$Correct\text{-}Result_{leader}(\gamma_0 \ldots \gamma_k, p)$ is true if and only if $\exists p^* \in V$ such that:
– $Unique(\gamma_k, p^*)$ and
– $\forall i \in \{i^*, ..., k\}, Unique(\gamma_i, p^*)$, where $i^* = \min\{i \in \{1, ..., k\} : \exists q \in V,$
$Result(\gamma_{i-1}(q), \gamma_i(q)) \wedge \exists l < i, Start(\gamma_l(q), \gamma_{l+1}(q))\}$.

The first item of the definition ensures that there exists a unique leader at the completion of a previously started leader-computation. The second item ensures that all results obtained from started leader-computations are consistent, *i.e.*, the leader is the same.

4   Probabilistic Snap-Stabilizing Guaranteed Service Leader Election

We now deal with a problem having no deterministic solution: the *guaranteed service leader election in anonymous networks* [2]. We first propose a probabilistic snap-stabilizing solution, called $S_{\mathcal{GSLE}}$ (*Synchronous Guaranteed Service Leader Election*), which assumes a *synchronous* daemon. Then, we slightly modify the solution to obtain a probabilistically snap-stabilizing algorithm, called $\mathcal{A}_{\mathcal{GSLE}}$ (*Asynchronous Guaranteed Service Leader Election*), which works under an *unfair (distributed)* daemon.

First, note that, without an additional assumption on the system (*e.g.*, the knowledge of some upper bound on some network global parameter), there is no probabilistic guaranteed service leader election in our setting. We prove this claim by reducing the guaranteed service leader election to the ring-size counting problem, which has been proven to be probabilistically unsolvable in our setting [26]. So, following the ideas in [24], we assume that the processes know a bound B on n such that $B < n \leq 2B$.

4.1 Synchronous Settings

$\mathcal{S}_{\mathcal{GSLE}}$ is made of three modules — Election, Pulse, and Service — which run concurrently: at each local step, a process simultaneously executes an action of each module where it is enabled. Election is the main module. It uses the output of Pulse to perform probabilistic *self-stabilizing* leader election. In Election, each process p maintains a Boolean variable p.me, which states whether it is candidate for the election. The module executes in cycles. Each cycle computes a Boolean output oneLdr at each process, stating whether a unique leader exists; it is computed by testing whether there is a unique process p^* which is candidate in the configuration γ ending the cycle, *i.e.*, if the predicate $Unique(\gamma, p^*) \stackrel{\text{def}}{=} \gamma(p^*)$.me $\wedge \forall p \in V, p \neq p^* \Rightarrow \neg\gamma(p)$.me holds.

If there is no leader at the end of the cycle, the next cycle attempts to elect a leader by modifying the variables me. Once a cycle succeeds in electing a leader, all processes compute the output $true$ in their variable oneLdr and during the remaining cycles their variable me stays constant: once elected, the leader remains stable.

Conversely, if oneLdr is $false$ at the end of a cycle, then every process p randomly and synchronously chooses a new value for p.me: p resets p.me to v, where v is a random Boolean value which is $true$ with probability α_{vote}, respectively $false$ with probability $1 - \alpha_{vote}$. In other words, the new random Boolean value v of p.me follows a Bernoulli distribution of constant parameter α_{vote}, noted $v \hookrightarrow \mathcal{B}(\alpha_{vote})$ in the sequel. Hence, if there is not a leader at the end of a cycle, then a leader is elected during the next cycle with positive probability.

Processes should be synchronized in order to obtain a consistent output at the end of a cycle. This is the aim of the second module, Pulse, which is actually a *self-stabilizing synchronous unison* algorithm. In synchronous systems, a self-stabilizing unison consists in implementing a logical clock at each process such that, once the system is in a legitimate configuration, all local clocks have the same value and increment at each step; we denote by P_{SU} the predicate defining all legitimate configurations of the synchronous unison. Once Pulse achieves its legitimacy, all processes execute cycles synchronously. The output oneLdr computed during each cycle started in a configuration satisfying P_{SU} will be both consistent (*i.e.*, all processes will have the same value for oneLdr), and correct (*i.e.*, oneLdr will be $true$ if and only if there is unique leader in the system).

The composition of the two aforementioned modules is only probabilistically self-stabilizing. So, to ensure the safety part of $\mathcal{S}_{gs,leader}$, we cannot let a process directly evaluate its variable me to state whether it is the leader, even if oneLdr is currently $true$. To guarantee that, after starting a question, a process delivers a correct result, we use an additional module, Service. The aim of this module is to delay the processing of each question (service), so that the initiator is able to consult its variables me and oneLdr only when they are correctly evaluated. To that end, p should (at least) wait for the first cycle of Election started after the system has reached a configuration satisfying P_{SU}. After this waiting time, an initiator p can consult p.me and p.oneLdr at the end of each cycle; when p.oneLdr is $true$, it delivers the result p.me. Below, we give more details about the three modules of $S_{\mathcal{GSLE}}$.

Module Pulse. We consider a slightly updated version of the unison algorithm proposed in [7], which we call $\mathcal{U}$. Actually, we add a local observer into the program of $\mathcal{U}$. This observer will be used by Module Service to guarantee service.

$\mathcal{U}$ is a unison algorithm with a bounded number of clock values: the clock of every process takes a value in $\{-\kappa, ..., \xi - 1\}$; however the negative values are only used during the stabilization phase. Once $\mathcal{U}$ has stabilized, the values of the clocks increment using the function Φ from 0 to $\xi - 1$, then back to 0, and so forth. Consequently, $P_{SU} \overset{\text{def}}{=} \forall p, q \in V, p.\text{clock} = q.\text{clock} \wedge p.\text{clock} \geq 0$. In [5], $\mathcal{U}$ is shown to be self-stabilizing for the synchronous unison in any anonymous synchronous network if $\kappa \geq n - 2$ and $\xi \geq n + 1$. Here, processes do not know n, but they know a value B such that $n \leq 2B$. So, it is sufficient to take $\kappa = 2B - 2$ and $\xi \geq 2B + 1$, to guarantee the self-stabilization of $\mathcal{U}$ in any topology. Moreover, the stabilization time of $\mathcal{U}$, called ST, is shown in [5] to be less or equal to $n + \kappa + \mathcal{D}$ steps in synchronous settings, where $\mathcal{D}$ is the diameter of the network. So, $ST \leq 6B$ steps (or equivalently $6B$ rounds).

We add to $\mathcal{U}$ an observer in order to obtain a guaranteed service property: as explained before, we need a mechanism that allows any process p to locally decide whether the configuration satisfies P_{SU}. To achieve that, p needs only to wait at least $6B$ steps, because $ST \leq 6B$. So, we add a variable p.cnt, which takes a value in $\{0, ..., \text{CMax}\}$, where $\text{CMax} = 6B$. At each step, p.cnt is decremented if it is positive. We also add two functions that can be called in Module Service: $p.\text{init}()$ resets p.cnt to CMax; and $p.\text{OK}()$ returns $true$ if and only if p.cnt equals 0. Note that the local observers do not disturb the stabilization of $\mathcal{U}$, because they only write to a dedicated additional variable. Furthermore, starting from any configuration, for every process p, if $p.\text{init}()$ is called, $p.\text{OK}()$ returns $true$ CMax steps (resp. rounds) later and p has the guarantee that the configuration satisfies P_{SU}.

Module Election. This module (Algorithm 1) executes in cycles. Processes use their clocks in order to synchronize. Once all processes are synchronized, each cycle is performed in three phases. Each phase lasts φ steps and consists of an initialization step followed by a computation that is propagated to all processes. So, φ should be at least strictly greater than the diameter of the network: we set φ to $2B$. To easily distinguish each phase, we can set the size of the cycle to any value ξ greater or equal to $3\varphi = 6B$, a cycle starts when clocks reset to 0, and every process can determine in which phase it is thanks to its clock. For time complexity issues, we set ξ to exactly $6B$ since this also meets the condition for $\mathcal{U}$, $i.e.$, $\xi = 6B \geq 2B + 1$.

Each process p starts the $first\ phase$ of a cycle (Line 1) by resetting p.me and p.parent. The new value of p.me depends on the result of the previous cycle: if a process p believes that there is no unique leader ($i.e.$, p.oneLdr $= false$), p randomly chooses a new value for p.me to decide if it is candidate in the new phase; otherwise,

---

Algorithm 1 . Module `Election`, for every process p

Input: $p.\text{clock} \in \{-\kappa, ..., \xi - 1\}$: variable from Module `Pulse`
Variables:
$p.\text{me}, p.\text{oneLdr}$: Boolean
$p.\text{parent} \in \mathcal{N}_p \cup \{\text{null}\}$
$p.\text{stSize} \in \{1, ..., 2B\}$
Macros:
cmpMe $= \textbf{if } p.\text{oneLdr} \textbf{ then } p.\text{me} \textbf{ else } v \hookrightarrow \mathcal{B}(\alpha_{vote})$
branches $= \{q \in \mathcal{N}_p : q.\text{me} \vee q.\text{parent} \neq \text{null}\}$
cmpPar $= \textbf{if } p.\text{me} \vee p.\text{parent} \neq \text{null} \vee \text{branches} = \emptyset \textbf{ then } p.\text{parent} \textbf{ else } q \in \text{branches}$
children $= \{q \in \mathcal{N}_p : q.\text{parent} = p\}$
Actions:
1: $p.\text{clock} = \xi - 1$ $\mapsto$ $p.\text{me} \leftarrow \text{cmpMe}; p.\text{parent} \leftarrow \text{null}$
2: $p.\text{clock} \in \{0, ..., \varphi - 2\}$ $\mapsto$ $p.\text{parent} \leftarrow \text{cmpPar}$
3: $p.\text{clock} = \varphi - 1$ $\mapsto$ $p.\text{stSize} \leftarrow 1$
4: $p.\text{clock} \in \{\varphi, ..., 2\varphi - 2\}$ $\mapsto$ $p.\text{stSize} \leftarrow 1 + \sum_{q \in \text{children}} q.\text{stSize}$
5: $p.\text{clock} = 2\varphi - 1$ $\mapsto$ $p.\text{me} \leftarrow p.\text{me} \wedge p.\text{stSize} > B; p.\text{oneLdr} \leftarrow p.\text{me}$
6: $p.\text{clock} \in \{2\varphi, ..., 3\varphi - 2\}$ $\mapsto$ $p.\text{oneLdr} \leftarrow p.\text{oneLdr} \vee \bigvee_{q \in \mathcal{N}_p} q.\text{oneLdr}$

$p.\text{me}$ remains unchanged. The remainder of the phase (Line 2) consists in building a forest, where a process r is a tree root if and only if $r.\text{me} = true$. In the *second phase* of the cycle (Lines 3 and 4), each candidate (*i.e.*, each process whose variable me is $true$) computes the number of nodes in its own tree. Finally, the initialization step of the *third phase* (Line 5) is crucial for the candidates, if any. For every candidate p, if p has more than B nodes in its tree, a majority of nodes are in its tree since $n \leq 2B$. In that case, p is the only candidate in that situation. Consequently p is the leader and it sets both $p.\text{oneLdr}$ and $p.\text{me}$ to $true$. In either case, both $p.\text{oneLdr}$ and $p.\text{me}$ are set to $false$. All non-candidate processes also set their variables oneLdr and me to $false$ in this initialization step. The remainder of the phase (Line 6) allow propagation of the result to all processes so that when the next cycle begins, every process satisfies oneLdr $= true$ if and only if a unique leader is elected.

Module `Service`. Module `Service` (Algorithm 2) achieves snap-stabilizing guaranteed service. When a process p is available ($p.\text{status} = \text{Out}$, *i.e.*, p is not currently processing a service) and when it is requested (*i.e.*, $Request(s) \overset{\text{def}}{=} s.\langle \text{need} \rangle()$), it starts the computation of the service by switching $p.\text{status}$ to Wait (*i.e.*, $Start(s, s') \overset{\text{def}}{=} s.\text{status} = \text{Out} \wedge s'.\text{status} = \text{Wait}$) and resetting the observation in Pulse (Line 7). Then, p waits until $p.\text{OK}() \wedge p.\text{clock} = \xi - 1$: this waiting phase ensures that p will only consider cycles fully executed after the stabilization of Pulse. When this period has elapsed, p switches $p.\text{status}$ from Wait to In (Line 8), meaning that it is now allowed to consider the outputs computed by Module `Election`, which are available only at cycle completions. So, p delivers a result ($p.\text{me}$) only when $p.\text{oneLdr}$ is $true$ at the end of such a cycle (Line 9); in this case p switches $p.\text{status}$ from In to Out to inform the application of the availability of the result (*i.e.*, *Result*(s, s') $\overset{\text{def}}{=}$ s.status $=$ In $\wedge$ s'.status $=$ Out). Note that, from the application point of view, this result is guaranteed *provided that* its request has been properly handled and the corresponding service properly started (Line 7).

Algorithm 2 . Module `Service`, for every process p

Inputs:

p.clock $\in \{-\kappa, ..., \xi - 1\}$: variable from Module `Pulse`

p.me, p.oneLdr: Boolean   : variables from Module `Election`

init(), OK()   : functions from Module `Pulse`

$\langle$need$\rangle$(), $\langle$deliver$\rangle$(*Boolean*) : functions from the application

Variable: p.status $\in \{$Out, Wait, In$\}$

Actions:

7:   p.status $=$ Out $\wedge$ p.$\langle$need$\rangle$() $\mapsto$ p.status $\leftarrow$ Wait; p.init()

8:   p.status $=$ Wait $\wedge$ p.OK() $\wedge$ p.clock $= \xi - 1$ $\mapsto$ p.status $\leftarrow$ In

9:   p.status $=$ In $\wedge p$.clock $= 3\varphi - 1 \wedge p$.oneLdr $\mapsto$ p.status $\leftarrow$ Out; p.$\langle$deliver$\rangle$(p.me)

Complexity of $\mathcal{S_{GSLE}}$. The time complexity of a snap-stabilizing algorithm is measured in terms of *delay*, *response time*, and *service time*. The delay corresponds to the maximum time, starting from any configuration, before any process p starts a service (p.status $\leftarrow$ Wait). The response time is the maximum time between the start of a service (p.status $\leftarrow$ Wait) and its completion (p.status $\leftarrow$ Out), which also corresponds to the delivery of the result. The service time is the sum of the delay and the response time. Since $\mathcal{S_{GSLE}}$ is probabilistic, we give expected values for all these measures.

Assume that an application at process p needs a service, *i.e.*, p.$\langle$need$\rangle$() is *true*, and that the application is continuously requesting until p starts the service. If p.status $=$ Out, p starts immediately. If p.status $=$ In, the start is delayed until the completion of the current service (until p.status $\leftarrow$ Out). If p.status $=$ Wait, p should first switch p.status from Wait to In and then from In to Out before starting. This means that the *delay*, *response time*, and *service time* are of the same order of magnitude, and depend on:

T1: *The time p spends before switching p.status from Out to Wait, when p.$\langle$need$\rangle$() = true:* 1 round.

T2: *The time p spends before switching p.status from Wait to In:* at most CMax $+ \xi - 1 = 12B - 1$ rounds.

T3: *The expected time p spends before switching p.status from In to Out.*

Time **T3** is bounded by the stabilization time ST of $\mathcal{U}$ plus the length ξ of one synchronized cycle (at the first configuration satisfying P_{SU}, a cycle may already be in progress), plus the expected number of rounds used to elect a leader once synchronization is achieved. This latter number is equal to the product of ξ and the expected number EC of synchronized cycles that should be executed to elect a leader. Overall, **T3** is less or equal to $ST + (1 + EC)\xi$ rounds with $ST \leq 6B$ and $\xi = 6B$.

The value EC depends on α_{vote}. The random choices made in each cycle are independent, so the number of synchronized cycles needed to elect a leader follows a geometric distribution with parameter PE, where PE is the probability of electing a leader in one cycle; and $EC = \frac{1}{PE}$. Now, if exactly one process randomly chooses $true$ in its variable me during a synchronized cycle, then a leader is elected during that cycle. So, the probability $P1$ of that event satisfies $P1 \leq PE$, and consequently, $EC \leq \frac{1}{P1}$. Furthermore, we can show that $P1 = n\alpha_{vote}(1 - \alpha_{vote})^{n-1}$, and $P1$ is maximal for $\alpha_{vote} = \frac{1}{n}$. Considering the knowledge of processes (i.e., $B < n \leq 2B$), the best choice for α_{vote} is in $[\frac{1}{2B}, \frac{1}{B+1}]$. In that case, we can show that $\frac{1}{P1} \leq \frac{e^2}{2}$, where e is the Euler constant. So, $EC \leq \frac{e^2}{2} \leq 3.70$ and we can conclude that the expected delay, response time, and service time are all $O(B)$ rounds, i.e., $O(n)$ rounds.

Theorem 1. $\mathcal{S}_{\mathcal{GSLE}}$ *is probabilistically snap-stabilizing w.r.t.* $\mathcal{S}_{gs,leader}$ *in anonymous synchronous networks. If* $\alpha_{vote} \in [\frac{1}{2B}, \frac{1}{B+1}]$, *the expected delay, response, and service times of* $\mathcal{S}_{\mathcal{GSLE}}$ *are each* $O(n)$ *rounds.*

4.2 Asynchronous Settings

We now assume an unfair daemon: $\mathcal{S}_{\mathcal{GSLE}}$ should be adapted to take asynchrony into account, and we call the new version $\mathcal{A}_{\mathcal{GSLE}}$. As before, $\mathcal{A}_{\mathcal{GSLE}}$ is made of the same three modules, which are slightly modified. The module Pulse uses the same unison algorithm $\mathcal{U}$, but the parameters and the observers are adapted to handle asynchrony. The module Election is almost the same (in particular $\varphi = 2B$), but the reading of shared variables must be carefully managed in order to emulate the synchronous executions of the Election cycles. Finally, the module Service is left unchanged.

Asynchronous Unison. In asynchronous settings, the strict clock synchronization can no longer be assumed. The asynchronous version of the unison specification is relaxed as follows: the clocks of every two neighboring processes should not differ from more than one, and each process should increment its clock infinitely often. In [7], $\mathcal{U}$ is proven to be self-stabilizing for this specification under an unfair daemon in any anonymous network if $\kappa \geq n - 2$ and $\xi \geq n + 1$ (the same requirement as for the synchronous unison). We use the same value of κ as in $\mathcal{S}_{\mathcal{GSLE}}$, i.e., $2B - 2$. Then, note that in [5] (Theorem 61, page 104), $\mathcal{U}$ is proven to stabilize in at most $n + \kappa \leq 4B$ rounds. Moreover, its legitimate configurations are defined to be all configurations satisfying $P_{AU} \stackrel{\text{def}}{=} \forall p, q \in V, |p.\texttt{clock} - q.\texttt{clock}| \leq 1 \wedge p.\texttt{clock} \geq 0$.

Emulate Synchronous Cycles. Assume that the system is in a configuration satisfying P_{AU}. When a process p increments $p.\texttt{clock}$ from x to $\Phi(x)$, each neighbor q of p has either the same clock value ($q.\texttt{clock} = x$) or is one tick ahead ($q.\texttt{clock} = \Phi(x)$). In the former case, p can execute a step of Election, making use of the current local state of q. In the latter case, p should make use of the previous state of q (when $q.\texttt{clock}$ was equal to x). In order to do so, we modify the reading of variables of Election as follows. Each process p is now equipped with an additional vector variable $p.\texttt{prev}$, in which, at each clock increment, it saves its current local state w.r.t. Module Election before making any *writing* in that module. Furthermore, each direct *reading* of some process p to any Election variable v of one of its neighbors q is replaced by a call to the function $p.\text{read}(v, q)$, which returns $q.v$ if $p.\text{clock} = q.\text{clock}$; $q.\text{prev}.v$, otherwise.

Local Observers. We also modify the observers in Pulse since (1) waiting for $\text{CMax} = 6B$ local steps is no longer sufficient to guarantee that the system has reached a configuration satisfying P_{AU}; and (2) the result of a full cycle can be guaranteed only if all processes have reached some synchronization barrier. We can show that this barrier is reached after any process increments its clock at least $4\mathcal{D}$ times from any legitimate configuration.

We could used the upper bound given in [12] to ensure that the system reached a configuration satisfying P_{AU}. However, this bound is in $\Theta(\mathcal{D}n^3)$ steps. So, this would drastically impact the time complexity of our algorithm.

Instead, we borrow the ideas given in [6] by using the following result: If $p.\text{clock}$ successively takes values $u, u + 1, ..., u + (2\mathcal{D} + 1)$ between configurations γ_{t_0} and $\gamma_{t_{2\mathcal{D}+1}}$ with $\forall i \in \{1, ..., 2\mathcal{D} + 1\}$, $u + i > 0$, then every other process executes at least one step between configurations γ_{t_0} and $\gamma_{t_{2\mathcal{D}+1}}$.

This result provides a mechanism allowing a process to locally observe whether at least one round has elapsed. Indeed, by definition, if a process observes that all processes execute at least one step, then at least one round has elapsed. So, to decide that the configuration satisfies P_{AU}, a process p should observe that (i) all processes execute at least $n + \kappa$ rounds (the actual stabilization time of $\mathcal{U}$ for the asynchronous specification). In addition, (ii) p should increment its clock at least $4\mathcal{D}$ times after these rounds. So, it is sufficient that p counts $(2\mathcal{D} + 1) \times (n + \kappa) + 4\mathcal{D} \leq 16B^2 + 12B$ *consecutive positive (local) increments* to ensure both (i) and (ii).

We have modified the local observers by first respectively setting ξ and CMax to $16B^2 + 12B + 1$ and $16B^2 + 12B$. The function init() and OK() remain unchanged, but the way cnt is modified is slightly more complex. Indeed, when cnt reaches 0, CMax consecutive positive increments of the clock must have occurred. Now, $p.\text{clock}$ may become non-positive for two reasons. (1) During the stabilization phase of $\mathcal{U}$, p may set $p.\text{clock}$ to a negative value; or (2) p may "normally" reset $p.\text{clock}$ from $\xi - 1$ to 0. To handle Case (1), p also resets $p.\text{cnt}$ to CMax each time it sets $p.\text{clock}$ to a negative value (*i.e.*, we add $p.\text{cnt} \leftarrow$ CMax in the statement of the reset action of $\mathcal{U}$) and p does not decrement $p.\text{cnt}$ while $p.\text{clock}$ is negative. For Case (2), p starts decrementing $p.\text{cnt}$ only when $p.\text{clock} = 0$; since $\xi >$ CMax, the case cannot occur. Hence, at each local tick, $p.\text{cnt}$ is decremented only if $p.\text{cnt} > 0 \wedge (p.\text{cnt} = \text{CMax} \Rightarrow p.\text{clock} = 0)$.

Complexity of $\mathcal{A}_{\mathcal{GSLE}}$. As in the synchronous version $\mathcal{S}_{\mathcal{GSLE}}$, the delay, response time, and service time of $\mathcal{A}_{\mathcal{GSLE}}$ are of the same order of magnitude, and depend on **T1**, **T2**, and **T3**, as defined in Section 4.1. Again, we assume that when at some process p, $p.\langle\text{need}\rangle()$ is continuously *true* until p starts the service. So, **T1** is performed in at most one round. Then, to evaluate **T2** and **T3**, we should remark that, contrary to the synchronous case, a process does not advance its local clock at every round, even when the asynchronous unison specification is achieved. However, we can use the lemma given in [11], which claims that once P_{AU} holds, every process advances its clock at least $\mathcal{D}$ ticks during any $2\mathcal{D}$ consecutive rounds.

Consider **T2**. In the worst case, we need that $\mathcal{U}$ first stabilizes. Then, p may have to advance its local clock at most $\xi - 1$ ticks before starting to decrement $p.\mathtt{cnt}$. This latter counter reaches 0 at most CMax ticks later. Finally, once $p.\mathtt{cnt} = 0$, p may have to advance its local clock up to $\xi - 1$ times before satisfying $p.\mathtt{clock} = 3\varphi - 1$ and executing $p.\mathtt{status} \leftarrow \mathtt{Out}$ at its next tick. Hence, this complexity is bounded by $n + \kappa + \frac{2\mathcal{D}(\mathtt{CMax}+2\xi-1)}{\mathcal{D}} = O(n^2)$ rounds.

Consider **T3**. As in the synchronous case, this expected time is bounded by the stabilization time of $\mathcal{U}$ plus the product between $EC+1$ and the number of rounds to execute a synchronized cycle. Just as in the synchronous case, the best choice is to choose α_{vote} in $[\frac{1}{2B}, \frac{1}{B+1}]$. In this case, we still have $EC \leq \frac{e^2}{2} \leq 3.70$. Moreover, each synchronized cycle is executed in at most $2\xi = O(n^2)$ rounds. Hence, the time complexity of **T3** is also $O(n^2)$ rounds, and we have the following result.

Theorem 2. *With an unfair daemon, $\mathcal{A}_{\mathcal{GSLE}}$ is probabilistically snap-stabilizing w.r.t. $\mathcal{S}_{gs,leader}$ for anonymous networks. If $\alpha_{vote} \in [\frac{1}{2B}, \frac{1}{B+1}]$, its expected delay, response, and service times are each $O(n^2)$ rounds.*

If we add the assumption that processes know an upper bound D on the diameter $\mathcal{D}$ of the network, then $\mathcal{A}_{\mathcal{GSLE}}$ can be modified so that its expected time complexities are reduced to $O(D.n)$ rounds, by setting ξ and CMax to $8DB + 4B + 4D + 1$ and $8DB + 4B + 4D$, respectively.

5   Conclusion

We have introduced probabilistic snap-stabilization. Our goal is to relax (deterministic) snap-stabilization without altering its strong safety guarantees. We adopt a Las Vegas approach: after the end of faults, a probabilistic snap-stabilizing algorithm immediately satisfies its safety property; whereas its liveness property is ensured with probability 1. (It could be worth investigating if the Monte Carlo approach can be interesting.)

We implement this new concept in two algorithms which solve the guaranteed service leader election in arbitrary anonymous networks, a problem having neither self- nor snap deterministic solutions. Our first algorithm assumes a synchronous daemon, while the second works under a distributed unfair daemon, the weakest scheduling assumption. Note that these two algorithms are also self-stabilizing for the leader election problem.

These two algorithms show that probabilistic snap-stabilization is more expressive than its deterministic counterpart. Note that one can easily modify our guaranteed service leader election to obtain a guaranteed service algorithm whose result is the guarantee that the whole network has been identified. Then, using this algorithm, we can mimic the behavior of an identified network and emulate the transformer proposed in [9]. As a consequence, every (non-stabilizing) algorithm that can be made (deterministically) snap-stabilizing in an identified network by the transformer of [9] can be also automatically turned into probabilistic snap-stabilizing guaranteed service algorithm working in an anonymous network.

References

1. Alpern, B., Schneider, F.B.: Defining liveness. Inf. Process. Lett. 21(4), 181–185 (1985)
2. Angluin, D.: Local and global properties in networks of processors (extended abstract). In: 12th Annual ACM Symposium on Theory of Computing, pp. 82–93. ACM (1980)
3. Beauquier, J., Genolini, C., Kutten, S.: k-stabilization of reactive tasks. In: PODC, p. 318 (1998)
4. Beauquier, J., Gradinariu, M., Johnen, C.: Randomized self-stabilizing and space optimal leader election under arbitrary scheduler on rings. Dist. Comp. 20(1), 75–93 (2007)
5. Boulinier, C.: L'unisson. Ph.D. thesis, Université de Picardie Jules Verne (2007)
6. Boulinier, C., Levert, M., Petit, F.: Snap-stabilizing waves in anonymous networks. In: Rao, S., Chatterjee, M., Jayanti, P., Murthy, C.S.R., Saha, S.K. (eds.) ICDCN 2008. LNCS, vol. 4904, pp. 191–202. Springer, Heidelberg (2008)
7. Boulinier, C., Petit, F., Villain, V.: When graph theory helps self-stabilization. In: PODC, pp. 150–159 (2004)
8. Bui, A., Datta, A.K., Petit, F., Villain, V.: Snap-stabilization and PIF in tree networks. Dist. Comp. 20(1), 3–19 (2007)
9. Cournier, A., Datta, A.K., Petit, F., Villain, V.: Enabling snap-stabilization. In: ICDCS, pp. 12–19 (2003)
10. Cournier, A., Devismes, S., Villain, V.: Snap-stabilizing pif and useless computations. In: ICPADS, pp. 39–48 (2006)
11. Datta, A., Larmore, L., Devismes, S., Heurtefeux, K., Rivierre, Y.: Self-stabilizing small k-dominating sets. International Journal of Networking and Computing 3(1) (2013)
12. Devismes, S., Petit, F.: On efficiency of unison. In: TADDS, pp. 20–25 (2012)
13. Devismes, S., Tixeuil, S., Yamashita, M.: Weak vs. self vs. probabilistic stabilization. In: ICDCS, pp. 681–688 (2008)
14. Dijkstra, E.W.: Self-Stabilizing Systems in Spite of Distributed Control. Commun. ACM 17, 643–644 (1974)
15. Dolev, S., Israeli, A., Moran, S.: Uniform Dynamic Self-Stabilizing Leader Election. IEEE Trans. Parallel Distrib. Syst. 8, 424–440 (1997)
16. Dolev, S., Herman, T.: Superstabilizing protocols for dynamic distributed systems (abstract). In: PODC, p. 255 (1995)
17. Duflot, M., Fribourg, L., Picaronny, C.: Randomized finite-state distributed algorithms as markov chains. In: Welch, J.L. (ed.) DISC 2001. LNCS, vol. 2180, pp. 240–254. Springer, Heidelberg (2001)
18. Durrett, R.: Probability, theory and examples, Cambridge (2010)
19. Ghosh, S., Gupta, A., Herman, T., Pemmaraju, S.V.: Fault-containing self-stabilizing algorithms. In: PODC, pp. 45–54 (1996)
20. Gouda, M.G.: The theory of weak stabilization. In: Datta, A.K., Herman, T. (eds.) WSS 2001. LNCS, vol. 2194, pp. 114–123. Springer, Heidelberg (2001)
21. Herman, T.: Probabilistic self-stabilization. Inf. Proc. Letters 35(2), 63–67 (1990)
22. Israeli, A., Jalfon, M.: Token management schemes and random walks yield self-stabilizing mutual exclusion. In: PODC, pp. 119–131 (1990)
23. Manna, Z., Pnueli, A.: A hierarchy of temporal properties. In: PODC, pp. 377–410 (1990)
24. Matias, Y., Afek, Y.: Simple and efficient election algorithms for anonymous networks. In: WDAG, pp. 183–194 (1989)
25. Puterman, M.L.: Markov Decision Processes: Discrete Stochastic Dynamic Programming, 1st edn. John Wiley & Sons, Inc. (1994)
26. Tel, G.: Introduction to Distributed Algorithms, 2nd edn. Cambridge University Press (2001)
27. Yamashita, M., Kameda, T.: Computing on anonymous networks: Part i-characterizing the solvable cases. IEEE Trans. Parallel Distrib. Syst. 7(1), 69–89 (1996)

Backward-Compatible Cooperation
of Heterogeneous P2P Systems

Hoang Giang Ngo[1,2,3], Luigi Liquori[1], and Chan Hung Nguyen[4]

[1] National Institute for Research in Computer Science and Control, France
{giang.ngo_hoang,luigi.liquori}@inria.fr
[2] Université de Nice Sophia-Antipolis, France
[3] Hanoi University of Science and Technology, Vietnam
[4] Vietnam Research Institute of Electronics, Informatics and Automation, Vietnam
hungnc@vielina.com

Abstract. Peer-to-peer (P2P) systems are used by millions of users everyday. In many scenarios, it is desirable for the users from different P2P systems to communicate and exchange content resources with each other. This requires co-operation between the P2P systems, which is often difficult or impossible, due to the two following reasons. First, we have the lack of a dedicated routing infrastructure throughout these systems, caused by the incompatibilities in overlay networks on top of which they are built. Second, there are incompatibilities in the application protocols of these systems. In this paper, we introduce a new model for backward-compatible co-operation between heterogeneous P2P systems. The routing across systems is enabled by introducing a super-overlay formed by a small subset of peers from every system, which run an overlay protocol called OGP (*Overlay Gateway Protocol*). The incompatibilities in the application protocols are solved by a co-operation application, running on top of OGP, bridging these systems at interface level. As a real application, we present a protocol named Inter-network File-sharing Protocol (IFP), running on top of OGP, aimed at co-operation of P2P file-sharing networks. The experimental results performed on the large-scale Grid5000 platform show our model to be *efficient* and *scalable*.

1 Introduction

Nowadays, many distributed systems, such e.g. those involving P2P file sharing, P2P instant messaging, cloud computing etc, are built on top of various overlay networks. These overlay networks can differ from each other in many aspects, such as topologies, routing algorithms, types of queries, and message-encoding algorithms, and this differentiation propagates into the application protocols built on top of these overlay networks, as well. These particularities result in an *overall incompatibility* of P2P systems, and impede their cooperation. As for our motivation, there are clear advantages in facilitating the cooperation of these systems, such as increased content resources, easily achievable content redundancy, and saved storage.

In this paper, we introduce a new model targeting cooperation of P2P systems. The model consists of two parts, which bridge the involved systems at the routing and application layers, respectively. The first part is the OGP routing framework, including

M. Chatterjee et al. (Eds.): ICDCN 2014, LNCS 8314, pp. 287–301, 2014.

the OGP protocol, an extension of Kademlia [1], which allows efficient routing among heterogeneous overlay networks. OGP is run only by a small number of peers from each of the standard overlays, in addition to their native protocols. These peers form a super-overlay (the OGP overlay) equipped with efficient algorithms to perform unicast, broadcast, and multicast of messages from one standard overlay to the others. Peers forming the OGP overlay can reach across standard overlays, and act as gateways for peers especially created for taking advantage of OGP which run a *lightweight version of the* OGP *protocol*. The OGP and lightweight OGP protocols together form a framework for inter-routing between heterogeneous standard overlays. The idea of OGP was briefly introduced in our poster paper [2].

The second part of the model is a cooperation application that makes use of the OGP routing framework, and is responsible for bridging the P2P systems at the application layer with tasks such as transcoding the messages and data from formats of the P2P systems to intermediary formats and vice versa. Since the particular tasks of the cooperation application depends on the application domain, in this paper we only describe the principles of the cooperation application and introduce the IFP protocol for cooperation of heterogeneous P2P file-sharing systems as an example.

Our original approach ensures *backward-compatibility*, in the sense that the peers, which are unaware of new protocols, can continue to operate normally. As such, the contribution of our paper is twofold. First is the introduction of a new model for cooperation between heterogeneous P2P systems. Second is a concrete example of the model for cooperation of heterogeneous P2P file-sharing networks.

The rest of the paper is structured as follows: in Section 2, we survey the related work. Section 3 presents the system model, which was the motivation of this paper. The routing framework based on OGP and lightweight OGP protocols and the cooperation application are described in Section 4. The IFP protocol for cooperation P2P file-sharing networks is described in Section 5. Section 6 evaluates the model. Finally, in Section 7, we present our conclusions and outline future work.

2   Related Work

On Cooperation of P2P Systems. Cooperation between P2P systems and inter-overlay routing has served as an inspiration to a number of research efforts. In [3], the authors introduced a model for cooperation between file-sharing networks, i.e. unstructured overlays, with purely *flooding-based* queries using the logical links established by several pairs of peers from two networks. In [4–7], the authors deal with inter-overlay routing between *Distributed Hash Tables* (DHT's), i.e. structured overlays, by using co-located nodes, i.e. nodes belonging to multiple overlays at the same time, as gateways forwarding messages between overlays. The co-located nodes also perform the transcoding of queries between overlays. In [4], the original queries from peers in one DHT are sent to the trackers that, in turn, forward them to co-located nodes, in order to reach other DHT's. In [5, 6] the messages from one DHT are forwarded to others only if they randomly touch the co-located nodes while in [7], the co-located nodes have some auto discovery mechanisms to detect each other, thus the original messages can be sent directly between them. In all previous solutions, the transcoding of messages between P2P systems is built-in function of the routing protocols thus makes these solutions less practical. By separating the inter-overlay routing function and application bridging function, our solution achieve more flexible and thus more practical. This is the fundamental difference between our model and others.

The main features of the inter-overlay routing framework in our model are as following: (i) it allows for inter-routing over *heterogeneous* overlays, including both structured and unstructured overlays. Previous works can only inter-routing between either unstructured overlays [3] or structured overlays [4–7]; (ii) it guarantees backward compatibility. The models in [3,4,7] also allow the backward compatibility while the models proposed by [5,6] require the modification of all peers in overlays; (iii) it features *better control over routing*, by allowing the delivery of messages to destination overlays without duplication. In previous works, where there was no control on which overlays will receive the query and, mostly, a query could reach an overlay multiple times, triggering numerous duplicated lookup processes, while not reaching some other overlays.

On Unicast, Broadcast and Multicast in OGP. Historically, unicast, multicast and broadcast in a DHT respectively denote the sending of a message to a peer, to a group of peers, and to all of the peers in that DHT. In OGP, we introduce new schemes of unicast, multicast and broadcast. OGP categorizes all peers belonging to one standard overlay into a group. The unicast, multicast and broadcast in OGP respectively denote the sending of a message to a group, to a number of groups, and to all of the groups in the OGP overlay. In each group, only one random node receives the message.

On Hierarchical Overlays vs. OGP. Hierarchical overlays aim at bringing a hierarchical structure into flat DHT s. In these overlays, peers are categorized into groups or netted groups, and each of these groups is a DHT. The routing are key-based with a unique hash function. OGP, along with standard overlays can be seen as a hierarchy of heterogeneous overlays. The standard overlays can be structured or unstructured and can use different routing schemes. The OGP overlay itself categorizes peers belonging to the same standard overlay into one group which is not a DHT. Therefore, the OGP approach does not fit the description of a hierarchical overlay.

3 System Model

3.1 Classification of Peers and Inter-routing Schemes

In our model, there are three kind of peers:

Full OGP peers, hereafter denoted as FOGP peers, simultaneously belong to one P2P system and the OGP overlay. In addition to their native protocols, they also run the OGP protocol and the cooperation protocol. They route messages from one P2P system to the others via the OGP overlay and serve as gateways for lightweight OGP peers to reach P2P systems to which they do not belong.

Lightweight OGP peers, denoted as LOGP peers, take advantage of the inter-overlay routing provided by the OGP overlay. They belong only to one P2P system, do not participate in the OGP overlay, but keep a list of FOGP peers. In addition to their native protocols, they run the lightweight OGP protocol and the cooperation protocol. LOGP

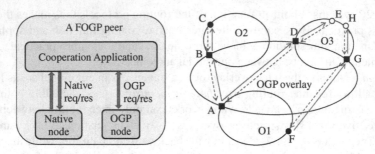

Fig. 1. (a) A FOGP peer (b) Examples of cooperation

peers are introduced: (i) to reach P2P systems they are not members of with low cost in terms of power processing and bandwidth, and (ii) to improve the scalability of the cooperation system by reducing the number of FOGP peers and the size of OGP overlay. **Blind peers** are peers that belong to only one P2P system, are not aware of the existence of the new protocols and use only their native protocols.

The inter-routing algorithms are the heart of OGP protocol, including OGP *unicast*, OGP *multicast* and OGP *broadcast*. A FOGP peer can use any of these schemes. For the sake of brevity, the operation of routing a request to a random FOGP peer belonging to the destination standard overlay is hereby described as routing that request to the destination overlay. OGP *unicast* allows FOGP peers route requests into only one destination overlay different from the one the request originated from. With OGP *multicast*, a FOGP peer can selectively choose multiple destination overlays, and all of the responses are returned to the original sender. In OGP *broadcast*, all standard overlays are chosen as destination, and all of the responses are returned to the sender.

3.2 Structure of A FOGP Peer

A FOGP peer, see Figure 1(a), has several components:

A **Native node** participates in the P2P system to which the FOGP peer belongs, launches requests on this P2P system and returns the results to the cooperation application.

An OGP **Node** participates in the OGP overlay and provides unicast, multicast and broadcast inter-routing for the cooperation application.

The **Cooperation application** can launch the request on a P2P system via the Native node, on the OGP overlay via the OGP node, and performs other tasks. One of them is transcoding of messages and data at interface level between formats of P2P systems and intermediary formats defined by itself.

3.3 Cooperation Examples

In Figure 1(b), two scenarios are shown to illustrate the cooperation of three P2P systems in which a FOGP peer and a LOGP peer lookup information at overlays they are not members of. The three smaller ovals, denoted by 01, 02 and 03, represent standard overlays the P2P systems based on, while the largest oval represents the OGP overlay. The black squares A, B, D, and G represent FOGP peers, the black circles F, and C represent LOGP peers, while the white circles E, and H represent blind peers. Solid lines represent requests, while dashed lines represent responses.

First Scenario. The FOGP peer A is looking for some information which is located at the LOGP peer C in overlay O2 and the blind peers E in the overlay O3. A send the request to the FOGP peer B and the FOGP peer D, belonging to O2 and O3 respectively, via its OGP node, using OGP broadcast routing. Upon receiving the request, B and D reconstruct the request to be in accordance with the possibly different format defined by the native protocols of O2 and O3 respectively, then forward it to C and E via their Native nodes. C and E then send the responses back to B and D, which reconstruct the responses to follow the format defined by cooperation protocol, and send it, along with their contact information for later communication, back to A, via their OGP nodes.

Second Scenario. The LOGP peer F, belonging to overlay O1, is looking for some information located at the blind peer H in overlay O3 . It forwards, via OGP node, using OGP unicast routing, the message to G which is a FOGP peer in overlay O3. Upon receiving the message, G converts the message in accordance with the native protocol of O3, and forwards it to H via its Native node. The return path takes us back through G to F, following the native protocol of O3 first, and then the OGP protocol.

3.4   Potential Applications

Our model can used for cooperating many distributed applications, such as:

File-Sharing Applications. Many isolated file-sharing networks currently co-exist in the Internet, are based on various incompatible overlay protocols, and use incompatible mechanisms for downloading and uploading files [9]. By having a number of peers in each involved file-sharing network running the OGP protocol, an OGP overlay can be established to inter-connect these networks. The searching and exchanging files over networks are performed by cooperation application on top of this infrastructure. In Section 5 we develop a complete solution for cooperation of P2P file-sharing networks.

Instant Messaging (IM) Applications. There are many instant messaging networks with incompatible instant messaging protocols [10]. Currently, to have these networks cooperate, one can combine the many disparate protocols inside the IM client application or inside the IM server application. Our model provides another promising solution.

Cloud-Based Applications. Cloud systems such as Amazon EC2, or NoSql databases, such as Amazon SimpleDB [11] or Cassandra [12] or Google BigTable [13] usually rely on a computer cluster; the OGP framework can be used to form a routing infrastructure over the existing cloud systems while the cooperation applications on top of the OGP framework enable the exchanging data between these systems, while resolving incompatibilities.

4   System Description

In this section, we describe the OGP routing framework consisting of OGP and lightweight OGP protocols and cooperation application running on top OGP framework.

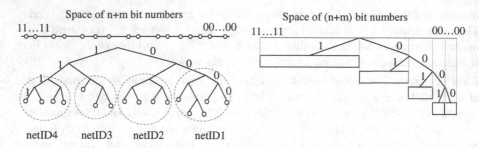

Fig. 2. (a) A binary tree of FOGP peers with $n=2$ (b) Routing table of a FOGP peer

4.1   OGP **Protocol: ID Assignment and Routing Table**

OGP identifies each standard overlay by a unique n-bit number we denote by netID. A FOGP peer is assigned an unique $(n+m)$-bit identifier, denoted by ID, consisting of two parts: the n-bit identifier of the standard overlay to which that peer belongs (netID), and a random m-bit number denoted by nodeID. Given this, and using "|" as a concatenation operator, we have that: ID=netID | nodeID.

A FOGP peer calculates the XOR distances, which is defined in [1], from itself to other FOGP peers and uses these distances to internally represent these nodes as a binary tree with the leaves of the tree are the shortest unique prefix of these distances. One important property of this binary tree is that all FOGP peers connected to the same standard overlay share a single subtree. Let the identifier of the current node be netIDi | nodeID. By properties of the XOR distances, we can easily see that the distance between the current node and any of the peers connected to the same overlay will share the same n-bit prefix, and, therefore, the same subtree.

Figure 2(a) illustrate the binary tree representing FOGP peers from the view of the FOGP peer whose distance metric is 00...00, while Figure 2(b) illustrates the routing table of a FOGP peer with distance from itself is 00...000. In the Figure, we have that $n=2$, i.e. netID is represented by 2 bits. Here, FOGP peers can belong to one of the four standard overlays, whose identifiers are netID1, netID2, netID3, and netID4.

We refer to the set of all $(n+m)$-bit numbers as the *distance space*, as they represent all of the possible distances between nodes in the OGP protocol. The routing table of FOGP peer is the same as the one of Kademlia peer. A FOGP peer keeps contact information for k nodes of distance between 2^i and 2^{i+1} from itself, with $0\leq i<(n+m)$. These lists are called k-buckets that each of which cover a range of distance space and they, together, cover the whole distance spaces. We also refer the range of distance space covered by one k-buckets as a final space.

An FOGP peer keeps a fix-sized list of other FOGP nodes, belonging to the same n-level subtree with it, for cooperation application to exploit.

4.2   OGP **Protocol: Routing Schemes**

Definitions. A n-level subtree of the OGP binary tree (Figure 2(a)) is a subtree whose prefix length equals n: all nodes connected to one standard overlay belong to a n-

level subtree. From now on, by "sending a message to a subtree" we mean "sending a message to a random node belonging to the said subtree".

OGP provides three kinds of routing, namely: (i) n-level unicast, (ii) n-level multicast, and (iii) n-level broadcast which are used by a FOGP peer to, respectively, send a message to an n-level subtree, to a group of n-level subtrees, to all of the n-level subtrees that do not contain the FOGP peer. In all of the cases, each n-level subtree only receives one message. All the final subspaces, that together cover a n-level subtree with no overlap, are represented by a subspace which covers this n-level subtree.

The *Range* of a distance space S, denoted by ρ_S, is the XOR between the maximal (UB) and minimal (LB) numbers in S: $\rho_S = UB \oplus LB$.

The *Depth* of a distance space S in the routing tree of a FOGP peer, denoted by δ_S, is the number of bits of the space's prefix in that tree. From now on by "sending a message to a subspace" we mean "sending a message to a random node belonging to the said subspace". What follows are the routing schemes provided by the OGP protocol.

First Routing: n-Level Unicast. The n-level unicast is a greedy algorithm aimed at sending a message to an n-level subtree, knowing its n-bit prefix P_n. The sending node, which is a FOGP node and has the identifier ID_0, first generates an m-bit random number R_m and concatenates it to P_n to form an $(n+m)$-bit identifier $ID = P_n \cdot 2^n + R_m$.

The initiator node then sends a REPLICATE(message, ID) request to the FOGP node in its routing table closest to $ID' = ID \oplus ID_0$. Upon receiving the REPLICATE request, the recipient node checks if its identifier ID_i and ID have the same n-bit prefix. If so, the unicast is completed. Otherwise, the recipient node forwards the REPLICATE request to the FOGP node in its routing table closest to $ID' = ID \oplus ID_i$. If there is no node in its routing table closer to ID' than itself, the recipient node drops the request.

Discussion and analysis. By this algorithm, the message jumps from one n-level subtree to an other n-level subtree to approach closer and closer to the destination n-level subtree. At each n-level subtree, the request touches only one node. Hence, we can assume that each n-level subtree is a virtual node in the overlay with n-bit identifier space. The distance of the message from the destination n-level subtree is reduced at least twice per round of request sending. Assume that the number of n-level subtrees in OGP overlay is K. After $log_2 K$ rounds of sending the request, i.e. message traverses through $log_2 K$ hops, the distance from the message to the destination subtree is $\frac{2^n}{2^{log_2 K}} = \frac{2^n}{K}$. Because the n-bit prefixes of n-level subtrees are random numbers, the number of the n-level subtrees belonging to the above distance from the destination n-level subtree is 1, with high probability. That n-level subtree is the destination n-level subtree itself. Thus, it takes $O(log_2 K)$ hops to reach the destination.

Second Routing: n-Level Broadcast. This mechanism is used by a FOGP node to send a message to all n-level subtrees to which it does not belong. The main idea is that the initiator node sends the replication message to every subspaces in its routing table that does not contain the sending node and contains at least one n-level subtree. These destination subspaces, together, cover the entire distance space with no overlap. The node, receiving the message, belonging to a destination subspace, is responsible for the further broadcast of the message in this subspace, by repeating the sending operation of the initiator node, except that the entire distance space is replaced by the destination subspace. In all cases, a recipient node always excludes the subspace covers the n-level subtree containing it which already received the message from its responsible space before continuing to send the message. A node stops sending messages if the space it is responsible for has only one n-level subtree. The entire process stops when all of the n-level subtrees have received the message. The n-level broadcast algorithm can be sketched as follows:

The initiator node sends the REPLICATE(message, ρ_i) request to every subspaces S_i in its routing table which satisfy the following conditions: (i) $\delta_{S_i} \leq n$, and (ii) S_i does not contains the initiator node, where ρ_i is the range of the subspace S_i which will receive the message.

The recipient node, i.e. the node which has received the REPLICATE(message, ρ_i) request, sends the REPLICATE(message, ρ_j) request to every subspace S_j in its routing table which belongs to the distance ρ_i from the recipient, and satisfies the following conditions: (i) $\delta_{S_i} \leq n$, and (ii) S_j does not contains the recipient node; where ρ_j is the range of the subspace S_j which will receive the message.

The above process finishes once all n-level subtrees have received the message.

Discussion and Analysis. Similar to the unicast algorithm, the message also touches only one node per subtree in broadcast scheme. Thus the n-level subtrees can be seen as virtual nodes in the n-bits overlay. The distance of the message from the destination n-level subtree is also reduced at least twice per round of request sending. Therefore, similar to unicast algorithm, n-level broadcast scheme takes $O(log_2 K)$ hops to reach the destination with high probability.

Third Routing: n-Level Multicast. Due to lack of space, we only present the main idea of this mechanism. n-level multicast is an algorithm used by a FOGP node to send a message to a group of n-level subtrees on the OGP overlay of which it is not a member. The multicast algorithm is similar to the broadcast algorithm, with the following general idea: a node is responsible for multicasting the message within a certain distance space. To perform this task, the node divides that distance space into *multiple subspaces with no overlap*. Each subspace contains at least one n-level subtree. For each subspace that overlaps with the multicast group, if the routing table contains a contact belonging to both the subspace and the multicast group, that contact is chosen. Otherwise, the node chooses a contact belonging to that subspace which is closest to the multicast group, i.e. the node whose n-bit prefix is closest to n-bit prefix of one of subtrees belonging to the multicast group. It then sends the message to the chosen node and asks the chosen node to be responsible for multicasting the message to the n-level subtrees belonging to both that subspace and the multicast group. The above process continues until all n-level subtrees in the multicast group have received the message.

Discussion and Analysis. Using the same analysis with broadcast and unicast algorithm discussions, it takes $O(log_2 K)$ hops to multicast the message to the destination n-level subtrees with high probability. In summary, the routing cost in three OGP routing algorithms are the same and are $O(log_2 K)$. We notice that the routing cost only depend on the number of n-level subtrees, i.e. K, and doesn't depend on the number of FOGP nodes.

4.3 Lightweight OGP Protocol and Cooperation Application

The lightweight OGP protocol is performed by LOGP peers to communicate with FOGP peers. A LOGP peer maintains a routing list, which is a fixed-size list containing information about some FOGP peers in the OGP overlay by periodically asking for the routing table of FOGP peers in its routing list and then using the information in these routing table for updating the routing list. At the bootstrap time, a LOGP peer known some bootstrap FOGP peers via external mechanisms such as from websites. A LOGP peer sends messages to standard overlays of which it is not member by simply sending these messages to the first FOGP peer in its routing list which will forward its messages.

The cooperation application in a FOGP peer is built on top of the OGP routing layer, and is responsible for following tasks: (i) launching the delivery of requests to P2P systems via the Native node or the OGP node or both and receiving results from these nodes, and (ii) transcoding of messages and data between formats of P2P systems and the intermediary formats defined by itself, and (iii) communication with each other. While the first and the third tasks can be achieved easily, the intermediary formats, in the second task, vary from application to application. Therefore, we cannot introduce a common intermediary formats. As a case study, we show in the next section the IFP protocol, running on the top of OGP, which is an application allowing heterogeneous P2P file-sharing networks to cooperate, together with the respective intermediary formats.

5 Case Study: Cooperation of P2P File Sharing Networks

We introduce the IFP protocol for cooperation between heterogeneous P2P file sharing networks. The IFP constitutes two schemes of cooperation, namely inter-network downloading and inter-network uploading, allowing users to download files from and upload files to P2P file-sharing networks, respectively.

The IFP protocol is responsible for the following tasks: (i) launching the processes of searching, downloading and uploading files on P2P file-sharing network contains the peer and receiving the results via the Native node, (ii) launching the delivering of search requests or upload requests to P2P file-sharing networks don't contain the peer and receiving the results from these networks via the OGP node, (iii) transcoding of search requests, search results, download requests and upload requests between the formats defined by P2P file-sharing networks and the intermediary formats defined by IFP, (iv) delivery of download requests on P2P file-sharing networks don't contain the peer and exchanging files, and (v) communicating with, and transferring the files between FOGP nodes.

5.1 Inter-network Downloading

Transcoding of Messages. IFP defines its own formats for the search request, the search result and the download request. The transcoding of these messages between IFP format and formats of P2P file-sharing networks happens at the FOGP gateways.

Most of P2P file-sharing networks have search capability with keyword search. The search criteria can include file attributes. One exception is BitTorrent which does not have search capability. However, BitTorrent users can still search the torrent files from websites using keywords. Therefore, IFP defines its search request containing keywords and file attributes; the search result contains the notification of no search capability in case of BitTorrent or the list of matched files along with attributes in other cases; the download request contains the torrent file in case the destination network is BitTorrent and information of the expected file in other cases. These messages are show in Figure 3.

Algorithm. The IFP protocol functions as follows:

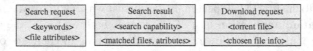

Fig. 3. Formats of search messages defined by IFP

Step 1: The *initiator* peer sends the search request to destination networks via its OGP node. The case that the *initiator* search files on its network is trivial, thus is not shown.
Step 2: A *recipient* peer, which is a FOGP peer belonging to the destination network, upon receiving the search request, acts as follows: if the destination network is BitTorrent, the *recipient* return BitTorrent indication i.e. no search capability. Otherwise, the *recipient* converts the search request from IFP format to the format defined by the destination network. It then launches the search on this network via its Native node. Upon receiving the search result, the *recipient* convert the this result to the IFP format and then sends the result along with its information to the *initiator* via its OGP node.
Step 3: Upon receiving the search result from the *recipient* peer, if the result indicates the destination network as BitTorrent, then the user search and download the torrent file from a website, and directly send the torrent file to the *recipient* in the download request. Otherwise, if the sought file exists on the destination network, the *initiator* peer directly contacts the *recipient* asking it to retrieve the file.
Step 4: The *recipient* peer, upon receiving the download request, retrieves the list of peers hosting the file via its Native node. If the destination network supports multiple-source download, the *recipient* peer can ask some other FOGP peer belonging to destination network, which are in its FOGP peer list, to download some parts of the file. Otherwise, it is responsible for downloading the entire file using its Native node.
Step 5: The FOGP peer, upon receiving the request for downloading some parts of the file, downloads these parts via its Native node.
Step 6: Upon receiving the file or file parts from the hosting peers after issuing the download request, the recipients send the file or file parts back to the *initiator* node and the information for joining the parts is sent along with these parts.

5.2   Inter-network Uploading

Algorithm. The processes of inter-network uploading is as follows:

Step 1: The *initiator*, which is a FOGP or a LOGP peer sends the upload request to *recipients* which are FOGP peers belonging to a group of networks that the *initiator* wants to replicate the file to, via its OGP node.

Step 2: Upon receiving the request, a *recipient* sends the response notifying the *initiator* whether the upload request is accepted or not via its OGP node.

Step 3: Upon receiving the notification, if the upload request is accepted, the *initiator* peer sends the file to the *recipient*.

Step 4: Upon receiving the file, if the recipient's network is BitTorrent, the *recipient* creates a torrent file for the file and registers the torrent file with some trackers, using its Native node. Then the *recipient* sends the torrent file back to the *initiator*. If the *recipient*'s network isn't BitTorrent, it uploads the file to its standard network using the Native node and send the acknowledgement back to the *initiator*.

6   Evaluation

6.1   Metrics

We first evaluate the OGP routing framework in three following aspects: routing efficiency, routing cost, and traffic generated by OGP and lightweight OGP protocol. Then, we evaluate the efficiency of cooperation of P2P file-sharing networks.

OGP Framework. The routing efficiency is characterized by the metrics R^{fogp}, R^{fogp}_{lookup}, R^{logp} and R^{logp}_{lookup} defined as follows. R^{fogp} is the success ratio for requests sent from a FOGP peer to the standard overlay containing the requested data and then back to the originator. R^{logp} is success ratio of request sent to a FOGP peer from a LOGP peer and the corresponding response is turned back. R^{fogp}_{lookup} and R^{logp}_{lookup} are the success ratios of inter-overlay lookups initiated by FOGP and LOGP peers, respectively.

The routing cost is represented by P^{fogp} metric which is the number of hops on OGP overlay that a request passed in a successful routing. The bandwidth generated by OGP and lightweight OGP protocols in a FOGP peer and a LOGP peer respectively during one minute are denoted by T^{fogp} and T^{logp}.

Cooperation of P2P File-Sharing Networks. The cooperation efficiency is characterized by the metrics $R^{fogp}_{download}$, $R^{logp}_{download}$, R^{fogp}_{upload} and R^{logp}_{upload} defined as follows : $R^{fogp}_{download}$ and $R^{logp}_{download}$ are the ratios of a FOGP peer and a LOGP peer, respectively, successfully download a file which does not exist in the peer's network but exists in other networks. The two metrics, R^{fogp}_{upload} and R^{logp}_{upload}, are the ratios of a FOGP peer and a LOGP peer, respectively, successfully upload their files to networks of which they are not members.

6.2   Setup

To evaluate the OGP framework, a complete system, in which the OGP overlay is used to interconnect twenty 50-node networks of three types Kademlia, Chord [8] and Gnutella [14] has been deployed. Random unique data is distributed across all of the standard overlays. The FOGP and LOGP peers periodically looked up a random piece of data on any of the standard overlays of which they are not members. To evaluate the cooperation of P2P file-sharing networks, we deployed a complete system in which OGP, lightweight OGP and IFP protocols are used to cooperating three P2P file-sharing networks: BitTorrent, Gnutella-based and Kademlia-based which represent for three

Table 1. Values of experimental parameters

Experimental parameters	Evaluation 1		Evaluation 2	
	Scenario 1	Scenario 2	Scenario 1	Scenario 2
% of FOGP peers	6, 10, 20, 30	10, 20	3, 6, 10, 20, 30	6, 10
% of LOGP peers	0	10, 20, 40, 60	0	10, 20, 40, 60
Type of networks	Kademlia, Chord, Gnutella		BitTorrent, Kademlia-based, Gnutella	
No. of networks	20		3	
No. of nodes per network	50		100	
Lifetime mean (second)	3600			

typical kinds of P2P file-sharing networks currently: (i) the network without search capability, (ii) the network with the flooding search and (iii) the network with DHT search, respectively. The FOGP peers and LOGP peers periodically download/upload random files from/to the networks of which they are not members.

The experimental platform is French Grid5000. All experiments are performed in churn condition with the lifetime mean of nodes is set to 3600 seconds and follows the Pareto distribution. Each experiment includes 3 successive phases: *1: initial phase*, *2:stabilizing phase* and *3:evaluation phase* in which *1:*nodes are created and join overlays; *2:*the system becomes stable; *3:*the statistics are collected. The duration of each of two last phases is T with T is the lifetime mean of a node in that experiment. Each experiment is run 5 times. Average values and standard deviations of the metrics are plotted in the figures. The experimental parameters are illustrated in Table 1.

6.3 Experiment Results: Efficiency

This section evaluates the routing efficiency of OGP framework which is characterized by R^{fogp}, R^{fogp}_{lookup}, R^{logp} and R^{logp}_{lookup} metrics and the efficiency of cooperating P2P file-sharing networks, represented by $R^{fogp}_{download}$, $R^{logp}_{download}$, R^{fogp}_{upload} and R^{logp}_{upload}. The values of the metrics for FOGP and LOGP peers are illustrated in Figure 4 and in Figure 5.

Figure 4 shows the four lines: $R^{fogp}_{download}$, R^{fogp}_{upload}, R^{fogp}_{lookup} and R^{fogp} share mostly the same trend. The two lines R^{fogp} and R^{fogp}_{lookup}, dramatically increase from 83% to 97% and from 81% to 95% then slightly vary in the range from 97% to 99% and from 95% to 97 % as the percentage of FOGP peer increase from 6% to 10% and then to 30%. Similarly, the two lines $R^{fogp}_{download}$ and R^{fogp}_{upload}, come from 92 % to 97% and from 95% to 99%; then slightly vary in the range from 97% to 99% and from 99% to 100% as the percentage of FOGP peer increase from 3% to 6% and then to 30%.

Analysis and discussion. The OGP protocol achieves routing efficiency in the interconnecting system of 20 overlays with only a small percentage of FOGP, namely 10%, while the cooperation of 3 file-sharing network achieve efficiency with even smaller % of FOGP peers (6%). In the first evaluation, the R^{fogp} and R^{fogp}_{lookup} are not less than 97% and 95% while in the second, $R^{fogp}_{download}$ and R^{fogp}_{upload} are not less than 97% and 99%. The reason for these results is as follow: with 6% of FOGP peers in the first evaluation and with 3% of FOGP peers in the second one, the number of FOGP peers per overlay is 3 in both evaluations, meaning that there are 3 gateways to enter each standard overlay.

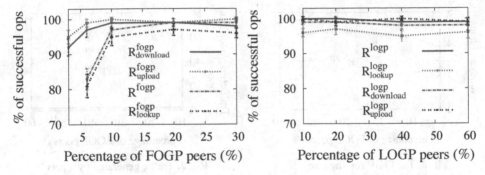

Fig. 4. Operation efficiency of FOGP peer   **Fig. 5.** Operation efficiency of LOGP peer

In a churn environment, some gateways can go down for at certain time. During this time, some other FOGP peers do not have any backup gateways for the downed gateways in their routing tables, as the number of gateways to enter an standard overlay is only 3. With 10% of FOGP peers in the first evaluation, and 6% in the second one, there are 5 and 6 gateways to enter a standard overlay, respectively, and these numbers appears to be sufficient for the FOGP peers to build their routing table with quite enough backup.

Figure 5 shows that, with the percentage of FOGP peers is set to 10%, the two lines R^{logp} and R^{logp}_{lookup} vary from 99% to 100% and from 95% to 97% when the percentage of LOGP peers comes from 10% to 60%. On the other hand, the $R^{logp}_{download}$ and R^{logp}_{upload} values slightly vary in the range from 98% to 99% and from 99% to 100% respectively with percentage of FOGP peers is set to 6%. The experimental results in the cases that the % of FOGP peers is set to 20% in the first evaluation and 10% in the second one are similar to those in the illustrated cases that the % of FOGP peers is set to 10% and 6% respectively, thus are not shown in the figure for the sake of clarity.

Analysis and discussion. The experiments shows an important results. The LOGP protocol achieves highly routing efficiency, namely R^{logp} is nearly 100% for all percentage of LOGP. Because the LOGP peers rely on FOGP peers for inter-overlay cooperation, this means that LOGP peers perform the inter-overlay operations with the efficiency nearly the same as the efficiency of FOGP peers.

6.4 Routing Cost

Figure 6 shows values of the P^{fogp} metric, i.e. the number of hops on OGP overlay that a request passed in a successful routing in the first evaluation, increase from 3.9 to 4.2 and then slightly vary in the range from 4.2 to 4.4 when the percentage of FOGP peers increase from 5% to 10% and then to 30% respectively.

Analysis and discussion. The experiment results confirm the evaluation of routing cost on OGP overlay. In our experiments, $K=20$, thus the expected value of P^{fogp} is $O(log_2 20)$ or approximately 4.3 hops, i.e. a constant. The experiment shown that the values of P^{fogp} is approximately the expected constant when the percentage of FOGP nodes is larger than 10% while smaller than expected constant with the 6% of FOGP.

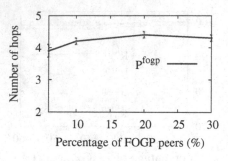

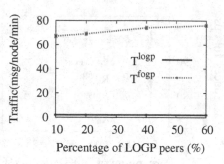

Fig. 6. The OGP routing cost **Fig. 7.** Traffic generated by a peer

The reason is the following: in churn environment, the routing with more hops fails at higher probability than the routing with less hops (each hop has a certain probability of failure). In our experiment, at 6% of FOGP peers, the ratios of success routing, i.e. R^{fogp}, are only 83%. This means the number of routing with more hops which fails is considerably higher than the number of routing with less hops which fails. Hence the average hops of success routing, i.e. P^{fogp}, is lower than the expected constant.

6.5 Generated Traffic

In Figure 7, the two lines T^{fogp} and T^{logp}, respectively, represent the traffic generated by OGP and LOGP protocols in a peer during one minute while the percentage of LOGP peers increase from 10% to 60% and the percentage of FOGP peer is 10%. As the percentage of LOGP peers increase from 10% to 60%, the T^{fogp} increase from 67 to 76 messages/node/minute while the T^{logp} is a horizontal line at the traffic of 2 messages/node/minute.

Analysis and discussion. The LOGP protocol generates little traffic (2 messages/node /minute), which also does not depend on the percentage of LOGP peers in the lookup system. On the other hand, traffic generated by a FOGP peer increases only 13% as the percentage of LOGP peers increases from 10% to 60%. These results show that our model is scalable in terms of generated traffic.

7 Conclusions and Future Work

In this paper, we have introduced an efficient model for cooperation of heterogeneous P2P systems. The model consists of the OGP framework for inter-overlay routing and the cooperation application on top of the OGP framework, bridging these P2P systems at application level. We also introduce the IFP protocol, which, along with OGP framework, enables the cooperation of heterogenous P2P file-sharing networks.

The evaluations show that having a small number of FOGP peers, namely not less than about 5 FOGP peers per network, is sufficient for achieving routing efficiency in 20 inter-connected overlays and achieving efficiency in the cooperation of 3 different P2P file-sharing networks. The experiments confirm that the routing cost on the OGP overlay is logarithmic to the number of overlays inter-connected by the OGP overlay.

We also notice that the LOGP peers need only one hop to reach FOGP peers. The experiments also show that the traffic generated by a FOGP peer increases only 13% as the percentage of LOGP peer rises from 10% to 60%, while a LOGP peer generates the traffic nearly as same as that generated by a blind peer (only 2 messages larger than the blind peer). These, coupled with control over the routing between standard overlays, make our model scalable. The experiment results show that the LOGP peers achieve routing efficiency is nearly the same as the FOGP peer, namely R^{logp} is not less than 99%. As a matter of fact, we can see that the LOGP peers achieve nearly the same routing efficiency and cooperation efficiency, while paying a small cost.

Our further work on this topic is a solution aimed towards a real-world P2P file-sharing network and a model for cooperation of P2P instant messaging networks.

Acknowledgements. The authors are grateful to Petar Maksimović for a careful reading of the paper and Vincenzo Ciancaglini for the useful discussions.

References

1. Maymounkov, P., Mazières, D.: Kademlia: A Peer-to-Peer Information System Based on the XOR Metric. In: Druschel, P., Kaashoek, M.F., Rowstron, A. (eds.) IPTPS 2002. LNCS, vol. 2429, pp. 53–65. Springer, Heidelberg (2002)
2. Ngo, G., Liquori, L., Ciancaglini, V., Maksimovic, P., Nguyen, H.: A backward-compatible protocol for inter-routing over heterogeneous overlay networks. In: 28th Annual ACM Symposium on Applied Computing, pp. 649–651 (2013)
3. Konishi, J., Wakamiya, N., Murata, M.: Proposal and evaluation of a cooperative mechanism for pure P2P file sharing networks. In: Ijspeert, A.J., Masuzawa, T., Kusumoto, S. (eds.) BioADIT 2006. LNCS, vol. 3853, pp. 33–47. Springer, Heidelberg (2006)
4. Cheng, L.: Bridging Distributed Hash Tables in Wireless Ad-Hoc Networks. In: IEEE Global Telecommunications Conference 2007, pp.5159-5163 (2007)
5. Liquori, L., Tedeschi, C., Bongiovanni, F.: Babelchord: A Social Tower of Dht-based Overlay Networks. In: IEEE Symposium on Computers and Communications, pp. 307–312 (2009)
6. Liquori, L., Tedeschi, C., Vanni, L., Bongiovanni, F., Ciancaglini, V., Marinković, B.: Synapse: A scalable protocol for interconnecting heterogeneous overlay networks. In: Crovella, M., Feeney, L.M., Rubenstein, D., Raghavan, S.V. (eds.) NETWORKING 2010. LNCS, vol. 6091, pp. 67–82. Springer, Heidelberg (2010)
7. Ciancaglini, V., Liquori, L., Hoang, G.N., Maksimović, P.: An extension and cooperation mechanism for heterogeneous overlay networks. In: Becvar, Z., Bestak, R., Kencl, L. (eds.) NETWORKING 2012 Workshops. LNCS, vol. 7291, pp. 10–18. Springer, Heidelberg (2012)
8. Stoica, I., Morris, R., Karger, D., Kaashoek, M.F., Balakrishnan, H.: Chord: A scalable peer-to-peer lookup service for internet applications. In: Conference on Applications, Technologies, Architectures, and Protocols for Computer Communications 2001, pp. 149–160 (2001)
9. Wikipedia: Comparison of file sharing applications, http://en.wikipedia.org/wiki/Comparison_of_file_sharing_applications
10. Wikipedia: Comparison of instant messaging protocols, http://en.wikipedia.org/wiki/Comparison_of_instant_messaging_protocols
11. Amazon: simpledb, http://aws.amazon.com/simpledb/
12. The Apache Cassandra project, http://cassandra.apache.org/
13. The BigTable Data Storage system. Wikipedia, http://en.wikipedia.org/wiki/BigTable
14. Gnutella. Wikipedia, http://en.wikipedia.org/wiki/Gnutella

Towards a Peer-to-Peer Bandwidth Marketplace

Mihai Capotă, Johan Pouwelse, and Dick Epema

Delft University of Technology, The Netherlands

Abstract. Peer-to-peer systems are a popular means of transferring files over the Internet, accounting for a third of the upload bandwidth of end users as of 2013. However, recent studies have highlighted that peer-to-peer systems are affected by a lack of balance between the supply and demand of bandwidth. This imbalance stems from the skewed popularity distribution of the files transfered in the system; newly released files may exhibit an undersupply of bandwidth while older ones may exhibit oversupply. In this work, we introduce a *bandwidth marketplace* for peers, with the aim of aligning supply and demand without the need for human intervention. Peers constantly monitor their performance and gossip with each other about undersupplied files. Peers with idle upload bandwidth that learn about an undersupplied file can autonomously start a special *help mode* download, with the goal of supplying as much upload bandwidth as possible to the other peers. We present an analytical model of help mode downloading and derive from it bounds for the performance of helper peers. Furthermore, we evaluate a recent existing implementation of help mode in Libtorrent, a popular BitTorrent library. Our tests show that Libtorrent help mode is effective at alleviating undersupply, although its performance relative to our model can be improved.

1 Introduction

Measurements from 2013 show that peer-to-peer (P2P) file transfer systems continue to be very popular, generating a third of the end user upload traffic over the Internet [15]. Systems like BitTorrent and its descendants (uTP, Swift)—based on the breaking up of files into small pieces to enable multi-peer, or *swarm*, collaboration—are very efficient at transferring files. At the same time, they are susceptible to bad performance caused by flash crowds—sudden surges in the popularity of files—and other types of supply and demand misalignments. In fact, recent studies [9,10] have documented severe imbalances in existing in P2P file transfer communities, with some peers experiencing limited download speeds while other peers that are willing to donate their upload bandwidth are waiting idle. The problem stems from the matching of supply and demand, which is exclusively file-based, i.e., communication between peers only takes place in the context of the file being transferred.

In this paper, we introduce the design of a *bandwidth marketplace*, where peers can initiate cross-files bandwidth trades without human oversight. Peers independently monitor the supply and demand of individual files and alert other peers when they discover an undersupply situation. Idle peers can respond to

M. Chatterjee et al. (Eds.): ICDCN 2014, LNCS 8314, pp. 302–316, 2014.

these alerts and alleviate the undersupply by providing their upload bandwidth using a *helper algorithm*.

To study the behavior of helpers, we develop an analytical model based on the BitTorrent fluid model [14,8]. Using our model, we identify several bottlenecks that can affect the download performance of peers. We show that the bandwidth marketplace we design can increase the performance in most typical situations, but conclude there are cases where performance improvements are impossible.

We identify an existing algorithm, part of Libtorrent [1], that can be used by bandwidth marketplace helpers and present it in detail in Section 4. To study the behavior of the algorithm, we test it in a lab environment through experiments emulating two different types of oversupply, one static and one with dynamic peer arrival. The experiments are not simulations, they involve proper purposefully instrumented clients run by up to 210 peers.

The contribution of our paper is threefold. First, we design a bandwidth marketplace that facilitates matching of bandwidth supply and demand in P2P file transfer systems. The design is completely decentralized, incentives compatible, and permits each participating peer to maintain its autonomy. Second, we develop a model to for the behavior of helper peers within swarms. We derive using the model performance bounds for the general operation of swarms and for the performance impact helpers can have. Third, we present and evaluate an algorithm recently included in Libtorrent which can be used by helpers. We show using realistic experiments that include actual running P2P clients that it fulfils the requirements of a bandwidth marketplace helper algorithm.

2   Bandwidth Marketplace Design

As a prerequisite, the bandwidth marketplace design depends upon the existence of a credit system, e.g., as used by private communities [9], to incentivize users to contribute upload bandwidth across swarms. The plain BitTorrent tit-for-tat incentive mechanism is not sufficient. In tit-for-tat, peers that are downloading a file, called *leechers*, are incentivized to upload fast so they can download fast. However, *seeders*—peers that continue uploading after finishing downloading— are not incentivized at all.

Our design is based on a decentralized algorithm, executed independently by all peers in the system. This is summarized in Figure 1. The operations executed in the algorithm are as follows:

1. All peers constantly monitor their own download progress to detect a potential supply shortage, as in swarm A in the figure. Whenever their download speed drops below a percentage of their historical download speed, they use MultiQ [11] to detect the real upload bandwidth of seeders in the swarm. If they determine that the low download speed is caused by a leecher bottleneck (i.e., the seeders are fast, but the leechers cannot replicate the data they receive from seeders fast enough, Section 3.3) they execute the next operation in the algorithm.

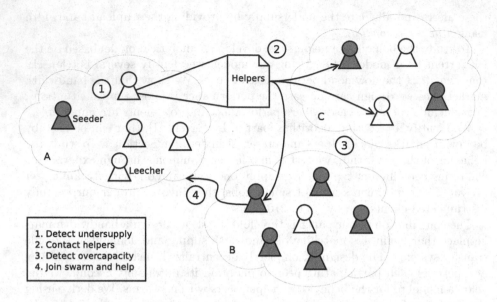

Fig. 1. Overview of bandwidth marketplace operation

2. A peer that identifies an undersupplied swarm broadcasts a help request containing the swarm ID to a limited set of marketplace partners, called its set of *helpers*. The set is bootstrapped with the best tit-for-tat partners from existing swarms. The helpers are ranked according to their responses to past requests. New helpers are optimistically added constantly to replace badly performing helpers, in order to improve the chances of receiving help, similarly to the way BitTorrent discovers new partners through optimistic unchoking.

3. All peers listen for help requests, but are free to act upon them autonomously. If a peer has a lower upload bandwidth utilization compared to historical values, for example because it is only part of oversupplied swarms, like swarm B in the figure, it joins the undersupplied swarm as a helper. Note that this does not imply connecting directly to the peer that sends the help requests. The helper simply offers its excess upload bandwidth to the swarm, which inevitably also benefits the requester. Helpers keep track of the their own upload in the new swarm and use it to rank requesting peers in the future. Peers that request help in severely undersupplied swarms are helped more frequently than those who request help in swarms that are not only mildly undersupplied; this also provides security against malicious peers. Peers that are part of balanced swarms, like swarm C in the figure, ignore the help requests.

4. As a helper, a peer tries to upload as much as possible in the swarm while downloading as little as possible. Ideally, adding helpers to a swarm should have the same effect as increasing the upload bandwidth of existing peers in the swarm. We investigate the behavior of helper algorithms in general in Section 3 and we present an existing helper algorithm recently introduced by Libtorrent in Section 4.

3 Model

In this section, we present a model for predicting the performance of helper algorithms using analytically derived bounds, starting from the well established BitTorrent fluid models [14,8]. We describe corner cases of peer interaction and show how adding helpers to the system changes performance.

3.1 Overview

Consider a system of identical peers with a download bandwidth much greater than their upload bandwidth. According to the fluid model of Guo et al. [8], the download speed of a leecher at time t is

$$u(t) = \mu \frac{\eta_x x(t) + y(t)}{x(t)} \tag{1}$$

where μ is the upload bandwidth, η_x is the effectiveness of leecher upload (i.e., the fraction of upload bandwidth leechers are able to use), x is the number of leechers, and y is the number of seeders.

Considering further that leechers have upload bandwidth μ_x different from the upload bandwidth of seeders μ_y, download speed becomes

$$u(t) = \frac{\eta_x \mu_x x(t) + \mu_y y(t)}{x(t)} \tag{2}$$

We introduce helper peers and model their population through $z(t)$. Each helper has upload bandwidth u_z. Helpers have a different effectiveness in using their upload bandwidth than leechers, which we denote η_z. Adding helpers to the system generates a certain increase in download requests, modeled through parameter ϵ, which can vary from 0 (minimal effect) to 1 (helper downloads everything at full speed just like a leecher). The goal of the helper algorithm is to maximize η_z while minimizing ϵ. The download speed of leechers becomes

$$u(t) = \frac{\eta_x \mu_x x(t) + \mu_y y(t) + \eta_z \mu_z z(t)}{x(t) + \epsilon z(t)} \tag{3}$$

We summarize the notation used in the model in Table 1.

3.2 Swarm Bootstrapping

We define the bootstrapping phase of the swarm as the time before any of the leechers and helpers download a complete piece from the seeder. During this phase, $\eta_x = 0$ because leechers have no pieces to upload to one another. Similarly, $\eta_z = 0$. Thus

$$u(t) = \frac{\mu_y y(t)}{x(t) + \epsilon z(t)} \tag{4}$$

It is especially important for the helper algorithm to recognize and adapt to this phase of the swarm lifetime so that the duration of the phase is minimized and the swarm moves to the phase when leechers and helpers can contribute upload bandwidth.

Table 1. Model notation

Number of leechers	$x(t)$
Number of seeders	$y(t)$
Number of helpers	$z(t)$
Leecher upload bandwidth	μ_x
Seeder upload bandwidth	μ_y
Helper upload bandwidth	μ_z
Leecher effectiveness	η_x
Helper effectiveness	η_z
Helper download effect	ϵ

3.3   Download Speed Bottlenecks

The leecher upload speed is determined by one of the three mutually exclusive bottlenecks that can exist in the system.

The first is a seeder bottleneck (SB), when the aggregate upload speed of the seeders is slower that the upload speed of a leecher, $\mu_y y(t) < \mu_x$. In other words, the leechers in the swarm can replicate among themselves the pieces they receive from the seeders faster than the seeders can upload the pieces. In this case, in the absence of helpers, the download speed is bound by:

$$u_{SB}(t) = \mu_y y(t) \tag{5}$$

Helpers can not increase the leecher upload speed in this situation. The best a helper algorithm can do is maintain an ϵ as low as possible so $u(t)$ does not decrease.

The second bottleneck is the leechers bottleneck (LB). In this case, $\mu_x < \mu_y y(t)$, so that seeders can upload data faster than leechers can distribute it among themselves. Qiu and Srikant [14] show that leecher upload effectiveness is very high:

$$\eta_x \approx 1 - \left(\frac{\log N}{N} \right)^k \tag{6}$$

where N is the number of file pieces and k is the number of connections each peer has. In practice, with files having at least hundreds of pieces and peers having tens of connections, η_x is considered 1, which is confirmed by actual measurements [12]. In the absence of helpers, the download speed is bound by:

$$u_{LB}(t) = \frac{\mu_x x(t) + \mu_y y(t)}{x(t)} \tag{7}$$

Adding helpers to a swarm operating in this regime can increase download speed up to the limit given by the upload speed of the seeders (Equation 5). Thus, the speedup helpers can achieve is bounded by:

$$S_{b_1} = \frac{\mu_y y(t) x(t)}{\mu_x x(t) + \mu_y y(t)} \tag{8}$$

Introducing helpers into the system can create a helper bottleneck (HB), derived from the total upload bandwidth that helpers add to the swarm. Consider the ideal situation where helpers do not download anything ($\epsilon = 0$) and use their full upload bandwidth ($\eta_z = 1$) (not possible in reality). The download speed is:

$$u_{\text{HB}}(t) = \frac{\mu_x x(t) + \mu_y y(t) + \mu_z z(t)}{x(t)} \tag{9}$$

Thus, the second speedup bound is:

$$S_{b_2} = \frac{\mu_x x(t) + \mu_y y(t) + \mu_z z(t)}{\mu_x x(t) + \mu_y y(t)} \tag{10}$$

We compute $z_{\max}(t)$, the maximum useful number of helpers. Having more than $z_{\max}(t)$ helpers does not increase download speed any further. Starting from the two download speed bottlenecks, $u_{\text{SB}}(t)$ 5 and $u_{\text{HB}}(t)$ 9:

$$\mu_y y(t) = \frac{\mu_x x(t) + \mu_y y(t) + \mu_z z_{\max}(t)}{x(t)} \tag{11}$$

$$z_{\max}(t) = \frac{\mu_y y(t)(x(t) - 1) - \mu_x x(t)}{\mu_z} \tag{12}$$

4   Libtorrent Helper Algorithm

Libtorrent [1] is a library implementing the BitTorrent protocol designed to be used by third-party BitTorrent clients. In its latest major version (0.16), it introduced a *share mode* for downloading, where file pieces are downloaded only when a heuristic determines it is possible to upload them to other leechers. Like many other BitTorrent engines, Libtorrent supports choosing a subset of files to download from a multi-file torrent. Internally, the choice is implemented through a bitmap which marks each file piece for download or not. This bitmap is also used in share mode. Initially, the bitmap is empty, so Libtorrent does not download any data. The bitmap is updated by Algorithm 1, which is triggered by new peer connections, the closing of connections, the completion of piece downloads, and various other events. The parameters are controlled by Libtorrent code, except for T, which we set to 1, so the upload is at least equal to the download.

The algorithm tries to heuristically estimate the feasibility of downloading one of the rarest pieces observed at neighboring peers. It starts by counting the total number of pieces missing at neighboring leechers (Line 4). Only the number of pieces is taken into consideration, not their IDs; however, given the random rarest first piece picking policy of BitTorrent clients [5], it is very likely that the sets of missing pieces of leechers are disjoint, hence the choice of not storing piece IDs. Note that other helpers are not taken into consideration when counting missing pieces. The number of missing pieces is decreased considering each seeder can upload a number of pieces given by parameter B while the helper is downloading one piece. If this results in no missing pieces being left

---

Algorithm 1. Libtorrent helper algorithm for piece selection

Require: B, T, S, D

1: $missing\_pieces = 0$
2: **for all** $p \in connected\_peers$ **do**
3:   **if** p is a leecher **then**
4:     $missing\_pieces$ += $total\_pieces - pieces(p)$
5:   **end if**
6: **end for**
7: $missing\_pieces$ -= $B \times |connected\_seeders|$
8: **if** $missing\_piece \leq 0$ **then**
9:   **return**
10: **end if**
11: **if** $|connected\_seeders|/|connected\_peers| > S$ **then**
12:   disconnect excess seeders
13: **end if**
14: **if** $downloaded \times T > uploaded$ **then**
15:   **return**
16: **end if**
17: **if** $downloading \times D > downloaded$ **then**
18:   **return**
19: **end if**
20: **if** $|connected\_peers| - min(piece\_rarities) < T$ **then**
21:   **return**
22: **end if**
23: download $random(rarest\_pieces)$

---

among the connected leechers, the algorithm returns and the helper does not start downloading another piece.

Next, the helper examines the type of peers it is connected to (Line 11). Having seeders take up a too high proportion of all connections is detrimental to the chances of uploading, because seeders are never interested in new pieces. However being connected to some seeders is beneficial overall, because it offers the opportunity to download pieces that are rare among leechers. The parameter S controls the proportion of seeder connections; it depends on a number of factors, like the total number of connected peers and the maximum number of connections allowed. In case the helper is connected to too many seeders, it disconnects some of them.

The algorithm checks the upload and download statistics to make sure the sharing ratio remains above the target given by parameter T. Note that this check does not stop the bootstrapping of the helper (the sharing ratio while downloading the first piece is inevitably 0), because it only involves fully downloaded pieces. This check is a feedback mechanism that stops the download of new pieces if the upload is not proceeding as expected. Furthermore, there is also a check on the pieces whose download is in progress, controlled by parameter D (Line 17), which ensures the helper does not request too many pieces at the same time.

Finally, the availability of the rarest pieces is computed and compared to the number of connected peers to ensure there are enough peers potentially interested in a future download (Line 20). One piece is selected at random from the set of rarest pieces and is marked for download.

5   Evaluation

We evaluate the helper algorithm in a controlled environment using a Libtorrent-based BitTorrent client through a static experiment where we compare the performance of the client to the bound given by the model in Section 3, and a dynamic experiment in which we replicate a flash crowd peer arrival pattern.

5.1   Experimental Setup

The experimental setup is based on the P2P Test Framework [2], a collection of scripts that facilitates testing P2P clients in controlled conditions. We build a C++ BitTorrent client based on Libtorrent that supports share-mode peers acting as helpers, starting from the minimal client included in the framework.

The common parameters of our experiments are summarized in Table 2. We only limit the upload bandwidth of peers and leave the download unconstrained, in accordance with the model we use [14,8] and typical ISP connections which are highly asymmetrical. All clients are stopped after the given run time. Considering the file size and upload bandwidths we use, this means no leechers become seeders. In other words, our results describe exclusively the transient undersupplied phase of the swarm during which helpers have the biggest impact.

The number of peers is sufficient to allow choking to occur given the usual number of upload slots, 5 [5]; experiments using less peers would be unrealistic because peers would always upload to each other. The run time is chosen to allow sufficient choke rounds between peers to minimize outliers, which is visible in the low standard deviation of the results.

Table 2. Experiment parameters

Parameter	Experiment	
	Static	Dynamic
File size [GiB]	1	1
Number of seeders	1	1
Seeder bandwidth [KiB/s]	1000–5000	5000
Number of leechers	20	70
Leecher bandwidth [KiB/s]	1000	1000
Number of helpers	10–70	70
Helper bandwidth [KiB/s]	500–3500	1000
Run time [s]	200	300

5.2   Static Experiment

In the first experiment, which we call static, we observe a swarm for the first 200 seconds of its lifetime. The swarm has a single seeder, which is the content injector in this case, and uses the Libtorrent version of the efficient super-seeding algorithm [4]. There are 20 identical leechers in the swarm with an upload bandwidth of 1000 KiB/s and they all join at the beginning.

The baseline performance in our evaluation is given by the normal BitTorrent execution. We start the seeder and leechers and record the mean leecher download speed over the duration of the experiment. We compare the baseline with the effect of introducing helpers originating from our bandwidth marketplace. We again record the mean download speed of the original leechers, which is now affected by the additional helpers. In this experiment, all additional helpers are added to the swarm at the same time, 30 seconds after the start, to simulate the delay introduced by the bandwidth marketplace protocol.

Along with the additional helpers running the Libtorrent helper algorithm, we use two other types of additional peers, in order to give insight into the performance of the Libtorrent helper algorithm. First, to replicate a naive approach to designing a bandwidth marketplace, where additional peers trying to help are actually normal peers, we inject peers running the normal leecher algorithm. Second, we simulate the addition of ideal helpers using the model bound for the download speed (Equation 9); this ideal bound provides a performance target for helper algorithms, although it cannot be reached by an actual implementation.

We first explore the leecher bottleneck case, when download speed is constrained by the upload speed of leechers. To reproduce this bottleneck, we set the seeder upload bandwidth to 5000 KiB/s, corresponding to a well provisioned content injector.

Figure 2 shows the effect of adding additional peers compared to the baseline BitTorrent performance. The maximum number of additional peers used is 70, (it must be less the $z_{max} = 75$, Equation 12), and the minimum number is 10, half the number of leechers. All additional peers have the same bandwidth, 1000 KiB/s, which is equal to that of the leechers. The Libtorrent helper algorithm is successful in alleviating undersupply in the swarm. It shifts the bottleneck from a leecher bottleneck to a helper bottleneck. The addition of helpers produces a linear effect from 10 to 50 helpers, when leecher download speed is more than twice as high as the baseline speed. Adding more helpers gives diminishing returns; the download speed increase from 50 to 70 helpers is sub-linear. Examining the use of normal peers as additional peers, we note that it does not improve the performance of the original leechers. This is in accordance with our model, which predicts the slight drop in performance visible in the figure caused by the division of seeder bandwidth to more peers (x increased in Equation 7).

The simulated ideal performance bound shown in the figure is approximately twice as high as the performance generated by Libtorrent helpers, in the 10–50 additional peers range. To investigate the cause of this difference, we analyze the bandwidth usage of Libtorrent helpers in Figure 3. The mean upload and download speed of helpers can be used to approximate parameters η_z and ϵ in

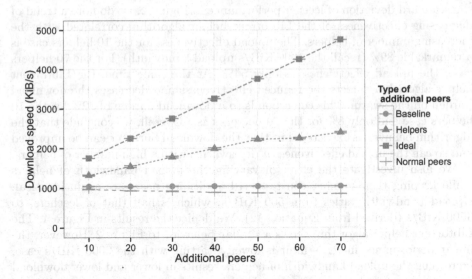

Fig. 2. Effect of number of additional peers on mean download speed of original leechers in swarm for static experiment (standard deviation error bars, $n = 20$)

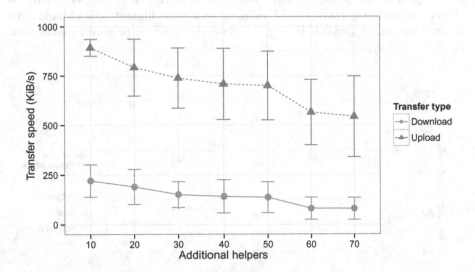

Fig. 3. Effect of number of helpers on their own mean download and upload speed (standard deviation error bars, n indicated by horizontal axis)

Equation 3. While the standard deviation of these mean speeds is not as low as the standard deviation of leecher performance in Figure 2, we do note a trend of decreasing effectiveness of the Libtorrent helper algorithm correlated with the increasing number of helpers. The upload effectiveness for the 10 helpers case is a remarkable 89% (recall the 1000 KiB/s upload bandwidth). For the 70 helpers case, the upload effectiveness is only 54%. At the same time, the Libtorrent helper algorithm detects the reduced effectiveness and decreases the download burden on the swarm. This corresponds to a download burden of 22% for the 10 helpers case and only 8% for the 70 helpers case. Overall, we conclude that the algorithm behaves as expected, but that the download burden ϵ can be improved and so can the upload effectiveness η_z for swarms with a high number of helpers.

We also investigate the effect of varying the upload bandwidth of helpers while keeping their number constant. All additional peers are again identical. Upload bandwidth varies from 500 KiB/s, which is half that of leechers, to 3500 KiB/s (derived from Equation 12). We depict the results in Figure 4. The Libtorrent helper algorithm shows a similar behavior to Figure 2. However, the linear performance increase limit is lower. Starting with the 2000 KiB/s case, increasing the upload bandwidth of helpers results in lower and lower download speed increases for leechers. On the other hand, using normal peers as additional peers has the potential to generate good results. If low bandwidth peers (500 KiB/s) are used, there is a performance drop. Starting with moderately fast peers (1500 KiB/s) though, there is a positive effect on the download speed of the original leechers. At the same time, we note that it is still better to use helpers instead of normal peers; even considering the highest upload bandwidth in the experiment (3500 KiB/s), they generate a bigger performance increase, 112% vs. 70%.

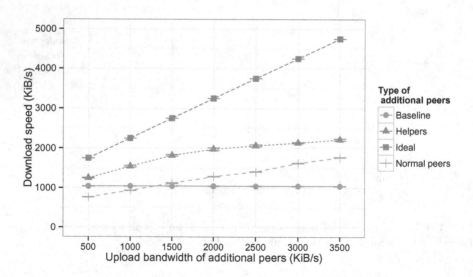

Fig. 4. Effect of upload bandwidth of additional peers on mean download speed of original leechers in swarm (standard deviation error bars, $n = 20$)

Figure 5 shows the effect of helper upload speed on their upload effectiveness and their download burden on the swarm. For low bandwidth helpers, the effectiveness is very high. Starting from 2000 KiB/s, however, it flattens out. This is accompanied by a decrease in download burden, so the actual effect on leecher performance is still positive.

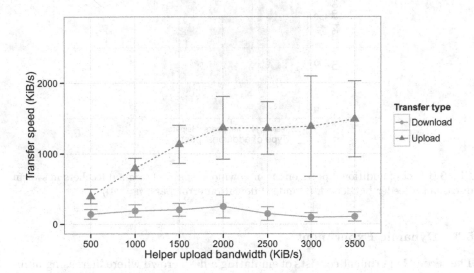

Fig. 5. Effect of upload bandwidth of helpers on their own mean download and upload speed (standard deviation error bars, $n = 20$)

While in practice the leecher bottleneck case we explored so far is most common, we also investigate the seeder bottleneck case. For this, we set the seeder upload speed to 1000 KiB/s, equal to that of leechers, generating a seeder bottleneck slightly lower than the theoretical swarm dissemination speed of 1050 KiB/s (Equation 7). Figure 6 shows the results. Recall from Section 3.3 that even ideal helpers cannot increase leecher download speed in this case, because it is strictly bounded by the upload speed of the under-provision seeder. The additional peers have an upload bandwidth of 1000 KiB/s, just like the leechers. Note that the baseline performance does not coincide with the model, due to overhead in the practical implementation of the protocol. The Libtorrent helper algorithm performs ideally, generating no download burden on the swarm and keeping the download speed of leechers unchanged. On the other hand, adding normal peers to the swarm causes a significant performance drop. This is due to the bootstrapping period (Section 3.2) which lasts for approximately 10% of our experiment.

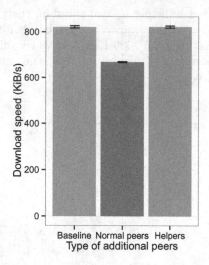

Fig. 6. Effect of additional peers on mean download speed of original leechers in swarm in case of a seeder bottleneck (standard deviation error bars, $n = 20$)

5.3   Dynamic Experiment

The second experiment consists of emulating a flash crowd where increasing numbers of leechers join the swarm. To record the baseline BitTorrent performance, we create 5 waves of leechers spaced 30 seconds apart, starting at the beginning of the experiment. The number of leechers in each wave is 10, 12, 14, 16, and 18, respectively. All leechers have the same upload bandwidth, 1000 KiB/s, while the seeder has 5000 KiB/s, meaning the performance bottleneck is caused by the leechers. The experiment lasts for 300 seconds and no leecher finishes downloading. We report the mean download speed of leechers grouped by their join time, to see if the join time has an effect on performance.

To test the effect of helpers, we consider that each leecher determines two helpers to join the swarm. All helpers have the same upload bandwidth of leechers, 1000 KiB/s. Each helper joins the swarm 10 seconds after the leecher that summons it. Figure 7 shows the results.

The baseline performance of early leechers is better than that of late leechers, because early leechers benefit from a higher bandwidth allocation from the seeder. The Libtorrent helper algorithm works very well in this dynamic flash crowd situation, which is the ideal use case for the bandwidth marketplace. The presence of helpers more than offsets the performance decrease of leechers joining the swarm in the middle of the experiment, in the 30 and 60 seconds waves. These leechers benefit from the presence of helpers summoned by previous waves of leechers; these helpers had already downloaded pieces and are ready to share them. Specifically, the download speed of leechers in the 60 seconds wave almost

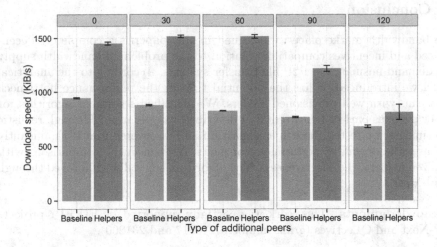

Fig. 7. Effect of helpers considering arrival time of leecher waves in seconds (standard deviation error bars, $n = 10 + wave \times 2$ for baseline, double for helpers)

doubles from 827 KiB/s to 1518 KiB/s. The leechers arriving latest do not have the chance to encounter enough helpers before the experiment ends, hence their lower performance.

6 Related Work

Several designs have been proposed to solve the supply and demand problem in P2P file transfer systems. None of them have seen wide scale adoption, and plain BitTorrent continues to be very popular. Compared to previous work, our solution is decentralized, incentives compatible, and based on a simple algorithm that does not require user intervention. Garbacki et al. [7] attempt to solve the problem using "bandwidth borrowing". While effective, their solution has a clear scalability problem, as a peer can only recuperate bandwidth from its debtors. Aperjis et al.[3] propose PACE, a credit-based system for multilateral transfers, where each peer asks for a specific price for its services. The main problem with the design of PACE is the complexity of the pricing algorithm which, although allegedly simple, does take into account complex parameters like "network-friendly" behavior. Peterson and Sirer [13] propose Antfarm, a P2P system that efficiently balances bandwidth supply and demand. Antfarm, however, is not a truly decentralized solution, relying instead on a central server coordinating peer actions. Wu et al. [16] design a solution specific to video-streaming where peers are assigned to static groups responsible for certain streams. Again, the grouping of peers is done by a centralized server. Most recently, Dán and Carlsson [6] propose the merging of under- and oversupplied swarms with good results. However, their design also includes centralized servers, used for merging swarms.

7   Conclusion

The bandwidth marketplace we designed in this paper is a completely decentralized and incentives compatible solution to the problem of bandwidth supply and demand mismatch in P2P file transfer systems. According to the analytical model we introduced, it has the potential to shift the performance bottleneck in swarms with well provisioned seeders. We identified a suitable algorithm for helper peers as part of Libtorrent and described its operation. Through realistic experiments, we tested the helper algorithm and discovered that it significantly increases the download performance of peers. As seen in the comparisons with idealized helpers, the effectiveness of the algorithm can still be improved through future work.

Acknowledgments. This work was partially supported by EU FP7 projects P2P-Next and QLectives (grant numbers 216217 and 231200).

References

1. Libtorrent, http://libtorrent.com
2. P2P Test Framework, https://github.com/schaap/p2p-testframework
3. Aperjis, C., Freedman, M.J., Johari, R.: Peer-assisted content distribution with prices. In: CONEXT, pp. 1–12. ACM (2008)
4. Chen, Z., Chen, Y., Lin, C., Nivargi, V., Cao, P.: Experimental Analysis of Super-Seeding in BitTorrent. In: ICC, pp. 65–69. IEEE (2008)
5. Cohen, B.: Incentives build robustness in BitTorrent. In: P2PEcon (2003)
6. Dán, G., Carlsson, N.: Centralized and Distributed Protocols for Tracker-Based Dynamic Swarm Management. IEEE/ACM TON 21(1), 297–310 (2013)
7. Garbacki, P., Epema, D., Van Steen, M.: An amortized tit-for-tat protocol for exchanging bandwidth instead of content in p2p networks. In: SASO. IEEE (2007)
8. Guo, L., Chen, S., Xiao, Z., Tan, E., Ding, X., Zhang, X.: A performance study of BitTorrent-like peer-to-peer systems. IEEE JSAC 25(1), 155–169 (2007)
9. Jia, A.L., Chen, X., Chu, X., Pouwelse, J.A., Epema, D.H.J.: How to Survive and Thrive in a Private BitTorrent Community. In: Frey, D., Raynal, M., Sarkar, S., Shyamasundar, R.K., Sinha, P. (eds.) ICDCN 2013. LNCS, vol. 7730, pp. 270–284. Springer, Heidelberg (2013)
10. Kash, I.A., Lai, J.K., Zhang, H., Zohar, A.: Economics of BitTorrent communities. In: WWW, pp. 221–230. ACM (2012)
11. Katti, S., Katabi, D., Blake, C., Kohler, E., Strauss, J.: MultiQ. In: IMC, pp. 245–250. ACM (2004)
12. Legout, A., Liogkas, N., Kohler, E., Zhang, L.: Clustering and sharing incentives in BitTorrent systems. In: SIGMETRICS, pp. 301–312. ACM (2007)
13. Peterson, R.S., Sirer, E.G.: Antfarm: efficient content distribution with managed swarms. NSDI, pp. 107–122. USENIX (2009)
14. Qiu, D., Srikant, R.: Modeling and performance analysis of BitTorrent-like peer-to-peer networks. ACM SIGCOMM Comput. Commun. Rev. 34(4), 367–378 (2004)
15. Sandvine: Global Internet Phenomena Report 1H2013
16. Wu, D., Liu, Y., Ross, K.W.: Modeling and analysis of multichannel P2P live video systems. IEEE/ACM TON 18(4), 1248–1260 (2010)

A Fault Tolerant Parallel Computing Scheme of Scalar Multiplication for Wireless Sensor Networks

Yanbo Shou[1] and Hervé Guyennet[1]

University of Franche-Comté, Besançon, France
{yshou,hguyennet}@femto-st.fr

Abstract. In event-driven sensor networks, when a critical event occurs, sensors should transmit messages back to base station in a secure and reliable manner. We choose Elliptic Curve Cryptography to secure the network since it offers faster computation and good security with shorter keys. In order to minimize the running time, we propose to split and distribute the computation of scalar multiplications by involving neighboring nodes in this operation. In order to improve the reliability, we have also proposed a fault tolerance mechanism. It uses half of the available cluster members as backup nodes which take over the work of faulty nodes in case of system failure. Parallel computing does consume more resources, but the results of simulation show that the computation can be significantly accelerated. This method is designed specially for applications where running time is the most important factor.

Keywords: Wireless sensor networks, Elliptic curves, Scalar multiplication, Parallel computing, Fault tolerance.

1 Introduction

The advances of micro-electro-mechanical technology in recent years have enabled the fast development of smart sensor node. A sensor node is small electronic device which is usually composed of processing, sensing, radio communication and power supply units [1,2]. It is programmable and is able to collect environmental data and communicate with other sensor nodes by using wireless technologies. Such sensor nodes have limited resources and are often battery-operated, they are not designed to handle complicated tasks and that's why a sensor node rarely works alone. Sensor nodes are supposed be deployed massively and be programmed to form automatically a fully functional network, called wireless sensor network.

Ideally, a sensor network consists of a large number of low-cost and low-power sensor nodes, which are interconnected with each other and operate in unattended manner. This kind of networks are often deployed in inaccessible and hostile zones where human interventions are not always possible. Today we can find a wide range of applications using wireless sensor technologies, such as

M. Chatterjee et al. (Eds.): ICDCN 2014, LNCS 8314, pp. 317–331, 2014.

environment monitoring, industrial sensing, medical care and military surveillance [3,4,5,6,7].

However sensor nodes are quite fragile and are vulnerable to various attacks due to the lack of resources and unreliability of wireless communication. [8] gives a detailed presentation of almost all possible attacks in wireless sensor networks. An efficient way to protect sensor networks is to use cryptographic techniques [8,9]. On one hand, symmetric cryptographic algorithms are usually computational less expensive and easier to implement in hardware and software, but as we use the same key for data encryption and decryption, the key management in sensor networks becomes a challenging issue. On the other hand, asymmetric algorithms need more complicated computation, but as we use two different keys respectively for encryption and decryption, a compromised node can not provide clue to the private keys of other nodes.

In this paper we choose *Elliptic Curve Cryptography* (ECC) to secure the communications in sensor networks. It has become recently one of the most famous asymmetric cryptographic mechanism because of its shorter key length requirement and faster computation compared with other asymmetric mechanisms, such as RSA [10]. ECC has successfully attracted the interest of researchers, especially in the domain of embedded system where most of the devices have strict resource restriction.

The performance of ECC can be significantly improved by using mathematical tools, such as NAF, windowed method, projective coordinates [11]. Besides traditional algorithmic optimization, parallel computing is an other choice for accelerating the computation on elliptic curves. The computation task is split into smaller independent ones which are then distributed to neighboring sensor nodes and carried out simultaneously. However, sensor nodes communicate with each other through wireless connection, which is considered as unreliable and sensitive to radio interference. In addition, sensor nodes might suffer external attacks during computation. In this paper we present our new fault tolerant parallel computing scheme for elliptic curve cryptography in wireless sensor networks, which is actually the following of our research published in [12].

The rest of the paper is organized as follows. Section 2 presents basic concepts of ECC, and section 3 describes our parallel computing scheme. In section 4 and 5 we present possible fault tolerance issues and the related work. In section 6, we propose a fault tolerance mechanism designed specially for our parallel computing scheme, then it is tested by a simulator and the results are illustrated in 7. Section 8 concludes the paper.

2   Basic Concepts of Elliptic Curve

Elliptic curve cryptography (ECC) is an approach to public-key cryptography which is proposed independently by Koblitz [13] and Miller [14] in the 80's. It's suitable for creating lightweight and efficient cryptosystem, especially for embedded systems which have limited resources. Experiments prove that a 160-bit elliptic curve key can provide the same security robustness as a 1024-bit RSA key [15].

In cryptography we work with the curves which are defined over finite field $\mathbb{F}_q$ where $q = p^m$. p is a prime number, called the characteristic of $\mathbb{F}$. $\mathbb{F}$ is finite prime field when $m = 1$ and $p \neq 2, 3$, which is also the configuration that we use in this paper. Such curves can be represented by the simplified Weierstrass equation (see formula 1).

$$y^2 = x^3 + ax + b \tag{1}$$

whose discriminant $\Delta = -16(4a^3 + 27b^2)$ and $\Delta \neq 0$.

All points on an elliptic curve, including the point at infinity, constitute an abelian group whose law is point addition, denoted by $+$, which combines 2 points on the curve to form a third point which is on the same curve. Suppose that $P_1(x_1, y_1)$ and $P_2(x_2, y_2)$ are 2 points on an elliptic curve, then $P_3(x_3, y_3) = P_1(x_1, y_1) + P_2(x_2, y_2)$ can be calculated by using the formulas 2 and 3.

$$\begin{cases} x_3 = s^2 - x_1 - x_2 \\ y_3 = s(x_1 - x_3) - y_1 \end{cases} \tag{2}$$

where

$$s = \begin{cases} (y_2 - y_1)/(x_2 - x_1) & \text{if } P_1 \neq P_2 \\ (3x_1^2 + a)/2y_1 & \text{if } P_1 = P_2 \end{cases} \tag{3}$$

Based on point addition, we may also perform point multiplication, also called scalar multiplication. For example $Q = kP$, where Q and P are 2 points on an elliptic curve, and k is a big integer. The most basic method to calculate kP is using Double-and-Add algorithm [16].

The security of ECC relies on the difficulty of solving the discrete logarithm problem. For $Q = kP$, given points Q and P, it's extremely difficult to compute the value of k if it's big enough. However it's not always easy to transform the data we want to protect into a point on elliptic curve. Thus in most of the cases, we only use ECC to establish a shared key between both parties, then we can use a symmetric-key cryptographic algorithm to encrypt our data.

A example of key exchange protocol is Elliptic Curve Diffie-Hellman [17]. Suppose that Alice and Bob share the same elliptic curve E whose generator point is G. To establish a shared key, Alice computes and sends her public key $Q_A = s_A G$ to Bob where s_A is her private key, meanwhile Bob sends $Q_B = s_B G$ to Alice where s_B is his private key. Then the shared key $K_{AB} = s_A Q_B = s_B Q_A = s_A s_B G$.

We can notice that the scalar multiplication is the most essential operation on elliptic curve, and it's also the most computationally intensive operation we need to perform. It is obvious that this kind of computation is too complicated for sensor nodes, performance optimization is then absolutely necessary.

3   Parallel Scalar Multiplication in WSN

We suppose that in a cluster based sensor network, cluster members send periodically environmental data to their cluster head which is responsible for data processing. Whenever a critical event is detected, the cluster head has to warn the base station as fast as possible in a secure and reliable manner.

Our parallel scalar multiplication method is based on the idea of [18] which doesn't need shared memory and offers an efficient scalar decomposition. For example we need to compute $Q = kG$ where Q and G are 2 points on an elliptic curve, and k is a large integer of length l which can be represented in binary $k = \sum_{i=0}^{l-1} k_i 2^i$. The cluster head splits k into n blocks B_i of $b = \lfloor \frac{l}{n} \rfloor$ bits according to the number of available cluster members.

$$B_i = \sum_{j=ib}^{(i+1)b-1} k_j 2^j$$

As all sensor nodes share the same elliptic curve which is configured and preloaded before deployment, then it is possible to precompute points $G_i = 2^{ib}G$ where G is the generator point. Thus the computation of kP can be rewritten in the following manner.

$$Q = kG = \sum_{i=0}^{l-1} k_i 2^i$$
$$= Q_0 + Q_1 + \ldots + Q_{n-1}$$
$$= B_0 G + B_1 2^b G + \ldots + B_{n-1} 2^{b(n-1)} G \qquad (4)$$

We can notice in equation 4 that each Q_i can be considered as an independent task and can be treated separately. The entire process of parallel computing is graphically illustrated in figure 1.

1. Cluster members send data to cluster head periodically.
2. Cluster head detects a critical event. It broadcasts a call for parallel computing and then waits for responses.
3. Available cluster members send positive responses back to cluster head and become *Slave nodes* of parallel computing.
4. Cluster head decomposes the computation according to the number of available slaves. Then it sends the tasks to slaves, and it becomes the *Master node* of parallel computing.
5. Slaves complete the task and send the results back to their master.
6. Master nodes combines received results to obtain the final result, by which the master can encrypt its message and send it to the node of next hop.

As we can see that the parallel scalar multiplication on elliptic curve is a complicated operation, and every step must be carried out carefully. Moreover, the process needs reliable wireless communication which is not always possible in wireless sensor networks.

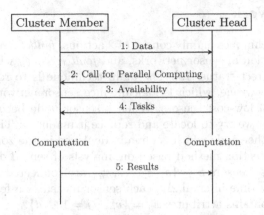

Fig. 1. Parallel Scalar Multiplication Process

4   Fault Tolerance Issues

Three terms have been introduced in [19] in order to explain the fault tolerance issues in wireless sensor networks.

A *fault* is a defect causing an *error*, which represents an incorrect status of system. Such erroneous status may lead the entire network to a *failure* in which the system deviates from its specification and loses its intended functionality.

As we know, sensor nodes are prone to suffer various faults and attacks[1,2]. There are many different types of fault in wireless sensor networks, it is extremely hard to design a fault tolerance technique which solves all kinds of problem. For our parallel computing scheme, we have identified three main possible errors during computation.

– *Missing result* : The master node needs to receive every single result from its slaves to form the final result. Missing results will make the master unable to complete the parallel computing. The missing result may due to various faults such as battery depletion, radio interference and physical attack.
– *Incorrect result* : The results sent back to master node might be wrong because of low battery level, radio interference and other internal errors of sensor nodes. If the master node computes the final result based on incorrect slave results, the entire encryption process will fail.
– *Faulty cluster head* : The cluster head plays the role of master node during parallel computing, if the cluster head becomes faulty in the course of task distribution and results reception, the parallel computing process has to be aborted.

As we can notice that either of these errors may cause the parallel computing scheme to fail. Before elaborating our fault tolerance mechanism, we will see in the following section a few fault tolerance techniques proposed in literature.

5   Related Work

Fault tolerance techniques mainly consist of 2 actions, *fault detection* which aims to detect malfunction in sensor networks, and *fault recovery* which recovers the system from incorrect status [19]. The main technique is to replace the faulty component by a new one, which is logical, since sensor network is constituted of large number of low-cost sensors. When a sensor node becomes faulty, it is worth nothing that we try to locate and replace it manually. The best way is to replace it by an other node which is already deployed in the zone.

An anomaly detection method based on analysis of sensed data is presented in [20]. We suppose sensors $S = \{s_1, s_2, \ldots, s_n\}$ are connected in a hierarchical topology. At every time interval Δ_k, each sensor measures a feature vector x_k^i, and very vector contains attributes $x_k^i = \{v_{kj}^i : j = 1 \ldots d\}$.

Two approaches are presented, in centralized way, every sensor sends its measured vectors $X_i = \{x_k^i : k = 1 \ldots m\}$ to its immediate parent, which merges the received data with its own vectors and then sends them to its parent. All vectors are sent back step by step to the gateway node, on which a clustering algorithm [21] is executed. Vectors belonging to a cluster are kept, the others are discarded. The inconvenience of this approach is the big data transmission load which may reduce the lifetime of the network. In distributed way, the clustering algorithm is applied at every step, only necessary statistics are sent to the next step for following analysis. Thus the volume of data to transmit can be considerably reduced.

An other method to identify faulty node is to launch a vote. In [22] sensors are deployed randomly in a zone, and we suppose that every sensor has at least 3 neighbors. Sensors are considered as neighboring sensors if they're in the radio range of each other, and each sensor broadcasts periodically to the neighbors its measured data which is then stored in their memory.

Sensors deployed in the same area are supposed to have similar measured values. A sensor S_i is interested in history data when more then half of its neighbors have significantly different values. It can use $\Delta d_{ij}^{\Delta t_l}$ which represents the difference between measured value of sensor S_i and S_j from time t_{l+1} to t_l. The status of the sensor T_i is likely faulty (LF) if the measurements change over time significantly.

The status of sensor S_i is good(GD) if $\forall S_j \in N(S_i)$ and $T_j = LG$ (likely good), $\sum(1 - c_{ij}) - \sum c_{ij} \geq \lceil |N(S_i)|/2 \rceil$, where $N(S_i)$ represents all neighbors of S_i and c_{ij} is a test result generated by S_i and its neighbors. $c_{ij} = 0$ if S_i and S_j have the same status, otherwise $c_{ij} = 1$.

In [23], a fault tolerant clustering mechanism is proposed for sensor networks. Cluster heads evaluate their status and diffuse status update messages to other cluster heads through inter-cluster communication. Faulty cluster head can be identified by vote of all cluster heads. Once the identification is done, the network pass to the next step, system recovery.

If a cluster head becomes faulty, all its cluster members are then divided into smaller groups and merged with neighboring clusters. A sensor S_j belongs to cluster head G_i if $S_i \in RSet_{G_i} \Leftrightarrow (R_{G_i} > d_{S_j \rightarrow G_i}) \wedge (R_{S_{j.max}} > d_{S_j \rightarrow G_i})$ where

$RSet_{G_i}$ is the range set of G_i, $d_{S_j \rightarrow G_i}$ is the distance between G_i and S_j, R_{G_i} and $R_{S_{j,max}}$ are respectively the ranges of G_i and S_j. Once S_j is assigned to G_i, a final set $FSet_{G_i}$ is constructed based on minimum communication cost between sensors and cluster head.

A cluster head can still construct a backup set, denoted $BSet$, containing sensors which belong to its $RSet$, but not its $FSet$. $S_j \in BSet_{G_i} \Leftrightarrow (S_j \in RSet_{G_i}) \wedge (S_j \notin FSet_{G_i})$. If the cluster head of S_j becomes faulty, it can be recovered if it's present in an other cluster head's $BSet$.

In a landslide monitoring application presented in [24], sensors are formed in clusters which contain a cluster head (CH) and a node leader (NL). The NL aggregates the data collected from other members and sends it to CH, which will then forward the data to base station via multi-hop transmission.

For fault tolerance purpose, the intersection zone of 2 overlapping clusters is considered as a sub cluster, which contains only a NL. When a CH is failed, its NL will send the latest aggregated data to the NL of the sub cluster, then the data will be forwarded to the CH of the other cluster. If NL is failed, its CH will take over its work, and a NL election algorithm will be executed at the same time.

We can notice that in sensor networks, one sensor node is barely able to detect system malfunction or recover the network from faulty status alone. The idea of sensor networks is to make sensor nodes cooperate together to achieve a common goal. For fault tolerance, sensor nodes should also work collectively for fault detection and system recovery. We can also see that the basic method of system recovery is to prepare a backup node which takes over the work of the faulty node.

6 Countermeasures against Sensor Node Failure

According to [25], fault tolerance techniques can be designed for and applied to (from lowest to highest) hardware, system software, middleware and application layers. Generally speaking, techniques designed for lower layer, such as hardware layer, are more generic, which means they can usually be applied to different applications. However higher layer techniques are more application-specific, a fault tolerance method is designed specially for a particular application, and it can hardly be used in other applications.

Certainly, fault tolerance methods for application layer are not as portable as the other ones designed for lower layers, but they can be carefully tailored to meet the specific needs of applications. For our parallel computing scheme, we have decided to design and deploy our fault tolerance technique on application layer.

Our fault tolerance method is also based on the idea of backup nodes. Suppose that there are n available members in a cluster, and the cluster head CH needs to perform a parallel scalar multiplication. Instead of involve all available cluster members in parallel computing, we use only $\lfloor \frac{n}{2} \rfloor$ members for parallel computing, the rest of cluster members are used as backup nodes. If the probability of a member becomes faulty is p, which is also the probability that a parallel scalar multiplication fails. The use of backup node can reduce the probability of system failure to $p/2$.

The selection of slaves nodes and of backup nodes is driven by algorithm 1 where L_a is the list of all available cluster members, L_s and L_b are respectively the lists of selected slave nodes and backup nodes.

Algorithm 1. Algorithm of backup selection

Data: L_a
Result: L_s, L_b
Sort(L_a);
forall the $\varphi \in L_a$ **do**
    $\omega \leftarrow getBackup(\varphi)$;
    $L_a \leftarrow L_a - \varphi$;
    $L_a \leftarrow L_a - \omega$;
    $L_s \leftarrow L_s + \varphi$;
    $L_b \leftarrow L_b + \omega$;
end

Before node selection, we sort L_a by the number of its available neighbors in ascending order, since we want the φ having the least neighbors to choose its backup node first. $getBackup()$ is a function which returns the most suitable backup node for φ. Every ω evaluated by multiple parameters, such as RSSI, remaining energy, distance to φ. We always choose a backup node having the most reliable connection.

As we have explained in our last paper [12], to avoid large radio communication overhead, the number of slave nodes participating in parallel computing should be limited at less than 5. Thus the possibility for performing fault tolerant parallel scalar multiplication depends on the number of available cluster members, denoted by n :

- $n \in [0, 1]$: Unable to perform fault tolerant parallel computing.
- $n \in]1, 8[$: Parallel computing using $\lfloor \frac{n}{2} \rfloor$ slaves and $\lfloor \frac{n}{2} \rfloor$ backup nodes.
- $n \in [8, \infty]$: Parallel computing using 4 slaves and 4 backup nodes.

6.1   Result Detection

To deal with the missing result error, we ask the backup node to prepare an other copy of result for the slave that it's monitoring. We can see in figure 2 that tasks are sent not only to slave nodes, but also to backup nodes. Both slave node and backup node have the same task. After computation, if a backup node *detects* that the slave node doesn't send result back to master node, it will send its local copy instead of the slave.

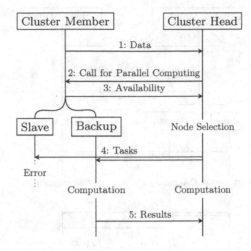

Fig. 2. Parallel scalar multiplication with result detection

Suppose that all cluster members have the same distance to their cluster head. The energy cost of wireless transmission is a function of message size m and distance d, $E_{T_x} = e(m, d)$, and the energy cost of reception is a constant E_{R_x}. We may notice that the parallel scalar multiplication with result detection doesn't consume more energy than the original parallel computing scheme. However, the fault tolerant version takes a little more time, since backup nodes have to wait a small period before sending its result.

6.2   Result Verification

For incorrect result error, the slave node does send result back to its master, but an incorrect one. Just like the case of missing result, both slave node and backup node have the same task.

Backup node is supposed to *verify* the result sent by the slave node. When slave node sends its result, as the backup node is in its radio range, it can also receive the result. Backup node compares the result with its local one. If the results are different, the backup node will send immediately a warning message to their master node so that the result is discarded, and the task in question will be repeated locally by the master node.

When no fault occurs, the system consumes almost the same energy and time than the original version. But when some slave nodes become faulty, the energy and time cost is proportional to the number of faulty nodes.

For the third case, when cluster head is faulty, the system has to execute a cluster head election algorithm such as the one described in [26].

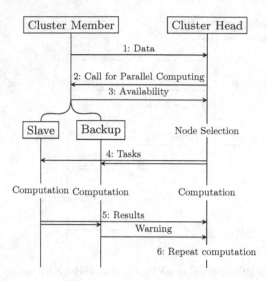

Fig. 3. Parallel scalar multiplication with result verification

7   Simulation and Performance Evaluation

To assess the performance of our method, we have created a simulator in Java which estimates the running time and the energy cost of our fault tolerant parallel computing scheme.

The simulator creates a random sensor cluster in an ideal free space without obstacle, and asks the cluster members to perform parallel scalar multiplications. We suppose that the cluster uses a TDMA based MAC protocol which allows only one sensor to send data at a time. Moreover, all nodes share the same elliptic curve which is defined over a finite prime field and uses $NIST_{192}$ recommended parameters [16].

We also suppose that the sensor nodes communicate with each other using Zigbee protocol whose throughput is studied in [27]. As in sensor networks, most of the energy is consumed during wireless communication, only the energy cost of radio communication is taken into account, and the formula for energy cost estimation is presented in [26] and [28]. In addition, the running time of scalar multiplication is estimated based on the results published in our last paper [12].

The simulator mainly focus on the execution of our parallel computing protocol. Our goal is not to retrieve the precise values of the running time and the energy cost, but to illustrate the impact of our fault tolerance method on the parallel computing scheme. Tests are run is three different cases:

- There are just enough nodes for parallel computing without fault tolerance, but not enough to have a backup node for each slave participating in computation.
- There are enough nodes for parallel computing with the proposed fault tolerance mechanism activated.

- There are enough nodes for fault tolerant parallel computing, but faults occur during the computation.

In our last paper, we have concluded that for efficiency reasons, the maximum number of slaves participating in computation should be limited at 4. We define that n is the number of available cluster members, and the tables 1 and 2 contain the simulation results of the first case where $n \leq 4$.

Table 1. Performance of the parallel computing scheme ($n \leq 4$)

Nb of cluster members	Running time (ms)	Energy cost (mJ)
0	2308.77	0.06639066
1	1158.88	0.17869498
2	777.75	0.27243610
3	588.81	0.34194090
4	476.75	0.41024986

Table 2. Performance of the fault tolerant parallel computing scheme ($n \leq 4$)

Nb of cluster members	Running time (ms)	Energy cost (mJ)
0	2308.70	0.06639066
1	2308.77	0.06639066
2	1159.01	0.16637882
3	1159.01	0.16637882
4	778.01	0.24765018

The results are also graphically illustrated in figures 4. As the node usage is doubled when our fault tolerance method is applied, so on the one hand, only $\lfloor n/2 \rfloor$ nodes can participate in parallel computing and it takes more time to finish the tasks, on the other hand backup nodes don't need to communicate with the cluster head when no fault occurs, the cluster can consumes less energy.

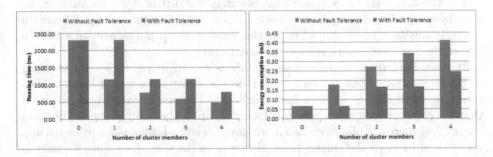

Fig. 4. Running time (ms) and energy cost (mJ) ($n \leq 4$)

In the second case where $n \leq 8$ which means the cluster head always has enough slaves to perform parallel scalar multiplication no matter if our fault tolerance method is used.

Table 3. Performance of the fault tolerant parallel computing scheme ($n \leq 8$)

Nb of slaves	Running time (ms)	Energy cost (mJ)
0	2308.70	0.06639066
1	1159.01	0.16637882
2	778.01	0.24765018
3	589.20	0.34410666
4	477.27	0.43921370

As we can see in table 3 and in figure 5, when our fault tolerance method is used, the cluster needs slightly more time to complete the computation, since more nodes are involved in parallel computing, and backup nodes also need to receive tasks from cluster head during task distribution. The total energy cost increases gradually with increase in number of slaves. The difference of energy cost between the tests with and without fault tolerance is mainly due to the randomness of node deployment.

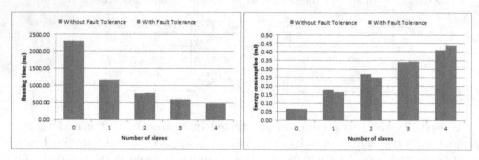

Fig. 5. Running time (ms) and energy consumption (mJ) ($n \leq 8$)

For the 3rd test, we suppose that we may use up to 4 slaves to perform parallel computing, and each slave has a backup node. Some slaves don't function properly during the computation, in this case, backup nodes are supposed to detect the fault and try to recover the computation.

When a backup node detects an erroneous result, it has to send a warning to the cluster head, and the latter will redo the faulty slave's task locally. Thus compared with results without faulty node, we can see in table 4 and figure 6 that the cluster needs more time and energy to finish the computation. The total energy cost increases slightly when more slaves become faulty, since more backup nodes need to warn the cluster head. However as the size of warning message is relatively smaller, the energy cost doesn't increase very fast, its value remains between $0.44mJ$ and $0.45mJ$.

A backup node is also supposed to send result back to cluster head when the slave that it's monitoring doesn't respond at all. However we can notice in table 5 that the running time doesn't increase when more slaves become faulty, since all backup nodes monitor the behavior of slaves and react simultaneously.

Table 4. Performance of the fault tolerance method when erroneous result occurs

Nb of faulty slaves	Running time (ms)	Energy cost (mJ)
0	477.27	0.43921370
1	938.86	0.44161946
2	1400.44	0.44564062
3	1862.03	0.44965998
4	2323.61	0.45207022

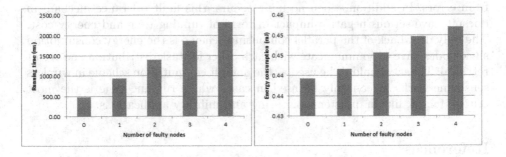

Fig. 6. Performance of the fault tolerance method when erroneous result occurs

Table 5. Performance of the fault tolerance method when missing result occurs

Nb of faulty slaves	Running time (ms)	Energy cost (mJ)
0	477.27	0.43921370
1	517.27	0.43859930
2	517.27	0.47736890
3	517.27	0.49638458
4	517.27	0.47632058

The irregularity of energy cost in figure 7 is due to the random deployment of sensor nodes. In our power model, the energy consumption is proportional to the distance of wireless communication.

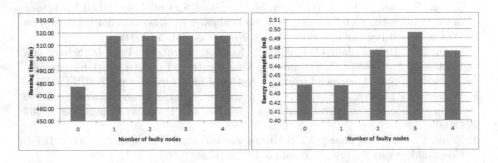

Fig. 7. Performance of the fault tolerance method when missing result occurs

8   Conclusion

In this paper we have proposed parallel computing scheme to accelerate the scalar multiplication on elliptic curves, we have also designed a fault tolerance mechanism which can significantly improve the reliability of the system. We have tested our method by using a simulator, and the results show a considerable acceleration of computation. Even in case of anomaly, such as sensor failure and incorrect result, the system is still able to detect the error and recover the system from errors. In addition, when no fault occurs, this fault tolerance mechanism doesn't have serious negative impact in term of running time and energy cost. The only drawback of the parallel computing scheme is the energy consumption since nodes have to communicate with each other for task distribution and result retrieval. Thus it shouldn't be used as the default computation scheme in wireless sensor networks. it can only be used in cases where running time is the most critical factor, like in disaster monitoring and military applications.

References

1. Akyildiz, I.F., Su, W., Sankarasubramaniam, Y., Cayirci, E.: Wireless sensor networks: a survey. Computer Networks 38(4), 393–422 (2002)
2. Yick, J., Mukherjee, B., Ghosal, D.: Wireless sensor network survey. Computer Networks 52(12), 2292–2330 (2008)
3. Werner-Allen, G., Lorincz, K., Ruiz, M., Marcillo, O., Johnson, J., Lees, J., Welsh, M.: Deploying a wireless sensor network on an active volcano. IEEE Internet Computing 10(2), 18–25 (2006)
4. Kim, S., Pakzad, S., Culler, D., Demmel, J., Fenves, G., Glaser, S., Turon, M.: Wireless sensor networks for structural health monitoring. In: Proceedings of the 4th International Conference on Embedded Networked Sensor Systems, pp. 427–428. ACM (2006)
5. Baker, C.R., Armijo, K., Belka, S., Benhabib, M., Bhargava, V., Burkhart, N., Der Minassians, A., Dervisoglu, G., Gutnik, L., Haick, M.B., et al.: Wireless sensor networks for home health care. In: 21st International Conference on Advanced Information Networking and Applications Workshops, AINA 2007, vol. 2, pp. 832–837. IEEE (2007)
6. Malan, D., Fulford-Jones, T., Welsh, M., Moulton, S.: Codeblue: An ad hoc sensor network infrastructure for emergency medical care. In: International Workshop on Wearable and Implantable Body Sensor Networks, vol. 5 (2004)
7. Gosnell, T., Hall, J., Jam, C., Knapp, D., Koenig, Z., Luke, S., Pohl, B., Schach von Wittenau, A., Wolford, J.: Gamma-ray identification of nuclear weapon materials. Technical report, Lawrence Livermore National Lab, Livermore, CA, US (1997)
8. Walters, J.P., Liang, Z., Shi, W., Chaudhary, V.: Wireless sensor network security: A survey. Security in Distributed, Grid, Mobile, and Pervasive Computing 1, 367 (2007)
9. Zhou, Y., Fang, Y., Zhang, Y.: Securing wireless sensor networks: a survey. IEEE Communications Surveys & Tutorials 10(3), 6–28 (2008)
10. Rivest, R.L., Shamir, A., Adleman, L.: A method for obtaining digital signatures and public-key cryptosystems. Communications of the ACM 21(2), 120–126 (1978)

11. Gordon, D.M.: A survey of fast exponentiation methods. Journal of Algorithms 27(1), 129–146 (1998)
12. Shou, Y., Guyennet, H., Lehsaini, M.: Parallel scalar multiplication on elliptic curves in wireless sensor networks. In: Frey, D., Raynal, M., Sarkar, S., Shyamasundar, R.K., Sinha, P. (eds.) ICDCN 2013. LNCS, vol. 7730, pp. 300–314. Springer, Heidelberg (2013)
13. Koblitz, N.: Elliptic curve cryptosystems. Mathematics of Computation 48(177), 203–209 (1987)
14. Miller, V.S.: Use of elliptic curves in cryptography. In: Williams, H.C. (ed.) CRYPTO 1985. LNCS, vol. 218, pp. 417–426. Springer, Heidelberg (1986)
15. Gura, N., Patel, A., Wander, A., Eberle, H., Shantz, S.C.: Comparing elliptic curve cryptography and RSA on 8-bit cPUs. In: Joye, M., Quisquater, J.-J. (eds.) CHES 2004. LNCS, vol. 3156, pp. 119–132. Springer, Heidelberg (2004)
16. Hankerson, D., Vanstone, S., Menezes, A.: Guide to elliptic curve cryptography. Springer-Verlag New York Inc. (2004)
17. Diffie, W., Hellman, M.: New directions in cryptography. IEEE Transactions on Information Theory 22(6), 644–654 (1976)
18. Lim, C.H., Lee, P.J.: More flexible exponentiation with precomputation. In: Desmedt, Y.G. (ed.) CRYPTO 1994. LNCS, vol. 839, pp. 95–107. Springer, Heidelberg (1994)
19. Mishra, S., Jena, L., Pradhan, A.: Fault tolerance in wireless sensor networks. International Journal 2(10), 146–153 (2012)
20. Rajasegarar, S., Leckie, C., Palaniswami, M., Bezdek, J.C.: Distributed anomaly detection in wireless sensor networks. In: 10th IEEE Singapore International Conference on Communication systems, ICCS 2006, pp. 1–5. IEEE (2006)
21. Eskin, E., Arnold, A., Prerau, M., Portnoy, L., Stolfo, S.: A geometric framework for unsupervised anomaly detection. In: Barbará, D., Jajodia, S. (eds.) Applications of Data Mining in Computer Security. Advances in Information Security, vol. 6, pp. 77–101. Springer, US (2002)
22. Chen, J., Kher, S., Somani, A.: Distributed fault detection of wireless sensor networks. In: Proceedings of the 2006 Workshop on Dependability Issues in Wireless Ad hoc Networks and Sensor Networks, pp. 65–72. ACM (2006)
23. Gupta, G., Younis, M.: Fault-tolerant clustering of wireless sensor networks. In: 2003 IEEE Wireless Communications and Networking, WCNC 2003, pp. 1579–1584. IEEE (2003)
24. Raj, R., Ramesh, M.V., Kumar, S.: Fault tolerant clustering approaches in wireless sensor network for landslide area monitoring. In: Proceedings of the 2008 International Conference on Wireless Networks (ICWN 2008), vol. 1, pp. 107–113 (2008)
25. Koushanfar, F., Potkonjak, M., Sangiovanni-vincentelli, A.: Fault tolerance in wireless sensor networks. In: Handbook of Sensor Networks: Compact Wireless and Wired Sensing Systems (2004)
26. Heinzelman, W.R., Chandrakasan, A., Balakrishnan, H.: Energy-efficient communication protocol for wireless microsensor networks. In: Proceedings of the 33rd Annual Hawaii International Conference on System Sciences. IEEE (2000)
27. Burchfield, T.R., Venkatesan, S., Weiner, D.: Maximizing throughput in zigbee wireless networks through analysis, simulations and implementations. In: Proceedings of the International Workshop on Localized Algorithms and Protocols for Wireless Sensor Networks Santa Fe, pp. 15–29. Citeseer, New Mexico (2007)
28. Heinzelman, W.B., Chandrakasan, A.P., Balakrishnan, H., et al.: An application-specific protocol architecture for wireless microsensor networks. IEEE Transactions on Wireless Communications 1(4), 660–670 (2002)

Conflict Resolution in Heterogeneous Co-allied MANET: A Formal Approach

Soumya Maity and Soumya K. Ghosh

School of Information Technology
Indian Institute of Technology Kharagpur
India 721302
{soumyam,skg}@iitkgp.ac.in

Abstract. Implementing a conflict free access control policies for coallied networks where different organizations involve for a common goal is becoming important. In mission-critical scenarios, different organizational networks cooperate to form a single mobile ad hoc network to implement their respective operations. These teams (or quads) are operated under different set of local policies for their own security, which results heterogeneity in access control. Each team wants to preserve its access control policies at maximum level. Moreover, a set of *allied policies* governs the interaction among the different teams, which may conflict with their local policies. In mobile ad hoc networks this becomes more challenging due to absence of network perimeter and mobility. In addition, the policy rules may have local and transitive conflicts. To achieve successful completion of the mission, compromising with the stringency of the enforcement of the conflicting rules for the quads may be required. In this paper, we propose a formal method to find the optimal negotiation of the policy rules to preserve the mission. The efficacy of the work lies on optimizing the enforcement of access control policies to achieve the coalition instead of negating the policy.

Keywords: Policy Negotiation, MANET, Access Control.

1 Introduction

The co-allied networks or teams are referred as *quad*. Each quad has its own access control policies according to the different types of security requirements. Each node follows a set of security protocols to implement the specifications. So, on basis of local policy, the network is *heterogeneous*. However, the collection or summation of these distributed implementations may violate the overall security. There may exist hidden access paths for the transitive property of the access policies. Moreover, the dynamic topology, changing values of trust relation, and absence of network perimeter increases the chance of security violations. As an example, a given topology may ensure the implementation to be conforming the specification, but a certain change in topology due to the mobility of the nodes may create a violation.

M. Chatterjee et al. (Eds.): ICDCN 2014, LNCS 8314, pp. 332–346, 2014.

In this paper, a formal mechanism to find the optimized set of trust-based policy implementation for consolidated policies has been proposed. As formal verification is a promising approach to correctly and completely verify implementation with specification, the problem has been modeled to a satisfiability problem. The efficiency of this approach has been discussed later. We have formally modeled the network and the policies (both local and allied). We have modeled the implementation of each policy in a varying range of strictness of enforcement. The highest level of implementation is keeping the rule as it is without compromising and lowest level of implementation is removing the policy rule from the quad. The framework finds the solution with highest level of enforcement of each of the policy rule that does not conflict with allied policy.

1.1 Motivating Example

MANET is actively used in mission critical scenario where people from different organizations with different domain of expertise, work together for a rescue mission. In that scenario, each of them require different set of policies for their operation. Reachability and avoidance of disconnectivity are critical issues.

We have taken an example of coallied MANET where coalition has been formed between three organizations, namely Quad1, Quad2 and Quad3. For simplicity of this example, we assume that only service running in each note is *getLocation()*, which gives the present coordinate of the requested node.

Each of the nodes can request another node to share its current location, and the requested node sends back its own location. There is a policy enforced on all the nodes of Quad1: "`Share the location information with nodes which are only from the same quad if there is a trusted route`". Now, for the coalition between the Quad1, Quad2 and Quad3 requires an allied policy, "`Nodes of Quad2 needs to know the area where a node from Quad1 is located.`" Logically, the former local policy of Quad1 is conflicting the allied policy. Hence, Quad1 needs to compromise with the policy. Just removing or negating the local policy from Quad1 is not a desirable solution. Moreover, transitivity of policy rules, mobility of the nodes, and variation of trust values over time lead to conflicts in policies. Our framework checks for such conflicts and suggests the optimal implementation. In this case, our system proposes a better solution to implement an optimized *conciliated policy* as,

"`Share the exact location information nodes from Quad1 if there is a trusted route.`
`or`
`Share approximate location (like a defined boundary) information with Quad2 if there is very high trust value of the requesting node`"

Instead of negating the policy itself, our framework find an optimal concilliation by negotiating with the stringency the implementation level of the policy. The rest of the paper is organized as follows. Section 2 describes the overview of the proposed formal system. The system has three units, each of the units are elaborately explained. The formal modeling of network instance and network access policies are explained in section 2.1 and 2.2 respectively. Section 2.3

represents the process of optimization of conciliated policies. The implementation and analysis on the results are shown in section 3. Related works are written in section 4 with the differences between those aproaches with oours. Section 5 concludes the paper with remarks and future direction of the work.

2   Overview of Proposed Formal System

Satisfiability (SAT) based formal framework for generating negotiated policy rules between the quads (allied parties) has been proposed in this work. The input to this framework is the different parameters of the network at particular instance of time. The output is an optimal conciliated policy implementation. It has three modules(refer to figure.1), namely (A) *Network Instance Modeler*, (B) *Network Access Modeler* and (C) *Access Control Optimizer*.

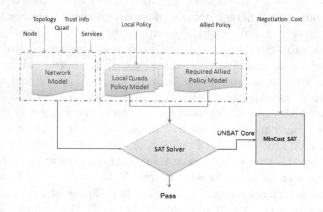

Fig. 1. Architecture of Proposed System

The *Network Instance Modeler* parses the specification and generates a formal model of the network instance which represents the network topology. As the nodes are mobile, the topology is constantly changing. Taking a snapshot at a particular instance is not enough. Hence, the network model should capture the mobility. We have used a mobility model to generate a valid set of the topologies that the network follows. We call this set as *Closure of Topology*. The topology comprises of various network resources. The network resources and their properties have been encoded into Boolean logic. In this work we are not proposing a completely new mobility model. For simulation random way-point model [1] has been considered. For the purpose of verification using Boolean satisfiability (SAT) based decision procedure, our framework converts the network instance model into Conjugal Normal Form (CNF) clauses [2].

The local policy specifications are encoded into Boolean logic by the *Network Access Modeler*. The allied policy requirement is also modeled under the same formalism and converted into CNF clauses. Finally, our framework uses zChaff SAT solver for checking the satisfiability of the conjunction of these CNF clauses. The satisfiable result (i.e., does not find any counter-example) indicates that there is no violation of policies or the policies are non-conflicting and consolidatable. Otherwise, the conflicting policies from unsatisfiable core are extracted. Each of the possible implementation level of the conflicting policies are assigned with a numeric weight. Finally, these implementation levels along with the allied policy are modeled as a Minimum-Cost SAT problem [3] [4] for generating optimized policy negotiation. The satisfiable instance of the *Min-Cost SAT* represents the conflict-free conciliated policy implementation with minimal cost. It systematically generates the optimal solution by iterating the *Min-Cost SAT* procedure for all the conflicting rules.

2.1 Network Instance Modeler

Instance Modeler (NIM) is responsibe for converting the network instance into boolean clauses. For this purpose, we have modeled the network instance.

A MANET is a network formed by n nodes (n being a real positive number). N denotes the set nodes. Every node has a unique ID ($N_{id} \in N$) and a Quad ($q \in Q$). The unique ID is an address within a fixed global address space. The quad is one the set of allied parties (Q). We assume a random distribution of the node IDs. This distribution is ensured by mapping some device specific address, e.g. such as Internet host names, IP addresses, or MAC addresses, to the node IDs using a strong hash function (not further specified here). Consider the resulting addresses as given by a static mapping from nodes to some abstract domain of addresses. The underlying network protocols ensures that Node $N_i \in N$ can send data packet to another node $N_j \in N, i \neq j$ if N_j is reachable to N_i.

Definition 1 (Network Instance). A Network Instance NI is defined as two tuples $\langle N, I \rangle$, where N is the set of finite hosts, and I is the connectivity matrix of all the nodes in N.

A node $n \in N$ has two attributes, ID and Quad. $n.ID$ is a positive real number i such that $\forall n' \in \{N - n\} \mid n'.ID \neq i$. In the paper n_i conventionally represents $n_i \in N \wedge N_i.ID = i$. Q is the set of the identifiers of the allied parties. $n.Quad$ must be in Q. Connectivity matrix I is a $|N| \times |N|$ matrix where the non diagonal entries $a_{ij} = 1$ if n_j is in the radio range of n_i, eventually n_i can directly communicate with n_j, else $a_{ij} = 0$. If $a_{ij} = 0$ in I, then n_j is said to be a neighbor of n_i, denoted as $Neighbor(n_i, n_j)$.

A node $n \in N$ has some properties like mobility, trust, reachability and it can execute some functions like request, response, forward, discard, attack. We assumed our model to be closed under these properties and functions.

Property [Mobility]: Each node $n \in N$ has a coordinate identifying its geographic position on the plane. As nodes may move, their positions change over time. The current position of a node is always known. The position of n is defined by $POS(n)$. Mobility of a node n after time interval t, denoted as $\mu(n, t)$ is the property of the node n for which the value of $POS(n)$ at t=0 may differ from the value of $POS(n)$ at t=t. As the position the of the nodes changes, the connectivity matrix also changes. So, if at time instance t=0, the Connectivity Matrix was $I(0)$ and at time = t, due to the mobility of the nodes, Connectivity Matrix becomes $I(t)$. $I(0) \leadsto_t I(t)$ denotes the connectivity matrix $I(0)$ changed to $I(t)$ after time interval t. Mobility of a network instance $\Upsilon_{NI}(N, I, t)$ is defined as $(\forall n \in N, \sum \mu(n, t) \Rightarrow I(0) \leadsto_t I(t)) \Rightarrow NI'(N, I(t), t)$. All the possible values of $I(t)$ comprises to form a set of connectivity matrices called *Closure of Topology (I*)*.

We model the impact of mobility, deletions and additions of nodes by representing the network topology at any point in time with a NN adjacency matrix denoted by $I(t)$.

a_{ij}^* is defined as, $\bigvee\limits_{t=0}^{t} a_{ij}(t)$ That means, if at any point of time node i and node j are directly connected, $a_{ij}^* = 1$, otherwise 0.

Closure of topology I^* is defined by the matrix,

$$
I^* = \begin{bmatrix}
a_{11}^* & a_{12}^* & a_{13}^* & \cdots & a_{1n}^* \\
a_{21}^* & a_{22}^* & a_{23}^* & \cdots & a_{2n}^* \\
a_{31}^* & a_{32}^* & a_{33}^* & \cdots & a_{3n}^* \\
\cdot & \cdot & \cdot & & \cdot \\
\cdot & \cdot & \cdot & & \cdot \\
\cdot & \cdot & \cdot & & \cdot \\
a_{n1}^* & a_{n2}^* & a_{n3}^* & \cdots & a_{nn}^*
\end{bmatrix}
$$

This matrix captures the topology of the network over time interval t. Hence, this matrix is used for modeling the network instead of a snapshot of the topology at a particular instance.

Property [Trust]: All the nodes in the network might not be equally trustworthy.A proper trust model based on recommendation, behavioral analysis, central certification etc assigns a trust value to a node with respect to a particular node. A number of trust models have been proposed by the researcher that are able to quantitatively calculate trust value of other nodes over time. Proposing a new trust model is not in the scope of this paper. We assume an underlying trust model gives a trust value of all other nodes with respect to a given nodes. The range of trust value is scaled in 0 to 1. The detail trust model has been described in our previous work [5]. The underlying trust model ensures that each node N_i measures trust value $\tau(n_i, n_j)$ of another node N_j based on the basis a set of evidences E_i. These evidences E_i are captured by individual nodes N_i. On the basis of the set of trust values ($T = \tau_{n_i}(n_j), \forall i \forall j, i \neq j$), the node performs certain actions or takes certain decisions, denoted as A_i. Trust $\tau(n_i, n_j)$ of a node n_j with respect to node N_i is defined as a real number within range [0,1]. $\tau(n_i, n_j) = 0$ denotes n_j is not trustworthy to n_i. The untrustworthiness $u(n_i, n_j)$ of n_j with respect to n_i is defined as $(1 - \tau(n_i, n_j))$.

Property [Reachability]: A node $n_i \in N$ is said to be *reachable* to $n_j \in N$ if n_i can communicate with n_j, directly or indirectly. It is denoted as $Reachable(n_i, n_j)$.

The necessary condition for every node must hold a reachability property with at least another node n_i that also holds this necessary condition.

$Reachable(n_i, n_j) \Rightarrow Neighbor(n_i, n_j) \lor \exists n_1 \exists n_2 \exists n_3 ... \exists n_x, x < |N| \mid (Neighbor(n_i, n_1) \land Neighbor(n_2, n_3) \land ... \land Neighbor(n_{x-1}, n_x) \land Neighbor(n_x, n_j))$.

Thus it can be deduced that, $Neighbor(n_i, n_j)$ corresponds to direct reachability. $Reachable(n_i, n_j)$ also eventually implies that there is a valid *route* (refer to Definition 2) from n_i to n_j.

Definition 2 (Route). Route $R(n_i, n_j)$ is defined as an ordered set of nodes that forward the network traffic from $n_i \in N$ to $n_j \in N$ if $Reachable(n_i, n_j)$. From the definition of reachability, $\exists n_1 \exists n_2 \exists n_3 ... \exists n_x, x < |N| \mid (Neighbor(n_i, n_1) \land Neighbor(n_2, n_3) \land ... \land Neighbor(n_{x-1}, n_x) \land Neighbor(n_x, n_j))$, the ordered set $\{n_i, n_1, n_2, ...n_x, n_j\}$ is the Route $R(n_i, n_j)$.

Definition 3 (Trust of a Route). Trust of a route is a quantitative measure of how trustworthy the route is. For a route $R(n_i, n_j)$ any member n_x of ordered set $\{n_i, n_1, n_2, ...n_x, ...n_j\}$ has a particular trust value with respect to n_i, $\tau(n_x, n_j)$. Set U, represents the untrustworthiness of all the members of $R(n_i, n_j)$ with respect to its previous one, i.e $U = \forall n_x \in R(n_(i+1), n_j), (1 - \tau(n_x, n(x-1)))$. Now the Trust of the route $R(n_i, n_j)$ is defined as $T_{R(n_i, n_j)} = 1 - (u_i \times u_i + 1 \times ....u_j)$.

2.1.1 Reduction in Boolean Model

The boolean reduction process starts with mapping of the Network Instance into boolean variables. The network instance has components like quads, nodes, connectivity matrix and trust matrix. If there are q number of quads, $\lceil \log_2 q \rceil$ bits are required to represent it. For our case we have assumed 16 quads. Thus, four boolean variables namely q_3, q_2, q_1, q_0 are required to represent a quad. Similarly, if a quad has maximum 128 nodes, seven boolean variables, $n_6..., n_1, n_0$ are used to represent a node. Function $\mathcal{FQ}(q3, q_2, q_1, q_0)$ represents a quad or a set of quads and function $\mathcal{FN}(n_6, ...n_1, n_0)$ represents the nodes. So, $\mathcal{FNode} := \mathcal{FQ} \land \mathcal{FN}$ can uniquely represent a set of nodes in the network. A function represents a network resource means, it gives an output TRUE value if that resource exists, it gives FALSE otherwise. Just as an example if, 0101 is a quad, then $\mathcal{FQ} \Leftrightarrow \neg q_3 \land q_2 \land \neg q_2 \land q_1$. Each of the services is represented by variables $r_0, r_1...r_7$. Boolean function $\mathcal{FServ}$ on the variables $r_0, r_2...$ represents services in the network. The function $\mathcal{FI} : \mathcal{FNode} X \mathcal{FNode} \rightarrow 0, 1$ is defined to check neighborhood of a node from $\mathcal{P}$. The underlying trust model gives the trust matrix T, as defined in Section 2.1. Just like the connectivity matrix, trust matrix is also represented by $\mathcal{T}(t_0, t_1, t_2, t_3....t_n)$. The function $\mathcal{FT} : \mathcal{FNode} X \mathcal{FNode} \rightarrow 0, 1$ is defined to get the trust value of a node with respect to another from the $\mathcal{T}$. Output of $\mathcal{FT}$ is $TRUE$ if trust value $\tau \leq C, 0 < C < 1$ and $FALSE$ otherwise. This is how the network instance is reduced to boolean clauses. Table 1 shows procedure and an example for boolean reduction of network.

Table 1. Boolean mapping of the Model

Quad(Q) : $\mathcal{FQ}(q_0, q_1, ...q_4)$
Node(N) : $\mathcal{FN}(d_0, d_1, ..., d_6)$
Service(P) : $\mathcal{FP}(r_0, r_1..., r_7)$
ConnectivityMatrix(I) : $I(p_0, p_1, ...p_144)$
TrustMatrix(T) : $\mathcal{T}(t_0, t_1, ...t_144)$

Procedure Reduce_Network_Instance()
Input: Network Instance NI
Output: Boolean Reduction of Network Instance M
BEGIN
1.   For all nodes
2. $Node \Leftrightarrow Node \vee \left(\mathcal{FQ}(q_0, q_1...q_4) \wedge \mathcal{FN}(n_0, n_1...n_7) \wedge \mathcal{FServ}(r_0, r_1..r_7) \right)$
3. $I \Leftrightarrow \mathcal{FI}(p_0, p_1...p_144)$
4. $T \Leftrightarrow \mathcal{T}(t_0, t_1, ...t_{144})$
5. $G \Leftrightarrow Node \wedge I \wedge T$
6.   Return M
7.END

Example: Boolean Reduction of a Network Instance
Input:
Network Specification, Closure of Topology and Trust Values
Output:
$q1 \Leftrightarrow \neg q_1 \wedge \neg q_0$; as, $q_1 = 00$
$q2 \Leftrightarrow \neg q_1 \wedge q_0$; as, $q_2 = 01$
$n1 \Leftrightarrow q_1 \wedge \neg n_1 \wedge \neg n_0$; as,$n_0 = 00$
$n2 \Leftrightarrow q_2 \neg q_1 \wedge q_0 \wedge \neg n_1 \wedge n_0$; as $n_2 = 01$.
$serv1 \Leftrightarrow \neg r_1 \wedge \neg r_0$
$serv2 \Leftrightarrow \neg r_1 \wedge r_0$
$serv3 \Leftrightarrow r_1 \wedge \neg r_0$
$N \Leftrightarrow n_1 \wedge \neg r_1 \vee n_2 \wedge (r_1 \wedge \neg r_0 \vee \neg r_1 \wedge r_0)$
$I \Leftrightarrow p_0 \wedge \neg p_1 \wedge p_2 \wedge p_3$
$T \Leftrightarrow t_0 \wedge \neg t_1 \wedge t_2 \neg t_3$;as $\tau(n_2, n_1) > C$, C is taken as 0.5
$M \Leftrightarrow N \wedge I \wedge T$

Note: For simplicity, less number of variables are considered for the example.

2.2   Network Access Modeler

Different policy rules are applied on Network Instance. Depending on the policy rules [6] a node takes the decision whether to reply to a request for a specific service or not. The access control on the network requires to be formally modeled for Network Access Modeler to deduce the Boolean clauses. The network access model represents the policies applied on the network. Policy rules are written for the quads. A policy rule P between a source node n_s and a destination node n_d defines whether n_d will respond positively for the request made by n_s for the service $serv$.

Definition 4 (Policy Rule). *Policy Rule P can be defined as four tuples,* $\langle SRC, DST, Serv, Condtion \rangle$ *along with an attribute Action* $\in \{+, -\}$, *where* $SRC, DST \subseteq N$ *and* $request(src, dst, Serv) \wedge src \in SRC \wedge dst \in DST$. *The Condition is a boolean function on the Network Instance (NI). Condition must be true for a valid Policy Rule. All* $dst \in DST$ *executes for the above mentioned request according to attribute Action.*

$(P.Action = `+') \Rightarrow response(dst, src, Serv) \wedge (P.Action = `-') \Rightarrow \neg response$ $(dst, src, Serv)$. Multiple conditions will be expressed as conjunction. There are four types of condition,

1) [Subsuming Condition]: The condition restricts the access on the basis of the source node that tries request for a service. A policy rule action may depend on the containment of the requesting node in a specified set of nodes. For a Policy Rule P, a subsuming condition is modeled as, $P.src \in N' \subseteq N$. Typically the set N' is a quad or a group of quads. As an example of such Subsuming Condition, the policy rule might be *Any node of Quad1 can access the exact position information of another node of Quad1. The Node n_3 of Quad2 can access exact information of any other nodes of Quad2. Other nodes of Quad2 are entitled to get the approximate location of the Quad2 devices."* This policy can be modeled as,

$P1 := \langle N_1, N_2, getExactLocation(), \forall n \in N_1, \forall n' \in N_2(n.quad == 1 \land n'.quad == 1)\rangle+$

All other rules are denied by default.

2) [Trust Condition]: The condition that controls the access on a service involving trust of the route or trust of the requesting nodes falls under this category. There is an assumption all the nodes have agreed upon a same trust model. Action of the policy rule $P_n \langle N_1, N_2, getExactLocation(), \forall n \in N_1, \forall n' \in N_2 T(n, n') \geq K \rangle$ allows the access from n to n' for service $getExactLocation()$ if, the trust of route between them has a value greater than K, where K is a positive real number. For our model, we have normalized K within the range of 0 to 10. $P_n \langle N_1, n', getExactLocation(), \forall n \in N_1, \tau(n', n) \geq K \rangle$ is such kind of policy rules. In our example the policy "N3 and N4 is permitted to access exact location information of devices from Quad2 if there is a route with minimum trust value 5 and requesting node can have trust value below 4. Otherwise U1 and U3 can access only an approximate location of any UK device" can be modeled as follows,

$P2 := \langle N_1, N_2, getExactLocation(), \forall n \in N_1, \forall n' \in N_2 T(n, n') \geq 5 \land \tau(n', n) \geq 4 \rangle+$. The other rules are by default deny.

3) [Event-based Condition]: Event-based condition controls the access to a service on occurrence of an event. Each event is represented by a boolean function. If the event happens, the function becomes true. For example, the nodes of Quad3 (assuming it is the Red Cross Society) can access the service $getExactLocation()$ only if a casualty happens. $IsCasualtyHappened()$ is the function that return boolean $True$ when casualty takes place in the area. The policy rule will modeled as,

$P3 := \langle n, n', getExactLocation(), n.quad == 3 \land \forall n' \in N \land IsCasualtyHappened()$

4) [Topology Condition]: Topology conditions restrict the access for certain spatial condition that affects the topology of the network. These kind of conditions are modeled based on two functions, $neighbor(n, n')$ and $reachable(n, n')$. The policy can be framed like "n_5 will share its exact location with n_6 if n_3 is not in its radio range". This can be modeled as,

$P4 := \langle n_6, n_5, getExactLocation(), \neg neighbor (n_6, n_3)\rangle+$.

Another example of this category is "n_7 and n_8 can access approximate location of any device of Quad1 if the intermediate nodes are from Quad1 only". This policy is reflected in our model as,

$P5 := \langle n_7, n_8, getApproxLocation(), \forall n \in R(n_7, n_8)n.quad == 1 \rangle +$ Topology condition also can be modeled using Connectivity Matrix I of the network instance.

2.2.1   Boolean Modeling of Policy Rules

Node policybase $P_n(n_i)$ of a node $n_i \in N$ is a set of policy rules such that, $\forall P, P.Dest = n_i \Leftrightarrow P \in P_n(n_i)$. Node Permitted Policybase $P_n^+(n_i) \subseteq P_n(n_i)$ of a node $n_i \in N$ is the set of policy rules for which, $\forall P \in P_n^+(n_i), P.Action =$ '+'. Similarly, Node Denied Policybase can be defined as $\forall P \in P_n^-(n_i) \subseteq P_n(n_i), P.Action =$ '−'. Quad Policy Set $P_q(Q_i)$ is $\forall n \in N \wedge n.quad = Q_1, \cup P_n(n)$. Similarly we can define Quad Permitted Policybase $P_q^+(Q_i)$ and Quad Denied policybase $P_q^-(Q_i)$.

Definition 5 (Consolidated Policy Model). Consolidated Policy Model M_c is the summation of all the policy rules. Consolidated Permitted Policybase P_c^+ may be defined as $\cup_{\forall Q} P_q^+(Q)$ and Consolidated Denied Policybase P_c^- is $\cup_{\forall Q} P_q^-(Q)$. Consolidated Permitted Policy Model M_c^+ is given by $\forall P_i \in P_c^+, \vee P_i$. Consolidated Denied Policy Model M_c^- is $\forall P_i \in P_c^-, \wedge P_i$. If there are n numbers of Permit Rules in the model, $M_c^+ := (P_1^+ \vee (P_2^+ \vee ... P_n^+)$. Similarly, for n' number of Deny rules, $M_c^- := (P_1^- \vee (P_2^- \vee ... P_n^-)$. Now Consolidated Policy Model M_c is defined as $(M_c^+ \wedge M_c^-)$.

The policy rules may have conflicts and redundancy. The policy refinement is necessary for a correct and sound Policy Model. The conflicts can be analyzed in our framework. There might be intra node conflicts, inter node conflicts or allied policy conflicts. *Intra node conflicts* is defined as $\exists P, P \in P \in P_n^+(n_i) \wedge P \in P \in P_n^-(n_i)$. Where as *inter rule conflicts* is $\exists P_1 \in P_n^+(n_1) \cap P_q^-(Q_i), \exists P_2 \in P_n^-(n_2) \cap P_q^-(Q_i), P_1.src == P_2.src \wedge P_1.dst, P_2.dst \in Q_i \wedge P_1.serv == P_2.serv \wedge P_1.condition = P_2.condition$. Inter rule conflict is a superset of intra rule conflicts as, $P_1.dst \equiv P_2.dst \Rightarrow n_1 \equiv n_2$.

Definition 6 (Allied Policy). Allied policy A of a network instance NI is the set of high level specification of the behaviors or access control mechanism set by the corresponding authorities of the allied quads. The allied policy A can be modeled as a set of abstract policy rules P' that are not specific to a node. A can be specified in natural language or any higher level specification language. The corresponding parser will map the semantics to low level policy rules.

Now, A is the expected or desired behavior of the consolidated policy. M_c is the consolidated policy model. We need to check if $A \wedge M_c$ is satisfiable or not. We will find the unsatisfiable core. The unsat-core contains the conflicting policies. If the boolean model is satisfied then the policies are non-conflicting thus there is no need for further optimization.

The boolean reduction of the network access model requires functional mapping of the rule components into boolean clauses. The procedure is explained with an example in table 2.

Table 2. Boolean mapping of the Policy Rule

Service(P):FP($r_0, r_1, ... r_8$) Src(SIP):FS($s_0, s_1, ... s_1 1$) Dst(DIP):FD($d_0, d_1 ..., d_1 1$) Condition(Cond):FC($c_0, c_1 ... c_3 2$) Action(g):$A(g)$
Procedure Reduce_Rule() **Input:** A Policy Rule r_i **Output:** Boolean Reduction of the rule r_i BEGIN 1. $P_i \Leftrightarrow FP_i(r_0, r_1, r_2 .. r_8) \wedge$ 2. $SIP_i \Leftrightarrow FS_i(s_0, s_1, ... s_1 1) \wedge$ 3. $DIP_i \Leftrightarrow FD_i(d_0, d_1, ..., d_1 1) \wedge$ 4. $Cond_i \Leftrightarrow FC_i(c_0, c_1, ... c_3 1) \wedge$ 5. $r_i \Leftrightarrow Serv_i \wedge SIP_i \wedge DIP_i \wedge Cond_i$ 6.   Return r_i END
Example: Boolean Reduction of a rule **Rule(r_1) :** **ALLOW** $\{n_1, n_3\}$, n_2, $serv1$ IF $trust(n_1) > .3$ $P_1 \equiv serv1 \Leftrightarrow (\neg r_1 \wedge r_0)$ $SIP_1 \equiv \{n_1, n_3\} \Leftrightarrow \neg s_0$; as $n_3 = 10$, $FS(s_1, s_0) = \neg s_0$ $DIP_1 \equiv n_2 \Leftrightarrow d_0 \wedge \neg d_1$ $Cond_i \equiv \{trust(n_1) > .3\} \Leftrightarrow \{\mathcal{FT}\_node(n_1) > .3\} \odot c_0$ $r_i \Leftrightarrow (P_1 \wedge SIP_1 \wedge DIP_1 \wedge Cond_1)$

2.3 Access Control Optimizer

PIO unit of the framework (refer to section 2) suggests the optimized policy which is required to achieve the coalition. All its possible implementation level has been assigned with weight. All those implementations along with the allied policy is modeled as a Minimum-Cost SAT problem [3].This unit models the policy base as a minimum-cost satisfiability problem [3] and uses min-cost sat-solver for analysis. This is an iterative process for each of the conflicting policy rule.

We have defined a range of enforcement levels of priority for the policy rules. Each of the policy rule can be enforced in one of these levels. The corresponding administrators decide the priority level of the rule. Each of the services are classified according to approximation level. Thus a service can be replied back with sharing the critical information fully or partly or none. As an example, if getLocation() is a service, getExactLocation(), getApproximateLocation(),noLocationInfo() etc are the approximation level of that service. The administrator of the quad determines these approximation level of a service.

Definition 7 (Enforcement Level of Policy Rules). Enforcement Level of a policy rule P $\rangle N', n_i, SERV, COND \langle \pm$, can be defined as a set of policy rules $\{P_1^*, P_2^*, P_3^* ... P_n^*\}$ such that, $P_1^* := P$ and $P_n^* := \rangle N', n_i, SERV \langle +$ (all permit) and $P_2^*, P_3^* ... P_{n-1}^*$ are the policy with same source and destination, but with varying approximation level of service (SERV) and strictness of condition (COND). Enforcement level of a policy can be written as $\rangle N', n_i, SERV_i, COND_i \langle \pm$. The administrator of the allied quads need to categorize all the enforcement level of a policy rule. The administrator also needs to assign cost for each of the enforcement level.

The cost of an enforcement level P_x^* is defined as the cost $c_x \in 1, 2, 3, 4, 5 \ldots 100$ that is associated to the it. If, P is a conflicting rule, $(P_1^* \vee P_2^* \vee P_3^* \ldots \vee P_n^*) \wedge A$ is the boolean function ϕ. The goal of the model is to find a variable assignment $X \in \{0, 1\}^n$ such that X satisfies the boolean formula ϕ and minimizes $C = \sum_{i=1}^{n} c_i x_i$, where $x_i \in \{0, 1\}$ and $1 \leq i \leq n$. In the satisfiability instance, set of all the P_i^* for which corresponding variables in X are true, is the desired conciliated policy. The process is repeated for each of the conflicting policy rules.

3   Experimentation

In this section, we show the performance analysis and feasibility studies of the proposed framework. We have tested our framework for more than 40 networks with varying loads and policy specifications. We focus our study on the time and space requirement for building and running the model. We study the effect of several parameters like, number of nodes, number of quads, number of policy rules, enforcement levels of each policy rules etc. We have varied the parameters to thoroughly test the network. A random topology is generated as a mesh for the tests. We have built a random policy generator that generates a number of policy rules for the testing. Zchaff [2] and its minimal cost zchaff extension [3] is used for model checking. Modeling time to generate the CNF and SAT execution time are the main performance concerns. Number of variables and clauses generated for the CNF, affect on the space complexity, which is a major feasibility concern. Typically, for 4 quads, each with 8 nodes in a network having total number of policy rules 100 and 5 enforcement levels, the parsing time is 0.009 second, SAT execution time is 0.005 seconds and number of variables used 232 and number of clauses are 856. We have evaluated our framework in 50 different test networks with more than 1000 nodes and 1000 randomly generated security policies. In each cases, the conflict analysis and optimal solution generation times lies within 14 seconds. In addition, the maximum space requirement for modeling and analysis is $1.4MB$. Impact of different parameters on the model is discussed bellow.

Impact of Network Size: Network size depends on number of quads and number of nodes. As we have modeled the nodes as boolean variables, n number of nodes can be represented by $\log_2 n$ boolean variables, we have varied the number of nodes as a power of 2. The number of variables used for the generating the CNF for SATsolver, the CNF generation time and SAT execution time with varying number of nodes and quads are plotted in Figure 2a. CNF generation time is polynomially increasing with network size as parsing time of the whole network increases for addition of each single bit. Where as SAT execution time is almost constant and space complexity becomes linear.

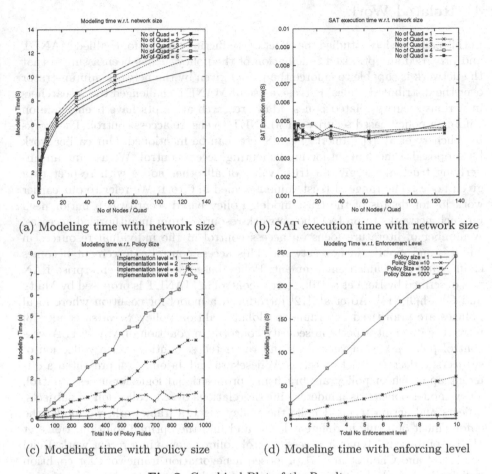

(a) Modeling time with network size   (b) SAT execution time with network size

(c) Modeling time with policy size   (d) Modeling time with enforcing level

Fig. 2. Graphical Plot of the Results

Impact of Policy Size: Policy size represents the summation of number of policy rules to each quads and the number of allied policies. Each of the policy rules is modeled into constant number of boolean variables. So the modeling time varies linearly with the number of policy rules. The figure 2c confirms the relation. Because it depends on the number of conflicting rules in policybase. As we have generated random rules, conflicts also occurs in irregular pattern.

Impact of Enforcement Level: Each of the policy rules may have different enforcement level. Maximum number of level is taken as 10. The minimum number of level enforced is 1, i.e. the rule cannot be compromised. Modeling the enforcement level maintains a linear proportion with policy rules (figure 2d). The space complexity follows the similar pattern of parsing time, as parsing for each level is almost constant. It can be noted that for lesser number of enforcement level, it gives better performance. Although, minimizing the level increases the probability of unsatisfiability, causing no optimal solution.

4   Related Work

In this paper we have studied the effect of conflicting policies for coallied MANET and proposed an optimized conciliation of the policy. It has been assumed that the network is capable to enforce the policy given by the network administrator over the distributed nodes. Pervasive use of MANET challenged the researchers in various security related issues. Many research attempts have been made on enforcing policy based security for MANET to ensure access control. The works by Alichery et al. [7], Mulert et al. [8] etc. can be mentioned. Our earlier work [9] proposed a mechanism for implementing access control. We assume an underlying trust model gives a trust value of all other nodes with respect to a given nodes. The range of trust value is scaled in 0 to 1. We refer to our earlier work [5] for details of the trust model. Policy based security is a major need for such networks to protect the network resources from unauthorized accesses. A number of literature focus on access control in the individual resources in wireless and mobile ad hoc network. This access control enforcement becomes challenging in co-allied environment. Policy based security for enterprise LAN was described by Bera et al [10]. Access control in MANET is proposed by Maity and Ghosh[9], [11]. Ao et al. [12] introduced a model for coalition where local policies are prioritized according to global coalition policy. Srivatsa et al. [13] introduce different aspects in security concerns in coalition of MANET. Access control policies have a very clear and restricted semantics over a collection of subjects, objects and action terms. Wijesekera and Jajodia [14] presented a different approach of policy algebra using propositional logic for access control. They model policies as nondeterministic relations over a collection of subjects, objects and action terms. Unlike the policy algebra framework, we model the enforcement of a rule in different levels and find the optimal solution. Helge et al. [15] proposed a dynamic access control policy algebra in a recent work. Beigi et al. [16] and Chen et al. [17] proposed a negotiation framework for coalition policies in MANET . Their work mainly based on an automated negotiation schemes using rule taxonomy. The proposed framework by Beigi et al. enables different network entities to collaborate and negotiate their offers in reaching a mutual goal. Our model is different from negotiation as we are trying to find the optimized enforcement of the conflicting policies instead of negotiating it. Moreover, the optimization strategy adds efficacy to our work.

5   Conclusion

In heterogeneous networks like co-allied MANET, conflicts may occur due to the agreements between the allied teams(quads) and enforcement of their existing security policies. In such mission critical networks, one of the major concerns is negotiating the security policies among allied parties. Instead of negating with policies, this formal framework establishes a novel approach of negotiation for compromising with the enforcement of the policy to the optimal level toward a successful coalition. However, in co-allied MANET environment, enforcement of these security requirements may conflict with allied policies framed by the mutual agreements among the co-allied parties (quads). In addition, these requirements may be temporal or static with fine-grained constraints(trust, mobility etc.). This paper has presented a formal framework for finding optimal conciliated policy enforcement in co-allied MANET. This framework formally models the network instances considering various nodes with their properties into Boolean logic. By reducing the local policy requirements of different nodes and the allied security policy under the same formalism, the framework verifies for conflicts between the local and allied policy constraints using zChaff SAT solver. Finally, the framework uses Minimal-Cost satisfiability analysis to find the optimal solution from the model. The time complexity varies linearly with policy and network size. Incorporating mobility models with the framework, managing and modeling temporal policies and field study of the implemented framework are the potential future directions of this work.

References

1. Bettstetter, C., Resta, G., Santi, P.: The node distribution of the random waypoint mobility model for wireless ad hoc networks. IEEE Transactions on Mobile Computing 2(3), 257–269 (2003)
2. Fu, Z., Marhajan, Y., Malik, S.: zchaff. Research Web Page. Princeton University, USA (March 2007), http://www.princeton.edu/~chaff/zchaff.html
3. Li, X.Y., et al.: Optimization algorithms for the minimum-cost satisfiability problem. North Carolina State University (2004)
4. Dillig, I., Dillig, T., McMillan, K.L., Aiken, A.: Minimum satisfying assignments for SMT. In: Madhusudan, P., Seshia, S.A. (eds.) CAV 2012. LNCS, vol. 7358, pp. 394–409. Springer, Heidelberg (2012)
5. Maity, S., Ghosh, S.K.: A cognitive trust model for access control framework in manet. In: Venkatakrishnan, V., Goswami, D. (eds.) ICISS 2012. LNCS, vol. 7671, pp. 75–88. Springer, Heidelberg (2012)
6. Zhao, H., Lobo, J., Roy, A., Bellovin, S.M.: Policy refinement of network services for MANETs. In: The 12th IFIP/IEEE International Symposium on Integrated Network Management (IM 2011), Dublin, Ireland (2011)
7. Alicherry, M., Keromytis, A.D.: DIPLOMA: Distributed Policy Enforcement Architecture for MANETs. In: Fourth International Conference on Network and System Security, pp. 89–98. IEEE (2011)
8. Von Mulert, J., Welch, I., Seah, W.K.G.: Security threats and solutions in manets: A case study using aodv and saodv. Journal of Network and Computer Applications 35(4), 1249–1259 (2012)
9. Maity, S., Ghosh, S.K.: Enforcement of access control policy for mobile ad hoc networks. In: Proceedings of the Fifth International Conference on Security of Information and Networks, pp. 47–52. ACM (2012)
10. Bera, P., Ghosh, S.K., Dasgupta, P.: Policy based security analysis in enterprise networks: A formal approach. IEEE Transactions on Network and Service Management 7(4), 231–243 (2010)
11. Maity, S., Bera, P., Ghosh, S.K.: A mobile ip based wlan security management framework with reconfigurable hardware acceleration. In: Proceedings of the 3rd International Conference on Security of Information and Networks, pp. 218–223. ACM (2010)

12. Ao, X., Minsky, N.H.: Flexible regulation of distributed coalitions. In: Snekkenes, E., Gollmann, D. (eds.) ESORICS 2003. LNCS, vol. 2808, pp. 39–60. Springer, Heidelberg (2003)
13. Srivatsa, M., Agrawal, D., Balfe, S.: Bootstrapping coalition manets. IBM Research Report RC24588 (2008)
14. Wijesekera, D., Jajodia, S.: A propositional policy algebra for access control. ACM Transactions on Information and System Security (TISSEC) 6(2), 286–325 (2003)
15. Janicke, H., Cau, A., Siewe, F., Zedan, H.: Dynamic access control policies: specification and verification. The Computer Journal 56(4), 440–463 (2013)
16. Beigi, M., Lobo, J., Grueneberg, K., Calo, S., Karat, J.: A negotiation framework for negotiation of coalition policies. In: 2010 IEEE International Symposium on Policies for Distributed Systems and Networks, pp. 133–136. IEEE (2010)
17. Chen, K., Qiu, X., Yang, Y., Rui, L.: Negotiation-based service self-management mechanism in the manets. In: 2011 13th Asia-Pacific Network Operations and Management Symposium (APNOMS), pp. 1–7. IEEE (2011)

Batch Method for Efficient Resource Sharing in Real-Time Multi-GPU Systems

Uri Verner, Avi Mendelson, and Assaf Schuster

Technion – Israel Institute of Technology
{uriv,avi.mendelson,assaf}@cs.technion.ac.il

Abstract. The performance of many GPU-based systems depends heavily on the effective bandwidth for transferring data between the processors. For real-time systems, the importance of data transfer rates may be even higher due to non-deterministic transfer times that limit the ability to satisfy response time requirements. We present a new method that allows real-time applications to make efficient use of the communication infrastructure in multi-GPU systems, while retaining the necessary execution time predictability. Our method is based on a new application interface for executing batch operations composed of multiple command streams that can be executed in parallel. The new interface provides the run-time with information it needs to optimize the communication and to reduce the execution time. The method is compliant with common scheduling algorithms, such as EDF and RM, as it provides accurate offline execution time prediction for jobs using their definition and system characteristics.

Experiments with two multi-GPU systems show that our method achieves 7.9x shorter execution time than the bandwidth allocation method, and 39 % higher image resolution than the time division method, for realistic applications.

1 Introduction

In high throughput data processing systems, the computational load is distributed across multiple interconnected processors. To efficiently execute data-parallel parts of the computation, such systems often make use of discrete GPUs and other compute accelerators. The data is collaboratively processed by the CPUs and accelerators, and transferred between their local memories as required by the algorithm.

The data processing operations in many real-time systems are modeled as collections of simple repetitive tasks that generate jobs in a predictable manner. The jobs are executed by offline schedulers, such as Earliest-Dealine-First (EDF) and Rate-Monotonic (RM), which have been extensively studied [1,2]. Such modeling allows execution times to be analyzed and schedule validity to be checked offline. In systems with a multi-processor platform with distributed memories, and particularly in GPU-based systems, the data processing includes data transfer and compute operations.

Modern systems handle communication among different components via a heterogeneous interconnect, which is composed of several linked communication domains, and may be shared by different data transfer operations. As a result, the effective throughput of a data transfer may depend not only on the physical characteristics of the links, but also on the concurrent data transfers that share resources with it. Unless executed in

M. Chatterjee et al. (Eds.): ICDCN 2014, LNCS 8314, pp. 347–362, 2014.

a controlled way, the resource contention may even cause the communication time to become unpredictable, and the utilization may become prohibitively low.

For real-time systems, where the worst-case execution time is important, the common methods for resource sharing include bandwidth allocation and time division. The bandwidth allocation method calls to divide the resource into a number of smaller portions, and to assign each of them to a task. The time division method calls to split the time domain into time-slots and to assign them to the tasks according to a given priority scheme. Each of these methods allows the system to make the communication time deterministic at the expense of underutilizing resources such as the bus bandwidth, since a resource that is assigned to a task but not fully utilized is not used by the other tasks. Underutilization of the resources could increase power consumption or even prevent the system from meeting real-time deadlines.

In this paper, we propose a new execution method for data transfers and distributed computations between the host (CPUs) and multiple devices (GPUs). The new proposed method is based on a new application/run-time interface that allows the application to define which parts of the multiple command streams of data transfer and compute operations can be considered as a single job (unit of work). From the application's point of view, all the command streams in a job start and complete execution at the same time. We show that using the additional information provided by the new proposed interface the run-time is able to execute data transfers and computations in a way that (1) exploits parallel execution, (2) efficiently utilizes the computation and communication resources, and (3) still provides predictable job execution times. Our measurements on two multi-GPU systems with realistic GPGPU applications show that the tested application achieved up to 7.9x shorter execution time using our method than the bandwidth allocation method, and up to 39 % higher image resolution than the time division method.

2   CPU and GPU Terminologies and Definitions

2.1   System Architecture

In this work, we will focus on a single-node multi-GPU system that includes one or more CPUs and a set of discrete GPUs, each of which has a local memory module and serves as a computational device. Figure 1 illustrates a possible architecture of such a system. The interconnect provides connectivity among the different components such as memories, processors, GPUs, etc., and consists of several communication domains, depicted in the figure by background blocks. Each domain consists of components that use the same architecture and protocol for communication. The domains are bridged by components that belong to several domains.

As the figure shows, the system consists of memory modules (MEM), CPUs, GPUs, and I/O Hubs (IOH). The I/O hubs bridge between the processor interconnect and PCI Express, and provide connectivity between PCI Express devices and the main memory modules; in some architectures, the I/O hubs are integrated into the CPUs. In addition to GPUs, other external devices may be connected via PCI Express; examples include compute accelerators such as Intel's Xeon Phi and high-throughput network cards.

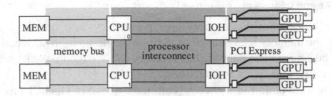

Fig. 1. System architecture of a multi-GPU system

In this work, we focus on GPU-based systems, but the proposed method can be extended to be used with other devices as well.

Each CPU accesses its local memory directly via the memory bus, while distant CPUs and I/O Hubs (IOH) access it indirectly via the processor interconnect, which is a set of high bandwidth full-duplex point-to-point links. Examples of such interconnects include Intel QuickPath Interconnect (QPI) and HyperTransport. Data transfers from and to GPU memory are executed by DMA controllers (a.k.a. DMA engines).

2.2 Aggregate Bandwidth

Theoretical bandwidth is the maximum rate at which data can be transferred over a communications network according to hardware specification. *Effective* bandwidth is the maximum measured throughput, which is typically lower than the theoretical bandwidth. In this paper we will also use the term *aggregate* bandwidth which is the total bandwidth over a number of data transfer routes, e.g., the aggregate bandwidth from main-memory to GPU0 and to GPU1.

The bandwidth of a route that traverses several communication domains is limited by the bandwidth in each of the domains. For example, the following table lists the (theoretical) bandwidth of the communication domains and their bus types in a Tyan FT72B7015 system:

Communication domain	Bus type	Bandwidth (GB/s)
memory bus	DDR3	32
processor interconnect	QPI	9.6
PCI Express bus	PCIe 2.0	8

One can see that QPI has higher bandwidth than PCIe 2.0. Therefore, the bandwidth from CPU0 to GPU0 (Fig. 1) is limited by PCI Express. However, the bottleneck for aggregate bandwidth is not necessarily in the bus with the smallest bandwidth. In the example, QPI is the bottleneck for the aggregate bandwidth from the main memory to GPUs 0 and 2 since each GPU uses a separate PCIe port.

2.3 GPU Commands in CUDA and OpenCL

The CUDA and OpenCL programming models provide functions for data transfer and kernel execution. For example, the CUDA function

```
cudaMemcpyAsync(dst,src,count,kind[,stream])
```

copies count bytes from the memory area pointed by src on the source device (CPU/GPU) to the memory area pointed by dst on the destination device; this function requires CPU buffers to be in page-locked memory [3]. We ignore the kind parameter since it is not used on the latest architectures.

CUDA defines the notion of a *stream* (command queue in OpenCL) as a sequence of commands that execute in order. The run-time can execute commands from different streams in any order. Event objects are inserted as bookmarks in a stream for monitoring the progress of execution. The application can query these objects when the execution order reaches the events. In the function above, the application can optionally provide a stream object to issue the operation to a stream. For clarity, we use the term *command stream*.

2.4 Sharing Resources in Real-Time Systems

The current interfaces for CUDA and OpenCL do not provide mechanisms for real-time execution. The interfaces do not define methods to specify deadlines for commands or command streams, or methods for predicting their execution times. Applications that schedule the program execution in heterogeneous architectures usually do a worst-case static analysis of the execution patterns in order to guarantee that the deadlines are met. The analysis is based on static resource sharing methods, such as static resource allocation or time division, and assumes that the worse case execution time (WCET) is known ahead of time for each job (computation or data transfer). Such a system can be suboptimal in terms of power and utilization, but also may cause the system to miss deadlines, as the following example indicates.

Consider a real-time production inspection system that has a CPU and four GPUs illustrated in Fig. 2. Every period of 50 ms, four images arrive to main memory, are copied to GPU memory, scanned for defects, and, for each image, a Boolean value is returned to main memory. This value denotes if defects were found. The image sizes are 32 MB, 128 MB, 128 MB, and 32 MB, and they are processed on GPUs 0-3, respectively, one image per GPU. The system is required to produce the result in main memory within 50 ms, i.e., before the next period starts. The throughput of a GPU for scanning an image is 10 GB/s (value chosen arbitrarily). The result transfer time is in the order of microseconds; for simplicity, we ignore it in the following time analysis.

Using the resource allocation method (bandwidth allocation) for sharing resources, each task is statically assigned a portion of the communication bandwidth. In this system, the bandwidth bottleneck (to all four GPUs) is 8 GB/s on the CPU-IOH link. Assuming equal bandwidth distribution, each stream is assigned 2 GB/s. Fig. 3a shows a timeline of the expected execution for this method. The processing time is computed as follows:

$$t_{bandw} = \frac{128\,\text{MB}}{2\,\text{GB/s}} + \frac{128\,\text{MB}}{10\,\text{GB/s}} = 76.8\,\text{ms}$$

The resulting time is longer than the 50 ms latency bound, so this approach does not guarantee that the latency constraints are satisfied.

Using time division, the full bandwidth is allocated to tasks for periods of time. The GPUs are allocated separately; hence, kernel executions may overlap. The order in which the system allocates bandwidth to the images is not strictly defined by the method; Fig. 3b shows a timeline for the scenario with the shortest expected processing time. This time exceeds the latency bound. The method does not utilize the bandwidth of the 8 GB/s CPU-IOH bus, but only of a 6 GB/s bus.

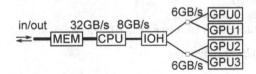

Fig. 2. Communication topology of explanatory example

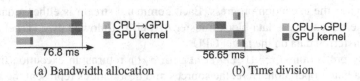

(a) Bandwidth allocation   (b) Time division

Fig. 3. Timeline of data processing for different resource sharing methods

One may notice that the incapability of the system to move allocated resources from one stream to another when they are not used, caused the system to miss the deadline. In the next section we present the batch allocation method that aims to ease this problem.

3   Batch Method for Data Transfer and Computations

In order to allow better utilization of the communication buses (and so, the entire system) while maintaining the ability to bound the execution time, we introduce a new run-time interface to the application (API). The new interface shifts from asynchronous command streams, as defined by CUDA and OpenCL, to batch operations that "bind" segments of multiple command streams together. It allows the system to optimize the execution, taking into account all the resources needed by the batch. From the point of view of the programmer, batch operations are executed atomically in issue order, but internally the run-time schedules the command stream segments concurrently, aiming to minimize the execution time.

Using the new interface, we will show that the run-time can provide two main services to the application: (1) better resource utilization, and (2) execution time prediction for a future batch operation. Such information can be used by the application to better schedule the batch operations in a way that meets system requirements (such as deadlines). It can also be used to dynamically control the execution, hence reducing the gap between the worst-case and actual execution times, and further improving the utilization of the system and its power consumption. Our new model is also compatible with the task model of classic scheduling algorithms, such as earliest-deadline-first (EDF) and rate-monotonic (RM).

3.1 Interface

We propose the use of the following API for batch operations:

```
    batchOp(dsts,srcs,sizes,kernels,n)
h = batchOpAsync(dsts,srcs,sizes,kernels,n)
b = batchOpQuery(h)
    batchOpSynchronize(h)
t = predictBatchLatency(dsts,srcs,sizes,kernels,n)
```

The API has three types of functions:

– Execution - batchOp() and batchOpAsync() execute a batch operation that contains n command streams. The function batchOp() is synchronous, while batchOpAsync() is asynchronous and returns a handler object h that the application uses to monitor the execution progress. Each command stream is either a data-block transfer, a kernel call, or a data-block transfer to a GPU followed by a kernel call that uses the transferred data on the target GPU.

– Latency prediction - predictBatchLatency() returns an execution time prediction for a batch operation. Here, the sources and destinations represent the memory modules, rather than specific addresses, such as GPU0 or MEM0 (local to CPU0).

– Progress monitoring - batchOpQuery(h) returns a boolean value indicating the completion status of an asynchronous batch operation, while batchOpSynchronize(h) blocks until the operation completes.

Using the API, the application can schedule data transfer operations and kernel calls, providing the run-time with the necessary information to use the interconnect and GPUs efficiently. In this work, we use a restricted model of a command stream: a stream is composed of a data transfer operation followed by a kernel call (both optional). This model does not limit the scheduling options for the application, as it may seem. We discuss this issue in greater detail in the Discussion and Related Work section.

3.2 Implementation

This section describes the implementation of the batch method for data transfer and kernel execution. The latency prediction algorithm is presented here and described in detail in the next section.

Execution. Calls to batchOp() and batchOpAsync() are processed in FIFO order. The execution algorithm schedules the command streams to execute in parallel with the goal of minimizing the execution time. For data transfers, it configures multiple DMA controllers to concurrently transfer data blocks that belong to different streams.

We propose a heuristic algorithm that aligns the *completion times* of the command streams. The algorithm computes when to start executing each command stream, such that the execution of all streams completes at the same time. The algorithm for computing the execution start times is described in the next section.

Two types of batch operations require special treatment:

1. If the batch operation contains command streams that use the same DMA controller, these operations cannot overlap, so the streams are merged by joining their data transfers and their kernels.
2. Data transfers between two GPUs that reside in different PCIe communication domains (e.g. GPUs 0 and 4 in Fig. 1) currently require staging in CPU memory, hence requiring a GPU→CPU and a CPU→GPU data transfer. These transfers may overlap, but the GPU→CPU must begin first. Therefore, after the initial schedule of the batch operations is computed, the algorithm checks whether the order of transfers is inverted and schedules the GPU→CPU earlier if necessary.

The heuristic algorithm limits the execution time to the longest command stream execution time and aims to achieve the highest throughput for this stream's data transfer. While the kernel execution time is independent of execution of other streams, the data transfer can be delayed due to contention. The algorithm delays the data transfers in the other streams to reduce bandwidth contention with the long stream and make them overlap with

Fig. 4. Timeline for the batch method

the kernel execution. Consider the example in Fig. 4; by aligning the completion times, the large blocks are delayed the least by contention with the small blocks, which reduces the execution time.

Latency prediction and run-time scheduling. To schedule the execution of data transfers and kernels in a batch operation, the run-time creates a timeline of start and completion events for the component operations (data transfers and kernel calls); the full algorithm is shown in Algorithm 1 in the appendix. This algorithm also computes the total execution time of the operation; i.e., it predicts the execution latency.

The event times are computed iteratively by simulating the execution. Since our execution method aligns the kernel *completion* times, the event times are computed from the batch completion time backwards. For simplicity of discussion, we consider the moment when the batch execution completes as $t = 0$, and count the time backwards.

Computing the start and completion times of kernels is trivial since they all start at time zero (on the reversed timeline) and execute in parallel for fixed amounts of time, given by the user. For data transfers, such computation is more complex, since it needs to take contention into account. It is assumed that the throughput of concurrent data transfers is constant as long as no transfer starts or completes; hence, it is constant between any two events. Next, we present an algorithm for computing the throughput of concurrent data transfers.

Model for bandwidth distribution for concurrent data transfers. We represent the interconnect topology as a weighted directed graph $G = (V, E, b)$, where a vertex $v \in V$ represents a component of the network, such as main-memory, a CPU, a GPU, or a routing component (controller, I/O hub, switch, etc.). A directed edge $e_{ij} \in E$ represents a unidirectional link from component n_i to component n_j, and the positive weight $b(e_{ij})$ represents its bandwidth.

The topology graph can be used to detect the bandwidth bottleneck along a path between two components and across multiple paths. For example, Fig. 5 illustrates the network topology graph of a Tyan FT72B7015 system with four GPUs. In this graph, the M0→GPU0 and M0→GPU1 paths both traverse the CPU0→IOH0 edge; hence the aggregate bandwidth on these two paths is 9.6 GB/s. The throughput of a data transfer is limited by the minimum edge weight $b(e)$ on its path in the graph. It may further be limited by concurrent data transfers that consume some of the bus bandwidth.

We use the *effective* bandwidth for the edge weights instead of the theoretical one; for worst-case analysis, a lower bound on the effective bandwidth is used.

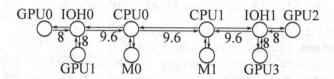

Fig. 5. Network topology graph of a Tyan FT72B7015 system with four GPUs. The edge weights denote the theoretical bandwidth of the link in GB/s.

3.3   Results for the Example in Sect. 2.4

Our example in Sect. 2.4 indicates that using the existing resource sharing mechanisms may lead to sub-optimal utilization of the shared resources and to a failure of the system (deadline miss). In this section, we return to this example and show that our method solves these problems for that case.

The batch method re-allocates the bandwidth during the execution in a predictable manner. Thus, the application is able to utilize the full 8 GB/s bandwidth, while still being able to validate that the execution completes within the given latency constraints. The application binds the CPU→GPU data block transfers and kernel calls into a batch operation, followed by another batch operation for the return values. The run-time executes the command streams concurrently, aiming for a minimum total execution time. Fig. 4 shows a timeline of the expected execution of a batch operation consisting of the data transfers and kernel calls for the four images. Due to the higher bandwidth, the operation completes after 44.8 ms, which is consistent with the given latency constraints. Thus the schedule is valid.

The example shows that our proposed method achieves shorter execution times than the existing methods by using the interconnect more efficiently.

4   Evaluation

To evaluate the batch method, we consider two applications running on two multi-GPU systems. We compare the batch method with two other bandwidth distribution methods: bandwidth allocation and time division.

For each system, we provide the system specification, find and analyze the effective bandwidth, and compare the performance using each of the methods in test case applications.

4.1 Baseline Configurations and Their Effective Bandwidth

In this section we describe two existing systems and use the techniques described in Sect. 3.2 to analyze their effective bandwidth.

Nehalem multi-GPU system
This system is a Tyan FT72B7015 server featuring the following components:
– Two 4-core Intel Xeon 5620 CPUs at 2.4 GHz, based on the Nehalem micro-architecture
– An Intel 5520/ICH10R chipset with a QPI processor interconnect at 4.8 GT/s (9.6 GB/s) and two I/O hubs, each with two PCIe 2.0 ports
– A total of 24 GB RAM in two modules
– Four NVIDIA Tesla C2050 GPUs, each with 3 GB of GDDR5 memory
The system runs Ubuntu 10.04 x64 Linux with CUDA SDK 5.0.

The batch method uses the effective aggregate bandwidth to compute the completion times of data transfers. In Sect. 3.2, we presented a method for computing the aggregate bandwidth from a topology graph with edge weights that represent bus bandwidth. We obtained the edge weights using a series of benchmarks. To find the effective bandwidth of a bus, we transferred 256 MiB (2^{28} bytes) data blocks between CPU0 and the GPUs in host-to-device (H2D), device-to-host (D2H), and bi-directional (Bi) modes on all the paths that traverse this bus, and measured the aggregate throughput for each direction (Fig. 7a). Using these measurements, we determined the effective bus bandwidths in Fig. 6a. For simplicity, we did not include the bi-directional bandwidth measurements in the figure.

The results show that the bus bandwidth is asymmetric; the effective H2D PCIe bandwidth is between 25 % and 50 % higher than the D2H bandwidth. We also see that the effective bandwidth to the remote GPUs is 20 % lower. Since the QPI bus has higher bandwidth than the PCIe bus, this indicates that the latency of the extra hop over QPI translates into throughput degradation. The H2D aggregate bandwidth scales up for two GPUs by 57 % for local GPUs (saturates the QPI bus), and by 33 % for remote GPUs. In contrast, the D2H bandwidth for two GPUs does not scale. For four GPUs, the H2D bandwidth does not scale further, but the aggregate D2H bandwidth lines up with the bandwidth of the local GPUs. We ascribe the reduced scaling to chipset limitations, except where the QPI bus was saturated. Since the GPUs only have one DMA engine, they are not able to get more bandwidth from bi-directional transfer, yet we see that for the local GPUs a bi-directional transfer is faster than an H2D transfer followed by a D2H.

Sandy Bridge multi-GPU system
This system features the following components:
– Two 6-core Intel Xeon E5-2667 CPUs at 2.9 GHz based on the Sandy Bridge micro-architecture
– An Intel C602 chipset w/ QPI at 8 GT/s (16 GB/s) and two PCIe 3.0 ports in each CPU
– 64 GB of RAM in two modules
– Two NVIDIA Tesla K10 cards, each with two GPU modules, connected by a PCIe switch, that include a GPU and 4 GB of GDDR5 memory.

The system runs Red Hat Ent. 6.2 Linux with CUDA SDK 5.0.

We determined the effective bus bandwidths shown in Fig. 6b using a series of benchmarks, as described for the Nehalem system. Figure 7b shows the benchmark results for the Sandy Bridge system.

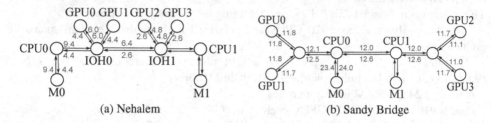

(a) Nehalem   (b) Sandy Bridge

Fig. 6. Topology graph showing effective bandwidth in GB/s

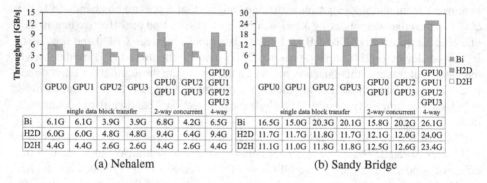

(a) Nehalem   (b) Sandy Bridge

Fig. 7. Bus bandwidth benchmark

The Sandy Bridge system has higher bandwidth than the Nehalem system as it uses PCIe 3.0. Moreover, the bandwidth in Sandy Bridge is symmetric and is similar for local and remote GPUs, unlike in the Nehalem system. The aggregate bandwidth to the GPU pairs is only slightly higher than for the individual GPUs; this is expected, as the GPUs share a PCIe bus. However, moving further to four GPUs, the bandwidth scales almost perfectly. For a single GPU, bi-directional transfers increase the bandwidth by 32 %-72 % over uni-directional transfers, while for all four GPUs, the increase in bandwidth is only 10 %.

4.2   Application Based Performance Evaluation

The evaluation we are providing in this section is based on two applications, one that represents a solution for a wide range of algorithms in areas such as signal processing and image processing, and the other which is motivated by an application we are developing as part of a consortium for inspection of 450 mm wafers called Metro 450.

Domain decomposition. In many scientific GPGPU applications that work on large datasets, the domain is decomposed into parts that fit in GPU memory. The application we examine uses two GPUs, and follows a common pattern in multi-GPU programming:

```
1: scatter 3.69 GB input data to 2 GPUs
2: repeat 100 times
3:   compute boundary points (1 ms)
4:   in parallel:
5:     GPUs exchange 295.2 MB boundaries
6:     compute internal points (23 ms)
7: gather output from GPUs
```

Table 1 shows the execution time using each of the bandwidth distribution methods. Using the batch method on the Sandy Bridge system, the application runs 7.9 times faster than using the bandwidth allocation method, and 2 times faster than using the time division method. On the Nehalem system, it runs 28 % faster than bandwidth allocation, and 15 % faster than time division.

While the batch method efficiently uses the available bandwidth, the bandwidth allocation splits the available bandwidth and conservatively assigns pieces to each data transfer; hence, when a data transfer is not actually being transmitted its bandwidth is lost. The time allocation method also does not fully utilize the available bandwidth, as without executing several data transfers concurrently, the system cannot fully utilize the available bandwidth.

Wafer inspection. In a real-time wafer inspection system, an image of a wafer arrives to main-memory every 25 ms, and is sent to the GPUs for defect detection. The defects on the wafer are distributed non-uniformly, so in order to balance the kernel execution times, the image is split between GPUs 0-3 as follows: 40 %, 10 %, 10 %, and 40 %. The four GPUs process the image at 10 GB/s.

The system is required to produce a defect report in main-memory every 60 ms, and its size equals that of the image. This requirement limits the resolution of wafer images processed by the system, yet the maximal resolution depends on the bandwidth distribution method. To calculate the maximum resolution for each of the methods, we take into account that the system uses the non-preemptive EDF scheduler, and check the validity of the schedule using the test described by Jeffay et. al. [4]. We use image size as a measure of the resolution.

Table 1 shows the maximum image sizes using each of the bandwidth distribution methods. The batch method achieves the highest average throughput by multiplexing the data transfers. On the Nehalem system, it supports 39 % higher image resolution than that of the bandwidth allocation method, because, when the short data transfers complete, it assigns some of the released bandwidth to the long transfers. It also achieves 37 % higher image resolution than the time division method by utilizing the aggregate bandwidth of multiple routes.

On Sandy Bridge, it supports 22 % higher image resolution than that of the bandwidth allocation method, because, when the short data transfers complete, it assigns

Table 1. Performance comparison of the different methods

	Domain decomposition (execution time)		Wafer inspection (image size – larger is better)	
	Nehalem	Sandy Bridge	Nehalem	Sandy Bridge
Batch method	20.03 sec	3.18 sec	82.46 MB	156.77 MB
B/W allocation	25.59 sec	25.19 sec	59.28 MB	128.10 MB
Time division	23.10 sec	6.43 sec	60.24 MB	112.58 MB

some of the released bandwidth to the long transfers. It also achieves 39 % higher image resolution than the time division method by utilizing the aggregate bandwidth of multiple routes.

4.3   Execution Time Prediction

A fundamental part of the batch method is the execution timeline computation algorithm described in Sect. 3.2. This algorithm is used both for scheduling the execution of batch operations and predicting their latency. Hence, precision is essential. We evaluate the algorithm's precision by (1) computing an execution timeline for selected batch operations; (2) executing the operations and recording the execution time of each command stream; and (3) comparing the execution times for each command stream and for the batch in total.

We ran two experiments on each system. On Nehalem, we executed the following batch operations:

Experiment 1 (Batch #1)	Experiment 2 (Batch #2)
256 MiB H2D (GPU0) + kernel (10 ms)	256 MiB D2H (GPU0)
128 MiB H2D (GPU1) + kernel (10 ms)	128 MiB D2H (GPU1)

On Sandy Bridge we executed similar experiments, but with four GPUs; the additional block sizes were 64 MiB and 32 MiB. Table 2 displays the results of the computations and measurements side by side, and shows the prediction error of the total execution time. The prediction error was no more that 3.6 % for all the tested cases. The table in that figure shows that the computed execution times of individual command streams are also similar to the recorded values.

We've shown that our algorithm correctly estimates command stream execution times for batch operations with different data transfer sizes that execute concurrently. Thus, it can be used for efficiently scheduling the execution of command streams and predicting the execution time of batch operations.

4.4   Throughput Computation vs. Measurement

In Sect. 3.2, we presented a method for computing the aggregate throughput using a topology graph of the system. The topology graph represents bus bandwidth as edge weights, allowing the computation of end-to-end throughput by finding the bottleneck. However, the computed throughput may differ from the actual throughput due to chipset

Table 2. Predicted vs. measured execution time for each command stream and for the entire batch

Configuration	Prediction					Measurement					
	S1	S2	S3	S4	Total	S1	S2	S3	S4	Total	Err
Nehalem H2D	60.71	38.46			60.71	60.94	38.64			60.94	**0.4 %**
Nehalem D2H	91.69	61.12			91.69	91.97	61.39			91.97	**0.3 %**
Sandy Bridge H2D	43.74	32.25	18.40	15.60	43.74	43.44	32.08	18.85	16.01	43.45	**0.7 %**
Sandy Bridge D2H	34.11	22.02	8.59	5.72	34.11	32.95	21.52	8.65	5.76	32.94	**3.6 %**

limitations. We evaluated the relative error of our algorithm by comparing the computed values with throughput measurements in a series of experiments with concurrent data transfers on the Sandy Bridge system.

For the experiments in Fig. 7b the error was 0 % for H2D and D2H, and 0 %–(-4) % for Bi. The error in these experiments was low, because the edge weights in the topology graph were set to match these measurements as much as possible. Interestingly, the weights could not fully match the Bi bandwidth measurements, and an error of 4 % was observed. In cases with two GPUs that do not appear in Fig. 7b, the maximum error was as follows: 0.7 % for H2D, 5.4 % for D2H, and 26 % for Bi. The error for the Bi transfers was high because the measured bandwidth did not fit the topology model. We attribute this result to chipset limitations.

To summarize, our algorithm efficiently calculated the expected throughput for uni-directional data transfers, but not for all bi-directional data transfers.

5   Discussion and Related Work

We have shown in Sect. 4.2 that our method is efficient in executing workloads of data transfers and computations. The experimental results show that it achieves up to 7.9 times better results than the bandwidth allocation method (execution time) and up to 39 % better results than the time division method (higher image resolution) in realistic applications. In Sect. 4.3, we have also shown that the batch execution time is predictable and that our latency prediction algorithm computes a close estimation of that execution time. Sufficient safety margins on bandwidth and setup time should be used to compensate for prediction errors where strict latency guarantees are required.

Communication scheduling that incorporates contention awareness has been studied in several works [5,6,7,8]. In all these works, the basic unit of communication is a message – a chunk of data that is sent from a source to a destination. In order to overcome bus contention issues when sending multiple messages, the proposed algorithms allocate bandwidth and/or communication time for each message. In this work, we proposed to extend the classic communication model by allowing multiple messages to be sent in one job. This extension allows the run-time to utilize the communication network more efficiently by optimizing the total job execution time, rather than the transfer time of each message. Our method provides an algorithm to predict the job execution time, which is required as part of the input to the scheduler.

Our method executes batch operations that are a collection of command stream segments containing data block transfers and kernel calls. However, we have limited each command stream segment to contain only a data transfer followed by a kernel call (both optional), forcing the application to divide longer streams into multiple batch operations. However, fine-grained scheduling can be achieved using two techniques: (1) dividing large data blocks into smaller chunks (also suggested in other works [9,10]), and (2) scheduling kernels in parallel with batch operations, without using the API. When using the second technique, the application needs to make sure that the kernel and the batch operation do not use the same GPU for computations. Using the techniques mentioned above, the application can make fine-grained scheduling decisions for data transfers and kernel calls. Our method uses execution time computations assuming no external factors that influence the execution time. Therefore, during the execution of a batch operation, the interconnect must be used exclusively by the execution algorithm.

In Sect. 3.2 we presented an algorithm for computing throughput using a topology graph of the system with edge weights that represent bus bandwidth. The precision evaluation in Sect. 4.4 shows that this method is effective for data transfers from the CPU to the GPUs and in the opposite direction, but not for bi-directional data transfers. Our experiments show that for bi-directional transfers, the results are not consistent with topology graph analysis. In applications with workloads where the throughput computation algorithm is not efficient, we recommend using a lookup table that contains the throughput values for any combination of data transfer routes that may be used in the application. The throughput values can be found using benchmarks. Since the batch operation execution uses the interconnect exclusively, the benchmark results are expected to be consistent with the throughput values during the execution.

RGEM [9] is a run-time execution model for soft real-time GPGPU applications. It divides data transfers into chunks to reduce blocking times and schedules the chunks according to given task priorities. Because this model uses blocking data block transfers, it is based on the time division bandwidth distribution scheme.

Verner et al. [11] presented a framework for processing data streams with hard real-time constraints. The framework abstracts the GPUs as a single device and transfers the data to all the GPUs collectively, thus utilizing the bandwidth of the shared bus. The authors demonstrate the importance of developing a data transfer mechanism that would provide efficient communication and execution time guarantees in order to achieve better scheduling opportunities.

Kato et al. [12] described a technique for low-latency communication between the GPU and other I/O devices. The technique allows the devices to communicate by writing directly to each other's memory, thus decreasing the transfer latency. However, since there is no centralized mechanism that schedules the data transfers, the transfer latency may be influenced by concurrent data transfers.

Several works [11,13,9] predicted the CPU-GPU data-transfer latencies using empirical performance models. The performance models were built upon data-transfer benchmarks for a range of transfer sizes.

6   Conclusion

In this paper, we have presented a new execution method for data transfers and computations in multi-GPU systems. Using this method, a real-time application can schedule and efficiently execute data transfers and kernel calls. The method executes jobs we call "batch operations" that include multiple data transfers and kernel calls that can be executed in parallel. The method also includes an algorithm for predicting the execution time of batch operations, which is made possible by executing them atomically. The method also implements a new and efficient execution algorithm for batch operations. Unlike existing execution methods that provide predictable execution times for individual data transfers and kernels calls at the cost of performance, our algorithm overlaps the execution of multiple data transfers and kernels, thus gaining efficient communication and compact execution.

Acknowledgments. The work was supported by the Metro 450 Israeli national consortium for inspection of 450 mm wafers.

References

1. Zapata, O.U.P., Alvarez, P.M.: EDF and RM multiprocessor scheduling algorithms: Survey and performance evaluation. Queue, pp. 1–24 (2005)
2. Baruah, S., Goossens, J.: Handbook of Scheduling: Algorithms, Models, and Performance Analysis. Chapman Hall/CRC Press (2004)
3. NVIDIA Corporation, CUDA API Reference Manual, version 5.0 (2012)
4. Jeffay, K., Stanat, D., Martel, C.: On non-preemptive scheduling of period and sporadic tasks. In: Real-Time Systems Symposium, pp. 129–139 (1991)
5. Lehoczky, J.P., Sha, L.: Performance of real-time bus scheduling algorithms. ACM SIGMETRICS Performance Evaluation Review 14, 44–53 (1986)
6. Natale, M., Meschi, A.: Scheduling messages with earliest deadline techniques. Real-Time Systems (1993), 255–285 (2001)
7. Sinnen, O., Sousa, L.A., Member, S.: Communication contention in task scheduling. IEEE Transactions on Parallel and Distributed Systems 16(6), 503–515 (2005)
8. Balman, M.: Data transfer scheduling with advance reservation and provisioning. Ph.D. dissertation, Louisiana State University (2010)
9. Kato, S., Lakshmanan, K.: RGEM: A responsive GPGPU execution model for runtime engines. In: Real-Time Systems Symposium (RTSS), pp. 57–66 (November 2011)
10. Basaran, C., Kang, K.-D.: Supporting preemptive task executions and memory copies in GPGPUs. In: Euromicro Conference on Real-Time Systems, pp. 287–296 (July 2012)
11. Verner, U., Schuster, A., Silberstein, M., Mendelson, A.: Scheduling processing of real-time data streams on heterogeneous multi-GPU systems. In: International Systems and Storage Conference (SYSTOR), pp. 1–12 (2012)
12. Kato, S., Aumiller, J., Brandt, S.: Zero-copy I/O processing for low-latency GPU computing. In: International Conference on Cyber-Physical Systems (ICCPS 2013), pp. 170–178 (2013)
13. Augonnet, C., Clet-Ortega, J., Thibault, S., Namyst, R.: Data-aware task scheduling on multi-accelerator based platforms. In: International Conference on Parallel and Distributed Systems (ICPADS), pp. 291–298 (2010)

Algorithm 1. Batch run-time scheduling algorithm (MATLAB)

```
function Batch
    %Batch = [ (dst1,src1,size1,kernel1),
    %           (dst2,src2,size2,kernel2),
    %           ...
    %           (dstN,srcN,sizeN,kernelN)]
    N=size(Batch,1)

    % Event times for each command stream
    % (kernel begin, kernel end, copy begin, copy end)
    StreamSched = zeros(N,4)
    StreamSched(1:N,2) = arrayfun(@KernelTime, Batch(1:N,4))
    StreamSched(1:N,3) = StreamSched(1:N,2)

    % Timeline of data transmission start times, which are equal to the
    % kernel completion times. Col #1: time, Col #2: id of command stream
    DataStart = [StreamSched(1:N,3), [1:N]']
    DataStart = sortrows(DataStart,1)    % sort by time

    % t is a time point that moves between event times as they are computed
    % Workload is the set of stream ids that have a data transfer in
    % progress. The initial values are set to the time when the first data
    % transfer starts executing
    t = DataStart(1,1)
    Workload = DataStart(1,2)
    for i = 2:size(DataStart,1)
        Tnext = DataStart(i,1)
        while (t < Tnext)
            [t,Workload,Completed,Batch] =
                    ComputeNextEvent(t,Tnext,Workload,Batch)
            StreamSched(Completed,4) = t
        end
        Workload = [Workload; DataStart(i,2)]
    end
    while (~isempty(Workload))
        [t,Workload,Completed,Batch] = ComputeNextEvent(t,inf,Workload,Batch)
        StreamSched(Completed,4) = t
    end
    % makespan is the time difference between first and last events
    makespan = t + SetupTime(Batch) % add setup time (usually very small)
    % reverse timeline
    Sched = makespan - StreamSched(:,end:-1:1)
end

function [CurTime,Workload,Completed,Batch] = ComputeNextEvent(Tstart,Tnext,
    Workload,Batch)
    if (length(Workload) == 0)
        CurTime = Tnext
        Completed = []
        return
    end
    % Get throughput for each data transfer in workload
    T = Throughput(Batch(Workload,:))
    sizes = [Batch{Workload,3}]'
    % Compute earliest completion time
    completion_times = sizes ./ T
    soonest = min(min(completion_times),Tnext-Tstart)
    CurTime = Tstart + soonest
    % Update remaining data to transfer in all active command streams
    sizes = sizes - soonest * T
    for ii = 1:length(Workload)
        Batch{Workload(ii),3} = sizes(ii)
    end
    % Completed is a list of completed data transfers
    Completed = Workload(sizes <= 0)
    Workload = Workload(sizes > 0)
end
```

Impairment-Aware Dynamic Routing
and Wavelength Assignment
in Translucent Optical WDM Networks

Sriharsha Varanasi, Subir Bandyopadhyay, and Arunita Jaekel

School of Computer Science, University of Windsor,
Windsor, ON N9B 3P4, Canada
{varanas,subir,arunita}@uwindsor.ca

Abstract. Imperfections in the optical fiber and other optical phenomena give rise to several physical layer impairments that degrade the
Quality of Transmission (QOT) of a propagating optical signal in WDM
networks. 3R regenerators are deployed to restore the QOT of the optical
signal before it falls below a predetermined threshold value. In opaque
networks, these regenerators are installed in all the nodes. However as
the size of the network increases, several practical issues related to regenerators such as installation costs, power consumption, physical space
requirements, upgradability, operation and maintenance costs etc. have
to be considered. In view of these practical constraints, the trend has
been to move towards the low cost translucent networks, in which the 3R
regenerators are sparsely yet strategically placed in the network. We propose a new approach to solve the Impairment-Aware Routing and Wavelength Assignment (IA-RWA) problem under dynamic network traffic
conditions, assuming a given sparse placement of the regeneration capable nodes. Since 3R regenerators use Optical-to-Electrical-to-Optical
(OEO) conversion to restore the optical signal quality, which is an expensive operation, the objective of our IA-RWA approach is to find a
solution that involves the fewest possible number of regenerators. Our
approach is based on the A* (Best First Search) algorithm and guarantees an optimal solution (if it exists).

1 Introduction

In *Wavelength Division Multiplexing* (WDM) Optical networks, data is transmitted in the form of optical signals over optical level connections called *lightpaths*.
The entire bandwidth available for transmission is divided into non-overlapping
ranges of wavelengths, called *channels* [1] and each optical signal is allotted
a unique channel. *Route and Wavelength Assignment* (RWA) is the process of
establishing a lightpath that involves finding i) a route through the network
and ii) a channel which is not used by any other lightpath using any edge in
this route [2]. Imperfections in the optical fiber, component vulnerabilities and
other optical phenomena give rise to several *Physical Layer Impairments* (PLIs),
which degrade the Quality of Transmission (QOT) of a propagating optical signal. Some of the important PLIs include Optical Noise, Amplified Spontaneous

M. Chatterjee et al. (Eds.): ICDCN 2014, LNCS 8314, pp. 363–377, 2014.
© Springer-Verlag Berlin Heidelberg 2014

Emission (ASE), Chromatic Dispersion (CD) and Polarization Mode Dispersion (PMD) [3], Cross-Phase Modulation (XPM), Switch Crosstalk (XT) and Four Wave Mixing (FWM) [4]. PLIs can be classified into two categories [4] as follows. *Class 1 impairments* affect a lightpath individually and are not dependant on the existence of other lightpaths in the network. *Class 2 impairments* are generated mainly due to the interference between lightpaths. RWA which takes into account the PLIs is called *Impairment-Aware RWA* (IA-RWA). In order to ensure proper communication, the optical signal needs to undergo 3R regeneration (Reamplification, Reshaping and Retiming) [5] before its QOT falls below a predefined threshold value. 3R regenerators typically use Optical-to-Electrical-to-Optical (OEO) conversion [5] to restore the degraded signal quality. The maximum distance an optical signal can travel before it needs 3R regeneration is called *Optical Reach* [6]. In an *opaque* network, all the network nodes are capable of providing 3R regeneration. To reduce installation costs, power consumption and physical space required, *translucent* optical networks [7], where relatively few network nodes are capable of 3R regeneration, are receiving attention.

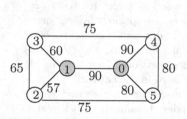

Fig. 1. A translucent optical network

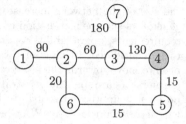

Fig. 2. Occurrence of loops in lightpaths

A lightpath which does not involve (involves) 3R regeneration is called a *transparent* (*translucent*) lightpath. A translucent lightpath may be viewed as having two or more components, where each component is a transparent lightpath. We will call each such transparent component a *segment*. Fig. 1 shows a translucent network, where nodes 0 and 1 are capable of 3R-regeneration. A translucent lightpath having route $3 \rightarrow 2 \rightarrow 1 \rightarrow 0 \rightarrow 4 \rightarrow 5$, with regeneration at nodes 1 and 0, consists of 3 transparent segments, having routes $3 \rightarrow 2 \rightarrow 1, 1 \rightarrow 0$ and $0 \rightarrow 4 \rightarrow 5$. Unlike transparent lightpaths, a translucent lightpath may have loops. Fig. 2 shows a sample translucent network, where only node 4 is capable of 3R-regeneration. Assuming an optical reach of 300 km, an optical signal starting at node 1 cannot reach 7 without undergoing regeneration at node 4. The only possible translucent lightpath from 1 to 7 has the route $1 \rightarrow 2 \rightarrow 3 \rightarrow 4 \rightarrow 5 \rightarrow 6 \rightarrow 2 \rightarrow 3 \rightarrow 7$. In this case, the edge $2 \rightarrow 3$ is shared by the transparent segments using routes $1 \rightarrow 2 \rightarrow 3 \rightarrow 4$ and $4 \rightarrow 5 \rightarrow 6 \rightarrow 2 \rightarrow 3 \rightarrow 7$. As a result these segments cannot be assigned the same channel. This interesting feature was pointed out in [8].

We are considering *dynamic* lightpath allocation (DLA) [9] in this paper. In DLA, connection requests (each specified by a source s, a destination d and a duration of communication) arrive dynamically and we cannot predict the pattern of these requests. As a result, it is not possible to determine, in advance, which nodes may need 3R regeneration capability. In translucent networks where DLA is used, there are two phases: i) the *Regenerator Placement Problem (RPP)* phase [8], which is carried out before the network starts operating and ii) the *Routing with Regenerators Problem (RRP)* [8], [9] phase, which is carried out only when the network is in operation. Given a WDM network topology, the objective of RPP is to identify the smallest possible subset of nodes ($\mathbb{N}$), which will have 3R regeneration capability, to ensure full connectivity. In other words, corresponding to every (source, destination) pair (s, d), a route for a translucent lightpath from s to d exists, such that the length of all segments of the lightpath is less than the optical reach. During the RRP phase, in response to a request for a connection from s to d, the objective is to set up, if possible, a transparent or a translucent lightpath from s to d. The attempt may fail due to i) network layer limitations (no available channel), ii) physical layer limitations, or iii) lack of regenerators. To conserve resources, algorithms for RRP attempt to minimize the number of regenerators used in the translucent lightpath from s to d.

In this paper, our focus is on the RRP phase and we propose a novel IA-RWA approach called Best First Search for Route and Wavelength Assignment (BFS-RWA). The interesting features of BFS-RWA are as follows:

- The BFS-RWA is based on the A^* algorithm and uses an admissible heuristic. Thus, an optimal solution, if it exists, is guaranteed. The approaches proposed in [10], [11], [12], [13] & [14] use a set of k pre-computed candidate paths (from the source to the destination of the connection request) to select a feasible route for the lightpath. These approaches use different criteria to construct the candidate set of paths such as: distance ([10],[12],[13]), minimum link sharing among paths ([10],[12],[14]), worst case class 2 impairments ([11]), and minimum number of hops ([13]). The authors in [5] assign weights to the network edges based on availability of regenerators and select the shortest path (computed using Dijkstra's algorithm) as the route for the lightpath. Previous works on RRP mentioned above use a limited set of candidate paths and may fail to select a feasible route. This becomes even more significant in large networks because there is a very large number of possible routes between each node pair. The BFS-RWA therefore is ideally suited to serve as a benchmark for any "fast" algorithm for RRP in IA-RWA.
- BFS-RWA allows the same edge to appear multiple times in a translucent lightpath, as shown in Fig. 2. Existing IA-RWA approaches considering class 2 impairments [5], [10], [11], [12], [13], and [14] do not handle this. To our knowledge, [8] is the only paper that takes this constraint into consideration. However, [8] does not consider class 2 impairments and restricts the search for a route to a pre-computed set of paths.
- Optical reach is a distance-based metric and only accounts for class 1 impairments. Class 2 impairments are not considered in the optical reach because

they cannot be quantified until the lightpaths are actually established. One possibility is to assume the worst case for class 2 impairments, following [11]. However, this increases the number of regenerators and hence the capital expenses, perhaps unnecessarily. The BFS-RWA allows us to study the impact of different regenerator placement strategies on the blocking probability [8].

2   A New Approach to Dynamic IA-RWA

In this section, we present our approach (BFS-RWA) to solve the Routing with Regenerators Problem (RRP). BFS-RWA uses the $A*$ [15] *Best First Search* Algorithm and constructs a search tree to find a feasible RWA solution for every new connection request from source s to destination d. The search starts by creating the root of the search tree, containing the source node s. The search continues until i) either d is reached and we conclude that there does not exist a better solution, or ii) we conclude that the destination d cannot be reached.

For clarity, we have used the term "route" to denote the sequence of fiber (s) used by a lightpath from s to d in the physical topology and the term "path" to denote the edges in the search tree from the root node (which corresponds to s) to the node corresponding to d. The BFS-RWA looks for the most "promising" path in the search tree in order to determine the best possible route, from s to d, for the lightpath. We have briefly outlined our approach for estimating the QOT in the Section 2.1. In subsequent sections, we have described the BFS-RWA.

2.1   Measuring Physical Layer Impairments

In order to determine the QOT of an optical signal during its propagation in the fiber, PLIs need to be quantified. We have developed a PLI tool, based on the analytical model proposed in [16], that considered both class 1 and class 2 impairments. The analytical model in [16] measures the QOT of an optical signal using the *Optical Signal to Noise Ratio (OSNR)* degradation concept. OSNR can be defined as the ratio of the total optical signal power to the total noise power (expressed in decibels, dB). The OSNR value at any node x along the route of an optical signal is calculated as follows:

$$OSNR_x = 10 \, log_{10}\left(\frac{P_x}{N_x}\right) dB \qquad (1)$$

where P_x and N_x represent the values of total signal and noise powers respectively at node x, measured in milliWatts (mW). The total optical noise power (N_x) is the sum of noise powers due to various class 1 and class 2 impairments [16]. If the OSNR value of the optical signal goes below a predetermined threshold value $(OSNR_{Th})$, then it becomes infeasible and needs 3R regeneration before it can travel further. Therefore the condition $OSNR_x > OSNR_{Th}$ must be satisfied. Due to lack of space, we have omitted details of this tool. We will refer to this tool as "*OSNR tool*" in this paper.

2.2   Notation Used in BFS-RWA

s (d) : the source (destination) of the new request for communication.

$\mathbb{N}$: the set of nodes in the physical topology equipped with 3R regenerators.

t^h : the best node in the search tree whose neighborhood is being explored.

n (t^n) : a node in the physical topology (search tree) that is currently being considered, where n is adjacent to h.

N_{reg}^n : number of regenerators used in the path from t^s to t^n.

$\mathcal{A}_{t^n}$ $(\mathcal{H}_{t^n}, \mathcal{T}_{t^n})$: the actual (respectively heuristic and total estimated) cost for a lightpath from node s to n (respectively from n to d, from s to d through n) using the path from t^s to t^n.

$OSNR_{t^n}(OSNR_{in})$: the OSNR value at node t^n(t^s or at any node where the lightpath undergoes regeneration).

$OSNR_{Threshold}$: the minimum acceptable OSNR value.

D_d^n : the length of the shortest route from n to d.

$\mathcal{N}$: set of potential next nodes for the search.

$\mathcal{L}$: RWA solution for communication from s to d.

r : the optical reach.

$\mathbb{C}_{t^n}$: a list of valid channel numbers for the segment to t^n.

Ψ : the list of segments in the proposed lightpath, where Ψ^k denotes the kth segment of Ψ, where the first segment starts from s.

num_segments : number of segments in Ψ.

PIG : the path intersection graph for the lightpath under consideration.

c : a channel number.

heuristic_cost(t^x) (*actual_cost(t^x)*) : function to compute the heuristic (actual) cost using equation 2 (3), given in section 3.2.

assign_channel(Ψ^k, c) : function assign channel c to segment Ψ^k.

calculate_OSNR_value(Ψ) : function to calculate, the QOT of all existing lightpaths as well as the proposed lightpath. It returns the lowest OSNR value among all these lightpaths.

check_for_shared_edges(Ψ) : function that returns true only if there is at least one common edge in any two segments of Ψ.

create_path_intersection_graph(Ψ) : function to create a path intersection graph, considering all the segments in Ψ.

colorable(PIG) : function that returns true if graph *PIG* can be colored.

create_node(t^h, n) (*create_regenerator_node(t^h, n)*) : function to create node (regenerator node) t^n, and insert it into the search tree as a child of node t^h. The function returns node t^n.

create_root_node(s) : function to create the root node t^s. The function returns t^s.

find_best_node_in_tree() : function that retrieves the leaf node t^h in the tree having the least total cost.

find_eligible_neighbours(t^h) : function to find all valid child nodes of t^h.

lightpath_feasible(t^h, t^n) : function that returns true iff the path from t^s to t^n through t^h may be used to set up a lightath from s to n.

generate_RWA_solution_using_search_tree(t^h) : function that returns the routes and the channels assigned to the segments of the new translucent lightath from s to d.

2.3   Details of BFS-RWA

Each node t^n in the search tree includes the following information:

1. a reference to node n in the physical topology,
2. Two types of costs, i) the actual cost $\mathcal{A}_{t^n}$, and ii) the heuristic cost $\mathcal{H}_{t^n}$,
3. If $n \in \mathbb{N}$, whether 3R regeneration is carried out at t^n,
4. The list of channel numbers $\mathbb{C}^n$ that may be used in the segment to node n.

We note that, in general, a number of nodes (t^x) in the tree may refer to the same node x in the physical topology. This is because a) the tree, in general, involves multiple route from s to d, through node x and b) the route of the light-path may involve loops as shown in Fig. 2. Since our objective is to minimize the total number of regenerators used, we determine the actual $(\mathcal{A}_{t^n})$ and heuristic $(\mathcal{H}_{t^n})$ costs in terms of the number of regenerators required as follows:

$$\mathcal{A}_{t^n} = N_{Reg}^n + \frac{OSNR_{in} - OSNR_n}{OSNR_{in} - OSNR_{Threshold}} \tag{2}$$

$$\mathcal{H}_{t^n} = \frac{D_d^n}{r} \tag{3}$$

$(OSNR_{in} - OSNR_{Threshold})$ is the amount of degradation in OSNR value before regeneration is needed. The ratio in (2) measures, in terms of a fraction of a regenerator, the extent of signal degradation in the current segment. The sum in Equation (2) represents the actual cost, in terms of the total number of regenerators required from t^s to t^n. The total estimated cost to go from node t^s to t^d through node t^n is $\mathcal{T}_{t^n} = \mathcal{A}_{t^n} + \mathcal{H}_{t^n}$, which guides the search in the A* algorithm. The A* algorithm generates an optimal solution (if it exists), if the value of $\mathcal{H}_{t^n}$ is an admissible heuristic [15].

Lemma 1. *The cost, $\mathcal{H}_{t^n}$, is an admissible heuristic.*

Proof. The numerator, D_d^n, in Equation (3) is the distance of the shortest route from n to d, so that the actual route used to go from n to d is at least as long as D_d^n. The denominator uses the optical reach r and hence ignores all class 2 impairments. If both class 1 and class 2 impairments are considered, the extent of signal degradation increases and hence the distance the signal can travel along fibers is further reduced. Therefore, r represents an upper bound. Hence, the heuristic cost, $\mathcal{H}_{t^n}$, gives a lower bound for the number of regenerators required to reach d from n. In other words, $\mathcal{H}_{t^n}$ is an admissible heuristic.   □

In lines $1-2$, the BFS-RWA (**Algorithm 1**) starts with node t^s as the root of the search tree. Line 3 sets the stage for the following iterative process, where t^h denotes the node whose neighborhood will be explored. Lines $5-27$ describe how the node, t^h, will be expanded. In line 5, $find\_eligible\_neighbours(t^h)$, finds the set of nodes adjacent to h in the physical topology and excludes from the set all nodes x such that a) there is no wavelength that is currently unused on the link $h \to x$, or b) t^x is an ancestor of t^h and appears in the same segment as t^h.

Algorithm 1. BFS-RWA

Input: New Request: $\mathcal{R} = (s, d)$, Network Topology, $\mathbb{N}$ (the set of regenerator nodes), Network State

Output: RWA Solution (if lightpath established), NULL (otherwise)

1:   $t^s \leftarrow create\_root\_node(s)$
2:   $\mathcal{T}_{t^s} \leftarrow heuristic\_cost(t^s)$
3:   $t^h \leftarrow find\_best\_node\_in\_tree()$
4:   **while** (true) **do**
5:     $\mathcal{N} \leftarrow find\_eligible\_neighbours(t^h)$
6:     **for each** $n \in \mathcal{N}$ **do**
7:       $t^n \leftarrow create\_node(t^h, n)$
8:       **if** $(lightpath\_feasible(t^h, t^n))$ **then**
9:         $\mathcal{A}_{t^n} \leftarrow actual\_cost(t^h, t^n)$
10:        $\mathcal{H}_{t^n} \leftarrow heuristic\_cost(t^n)$
11:        $\mathcal{T}_{t^n} \leftarrow \mathcal{A}_{t^n} + \mathcal{H}_{t^n}$
12:       **if** $(n \in \mathbb{N})$ **then**
13:         $t^n \leftarrow create\_regenerator\_node(t^h, n)$
14:         $\mathcal{A}_{t^n} \leftarrow \lceil actual\_cost(t^h, t^n) \rceil$
15:         $\mathcal{T}_{t^n} \leftarrow \mathcal{A}_{t^n} + \mathcal{H}_{t^n}$
16:       **end if**
17:       **else**
18:         $delete\_node(t^n)$
19:       **end if**
20:     **end for**
21:     $t^h \leftarrow find\_best\_node\_in\_tree()$
22:     **if** $(t^h$ is $NULL)$ **then**
23:       **return** NULL // The request for communication has to be blocked.
24:     **else if** $(reached\_destination(t^h))$ **then**
25:       $\mathcal{L} \leftarrow generate\_RWA\_solution\_using\_search\_tree(t^h)$
26:       **return** $\mathcal{L}$ // The request can be handled using the lightpath $\mathcal{L}$
27:     **end if**
28:   **end while**

---

find_eligible_neighbours allows a node x to appear more than once in a translucent lightpath if these occurrences are in different segments (Fig. 2 shows an example). However, a loop in the same segment cannot happen.

Lines 6 – 20 define an iterative process, which has to be repeated for each element in $\mathcal{N}$. In line 8, $lightpath\_feasible(t^h, t^n)$ checks whether it is feasible (in terms of channel assignment and QOT) to set up a lightpath, using a path from t^s to t^n through t^h, in the presence of all other existing lightpaths. If so, lines 9 – 11 compute the total cost of node t^n. Lines 12 – 16 consider the possibility that node n is capable of 3R regeneration. If so, another child of node t^h is created (line 13). This new child of t^h uses 3R regeneration and starts a new segment, having a OSNR value of $OSNR_{in}$. The ceiling function in line 14 means that the second term in equation 2 is replaced by 1. If the condition in line 8 is not satisfied, it means that t^n created in line 7 cannot be a child of t^h and is deleted in line 18.

Line 21 finds the next best node, t^h, to explore (i.e., the leaf node with the least total estimated cost). If this node cannot be found, the search has failed (line 23). If node t^h corresponds to d, the search terminates and returns the RWA solution (i.e., the route and the channel number(s) for all segment(s)).

Algorithm 2 describes function $lightpath\_feasible(t^h, t^n)$ and is discussed below. As mentioned before, every node (t^x) in the search tree maintains a list of channels, $(\mathbb{C}_{t^x})$, which can be assigned to the segment, ending in node t^x. In lines $1 - 5$, the intent is to determine the set of channels, $\mathbb{C}_{t^n}$ (i.e., the set of channels for the last segment so far). Those channels that are in use on the fiber $h \to n$, cannot be assigned to this segment. If node t^h is being used for regeneration (lines $1 - 2$), a new segment starts from t^h. Otherwise (lines $3 - 4$), the same segment from t^h continues to node t^n. In line 6, function $construct\_transparent\_segments(t^s, t^n)$, returns the set, Ψ, of all transparent segments (Ψ) of the proposed translucent lightpath.

Lines $7 - 12$ define an iterative process, which is repeated for every channel in set $\mathbb{C}_{t^n}$. In line 8, $assign\_channel(\Psi^{num\_segments}, c)$ assigns channel c to the last segment $(\Psi^{num\_segments})$ of the proposed lightpath. In line 9, our OSNR tool determines the feasibility of the proposed lightpath. The OSNR tool has access to the network state information, which includes the set of existing lightpaths. The OSNR tool measures the degradation of optical signals in all the lightpaths (including the new lightpath under consideration and the existing lightpaths) and returns the final OSNR value of the optical signal that has degraded the most. If this OSNR value is less than the $OSNR_{Th}$ for the network, then there is at least 1 lightpath that is infeasible. Therefore, channel c is not a valid assignment for $\Psi^{num\_segments}$, and is excluded from $\mathbb{C}_{t^n}$ in line 10.

After these iterations, if $\mathbb{C}_{t^n}$ becomes empty (line 13), it means that node t^h cannot be expanded to t^n in the search tree and $lightpath\_feasible(t^h, t^n)$ returns false. Otherwise, it means that channels are available to go from t^h to t^n. At this stage, the proposed lightpath is checked to see if any edge is shared by two or more segments (line 16). If there is at least one such shared edge, the technique described in [8] is used to ensure that such segments are not assigned the same channel. As done in [8], a path intersection graph (PIG) is created and list coloring [17] is used to color the graph (lines $17 - 20$). The segments of the proposed lightpath become nodes in the PIG and any 2 nodes in the PIG are connected by a link if the corresponding segments share an edge. Each node in the PIG is assigned a list of colors, where each color represents a channel that may be used for the corresponding segment. The objective is that each node in the PIG should be colored, using one of the colors in the list for that node. If the list coloring is successful, it means a valid channel assignment is possible for all the transparent segments and $lightpath\_feasible(t^h, t^n)$ returns true (Line 19). Otherwise returns false (Line 21).

In our network simulations we observed that, the translucent lightpaths that were established had no more than 2 shared edges. As a result, the corresponding path intersection graph (PIG) is a trivial one and any simple greedy algorithm can be used to color the PIG optimally. Hence, the usage of graph coloring technique in **Algorithm 2** does not affect the optimality of the final RWA solution.

Algorithm 2. lightpath_feasible(t^h, t^n)

Output: true (if feasible), false (otherwise)
1: **if** (t^h is used for 3R-regeneration) **then**
2:     $\mathbb{C}_{t^n} \leftarrow \{\, c \mid c$ *is an unused channel on fiber* $h \rightarrow n \,\}$
3: **else**
4:     $\mathbb{C}_{t^n} \leftarrow \mathbb{C}_{t^h} - \{\, c \mid c$ *is a used channel on fiber* $h \rightarrow n \,\}$
5: **end if**
6: $(\Psi, num\_segments) \leftarrow construct\_transparent\_segments(t^s, t^n)$
7: **for each** $c \in \mathbb{C}_{t^n}$ **do**
8:     $assign\_channel(\Psi^{num\_segments}, c)$
9:     **if** $(calculate\_OSNR\_value(\Psi) < OSNR^{Threshold})$ **then**
10:         $\mathbb{C}_{t^n} \leftarrow \mathbb{C}_{t^n} - \{c\}$
11:     **end if**
12: **end for**
13: **if** ($\mathbb{C}_{t^n}$ *is* $\emptyset$) **then**
14:     **return** false
15: **else**
16:     **if** $(check\_for\_shared\_edges(\Psi))$ **then**
17:         $PIG \leftarrow create\_path\_intersection\_graph(\Psi)$
18:         **if** $(colorable(PIG))$ **then**
19:             **return** true
20:         **end if**
21:         **return** false
22:     **end if**
23:     **return** true
24: **end if**

2.4   Example

Let there be a new connection request from $s = 3$ to $d = 5$ for the network given in Fig. 1. Fig. 3(a) shows the search tree, constructed using BFS-RWA, after a few iterations of the while loop starting at line 4 of Algorithm 1. Each node in the tree is shown using a circle enclosing the corresponding node number in the physical topology. The total estimated cost for each node in shown beside the node. A shaded node denotes that 3R regeneration will take place at that node. Additionally, selected nodes have been shown with a unique label(e.g., A, B, C) for convenience. Nodes marked with a X[1] in Fig. 3(a) are those that cannot be explored further in the search tree, either due the unavailability of channels (network layer constraints), or because of unacceptable QOT (physical

---

[1] Since nodes marked with a X in Fig. 3(a) correspond to nodes that cannot be explored further, they have been omitted from Fig. 3(b).

layer limitations). Table 1 shows the lightpaths in existence at the time when this new connection request is processed. Each fiber in the network supports 2 channels (c^0, c^1).

For the tree shown in Fig. 3(a), the node with label A has a total estimated cost of 1.60, which is the least among all leaf nodes in the tree. Therefore, in line 21 of Algorithm 1, $find\_best\_node\_in\_tree()$ returns node A, so that t^h has $h = 0$ and $\mathcal{T}_{t^0} = 1.60$. The conditions in lines 22 and 24 are not satisfied, so the next iteration of the while loop begins by exploring node A.

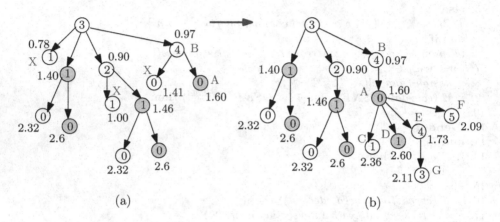

Fig. 3. Search tree after generating (a) node labelled A (b) node labelled G

Table 1. List of existing lightpaths

Lightpath Num.	Route	Channel
L1	$3 \to 1 \to 2$	c^0
L2	$1 \to 0$	c^1
L3	$3 \to 2$	c^0
L4	$2 \to 5$	c^1
L5	$4 \to 5$	c^0
L6	$4 \to 5$	c^1
L7	$1 \to 3$	c^0
L8	$1 \to 3$	c^1
L9	$1 \to 2$	c^1

Since A is shaded, a new segment starts from A. The set of nodes adjacent to node 0 in the physical topology is {1,4,5}. We note that node B in Fig. 3(b) is an ancestor of A but appears in a different segment. Therefore, we cannot exclude 4 from $\mathcal{N}$. Hence, in line 5, $find\_eligible\_neighbours(t^0)$ returns set $\mathcal{N} = \{1, 4, 5\}$. When $n = 1$, line 7 creates node C of Fig. 3(b). Function $lightpath\_feasible(t^0, t^1)$, in line 8, returns true, so that lines $9 - 16$ will be executed. In lines 9 – 11, the total estimated cost, for C, is calculated to be $\mathcal{T}_{t^1} = 2.36$. Since node 1 is capable of 3R regeneration, the condition in line 12 is satisfied. In lines 13 – 15, node D is created in a way similar to that for C. The process for $n = 4$ $(n = 5)$ is similar to that for C, giving node E (F) of Fig. 3(b). Since neither of the nodes 4 and 5 are capable of 3R regeneration, lines 13 – 15 are not applicable for E and F.

Even though node F in the search tree refers to the destination node 5 in the physical topology, the search proceeds, since the least cost node is currently E which will be selected for further exploration. In the next iteration, node G becomes a child of E, in a way just like C. In the following iteration, the lowest cost node is F. Since F refers to the destination node 5, the search has found the optimal solution. The routes for the segments of the established translucent lightpath are $3 \rightarrow 4 \rightarrow 0$ and $0 \rightarrow 5$. The channels assigned to these segments are c^1 and c^0 respectively. In line 25, this information is returned by $generate\_RWA\_solution\_using\_search\_tree(t^5)$.

3   Simulation and Results

In optical networks using DLA, the performance is measured in terms of the *lightpath blocking probability*, defined as the ratio of the number of lightpath requests that could not be satisfied (or blocked) to the total number of lightpath requests. In our experiments, we used synthetic network topologies of varying sizes (namely 15, 30 and 60 nodes) and 3 existing topologies, namely NSFNET (14 nodes), ARPANET (21 nodes) [18] and USANET (24 nodes) [19]. A link between two nodes in the network is assumed to be composed of 2 separate uni-directional optical fibers, where each fiber supports 32 channels.

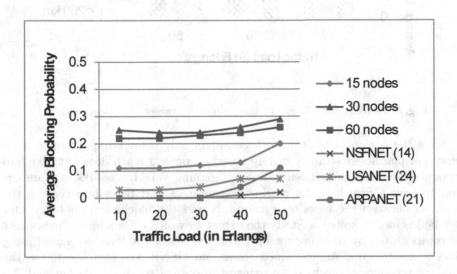

Fig. 4. Average Blocking Probability vs Traffic Load

The arrival of lightpath requests was assumed to follow a *Poisson distribution* and an *exponential distribution* was assumed for the duration of the lightpaths, after they have been established. The traffic load was measured in Erlangs (defined as the product of the request arrival rate and the average duration of the resulting lightpaths) and was varied by changing the request arrival rate. It was assumed that the average duration of the lightpaths was 3 minutes.

For synthetic networks, 5 different topologies were generated, for each size considered. For each value of the traffic load, 5 different sequences of requests for lightpaths were used. Each blocking probability reported in this section is, therefore, the average of 25 simulation runs. For each of the standard topologies, 5 different sequences of requests for lightpaths were used. For a given topology, to identify nodes which have 3R-regeneration capability, a branch and cut algorithm proposed in [20] was used. In our simulations, we have used an optical reach value of 300 km (calculated using the OSNR tool parameters, considering only class 1 impairments). Fig. 4 shows how the blocking probability changes when the traffic load is varied. For the standard (synthetic) topologies, a maximum of 10% (30%) of the requests were blocked.

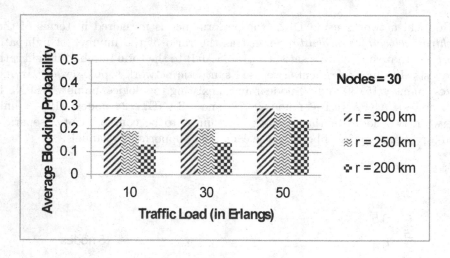

Fig. 5. Regenerator Placement using different values of optical reach (r)

Since the notion of optical reach considers only class 1 impairments, a regenerator placement strategy merely based on optical reach does not take into account the class 2 impairments. When designing WDM networks, it is important to have a firm basis for placing regenerators that takes into account the trade-off between the costs of regenerators and the blocking probability. Our test-bed is ideally suited to study the extent to which class 2 impairments may be compensated by reducing the optical reach below the level estimated using class 1 impairments. As mentioned above, our OSNR tool gave 300 km as the value of the optical reach. If we reduce the optical reach to 200 km and 250 km, we anticipated that the blocking probability will be reduced. We note that, when a lightpath undergoes 3R regeneration, implicitly wavelength conversion is available. It is known that wavelength converters have an effect on the blocking probability, since the wavelength continuity constraint [1] is relaxed at the node where 3R regeneration takes place. Thus, the reduction in the blocking probability is due to 2 factors - i) the possibility of wavelength conversion at the time of 3R-regeneration, and ii) the result of overestimating the class 1 impairments.

Fig. 5 shows the impact of using a reduced optical reach, during the RPP phase, on the blocking probability. For a traffic loads of 10, 30 and 50 Erlangs, the blocking decreased by 48%, 42% and 17% respectively, when we used an optical reach of 200 km, compared to the actual optical reach of 300 km (which was based on class 1 impairments only). The immediate effect of reducing the optical reach is an increase in the number of regeneration capable nodes. For instance, in the case of the 30 node network shown in Fig. 5, the number of regeneration capable nodes increased from 3 to 7 by changing the optical reach from 300 km to 200 km. This study shows the trade-off between the blocking probability and the number of regeneration capable nodes. In this series of experiments we assumed that each node, capable of 3R regeneration, has an unlimited number of regenerators available.

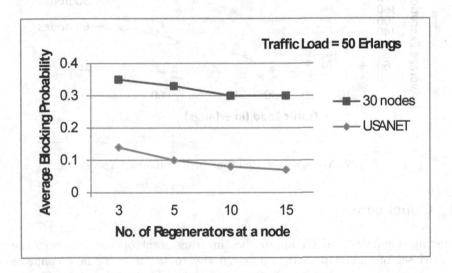

Fig. 6. Effect of varying the number of regenerators

It is not reasonable to place a very large number of regenerators at a node, if the likelihood of using them is very small. If this number is too small, some additional lightpath connection requests will be blocked, due to the lack of free regenerators. Fig. 6 shows the impact of varying the number of regenerators at each regeneration site, on the blocking probability. As expected, the blocking probability decreases, as the number of regenerators at the regeneration sites increases. This effect can be seen clearly in networks having 24-30 nodes. In small translucent networks, the number of regeneration sites is very small (usually 1 or 2) and the number of lightpaths requiring regeneration is also relatively low. As a result, the reduction in blocking probability is small.

Finally, Fig. 7 shows the average execution time of one complete simulation. One complete simulation means processing all requests for connections, for a given Erlang value, generated during an interval of one hour of network operation. The execution time was averaged over 25 simulations, using 5 randomly generated topologies. For small and medium sized networks, the execution times increase reasonably with traffic load. For large networks, the execution time grows rapidly with traffic. It is to be noted that, the main objective of formulating this approach was to present a benchmark, in terms of blocking probability, for any future fast algorithm to be developed.

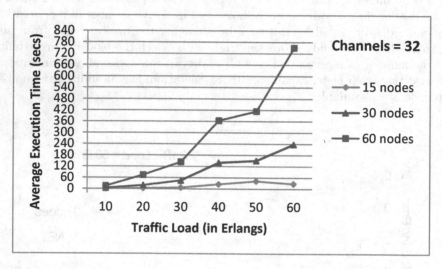

Fig. 7. Average execution time of 1 simulation(in secs)

4 Conclusions

Existing dynamic IA-RWA approaches in translucent optical networks use a limited set of candidate paths to assign the route for every new connection request. This leaves a number of other potential paths unexplored. In this paper we propose an IA-RWA approach (BFS-RWA) based on the A* algorithm that removes this limitation by performing an informed search of the solution space. To the best of our knowledge, this is the first approach to guarantee an optimal solution (if it exists) involving the fewest possible number of regenerators along the route for the lightpath. The BFS-RWA is also the first optimal algorithm that takes into account the occurrence of loops in translucent lightpaths.

Acknowledgements. This work was supported by a discovery grant from the Natural Sciences and Engineering Research Council of Canada (NSERC).

References

1. Bandyopadhyay, S.: Dissemination of Information in Optical Networks: From Technology to Algorithms. Springer (2008)
2. Chlamtac, I., Ganz, A., Karmi, G.: Lightpath communications: an approach to high bandwidth optical wan's. IEEE Trans. on Comm. 40(7), 1171–1182 (1992)
3. Ramaswami, R., Sivarajan, K., Sasaki, G.: Optical Networks: A Practical Perspective, 3rd edn. Morgan Kaufmann Publishers Inc. (2009)
4. Christodoulopoulos, K., Manousakis, K., Varvarigos, E., Angelou, M.: Considering physical layer impairments in offline rwa. IEEE Network 23(3), 26–33 (2009)
5. Yang, X., Ramamurthy, B.: Sparse regeneration in translucent wavelength-routed optical networks: Architecture, network design and wavelength routing. Photonic Network Communications 10(1), 39–53 (2005)
6. Sen, A., Murthy, S., Bandyopadhyay, S.: On sparse placement of regenerator nodes in translucent optical network. In: IEEE GLOBECOM, pp. 1–6 (2008)
7. Saradhi, C., Zaks, S., Fedrizzi, R., Zanardi, A., Salvadori, E.: Practical and deployment issues to be considered in regenerator placement and operation of translucent optical networks. In: ICTON, pp. 1–4 (2010)
8. Bandyopadhyay, S., Rahman, Q., Banerjee, S., Murthy, S., Sen, A.: Dynamic lightpath allocation in translucent wdm optical networks. In: IEEE ICC, pp. 1–6 (2009)
9. Azodolmolky, S., Angelou, M., Tomkos, I., Panayiotou, T., Ellinas, G., Antoniades, N.: Impairment-aware optical networking: A survey. In: WDM Systems and Networks, Optical Networks, pp. 443–479 (2012)
10. Yannuzzi, M., Quagliotti, M., Maier, G., Marin-Tordera, E., Masip-Bruin, X., Sanchez-Lopez, S., Sole-Pareta, J., Erangoli, W., Tamiri, G.: Performance of translucent optical networks under dynamic traffic and uncertain physical-layer information. In: ONDM, pp. 1–6 (2009)
11. Pachnicke, S., Luck, N., Krummrich, P.: Online physical-layer impairment-aware routing with quality of transmission constraints in translucent optical networks. In: ICTON, pp. 1–4 (2009)
12. Tordera, E., Martinez, R., Munoz, R., Casellas, R., Solé-Pareta, J.: Improving iarwa algorithms in translucent networks by regenerator allocation. In: ICTON, pp. 1–4 (2009)
13. Manousakis, K., Kokkinos, P., Christodoulopoulos, K., Varvarigos, E.: Joint online routing, wavelength assignment and regenerator allocation in translucent optical networks. Journal of Lightwave Technology 28(8), 1152–1163 (2010)
14. Zhao, J., Subramaniam, S., Brandt-Pearce, M.: Cross-layer rwa in translucent optical networks. In: IEEE ICC, pp. 3079–3083 (2012)
15. Russell, S., Norvig, P.: Artificial Intelligence: A Modern Approach, 2nd edn. Prentice Hall (1995)
16. Pereira, H., Chaves, D., Bastos-Filho, C., Martins-Filho, J.: Osnr model to consider physical layer impairments in transparent optical networks. Journal of Photonic Network Communications 18, 137–149 (2009)
17. Jensen, T.R., Toft, B.: Graph Coloring Problems. John Wiley & Sons (1995)
18. Kim, S., Zhang, X., Lumetta, S.S.: Rapid and efficient protection for all-optical wdm mesh networks. IEEE Jour. on Selected Areas in Comm. 25(9), 68–82 (2007)
19. Ye, Y., Chai, T., Cheng, T.H., Lu, C.: Algorithms for wavelength division multiplexed translucent optical networks. In: ICCS, pp. 361–365 (2004)
20. Rahman, Q.: Optimization of WDM Optical Networks. PhD thesis, School of Computer Science, University of Windsor, Windsor, ON, Canada (2012)

Mobility Aware Charge Scheduling of Electric Vehicles for Imbalance Reduction in Smart Grid

Joy Chandra Mukherjee and Arobinda Gupta

Department of Computer Science & Engineering,
Indian Institute of Technology, Kharagpur, India
{joy.cs,agupta}@cse.iitkgp.ernet.in

Abstract. Electric vehicles (EVs) are being introduced by different manufacturers as an environment-friendly alternative to vehicles with internal combustion engines. The number of EVs is expected to grow rapidly in the coming years which will act as distributed loads in the demand side of the smart grid. On the supply side, an aggregator has to predict a load schedule 12-36 hours in advance to charge the EVs and purchase energy accordingly from the day-ahead market. The goal of the aggregator is to schedule the charging of EVs at different charging stations so that the load prediction made by the aggregator are met and the energy imbalance between the energy purchased and the energy consumed by the EVs is minimized. In this work, we refer to this problem as the *Maximum Energy Usage EV Charging Problem* where mobile EVs communicate their charging preferences apriori to the aggregator and the aggregator schedules EVs to different charging stations in their route so that it incurs maximum energy usage (and therefore, minimum energy imbalance). We first prove that the problem is NP-complete. A pseudo-polynomial algorithm is proposed for a restricted version of the problem that can act as an upper bound for the solution of the general problem. A greedy heuristic is then proposed to solve the problem. Detailed simulation results in different city traffic scenarios show that the usage of energy achieved by the heuristic proposed is close to the upper bound proved.

Keywords: Electric Vehicle, Scheduling, VANET, Smart Grid.

1 Introduction

As an eco-friendly and cost-effective alternative over conventional vehicles driven by internal combustion engines, the use of electric vehicles (EV) have received significant importance in recent times. However, large scale adoption of EVs comes with new challenges. Though their operating costs are less, EVs are still more expensive to buy than ICE vehicles. In addition, EVs consume comparatively high power from the grid during charging. Therefore, uncoordinated charging of a large number of EVs can have an adverse impact on the grid operation (power outages, unacceptable voltage fluctuations) [5]. Hence, charge scheduling of EVs in smart grid is an important problem.

Majority of the EVs will be connected to the Internet through VANET, Wi-Fi, or cellular network. The Internet-enabled communication enables EVs to be clubbed into different groups of varying sizes by *aggregators* so that each group can be treated as

M. Chatterjee et al. (Eds.): ICDCN 2014, LNCS 8314, pp. 378–392, 2014.

a dispatchable load to the grid. An aggregator is a central entity that controls the actual charging decision of the EVs in its group. The aggregator has to predict a load schedule 12-36 hours in advance to charge the EVs and purchase energy accordingly from the day-ahead market. The EVs communicate their charging preferences such as time within which they want to be charged, their preferable charging spots, their route information, their maximum battery capacity, initial state-of-charge (SOC) of battery, desired SOC etc. to the aggregator beforehand. The aggregator, based on several grid constraints, user constraints, and mobility parameters, determines the charge schedule and communicates the schedule back to the individual EV. The goal of the aggregator is to minimize the energy imbalance between the energy purchased from the day-ahead market and the actual energy consumed by the EVs for charging while avoiding grid overload.

In this paper, we assume that an EV communicates its charging preferences to an aggregator at the beginning of its journey through the vehicular ad-hoc network (VANET) [3] infrastructure. Typically, VANET environments consist of moving vehicles and roadside infrastructure (road-side units or RSUs), with potential communication both between vehicles and between a vehicle and an RSU. The RSUs are usually connected to the internet through some backbone network. EVs moving along the roads in a city communicate their trajectory information, charging requirements (initial state-of-charge, maximum battery capacity, validity period or deadline, charging spot preferences) through RSUs to the aggregator. The aggregator schedules the charging plan of EVs (EV id, charging station, start and end time of charging, charging energy) in advance and communicates back to the EVs through RSUs. We have formulated the problem as an optimization problem called the *Maximum Energy Usage EV Charging Problem* which addresses the issue of scheduling the EVs to different charging stations in its route while maximizing the energy usage (and hence minimizing the energy imbalance) of the aggregator. We first prove that the problem is NP-complete. We then propose a pseudo-polynomial algorithm for a restricted version of the problem that will act as an upper bound for the problem. A greedy heuristic algorithm is proposed to solve the problem. Detailed simulation results of realistic traffic scenarios for two different cities (Tokyo and San Francisco) are presented to show that the usage of energy achieved by the heuristics proposed is close to the upper bound proved.

The rest of this paper is organized as follows. Section 2 discusses some related works. The *Maximum Energy Usage EV Charging Problem* is described in Section 3. The problem is then proved to be NP-complete in Section 4. Section 5 presents a pseudo-polynomial algorithm for a restricted version of the problem. Section 6 presents a greedy heuristic algorithm for the original problem. Section 7 presents the simulation results. Finally, Section 8 concludes the paper.

2   Related Works

Uncoordinated charging of a large number of EVs can have an adverse impact on the grid operation (power outages, unacceptable voltage fluctuations) [5]. Therefore, smart grid allows EVs to coordinate their charging operations that can improve frequency regulation [8], reduce energy imbalances [18], smooth out intermittent power generation from renewable energy sources, and make the electric power usage more efficient [4],[17].

There have been many works reported in the area of charge scheduling for EVs in the last few years. While all of them address the same basic problem, there is a wide variation in the environment in which they operate, parameters and constraints handled, and methodology employed for deriving the charge schedule. Unidirectional power flow model assumes that power flows only from the grid to EVs (G2V) when the EVs charge [8], [16], [14], [13], [2]. In the bidirectional power flow model, power flow is possible in both directions (V2G), but simultaneous charging and discharging of an EV battery is not allowed [15], [9], [10], [20]. Majority of the works on charge scheduling use centralized charging [12], [2], [11], [19], [6], [16], [14], [13], where the optimization of EV charge scheduling is done centrally at the aggregator after collecting information about power requirement of the EVs. None of these works consider the EVs' mobility aspects apart from the arrival and departure time in a specific parking lot. In this work, we consider the EVs' location at different point in time in their trajectory along with their varying charge requirement across different locations.

To the best of our knowledge, Vandael et al. [18] are the first to address the problem of imbalance reduction in smart grid by means of EVs. They propose a multi-agent solution to the above problem. Their approach is based on the assumption that since the EVs are parked most of the time, shifting their charging operation in time before their intended departure from the parking lot reduces the imbalance caused by unpredictable generation. However, their approach can not take advantage of the mobility of EVs which allows the possibility of EVs to be charged in one of the preferred charging stations in their way. In this work, we take advantage of the mobility information of EVs to schedule their charging in different charging stations.

3 Maximum Energy Usage EV Charging Problem

Each electric vehicle (EV) communicates its route information, its average speed, driver's charging station preferences, and charge status of its battery at the beginning of its journey via RSUs to the aggregator. The set of EVs is represented by H ($|H| = n$). The set of charging stations is represented by S ($|S| = m$). The route information of an EV h is represented as a tuple $\langle l_1^h, l_2^h, \ldots, l_r^h \rangle$, where $l_i^h \in L$ is an important location in h's trajectory, and L denotes the set of important locations in the city. The charge status of an EV h includes its maximum battery capacity (mc_h) and initial SOC ($ISOC_h$) of its battery. At the start of a journey, an EV h may communicate several preferential information regarding its charging requirements such as the desired SOC ($FSOC_h$) after charging, willingness to charge ($w_{hs} = 1$ denotes its willingness to charge at a charging station s, and $w_{hs} = 0$ denotes that h is not willing to charge at a charging station s). We assume that the rate of charging (nr) is constant for all EVs. Each charging station s has n_s number of charging outlets.

Each aggregator contracts the grid operator for purchasing energy from the day-ahead market for charging EVs from different charging stations. Let cap be the energy capacity that an aggregator has purchased from the day-ahead market.

Given a city map, the route information, the location-charging station mapping, and the average speed of the vehicle, the tentative arrival times of an EV and their current state-of-charge ($CSOC_{hs}$) in each charging station can be estimated. Also, we assume that an EV can charge only once in any one of the charging stations in its route in a single trip. Therefore, the charging requirement status of an EV h at a charging station s can be represented as a tuple $\langle h, s, st_{hs}, et_{hs}, ec_{hs} \rangle$, where $ec_{hs} = (FSOC_h - CSOC_{hs}) * mc_h$ is the energy consumption of EV h at charging station s, st_{hs} and $et_{sh} = st_{hs} + ec_{hs}/nr$ are the start and end time of charging of EV h at charging station s.

The objective is to schedule the charging so as to maximize the energy usage by the EVs. The total charging time T is divided into T timeslots, where $[0-1]$ denotes the 1st timeslot, $[1-2]$ denotes the 2nd timeslot, ..., and $[T-1, T]$ denotes the Tth timeslot. The output is a set of variables $\{x_{hst}\}$, where $x_{hst} = 1$ indicates that the EV h is scheduled for charging at the charging station s in time slot $[t-1, t]$; $x_{hst} = 0$ means otherwise. The problem is formally specified as follows:

$$\text{maximize } I' = \sum_{h \in H} \sum_{s \in S} ec_{hs} * w_{hs} * \prod_{t=st_{hs}}^{et_{hs}} x_{hst}$$

subject to the following conditions

$$\forall h \in H \; \forall s \in S \; \forall t \in [1, T] \quad x_{hst} \in \{0, 1\} \tag{1}$$

$$\forall h \in H \; \forall s \in S \quad w_{hs} \in \{0, 1\} \tag{2}$$

$$\sum_{h \in H} \sum_{s \in S} w_{hs} * \prod_{t=st_{hs}}^{et_{hs}} x_{hst} \leq n \tag{3}$$

$$\sum_{h \in H} \sum_{s \in S} ec_{hs} * w_{hs} * \prod_{t=st_{hs}}^{et_{hs}} x_{hst} \leq cap \tag{4}$$

$$\forall s \in S \; \forall t \in [1, T] \sum_{h \in H} w_{hs} * x_{hst} \leq n_s \tag{5}$$

$$\forall h \in H \; \sum_{s \in S} w_{hs} * \sum_{t=1}^{T} x_{hst} = \sum_{s \in S} w_{hs} * ((et_{hs} - st_{hs}) * \prod_{t=st_{sh}}^{et_{sh}} x_{hst}) \tag{6}$$

$$\forall h \in H \; \sum_{s \in S} w_{hs} * \prod_{t=st_{sh}}^{et_{sh}} x_{hst} \leq 1 \tag{7}$$

$$\forall h \in H \; \forall s \in S \; \forall t \in [1, st_{hs}) \quad x_{hst} = 0 \tag{8}$$

$$\forall h \in H \; \forall s \in S \; \forall t \in (et_{hs}, T] \quad x_{hst} = 0 \tag{9}$$

Constraint 3 indicates that the number of EVs that can be charged by an aggregator is upper-bounded by n. Constraint 4 tells that the total charging power of all the EVs is upper bounded by the energy capacity of the aggregator. A charging station can handle the charging activity of a finite number of EVs bounded from above by the number of the charge outlets it has (Constraint 5). We assume that the charging activity for a vehicle is non-preemptive i.e. the charging activity of an EV continues till it has reached its desired SOC ($FSOC_h$) (Constraint 6). We assume that only one charging station is used for a given EV h for its charging (Constraint 7). For a given EV and a charging station, a specific time duration is used for charging (Constraint 8, 9).

We refer this problem as the *Bounded Maximum Energy Usage EV Charging Problem (BMEVC)*. We will prove the NP-completeness of *BMEVC* in the next section.

4   NP-Completeness of the BMEVC Problem

In this section, we first define a restricted version of the *BMEVC* problem, where we assume that the number of charge outlets at a charging station s is unbounded ($n_s = \infty$), i.e., any number of EVs can be charged from s simultaneously. We refer to this restricted version of the *BMEVC* problem as the *Unbounded Maximum Energy Usage EV Charging Problem (UMEVC)*. The output of *UMEVC* is a set of variables $\{x_{hs}\}$, where $x_{hs} = 1$ indicates that the EV h is scheduled for charging at the charging station s; $x_{hs} = 0$ means otherwise. Then, we show that the *UMEVC* problem is NP-complete by reducing it from the *Partition Problem (PP)* [7] which is known to be an NP-Complete problem. Clearly, this also implies that *BMEVC* problem is NP-Complete.

The *UMEVC* problem is defined as follows:

$$\text{maximize } I'' = \sum_{h \in H} \sum_{s \in S} ec_{hs} * w_{hs} * x_{hs}$$

subject to the conditions (1) $\forall h \in H \; \forall s \in S \;\; w_{hs}, x_{hs} \in \{0, 1\}$, (2) $\sum_{h \in H} \sum_{s \in S} w_{hs} * x_{hs} \leq n$,

(3) $I'' \leq cap$, and (4) $\forall h \in H \; \sum_{s \in S} w_{hs} * x_{hs} \leq 1$.

The decision version of *UMEVC problem* (D-UMEVC) is to decide that given a non-negative integer cap', whether there exists an assignment of 0 or 1 to the set of variable x_{hs} such that $I'' \geq cap'$.

The *Partition Problem* (PP) is defined as follows:

[PP]: *Given a finite multiset* $A = \{a_1, a_2, \ldots, a_n\}$ *of n positive integers with* $T = \sum_{a_i \in A} a_i$, *is there a subset* $A' \subseteq A$ *such that* $\sum_{a_i \in A'} a_i = \sum_{a_i \in A - A'} a_i = T/2$?

Theorem 1. *The D-UMEVC problem is NP-complete.*

Proof. We start by arguing that D-UMEVC $\in$ NP. Given a certificate for the problem, we can calculate the total charging energy consumption by the EVs by multiplying x_{hs} to ec_{hs} and w_{hs}. Then, the total energy consumption can be checked whether it is less than or equal to cap, and whether it is greater than or equal to cap'. Next, we can check whether the sum of all the x_{hs} values is less than or equal to n, and for a given h, whether the sum of all the x_{hs} values is less than or equal to 1. Thus, the certificate can be verified in polynomial time.

Now we prove that D-UMEVC is NP-hard by showing that PP $\leq_P$ D-UMEVC. The reduction algorithm takes an instance of the PP, and produces an instance of the D-UMEVC in polynomial time as follows:

Let, $A = \{a_1, a_2, \ldots, a_n\}$ be an input instance of n positive integers for PP with $T = \sum_{a_i \in A} a_i$. Then, the instance B of D-UMEVC is defined by setting (1) $H = \{1, 2, \ldots, n\}$ i.e. $|H| = |A| = n$, (2) $S = \{s\}$, (3) For each $h \in H$ and for $s \in S$, $ec_{hs} = 2 * a_h$, (4) For each $h \in H$ and for $s \in S$, $w_{hs} = 1$, (5) $cap' = T$, and (6) $cap = T$.

We first show that a solution of PP gives a solution of D-UMEVC. Let $A' = \{a'_1, a'_2, ..., a'_k\}$ be an output instance of PP with cost equal to $T/2$. By our reduction, each a'_h corresponds to $1/2$ the charging energy ec_{hs}. The output instance of D-UMEVC B', denoted by $\{x_{hs}\}$, is constructed as follows:

$$x_{hs} = \begin{cases} 1 & \text{if } \exists h \in [1..k] \text{ such that } a'_h \in A' \\ 0 & \text{otherwise} \end{cases}$$

Since A' is a solution of PP, $\sum_{a'_h \in A'} a'_h = T/2$. This implies $\sum_{a_h \in A} \sum_{s \in S} a_h * w_{hs} * x_{hs} = T/2$. This implies $\sum_{h \in H} \sum_{s \in S} 2 * a_h * w_{hs} * x_{hs} \leq T$. This implies $\sum_{h \in H} \sum_{s \in S} ec_{hs} * w_{hs} * x_{hs} \leq cap$. Similarly, $\sum_{a_h \in A} \sum_{s \in S} a_h * w_{hs} * x_{hs} = T/2$. This implies $\sum_{h \in H} \sum_{s \in S} 2 * a_h * w_{hs} * x_{hs} \geq T$. This implies $\sum_{h \in H} \sum_{s \in S} ec_{hs} * w_{hs} * x_{hs} \geq cap'$. Hence, B' is a valid solution of D-UMEVC. Hence, a solution of PP gives a solution of D-UMEVC.

We next show that a solution of D-UMEVC gives a solution of PP. Suppose that $B' = \{x_{hs}\}$ has a value less than or equal to cap, and greater than or equal to cap', i.e., $\sum_{h \in H} \sum_{s \in S} ec_{hs} * w_{hs} * x_{hs} \leq cap$, and $\sum_{h \in H} \sum_{s \in S} ec_{hs} * w_{hs} * x_{hs} \geq cap'$.

From this, we construct A' as follows. Any $a'_h = ec_{hs}/2$ is included in A' if and only if $x_{hs} = 1$ for some EV h and the charging station s. Let $A' = \{a'_1, a'_2, ..., a'_k\}$.

Since $\{x_{hs}\}$ is a solution of D-UMEVC, $\sum_{h \in H} \sum_{s \in S} ec_{hs} * w_{hs} * x_{hs} \leq cap$. This implies $\sum_{a'_h \in A'} 2 * a'_h \leq T$. This implies $\sum_{a'_h \in A'} a'_h \leq T/2$. Similarly, $\sum_{h \in H} \sum_{s \in S} ec_{hs} * w_{hs} * x_{hs} \geq cap'$. This implies $\sum_{a'_h \in A'} 2 * a'_h \geq T$. This implies $\sum_{a'_h \in A'} a'_h \geq T/2$. Therefore, $\sum_{a'_h \in A'} a'_h = T/2$. Hence, A' is a valid solution of PP. Hence, a solution of D-UMEVC gives a solution of PP.

Hence, we have shown that for the reduction proposed, a valid solution of PP gives a valid solution of D-UMEVC and a valid solution of D-UMEVC gives a valid solution of PP. Hence, D-UMEVC is NP-complete. $\square$

5   Pseudo-Polynomial Algorithm for the UMEVC Problem

In this section, we propose a dynamic programming based pseudo-polynomial algorithm for the *UMEVC* problem that gives the optimal solution to the problem. The solution will act as an upper bound of any solution for the original *BMEVC* problem. The input to the algorithm is an array $ec[1+n][1+m]$ of elements, where $ec[h][s]$ is the maximum energy consumed by h^{th} EV in charging station s, where $ec[h][0] = 0$ for $h = 0, 1, ..., n$ and $ec[0][s] = 0$ for $s = 0, 1, ..., m$. cap is the total energy purchased by the aggregator. The output is stored in another array, called $optimum[1+n][1+cap]$, where $optimum[h][c]$ is the maximum energy consumed by the EVs numbered from 1 to h that is $\leq c$. Finally, $optimum[n][cap]$ returns the total energy consumed by the EVs that is less than or equal to cap, where cap is the total purchased energy. The optimal value of the solution to *UMEVC* is calculated recursively as follows:

$$optimum[h][c] =$$

$$
\begin{cases}
\quad\quad\quad 0 & \text{for } c = 0 \text{ and } h = 0, 1, \ldots, n \\
\quad\quad\quad 0 & \text{for } h = 0 \text{ and } c = 0, 1, \ldots, cap \\
MAX\{optimum[h-1][c], MAX_{s=1..m}ec[h][s] & \\
\quad +optimum[h-1][j-ec[h][s]]\} & \text{for } h = 1, \ldots, n \text{ and } c = 1, \ldots, cap
\end{cases}
$$

Theorem 2. $optimum[n][cap]$ *gives the optimal energy value consumed by EVs numbered from 1 to n for the UMEVC problem.*

Proof. We prove our claim by induction.

   Basis Step:

1. $\forall h \in [0..n]\ optimum[h][0] = 0$: Since the aggregator does not purchase any energy, i.e., $c = 0$, the charging requirements of any EV can not be fulfilled. Hence, the base case is trivially proved.

2. $\forall c \in [0..cap]\ optimum[0][c] = 0$: Since there is no EV ready for charging, i.e., $h = 0$, the aggregator will not be able to use any energy that it has purchased. Hence, the base case is trivially proved.

Induction Step: Let optimum[i][j] be the maximum energy consumed by the EVs numbered from 1 to i that is $\leq j$ for all $i < h$ and for all $j <= c$. We have to prove that optimum[h][c] stores the maximum energy consumed by the EVs numbered from 1 to h that is $\leq c$.

In the optimal solution value, either EV h is selected for charging or not.

Case 1: *If EV h is not selected in the optimal solution:* $optimum[h][c] = optimum[h-1][c]$.

Case 2: *If EV h is selected in the optimal solution:* Consider any charging station s where the EV h can be charged with energy $ec[h][s]$. If $ec[h][s]$ is in the solution (i.e. EV h is charged at charging station s), then $c - ec[h][s]$ is the remaining energy that the aggregator will use to optimally charge the EVs numbered from 1 to $h - 1$. By induction hypothesis, that optimal value is stored in $optimum[h-1][c - ec[h][s]]$. Therefore, the best solution value possible considering $ec[h][s]$ in the solution (i.e. EV h is charged at charging station s) is $ec[h][s] + optimum[h-1][c - ec[h][s]]$. Since, we take the maximum MAX of the best solution values over all the charging stations where EV h can charge, the maximum value MAX gives the best solution possible if we consider EV h's charging in the solution. Hence, $M = MAX_{s=1..m}(ec[h][s] + optimum[h-1][c - ec[h][s]])$.

Therefore, $optimum[h][c] = MAX(optimum[h-1][c], M)$. This implies that $optimum[h][c] = MAX(optimum[h-1][c], MAX_{s=1..m}(ec[h][s] + optimum[h-1][c - ec[h][s]]))$. □

The time complexity of the algorithm is $O(cap * n * m)$.

6   Greedy Heuristic for BMEVC Problem

In this section, we propose a centralized greedy algorithm for the *BMEVC* problem that can be used by the aggregator. Formally, the input to the algorithm is a list *list* of elements, where each element is a tuple $\langle h, s, ec[h][s], st[h][s], et[h][s] \rangle$ that denotes if the

EV h is selected to charge at the charging station s, the amount of energy required for its charging will be $ec[h][s]$ with $st[h][s]$ and $et[h][s]$ as the start and end time of charging respectively. cap is the total energy purchased by the aggregator. The maximum number of EVs that can be charged at the charging station s is upper-bounded by an integer $outlet[s]$. The output comprises of a subset of the elements in $list$ that satisfies all the constraints of the problem stated earlier, and returns the total energy consumed $totalEnergy$ by the EVs.

The pseudo code for the greedy algorithm is given in Algorithm 1. rem denotes the remaining energy left for charging the EVs not yet charged. Initially, rem is equal to the energy cap purchased by the aggregator. $allot[h]$ denotes the charging station used by EV h for its charging. Initially, $allot[h]$ is set to zero for all h. At the beginning of each pass of the algorithm, $time[s][t]$ indicates the number of EVs allocated for charging at the charging station s at time t. The algorithm works as follows. First, the elements of the $list$ are sorted in non-increasing order of the energy consumed ($ec[h][s]$) of the EVs (Line 5). In each pass of the algorithm, the element with the maximum energy is chosen in the solution provided (i) the energy requirement for the EV is less than or equal to rem (Line 7), (ii) the EV is not selected by the algorithm in any earlier pass (Line 8), and (iii) there is at least one charging outlet available for the EV to charge in that given duration at the charging station (Lines 9-16). The remaining energy capacity available to the aggregator rem is updated by subtracting the maximum energy selected from rem (Line 17). $allot[h]$ for the EV h is updated to s, the charging station where h will be charged (Line 18). Also, $time[s][t]$ is incremented by one for each $t \in [st[h][s], et[h][s]]$ for the charging station s (Lines 19-21). The total energy $totalEnergy$ consumed for charging EVs is updated by adding the maximum energy selected in the pass to $totalEnergy$ (line 22). The process is repeated for all the elements in the $list$.

7   Simulation Results

We have performed detailed simulations on realistic traffic patterns to evaluate the performance of the proposed heuristic. To simulate the vehicular environment, we use city maps of Tokyo and San Francisco available from [1]. A city is divided into a 7×15 grid, where each grid-cell represents a zone of area about 25 km^2. Each zone is characterized either as a busy zone (e.g. downtown or shopping district) or a less-busy zone depending on the number of four-road junctions in a zone, with zones with the number above a threshold being marked as busy zones.

The charging stations are placed in some of these junctions, with the exact placement depending on the experiments done. The distance between two locations in a city is calculated using *All Pair Shortest Path* algorithm. The zone from where a vehicle starts from is called its *source zone*. Similarly, the zone where the destination lies is called its *destination zone*. Given the source zone and the destination zone of a vehicle, two locations are picked from each zone as its start and end location of journey. The route of a vehicle is the set of locations in its shortest path from the start location to the end location. For a given zone, each charging station serves a subset of locations in that zone. Since an EV passes by a set of locations in the city, we pick the charging stations uniquely from the location-charging station mapping appropriate for the EV. The number of outlets in a charging station depends on the zone it is situated in.

Algorithm 1. Bounded Maximum Energy Usage EV Charging (BMEVC)

```
1:  rem ← cap;
2:  allot[1..n] ← 0;
3:  time[1..m][1..T] ← 0;
4:  totalEnergy ← 0;
5:  list ← Sort ec[h][s] in non-increasing order ∀ h ∀ s such that ec[h][s] ≠ ∞;
6:  for all (i ← 1; i ≤ list.length(); i ← i + 1) do
7:      if (list[i].ec ≤ rem) then
8:          if (allot[list[i].h] = 0) then
9:              flag ← true;
10:             for all (t ← list[i].st; t ≤ list[i].et; t ← t + 1) do
11:                 if (time[list[i].s][t] = outlet[list[i].s]) then
12:                     flag ← false;
13:                     break;
14:                 end if
15:             end for
16:             if (flag = true) then
17:                 rem ← rem − list[i].ec;
18:                 allot[list[i].h] ← list[i].s;
19:                 for all (t ← list[i].st; t ≤ list[i].et; t ← t + 1) do
20:                     time[list[i].s][t] ← time[list[i].s][t] + 1;
21:                 end for
22:                 totalEnergy ← totalEnergy + list[i].ec;
23:                 print EV list[i].h is charged at charging station list[i].s from list[i].st to list[i].et
                      by list[i].ec;
24:             end if
25:         end if
26:     end if
27: end for
28: return totalEnergy;
```

For a given EV h, the maximum battery capacity (mc_h) varies between 20-30 KW. The rate of charging (nr) is constant and fixed at 60 KW/hr. The total capacity purchased by the aggregator cap is 45 MW. The initial SOC ($ISOC_h$) varies between 40-50%. The SOC of an EV in the next charging station decreases proportionally with the distance from the source. The $FSOC_h$ value varies between 90-100%.

The time of reaching the first charging station by an EV varies randomly between 1 to 10 minutes from the beginning of simulation (from the simulation data, a typical journey from a source to a destination has been seen to take between 20-50 minutes). The st_{hs} values are generated in the order the charging stations are encountered in the route of EV h, and the starting st_{hs} value, and are proportional to the shortest path distance between them. The average speed of the vehicle is between 20 km/h to 60 km/h. The charging station ids are integers starting from 1 to the number of charging stations ($|S|$). The EV ids are integers starting from 1 to the number of EVs ($|H|$). All results reported are the average of at least 50 runs.

In this paper, three types of charging stations' placements are considered:

Zone Independent Uniform Placement Scheme: In this setting, the charging stations are uniformly distributed in all zones. In each zone, every charging station will serve equal number of locations in that zone.

Zone Dependent Uniform Placement Scheme: In this setting, 33% of the charging stations are uniformly distributed in all the busy zones and the remaining 67% are uniformly distributed in the less-busy zones. In each zone, every charging station will serve equal number of locations in that zone.

Zone Dependent Nonuniform Placement Scheme: In this setting, 33% of the charging stations are non-uniformly distributed in all the busy zones and the remaining 67% are uniformly distributed in the less-busy zones. Out of these 33% charging stations in the busy zones, each one-third of the busy zones chosen randomly have 50%, 30%, and 20% of the charging stations distributed uniformly. The reason for nonuniform placement of charging stations among busy zones is the varying amount of traffic (number of EVs) passing through those zones.

The following traffic patterns are generated:

Random Traffic: This scenario represents many vehicles moving from one end of the city to the other end in both directions. We randomly choose 5 to 7 different zones from the first two columns as source zones, and choose 5 to 7 different zones from the last two columns as destination zones for half of the EVs. The remaining EVs are traversed in the other direction with source and destination zones reversed.

Traffic towards busy zones: This scenario represents many vehicles moving towards some central location like the downtown of a city. 4-5 source zones are selected randomly from the less-busy zones and 3-4 destination zones are picked randomly from the busy zones.

Traffic from busy zones: This scenario represents vehicles diverging from a zone, for example, when people return to different parts of the city from the office district in the evening. 4-5 destination zones are selected randomly from the less-busy zones and 3-4 source zones are picked randomly from the busy zones.

In the simulation, the following five scenarios are considered based on the traffic pattern and charging station placement.

Scenario 1: Random traffic with Zone Independent Uniform Placement Scheme

Scenario 2: Traffic from busy zones with Zone Dependent Uniform Placement Scheme

Scenario 3: Traffic towards busy zones with Zone Dependent Uniform Placement Scheme

Scenario 4: Traffic from busy zones with Zone Dependent Nonuniform Placement Scheme

Scenario 5: Traffic towards busy zones with Zone Dependent Nonuniform Placement Scheme

We analyze how the percentage of energy consumed varies with the number of EVs and charging stations for all scenarios, and compare the performance of the heuristic to the upper bound (denoted in the graphs as *UMEVC*) result that forms a good

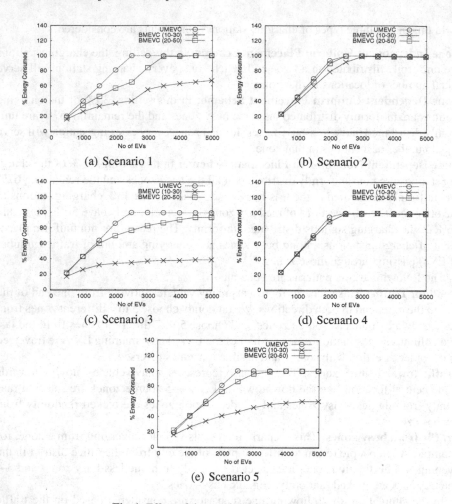

Fig. 1. Effect of the number of electric vehicles

reference for comparison. Due to lack of space, only the performance graphs for Tokyo are shown. Similar trends are seen in the results for San Francisco also. In each scenario, the number of outlets in a charging station in a busy and a less-busy zone are set to 30 and 10 respectively for one experiment (denoted in the graphs as *BMEVC (10-30)*, and to 50 and 20 respectively in another (denoted in the graphs as *BMEVC (20-50)*.

Effect of the number of EVs

For these experiments, 525 charging stations are placed in different zones of Tokyo with the exact placement depending on the scenario studied. Figure 1(a) to Figure 1(e) show how the % of energy consumption varies with the number of EVs for five different scenarios. As expected, the energy consumed for charging EVs shows a non-decreasing trend with increasing number of EVs for all scenarios. In all cases, an analysis of the simulation data shows that the charging stations that are used for charging EVs belong to the source zones or the zones nearer to them. EVs with low SOC in their battery are anyway charged in the source zone or the zones in the immediate neighborhood. The EVs with relatively high SOC are scheduled in 2-3 zones away from the source zones.

In all five scenarios, the performances of *UMEVC* are identical in the percentage of energy consumed by the EVs. Since the number of outlets are unbounded for any charging station, the number of charging stations in a zone does not affect the performances. Simulation log shows that 100% EVs are charged when the number of EVs are below a threshold (in our case 2500); the energy imbalance occurs due to the fact that no more EVs are left for charging. When the number of EVs is 2500, 100% energy is used to charge almost all the EVs. Beyond that point, the energy usage is 100%, and the number of EVs charged are almost constant (approximately 2500).

In Scenario 2 (Figure 1(b)) and Scenario 4 (Figure 1(d)), the % of energy consumption of *BMEVC (10-30)*, *BMEVC (20-50)* and *UMEVC* are almost identical, and the reason is majority of EVs are charged in the busy zones (6-7) with large number of charging stations (each with higher number of charge outlets) in their path. From simulation log, it is seen that 100% EVs are charged for less than 2500 EVs beyond which any increase in the number of EVs does not increase the number of EVs charged.

In Scenario 1 (Figure 1(a)), Scenario 3 (Figure 1(c)) and Scenario 5 (Figure 1(e)), *UMEVC* has shown identical performance to *BMEVC (20-50)* (100% EVs are charged with 60% energy usage) for lower number of EVs ($\leq$ 1500) since all the EVs can be accommodated in the charging stations in the source zones and other zones in the vicinity. For higher number of EVs (between 1500 and 3500), *UMEVC* performs better than *BMEVC (20-50)*, since less number of EVs can be accommodated for lack of charge outlets, and hence the energy usage is much better for *UMEVC*. Beyond 3500, the performance of *UMEVC* and *BMEVC (20-50)* are constant in terms of energy usage (100% for *UMEVC* and 90% for *BMEVC (20-50)*). From simulation log, it is clear that the number of EVs charged in these scenarios is also constant (2500 for *UMEVC* and 1800 for *BMEVC (20-50)*). Beyond 3500, no more EVs are charged in case of *UMEVC* since the aggregator capacity is fully utilized, and in case of *BMEVC (20-50)*, no more EVs are charged since all the charge outlets are used. The performances of *BMEVC (10-30)* are much poorer than *BMEVC (20-50)* for less number of outlets.

The presence of higher number of charging stations in and near the source zones causes the better performance. For lower number of EVs, the aggregator will schedule the EVs to charging stations as far as possible from the source zones, since all of them will anyway gets charged with zero energy imbalance. After a threshold number of EVs (in this case 2500), the aggregator's goal will always be met.

Effect of the number of charging stations

Figure 2(a) to Figure 2(e) show how the % of energy consumption varies with the number of charging stations for five different scenarios while keeping the number of EVs constant at 5000. In all scenarios, the entire energy purchased by the aggregator is consumed by the EVs for the unbounded case for similar reasons stated before. Relatively

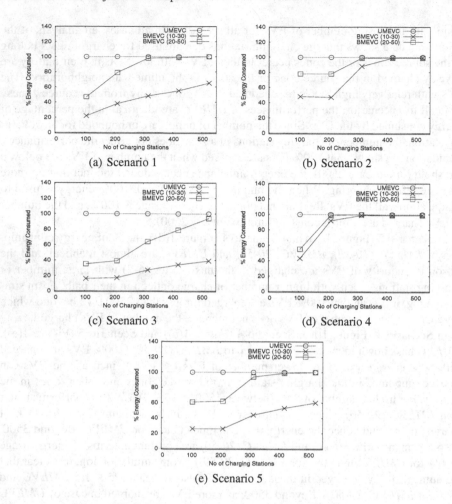

Fig. 2. Effect of the number of charging stations

small number of charging stations (10-12) situated in the source zones or the zones in their vicinity are used to charge majority of the EVs until the energy imbalance is close to zero. In all cases, it is observed from the simulation log that around 50% of the total EVs are charged in the unbounded case. The others are not charged due to the fact that there is not enough energy available to the aggregator to charge them.

For higher number of charging stations ($>$ 300), the energy consumption in Scenario 2 (Figure 2(b)) and Scenario 4 (Figure 2(d)) are almost identical for *BMEVC (10-30)*, *BMEVC (20-50)* and *UMEVC* since the majority of EVs are charged in the busy zones (6-7) with large number of charging stations (each with higher number of charge outlets) in their path. The availability of higher number of charging stations in busy zones in Scenario 4 than Scenario 2 causes the energy consumption in Scenario 4 to reach 100% much earlier than that in Scenario 2. Simulation log shows that 50% of the EVs are charged in these Scenarios for charging stations $>$ 300.

For lower number of charging stations (around 200), % of energy consumption in Scenario 4 is better than Scenario 2 in case of *BMEVC (20-50)* and *BMEVC (10-30)* because of the higher density of charging stations in busy zones in Scenario 4. Simulation log reveals that more EVs are charged in Scenario 4 than in Scenario 2 for *BMEVC (20-50)* and *BMEVC (10-30)* for lower number of charging stations. (Scenario 4: *BMEVC (20-50)* (50%) and *BMEVC (10-30)* (45%), Scenario 2: *BMEVC (20-50)* (40%) and *BMEVC (10-30)* (20%)).

For higher number of charging stations ($\geq$ 300), the energy imbalance reaches zero much earlier in Scenario 5 (Figure 2(e)) than in Scenario 3 (Figure 2(c)) for *BMEVC (20-50)* because of the higher number of charging stations in busy zones appeared in the midway of EVs' journey. Also, higher number of EVs are charged in Scenario 5 (45%) than Scenario 3 (40%) as evident from the log. In both of these scenarios, *BMEVC (20-50)* performs better than *BMEVC (10-30)* for higher number of charge outlets. Scenario 1 (Figure 2(a)) performs similar to Scenario 5 and better than Scenario 3 for higher number of charging stations. The uniform distribution of charging stations across all the zones in Scenario 1 and the higher density of charging stations in busy zones in Scenario 5 justify the result.

For lower number of charging stations (around 200), % of energy consumption in Scenario 5 is better than Scenario 3 in case of *BMEVC (20-50)* and *BMEVC (10-30)* because of the higher density of charging stations in busy zones in Scenario 5. Simulation log reveals that more EVs are charged in Scenario 5 than in Scenario 3 for *BMEVC (20-50)* and *BMEVC (10-30)* for lower number of charging stations. (Scenario 5: *BMEVC (20-50)* (30%) and *BMEVC (10-30)* (15%), Scenario 3: *BMEVC (20-50)* (25%) and *BMEVC (10-30)* (10%)). Scenario 1 (Figure 2(a)) performs better than Scenario 5 and Scenario 3 for lower number of charging stations. The uniform distribution of charging stations in the zones increases the opportunity to charge the EVs across all the zones.

On analyzing the results, it is evident that the energy consumption by EVs is predominantly influenced by the distribution of the charging stations and the number of charge outlets in each of the charging stations in the busy zones where the congestion is relatively high. A higher number of charging stations with large number of outlets potentially increase the number of EVs charged while decreasing the energy imbalance.

8   Conclusion

In this paper, we have proposed a greedy algorithm that the aggregator will execute to schedule the EVs for charging in one of their preferred charging stations in their way to destination. We have formulated and studied a problem for maximizing the energy usage by the aggregator for charging the EVs. The work is hoped to be the first to explore the mobility aspects of EVs to schedule their charging so that the energy imbalance is minimal. Since the average traffic flow across the busy zones are expected to be much higher than the less-busy zones in general, the placement of higher number of charging stations with large number of charge outlets in busy zones and zones in their vicinity will reduce the energy imbalance considerably.

References

1. http://www.openstreetmap.org/
2. Al-Awami, A.T., Sortomme, E.: Coordinating vehicle-to-grid services with energy trading. IEEE Transactions on Smart Grid 3(1), 453–462 (2012)
3. Bai, F., Krishnan, H., Sadekar, V., Holl, G., Elbatt, T.: Towards characterizing and classifying communication-based automotive applications from a wireless networking perspective. In: IEEE Workshop on Automotive Networking and Applications, AutoNet (2006)
4. Boulanger, A.G., Chu, A., Maxx, S., Waltz, D.: Vehicle electrification: Status and issues. Proceedings of the IEEE 99(6), 1116–1138 (2011)
5. Clement-Nyns, K., Haesen, E., Driesen, J.: The impact of charging plug-in hybrid electric vehicles on a residential distribution grid. IEEE Transactions on Power Systems 25(1), 371–380 (2010)
6. Erol-Kantarci, M., Mouftah, H.T.: Prediction-based charging of phevs from the smart grid with dynamic pricing. In: LCN, pp. 1032–1039 (2010)
7. Garey, M.R., Johnson, D.S.: Computers and Intractability: A Guide to the Theory of NP-Completeness. W.H. Freeman (1979)
8. Han, S., Han, S., Sezaki, K.: Development of an optimal vehicle-to-grid aggregator for frequency regulation. IEEE Transactions on Smart Grid 1(1), 65–72 (2010)
9. He, Y., Venkatesh, B., Guan, L.: Optimal scheduling for charging and discharging of electric vehicles. IEEE Transactions on Smart Grid 3(3), 1095–1105 (2012)
10. Khodayar, M.E., Wu, L., Shahidehpour, M.: Hourly coordination of electric vehicle operation and volatile wind power generation in scuc. IEEE Transactions on Smart Grid 3(3), 1271–1279 (2012)
11. Kim, H.-J., Lee, J., Park, G.-L.: Constraint-based charging scheduler design for electric vehicles. In: Pan, J.-S., Chen, S.-M., Nguyen, N.T. (eds.) ACIIDS 2012, Part III. LNCS, vol. 7198, pp. 266–275. Springer, Heidelberg (2012)
12. Lee, J., Kim, H.-J., Park, G.-L., Jeon, H.: Genetic algorithm-based charging task scheduler for electric vehicles in smart transportation. In: Pan, J.-S., Chen, S.-M., Nguyen, N.T. (eds.) ACIIDS 2012, Part I. LNCS, vol. 7196, pp. 208–217. Springer, Heidelberg (2012)
13. Sortomme, E., El-Sharkawi, M.A.: Optimal combined bidding of vehicle-to-grid ancillary services. IEEE Transactions on Smart Grid 3(1), 70–79 (2012)
14. Sortomme, E., El-Sharkawi, M.A.: Optimal charging strategies for unidirectional vehicle-to-grid. IEEE Transactions on Smart Grid 2(1), 131–138 (2011)
15. Sortomme, E., El-Sharkawi, M.A.: Optimal scheduling of vehicle-to-grid energy and ancillary services. IEEE Transactions on Smart Grid 3(1), 351–359 (2012)
16. Sortomme, E., Hindi, M.M., MacPherson, S.D.J., Venkata, S.S.: Coordinated charging of plug-in hybrid electric vehicles to minimize distribution system losses. IEEE Transactions on Smart Grid 2(1), 198–205 (2011)
17. Sundstrom, O., Binding, C.: Flexible charging optimization for electric vehicles considering distribution grid constraints. IEEE Transactions on Smart Grid 3(1), 26–37 (2012)
18. Vandael, S., Boucké, N., Holvoet, T., Craemer, K.D., Deconinck, G.: Decentralized coordination of plug-in hybrid vehicles for imbalance reduction in a smart grid. In: AAMAS, pp. 803–810 (2011)
19. Vasirani, M., Ossowski, S.: Lottery-based resource allocation for plug-in electric vehicle charging. In: 11th International Conference on Autonomous Agents and Multiagent Systems, pp. 1173–1174 (2012)
20. Wu, C., Mohsenian-Rad, H., Huang, J.: Vehicle-to-aggregator interaction game. IEEE Transactions on Smart Grid 3(1), 434–442 (2012)

Effective Scheduling to Tame Wireless Multi-Hop Forwarding

Chen Liu, Janelle Harms, and Mike H. MacGregor

Department of Computing Science, University of Alberta,
2-32 Athabasca Hall, Edmonton, Alberta, Canada T6G2E8
{cliu2,janelleh,mike.macgregor}@ualberta.ca

Abstract. Multi-hop forwarding extends wireless coverage and provides inexpensive Internet access. However, due to co-existing intra-path and inter-path interference in wireless networks, multi-hop forwarding significantly degrades network performance (e.g. throughput, reliability and fairness etc.). In response to this challenge, we propose a unique solution, hybrid TDMA/CSMA, as a medium access control method to effectively handle a wide range of complicated interference scenarios under the impact of dynamic traffic. Our simulation results demonstrate that hybrid TDMA/CSMA significantly reduces packet loss rate, and increases throughput as well as fairness.

Keywords: Multi-Hop Forwarding, Medium Access Control, Scheduling.

1 Introduction

Wireless multi-hop forwarding is a promising paradigm to provide ubiquitous and inexpensive network coverage, and has been widely adopted in wireless mesh, sensor and vehicular networks. Key applications include wireless video surveillance, tactical edge networks, emergency response, and extended Internet access for rural areas etc. Despite diverse application scenarios, a fundamental challenge associated with wireless multi-hop forwarding is how to alleviate the significantly degraded network performance such as poor throughput and low reliability. This is because propagating traffic over a long distance via a path composed of multiple geographically distributed nodes causes chaotic bandwidth competition among transmission between different paths, and within the same path. Depending on the underlying routing topology, a multi-hop path may compete with different paths along its trajectory. Additionally, intra-path interference transforms expected coordination among nodes within the same path into unwanted competition. Such uncontrolled competition can lead to unfair and inefficient resource consumption. Furthermore, dynamic traffic patterns add another dimension of complication in addition to aggravated interference. Without carefully managing the scarce bandwidth resource and handling complicated competition scenarios, it is impossible to provide any level of performance guarantee. In response to this challenge, we propose a unique scheduling algorithm,

M. Chatterjee et al. (Eds.): ICDCN 2014, LNCS 8314, pp. 393–407, 2014.
© Springer-Verlag Berlin Heidelberg 2014

Hybrid TDMA/CSMA, which significantly improves network throughput, reliability and fairness with very low control overhead. To the best of our knowledge, the proposed scheduling algorithm is the first effort to jointly consider two important sources of dynamics: time-varying traffic patterns and a wide range of complicated wireless interference scenarios.

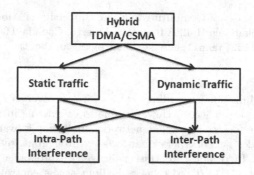

Fig. 1. Hybrid TDMA/CSMA

Existing methods provide piecewise solutions to the multi-hop forwarding problems. TDMA-style (time division medium access) approaches aim to achieve conflict-free transmission via centralized scheduling. For example, coloring algorithms are used in [1][2]. However, TDMA requires complex computation, centralized control, and frequent updates upon network and traffic changes. In contrast, CSMA is a distributed method that allows nodes to contend for medium access whenever they have data to transmit. CSMA-like (carrier sensing multiple access) methods are simple in computation, adaptable to network and traffic changes, but less effective than TDMA in reducing collisions. Efforts are also made to combine TDMA and CSMA. For example, Z-MAC invokes CSMA when traffic load is light, and applies TDMA with heavier traffic [2] to reduce energy consumption. However, these methods do not differentiate various interference scenarios and can lead to inefficient resource utilization.

In comparison, we tackle the unique challenges inherent to multi-hop forwarding from the perspective of how to comprehensively treat the interaction among various interference scenarios, under the impact of dynamic traffic with minimum efforts, in terms of computational complexity and control overhead. The proposed hybrid TDMA/CSMA makes the following contributions.

- **First,** our method jointly handles the interaction between dynamic traffic pattern and complicated multi-hop interference as shown in Fig. 1.
- **Second,** our method differentiates the causes of various interference scenarios and provides a comprehensive mechanism to handle their dynamic combination. In Fig. 2, we show the schematic hierarchy of the complex multi-hop interference that hybrid TDMA/CSMA handles.
- **Third,** our method also improves bandwidth utilization fairness by transforming unwanted competition into coordinated transmissions.

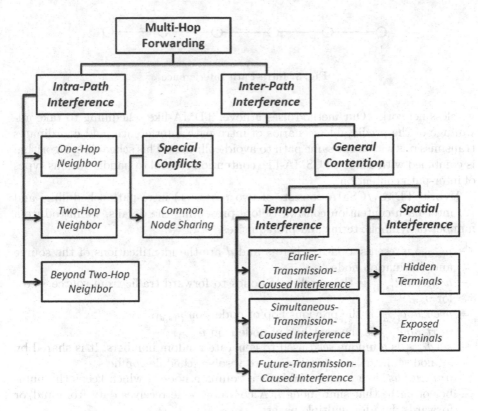

Fig. 2. Complex Interference Scenarios in Wireless Multi-Hop Networks

- **Fourth,** the proposed algorithm significantly improves multi-hop forwarding performance with low computation complexity and minimum control overhead.

Before diving into details, we would like to clarify the scope of this paper. First, we aim to tackle the fundamental challenge of wireless multi-hop forwarding which is common for diverse application scenarios. Therefore, we start with a generalized networking setup, and will target more specific application scenarios in the next stage. Second, in this paper, we mainly focus on improving transmission reliability, network throughput and fairness, and leave energy and delay related issues in the follow-up work [4]. Third, because the problem is difficult enough as is, we will consider mobility in the next step. In the rest of this paper, details of the proposed hybrid TDMA/CSMA are described in Section 2. Performance evaluation and conclusions are given in Sections 3 and 4.

2   Hybrid TDMA/CSMA

Hybrid TDMA/CSMA serves as the medium access control layer, and aims to effectively manage co-existing intra-path and inter-path interference in multi-hop

Fig. 3. Intra-Path Interference

wireless networks. Our method uses a novel TDMA-like scheduling to take advantage of the predictable scenarios of intra-path interference, and coordinates transmissions within the same path to avoid collisions. This scheduling algorithm is combined with a slotted CSMA-like contention control to handle various types of inter-path contention.

Hybrid TDMA/CSMA consists of two parts: (1) intra-path scheduling; and (2) inter-path contention control. Before presenting the details, we introduce a number of symbols, terms and prerequisites.

- $p_{(s,d)}$ represents a path, where s and d are the identifications of the source and destination node.
- $hop\_count^i_{(s,d)}$ is the number of nodes to forward traffic from source s to i for $p_{s,d}$.
- $prev\_hop^i_{(s,d)}$ is the previous hop of node i on $p_{(s,d)}$.
- $next\_hop^i_{(s,d)}$ is the next hop of node i on $p_{(s,d)}$.
- $seed_{(s,d)}$ is a unique seed used to generate random numbers. It is shared by all nodes on the same path $p_{(s,d)}$ to resolve schedule conflicts.
- num_paths_i is a local variable at a common node i, which keeps the number of paths that share node i. A common node receives data from and/or forwards data for multiple paths.
- $num\_share^i_{(s,d,j)}$ is a local record at node i of the number of paths that share a common node j ($i \neq j$). Both node i and j are neighbors within two hops, and forward data for path $p_{(s,d)}$.
- $num\_share\_map_i$ is a local map at node i that records all $num\_share^i_{(s,d,j)}$. We use (s,d,j) as the key, because a path may share different common nodes with different paths.
- $max\_num\_share_i$ is the current largest value recorded in $num\_share\_map_i$.

We assume that the above information is initialized before the scheduling algorithm starts via the following method. First, $hop\_count^i_{(s,d)}$, $prev\_hop^i_{(s,d)}$, $next\_hop^i_{(s,d)}$ and $seed_{(s,d)}$ can be easily obtained by sending an initialization message along each path $p_{(s,d)}$ after the routing phase. Node i keeps monitoring the number of paths it forwards/receives data for/from, and updates num_path_i when a change occurs. The common node map $num\_share\_map_i$ is initially empty. We describe how to update $num\_share^i_{(s,d,j)}$, $num\_share\_map_i$ and $max\_num\_share_i$ for both fixed and dynamic traffic in Section 2.2.

2.1   Intra-path Scheduling

When traffic is forwarded in a multi-hop manner, the transmissions between different nodes along the same path may interfere. For instance, if node A and

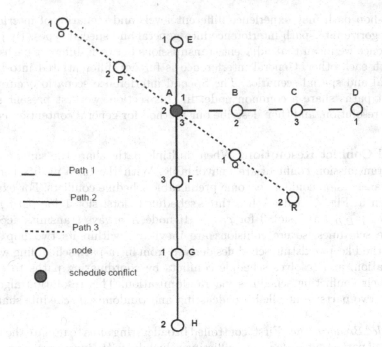

Fig. 4. Common Node Scheduling with Fixed Traffic

C transmit at the same time for $p_{A,F}$, collisions will happen at B (see Fig. 3). Intra-path scheduling aims to minimize collisions caused by such self interference. This algorithm takes advantage of the predictable self-obstructive conflicts within a scope of three hops, and enables a node i to infer its path-wise transmission schedule $sched^i_{(s,d)}$ locally. Specifically, if $hop\_count^i_{(s,d)}$ can be divided by 3, then $sched^i_{(s,d)}$ equals 3; otherwise, $sched^i_{(s,d)}$ equals $hop\_count^i_{(s,d)}\%3$. For example, $sched^i_{(s,d)}$ for A, B, C, D, E, and F are 1, 2, 3, 1, 2 ,3 (Fig. 3). These schedules eliminate collisions caused by intra-path interference, if the routing algorithm guarantees that nodes beyond two hops on the same path do not interfere with each other. Otherwise, our algorithm reduces intra-path collisions by guaranteeing that no self-obstructive transmissions occur within every three hops, and leaves interference beyond two hops away to be handled by a slotted CSMA/CA-like algorithm (see Section 2.2). Compared with graph-based TDMA scheduling [1] [2], our intra-path scheduling requires no message passing after the inital set up to infer local schedules. Furthermore, this algorithm transforms unwanted competition within the same path to coordinated transmissions.

2.2 Inter-path Contention Control

Compared to intra-path interference, transmission conflicts between different paths is less predictable in terms of when they occur and where the interference comes from. Depending on routing topology and traffic pattern, the nodes along a multi-hop path may experience different levels and scenarios of interference. We categorize inter-path interference into general and special types. By general interference we mean that adjacent transmissions between different paths interfere with each other. General interference is further differentiated into various temporal and spatial scenarios. The Special interference scenario occurs when different paths share a common node. In this section, we first present special conflict resolution, and then describe our method for general contention control.

Special Conflict Resolution. When multiple paths share the same common node, transmission conflicts are unavoidable. With the intra-path scheduling, these transmission conflicts become predictable schedule conflicts. For example, as shown in Fig. 4, node A has three scheduled slots: slot 1 for path $p_{(A,D)}$, slot 2 for $p_{(E,H)}$, and slot 3 for $p_{(O,R)}$. If node A always transmits according to these schedules, severe collisions are inevitable within its two hop range. Our method keeps existing schedules derived from intra-path scheduling without modification, and resolves schedule conflicts by coordinating paths to equally share their conflicting schedules via randomization. This resolution algorithm includes two parts: controlled broadcasting and randomized schedule sharing.

Controlled Broadcasting. First, controlled broadcasting aims to update the largest number of paths that node i has conflicting schedules with, $max\_num\_share_i$. Because a node may be within the two hop range of more than one common node, we keep a map $num\_share\_map_i$ at node i to record these common nodes and the number of paths they forward data for and/or receive data from. Because schedule conflicts only occur within the two hop range of each common node according to intra-path scheduling, we use a two hop broadcast to reduce overhead.

In the case of fixed traffic, this controlled broadcasting is invoked during system initialization after routing. Specifically, a common node j broadcasts a message that includes num_paths_j and the identifications of all the paths that share j. To achieve controlled broadcast, a counter field is included in . the broadcast message. This counter is initially set to two by a common node, and is updated by subtracting one each time it is received. After receiving this broadcast, a neighbor i first checks whether it belongs to a path $p_{(s,d)}$ that is included in the message, and either $prev\_hop^i_{(s,d)} = j$ or $next\_hop^i_{(s,d)} = j$ is satisfied. If these conditions are satisfied, i creates a record of $num\_share^i_{(s,d,j)} = num\_paths_j$ for j; inserts it to $num\_share\_map_i$; subtracts the value of the counter field by one. If the updated counter value equals one, i broadcasts this message. Otherwise, i discards the message.

For dynamic traffic, the same algorithm is invoked when a new/old path joins/leaves the network. By monitoring local traffic, an affected common node i detects these changes, updates num_path_i, and starts controlled broadcasting. An affected neighbor j updates the common node map $num\_share\_map_j$ and $max\_num\_share_j$ upon receiving such a message. The derived $max\_num\_share_i$ will be used in part 2.2.

Randomized Schedule Sharing. The second part of special conflict resolution aims to share conflicting schedules via randomization. Specifically, we assign each node $p\_share^i_{(s,d)}$, the schedule probability that node i transmits during its scheduled slot for path $p_{(s,d)}$. If $max\_num\_share_i \geq 1$, the transmission schedule of node i for path $p_{(s,d)}$ is conflicting with $(max\_num\_share_i - 1)$ other paths, and should share this conflicting schedule with a probability of $p\_share^i_{(s,d)} = 1/max\_num\_share_i$. Otherwise, node i has no conflicting schedules with any path, and always transmits during its scheduled slot. Therefore, $max\_num\_share_i$ allows randomization among multiple paths that share a common node to reduce conflict. Furthermore, we use a unique $seed_{(s,d)}$ for each path that allows intra-path scheduling to keep track of when to transmit, and therefore guarantees that during each round of slot 1, 2 and 3, the common node and its two hop intra-path nodes make non-conflicting decisions regarding whether to transmit during their designated slots. For instance, for path 1 in round n, if A does not transmit in slot 1, B, C and D do not transmit in slot 2, 3, and 1 respectively.

General Contention Control. Besides transmission conflicts caused by sharing a common node, general interference between adjacent transmissions is the fundamental contributor to inter-path competition. We categorize general interference scenarios into temporal and spatial types. Temporal scenarios include interference caused by earlier, simultaneous and future transmissions. Spatial scenarios cover both hidden and exposed terminals. Due to the dynamic nature of general interference, we propose a CSMA/CA-like contention control that is simple in computation, light in control overhead, and adaptable to dynamic network conditions.

Temporal Contention Control. First, we use a slotted CSMA/CA-like method to avoid collisions caused by earlier, simultaneous and future transmissions. Specifically, time is slotted and each slot equals the transmission period of a pair of data and acknowledgment packets, as well as contention overhead. The contention overhead includes a maximum contention window, interframe spaces and propagation delay. Before starting a transmission, a node first determines whether the medium is occupied by earlier transmissions via physical carrier sensing. If yes, the node waits until the occupation is over. Upon an idle medium, a node avoids simultaneous transmissions by selecting a random period within the contention window $cwin_i$ to back off at the beginning of this scheduled slot. Random back-off reduces the possibility that multiple transmissions start at the same time. Furthermore, no transmission can start after the maximum contention window expires during each slot. This limits the period when future-transmission-caused interference may occur. If a collision occurs, retransmissions are adopted to improve reliability. Unlike CSMA/CA, our method does not exponentially increase the contention window after a failed transmission. This is because every retransmission only starts in the next scheduled slot, and the waiting time is longer than the transmission time of a data packet.

Spatial Contention Control. In space, interference scenarios include hidden or exposed terminals. Hidden terminals occur when two transmissions fail due to undetected mutual interference. In contrast, exposed terminals occur when two transmissions do not proceed in parallel due to mistaking each other as interference. Our spatial contention control handles both scenarios. First, we avoid exposed terminals by setting the carrier sensing range equal to the transmission range. Upon overhearing a packet *pkt_ovrd* within the transmission range, node i checks whether the transmission of *pkt_ovrd* and i's pending transmission *pkt_nxt* (e.g. the first packet from i's queue) will form exposed terminals. We assume each packet carries the location information of its sender and receiver. Specifically, i retrieves the locations of itself and three other nodes: *pkt_nxt*'s receiver (denoted *nxt_rcv*) by reading the receiver field of *pkt_nxt*; *pkt_ovrd*'s sender (denoted *snd_ovrd*) and receiver (denoted *rcv_ovrd*) from the corresponding fields. Based on this information, we estimate the signal strength at *nxt_rcv* and *rcv_ovrd*, if *pkt_ovrd* and *pkt_nxt* proceed in parallel. If the signal strength is lower than a commonly used threshold 10 dB, i is allowed to contend for transmission right away. Otherwise, i waits until the medium becomes idle.

Second, we use a probabilistic contention method to reduce hidden terminals. Because the carrier sensing range is reduced to help detect exposed terminals, physical carrier sensing detects an idle medium, even when hidden terminals occur. Therefore, we introduce the idleness probability (p_i^{idle}) to enable a node to decide not to contend for transmission when physical carrier sensing detects an idle medium. p^{idle} can be adjusted according to the severity of hidden terminals, in terms of the number of collisions over a period. The more often hidden terminals occur, the higher p^{idle} should be. We dynamically adjust p^{idle} via the method we previously proposed in [3].

2.3   The Complete Algorithm and Complexity/Overhead Analysis

Hybrid TDMA/CSMA combines intra-path scheduling and inter-path contention control to provide medium access control for multi-hop wireless networks. During system initialization, the controlled broadcasting is called by each common node. After the routing phase, time is slotted and each slot is assigned a number 1, 2 or 3 according to intra-path scheduling. Node i contends for medium access at its scheduled slot by following the special contention control. If i has no schedule conflicts with other nodes or randomized schedule sharing allows i to transmit, it invokes general contention control to avoid collisions. Otherwise, i waits for the next scheduled slot.

This algorithm requires computations at two places. First, intra-path schedules are inferred locally via a modulo operation. Second, special conflict resolution requires that each node computes a schedule probability via a simple division, and determines whether to transmit by comparing a random number with the schedule probability. Message passing is only required for controlled broadcasting during initialization. Assuming m common nodes in a network of size n and the neighbor degree of each node is d, the first hop broadcast requires m messages. Because not all neighbors of a common node are on affected paths, we assume k neighbors of each common node are involved in the second hop broadcasting on average ($k \leq d$). Therefore, for average cases, the second hop broadcast requires k messages, and the message complexity is $O(m \cdot k)$. In the worst case scenario, all d neighbors of each common node transmit, and the message complexity is $O(m \cdot d)$.

3 Performance Evaluation

3.1 Implementation

We implement hybrid TDMA/CSMA in ns2 by modifying the basic access method CSMA/CA of IEEE 802.11b. Specifically, time is divided into slots. If a node i has a packet for path $p_{(s,d)}$ to send and the current slot is i's designated turn according to hybrid TDMA/CSMA scheduling, node i starts backing off with a probability $1 - p_{(i,s,d)}^{idle}$, and waits for the propagation delay of one packet with a probability $p_{(i,s,d)}^{idle}$. The back-off period is randomly selected within the contention window $cwin_{(i,s,d)}$. Second, to improve the simulation accuracy, we added a SINR-based collision model with aggregate interference [5] to the IEEE 802.11 implementation in ns2. The aggregate interference experienced by a node at a particular time is computed as the total signal strength it receives from all active transmissions at that time. Furthermore, a preamble detection function is also added in ns2.

3.2 Simulation Setup

We simulate a 800-by-800 m^2 network with 200 nodes that are randomly deployed. The routing topology is formed by randomly selected a number of source and destination pairs, and find the shortest path between each pair of source and destination nodes via the Dijkstra's algorithm [6]. Due to the random selection process, these paths vary in terms of length, overlapping degree and interference level. To capture the diversity of interference scenarios and common node sharing, we generate 16 different routing topologies and give a comprehensive evaluation of the proposed scheduling algorithm. Furthermore, the number of multi-hop paths (e.g. 10, 15 and 20) is also varied to increase diversity. Following the convention, traffic is generated at each source node according to the Poisson distribution. Each experiment spans 15 minutes.

We carry out two experiments to evaluate hybrid TDMA/CSMA in both random and controlled topologies. As an initial study, we aim to evaluate whether Hybrid TDMA/CSMA effectively handles various interference scenarios as it was designed for. Because hidden and exposed terminals are good indicators of under-controlling and over-controlling interference, we compare with Hybrid TDMA/CSMA (denoted HS in figure) with two configurations of CSMA/CA: CSMA/CA-ED (denoted EC) and CSMA/CA-HD (denoted HC). These two configurations represent the scenarios when exposed and hidden terminals dominate respectively. CSMA/CA-ED fixes the physical carrier sensing range to twice the

Table 1. Fixed Parameters

Parameter	Value
Transmission range	200 meters
HS Carrier sensing range	200 meters
HC Carrier sensing range	200 meters
EC Carrier sensing range	400 meters
Transmit power	0.2818 W
Minimum contention window	640 μs
Maximum contention window	20460 μs
Offered load	50 pps
Packet size	512 bytes
Channel capacity	1 Mbps
running time	30 minutes

transmission range to reduce hidden terminals. CSMA/CA-HD reduces exposed terminals by setting the carrier sensing range equal to the transmission range. We will implement other hybrid scheduling schemes such as Z-MAC to further evaluate the effectiveness of the proposed scheduling algorithm in the near future.

These experiments are carried out under different network topologies, traffic loads and interference levels. Performance is evaluated according to four metrics: packet loss rate, fairness, end-to-end delay and aggregate network throughput. As a convention, we use the widely adopted Jain's index to calculate fairness. Other fixed system parameters are listed in Table 1.

3.3 Experiments in Random Topologies

The first set of experiments are carried out in sixteen different routing topologies with a fixed offered load of 50 pps. Each topology is generated by randomly selecting fifteen multi-hop paths via Dijkstra's algorithm [6]. For visual clarity, we sort each sub-plot in Fig. 5 according to the performance of CSMA/CA-HD. Please note that the reason we use a line graph is for easy comparison. There is no correlations between the points along each line. Experiments are repeated with randomly generated Poisson traffic for ten times over each topology. Because the resultant confidence intervals are small, we did not include them in the already crowded figure, Fig. 5. We do present confidence intervals in the experiments of controlled topologies in Section 3.4. It needs to be noted that we use the line presentation in Fig. 5 only for easier visual comparison. A line, in this case, does indicate any relation among different topologies.

First, hybrid TDMA/CSMA (HS) reduces the packet loss rate significantly in all sixteen topologies as shown in Fig. 5. This is because HS minimizes collisions within the same path via intra-path scheduling; and reduces collisions between different paths caused by scheduling conflicts and various temporal and spatial interference. In comparison, CSMA/CA-HD (HC) incurs the highest packet loss rate because its physical carrier sensing range equals transmission range.

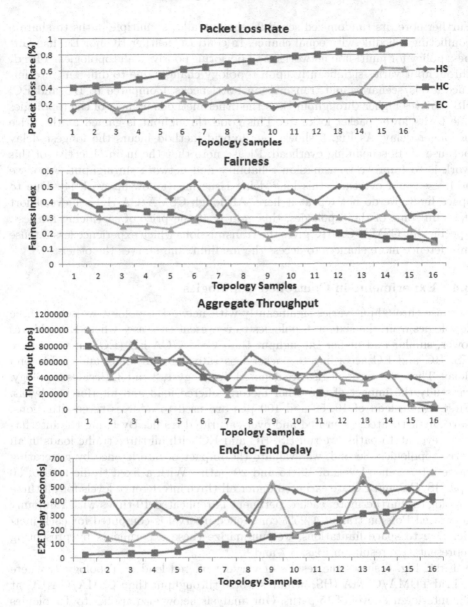

Fig. 5. Random Topologies

Consequently, it experiences significant packet loss caused by hidden terminals as well as intra-path interference and congestion. Although the larger carrier sensing range of CSMA-ED (EC) helps to reduce the occurrence of hidden terminals, our hybrid TDMA/CSMA outperforms EC in most of the cases. **Second,** our hybrid method improves fairness by transforming unwanted competition within the same path into coordinated transmission via intra-path scheduling.

Furthermore, its randomized schedule sharing allows multiple paths to share a conflicting schedule with equal chance. In contrast, neither HC nor EC has fairness policy for multi-hop networks, and performs poorly in all topologies. **Third,** throughput varies significantly upon topology changes due to different interference levels/scenarios and transmission bottlenecks. Compared to HC and EC, HS achieves higher throughput than the other methods in most of the topologies due to its lower packet loss rate. This good throughput is gained at the price of longer delay. As Fig. 5 shows, our hybrid method incurs the longest delay because of its scheduling overhead. Please note that the main objective of this work is to improve transmission reliability and network throughput. Also, we addressed and overcame this long delay issue in a follow-up work [4]. Due to space limit, we do not repeat it here. Although CSMA/CA-HC achieves short delay in some of the topologies, this gain is at the price of sacrificing fairness. Specifically, CSMA/CA-HC gives the transmissions which experience less intense interference more chances to access the medium, and starves the others.

3.4   Experiments in Controlled Topologies

Because throughput varies significantly with network topology, we select three topologies from the sixteen topologies to represent the cases where HS achieves lower, similar and higher throughput than CSMA/CA-ED (EC), and compare HS, HC and EC according to packet loss rate, fairness index and end-to-end delay. These three topologies are denoted Topology 1, 2 and 3. Besides topology, we study the impact of two other factors: offered load and interference levels. First, traffic load of 10, 50 and 100 pps are used to address three situations: partially saturated, saturated and over-saturated traffic. By fixing the interference level at 15 paths, we run HS, HC and EC with all three traffic loads in all three topologies. Second, we evaluate the impact of interference by generating three interference levels of 10, 15 and 20 paths. With a fixed traffic load of 50 pps, HS, HC and EC are executed under all three interference levels for all three topologies. Furthermore, each experiment is replicated 10 times with randomly generated Poisson traffic. A 95% confidence interval is computed for each metric. Due to space limitations, we summarize these experiments by presenting representative results in Figs. 6 7 and 8.

First, Fig. 6 shows the results of varying offered load in Topology 1, where hybrid TDMA/CSMA (HS) achieves worse throughput than CSMA/CA-HC at the interference level of 15 paths. Our analysis below also applies to Topologies 2 and 3. **Packet loss rate:** HS consistently achieves the lowest packet loss rate under different traffic load, because hybrid TDMA/CSMA significantly reduces collisions by handling various interference scenarios. CSMA/CA-HC alleviates hidden terminals and ranks second. EC incurs higher packet loss rate than HC because its aggressive transmission leads to more collisions caused by hidden terminals. **Fairness:** Our hybrid method remains the fairest with different traffic load, which attributes to coordinated intra-path transmission. EC and HC inherit the unfair nature of CSMA/CA and perform poorly in most cases. **End-to-end delay:** Hybrid TDMA/CSMA incurs longer delay than CSMA/CA-HC

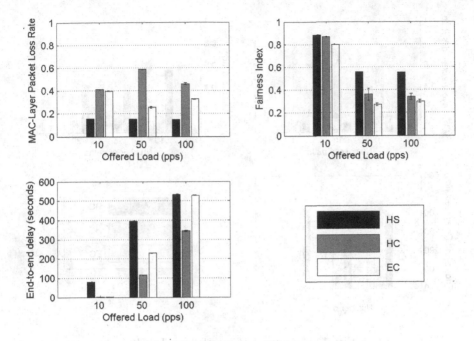

Fig. 6. The Impact of Offered Load

and CSMA/CA-EC because its scheduling overhead increases queue delay. In this paper, delay is not the main focus, and we address this issue in [4]. The shorter end-to-end delay of HC is because most packets are dropped rather than being delivered to the destination. Furthermore, HC's shorter delay is at the cost of fairness by starving the transmissions which experiences more intense interference higher chances to access the medium.

Second, Fig. 7 shows the results of varying interference levels with a fixed offered load (50 pps) and network topology (Topology 1). The analysis below can also be applied to Topology 2 and 3. **Packet loss rate:** Hybrid TDMA/CSMA (HS) achieves lower packet loss rate than HC and EC under different levels of interference, which again demonstrates that HS is effective for handling various interference scenarios. Different interference levels do not change the fact that HC experience more packet loss than EC, because it cannot handle hidden terminals. **Fairness:** Despite interference increases, our hybrid method remains the fairest among all four methods by transforming unwanted competition within the same path into coordinated transmission via intra-path scheduling. In contrast, HC and EC consistently perform poorly in fairness with different interference levels. **End-to-end delay:** The good performance of hybrid TDMA/CSMA in terms of higher throughput, lower packet loss and better fairness is achieved by trading off end-to-end delay. Once gain, we do not focus on delay minimization here. Please see the follow-up improvement in [4]. As shown in Fig 7 HS incurs longer delay than HC and EC under different interference levels. In contrast, HC and EC experience shorter delay by sacrificing fairness and throughput.

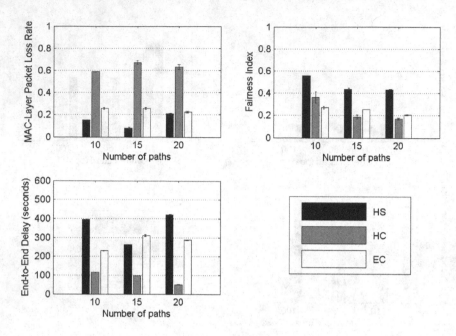

Fig. 7. The Impact of Interference Levels

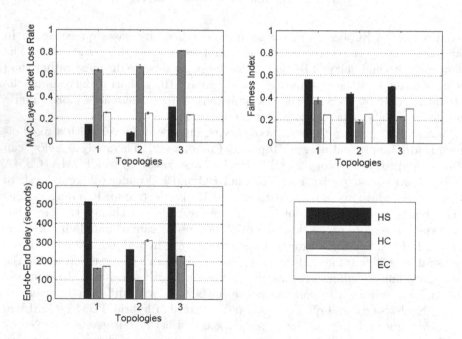

Fig. 8. The Impact of Topologies

At last, Fig. 8 shows the results of varying network topologies with an offered load of 50 pps and interference level of 15 paths. These results validate our analysis in Section 3.3. HS achieves better packet loss rate, higher fairness and higher throughput in all three topologies. We overcome the drawback of hybrid TDMA/CSMA in terms of long end-to-end delay via a novel congestion-collision control proposed in our follow-up work [4].

4   Conclusions

Multi-hop forwarding extends wireless coverage at the expense of degrading performance. To tackle unique multi-hop challenges, we propose a novel solution, hybrid TDMA/CSMA, as a medium access control method to handle co-existing intra-path and inter-path interference under the impact of dynamic traffic. Compared with previous work, Hybrid TDMA/CSMA is the only work that comprehensively handles a wide range of complex interference scenarios. Hybrid TDMA/CSMA introduces a very simple and pure local per-path schedule algorithm to coordinate transmissions within the same path; solves schedule conflicts caused by common nodes by coordinating different paths to share conflicting schedules via randomization and controlled two-hop broadcasting; handles various temporal and spatial contention by a slotted adjustable CSMA/CA. **Second,** the proposed algorithm jointly handles dynamic traffic and complicated multi-hop interference. **Third,** our method also improves bandwidth utilization fairness by transforming unwanted competition into coordinated transmission. Our simulation results demonstrate that hybrid TDMA/CSMA achieves lower packet loss rate, higher throughput and better fairness compared two alternative approaches. In the future work, we will extend Hybrid TDMA/CSMA to handle mobility scenarios, and apply this method in different application scenarios.

References

1. Ephremedis, A., Truong, T.: A Distributed Algorithm for Efficient and Interference Free Broadcasting in Radio Networks. In: IEEE INFOCOM 1988 - The Conference on Computer Communications, pp. 1119–1124. IEEE Press, New Orleans (1998)
2. Rhee, I., Warrier, A., Min, J., Xu, L.: DRAND: Distributed Randomized TDMA Scheduling for Wireless Ad-Hoc Networks. In: 7th ACM International Symposium on Mobile Ad Hoc Networking and Computing, pp. 190–201. ACM Press, New York (2006)
3. Liu, C., Harms, J., MacGregor, M.H.: MG-Local: A Multivariable Control Framework for Optimal Wireless Resource Management. In: 23rd International Teletraffic Congress, pp. 230–237. IEEE Press, San Francisco (2011)
4. Liu, C.: An Innovative MultiVariable Control Framework for Effective Wireless Resource Management. Ph.D. dissertation. University of Alberta (2012)
5. Prado Pavon, J., Choi, S.: Link adaptation strategy for IEEE 802.11 WLAN via received signal strength measurement. In: IEEE International Conference on Communications, pp. 1108–1113. IEEE Press, Alaska (2003)
6. Cormen, T.H., Leiserson, C.E., Rivest, R.L., Stein, C.: Introduction to Algorithms, 3rd edn. MIT Press, Cambridge (2009)

Dynamic Gateway Selection
for Load Balancing in LTE Networks

Sakshi Patni and Krishna M. Sivalingam*

Department of CSE, Indian Institute of Technology Madras,
Chennai 600036, India
{sakshi.patni89,krishna.sivalingam}@gmail.com,
skrishnam@iitm.ac.in

Abstract. In this paper, we consider a Long Term Evolution (LTE) network with multiple Packet Gateways (P-GWs), multiple User Equipments (UEs) and a single Mobility Management Entity (MME). The P-GW connects the UE to the external networks. The sessions are created between the User Equipment (UE) and the P-GW via Serving Gateway (S-GW). The MME selects the P-GW and the S-GW for the sessions and handles the control signaling. Multiple P-GWs handle these packets and transfer them to the external packet data networks. Thus, based on how the sessions are established, different gateways may have to handle different amount of load. If proper load balancing algorithms are not used, the load on some gateways may be higher than others leading to Quality of Service (QoS) degradation for the users. We propose a Linear Programming formulation of the problem and four different heuristics: Load Balancing Threshold (LBT); Static APN Associated Weights (SAAW); Dynamic Weights (DW); and Entropy Based Assignment (EBA). The entropy function provides an accurate measure of the difference in the load on the gateways. It measures the uncertainty or randomness in the outcome of an experiment. The performance studies show that the EBA algorithm provides 18% performance improvement for networks consisting of 1,00,000 users, 12 APNs and 50 P-GWs.

Keywords: LTE, Packet Gateway, Mobility Management Entity, Access Point Names, Load Balancing.

1 Introduction

Long Term Evolution (LTE) is a fourth generation mobile technology that can provide data rates up to 100 Mbps on the downlink and 50 Mbps on the uplink [1,2]. An LTE serving region, called the cell, consists of several user equipment (UE) devices connected to the network through a base station referred to as the *enodeB*. The enodeB in turn uses a Packet Gateway (P-GW) for forwarding UE data to the Internet. The data path between the UE and P-GW is established through a Serving Gateway (S-GW) while the control path is established through Mobility Management Entity (MME).

---

* This work as partly supported by DST-EPSRC funded India-UK Advanced Technology Centre of Excellence in Next Generation Networks, Systems and Services (IU-ATC).

M. Chatterjee et al. (Eds.): ICDCN 2014, LNCS 8314, pp. 408–422, 2014.
© Springer-Verlag Berlin Heidelberg 2014

All the data traffic from the UE to the external packet data networks flow through the P-GW. The P-GW for a particular UE or a connection is selected by the MME during connection establishment. After connection establishment, the data flows through that particular P-GW.

The Access Point Name (APN) is a configurable identifier used mostly in packet data networks to specify the network the UE wants to connect to. Each APN is associated with a number of P-GWs. So, when a connection request comes from a UE using a particular APN, the connection is established on one of the P-GWs that the APN is configured to use.

Each P-GW has limited capacity in terms of their link capacity, memory, CPU speed, buffer space and IP address pool. When any of these resources are used completely, no more connections can be set up through that P-GW. The load on the P-GW can be measured with respect to different parameters. The amount of link capacity used, the number of IP addresses used from its IP address pool, the queue length at the P-GW are different ways to measure the load on the P-GW. The load on the P-GW directly governs the response time of the packet at the P-GW. Thus, load balancing techniques are used to ensure that all the P-GWs are balanced and have approximately similar load at all times. The focus of this paper is to develop efficient load balancing algorithms that assign APNs to the most suitable P-GW.

Existing load balancing algorithms use static weights for the P-GWs and try to balance the load using weights based on capacities relative to other P-GWs. For example, assume that there are three P-GWs with respective bandwidths of 1 Gbps, 2 Gbps and 750 Mbps. The weights given by the static algorithm will be 1, 2 and 0.75. This kind of load balancing is usually done for traffic associated with bearers of QCI value of 9 which have delay budget of 300 ms [3]. Since different P-GWs will be associated with different number of APNs and different APNs may have different number of active users, this measure may not always lead to optimal load balancing. Thus, in this paper, dynamic load balancing algorithms are proposed to provide a better distribution of the load on the gateways.

In the algorithms proposed in this paper, the gateways are assigned weights that depend on different metrics used by the MME. The weights can be either static or dynamic. In case of dynamic weights, the weight changes based on the load conditions of the P-GWs. The changes in the load are informed to the MME by the P-GWs through a special interface or through SNMP MIBs. This information can be sent either periodically or non-periodically. The performance and the overhead differ based on the scheme used for sending load updates. Thus, there exists a trade-off between load balancing and overhead. To improve load balancing, periodic updates are required which increase the overhead.

A Linear Programming formulation (LP) and four load algorithms are proposed for balancing the load among the P-GWs. The algorithms proposed are: Load Balancing Threshold (LBT), Static APN Associated Weights (SAAW), Dynamic Weights (DW) and Entropy Based Assignment (EBA). The LBT algorithm uses different threshold intervals for sending the load updates from the P-GWs to the MME. The SAAW algorithm uses static weights for the P-GWs. Only certain P-GWs can be used for connections from a particular APN. The EBA algorithm uses entropy function to see which P-GW to use for a connection.

Simulation studies have been used to study the performance of the algorithms. The SAAW algorithm improves the performance of the static algorithm by 13% and requires no overhead for sending load updates from the P-GW to the MME. If the number of active users keep changing frequently, then the DW algorithm gives an exact measure of the load on the P-GW. The EBA algorithm can improve performance as high as 18% for large topologies of 1,00,000 users, 12 APNs and 12 P-GWs.

2   Background and Related Work

This section describes briefly LTE, its architecture, and the basic load balancing techniques.

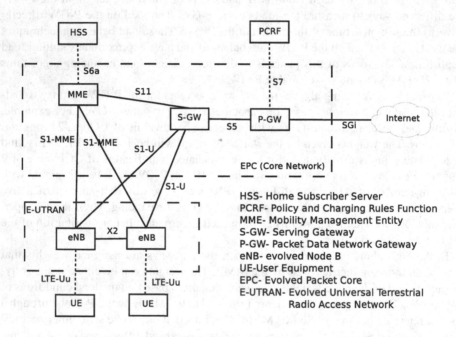

Fig. 1. LTE System Architecture

2.1   Long Term Evolution (LTE)

Long Term Evolution (LTE) [1,2], a 4G technology, was developed by Universal Mobile Telecommunication System (UMTS). The technology supports higher data rates as compared to 3G and other mobile networks. The control and user plane latencies are also comparatively low and thus improve the overall performance of the system. The system architecture of LTE is presented in Fig. 1. Here, evolved NodeBs (eNBs) are the base stations to which the User Equipments (UEs) connect to. The Core Network

(CN) of LTE consists of Mobility Management Entity (MME), Serving Gateway (S-GW) and Packet Data Network Gateway (PDN-GW or P-GW). The MME takes care of user mobility, intra-LTE handover and user authentication. The S-GW is responsible for supporting handover between the LTE nodes and the other 3GPP technologies. The P-GW is used to connect to the external packet data networks. The data path between the UE and the P-GW is established through S-GW and the control path is established through MME. The Home Subscriber Server (HSS) maintains all the user information which is used by MME for authentication and authorization. The Policy Charging and Rules Function (PCRF) is used to charge the users according to the services used by them.

The P-GW or PDN-GW is the network entity that provides access to external packet data networks such as Internet or IP Multimedia Subsystem (IMS) networks. These entities provide the functions such as packet filtering, providing Quality of service (QoS), IP address allocation, charging and policy enforcement via the PCRF. For each UE associated with the Evolved Packet System (EPS), there is at least one P-GW providing access to the requested PDN. If a UE is accessing multiple PDNs, there may be more than one P-GW for that UE.

The Mobility Management Entity (MME) exchanges the control signals with the UE through Non-Access Stratum (NAS) signaling. It is also responsible for the selection of S-GW and P-GW. The MME keeps track of the location of the UE by Tracking Area Update (TAU) of the user. It also selects other MMEs for handover.

2.2 Bearer Establishment

A bearer uniquely identifies the flows which receive a common treatment between the UE and the P-GW. A unique bearer exists for each combination of a particular QoS and IP address of the terminal. A Guaranteed Bit Rate (GBR) bearer [2] is associated with a dedicated EPS bearer and provides a guaranteed minimum transmission rate in order to offer constant bit rate services for applications such as interactive voice that require deterministic low delay service treatment. For a group of non-GBR bearers, Aggregate Maximum Bit Rate (AMBR) [2] denotes the bit rate of traffic for a group of bearers destined for a particular PDN. The Aggregate Maximum Bit Rate is typically assigned to a group of Best Effort service data flows over the Default EPS bearer.

When a UE initially attaches to the network, a default bearer is established between the UE and the P-GW. This bearer always remains established to provide always on-connectivity to the UE. This default bearer is always non-GBR since it will remain established for long periods. Any additional EPS bearer that is established to the same PDN is referred to as a dedicated bearer.

A UE/user needs to register with the network to receive certain services. This registration is described as Network Attachment. The always-on IP connectivity for UE/users of the EPS is enabled by establishing a default EPS bearer during Network Attachment. The PCC rules applied to the default EPS bearer may be predefined in the PDN-GW and activated in the attachment by the PDN-GW itself. The Attach procedure may trigger one or multiple Dedicated Bearer Establishment procedures to establish dedicated EPS bearer(s) for that UE. During the attach procedure, the UE may request for an IP address allocation.

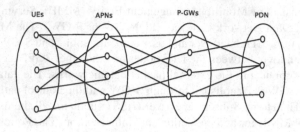

Fig. 2. UE, APN and P-GW Association

2.3 APN and P-GW Association

The Access Point Name (APN) is a configurable identifier which is used in packet data systems to identify the packet data network to which a UE wants to connect to. The UEs always use the APN to connect to a PDN. If the APN is not present in the request, the MME gets the default APN from the HSS and uses it for the connection. A UE can also use multiple APNs to connect to different PDNs for different services including IMS and Internet. The Mobility Anchor Gateway (MAG) function on the S-GW can maintain multiple PDN connections for the same user session. Each APN is associated with a number of P-GWs to connect the UE to the PDN. The MME while selecting the P-GW using "PDN-GW selection function" uses the APN to get the list of allowed P-GWs for that APN. The association between the UEs, APNs and P-GWs is shown in Fig. 2. Also, each UE can have multiple sessions over each APN.

2.4 Load Balancing among P-GWs

There are two existing commonly-used methods discussed for load balancing among P-GWs: static load balancing and inter-GW load balancing as explained below.

Static Load Balancing. The basic method [2] uses static weights for the P-GW based on its capacity relative to other P-GWs. These weights are given to the P-GWs so that the traffic can be distributed according to the capacities of the P-GWs. Thus, if the capacities of the P-GWs 1, 2, 3 and 4 are 1 Gbps, 2 Gbps, 750 Mbps and 900 Mbps, the weights assigned to them will be 1, 2, 0.75 and 0.9.

Inter-GW Load Balancing. In [4], the author has proposed inter-Gateway load balancing approaches. The P-GW transfers the connection to other P-GWs if the load on it is more than other P-GWs. Two types of load balancing approaches are discussed: centralized and distributed. In centralized inter-GW load balancing, all the GWs report their load conditions to a control plane gateway (CP_GW). The CP_GW takes decision about transferring connections from one GW to another depending on their load conditions. In distributed inter-GW load balancing, all the GWs exchange load information with their neighbors, so that they all know about the load conditions on each other.

If one of the GWs experiences heavy load, they ask their less loaded neighbors if they can accept some handovers from it. After getting a positive acknowledgement from its neighbor, the GW can transfer some connections to the other GW.

We next present some basic definitions for entropy that is used in subsequent sections.

2.5 Entropy

Given a probability distribution, there is some uncertainty associated with it. According to the maximum-entropy principle, given some partial information about a random variable, we should choose that probability distribution for it, which is consistent with the given information, but has otherwise maximum uncertainty associated with it. Shannon suggested the following function to measure entropy:

$$H_n(p_1, p_2, ..., p_n) = -\sum_{i=1}^{n} p_i \ln p_i \tag{1}$$

3   Proposed Load Balancing Algorithms

This section presents the proposed load balancing algorithms.

3.1   Load Definition

The metric used to quantify load balancing is a P-GW's carried load relative to its bandwidth. The bandwidth of the P-GW is defined as the amount of data it can transfer or handle per unit time. Different P-GWs may have different bandwidths depending on their configuration. The load on a P-GW is defined as the fraction of the bandwidth that is being used. More specifically, the used bandwidth can be measured as a combination of GBR for the dedicated bearers and AMBR for the default bearers. The amount of bandwidth reserved for the dedicated bearers are based on the number of APNs that share that P-GW, the number of UEs using that P-GW and the number of sessions or bearers each UE has on that P-GW. Similarly, Aggregate Maximum Bit Rate (AMBR) is defined as the bit rate allocated to a group of default bearers for a UE using an APN. Thus, the load is defined as:

$$L = \sum_{a_i \in \text{APN}} \sum_{u_j \in \text{UE}} \sum_{b_k \in \text{bearer}} \text{GBR}(a_i, u_j, b_k) + \sum_{a_i \in \text{APN}} \sum_{u_j \in \text{UE}} \text{AMBR}(a_i, u_j) \tag{2}$$

Let B denote the capacity or the bandwidth of the P-GW. Then, the fraction of the bandwidth utilization of the P-GW is defined as:

$$\delta = \frac{L}{B} \tag{3}$$

In the algorithms proposed, the major factor used for measuring load will be the bandwidth utilization of the P-GW, i.e. δ; the term *load* may be used interchangeably with δ.

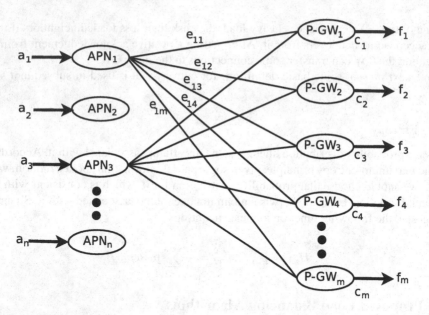

Fig. 3. Linear Programming Formulation for Load Balancing

3.2 Linear Programming Model

The load balancing problem can be modeled as a linear programming (LP) problem. If the problem can be formulated as an LP problem, exact values for the loads on all the P-GWs can be given and all the P-GWs will have equal amount of load. The LP formulation is shown in Fig. 3. The figure shows the APNs generating and sending the traffic to the P-GWs. Assume there are m P-GWs and n APNs. The traffic coming from each APN is described as a_i which is calculated as:

$$a_i = A_i \sum_{j=1}^{k} S_{ij} \lambda_{ij} \tag{4}$$

Here, A_i is the number of active users using the APN_i, k denotes the total types of sessions, S_{ij} denotes the average number of sessions of type j at APN_i and λ_{ij} denotes the arrival rate of session S_{ij} at APN_i. The total traffic at each APN can change as the number of active users and the average number of sessions change. This information has to be periodically updated based on the past history of the users.

The total inflow at j^{th} P-GW is denoted as f_j and the capacity is denoted as c_j. The problem here is to distribute the load or incoming traffic from all the APNs to the P-GWs such that the load on all the P-GWs is approximately same. For distribution of the loads, a weight is associated from each APN to each P-GW. The APN_1 is connected to all the P-GWs as can be seen in Fig. 3 with weights e_{11}, e_{12}, ..., e_{1m}. If some P-GWs are not associated with a particular APN, then the weight of that P-GW can be zero. The weights actually denote the amount of traffic that should flow from the APN to the P-GWs. The incoming traffic on the P-GWs should be proportional to their capacities.

This is measured through load on the P-GW which is the ratio of the total incoming flow to the total capacity of the P-GW. The load on the jth P-GW is given as:

$$\delta_j = \frac{f_j}{c_j} \tag{5}$$

The formulation for the load balancing among the P-GWs is given as:

$$\text{minimize} \quad F = max\left(\frac{f_j}{c_j}\right) \quad 1 \leq j \leq m \tag{6a}$$

$$\text{subject to} \sum_{j=1}^{m} e_{ij} = a_i \quad \forall 1 \leq i \leq n \tag{6b}$$

$$\sum_{i=1}^{n} e_{ij} = f_j \quad \forall 1 \leq j \leq m \tag{6c}$$

$$f_j \leq c_j \quad \forall 1 \leq j \leq m \tag{6d}$$

$$e_{ij} \geq 0 \quad \forall 1 \leq i \leq n \quad \forall 1 \leq j \leq m \tag{6e}$$

The link utilization or the objective function will always have value between 0 and 1. The problem of Eq. 6 is not an LP since the objective function is non-linear. These kind of functions are known as piece-wise linear functions.

Example: Consider the following example with the number of APNs and P-GWs set to 3 each. Assume that the incoming traffic is calculated on the basis of number of active users, average number of sessions per user and the arrival rate of each type of session. Let the incoming traffic be 100 Mbps from APN_1, 50 Mbps from APN_2 and 200 Mbps from APN_3. Let the capacities of the P-GWs be 200 Mbps, 300 Mbps and 400 Mbps respectively. Using Matlab, the values of the variables e_{11} to e_{33} are found to be 52.59, 47.42, 0, 25.19, 0, 24.81, 0, 69.26 and 130.74 respectively. The values of f/c for the P-GWs 1, 2 and 3 are 0.38. Additional details and results for the above formulation are available in [5].

However, the above formulation does not scale to large number of entities. Another problem with LP formulation is that the amount of total incoming traffic can only be predicted to a certain extent which limits the amount of load balancing that can be achieved. Hence, several heuristics are proposed in this paper.

3.3 Load Balancing Threshold Algorithm (LBT)

In this algorithm, a min-heap is maintained for each of the APN at the MME or HSS. The heap will contain all the P-GWs that can be used for that APN. The weights of all the P-GWs are initialized to 1. When a connection request with bit-rate b arrives to the MME from a UE, depending on the APN used by the UE for that connection, the MME accesses the corresponding heap. The MME then accesses the root of the heap and assigns the connection to the P-GW at the root of the heap. The load on the P-GW increases with the increase in the number of connections. The P-GW keeps monitoring its load and sends an update to the MME as the load crosses a threshold value. Based on the threshold value crossed, the MME updates the weight of the P-GW in all the APNs. The threshold values are defined as intervals having a lower threshold and an upper threshold. If the load on the P-GW crosses an upper threshold of one interval and goes into another interval, the weight at the MME for that P-GW in all APNs is increased.

A sample set of threshold values and their corresponding weights are defined in Table 1. Thus, initially the weights of all the P-GWs will be 1. When the load on any P-GW becomes greater than 1/3, then the weight of that P-GW increases to 2. If it becomes greater than 2/3, the weight becomes 3 and so on. If the load after being greater than 2/3 becomes less than 1/3 for a P-GW, then the weight of that P-GW also decreases and becomes 2.

Table 1. Sample weight factors based on load values

Load	Indicative Weight
< 1/3	1
≥ 1/3	2
≥ 2/3	3
≥ 7/9	4
≥ 8/9	5

The thresholds used can change depending on the amount of load balancing needed at the cost of increased signaling cost. The cost and load balancing trade-off is examined later.

3.4 Static APN Associated Weights Algorithm (SAAW)

This algorithm considers the different APNs a P-GW is associated with and also considers their weight defined by their priority. Suppose each APN at GW_i have weights associated with them. Let them be $v_1, v_2, ..., v_k$. Assume that the bandwidth of GW_i is B_i. For the implementation purpose, it is assumed that the weights are equal for all APNs. For each APN j with weight v_j at GW_i, the weight W_{ij} for the P-GW is given as:

$$W_{ij} = \frac{v_j}{\sum_k v_k} \times B_i \tag{7}$$

Based on the above equation, the P-GWs are assigned weights in the APNs. The weights are based on the bandwidth of the gateway and the number of APNs a P-GW is associated with. If the number of active users in each APN is different, then the weights for the P-GWs are slightly modified to include the information related to the number of UEs. Assume that a P-GW is shared by k different APNs with number of active users $u_1, u_2, ..., u_k$. Then, the weight of the Eq. 7 is modified to:

$$W_{ij} = \frac{v_j}{\sum_k v_k} \times \frac{u_j}{\sum_k u_k} \times B_i \tag{8}$$

3.5 Dynamic Weights Algorithm (DW)

The initial weights are given to the P-GWs as shown in Eq. 7. The SAAW algorithm will work well if the connections established are not terminated or terminate according to some pattern. The connections terminate randomly and thus the load on the P-GWs changes in a non-deterministic manner. Hence, if we change the weight of the P-GWs dynamically according to the load, then the load distribution will be uniform. The dynamic weights for the P-GW is given as:

$$w_{ij} = W_{ij} \times (1 - \delta) \tag{9}$$

The weight of the P-GW changes based on the load on the P-GW. When the load increases, the factor $1 - \delta$ decreases and the weight of the P-GW decreases than the initial weight and other P-GWs having lesser load will have more chances of getting selected. As the load increases and approaches 1, the weight factor approaches 0 and the P-GW will have less chances of getting selected.

3.6 Entropy Based Assignment (EBA)

The performance of the algorithms is measured with the help of an entropy function, with p_i defined as

$$p_i = \frac{\delta_i}{\sum_j \delta_j} \tag{10}$$

where

$$p_1 + p_2 + \dots + p_n = 1 \tag{11}$$

Here, the load on each P-GW is normalized with respect to the total load of all P-GWs. Also, if the load on all the P-GWs is the same, then $p_1 = p_2 = \dots = p_n = \frac{1}{n}$ and

$$H_n(p_1, p_2, \dots, p_n) = \sum_i -p_i \ln p_i = \ln n \tag{12}$$

which is the maximum value for the Shannon's Entropy function. Thus, if all the P-GWs are equally balanced or have the same amount of load, the value of the Entropy function will be maximum and will be equal to $\ln n$. If one of the $p_i = 1$, then

$$H_n(p_1, p_2, \dots, p_n) = \sum_i -p_i \ln p_i = 0 \tag{13}$$

which is the minimum value of the entropy function. Thus, if all the connections are on the same P-GW, then the entropy function will be zero. Therefore, in the load balancing algorithms, the performance of the algorithms can be measured as the value of the entropy function changes.

The earlier three heuristics consider various factors and then calculate the weight of the P-GW in an APN to get selected. The entropy function is used to see how balanced the P-GWs are with respect to each other. The P-GWs in the previous algorithms were not equally balanced because of the different weights of the APNs. Hence, instead of using other methods, entropy function can itself be used to select a P-GW for a connection. Thus, when a new connection or a session is to be established with a particular APN, the P-GW which increases the entropy to a greater extent is selected by the MME. The time required to select a P-GW in this case is $O(n)$ where n is the number of P-GWs that can be selected for that APN. Therefore, the entropy function gives an accurate measure of the difference in loads on different P-GWs and the most appropriate P-GW for a given session is selected.

Additional details and examples for the above heuristics are available in [5].

4   Performance Analysis

To perform simulations, a Java based model of the system was written. The simulation setup used for the modeling of the algorithms use multiple UEs, multiple APNs and multiple P-GWs. Each UE can use only those APNs which it is configured to use. The APNs will be associated with some P-GWs. Only these P-GWs can be selected by the MME for the connection coming from that APN. Each P-GW can have incoming traffic from the UEs of multiple APNs i.e. each P-GW is also associated with multiple APNs and serves users from each one of them. The simulation is run for different times with varying number of users, APNs and P-GWs. Two kind of scenarios are simulated- one in which no connection is terminated and one in which connections are terminated within the simulation time. The P-GWs are selected for each connection instead of each user. Thus, the granularity for selecting a P-GW is session or connection based.

The number of connections in each second is approximately the ratio of the total number of sessions (average number of sessions × total number of users) to the simulation time. Each time a connection is set-up on a P-GW, the load is updated and the entropy is calculated after every second. The simulation runs on discrete time intervals.

4.1   Parameters and Metrics

The parameters used for simulating the analysis are presented in Table 2. The number of UEs, number of APNs and number of P-GWs are varied. The bandwidth of the P-GWs are set to either 1 Gbps, 2 Gbps or 750 Mbps. Different termination time is set for connections in the scenarios where connections are terminated. Each simulation experiment is run for 500 seconds.

Table 2. Parameters

Parameter	Description
P-GW bandwidth	1 Gbps, 2 Gbps or 750 Mbps
Average number of sessions per user	3
Simulation time	500 seconds
Bit rate for video traffic	64 Kbps
Bit rate for VoIP call	17 Kbps
Bit rate for video streaming	12 Kbps
Bit rate for live streaming	64 Kbps
Bit rate for gaming applications	100 Kbps

The metrics analyzed are the entropy function value that captures the load balancing; and the costs involved in some of the algorithms for dynamic weight update. The cost is based on the number of times the update is to be sent to the MME by the P-GW.

4.2 Results

The performance results for the different algorithms are shown in this section.

LBT algorithm: The LBT algorithm which uses the thresholds for sending the updates to the MME is not compared to any other algorithm for performance since defining the thresholds means reducing the load balancing. Three threshold based schemes are used for showing the signaling cost to entropy value trade-off. The first scheme uses unequal threshold interval size. The threshold intervals used are in the set $\{0.3, 0.6, 0.7, 0.8, 1.0\}$. The second scheme uses threshold intervals of size 0.2. Thus, the intervals are $\{0.2, 0.4, 0.6, 0.8, 1.0\}$. The last scheme uses threshold intervals of size 0.1. These three schemes are compared with each other for signaling cost and entropy values.

The results are shown in Fig. 4 for the entropy difference in the values. Fig. 5 shows the signaling cost involved when different schemes are used. Thus, the trade-off can be easily seen from both the figures. The entropy value is high for the intervals of size 0.1 but the cost involved is also high. The signaling cost specifies the number of times the update is to be sent to the MME or the HSS when the threshold interval is being crossed.

The simulations are run for 1,00,000 users, 12 APNs and 50 P-GWs. Fig. 5 shows four different cases where two cases are for 1,00,000 users and two are for 50,000 users, 12 APNs and 50 P-GWs. Each case is shown for two different types: one in which connections are terminated and one in which they are not. The legends WTT and WT respectively represent 'Without Termination' and 'With Termination'. Both the cases perform approximately the same in case of entropy values but the value of the entropy starts decreasing at the end in case of terminating connections. In case of signaling cost, the signaling cost is less when connections are terminated since the load on the P-GWs rarely crosses the thresholds and typically remains in one threshold interval for a long time.

Performance Comparison. The simulations are run for random topologies. The number of UEs are 1,00,000, number of P-GWs are 50, the number of APNs are 12 and the number of MME is 1. The simulation is run for 500 time units where each time unit is 1 second. The average number of sessions that each UE can establish is 3. The simulations are run for two cases: one in which no connection is terminated and the other in which connections are terminated after some time. The time after which the connections terminate are selected randomly. The results are shown in Fig. 6. The average entropy values are 3.78, 3.83, 3.83 and 3.88 for static algorithm, SAAW algorithm, DW algorithm and EBA algorithm respectively when connections are terminated. Thus, the overall performance improvement from static algorithm to EBA algorithm is 10% whereas the SAAW and DW algorithm improves the static algorithm by 5%.

In a mobile network, the number of users associated with different APNs is usually different. Hence, the experiments are run for cases where different APNs have different

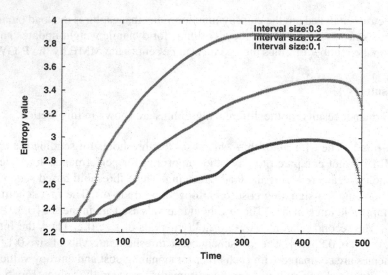

Fig. 4. Performance of LBT algorithm with 1,00,000 users, 12 APNs and 50 P-GWs

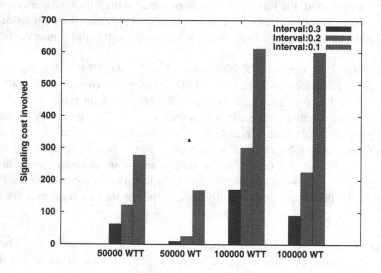

Fig. 5. Signaling cost for sending updates in LBT

number of UEs associated with them. Some APNs will be corporate APNs and will have less number of users associated with it than other mobile operators APNs. The simulation here is run for 1,00,000 users, 12 APNs and 50 P-GWs. The entropy value varying with time is shown in Fig. 7. The figure shows the case where connections are terminated randomly since the algorithm performs the same in both the cases. The performance improvement achieved is 19% for EBA algorithm, 13% for SAAW algorithm and 8% for DW algorithm as compared to the static algorithm.

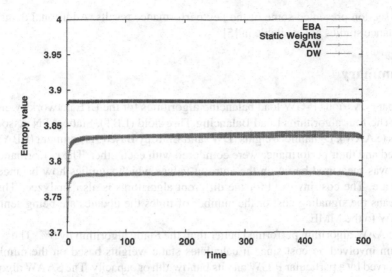

Fig. 6. Comparative analysis for 1,00,000 users, 12 APNs and 50 P-GWs

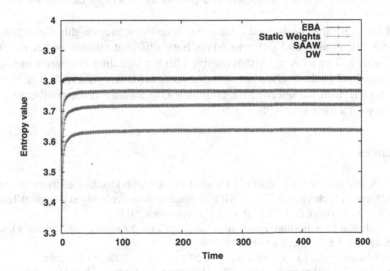

Fig. 7. Comparative analysis with different UEs in each APN

The DW algorithm in this case does not perform as well as SAAW algorithm. This is because in the latter scheme, the weights are calculated on the basis of number of active UEs associated with an APN and the number of APNs associated with a P-GW. Thus, the algorithm performs well as long as the number of active users are actually what is being predicted. In case of DW algorithm, the weights change dynamically and thus, does not reflect the number of active UEs information anymore. Thus, the SAAW algorithm performs better in this case.

This section presented some of the key performance results. Additional details and performance studies are available in [5].

5 Summary

In this paper, various P-GW load balancing algorithms for the LTE networks were presented. The four algorithms Load Balancing Threshold (LBT), Static APN Associated Weights (SAAW), Dynamic Weights (DW) and Entropy Based Assignment (EBA) were described and their performance were compared with each other. The performance difference was measured based on the entropy values which signifies how balanced the P-GWs are. The cost involved for the different algorithms is also analyzed. The cost here means the signaling cost or the number of times the updates are being sent from the P-GW to the MME.

The SAAW algorithm performed better than the Static algorithm by 5%. The SAAW algorithm involved no cost since it calculates static weights based on the number of APNs served by a particular P-GW and its bandwidth or capacity. The SAAW algorithm performed 13% better than the static algorithm when the approximate number of active users in each APN is also considered as a parameter in weight calculation for the P-GWs.

The EBA algorithm performed 19% better than the static weights algorithm when only one MME is used and different APNs have different number of active UEs associated with it. The EBA algorithm involved higher signaling cost since the updates related to the load on the P-GWs have to be sent to the MME or the HSS. The algorithm also needs $O(n)$ time for selecting the optimal P-GW where n is the number of P-GWs associated with a particular APN.

References

1. Ghosh, A., Ratasuk, R.: Essentials of LTE and LTE-A. Cambridge University Press (2011)
2. 3GPP, "General Packet Radio Service (GPRS) enhancements for Evolved Universal Terrestrial Radio Access Network (E-UTRAN) access" (September 2011)
3. 3GPP Technical Specification, Policy and Charging Control Architecture (Release 8), ser. TS, no. TS 23.203, V8.3.1 (September 2009), http://www.quintillion.co.jp/3GPP/Specs/23203-31.pdf
4. Xue, C., Luo, J., Halfmann, R., Schulz, E., Hartmann, C.: Inter GW Load Balancing for Next Generation Mobile Networks with Flat Architecture. In: Proc. IEEE Vehicular Technology Conference (VTC), pp. 1–5 (April 2009)
5. Patni, S.: Dynamic gateway selection for load balancing in LTE networks. Master's thesis, Department of CSE, Indian Institute of Technology Madras (2013)

Exploiting Scalable Video Coding for Content Aware Downlink Video Delivery over LTE

Ahmed Ahmedin[1], Kartik Pandit[1], Dipak Ghosal[1], and Amitabha Ghosh[2,*]

[1] Department of Computer Science, University of California, Davis, CA
{kdpandit,ahmedin,dghosal}@ucdavis.edu
[2] UtopiaCompression Corporation, Los Angeles, CA
amitabhg@utopiacompression.com

Abstract. We propose a content aware scheduler to allocate resources for video delivery on the downlink of a Long Term Evolution (LTE) network. We consider multiple users subscribe to a video streaming service, and request videos encoded in H.264 Scalable Video Coding format. The scheduler maximizes the average video quality across all users by assigning resource blocks based on their device capabilities, link qualities, and available resources. We measure video quality using two full reference metrics: peak signal-to-noise ratio (PSNR) and structural similarity (SSIM) index. We formulate the video delivery problem first as an integer linear program (ILP), and then reduce it to the multiple choice knapsack problem (MCKP). To solve the MCKP, we propose two fast heuristics with reduced processing overhead at the eNodeB, and a fully polynomial-time approximate scheme (FPTAS) using dynamic programming and profit-scaling. Our evaluation results indicate that the heuristics are within a factor of $\frac{1}{2}$, and the FPTAS is very close to the optimal obtained from an ILP solver. We also propose a signaling mechanism to implement the content aware scheduler in existing LTE systems, and evaluate the impact of signaling delay on video distortion using both indoor and outdoor measurements collected from AT&T and T-Mobile networks.

Keywords: LTE, Scalable Video Coding, content aware optimization, scheduler, network optimization, FPTAS, water-filling.

1 Introduction

The continuous growth in cellular data traffic is encouraging service providers to introduce new services and compete with each other to deliver the highest quality at the lowest price. Multimedia delivery is one of the most rapidly evolving services, as smart handheld devices (e.g., iPhone, iPad, tablet) and high-speed 4G technologies (e.g., LTE, WiMAX) are fast getting adopted [1]. It is projected that 70% of the cellular data traffic will be from video by 2016 [2].

The user equipments (UEs) in a cellular network can be very diverse, ranging from battery and hardware constrained cell phones, to more powerful tablets

---

* A. Ghosh did this work as a postdoctoral research associate at Princeton University.

M. Chatterjee et al. (Eds.): ICDCN 2014, LNCS 8314, pp. 423–437, 2014.
© Springer-Verlag Berlin Heidelberg 2014

with sophisticated transcoding features. Different users are also susceptible to different video qualities due to limited bandwidth and random channel variations resulting from shadowing, multipath fading, etc. These factors can cause the UE buffer to underflow during video playback. The eNodeB (term used for LTE base transceiver station) can also run out of resources without satisfying all the requests. In particular, when a large number users demand high quality videos at the same time, severe buffer underflows may occur for multiple users.

The H.264 Scalable Video Coding (SVC) [8] has emerged as a suitable coding standard for compressing high-quality video bitstreams. It supports a variety of devices using three different scalability options: (1) temporal scalability, where complete frames can be dropped from a video using motion dependencies; (2) spatial scalability, where videos are encoded at multiple resolutions; and (3) quality scalability, where decoded samples of lower qualities can be used to predict samples of higher qualities to reduce the bit rate required to encode the higher qualities. A UE can use any of these scalability options, or combine them based on the type of the video and user requirements. By leveraging multiple profiles supported by SVC that differ in compression, bit rate, and size, the video quality can be adapted based on link quality, device capability, and available resource blocks (referred to as physical resource blocks or PRBs in LTE).

There has been a lot of work in content aware networking for wireless video delivery, including choosing the best network code for video transmission over mesh networks [3], cross-layer solution with more protection for packets carrying important parts (e.g., I-frames) [4], and streaming SVC videos over WiMAX [7]. A similar method to [4] for content aware video delivery on the uplink of a wideband code division multiple access (WCDMA) network is proposed in [6]. Video frame scheduling under deadline constraints in the downlink is discussed in [5], while SVC tools for wireless are introduced in [8]. The performance of SVC over LTE is characterized in [9].

In this paper, we present a content aware PRB scheduler to deliver SVC encoded videos to multiple users on the downlink of an LTE network. Our goal is to maximize the average video quality across all users for a fixed number of PRBs. The PRB scheduler in the eNodeB decides the profile levels of the videos, and the number of PRBs to assign to each user depending on its decoding capability and link quality between the eNodeB and the UE. We assume that these link qualities can be estimated from feedback signals, such as channel quality indicator (CQI) and hybrid automatic repeat request (HARQ).

Our key contributions are the following:

- We formulate the PRB scheduling problem as an integer linear problem (ILP), and reduce it to the multiple choice knapsack problem (MCKP) [15].
- We propose a greedy heuristic and a water-filling heuristic to solve the MCKP with reducing processing complexity at the eNodeB.
- We also propose a fully polynomial-time approximation scheme (FPTAS) using dynamic programming and profit-scaling to solve the MCKP.
- We compare the performance of the heuristics and the FPTAS with the optimal by solving the ILP using CPLEX [18], a state-of-the-art ILP solver

developed by IBM. Our results indicate that the heuristics perform within a factor of $\frac{1}{2}$, and the FPTAS is very close to the optimal.
- We propose a signaling mechanism to implement the content aware PRB scheduler in an existing LTE system, and evaluate the impact of signaling delay on video distortion using both indoor and outdoor (urban and suburban) measurements collected from AT&T and T-Mobile networks.

The rest of the paper is organized as follows. In Section 2, we describe our system model and formulate the PRB scheduling problem. In Section 3, we first map the PRB scheduling problem to the MCKP, and present two heuristics and an FPTAS to solve the MCKP. Section 4 presents our evaluation results of the proposed heuristics and the FPTAS. In Section 5, we describe a signaling mechanism to implement the content aware PRB scheduler in an existing LTE system, and also present our evaluation results of this modified architecture based on measurement data. Finally, we conclude in Section 6.

2 LTE System Model

In this section, we first describe a high-level architecture of the content aware PRB scheduler in an LTE downlink, and define two video quality metrics. We then present the LTE video model and formulate the PRB scheduling problem.

2.1 Content Aware LTE Downlink Architecture

We consider the downlink of a single eNodeB in an LTE network where multiple users request SVC-encoded videos from a video server (e.g., YouTube). The Core Network (CN) establishes a non-guaranteed bit rate Evolved Packet System (EPS) bearer that provides Internet Protocol (IP) services to the UEs. The scheduler at the eNodeB allocates a certain number of PRBs to send the video as a unicast to each UE. A schematic diagram of this architecture is shown in Figure 1. The solid lines indicate different interfaces that already exist between different nodes in the EPS bearer. The dotted lines are the new conceptual interfaces we propose, the implementation of which is described in Section 5.

We envision that the content aware PRB scheduler is conceptually associated with the eNodeB. When a UE requests a video, the video server responds with the quality and transcoding information of that video. The eNodeB obtains this information from the UE, and sends it along with the set of available PRBs to the PRB scheduler. The PRB scheduler also obtains the channel quality from the UE, and then computes the number of PRBs and a video rate to be assigned to the UE corresponding to an SVC profile level. The profile level is sent to the UE, and the PRB assignment is sent to the scheduler at the eNodeB. The scheduler then allocates the assigned number of PRBs to the video flow.

In the downlink physical layer, LTE uses orthogonal frequency-division multiple access (OFDMA), and allocates radio resources in both time and frequency domains. The time domain is divided into LTE downlink frames, which are split

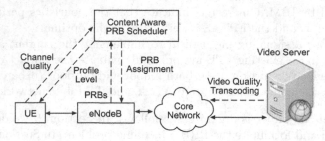

Fig. 1. A content aware architecture for video delivery over LTE downlink. The solid lines indicate interfaces that already exist in an LTE system; the dotted lines are the new conceptual interfaces proposed to implement the PRB scheduler.

into Transmission Time Intervals (TTIs), each of duration 1 millisecond (ms). The LTE downlink frame has a duration of 10 ms corresponding to 10 TTIs. Each TTI is further subdivided into two time slots, each of duration 0.5 ms, and each 0.5 ms time slot corresponds to 7 OFDM symbols. In the frequency domain, the available bandwidth is divided into subchannels of 180 kHz each, and each subchannel comprises 12 adjacent OFDM subcarriers. As the basic time-frequency unit in the scheduler, a PRB consists of one 0.5 ms time slot and one subchannel. The minimum unit of assignment for a UE is one PRB, and each one can be assigned to only a single UE. Additionally, the LTE downlink makes use of adaptive modulation and coding.

It is important to note that the content aware PRB scheduler only determines the number of PRBs needed for each UE, but not the specific PRBs that will finally be allocated. This job is left for a TTI level scheduler, which is a key component of the existing eNodeB design. Several TTI level schedulers that map PRBs to UEs have been studied in literature [27]. We propose to integrate the content aware PRB scheduler with any given TTI level scheduler using a two-level approach, similar to the one proposed in [28]. The PRB scheduler behaves like an upper-level scheduler, assigning the PRBs on a frame-by-frame basis. Within a frame, any TTI level scheduler that maximizes throughput or is proportionally fair can be used to map the PRBs to the UEs.

2.2 Video Quality Metrics

The content aware PRB scheduler requires the video quality and transcoding information to compute a PRB assignment. In this paper, we use two full-reference metrics that use the distortion-free version of a video as the reference. The first one is peak signal-to-noise ratio (PSNR) [24], and the second one is structural similarity (SSIM) index. For a video stream, these metrics are computed by averaging their values over all the video frames. For a frame of size $u \times v$ (in pixels), the PSNR of the ith frame can be computed as [24]:

$$\text{PSNR}(i) = 10 \log_{10} \left(\frac{\text{MAX}^2}{\text{MSE}(i)} \right), \tag{1}$$

where MAX is the maximum possible pixel value (typically, 255), and MSE is the mean square error, defined as:

$$\text{MSE}(i) = \frac{1}{uv} \sum_{k=0}^{u-1} \sum_{l=0}^{v-1} [I_i(k,l) - R_i(k,l)]^2, \tag{2}$$

where I_i and R_i represent the ith frames of the received video and reference video, respectively. Thus, the video PSNR is given by: $\text{VPSNR} = \frac{1}{m} \sum_{i=0}^{m} \text{PSNR}(i)$, where m is the total number of frames in the video.

The second metric SSIM takes into account the inter-dependency between different pixels, and, therefore, more consistent with the perception of the human eye [10]. The SSIM of the ith frame can be computed on two windows x and y as [24]:

$$\text{SSIM}_{x,y}(i) = \frac{(2\mu_x\mu_y + c_1)(2\sigma_{xy} + c_2)}{(\mu_x^2 + \mu_y^2 + c_1)(\sigma_x^2 + \sigma_y^2 + c_2)}, \tag{3}$$

where μ_x and σ_x^2 are the mean and variance, respectively, for window x; likewise, μ_y and σ_y^2 are the mean and variance, respectively, for window y. The covariance of x and y is σ_{xy}. The two variables c_1 and c_2 are to stabilize the division with weak denominator. Thus, the video SSIM is given by: $\text{VSSIM} = \frac{1}{m} \sum_{i=0}^{m} \text{SSIM}(i)$.

The SVC standard [8] defines 21 profiles that differ in capabilities and target specific classes of applications. The term "level" specifies a set of constraints indicating the required decoder performance for a certain profile, such as maximum picture resolution, frame rate, bit rate, etc. Table 1 shows the VPSNR and VSSIM values for the movie trailer MIB3 encoded at different SVC levels. The reference video is encoded at Baseline Level 4.

Table 1. MIB3 trailer attributes for different SVC levels

Levels/Attributes	VPSNR	VSSIM	Rate (Kbps)
L1.3 (96 × 72)	36.7617	0.72761	146
L2.2 (192 × 144)	37.684451	0.8625723	304
L3.0 (320 × 240)	38.36902	0.9254554	452
L4.0 (640 × 480)	Reference	Reference	1162

2.3 Video Model

We consider a total of N UEs and M available PRBs in the LTE system, with each PRB having a fixed bandwidth, denoted by B. Suppose each UE i can decode up to a set $L_i = \{l_{ij}\}$ of video profile levels. Each profile level $l_{ij} \in L_i$ requires a certain number α_{ij} of PRBs depending on channel conditions for smooth video playback without incurring buffer underflow. We assume that all the M PRBs are available to adapt the video quality only, and are not used for any other purpose, such as reliability or other application requirements. We assume that each UE i uses a forward error correction (FEC) code for protection, with coding rate T_i and modulation scheme m_i. Suppose $R_i(l_{ij})$ denotes the total downlink rate required for UE i to receive the video at level l_{ij} including all levels below it. This rate can be computed as [23]:

$$R_i(l_{ij}) = \alpha_{ij} m_i T_i B \log_2 \left(1 + \frac{Pg_i}{N_0} \right),\tag{4}$$

where P denotes the transmission power of the eNodeB; g_i is the channel gain from the eNodeB to UE i; and N_0 is the noise power. We assume that the channel gain g_i can be estimated using CQI measurements.

Suppose $Q_i(l_{ij})$ denotes the average quality observed while receiving the video at level l_{ij}. Since we measure video quality using VPSNR or VSSIM, $Q_i(l_{ij})$ accordingly refers to these quantities when UE i receives the video at level l_{ij}. We assume that there exists a monotonic, one-to-one relationship between the observed video quality and the corresponding rate.

2.4 PRB Scheduling Problem Formulation

We assume that the eNodeB is capable of sending videos at the basic profile level. To reduce distortion, however, a higher level is required, but at the expense of more number of PRBs. Depending on the link quality and available number of PRBs, the scheduler at the eNodeB chooses a certain level l_{ij}, and assigns the corresponding number α_{ij} of PRBs to each UE i. Suppose x_{ij} is a decision variable that is 1 if level l_{ij} is assigned to UE i, and 0 otherwise. We consider that these levels are chosen in such a way that it maximizes the average video quality over all UEs. We formulate this PRB assignment problem as:

$$\text{maximize} \sum_{i=1}^{N} \sum_{l_{ij} \in L_i} x_{ij} Q_i(l_{ij})$$

$$\text{subject to} \sum_{i=1}^{N} \sum_{l_{ij} \in L_i} x_{ij} \alpha_{ij} \leq M \tag{5}$$

$$\sum_{l_{ij} \in L_i} x_{ij} = 1, \ \forall i$$

$$\text{variables} \ x_{ij} \in \{0, 1\}, \ \forall i, \ \forall l_{ij} \in L_i$$

where the first constraint ensures that the total number of PRBs assigned to the UEs does not exceed the available number of PRBs, and the second constraint chooses exactly one profile level for each UE i. This is an ILP because of the integer variables x_{ij}, and, therefore, NP-hard.

3 Solutions to PRB Assignment Problem

In this Section, we first reduce the content aware PRB scheduling problem into the MCKP, and then present two fast heuristics and an FPTAS to solve it.

3.1 Reduction to Multiple-Choice Knapsack Problem

The PRB assignment problem (5) can be cast as the Multiple-Choice Knapsack Problem [15], which is a generalization of the classical 0-1 Knapsack Problem [13]. A similar reduction for video delivery over WiMAX is given in [7]. In MCKP, we are given a set of items subdivided into N mutually disjoint classes, $K_1, \ldots, K_N$, and a knapsack of total capacity c. Each item $j \in K_i$ has a profit p_{ij} and a weight w_{ij}. The goal is to choose exactly one item from each class so as to maximize the total profit without exceeding the capacity. The MCKP can be written as:

$$\text{maximize} \quad \sum_{i=1}^{N} \sum_{j \in K_i} p_{ij} y_{ij}$$

$$\text{subject to} \quad \sum_{i=1}^{N} \sum_{j \in K_i} w_{ij} y_{ij} \leq c \tag{6}$$

$$\sum_{j \in K_i} y_{ij} = 1, \quad \forall i$$

$$\text{variables} \quad y_{ij} \in \{0, 1\}, \quad \forall i, \; \forall j \in K_i$$

where y_{ij} is the decision variable that takes the value 1 if item j is chosen from class K_i, and 0 otherwise.

It is easy to see the mapping between the PRB assignment problem and the MCKP. The number of classes in the MCKP corresponds to the number of UEs, and the knapsack capacity c corresponds to the number M of available PRBs. The items in each class are the videos encoded at different profile levels. The decision variable y_{ij} corresponds to the variable x_{ij} that decides whether or not to choose level l_{ij} for UE i. The weight w_{ij} corresponds to the number of PRBs α_{ij} assigned to UE i, and the profit p_{ij} is the video quality $Q_i(l_{ij})$ experienced by UE i when receiving the video at level l_{ij}.

An important thing to decide is how frequently to solve the MCKP optimization, which defines the optimization horizon for the PRB assignment problem. The reason to consider this is the following: As channel conditions change over time, the solutions returned by the optimization might become stale if updated channel parameters are not used. Therefore, it is necessary to rerun the optimization whenever this happens, and also when the UEs start or end a video session. We discuss this issue in Section 5.

3.2 Fast Heuristics for PRB Assignment

The existing work on MCKP [15] offers various approximation algorithms that are not easily implementable in practical LTE networks. We propose two fast and simple heuristics that are easy to implement and show good performance.

The first heuristic (Algorithm 1) is a greedy algorithm similar to [16] with asymptotic worst-case running time $O(\sum_i |L_i|)$. The second heuristic (Algorithm 2) follows a technique similar to Water-Filling [22] by first assigning PRBs to the users with better channel conditions, and then distributing the rest of the PRBs to other users. Note that, typically the number of users served by a single eNodeB can be at most a few hundreds, and therefore, the sorting in both heuristics can be accomplished efficiently using any standard sorting algorithm.

Algorithm 1. Greedy heuristic for content aware PRB assignment.

1. For each UE i, sort the profile levels in increasing order of required PRBs. 2. Pick the UEs in a round robin fashion.
3. For each UE i, choose the highest level l_{ij*} from the sorted sequence that does not exceed the remaining PRB budget out of M total.

Algorithm 2. Water-Filling heuristic for content aware PRB assignment.

1. Sort the UEs in descending order of channel gains.
2. Pick the UEs from this sorted sequence starting from the first.
3. Follow steps 1, 2, and 3 in the Greedy heuristic, i.e., for each UE i, assign the highest profile level l_{ij*} that does not exceed the remaining PRB budget.

3.3   An FPTAS for MCKP Using Dynamic Programming

The classical 0-1 Knapsack Problem admits an FPTAS via dynamic programming and profit-scaling [16]. Using a similar approach, we present an FPTAS for the MCKP to solve the PRB assignment problem. We first formulate a dynamic program.

Let $y_i(q)$ denote the minimum weight of a solution to MCKP with total profit q, and classes $K_1, \ldots, K_i$. If no solution exists, we set $y_i(q) = c + 1$. We use an upper bound U to specify the termination point of this (finite horizon) dynamic program. We initialize $y_0(0) = 0$, and $y_0(q) = c + 1, \forall q = 1, \ldots, U$. Then, the recursion can be written as:

$$
y_i(q) = \min \begin{cases} y_{i-1}(q - p_{i1}) + w_{i1}, & 0 \leq q - p_{i1} \\ y_{i-1}(q - p_{i2}) + w_{i2}, & 0 \leq q - p_{i2} \\ \vdots \\ y_{i-1}(q - p_{in_i}) + w_{in_i}, & 0 \leq q - p_{in_i} \end{cases} \tag{7}
$$

where n_i is the number of items in class K_i.

If the argument to the min function is empty, it returns $c + 1$. The optimal profit is $\max\{q | y_N(q) \leq c\}$, with a runtime complexity $O(U \sum_{i=1}^{N} n_i) = O(nU)$, where $n = \sum_{i=1}^{N} n_i$, is the total number of videos across all classes. This type of recurrence admits an FPTAS [16]. The approach relies on appropriately scaling the profits in the above recursion. Accordingly, we define a new set of profits, $\tilde{p}_{ij} = \lfloor \frac{p_{ij}}{K} \rfloor$, with K appropriately chosen to satisfy the tight inequality $K \leq \frac{\epsilon z^*}{N}$, where z^* is the optimal value of the objective function in the MCKP, and ϵ is a positive quantity that decides the approximation factor. With this condition is satisfied, the DP has an approximation factor $(1 - \epsilon)$ [16]. The following analysis shows how to choose the value of K.

Let $p_{\max}$ be the item with the highest profit across all classes. If we choose $K = \frac{\epsilon p_{\max}}{N}$, then the above condition is clearly satisfied. Let the optimal value of the scaled problem be z_s^*. Then, it is clear that $z_s^* \leq N\tilde{p}_{\max}$, where $\tilde{p}_{\max} = \lfloor \frac{p_{\max}}{K} \rfloor$. Since $\tilde{p}_{\max} \leq \frac{p_{\max}}{K} = \frac{N}{\epsilon}$, we obtain $z_s^* \leq \frac{N^2}{\epsilon}$. Consequently, we can replace the upper bound U in the recursion by $\frac{N^2}{\epsilon}$. Since U can be computed in linear time, we get an overall running time of $O(\frac{nN^2}{\epsilon})$. The dynamic program using this technique of profit scaling is described in Algorithm 3. The objective value of the MCKP with the original profits can be obtained by examining the items that are chosen from each class in the solution of the algorithm.

Algorithm 3. Dynamic Program Scaling of Profits

Compute an upper bound U.
Set $y_0(0) = 0$, and $y_0(q) = c + 1$, $\forall q = 1, \ldots, U$.
for $i = 1, \ldots, N$ **do**
    for $q = U, \ldots, 0$ **do**
        $y_i(q) = \min_{j \in \{K_i | q \geq \tilde{p}_{ij}\}}(y_{i-1}(q - \tilde{p}_{ij}) + w_{ij})$.
$z_s^* = \max\{q | y_N(q) \leq x\}$.

---

4   Performance Evaluation

In this section, we compare the performance of the two heuristics and the FPTAS with the optimal obtained from CPLEX.

4.1   Experimental Setup

In our simulations, we uniformly distribute the UEs around the eNodeB, and randomly map each UE to a video. We use LTE system parameters defined in the 3GPP standard [21]. The focus of this study is primarily in measuring the performance at the physical and MAC layers. We acknowlege that different content distribution networks (CDNs) may employ different techniques at higher layers which might affect the metrics evaluated here. The transmission power P of the eNodeB is 46 dBm; the noise figure N_0 is 7 dB; the transmission frequency F is 925 MHz; the eNodeB antenna height h_b is 30 meters; and the UE antenna height h_m is 1.5 meters. We follow the path loss model described in [17], and use the statistical tool R [19] to generate the channel model. The path loss G for a UE that is d meters away from the eNodeB is given by:

$$G = 69.55 + 26.16 \log_{10}(F) - 13.82 \log_{10}(h_b)$$
$$-ch + (44.9 - 6.55 \log_{10}(h_b)) \log_{10}(d), \tag{8}$$

where the parameter ch depends on the city size. The number of available PRBs M in our simulation is set to 50, which is the same number of PRBs in an LTE frame when the channel bandwidth is 10 MHz. The spectral efficiency $m_i T_i$ for UE i depends on the CQI and is given in the LTE standard [21].

4.2   Simulation Results

In our simulation, we assume that a user experiences buffer underflow if it is not assigned the required number of PRBs to support a download data rate at least equal to the playback rate. We first compare the performance of the Greedy and the Water-Filling heuristics with the optimal. The results for VPSNR and VSSIM are averaged over 1000 iterations, where, at each iteration, we randomly map the UEs to the videos and generate channel conditions according to (8).

As shown in Figure 2(a) and 2(b), the three plots representing Greedy, Water-Filling, and Optimal follow a similar trend, i.e., the video quality decreases with increasing number of UEs. This is expected because the number of PRBs allocated per UE decreases with increasing number of UEs for a fixed PRB budget. We also note that the difference in VPSNR and VSSIM values obtained from the heuristics and those of the optimal increases with more number of users. However, the difference is less predominant for the Water-Filling algorithm than the Greedy one. This is because of the following: In the Greedy algorithm, the UEs are picked up at random and assigned PRBs for the highest profile level possible. In contrast, the Water-Filling algorithm first sorts the UEs in decreasing order of channel gains, and then assigns the PRBs corresponding to the highest levels. Thus, for the same rate requirement between two users, the user with good channel condition will need fewer PRBs in the Water-Filling algorithm, and, therefore, more PRBs will be left to satisfy the profile levels of other users. In the Greedy algorithm, the chance of picking up a user with good channel condition decreases as the number of users increases, and so it performs increasingly worse as compared to the Water-Filling algorithm for more number of users.

We now compare the performance of the FPTAS with the optimal obtained from CPLEX. As discussed before, the asymptotic running time of the FPTAS is $O(\frac{nN^2}{\epsilon})$, where n is the total number of videos, and ϵ decides the approximation factor, which is at least $(1 - \epsilon)$ in our implementation of the dynamic program. We applied the FPTAS for the same channel and video models for three different values of ϵ, namely, 0.25, 0.5, and 0.95. The results for VPSNR, shown only for $\epsilon = 0.5$ and $\epsilon = 0.95$ in Figure 3(a) and 3(b), respectively, indicate that the FPTAS performs very close to the optimal.

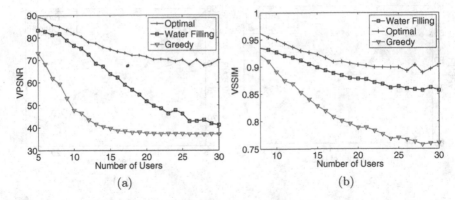

Fig. 2. Comparison of (a) VPSNR and (b) VSSIM obtained from the Greedy and Water-Filling heuristics with that of the optimal from CPLEX

5   Content Aware LTE Architecture and Signaling

In this section, we first propose a new signaling mechanism and a modification to the LTE architecture to implement the PRB scheduler. We then evaluate the performance of this modified architecture using measurement data.

5.1   Signaling Mechanism and Architecture Modification

We reuse the IP services of the EPS bearer to implement the content aware PRB scheduler. The signaling mechanism, as shown in Figure 4, takes place as follows: Upon receiving a video request from the UE, the video server responds with the levels, rates, and VPSNR/VSSIM information of that video. The UE sends this information to the eNodeB, which, in turn, forwards it to the PRB scheduler. The UE also sends the CQI and the Reference Symbol Received Power (RSRP) to the PRB scheduler. The PRB scheduler also obtains the set of available PRBs from the eNodeB, and then runs the optimization to compute the PRB assignment and the profile level assignment for each UE. The profile level is sent to the UE, while the PRB assignment is sent to the scheduler in the eNodeB. Finally, the UE requests the video at the assigned profile level from the video server.

We note that there can be delays associated with signaling that may affect the performance of the algorithm. This may require re-running the optimization. We show the effect of this delay under various channel scenarios, and give a method to choose when to re-run the optimization.

We propose to implement the PRB scheduler at two different places, motivated by the emerging trend of software defined networking (SDN) toward an open architecture at the switches and routers. The first is to include the PRB scheduler in the Mobility Management Entity (MME), where it can handle communications and negotiations between the server and the network. The MME

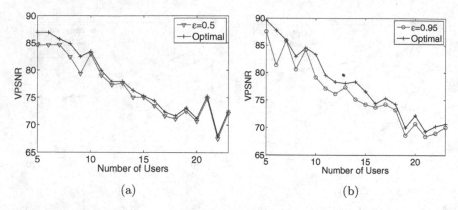

Fig. 3. Comparison of VPSNR obtained from the FPTAS and the optimal from CPLEX for different values of ϵ: (a) $\epsilon = 0.5$, and (b) $\epsilon = 0.95$

can keep track of the PRBs assigned to the UEs, and run the optimization with appropriate parameters during a handover. Although there is one instance of the PRB scheduler for each eNodeB, they are all located within a single MME. The PRB scheduler can also be placed at the eNodeB itself. However, this has some disadvantages, the biggest one being the difficulty of modifying every eNodeB to accommodate the PRB scheduler. We note that there is no security vulnerability of breaching user privacy in this modified architecture. The eNodeB treats each video simply as another flow, and it is the UE that requests a content aware profile level and PRB assignment.

5.2   Measurement Based Evaluation

We evaluate the performance of the modified architecture using real data sets collected from AT&T and T-Mobile networks by doing a drive-test and measuring delays using an Android device and Qualcomm eXtensible Diagnostic Monitor (QxDM) [20]. A sample plot for an outdoor suburban measurement data is shown in Figure 5. The plot captures four quantities: reference signal received power (RSRP), reference signal received quality (RSRQ), received signal strength indicator (RSSI), and CQI variation, as a time series for about 14 minutes. The data is then fit into a lognormal distribution, as shown in Figure 6(a), which is then used to obtain the urban data. The outdoor urban data is generated using the spatial channel model in [25].

The PRB scheduler depends on UE reports sent to the eNodeB. There is a network delay between the server and the UE, which can be tens to a few hundreds of milliseconds. Thus, depending on the environment, the channel conditions may change between the time the UEs request the video profile levels determined by the PRB scheduler, and the time the server starts sending the packets. As a result, the decisions taken by the scheduler may be obsolete.

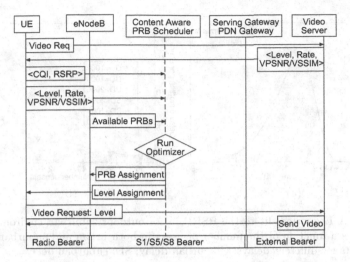

Fig. 4. Signaling to implement the content aware PRB scheduler in LTE

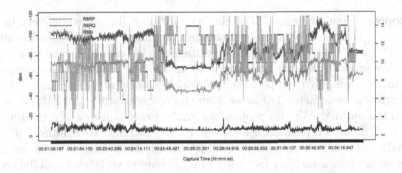

Fig. 5. RSRP, RSRQ, RSSI, and CQI data in an outdoor suburban environment

We measure this delay in AT&T and T-Mobile networks for different technologies. For an LTE network, the delay is 50-150 ms; for an HSDPA+ network it is 160-450 ms; and for an on-campus Wi-Fi network, the delay is 7-20 ms.

We evaluate the impact of this signaling delay on video distortion for both indoor and outdoor environments. Figure 6(b) shows the distortion per user in the outdoor for both urban and suburban areas. We observe that the impact of delay becomes more predominant with increasing number of users. We also see that the urban environment has more distortion than the suburban one. This is due to more severe variation in link quality in the urban environment than the suburban one, and can result from more multi-path fading, shadowing, and Doppler effect. The indoor environment has (plot not shown here) very little effect on distortion due to negligible variation in channel conditions.

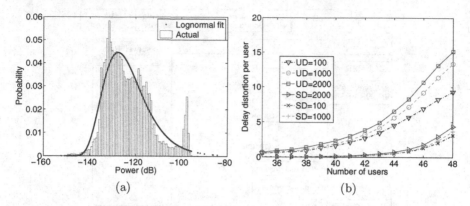

Fig. 6. (a) A Lognormal fit to the RSRP in an outdoor suburban environment; (b) Distortion as a function of the number of users in both urban and suburban outdoor environments for different delays; UD: urban delay; SD: suburban delay

6   Conclusion

We propose a content aware PRB scheduler for downlink video delivery in LTE based on SVC. The eNodeB in our scheme maximizes the average video quality across all users based on their link qualities, device capabilities, and available PRBs. We propose two fast heuristics and an FPTAS to solve this optimization problem, and compare their performance with the optimal. Our results show that the heuristics are a factor 1/2 away from the optimal, while the FPTAS is very close to the optimal. We also propose a signaling mechanism and a modification to the LTE architecture to implement the PRB scheduler. We evaluate the effect of signaling delay on this modified architecture using real measurement data. Our results show that, even after factoring in real channel variations and delays, the PRB scheduler still performs very well.

References

1. Driving, LTE.: Adoption: Mass-Market Pricing and a Large Device Ecosystem Emerge as Key Factors, Analysys Mason (2013)
2. Cisco Visual Networking Index: Global Mobile Data Traffic Forecast Update (2013)
3. Seferoglu, H., Markopoulou, A.: Video-Aware Opportunistic Network Coding over Wireless Networks. IEEE J. Select. Areas Commun. 27(5), 713–728 (2009)
4. Haghani, E., Ansari, N., Parekh, S., Colin, D.: Traffic-Aware Video Streaming in Broadband Wireless Networks. In: IEEE WCNC, pp. 1–6 (2010)
5. Zhu, X., Girod, B.: Distributed Media-Aware Rate Allocation for Wireless Video Streaming. IEEE Trans. Circuits Syst. Video Technol. 20(11), 1462–1474 (2010)
6. Pandit, K., Ghosh, A., Ghosal, D., Chiang, M.: Content Aware Optimization for Video Delivery over WCDMA. EURASIP J. Wirel. Commun. Netw. (2012)
7. Sharangi, S., Krishnamurti, R., Hefeeda, M.: Energy-Efficient Multicasting of Scalable Video Streams Over WiMAX Networks. IEEE Trans. Multimedia 13(1), 102–115 (2011)

8. Schwarz, H., Marpe, D., Wiegand, T.: Overview of the Scalable Video Coding Extension of the H.264/AVC Standard. IEEE Trans. Circuits Syst. Video Technol. 17(9), 1103–1121 (2007)
9. McDonagh, P., Vallati, C., Pande, A., Mohapatra, P., Perry, P., Mingozzi, E.: Investigation of scalable video delivery using H.264 SVC on an LTE network. In: IEEE WPMC, pp. 1–5 (2011)
10. Wang, Z., Bovik, A.C., Sheikh, H.R., Simoncelli, E.P.: Image Quality Assessment: From Error Visibility to Structural Similarity. IEEE Trans. Image Processing 13(4), 600–612 (2004)
11. Nikolaos, T., Boulgouris, N.V., Strintzis, M.G.: Optimized Transmission of JPEG2000 Streams over Wireless Channels. IEEE Trans. Image Processing 15(1), 54–67 (2006)
12. Pisinger, D.: A Minimal Algorithm for the Multiple Choice Knapsack Problem. Eur. J. Oper. Res. 83, 394–410 (1994)
13. Kellerer, H., Pferschy, U., Pisinger, D.: Knapsack Problems. Springer (2004)
14. Gens, G., Levner, E.: An Approximate Binary Search Algorithm for 0-1 MCKP. Information Processing Letters 67, 261–265 (1998)
15. Sinha, P., Zoltners, A.A.: The Multiple Choice Knapsack Problem. Operations Research 27(3), 503–515 (1979)
16. Lawler, E.L.: Fast Approximation Algorithms for Knapsack Problems. Mathematics of Operations Research 4(4), 339–356 (1979)
17. Holma, H., Toskala, A.: LTE for UMTS - OFDMA and SC-FDMA Based Radio Access. John Wiley & Sons (2009)
18. IBM CPLEX Optimizer, http://www-01.ibm.com/software/integration/optimization/cplex-optimizer/
19. The R Project for Statistical Computing, http://www.r-project.org/
20. Qualcomm eXtensible Diagnostic Monitor (QXDM Professional) (2007)
21. Requirements for further advancements for E-UTRA (LTE-Advanced), 3GPP TR 36.913, http://www.3gpp.org/ftp/Specs/html-info/36913.htm
22. Proakis, J.G.: Digital Communications. McGraw-Hill, New York (2001)
23. Cover, T.M., Thomas, J.A.: Elements of Information Theory. John Wiley & Sons (2006)
24. Bovik, A.C.: The Essential Guide to Video Processing. Elsevier (2009)
25. Radio Frequency (RF) Requirements for LTE Pico eNodeB. 3GPP TR 36.931
26. Sesia, S., Touffik, I., Baker, M.: LTE - The UMTS Long Term Evolution: From Theory to Practice. Wiley (2011)
27. Capozzi, F., Piro, G., Grieco, L.A., Boggia, G., Camarda, P.: Downlink Packet Scheduling in LTE Cellular Networks: Key Design Issues and a Survey. IEEE Communications Surveys and Tutorials 15(2), 678–700 (2013)
28. Piro, G., Grieco, L.A., Boggia, G., Camarda, P.: A Two-Level Scheduling Algorithm for QoS Support in the Downlink of LTE Cellular Networks. In: European Wireless Conference, pp. 246–253 (2010)

Stochastic Model for Cognitive Radio Networks under Jamming Attacks and Honeypot-Based Prevention*

Suman Bhunia[1], Xing Su[2], Shamik Sengupta[1], and Felisa Vázquez-Abad[2]

[1] University of Nevada, Reno, USA
{sbhunia,ssengupta}@unr.edu
[2] City University of New York, NY, USA
{xsu,FVazquez-Abad}@gc.cuny.edu

Abstract. Limited and dynamically available resources and "no right to protection from interference" in the open access dynamic spectrum access model bring forth a serious challenge of sustenance among the secondary networks and make them more susceptible to various spectrum etiquette attacks. Among these, the most common are jamming-based denial of service (DoS) attacks, which result in packet loss. The concept of a honeypot node or honeynode has been explored for wireless networks and has shown to be effective in attracting attacks, thus deterring the jammers from productive nodes. Yet a single dedicated honeynode, on account of its permanent idleness, is wasteful of an entire node as resource. In this paper, we seek to resolve this dilemma by dynamically selecting the honeynode for each transmission period, and we explore various methods of doing so. To begin with, we develop the first comprehensive queuing model for CRNs, which pose unique modeling challenges due to their periodic sensing and transmission cycles. We then build a simulation of CRNs under attack from jammers, introduce a series of strategies for honeynode assignment to combat these attacks, and assess the performance of each strategy. We find that the predictions of our mathematical model track closely with the results of our simulation experiments.

Keywords: Cognitive Radio, Honeypot, Stochastic Model, Queuing theory, queue with vacation.

1 Introduction

The conventional static spectrum allocation policy has resulted in suboptimal use of spectrum resource leading to over-utilization in some bands and under-utilization in others [1]. Such "artificial spectrum starvation" has led to the recent spectrum policy reform by the U.S. Federal Communication Commission (FCC). This reform, known as dynamic spectrum access (DSA), is expected to be achieved via the recently proposed concept of the cognitive radio (CR) [1].

---

* This research was supported by NSF CAREER grant CNS #1346600.

M. Chatterjee et al. (Eds.): ICDCN 2014, LNCS 8314, pp. 438–452, 2014.

The IEEE 802.22 is an emerging standard for CR-based wireless regional area networks (WRANs) [2]. The IEEE 802.22 standard aims at using DSA to allow the unused, licensed TV frequency spectrum to be used by unlicensed users on a non-interfering basis. To protect the primary incumbent services, IEEE 802.22 devices (e.g., base station and consumer premise equipment) are required to perform periodic spectrum sensing and evacuate promptly upon the return of the licensed users (as depicted in Fig. 1).

Even though the primary user protection mechanisms have been proactively specified, neither the secondary-secondary interaction mechanisms nor the protection of secondary devices/networks have been specifically defined or addressed in IEEE 802.22 standard. The "open" philosophy of the cognitive radio paradigm makes such networks susceptible to attacks by smart malicious user(s) that could even render the legitimate cognitive radios spectrum-less. Due to software reconfigurability, cognitive radios can even be manipulated to disrupt other secondary cognitive radio networks or legacy wireless networks with even greater impact than traditional hardware radios. There are several ways in which operations of cognitive radio networks can be jeopardized. Cognitive disruption through malicious channel fragmentation/aggregation/bonding, primary user emulation attack, multi-channel jamming or spectrum stealing through induced attack are just some of the examples that can severely cripple the cognitive radio networks. A number of defenses against such attacks have been attempted, among which the most effective is the so-called honeypot[3]. The concept of "Honeypot" in Cybercrime is defined as "a security resource whoś value lies in being probed, attacked or compromised". In Cybercrime defense, honeypots are being used as a camouflaging security tool with little or no actual production value to lure the attacker giving them a false sense of satisfaction thus bypassing (reducing) the attack impact and giving the defender a chance to retrieve valuable information about the attacker and attack activities. This node is called honeynode. Misra et al.[4] and Yek et al.[5] have proposed a honeypot-based attack detection and prevention mechanism for WLANs.

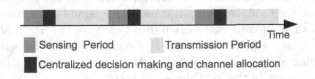

Sensing Period   Transmission Period

Centralized decision making and channel allocation

Fig. 1. Time domain representation of Cognitive Cycle

Several practical challenges however need to be co-opted and addressed to achieve such goal in uncoordinated DSA networks. Honeypot is not a "free-ride". While using a SU as honeynode potentially make the CRN robust but it also sacrifices the effective system throughput/QoS to some extent. How would the honeynode be chosen then? Who will be responsible ("honeynode" selection) for auxiliary communications and monitoring in honeynodes? To answer the above questions, we must however first understand the complexity of the CRN traffic behavior under DSA scenario (periodic sensing and transmission with channel switching due to primary arrival resulting in queuing with vacation). Consider a scenario wherein a user is conducting a number of simultaneous transmissions - say, videoconferencing, downloading a file using FTP, downloading large files from numerous seeders via torrent, periodically downloading data from a server with a widget, continuously synchronizing with a cloud server, and more. All these applications generate packets randomly and independently of other applications. The complex nature of data traffic makes it difficult to analyze the Quality of Service (QoS). CRNs, meanwhile, exhibit unique behavior patterns that remains yet to be investigated by any mathematical model. For example, the periodic sensing by SUs forces interruption of transmission, affecting end-to-end QoS by imposing delay and jitter on packet processing. The dynamic nature of spectrum access also introduces a particular complexity to CRN behavior. Thus, a major goal of this work is to model CRN service using stochastic analysis and use our model to estimate baseline performance indicators. Only then we can assess the performance of experimental honeypot selection algorithms.

The rest of the paper proceeds as follows: In Section 2, we discuss the motivation for our work, i.e. DoS attacks and honeypot limitations. Section 3 presents a mathematical model to estimate CRN performance using queue with fixed server vacation. We describe our simulation results and analysis in Section 4. Section 5 concludes the paper.

2   Motivation

2.1   Jamming Attack

In traditional wireless networks, the user of a particular channel has proprietary access to that channel and thus has the right to penalize any trespassers. The threat of penalty can discourage potential attackers. However, if a channel is being accessed by a CRN, the SUs are only borrowing the channel, and they have no grounds from which to fend off attackers. While PUs are able to discourage attackers, SUs are left vulnerable against malicious jamming / disruptive attacks [6]. Jamming can be broadly categorized into two types [4], [7]. In *physical layer jamming*, the attacker jams the channel of communication by sending strong noise or jamming signals. The *datalink / MAC layer jamming* targets several vulnerabilities present in the MAC layer protocol.

To see the effect of jamming, we run an experiment in our lab. Two computers are configured to communicate over a WLAN (IEEE 802.11-a, channel 36, central frequency: 5.18 GHz) with 54 mbps data rate. As the units are communicating in full throttle, we observe the Power Spectral Density (PSD) over the channel using the Wi-spy spectrum analyzer [8]. The PSD for normal communication (without jamming) can be seen in Fig. 2a, which shows that the transmission is using a 20 MHz channel and leaking energy to neighboring channels. Then we begin transmitting a very narrow band jamming signal of 2MHz from a third machine, also on channel 36. At the presence of the jamming signal, the

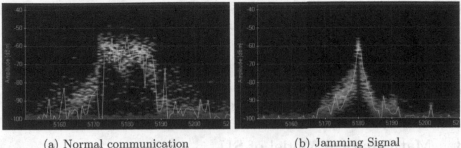

(a) Normal communication   (b) Jamming Signal

Fig. 2. PSD for data communication and jamming signal

actual transmission of the WLAN was stopped totally as can be observed in Fig. 2b: only the jamming signal is getting through. As the bandwidth is very narrow, this jamming costs very little power. However it is taking advantage of the vulnerability of IEEE 802.11 MAC (sensing the channel before transmission). When the legitimate transmitter senses that there is some energy on the channel, it refrains from transmission. In effect, the attacker successfully jams the channel with very little cost, denying service to the SU. Irrespective of the jamming technique, a target SU suffers a significant amount of data or packet loss and sometimes completely loses the channel. The CRN is a next-generation intelligent network, and it should incorporate a mechanism to mitigate, avoid or prevent these attacks.

2.2 Use of Honeypot in Avoiding Attacks

In CRN, honeypot mechanism can be deployed in SUs which act as normal data transmission. In order to attract the attacker to this channel, the honeynode tries to obtain the attacker's fingerprint. The authors of [3] and [5] have implemented honeypots to detect attacks on server and access-points in regular WLAN. They introduced fake access-point as honeypot nodes to guess the fingerprint of the attack. In [9] a learning mechanism is proposed to mitigate spoofing DoS attacks. Misra *et al* [4] implemented a channel surfing approach to mitigate jamming-based DoS attacks. Upon detecting an attack, the victim switches its transmission to a different channel.

When a honeypot mechanism is used consistently, the attacks will sometimes be trapped by honeypot, and sometimes can attack legitimate SUs. We define one parameter, that we call the *attractiveness of honeypot* (ξ) as the probability that the honeynode is the one to be attacked, conditional on observing a jamming attack[1]. Honeypot ensures less data loss at the cost of end-to-end delay. Some application can tolerate data loss but not delay and others the opposite.

---

[1] Understandably each honeypot strategy has a different ξ, and ξ also depends on the attacker's strategy. Calculating ξ on different strategy is beyond the scope of this paper.

The goal is to build a mathematical model that can estimate system performance before we actually apply honeypot. If honeypot degrades performance very badly and the system can tolerate some data loss then we can opt for not applying. The end-to-end delay in CR is mainly affected by queuing delay as processing, transmission and propagation delays are negligible compared to queuing delay. Our theoretical model focus on determining queuing delay. Then we concentrate on honynode selection mechanism to achieve better over-all system performance.

3   Mathematical Model of SU

3.1   Queuing Characteristics

In earlier telecommunication networks, voice packets were generated at fixed rates or at fixed burst sizes [10], [11]. For this kind of system the inter-arrival time is fixed and the value depends on the codec (voice digitization technique) used [10], [11] . Voice activity detection and Silence suppression techniques introduces randomness in packet arrival time. With the increase in usage of multimedia applications on smart-phones the nature of the traffic flow is very complex to model. Because of the independence between sources, a memoryless inter-arrival time may be a good model. This observation is supported by statistical analysis. The studies carried out in various experiments [12], [13], [14], [15] have concluded that when many different applications are merged, the packet arrival process tends to follow Poisson process. Fig. 3 provides an depiction of how packets from different applications flow to a queue. We use λ_i to denote the rate of the Poisson process of packet arrivals at SU labeled i, and $\{N_i(t); t \geq 0\}$ to denote the corresponding arrival process. When a single queue is analyzed, we drop the subindex i.

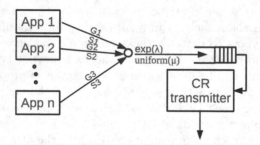

Fig. 3. Depiction of how packets are flowed to Queue

Data to be transmitted arrives at the different servers (corresponding to different SUs in a CRN) in packets. Each SU is modeled as a FCFS (first come-first served) queue with one server. Packets arrive according to a marked Poisson process with rate λ and "marks" specifying the packet size. In our model, the marks $\{Y_1, Y_2, \ldots\}$ are independent and identically distributed uniform random variables. The aggregate data arrival rate is thus $\lambda \mathbb{E}(Y)$. Each SU can transmit at a fixed rate r. Therefore, the service time of a packet size Y_n is, $S_n = Y_n/r$ and it has uniform distribution $U(\ell_1, \ell_2)$, with mean $\mathbb{E}(S) = (\ell_1 + \ell_2)/2$ and potential service rate, $\mu = 1/\mathbb{E}(S)$

During the transmission periods of length T_t, the model corresponds to a $M/G/1$ queue where the service time of consecutive packets are independent and identically distributed. During the sensing period of length T_s (and the transmission periods when it is chosen as a honeynode) our server stops servicing the queue, which nonetheless continues to accumulate arriving packets. Because the sensing period has deterministic size and frequency, the server model does not conform to the usual server with vacations ([16], [17]) where the server has the option to take vacations only at the end of busy periods. Instead, the sensing period acts as a "priority" customer whose inter-arrival rates and service times are deterministic. Under the assumption that the buffer is infinite, the effect of an attack during a transmission period when the SU is not a honeynode is that all packets transmitted in that slot are lost.

The two performance criteria of interest are the (stationary) average waiting time in queue per packet W_q, and the average packet drop rate PDR. In the case of infinite buffer PDR_i is also the long term probability that i'th SU is attacked, that we call θ_i.

3.2   Queuing Model with Vacations

In this section we assume that one SU is chosen to be "sacrificed" as a honenode at every transmission period. If a SU is chosen as a honeynode, then all the new arriving packets join the queue and wait until the next transmission period where the SU is not chosen as a honeynode. It is conceivable that intelligent policies include the possibility of regular transmissions without honeynode, and transmission periods with multiple honeynodes, but as a first step, we impose here that a SU (only one) be chosen at every transmission period. Let's consider there are N SUs in the CRN. Because the CRN works by assigning channel to SUs, we assume here w.l.o.g. that the there are more free channels than number of nodes or SUs in the network. Under the round robin policy, SUs are chosen as honeynode in a circular fashion, so one out of every N transmission periods becomes an "extended vacation" for the server. A random policy assigns the honeynode to i'th SU with probability p_i, independently of past assignments and of the state of the CRN. A random policy that targets fairness could be used by attempting to balance the utilization factors. Other random policies may be justified when they are used to increase the attractiveness of the honeypot, as we will discuss at the end of the paper. In a state dependent policy the centralized controller picks the SU according to the current values of the queues. These policies target a decrease in mean queuing delay.

We now calculate the *effective utilization factor* for the queue under the random policy. The amount of service time that must be postponed at the start of a sensing period is either 0 (when the server is idle at time of sensing) or it has the value of the random variable $\tilde{S}$ representing the fraction of service time that must be postponed. In steady state, if $\rho = \mathbb{P}(\text{the server is busy})$ then the server is not idle with probability ρ. When in steady state, the start of a sensing period may fall in in any subinterval of the current packet's service time with equal probability. Thus $\tilde{S} \sim U(\ell_1, S)$, where $S \sim U(\ell_1, \ell_2)^2$ represents the (random) amount of current service when the server is not idle.

Result: Assume that each queue is stable and call X the fraction of service that must be postponed at the start of a sensing period in steady state. Then:

$$\mathbb{E}(X) = \rho \left(\frac{\mathbb{E}(S) + \ell_1}{2} \right). \tag{1}$$

Let $a \geq 0$ be a non-negative constant. Then:

$$\mathbb{E}((a + X)^2) = a^2 + \rho \left(a\ell_1 + \frac{\ell_1^2}{3} + \frac{(3a+1)\ell_1}{3} \mathbb{E}(S) + \frac{\mathbb{E}(S^2)}{3} \right). \tag{2}$$

This result follows from straightforward calculation. Assuming that the queues are stable, the effective service rate for each of the SUs satisfies the equation:

$$\mu_i' = \mu \left(\frac{T_t - \rho_i \, 0.5(\mathbb{E}(S) + \ell_1)}{T_s + T_t} \right)(1 - p_i), \quad \rho_i = \frac{\lambda_i}{\mu_i'},$$

which yields an implicit equation for μ':

$$\mu_i'(T_t + T_s) = \mu \left(\mu T_t - 0.5 \frac{(\mathbb{E}(S) + \ell_1)\lambda_i}{\mu_i'} \right)(1 - p_i) \tag{3}$$

Solving the quadratic equation (3) gives values that depend on λ_i. In particular, if all SUs have equal probability of being chosen (p_i), then the reduced service rate is the same as in the round robin policy.

STATIONARY POLICIES. We now provide an analysis of the stationary queuing delay for the random (or round robin) policies. In this section we use our previous results that $\mathbb{E}(\tilde{S}) = 0.5 \, \rho_i \, \mathbb{E}(S)$ for each of the nodes. The analysis is done for each queue, and the subscript i will be dropped from our notation.

Theorem 1. *Suppose that i'th SU has incoming rate λ, and that it is chosen as a honeynode independently of the state of the queue, with long term frequency of p. Furthermore, assume that this queue is stable and ergodic and let X satisfy equations (1) and (2). Then the stationary delay in queue is:*

$$W_q = \frac{R}{1 - \lambda \mathbb{E}(S)(1 + \Delta)}, \tag{4}$$

where the stationary residual service time is:

$$R = \frac{\lambda \mathbb{E}(S^2)}{2} + \frac{\mathbb{E}(T_s + X)^2 (1 - p) + \mathbb{E}(T_s + T_t + X)^2 p}{2(T_s + T_t)} \tag{5}$$

---

[2] The symbol "$\sim$" means "has distribution".

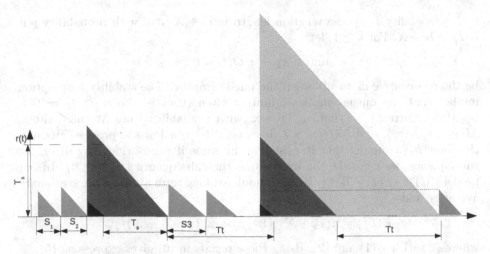

Fig. 4. Path of the residual service of customer currently in service, for the CRN model honeypot. Here, green indicates packet transmission, red is Channel sensing, yellow is Serving as honeypot and blue indicates, the node postpone current packet transmission as it can not be done within transmission period.

and the correction factor for the vacations is:

$$\Delta = \frac{T_s + \lambda \mathbb{E}(X) + pT_t}{(1-p)(T_t - \mathbb{E}(X))}.$$

Proof. We use the residual service approach [17,16] to calculate the stationary average delay in queue (assuming that it is well defined), as follows. Sensing periods of length T_s and honeynode periods of length T_t correspond to a "vacation" of the server, and are followed by transmission times of length T_t, during which consecutive packets with varying sizes enter service. Unlike the usual analysis of servers with vacations, here a vacation starts at deterministic times, and not necessarily at the end of busy periods. When not idle, the server can be in three different states: (a) a packet is being transmitted, (b) the server is on vacation, or (c) the current transmission is postponed and the server is waiting for the vacation.

Fig. 4 shows a typical path of the *residual* time until the completion of the current task (a service, a vacation, or the wait for the vacation), that we call $r(t)$. Under ergodicity, the stationary average residual service is the same as the long term average, given by:

$$R = \lim_{t \to \infty} \frac{1}{t} \int_0^t r(t) \, dt = \lim_{t \to \infty} \frac{1}{t} \left[\sum_{i=1}^{M(t)} \frac{S_i^2}{2} + \sum_{i=1}^{V(t)} \frac{L_i^2}{2} \right] \qquad (6)$$

where $M(t)$ is the number of arrivals that have entered service up to time t, $V(t)$ is the number of sensing periods up to time t, and L_i is the length of the i-th vacation. It follows that L_i are iid random variables with composite distribution:

with probability $1 - p$ the vacation length is $T_s + X$, and with probability p it is $T_s + T_t + X$. For $k \geq 1$, let

$$\tau_k = \min(t > \tau_{k-1} : Q(t) = 0); \quad \tau_0 \equiv 0$$

be the consecutive moments when the queue empties. The stability assumption implies that the queue empties infinitely often (that is, the state $Q = 0$ is positive recurrent), so that $\tau_k \to +\infty$ with probability one. At these times, $M(\tau_n) = N(\tau_n)$, and $N(t)/t \to \lambda$, because $N(\cdot)$ is a Poisson process. Because the limit R (assuming that it exists) is the same if we consider any divergent subsequence, we can take the limit along the subsequence $\{\tau_k; k \geq 0\}$. In our model $V(t)/t \to (T_s + T_t)^{-1}$. Under ergodicity, long term averages are stationary averages, and

$$\mathbb{E}(L_i^2) = \mathbb{E}(T_s + X)^2 (1 - p) + \mathbb{E}(T_s + T_t + X)^2 p,$$

where X satisfies (1) and (2). Using these results in (6) gives expression (5).

The rest of the argument is as follows. Because Poisson arrivals see time averages (PASTA), an arriving customer to a stationary queue will encounter N_q customers in queue, where N_q is a random variable that has the stationary distribution of the queue length. The average wait time is thus the sum of the expected service time of the N_q customers in queue, plus R, plus the contribution of the vacation periods during the waiting time. Call T the required service time for the customers in queue, then using Little's Law:

$$\mathbb{E}(T) = \mathbb{E}\left(\sum_{k=1}^{N_q} S_k\right) = \mathbb{E}(N_q \mathbb{E}(S)) = \lambda W_q \mathbb{E}(S).$$

Therefore, the stationary delay upon arrival at the queue will satisfy:

$$W_q = \lambda W_q \mathbb{E}(S) + R + v_s(T_s + \mathbb{E}(X)) + v_h T_t, \tag{7}$$

where v_s and v_h are the (expected) number of sensing and honeynode periods (respectively) that fall within the time required to transmit all the N_q customers in front of the new arrival. In the expression above we have used the fact that for every sensing period, the actual vacation time is not just T_s but we must add the lost time from the postponed service (if any). On average, the stationary contribution of this excess is $\mathbb{E}(X)$.

We now proceed to the calculation of v_s and v_h. In order to do so, we will use Wald's theorem. Given T, the actual number of (true) transmission periods required to provide the service for the N_q customers in queue is:

$$\nu_t = \min\left(n : \sum_{i=1}^{n}(T_t - X_i) \geq T\right), \tag{8}$$

where X_i is the fraction of postponed service at the i-th sensing period. This is a stopping time adapted to the filtration $\mathfrak{F}_n$ generated by $\{Z_i \equiv T_t - X_i, i \leq n\}$. In addition, Z_n is independent of $\mathfrak{F}_{n-1}$. For our model the random variables

$\{Z_n\}$ are bounded, thus absolutely integrable. It is straightforward to verify that $\mathbb{E}(X_n 1_{\{\nu_t < n\}}) = \mathbb{P}(\nu_t < n)\,\mathbb{E}(X)$, and finally, $\mathbb{E}(\nu_t) < \infty$, which follows because $\nu_t \leq T/(T_t - \ell_2)$ w.p.1. Under these conditions, Wald's Theorem ensures that

$$\mathbb{E}\left(\sum_{i=1}^{\nu_t} Z_i\right) = \mathbb{E}(\nu_t)(T_t - \mathbb{E}(X)).$$

Rewrite (8) as: $\sum_{i=1}^{\nu_t} Z_i \leq T < \sum_{i=1}^{\nu_t+1} Z_i$ and take expectations to get:

$$\frac{\mathbb{E}(T)}{T_t - \mathbb{E}(X)} - 1 < \mathbb{E}(\nu_t) \leq \frac{\mathbb{E}(T)}{T_t - \mathbb{E}(X)}.$$

In stationary state, we use the approximation $\mathbb{E}(\nu_t) = \lambda W_q \mathbb{E}(S)/(T_t - \mathbb{E}(X))$. In order to calculate v_s and v_h we reason as follows: given the number of honeynode periods, the number of sensing periods is the number of true transmission periods required to exhaust the time T, plus v_h, that is:

$$v_s = \mathbb{E}(\nu_t) + v_h = \mathbb{E}(\nu_t) + pv_s, \implies v_s = \frac{\mathbb{E}(\nu_t)}{1 - p}.$$

Replacing now these values in (7) and using $\mathbb{E}(T) = \lambda W_q \mathbb{E}(S)$, we obtain

$$W_q = \lambda W_q \mathbb{E}(S)\left(1 + \frac{T_s + \mathbb{E}(X)}{(1-p)(T_t - \mathbb{E}(X))} + p\frac{T_t}{(1-p)(T_t - \mathbb{E}(X))}\right) + R,$$

which yields (4), after some simple algebra.

3.3   State Dependent Policies

When a SU is chosen as a honeynode and it has an initial queue size of Q packets, the queue size at the beginning of the following transmission period is $Q + A$, where $A \sim \text{Poisson}(\lambda(T_s + T_t))$. For our model, we can solve recursions to approximate the probability that the queue empties within the following transmission period, or its expectation (details fall outside the scope of this paper and will be presented elsewhere). Strategies for honeynode allocation may include choosing the SU with largest probability of emptying. The particular case where all SUs have identical statistics (same arrival rates) is much simpler because it reduces to choosing the SU with minimal queue size, and no further calculations are necessary. However in the more realistic scenarios when λ_i are not only different but perhaps even slowly changing, it may prove essential to be able to calculate specific trade-offs between choosing honeynodes and avoiding attacks.

4   Simulation and Results

4.1   Simulation Parameters and Model

We coded a discrete event simulation written in Python in order to compare the three honeynode selection strategies mentioned in 3.2. All arrival rate (λ)

Table 1. Simulation Parameters

Parameter	Symbol	Value
Number of SU	N	20
Packet Service Time	S_n	$\sim U(0.1, 1.7)$ msec
Sensing Period	T_s	50 ms
Transmission Period	T_t	950 ms
Number of attacks / slot		1
Number of honeynodes /slot		20
Number of replication		30
Simulated time		5000000 msec
Warm-up time		100000 msec

are in millisecond domain and mean λ packets per millisecond. As a first step we consider in this paper equal arrival rates $\lambda_i = \lambda$ amongst the SUs. Under this assumption, the randomized and the queue dependent policies become a randomized policy with equal probabilities, and a minimum queue size policy, respectively. The data for our model is given in Table 1.

In all our simulations, we use the technique of antithetic random variables (ARN) for increased precision. For the infinite queue model where waiting and loss are monotone functions of the inter-arrival and service variables, ARN ensures variance reduction [18] (we used the inverse function method for generating random variables). For the finite buffer model, because some packets may be lost, it is no longer true that larger inter-arrivals (service times) always have a decreasing (increasing) effect on the delay. Although the theory does not ensure variance reduction for the finite buffer model, we verified by experimentation that this is the case.

Using a simulated time of 50,000 time slots means that the number of packets served in each SU is a random variable. For each replication of the simulation, we discarded the "warm up" data corresponding to the first 100 time slots. Preliminary simulations were used to choose these numbers, testing for stationarity and a satisfactory precision. For each replication or run of 50,000 slots we estimated the quantity $(1/N)\sum_i^n W_q(i)$ that we call the average wait time in the queues. We then used 30 independent replications to calculate 95% confidence intervals of the form:

$$\bar{W}_q \pm t_{29,0.975}\sqrt{\frac{\widehat{\mathrm{Var}(W_q)}}{30}},$$

where $\widehat{\mathrm{Var}(W_q)}$ is the sample variance from the 30 replications. In the plots that follow we do not report these intervals. In a typical simulation with $\lambda = 0.9$ and no honeynode the estimated average wait was 9.849 ± 0.097, which corresponds to a relative error of 1%.

4.2   Comparison of Approximations

Using parameters in Table 1, μ' can be calculated as in (3). When $\lambda \in [0.1, 0.9]$ and no honeynodes are assigned ($p_i = 0$) we get the range of values $\mu' \in$

[1.05513, 1.05551]. For random honeynode assignment ($p_i = 1/N$), the corresponding range is $\mu' \in [1.00283, 1.00320]$, ensuring stability for all queues. The analytical formulas available hold for the infinite buffer model and are as follows.

M/G/1 QUEUE. To obtain an expression for the stationary average delay or waiting time in the queue, a first crude approximation is to use the $M/G/1$ formulas with the effective rates λ and μ' [17].

PRIORITY MODEL. A second approximation is based on a $M/G/1$ priority queue [17]. The sensing operation is to be served in higher priority, and packet transmission is the lower priority job. Formula (9) estimates the stationary average queuing delay for a packet with service priority i, when all customer classes arrive according to independent Poisson processes.

$$W_q^i = \frac{\lambda_1 \mathbb{E}[S_1^2] + \cdots + \lambda_n \mathbb{E}[S_n^2]}{2 \prod_{j=i-1}^{i}(1 - \lambda_1 \mathbb{E}[S1] - \cdots - \lambda_j \mathbb{E}[Sj])} \tag{9}$$

This formula is only an approximation because the arrival rate of the "sensing" or high priority jobs is $\lambda_1 = (T_s + T_t)^{-1}$, and $S_1 = T_s$ is deterministic. Second high priority job is serving as honeynode where $\lambda_2 = p(T_s + T_t)^{-1}$ and $S_2 = T_t$, while $S_3 \sim U(0.1, 1.7)$ is the original packet service time distribution.

VACATION MODEL. This corresponds to our formula (4). When no honeynodes are assigned, we use $p_i = 0$. For the random honeynode assignment we used $p_i = 1/20$.

Fig. 5a and Fig. 5b show the results. The discrepancies are not very visible for smaller values of λ but they become more apparent for heavier traffic regimes, where the vacation formula seems to agree best with the simulated system, under the round robin strategy.

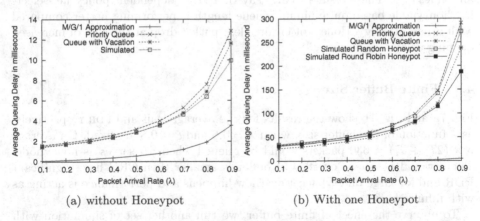

(a) without Honeypot   (b) With one Honeypot

Fig. 5. Average Queuing Delay for simple cognitive radio network

4.3   Comparison of Honeynode Assignment Strategies

Fig. 6a shows the average wait per packet as λ increases with fixed $\xi = 0.8$ and infinite buffer sizes. In infinite buffer systems there is no packet drop for queue overflow,

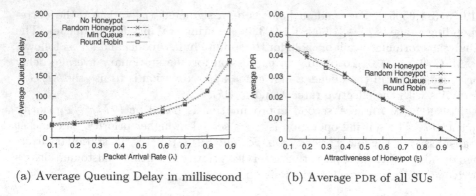

(a) Average Queuing Delay in millisecond   (b) Average PDR of all SUs

Fig. 6. Results for CRN with infinite buffer and $\lambda = 0.6$

and therefore PDR is independent of λ. The only cause of packet drop is the jamming attack. Simulation results reflects that with $\xi = 0.8$, having no honeynode gives PDR of 0.05 and with one honeynode, PDR is 0.01 for all values of λ.

For the infinite buffer model, if θ_i is the probability that i'th SU is attacked and p_i is the long term fraction of periods where SU_i is chosen as a honeypot (assuming stationarity), then $PDR_i = \theta_i((1 - p_i) + p_i(1 - \xi_i))$. When $\theta_i = p_i = 1/N$ and $N = 20$ we obtain the linear function $0.05(1 - 0.05\xi)$ as verified in Fig. 6b. The attractiveness (ξ) does not affect the queue size, which is only dependent on the strategy and the incoming rate λ. Simulation result shows average queuing delay for no honeypot, random honeypot, minimum queue and round-robin selection schemes are 3.54 ms, 72.55 ms, 62.1ms and 64.62 ms respectively for all values of ξ. These results clearly say that state dependent policy i.e. selecting honeynode based on minimum queue length is performing better compared with others strategy. Honeypot ensures less packet drop at the cost of increased queuing delay.

4.4   Finite Buffer Size

Fig. 7a and Fig. 7b show the results for the average wait and PDR respectively, as a function of the buffer size, when $\lambda = 0.6$ and $\xi = 0.8$ are fixed. On average $\lambda \times (2T_s + T_t) = 630$ packets would be queued when SU serves as honeynode. There would be queue overflow if buffer is smaller then CRN have significant PDR and for large buffer packet overflow happens and performance is acting as with infinite buffer.

To observe the effect of finite buffer, we run another set of simulation with buffer size as 400 packets for every SU. Fig. 8a and Fig. 8b shows the observed average queuing delay and PDR respectively. With low arrival rate λ (below a threshold) honeynode selection scheme based on minimum queue is performing better. This threshold value of λ should be Buffer Size$/(2T_S + T_t) = 0.381$ Because one SU can accumulate this amount of packets when serving as honeynode. When λ goes above the threshold, and when the SU is serving as honeynode,

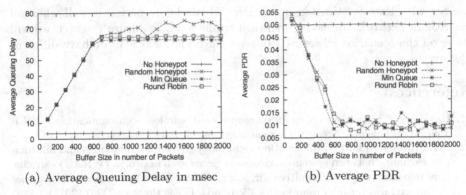

(a) Average Queuing Delay in msec   (b) Average PDR

Fig. 7. Results varying buffer size of SU with $\lambda = 0.6, \xi = 0.8$

it accumulate many packets so that the queue overflows which cause significant amount of PDR. Below this threshold SU behaves as infinite buffer model. These two graphs shows a good trade-off between Delay and PDR. With limited buffer and from the two figures it is clear that the administrator have to come to a conclusion at particular value of λ and ξ and specified buffer size, whether to apply honeypot or not. At higher value of λ and loss tolerant traffic (such as real time video) not having honeypot as it can not tolerate delay.

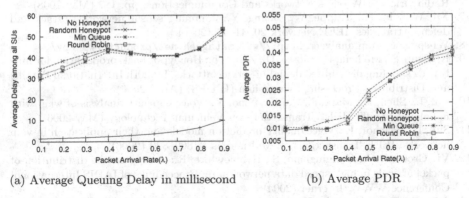

(a) Average Queuing Delay in millisecond   (b) Average PDR

Fig. 8. Results for CRN varying λ with $\xi = 0.8$ and Buffer of 400 packets

5   Conclusions and Future Work

In this paper we have presented a theoretical model to predict the performance of Cognitive Radio Network based on queuing model with fixed vacation. The model deals with the periodic sensing of cognitive cycle as fixed length vacation. Honeypot is well known to prevent jamming attack but assigning honeynode without considering queuing delay associated with it costs degradation of performance. Dynamic assignment of Honeynode is crucial from system performance perspective. We propose state dependent honeynode assignment scheme on every transmission cycle where the honeynode selection can be done by choosing the SU with lowest estimated queue size. This scheme performs well when all the SUs in network are having identical traffic load. In future research we will focus on the scenarios where SUs doesn't have identical load or have different QoS requirement.

References

1. Haykin, S.: Cognitive radio: brain-empowered wireless communications. IEEE Journal on Selected Areas in Communications 23, 201–220 (2005)
2. IEEE draft standard for information technology -telecommunications and information exchange between systems - wireless regional area networks (WRAN) - specific requirements - part 22: Cognitive wireless ran MAC & PHY specifications: Policies and procedures for operation in the TV bands, IEEE P802.22/D2.0 (2011)
3. Liu, Z., Chen, Y., Yu, W., Fu, X.: Generic network forensic data acquisition from household and small business wireless routers. In: IEEE International Symposium World of Wireless Mobile and Multimedia Networks (WoWMoM), pp. 1–6 (2010)
4. Misra, S., Dhurandher, S.K., Rayankula, A., Agrawal, D.: Using honeynodes for defense against jamming attacks in wireless infrastructure-based networks. Computers and Electrical Engineering 36(2), 367–382 (2010)
5. Yek, S.: Implementing network defence using deception in a wireless honeypot. In: 2nd Australian Computer Network, Information and Forensics Conference (2004)
6. Burbank, J.: Security in cognitive radio networks: The required evolution in approaches to wireless network security. In: 3rd International Conference on Cognitive Radio Oriented Wireless Networks and Communications, pp. 1–7 (May 2008)
7. Xu, W., Ma, K., Trappe, W., Zhang, Y.: Jamming sensor networks: attack and defense strategies. IEEE Network 20, 41–47 (2006)
8. Wi-spy spectrum analyzer, http://www.metageek.net/products/wi-spy/
9. Khattab, S., Melhem, R., Mosse, D., Znati, T.: Honeypot back-propagation for mitigating spoofing distributed denial-of-service attacks. In: 20th International Parallel and Distributed Processing Symposium (IPDPS) (April 2006)
10. Cai, L., Shen, X., Mark, J., Cai, L., Xiao, Y.: Voice capacity analysis of wlan with unbalanced traffic. IEEE Transactions on Vehicular Technology (May 2006)
11. Sun, L., Ifeachor, E.: Voice quality prediction models and their application in voip networks. IEEE Transactions on Multimedia 8, 809–820 (2006)
12. Vic Grout, D.O., Cunningham, S., Hebblewhite, R.: A note on the distribution of packet arrivals in high-speed data networks. In: Proceedings of IADIS International Conference WWW/Internet (2004)
13. Jain, R., Routhier, S.A.: Packet trains-measurements and a new model for computer network traffic. IEEE Journal on Selected Areas in Communication 6, 986–995 (1986)
14. Wilson, M.: A historical view of network traffic models, http://www.cse.wustl.edu/~jain/cse567-06/ftp/traffic_models2 (accessed: May 12, 2012)
15. Dennis Guster, D.R., Sundheim, R.: Evaluating computer network packet inter-arrival distributions. In: Encyclopedia of Information Science & Technology (2009)
16. Madan, K.C.: An m/g/1 queue with optional deterministic server vacations. Metron - International Journal of Statistics (3-4), 83–95 (1999)
17. Ross, S.M.: Introduction to Probability Models, 10th edn. Academic Press (December 2009)
18. Ross, S.M.: Simulation, 5th edn. Academic Press (October 2012)

InterCloud RAIDer: A Do-It-Yourself Multi-cloud Private Data Backup System

Chih Wei Ling and Anwitaman Datta*

Nanyang Technological University, Singapore
http://sands.sce.ntu.edu.sg/

Abstract. In this paper, we introduce InterCloud RAIDer, which realizes a multi-cloud private data backup system by composing (i) a data deduplication technique to reduce the overall storage overhead, (ii) erasure coding to achieve redundancy at low overhead, which is dispersed across multiple cloud services to realize fault-tolerance against individual service providers, specifically we use non-systematic instances of erasure codes to provide a basic level of privacy from individual cloud stores, and finally, (iii) a proof of data possession mechanism to detect misbehaving services - where we optimize the implementation by exploiting hash digests that are created in the prior deduplication phase. Apart from the uniqueness and non-triviality of putting these modules together, the system design also had to deal with artefacts and heterogeneity across different cloud storage services we used, namely Dropbox, Google drive and SkyDrive.

Keywords: backup, deduplication, erasure codes, proof-of-possession.

1 Introduction

Cloud based services have become an integral part for data storage and backup solutions used by many organizations as well as individuals. While the main commercial players generally provide robust and reliable service, guided both by the need to maintain good reputation as well as legal obligations, in this paper we explore an approach which enables the end-users to achieve better reliability and confidentiality while outsourcing their storage without being left to the mercy of the goodwill of any single service provider.

This is important, because, individual storage service providers may be compromised by hardware or software faults, e.g., Dropbox allowed password free access to data [20], Carbonite [21] and Microsoft lost customer data [22], or because a specific service provider may fall prey to hacking attack, e.g., Sony PlayStation Network [23] and LinkedIn [24], or a service may be compromised by malicious employees. Not to mention the issue of overzealous government agencies using or abusing legal instruments to access private data.

Likewise, when an user deletes his data from a service provider, there is no guarantee that all the copies that the service provider may have created (for

---

* This work was supported by A*Star TSRP grant 102 158 0038 for the pCloud project.

M. Chatterjee et al. (Eds.): ICDCN 2014, LNCS 8314, pp. 453–468, 2014.

fault-tolerance) are actually removed. Consequently, the exposure of data may persist beyond the period an user uses a specific service.

Storing only encrypted data can arguably deal with the confidentiality issue. However it does not prevent the problem of data loss. Creating a service which spreads the data across multiple clouds [25] is a logical way to achieve this.

Several prominent existing works embrace the latter idea, e.g., RACS (redundant array of cloud storage) [1] and DepSKY [2]. In order to keep the overhead of redundancy low, using erasure coding is a natural choice that is deployed by all such systems. Our work leverages the same broad ideas, but unlike these existing works, which demonstrate the concepts using services like Amazon S3, RackSpace, etc. that are aimed to cater to the businesses, we build a working system (InterCloud RAIDer[1]) using more 'plebeian' services such as Dropbox, Google Drive, SkyDrive, etc. which also cater to individual users, particularly by providing a stripped down service for free, which can then be augmented with more resources if needed, by paying. In doing so, we hope that InterCloud RAIDer can be readily utilized by individuals for personal use. A crucial challenge in realizing the system is to deal with the specific constraints posed by the limited and heterogenous APIs and functionalities these services provide.

In order to realize a wholesome system, we incorporate mechanisms for proof of data possession to determine that data stored with specific service providers are retained, and apply deduplication mechanisms in order to curtail the storage overhead. The constraints from the cloud service providers lead to peculiarities in achieving these functionalities, and our implementation experience reveals interesting insights pertaining to these. So to say, while the modular architecture is reasonably straightforward, the essence of this work is to instantiate these specific modules by taking into account the interplay and interference of the different design choices (e.g., to the best of our knowledge, deduplication is unique to our system w.r.to the above mentioned multi-cloud storage systems, and we will subsequently explore its synergy with proof of data possession mechanisms while discussing our design choices in building InterCloud RAIDer), and in presence of extrinsic artefacts as posed by the heterogeneous cloud service providers.

We use a non-systematic erasure code, which provides some natural obfuscation of the data being stored in the individual storage services. This approach is readily compatible with the deduplication mechanism, but does not provide the same kind of security as cryptography does. To keep the implementation simple, we did not add an encryption layer, but we will discuss how it could also be added if necessary while still retaining the other functionalities. Though the implementation is geared towards use by individuals for file backup, and uses commercial cloud services like Dropbox, the implementation can be easily generalized in two manner: (i) A reliable multi-cloud file system transparently providing a predefined set of interfaces, similar to Amazon S3 to be used by ap-

---

[1] The source code is available at http://code.google.com/p/intercloudraider/. The 'InterCloud' in the name refers to the use of multiple cloud services in our system, which are used to form a Redundant Array of Independent (virtual, cloud service based) Disks, i.e., RAID.

plications in a manner agnostic of the cloud-level distribution will allow diverse usage of the system. (ii) Mixing peer-to-peer or friend-to-friend 'crowdsourced' storage cloud [3] along with dedicated commercial cloud service providers, is expected to allow further robustness against various adversaries, while achieving agreeable quality of service. Such extensions comprise our future plans.

2   Preliminaries

InterCloud RAIDer is built on three techniques to achieve reliable and storage efficient data backup. The first is chunk-based deduplication [4–6, 10, 11], a method that breaks a file or data stream into a sequence of chunks and eliminates duplicate chunks by comparing the chunk hashes. The second is non-systematic erasure codes, which adds redundancy to stored file so that retrieving fully the file is possible even under the presence of faults. Using a non-systematic code provides some basic confidentiality of the data stored at different storage services. Encrypting the encoded data is an optional step (not implemented at present) that can be readily plugged in, in our system if stricter confidentiality guarantees are needed. The third is Provable Data Possession (PDP) [16–18], which provides the assurance to data owners that the data servers who claim to store the outsourced data from the owners, are actually storing the data. We next briefly summarize the specific instances of the respective techniques that we have employed in InterCloud RAIDer.

2.1   Chunk-Based Deduplication

Chunk-based deduplication has three main steps: chunking, indexing and deduplicating. Many chunking algorithms have been proposed and studied at length in the literature [5–9]. For an incoming data stream, the chunking step divides the stream into fixed or variable length chunks. We use the Two-Threshold Two-Divisor (TTTD) chunking algorithm [6] to subdivide the incoming data stream into a sequence of chunks. TTTD generates variable length chunks with smaller variation than other chunking algorithms and thus produces better deduplication ratio.

Then, a cryptographic hash function, such as MD5 [12] or SHA1 [13, 14], is used to hash the chunks at the indexing step. The chunks are identified by the hashes. By assuming that the collision probability is very low, chunks with the same hash and size are assumed to be identical. Since comparing hashes is faster than comparing the actual chunk contents, the deduplicating step can be executed efficiently. Only new chunks are stored and references are updated for duplicate chunks.

The naive and traditional way to implement deduplicating is to use full chunk index: a key-value index of all the stored chunks, where the key is a chunk's hash and the value holds metadata about that chunk, including where it is stored on disk. When an incoming chunk is to be stored, its hash is looked up in the full index, and the chunk is stored only if no entry is found for its hash. However, there are more sophisticated deduplicating techniques, such as Data Domain Deduplication File System [10] or Sparse Indexing [11], that solve the chunk-lookup disk bottleneck problem caused by full chunk index. We implement full chunk index given its simplicity.

2.2 Non-systematic (Homomorphic Self-repairing) Erasure Codes

An erasure code is a mapping, which creates $n > k$ symbols out of k input symbols, such that any k' (where $k' \geq k$ and $k' < n$) symbols can be used to reconstruct the inputs. A systematic erasure code is an erasure code in which the input data is embedded in encoded data. More precisely, for a systematic linear code, the generator matrix G can be expressed as $G = [I_k|A]$, where I_k is the identity matrix of size k. A non-systematic erasure code does not contain the input data in its encoded output. If systematic coding is used, then a server storing a systematic piece will be able to retrieve this part of the original input. When using non-systematic codes, without access to enough (code parameter k') encoded pieces at a single service provider, it is information theoretically impossible to infer the original input. Note that a strong adversary which has controls multiple such apparently independent services will be able to access the data as well. An additional layer of encryption may be employed to mitigate such information leak. However, in the current implementation we assume that only individual storage services can be individually and independently compromised, and hence bypass this computationally expensive step by using non-systematic erasure codes 'to kill two birds with a single stone'. Specifically, we use homomorphic self-repairing codes (HSRC) [19] to encode the chunks. In the current implementation, we do not exploit the 'repairability' property of HSRC, and hence any other non-systematic erasure code may also be used instead - but we aim to exploit the repairability property in future extensions, which we will discuss later when concluding the paper.

We denote finite fields by $\mathbb{F}$ and fields with q elements by $\mathbb{F}_q$. Let $\mathbf{o}$ be an object of size M, that is, $\mathbf{o} \in \mathbb{F}_{q^M}$. We can write

$$\mathbf{o} = (\mathbf{o}_1, ..., \mathbf{o}_k), \mathbf{o}_i \in \mathbb{F}_{q^{M/k}} \ . \tag{1}$$

Then a *homomorphic self-repairing code*, denoted by HSRC(n, k), is the code obtained by evaluating the polynomial

$$p(X) = \sum_{i=0}^{k-1} p_i X^{q^i} \in \mathbb{F}_{q^{M/k}}[X] \tag{2}$$

in n non-zero values $\alpha_1, ..., \alpha_n$ of $\mathbb{F}_{q^{M/k}}$ to get an n-dimensional codeword

$$(p(\alpha_1), ..., p(\alpha_n)), \tag{3}$$

where $p_i = \mathbf{o}_{i+1}$, $i = 0, ..., k-1$ and each $p(\alpha_i)$ is the ith encoded piece.

The resulting code does not have a deterministic value of k' - a compromise made n order to achieve good repairibility. This is a slightly tangential issue for the current work, and we instead use a concrete example of the code in order to explain how it works. Let $f(X) = X^8 + X^4 + X^3 + X^2 + 1 \in \mathbb{F}_2[X]$ be a primitive polynomial of degree 8 over $\mathbb{F}_2$ and α be a root of $f(X)$. Then a possible set to construct HSRC(7, 3) is the set $\{1, \alpha, \alpha^2, \alpha^{25} = 1 + \alpha, \alpha^{26} = \alpha + \alpha^2, \alpha^{50} = 1 + \alpha^2, \alpha^{198} = 1 + \alpha + \alpha^2\}$ and the corresponding generator matrix is

$$\begin{pmatrix} 1 & \alpha & \alpha^2 & \alpha^{25} & \alpha^{26} & \alpha^{50} & \alpha^{198} \\ 1 & \alpha^2 & \alpha^4 & \alpha^{50} & \alpha^{52} & \alpha^{100} & \alpha^{141} \\ 1 & \alpha^4 & \alpha^8 & \alpha^{100} & \alpha^{104} & \alpha^{200} & \alpha^{27} \end{pmatrix}.$$

Suppose that we have two input strings of three bytes each: 00000100 00000010 00000001 and 00000010 00000101 00000000. By identifying the strings as the elements of $\mathbb{F}_{256}$, we can rewrite them as the vectors $(\alpha^2, \alpha, 1)$ and $(\alpha, \alpha^2 + 1, 0)$ respectively. By multiplying the input strings with the first and second columns of G_{HSRC}, we have

$$\begin{aligned} (\alpha^2, \alpha, 1) * (1, 1, 1)^T &= \alpha^2 + \alpha + 1 = (\alpha, \alpha^2 + 1, 0) * (1, 1, 1)^T, \text{ and} \\ (\alpha^2, \alpha, 1) * (\alpha, \alpha^2, \alpha^4)^T &= \alpha^4 = (\alpha, \alpha^2 + 1, 0) * (\alpha, \alpha^2, \alpha^4)^T, \end{aligned}$$

so we see that for two distinct inputs, some of the resulting encoded blocks may be identical - thus illustrating that individual storage providers cannot discern between the inputs.

2.3 Provable Data Possession (PDP)

While dispersal of redundant data across multiple cloud provides fault tolerance and privacy against individual cloud service providers, it is also essential to ensure that the integrity of the outsourced data in not compromised at each such individual services, e.g., by illegitimate modifications or deletion. Accessing all the data all the time to check its integrity is impractical. This has led to the study of several provable data possession (PDP) techniques in recent years. We build upon a scheme proposed in [16], and modify it to better suit the expected workload for InterCloud RAIDer.

In the original scheme, a data object O is divided into a sequence of fixed-size blocks. Then a pseudo-random permutation g_k indexed on some secret key k is applied on the indices of blocks and a predetermined number of verification tokens are computed based on the contents of the permutated blocks. In our modified scheme, the chunk hashes that uniquely identify the variable-length chunks resulting from deduplication can be naturally used as a replacement of fixed-size blocks in the original scheme. This saves us a large amount of computations during the setup phase, since we only compute the tokens based on chunk hashes which are only tens of bytes (depending on what cryptographic hashing scheme is used), rather than the whole contents of chunks (which may up to tens of KBs). We also remove the authenticated encryption (AE) scheme from the original scheme, because we are storing the verification tokens at local storage of data owner.

The general idea is as follows. Consider a data repository D which contains d variable length chunks $D[1]$, ..., $D[d]$ and a chunk hash log L which contains cryptographic hashes $h_1 = H_1(D[1])$, ..., $h_d = H_1(D[d])$ that are listed sequentially, where H_1 is an arbitrary cryptographic hash function. We chose MD5_HMAC [15] as our pseudo-random function f and AES as the building block of our index permutator g.

During the setup phase, as shown in Figure 1, the token generator generates in advance t possible verification tokens and each token covers r random chunk hashes. To produce the ith token, where $1 \leq i \leq t$, we proceed as follows: First, generate two 16 bytes master keys W and Z by key generator. Store W and Z secretly at local storage of data owner. Then, generate a permutation key $k_i = f_W(i)$ and a challenge nonce $c_i = f_Z(i)$. Next, compute the set of indices $\{I_j \in [1, ..., d] : 1 \leq j \leq r\}$ where $I_j = g_{k_i}(j)$ by index permutator g. Finally, compute the token v_i using the formula:

$$v_i = H(c_i, h_{I_1}, ..., h_{I_r}) ,$$ (4)

where H is an arbitrary cryptographic hash and v_i is a stored locally secret.

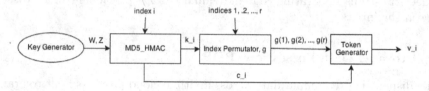

Fig. 1. A PDP Scheme

For the ith proof of data possession verification, we proceed as follows: First, regenerate the token key k_i and c_i by using the master keys W and Z. Then, compute $\{I_j \in [1, ..., d] : 1 \leq j \leq r\}$ as in setup phase and send GET requests to online stores to retrieve the chunks that are identified by h_{I_j}. Next, compute $h'_{I_j} = H_1(D'[I_j])$ where $1 \leq j \leq r$ (the chunks may be modified or deleted). Finally, compute v'_i as:

$$v'_i = H(c_i, h'_{I_1}, ..., h'_{I_r}) ,$$ (5)

where H is the arbitrary cryptographic hash function using in setup phase. If $v \neq v'$ then *reject*.

Now, we consider the probability that the hashes of missing or corrupted chunks are not included in the ith verification token. Assume that m is the number of chunks be deleted or modified. Then, the probability is given by

$$P = \left(1 - \frac{m}{d}\right)^r .$$ (6)

3   Design Considerations

The techniques explored in this work are generic, but the target users for the implementation are individuals with a small or moderate amount of data to backup, ranging between a few GBs up to a few tens of GBs. At the bottom-end of this volume range, the free capacity provided by services like Dropbox ought to be adequate, but efficient usage of the storage capacity is imperative to maximize utilization of the free services, or keep the additional costs low.

3.1   Cloud Service Providers

In order to realize the backup service over multiple cloud services, the proposed system has to encompass cloud stores from distinct service providers. The cloud Service providers (CSP), however, may use different APIs for access control and resource manipulation. This situation is complicated by the fact that distinct and sometimes mutually incompatible authentication and authorization standards are implemented by different CSPs. For example, as of July 2013, Dropbox is using OAuth1.0 while Google Drive and Skydrive are supporting OAuth2.0 as the recommended authentication mechanism for all of their APIs. However, OAuth2.0 is not backward compatible with OAuth1.0.

In addition, the CSPs may provide distinct file operations to their clients. Dropbox and Google Drive both support retrieving partial file content when a download request is forwarded to them, that is, users can specify to download only a certain contiguous range of the target file at cloud store without downloading the whole file. Put simply, they allow random accesses. However, Skydrive doesn't have this feature - Skydrive only allows file level access. Random access is essential in order to realize an efficient PDP scheme. To address this, in InterCloud RAIDer we upload the encoded pieces of non-duplicated chunks separately rather than upload a data package that contains all the pieces to be stored on cloud stores. This implies that a lot of network requests have to be made for uploading those pieces one by one, which has strong implications on the system's performance (in terms of latency) and its practicality.

Moreover, different CSPs may have different speeds for access control and resource manipulation. For a given block size, the file access interfaces provided by different CSPs with request method GET, PUT or POST may operate under different network speeds. Hence, it is crucial to choose an average chunk size for the system prudently.

3.2   Fixed vs. Variable Length Chunks

In a deduplication system, either fixed-size or content-based chunking can be used to determine the chunk boundaries — thus creating fixed or variable length chunks. The main advantage of fixed-size chunking is its simplicity in implementation. However, inserting or deleting even a single byte at the beginning of the file will shift all the remaining boundaries following the modification point, resulting in different chunks, knowing as boundary shifting problem. On an average, assuming writes at random locations, half the chunks would be different after every single byte modification to the file [6], and thereby reduce the overall deduplication ratio. Keeping updated the consequent changes in the associated metadata further accentuate the performance deterioration.

In contrast, content-based chunking has the advantage that the chunk sequence is more stable compared to fixed-size chunking under local modification [6]. Intuitively, given a file F, if we make a small modification on F to obtain F', stable under local modification means that after applying the chunking algorithm on both file versions, most of the chunks of F' are duplicates of the chunks of F. To support the dynamic nature of incremental backup system, content-based chunking is preferred over fixed-size chunking.

Average Chunk Size. Chunk size is one of the key design parameters. The choice of average chunk size is difficult because of its impact on the deduplication efficiency, network performance, and security. The smaller the chunks, the more duplicate chunks there will be and so the more efficient the deduplication technique employed in our system. On the other hand, the smaller the chunk size, there are more chunks to process during deduplication which means more times through the deduplication loop, and thus reduce the performance of deduplication. In addition, there will be more metadata of chunks to be maintained in local metadata log, and therefore increase the total cost of data maintenance.

As mentioned in Section 3.1, the APIs of different CSPs may operate under different network speeds. If we choose a smaller chunk size, there will be more number of chunks, and thus more PUT or GET requests have to be initiated to the CSPs for downloading or uploading, which will increase the total system operation time.

Suppose that we are using 4KB as the average chunk size and there is a 1TB of data on cloud store. Then there are approximately 2^{28} unique chunks. If we are using MD5 for indexing in deduplication, then we need 4GB of RAM for full chunk index. Moreover, as per Equation (6), if we have a larger total number of unique chunks, that is, $d = 2^{28}$, then we have to cover more random hashes in the verification tokens to provide better probability assurance provided that we want to give assurance based on amount of lost data rather than ratio between the affected chunks and total number of chunks. In both scenarios, using a smaller average chunk size increases the costs of deduplication and PDP scheme.

4   InterCloud RAIDer

InterCloud RAIDer stores some meta-information locally at the user client, while it outsources encoded data dispersed over multiple cloud service providers in a manner, such at none of the individual service providers can reconstruct the original files by using only data stored individually. The user client can also optionally store part of the encoded data. If the user wishes to access his outsourced data from another device, then he will have to carry the meta-information along.

One can imagine that the meta-information can be carried by the user on an USB storage device. Note that even if the device is lost, exposure of the meta-information is not adequate to gain access to the actual data, since the adversary will need the user's login credentials to gain access to the data stored at individual cloud services. However, in the current implementation, the onus of preserving a copy of the meta-information is still on the user, without which the backed-up data cannot be retrieved.

4.1   Architecture

The primary storage objects in the InterCloud RAIDer are the *files*, the *chunks*, the *encoded pieces* of chunks and their *metadata*. A file is a one-dimensional array of bytes. When a file data stream enters the system, simple metadata associated with the file, such as filename and size are generated and contained within a metadata structure (elaborated in next subsection). The data stream is then broken into a sequence of variable-length chunks by a chunking algorithm for deduplication. These chunks are identified by their contents. A cryptographic hash function is used to compute the hashes of the chunk contents and those hashes are used as the unique identifiers for chunks. Moreover, a file description that keeps track of the chunks mutual relation for constructing the retrieved file is generated. A chunk hash log is also constructed for the generated cryptographic hashes identifying the chunks.

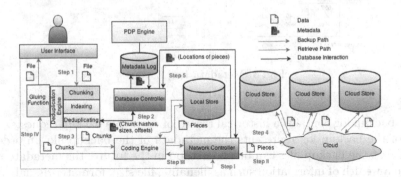

Fig. 2. InterCloud RAIDer Architecture

The software architecture is embodied in processes that execute on each user computer: a backup service interface, a deduplication engine, a coding engine, a database controller, a network controller and a PDP engine. The service interface accepts requests from users through a graphical user interface (GUI). A deduplication engine chunks and deduplicates a file object on backup request so that the identical chunks can be eliminated and thus achieve maximal storage efficiency. The coding engine adds redundancy to the unique chunks by encoding them with a non-systematic code. The network controller controls all the network requests to CSPs being used in our system. The PDP engine generates a predefined number of tokens for post-verification to assure the data owners that their outsourced data are indeed retained at the CSPs. The database controller keeps track and manages all the meta-information induced by those components.

The service interface consists of operations on storage objects, namely: *backup*, *retrieve*, *delete*, and *verify*; which we elaborate later in this section.

The meta-data is stored locally at the users, as is optionally a part of the encoded data. The rest of the data is dispersed across multiple CSPs. The current implementation uses Dropbox, Google Drive and SkyDrive.

4.2   Metadata Log Layout

The database controller maintains a metadata log in the local storage of system users. The metadata log (illustrated in Figure 3) contains three major types of metadata: the backup log, the file description table and the chunk hash log.

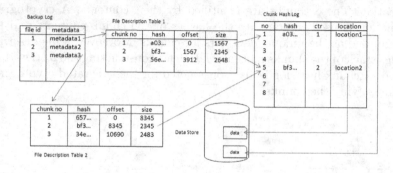

Fig. 3. Metadata Log Layout

The backup log contains a historical record of users' file backup requests. Each entry of the backup log represents the metadata of the backup file. In order to ensure that the backup files can be understood in the future, the metadata must contain a wealth of information such as filename, file size, format, original logical location at user computers, etc. Please note that every entry of the backup log is pointing to a file description table, which is generated by the database controller during deduplication.

The file description table contains 3 main fields: cryptographic hashes that uniquely identify the chunks, the offset of the chunks relative to the first byte of file data stream, and the chunk sizes. This table describes the arrangement of the variable length chunks that compose a file. For example, a file object could be divided into a sequence of variable-length chunks after chunking stage and then the chunks are hashed by a cryptographic hash function to a sequence of hashes in indexing stage. By listing the hash of every chunk in order, we provide a description of the file object. By using this description table, the file object can be reconstructed by fetching the constituting chunks. Depending on the number of files to which a specific chunk belongs, a corresponding count needs to be maintained, which is essential to determine whether a specific chunk should be removed (garbage collection) when files are deleted by the user.

4.3   System Interaction and Data Flow

We now describe how the InterCloud RAIDer modules and CSPs interact to realize data deduplication, data storage, data retrieval, and data verification.

Backup and Retrieve: In Figure 2, we illustrate the backup process through these numbered steps.

1. An user makes a file backup request to the system. The database controller generates metadata about the file and insert it into a backup log.
2. When the file data stream enters the deduplication engine, the engine chunks the data stream using TTTD (described in Section 2.1). At the indexing step, the chunks are hashed using a collision resistant hash function. We chose MD5 for this purpose, but any other cryptographic hash function could also be used instead. The MD5 hashes are used as the identifiers of the chunks since the probability of collision is negligible. A file description table as described earlier in Section 4.2 is accordingly created. Since the target system users are data owners with a small or moderate amount of data to be outsourced, the anticipated total number of chunks is relatively small compared to organizations and enterprises. Consider, for example, a store has 1TB of data (which is at the very upper range of our current targeted system usage) and the average chunk size is 32KB. Then there are roughly 2^{25} unique chunks. Assuming that we are using MD5 for indexing, then we need 512MB of RAM for deduplication. Hence, we choose to use full chunk index for deduplication, namely, the deduplication engine compares the incoming chunk hashes with the hashes in chunk hash log that be read and stored in RAM one at a time, and the new chunk is stored only if no entry is found for its hash in chunk hash log. However, more sophisticated techniques such as Data Domain Deduplication File System or Sparse Indexing can also be applied in order to achieve better deduplication performance. The database controller creates a new entry for a non-duplicate chunk in chunk hash log, and alternatively increases the reading of counters provided there was an existing identical chunk.
3. The non-duplicate chunks are passed to the coding engine. We chose the (7,3)-HSRC with the Galois Field $\mathbb{F}_{256}$ as the underlying field for the convenience of the byte operations in computer hardware, since $\mathbb{F}_{256}$ is corresponding to one byte. We also apply zero-padding to the non-duplicated chunks and up to two bytes are zero padded to the chunks so that the resulting block sizes are multiple of 3 bytes. On the average, if the average chunk size is 32KB, then the additional expense induced by zero-padding is one byte per 32KB, which is negligible.

4. After HSRC encoding, the encoded pieces of chunks are ready for storing. Suppose that we have three CSPs A, B, and C. We use the following allocation scheme for storing the encoded pieces on the CSPs: the system uploads two encoded pieces with the corresponding points 1 and α to storage provider A, two encoded pieces with the corresponding points α^2 and α^{26} to storage provider B, and two encoded pieces with the corresponding points α^{25} and α^{50} to storage provider C, and (optionally) stores the encoded pieces with the point α^{198} at user's local storage. The network controller is responsible for the network operations: it goes through the OAuth1.0 or OAuth2.0 authorization and authentication process to retrieve an access token from respective CSPs, and then uses the tokens to initiates multiple PUT or POST network requests to the CSPs to store the encoded pieces.

5. After completing the storage, the database controller keeps track of the locations of the encoded pieces in the chunk hash log for future reference.

For file retrieve, it is just the reverse steps of file backup and are indicated using roman numerals in the architecture Figure 2.

1. First, the users use the system GUI to choose an entry from the backup log for retrieving. The network controller will contact database controller to access necessary information, such as file description table or locations of encoded pieces on cloud, for file retrieving.

2. Then, the network controller initiate the network operations for connecting to the CSPs. By using the file description table and chunk hash log, the network controller will send multiple GET requests to the CSPs and download the necessary encoded pieces for decoding a chunk. If some encoded pieces are stored locally, only two other pieces are needed from a single CSP, otherwise multiple CSPs need to be contacted.

3. After that, the downloaded pieces (and the local encoded piece) are decoded by the Gaussian Elimination and Back Substitution at coding engine.

4. The retrieved chunks are then glued together to reconstruct the original file according to the arrangement of chunks in the file description table by gluing function, before returning the retrieved file to the user.

In addition, InterCloud RAIDer has several background processes - the most prominent one being the data integrity and retrievability checks (described in Section 2.3). There is also a garbage collection process, which needs to delete encoded blocks from all storage locations corresponding to files that are deleted by the user. Here, the main caution is to not inadvertently delete chunks that were duplicate across multiple files, and likewise, maintain the corresponding meta-data to determine when a chunk can indeed be garbage collected.

5 Experiments

We report the performance of InterCloud RAIDer from several aspects - looking at its overall performance, as well as micro-benchmarking the specific modules. As local user machine, an university PC running Windows 7 with 4GB RAM, and Intel CPU 6700 @ 2.66GHz was used for the experiments.

5.1   Impact of Chunk Size on Network Operations and Coding

By measuring the performance of InterCloud RAIDer that uses fixed-sized deduplication, we can narrow down the range of average chunk sizes to several candidates for optimality and then we will use these possible candidates to determine
the performance of InterCloud RAIDer in Section 5.2. We have performed several
series of experiments on a 1.12MB PDF file, 10.0MB DJVU file and 103.8MB
RMVB file. Due to space limitation, we report only the case of 1.12MB PDF
file, but the results scaled linearly with our experiments. While applying fixed-
size chunking, the file is subdivided into 12KB, 24KB, 48KB, 96KB, 192KB and
384KB fixed-size chunks (the words *chunk* and *block* are used interchangeably)
accordingly, and the chunks are passed to the remaining modules of InterCloud
RAIDer for further processing, namely, encoding the chunks by (7,3)-HSRC and
uploading the encoded pieces to cloud stores. After encoding, the sizes of the
encoded pieces are 4KB, 8KB, 16KB, 32KB, 64KB and 128KB respectively.
We measure the file access time, encoding time of (7,3)-HSRC, time of internal
metadata manipulation, uploading time to CSPs, and total backup time of the
1.12MB PDF file against encoded piece sizes. We have plotted the results in
Figure 4 with error bars by using 90% confidence interval.

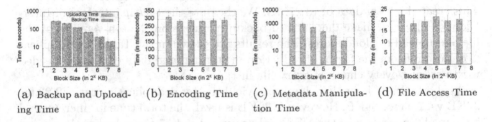

(a) Backup and Upload-   (b) Encoding Time   (c) Metadata Manipula-   (d) File Access Time
ing Time   tion Time

Fig. 4. File Backup: Measurements of 1.12MB PDF File

From Figure 4(b), we see that the encoding time is consistent, since encoding
is done byte wise, and only the absolute file size matters. Figures 4(a) and 4(c)
show that the backup, uploading or metadata manipulation time decrease with
increased chunk sizes. This is because fewer network requests are involved.

We also show in Figure 5 the file write time, decoding time of (7,3)-HSRC,
downloading time from CSPs, and total retrieval time vs. encoded piece sizes.
Note the huge discrepancy of network operation times across different service
providers. Similar behavior was also observed for data upload (not shown here).

Figure 5(c) shows the decoding time of the 1.12MB file by using Gaussian
Elimination and Back Substitution and it is more expensive than encoding.
This is because the Gaussian Elimination has arithmetic complexity of $O\left(n^3\right)$.
Similar to the trend of measurements in file backup, Figures 5(a) and 5(b) show
the decreasing trend when the chunk size is increasing. For both series of experiments, the network operations like uploading and downloading always are the
dominant factors in determining either the total backup or retrieve time.

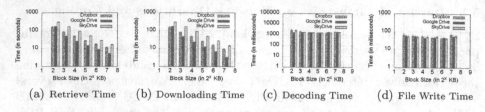

(a) Retrieve Time   (b) Downloading Time   (c) Decoding Time   (d) File Write Time

Fig. 5. File Retrieve: Measurements of 1.12MB PDF File

5.2   Deduplication in InterCloud RAIDer

While larger chunk size improves network operations, they have detrimental impact on deduplication as well as effectiveness of PDP. Based on the above experiments, we used variable length chunks with min/max thresholds configured to achieve mean sizes of 32KB and 64KB respectively, since they represent the middle of two extremes. We have chosen a real MS Word document with ten versions which were created by deleting, appending, or modifying the content from version to version. The modifications between two consecutive versions varied from 5% to 50% and the sizes of the versions ranged from 797KB to 1.71MB. This created a total data of 13.27MB. We then use the *backup* interface of Inter-Cloud RAIDer to make incremental backup requests on the ten versions of the file and upload to cloud stores. The results are shown in the Table 1. Deduplication ratio reflects the factor of reduction in storage (and data exchange) needed w.r.to storing every chunk of every file instance.

As shown Table 1, smaller chunk size yields better deduplication ratio, 2.23 for 32KB vs. 1.93 for 64KB. However, if 32KB is used, the total time for incremental backup of ten versions of the MS Word document is 1.55 times higher than using 64KB average chunk size.

Table 1. Comparison of 32KB and 64KB Average Chunk Sizes for Deduplication

Average chunk size	32KB	64KB
Total chunking time (in sec) for ten versions	41.90	46.40
Total time (in sec) of full chunk index for ten versions	1.69	1.22
Total metadata manipulation time (in sec) for ten versions	19.16	8.37
Total time (in minutes) of incremental backups for ten versions	14.35	9.23
Total data (in MB) to be uploaded after deduplication	5.939	6.871
Deduplication Ratio	2.23	1.93

5.3   Performance of PDP

We assess the overhead of the PDP setup phase by measuring the time to compute a verification token, and then summing up the overhead of the individual

Table 2. Computation Time of Each Verification Token Covering r Hashes

r	64	128	256	512	1024
Time (in ms) for computing a token	28	43	63	171	291

tokens to get overall cost. Each token contained r random hashes (see Section 2.3), and we tried up several values of r. The result is shown in Table 2.

The computations in verification phase are just repetition of the setup phase. If there are 1%, 2% or 5% corrupted chunks in data repository and data owners are seeking to have 99.9% detection probability, then the downloading time for the necessary random hashes are 25 mins, 13 mins and 5 mins respectively. The time estimates are based on 48KB fixed-size chunks being downloaded from the CSPs. This gives a rough estimate about the network overhead in our PDP scheme.

6 Concluding Remarks

We presented a holistic system which incorporates mechanisms for deduplication, data dispersal over multiple clouds and proof of data possession to facilitate back-up of private data in multicloud environment. The system design had to take into account the dependencies and constraints arising from the conflicting needs of the different modules, as well as the artefacts of the cloud service provider. The performance of the current implementation is modest, and while a more optimized implementation of the individual algorithms and modules can help improve it to certain extent, the performance shortcomings also expose the need to design more scalable algorithms for the individual tasks to achieve a better performing multi-cloud storage system while not using well provisioned cloud services in contrast to what is inherently assumed in designing systems like RACS [1] and DepSky [2].

The current version of InterCloud RAIDer implementation does not leverage on the repairability property of HSRC since the cloud stores used did not have computational power. We intend to extend the current implementation to work with other cloud services, as well as with P2P assisted hybrid architectures (similar as [26]) where the issues of repairability will be explored.

References

1. Abu-Libdeh, H., Princehouse, L., Weatherspoon, H.: RACS: A Case for Cloud Storage Diversity. In: SOCC (2010)
2. Bessani, A., Correia, M., Quaresma, B., Andre, F., Sousa, P.: DEPSKY: Dependable and Secure Storage in a Cloud-of-Clouds. In: EuroSys 2011 (2011)
3. Sharma, R., Datta, A., Dell'Amico, M.: An empirical study of availability in friend-to-friend storage systems. In: P2P (2011)
4. Hewlett-Packard, "Understanding the HP Data Deduplication Strategy: Why One Size Doesn't Fit Everyone" (2008),
   http://networkworld.com/documents/whitepaper/HPDataDeduper.pdf

5. Muthitacharoen, A., Chen, B., Mazieres, D.: A Low-bandwidth Network File System. In: SOSP (2001)
6. Eshghi, K., Tang, H.K.: A Framework for Analyzing and Improving Content-Based Chunking Algorithms. HP Labs Tech. Rep. HPL-2005-30(R.1) (2005)
7. Manber, U.: Finding Similar Files in a Large File System. USENIX ATC (2004)
8. Forman, G., Eshghi, K., Chiocchetti, S.: Finding Similar Files in Large Document Repositories. In: KDD (2005)
9. Quilan, S., Dorward, S.: Venti: A New Approach to Archival Storage. In: FAST (2002)
10. Zhu, B., Li, K., Patterson, H.: Avoiding the Disk Bottleneck in the Data Domain Deduplication File System. In: FAST (2008)
11. Lilibridge, M., Eshghi, K., Bhagwat, D., Deolaikar, V., Trezise, G., Campbell, P.: Sparse Indexing: Large Scale, Inline Deduplication Using Sampling and Locality. In: FAST (2009)
12. Rivest, R.: The MD5 Message-Digest Algorithm. IETF, Request For Comments (RFC) 1321 (1992), http://tools.ietf.org/html/rfc1321
13. National Institute of Standards and Technology, "Secure Hash Standard", FIPS 180-1 (1995), http://www.itl.nist.gov/fipspubs/fip180-1.htm
14. National Institute of Standards and Technology, "Secure Hash Standard", FIPS 180-4 (2012),
    http://csrc.nist.gov/publications/fips/fips180-4/fips-180-4.pdf
15. Bellare, M., Canetti, R., Krawczyk, H.: Keying Hash Functions for Message Authentication. In: Koblitz, N. (ed.) CRYPTO 1996. LNCS, vol. 1109, pp. 1–15. Springer, Heidelberg (1996)
16. Ateniese, G., Pietro, R.D., Mancini, L.V., Tsudik, G.: Scalable and Efficient Provable Data Possession. In: SecureComm (2008)
17. Ateniese, G., Burns, R., Curtmola, R., Herring, J., Kissner, L., Song, D.: Provable Data Possession at Untrusted Stores. In: CCS (2007)
18. Juels, A., Kaliski, B.: PORs: Proofs of Retrievability for Large Files. In: CCS 2007 (2007)
19. Oggier, F., Datta, A.: Self-repairing Homomorphic Codes for Distributed Storage Systems. In: Infocom 2011 (2011)
20. http://techcrunch.com/2011/06/20/dropbox-security-bug-made-passwords-optional-for-four-hours/
21. http://blogs.computerworld.com/carbonite_loses_7500_customers_files
22. http://gigaom.com/2009/10/10/when-cloud-fails-t-mobile-microsoft-lose-sidekick-customer-data/
23. http://www.pcworld.com/article/226128/Sony_Makes_it_Official_PlayStation_Network_Hacked.html
24. http://news.cnet.com/8301-1009_3-57448465-83/linkedin-confirms-passwords-were-compromised/
25. http://broadcast.oreilly.com/2011/04/the-aws-outage-the-clouds-shining-moment.html
26. http://www.spacemonkey.com/

Improved Heterogeneous Human Walk Mobility Model with Hub and Gateway Identification

Zunnun Narmawala[1] and Sanjay Srivastava[2]

[1] Institute of Technology, Nirma University, Ahmadabad, Gujarat, India
zunnun.narmawala@nirmauni.ac.in
[2] Dhirubhai Ambani Institute of Information and Communication Technology,
Gandhinagar, Gujarat, India
sanjay_srivastava@daiict.ac.in

Abstract. Heterogeneous Human Walk (HHW) model[1] mimics human mobility and is based on two important properties of social network: overlapping community structure and heterogeneous popularity. But, it does not produce heterogeneous local popularities of nodes in a community as observed in real mobility traces. Further, it does not consider Levy walk nature of human mobility which has significant impact on performance of protocols. We propose Improved Heterogeneous Human Walk (IHHW) model that correctly produces heterogeneous local popularities and also incorporates Levy walk nature of human mobility within overlapping community structure. As popular nodes are very useful for data dissemination, we also propose theoretical methods to identify popular nodes within community (hubs) and in entire network (gateways) from overlapping community structure itself. These nodes can act as hubs/gateways till overlapping community structure does not change. Our methods eliminate the need to identify and change these nodes dynamically when network is operational.

Keywords: Mobility model, Pocket Switched Network, Mobile Social Network, Overlapping Communities, Heterogeneous Popularity, Hub, Gateway.

1 Introduction

With the rapid growth of mobile hand-held devices with Bluetooth and adhoc WiFi connectivity, possibility of entirely new network paradigm has emerged in which encounters between these mobile devices can be exploited for opportunistic data transfer without using any fixed network infrastructure[2]. As these devices are carried by humans, their encounter patterns depend on human mobility patterns. So, knowledge of human movement behaviour can be exploited to make efficient forwarding decisions[3,4]. We call this network paradigm as Pocket Switched Network (PSN) or Mobile Social Network (MSN).

For this, various experimental projects are undertaken to collect encounter information of devices carried by humans[5,6]. These traces can be used in simulation to evaluate and analyze performance of different protocols. While this

M. Chatterjee et al. (Eds.): ICDCN 2014, LNCS 8314, pp. 469–483, 2014.

approach generates realistic mobility patterns, its usefulness is limited as performance of a protocol can not be evaluated for range of values for each of
the network parameters. None-the-less, from analysis of these traces, various
properties of human mobility are derived[5,6,7,8]. Well-known and widely used
mobility models such as Random Way Point (RWP)[9], Brownian Motion[10] do
not exhibit these statistical properties. So, trace-based mobility models such as
Levy Walk (LW)[7],TVC[11], SWIM[12] and SLAW[13] are proposed based on
these statistical properties. Although these models are able to reproduce statistical properties of real mobility traces, they assume that each node moves
independent of others.

But, movement of an individual is not independent. Humans belong to various
social communities like friends, family, co-workers etc.[14,15]. These social ties
significantly affect their movement. e.g. individuals meet others from the same
community more frequently than people of other community[16]. Mobility models such as CMM[16] and HCMM[17] incorporate this social aspect of human
mobility.

Individuals belong to multiple communities. i.e. communities in real social
network overlap[15]. Further, some nodes meet more nodes in the community
(locally popular nodes) or visit other communities more often than others (globally popular nodes). These properties have significant impact on the performance
of forwarding strategy. But, only Heterogeneous Human Walk (HHW) model[1]
attempts to incorporate these properties. HHW generates k-clique overlapping
community structure which satisfies common statistical features observed from
various social networks instead of extracting communities from real-life social
graph.

In this paper, our contributions are the following:

- We identify shortcomings of HHW model and propose an Improved Heterogeneous Human Walk (IHHW) model.
- We propose, using mathematical model, a method to identify nodes which
  can be used to reach high number of nodes in a community (hubs) in an
  overlapping community structure. In other words, we identify locally popular nodes from the given overlapping community structure apriori without
  accumulating past encounter information to identify them. The method is
  based on the fact that just knowing local degree of nodes is not enough to
  choose hub nodes because nodes may be member of multiple communities
  and so, how much time a node remains in a community is an important
  factor in choosing hub nodes.
- We propose, using mathematical model, a method to identify nodes which
  can be used to relay data between communities efficiently (gateways) in
  an overlapping community structure. In other words, we identify globally
  popular nodes from given community structure apriori without transmitting
  data between nodes to count how many times a node has acted as a relay
  node to detect gateways and without counting how frequently a node visits
  different communities.

The paper is organized as follows: In section 2, we discuss related work. In section 3, an overview of HHW model is given. In section 4, we describe shortcomings of HHW model and propose improvements. In section 5, identifying hub nodes of a community is described while section 6 describes a method to identify gateways of a community. Section 7 discusses simulation results and finally, we conclude in section 8.

2 Related Work

Based on whether social network dimension is incorporated in the mobility model or not, mobility models for MSN can be divided into two categories as discussed in [1]: Real-trace based models and Social-aware models.

2.1 Real-Trace Based Models

Following are the main properties of human mobility patterns as identified by analysis of various traces.

1. Inter-contact time follows truncated power-law distribution[3,5].
2. Pause-time follows power-law distribution[7].
3. Humans visit nearby locations more frequently compared to far-away locations[8].
4. Humans have location preferences and they periodically re-appear on these locations[8].
5. Speed at which humans move increases with distance to be traveled[7].

This type of models try to capture features of individual's independent movement observed from real traces. Working Day Mobility (WDM) model[18] incorporates properties numbered 1 and 4 in the above list by modeling individual's mobility during a day with home sub-model, office sub-model, transport-sub model and evening sub-model. Time Variant Community (TVC) model[11] incorporates properties 1 and 4. Small World In Motion (SWIM) model[12] incorporates all of the above properties. In this model, each node is assigned a randomly and uniformly chosen point over the network area called as home. For each node, a weight is assigned to each possible destination which grows with the popularity of the place and decreases with distance from home. This weight represents the probability for the node to choose that place as next destination. Self-similar Least Action Walk (SLAW) model[13] incorporates properties 1, 2 and 3.

2.2 Social-Aware Models

Following are the main properties derived from social network theory which affect human mobility.

1. Humans can be grouped into communities based on their social relationships[14].

2. Humans belong to multiple communities and so, communities overlap[15].
3. Different individuals have heterogeneous local popularity within community and heterogeneous global popularity in the social network[2].
4. Community size, number of communities in which a node is a member and overlap size approximately follow power-law distribution where overlap size is defined as number of individuals which are common in two communities[15].

Community-based Mobility Model (CMM)[16] groups nodes based on social relationships among individuals. This grouping is then mapped to a topographical space. Movement of nodes is influenced by strength of social ties among individuals which may also change in time. CMM uses Caveman model[19] as artificial Social Network Model (SNM) to generate community structure. Home-cell Community-based Mobility Model (HCMM)[17] assigns home-cell to each individual which is the location where people with whom the node shares social relationships are likely to be at some point in time. After each trip, node moves to home-cell with some probability. Both models incorporate only property 1 from the above list. These models also incorporate some of the properties derived from real traces. But, they do not incorporate properties 2, 3 and 4 from above list which are very important properties and have significant effect on the performance of the protocols. Heterogeneous Human Walk (HHW) model[1] incorporates all of above properties derived from social network theory. But, it does not incorporate important trace-based properties like human preference of nearby locations and dependence of speed at which humans move on distance to be traveled. Our model IHHW, which is the modification of HHW, incorporates all properties of above two lists which are derived from real-traces and from social network theory.

3 Overview of HHW Model

There are two options to generate overlapping community structure. First is to get social graph from some actual social network. After getting the social graph, one can apply algorithm similar to the one proposed in [15] to identify overlapping communities but it will significantly increase implementation and computational complexity and one has to collect large number of social graphs to analyse performance of protocols. Second option is to directly construct synthetic overlapping community structure which follows all the properties found in real social network. To achieve trade-off between reality and complexity, HHW uses second approach. In this approach, any number of different community structures can be generated using random variables.

For overlapping community structure, each individual n in the social network may belong to number of communities denoted as membership number MN_n. Further, any two communities x and y may share $S_{x,y}^{ov}$ individuals, defined as overlap size between two communities. Let us denote size of community x as S_x^{com} and probability distribution functions of membership number, overlap size and community size as P(MN), P(S^{ov}) and P(S^{com}-$(k-1)$) respectively where k

is clique size of community as defined in [15]. Based on analysis of various real social networks, Palla et al.[15] conclude that P(MN), P(S^{ov}) and P(S^{com}-(k - 1)) approximately follow power-law distribution P(x) $\sim$ x$^{-\tau}$, with exponents τ = PR^{MN}, τ = PR^{Osize} and τ = PR^{Csize}, respectively. Further, they report that, values of PR^{MN}, PR^{Osize} are not less than 2, and the value of PR^{Csize} is between 1 and 1.6. HHW model uses these statistical properties to artificially construct k-clique overlapping community structure. A k-clique is complete sub-graph of size k and k-clique community is union of all k-cliques that can be reached from one another through series of adjacent k-cliques where two k-cliques are adjacent if they share k − 1 nodes.

HHW model is composed of three components: 1) Establishing overlapping community structure and heterogeneous local degree 2) Mapping communities into geographical zones and 3) Driving individual motion. These components are explained in following three sub-sections.

3.1 Establishing k-Clique Overlapping Community Structure and Heterogeneous Local Degree

A day (or a week or any time duration) is divided into periods, and overlapping community structures are different in each of these periods but are the same in the same period of different days. Let us define nodes having membership number larger than 2, equals 2 and equals 1 as M-3 nodes, M-2 nodes and M-1 nodes respectively. Community structure for each period is constructed as follows:

1. Generate nodes' membership numbers such that they follow P(MN) with exponent PR^{MN}. Then, establish initial empty communities whose sizes S^{com} follow P(S^{com}-(k - 1)) with exponent PR^{Csize} such that $\sum_i MN_i = \sum_j S_j^{com}$.
2. Use all M-3 nodes to establish initial overlaps between pairs of communities.
3. Modify initial overlaps by allocating all M-2 nodes to communities such that overlaps' size follow P(S^{ov}) with exponent PR^{Osize}.
4. Allocate all M-1 nodes to unsaturated communities.

Please refer original paper[1] for detailed procedure of each step. Yang et al.[1] claim that local heterogeneous popularity is established by assigning heterogeneous local degrees to the nodes.

Generating Heterogeneous Local Degree. Let $Local_i^n$ denote local degree of node n in its community i where $Local_i^n \geq k - 1$ as per the definition of k-clique community. These values are generated such that they follow power-law distribution with exponent PR^{Local}.

3.2 Mapping Communities into Geographical Zones

To simulate n mobile nodes in two-dimensional square plane, the model divides the plane into grid of non-overlapping square cells. For each period, each community with size S^{com} is randomly associated with a zone composed of S^{com} connected cells. Each node n is randomly associated with $Local_i^n$ cells within the zone of its community i.

3.3 Driving Individual Motion

Initially, each node randomly selects one of all its associated cells and then it is located at random position inside that cell. To move, each node selects next goal inside one of its associated cells and then moves towards it by following straight path. When a node reaches its current goal, it waits for a power-law distribution pause time and then selects and moves towards next goal. At the start of the new period, overlapping community structure, corresponding associated zone and cells change. Now, after reaching its current goal, node selects next goal inside one of its newly associated cells of the new period.

The paper[1] demonstrates that nodes of this overlapping community structure exhibit global heterogeneous popularity and inter-contact time follows truncated power-law distribution.

4 Improved HHW Model

In this section, we discuss shortcomings of existing HHW model and propose our solution for each of them.

4.1 Incorporating Levy Walk Nature of Human Movement

In HHW, if a node is member of more than one community, then it will have associated cells of all those communities. As per the model, node chooses associated cell as next goal randomly with uniform distribution irrespective of the community of the associate cell. i.e. node chooses next goal irrespective of the distance it will have to travel. This is contrary to the finding that human prefer short distances over long distances or in other words, human movement can be characterized as Levy walk[7]. It is also counter-intuitive. For example, a postman has to visit multiple offices in more than two buildings to deliver posts. As per existing model, the postman will move from an office in a building to another office in another building with more probability than to the office in the same building.

As established in [7], distribution of distances covered in each flight by human follows power-law distribution having exponent less than 2.5 where flight can be defined as single displacement from one place to another place without a pause in between. We have incorporated this property in our model.

In IHHW, a node chooses an associated cell as next goal based on distance it will have to travel with power-law distribution instead of choosing it randomly with uniform distribution. We calculate distances at which all associated cells of a node are located from current cell from their location information and sort associated cells of a node based on these distances. Then, we generate a random variable (RV) which follows truncated power-law distribution $P(D)$ with exponent PR^D between minimum distance and maximum distance a node has to travel. We choose the associated cell as next goal whose distance from current cell is nearest to the value generated by the random variable. As RV will generate short distance values with higher probability than long-distance values, in our model, a node prefers short distances over long distances. As each community is associated with a zone composed of connected cells, distance between any two cells within a community will most probably be less than distance between any two cells of two different communities if simulation area is not too small. Therefore, a node will be choosing one of the associated cell of the community in which it is right now as its next goal with high probability compared to the associated cells of the node in other communities which is correct behaviour as we have seen in the postman example.

4.2 Treating Number of Cells and Number of Nodes in a Community as Separate Parameters

In HHW, each community with size S^{com} is associated with a zone composed of S^{com} connected cells. i.e. number of nodes (N) and number of cells (C) of a community are same. So, average number of nodes associated with a cell is equal to average local degree of a community (μ). One important effect of it is that a node, on an average, meets μ number of nodes in each cell it visits. So, local popularity of nodes increase with increase in local degree at the rate proportional to μ times rate of increase in local degree instead of increasing with same rate. As a result, there are high percentage of nodes with high local popularity than observed in real traces[2]. i.e. HHW generates too many locally popular nodes than expected. Further, μ increases with increase in community size because it follows truncated power-law distribution with maximum value equal to community size. So, the problem is aggravated in large communities.

In IHHW, we consider C and N as separate parameters. Let C_x be number of connected cells, μ_x be average local degree and N_x be number of nodes in community x. Let m be multiplier which decides denseness of all communities. Then,

$$C_x = m \times \mu_x \times N_x \tag{1}$$

4.3 Calculating Speed Based on Distance

In HHW, speed at which a node moves from one goal to next goal is chosen from given range uniformly regardless of the distance to be traveled. But, as found in [7], speed increases with increase in flight length because individuals use transportation to travel long distances instead of walking. They have also derived following relation between flight time (t) and flight length (l) from various real traces.

$$t = p \times l^{1-\eta}, 0 \le \eta \le 1 \tag{2}$$

From traces, Rhee et al.[7] have proposed $p = 30.55$ and $\eta = 0.89$ when $l < 500$ m, and $p = 0.76$ and $\eta = 0.28$ when $l \ge 500$ m. In IHHW, we also use this model to calculate speed at which a node should travel to next goal instead of choosing it uniformly from given range.

5   Identifying Hub Nodes in Overlapping Community Structure

Hub nodes of a community are nodes with high local popularity in that community and they are crucial to reach all nodes in the community efficiently. Identifying correct hub nodes is very important for the success of the protocol which aims to exploit heterogeneous local popularity. For non-overlapping community structure where each node is member of only one community, hub nodes are the nodes with high local degree but in overlapping community structure, if a node with high local degree in some community is also member of other communities then it is important to consider for how much fraction of time it will remain in that community. i.e. a node's popularity in a community is dependent not only on local degree but also on fraction of time it will spend in that community.

Hub nodes can be identified and changed dynamically from past encounter information using methods similar to those proposed in [2]. But, this approach involves considerable overhead. We identify hub nodes apriori from the overlapping community structure itself without having to accumulate and exchange encounter information when network is operational. These nodes act as permanent hub nodes of a community such that over the long run, they are more effective as hub nodes than other nodes of the community.

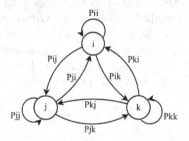

Fig. 1. Communities and movement of a node between communities represented as Markov Chain

To find out fraction of time for which a node will be in a particular community out of all communities in which it is a member, we model community structure as Markov chain. Communities are considered as states in Markov chain. Fig. 1 shows Markov chain of a node having membership in communities i, j and k. In the figure, P_{XY} with $X = i, j, k$ and $Y = i, j, k$ represents probability with which the node will travel from one community to another community or will remain in same community in the next flight. If we can find these probabilities, then steady state probability vector of the node will give fraction of time for which a node will be in a particular community. If locations of the communities are known, then we can calculate distances between them. It is known that human flight distances follow power-law distribution[7]. We can use this property to find out transition probabilities.

Let a node be a member of M communities and let it be currently in community $i = 0$. Assume that other communities are numbered from 1 to $M - 1$ in the increasing order of their distances from current community where distance between community i and j (d_{ij}) is defined as the distance from any one of the associated cells of the node in community i to nearest associated cell of the node in community j. Let probability of node movement from community i to community j is P_{ij}, minimum and maximum distance a node travels in a flight is $minD$ and $maxD$, d_0 is the maximum distance the node travels to reach some location within its community and D is power-law exponent. Then,

$$P_{ii} = \int_{minD}^{d_0} cx^{-D} dx$$

$$P_{ij} = \int_{d_{i(j-1)}}^{d_{ij}} cx^{-D} dx; i = 0; j = 1, 2, ..., M - 1 \tag{3}$$

Where $c = \dfrac{1}{\int_{minD}^{maxD} x^{-D} dx}$ is normalizing constant

Similarly, for each node, considering each of the communities in which it is member as its current community, distances to other communities can be found and thus entire transition matrix $\mathbf{P}$ for each node can be found. Let $\mathbf{w}$ be the steady state probability vector of this Markov chain then it is known that[20]

$$w_0 + w_1 + ... + w_{M-1} = 1$$
$$\mathbf{wP} = \mathbf{w} \tag{4}$$

From these equations, steady state vector $\mathbf{w}$ can be found which represents fraction of time for which the node will be in each community. Let for the node n in community i, theoretical estimate of local popularity be LPt_i^n, steady state vector be $\mathbf{w}^n$ and local degree be $Local_i^n$. Then,

$$LPt_i^n = w_i^n \times Local_i^n \tag{5}$$

Similarly, for all nodes in a community, LPt can be found. To choose nodes as hubs, we only need correct ordering of nodes based on their local popularity. LPt provides this correct ordering. Given percentage of nodes having higher value of LPt than other nodes of a community are identified as permanent hub nodes for that community.

6   Identifying Gateway Nodes in Overlapping Community Structure

Gateway nodes of a community are nodes with high global popularity and they are crucial to reach to other communities. Identifying correct gateway nodes is very important for the success of the protocol which aims to exploit heterogeneous global popularity.

As with hubs, we identify gateway nodes apriori from the overlapping community structure itself without having to count number of times each node visits different communities when network is operational. We identify permanent gateway nodes of a community such that over the long run, they are more effective as gateway nodes than other nodes of the community.

Intuitively, for a node to qualify as gateway node of a community x, it should move from one community to other community frequently and in this process, it should also visit community x sufficient number of times. Moreover, a node having membership in more number of communities should be preferred over a node having membership in less number of communities.

Mathematically, a node having less average self-transition probability is a good candidate for selection as gateway node. Let average self-transition probability of node n be P_{avg}^n, transition matrix of node n be $\mathbf{P}^n$ and M be number of communities in which node n is member. Then,

$$P_{avg}^n = \frac{1}{M} \sum_{i=0}^{i=M-1} P_{ii}^n \tag{6}$$

Similarly, a node having high transition probability from other communities to community x is a good candidate for selection as gateway for x. Let transition probability of node n from other communities to community x be T_x^n. Then,

$$T_x^n = \sum_{i=0;i \neq x}^{i=M-1} w_i^n \times P_{ix}^n \tag{7}$$

Let theoretical estimate of global popularity of node n in community i be GPt_i^n. Then,

$$GPt_i^n = (1 - P_{avg}^n) \times M \times T_i^n \times M \tag{8}$$

Similarly, for all nodes in a community, GPt can be found. To choose nodes as gateways, as with the case of hubs, we only need correct ordering of nodes based on their global popularity.

7   Simulation Results

We have implemented HHW and IHHW model in ONE simulator[21]. We have simulated the HHW model and IHHW model with following scenario. There are 200 nodes in a simulation plane of 5 Km x 5 Km, divided into a grid of 62,500 cells of 20 m x 20 m each. The transmission range of node is 20 m. For HHW, the speed of node is uniformly distributed between 1 and 6 m/s. For IHHW, speed follows Eq. 2. Pause-time is generated using truncated power-law distribution with exponent 2 between range 0 to 1000 sec. Warm up time is set to 1000 sec.

We generate 4-clique communities. i.e. with $k = 4$. We set $PR^{MN}=3$, $PR^{Osize}=2$, $PR^{Csize}=1.2$, $PR^{Local}=2.5$ and flight length exponent $PR^D=2$. All these values are in the range recommended for these exponents in literature from various real traces[7,14,15]. For comparison, we have used same community structures for both HHW and IHHW model.

To verify that in IHHW also, inter-contact time distribution is power-law, we have simulated HHW and IHHW model for two days and each day was divided in three identical periods of 8 hours each. We have generated three different overlapping community structures for each period using random variables which follow power-law distribution with different exponents for different quantities as specified earlier. Simulation result confirms that Complementary Cumulative Distribution Function (CCDF) of inter-contact time of IHHW matches with HHW which is shown to be matching with CCDF of inter-contact time of real traces[1]. Because of space constraint, we have not included the figure.

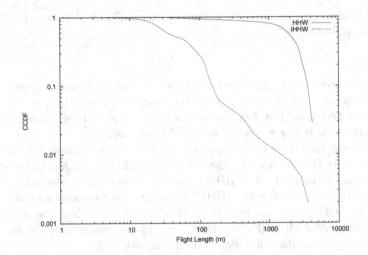

Fig. 2. CCDF of flight lengths

To show how a node with membership in multiple communities in HHW prefers long distances over short distances, we have selected a node which is member of 11 different communities and recorded flight lengths of all its flights both in HHW and IHHW. As shown in Fig. 2, flight lengths in IHHW follow power-law distribution while in HHW, flight lengths do not follow power-law distribution.

As shown in Fig. 3, in HHW, node takes high number of consecutive long flights. i.e. it jumps from one community to another community while in IHHW, the node moves within one community most of the time before jumping to other community.

In simulation, in order to measure local popularity, we have counted number of encounters between all pairs of nodes in a community. We define node's

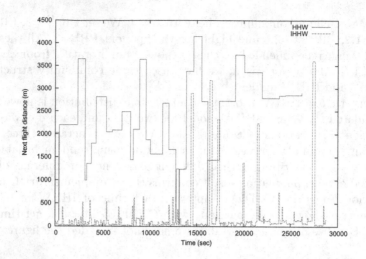

Fig. 3. Distance covered in each flight v/s Time (Large distance implies inter-community transition)

popularity as number of nodes which it has encountered more number of times than average number of encounters in the community. Further, we do not consider encounters that last less than 50 sec to discard those encounters which occur while node is moving from one cell to another.

Fig. 4 shows CCDF of local popularity of nodes in a community of size 70 in HHW and in IHHW with multiplier $m=1$, 2 and 3 (Eq. 1). As conjectured, it is evident from the figure that in HHW, there are too many nodes with high local popularity than expected while IHHW generates local popularities as expected. Further, in IHHW, with increase in value of m (i.e. with decrease in denseness) local popularity of all nodes decreases. So, by changing value of m, one can control local popularities of nodes in a community.

To validate steady sate probabilities found using Eq. 4, in simulation, we have kept log of amount of time a node has spent in each community in which it is member. Dividing these times by total simulation time gives fraction of time a node has spent in each community. It turns out that, these values are very closely matching with those found theoretically.

To validate our offline hub identification method, we have generated overlapping community structure with parameters specified at the start of this section. The implementation generated thirteen communities with some random seed. Then, using Eq. 5 we have calculated theoretical estimate of local popularity of all member nodes for each community and ordered them in separate list for each community. Further, as explained earlier in this section, we measured local popularities of nodes in each community in simulation and ordered them too. Then, we have used Spearman's rank correlation coefficient (ρ)[22] to measure difference between two ordered list. We have calculated ρ for each community and average of these values comes out to be 0.9890 where $\rho = 1$ means ordered

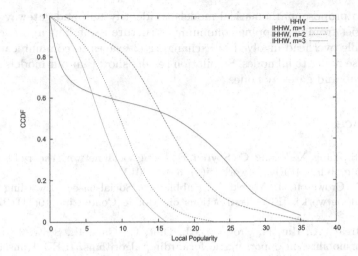

Fig. 4. CCDF of local popularity

list of our estimate is perfect monotone function of ordered list of measured local popularities. The result implies that our method identifies correct hub nodes.

To validate our offline gateway identification method, using Eq. 8, we have calculated theoretical estimate of global popularities of all member nodes for each community and ordered them in separate list for each community. In simulation, we have calculated global popularities of nodes in each community x by counting number of times a node has moved from one community to other community and scaled this number with membership number of the node and number of times it has visited community x as argued in section 6 and ordered them too. Average of values of ρ of different communities in this case comes out to be 0.9987 which implies that our method identifies correct gateway nodes.

8   Conclusion

Heterogeneous Human Walk (HHW) mobility model is based on heterogeneous centrality and overlapping community structure in social network. In this paper, we identify shortcomings of HHW model and propose IHHW with three modifications: incorporation of Levy walk nature of human mobility, treatment of number of cells and number of nodes in a community as independent parameters and calculation of speed based on distance to be traveled. Simulation results demonstrate that IHHW successfully generates flight lengths with power-law distribution while in HHW flight lengths are uniformly distributed. Further, movement of individuals in IHHW is as per rational human behaviour of preference of nearby locations over far-away locations while in HHW it is not. Results also establish that IHHW generates desired heterogeneous local popularity of nodes while HHW generates too many highly popular nodes.

We also propose mathematical models to identify hub and gateway nodes of communities from overlapping community structure itself. The approach avoids considerable overhead involved in exchanging messages to communicate identities of these nodes to all nodes. Simulation results show that our models correctly identify hub and gateway nodes.

References

1. Yang, S., Yang, X., Zhang, C., Spyrou, E.: Using social network theory for modeling human mobility. IEEE Network 24(5), 6–13 (2010)
2. Hui, P., Crowcroft, J., Yoneki, E.: Bubble rap: Social-based forwarding in delay-tolerant networks. IEEE Transactions on Mobile Computing 10(11), 1576–1589 (2011)
3. Chaintreau, A., Hui, P., Crowcroft, J., Diot, C., Gass, R., Scott, J.: Impact of human mobility on opportunistic forwarding algorithms. IEEE Transactions on Mobile Computing 6(6), 606–620 (2007)
4. Boldrini, C., Conti, M., Passarella, A.: Impact of social mobility on routing protocols for opportunistic networks. In: IEEE International Symposium on a World of Wireless, Mobile and Multimedia Networks, WoWMoM 2007, pp. 1–6. IEEE (2007)
5. Hui, P., Chaintreau, A., Scott, J., Gass, R., Crowcroft, J., Diot, C.: Pocket switched networks and human mobility in conference environments. In: Proceedings of the 2005 ACM SIGCOMM Workshop on Delay-Tolerant Networking, pp. 244–251. ACM (2005)
6. Eagle, N., Pentland, A.S.: Reality mining: sensing complex social systems. Personal and Ubiquitous Computing 10(4), 255–268 (2006)
7. Rhee, I., Shin, M., Hong, S., Lee, K., Kim, S.J., Chong, S.: On the levy-walk nature of human mobility. IEEE/ACM Transactions on Networking (TON) 19(3), 630–643 (2011)
8. Gonzalez, M.C., Hidalgo, C.A., Barabasi, A.L.: Understanding individual human mobility patterns. Nature 453(7196), 779–782 (2008)
9. Hyytiä, E., Koskinen, H., Lassila, P., Penttinen, A., Roszik, J., Virtamo, J.: Random waypoint model in wireless networks. In: Networks and Algorithms: Complexity in Physics and Computer Science, Helsinki (2005)
10. Groenevelt, R., Altman, E., Nain, P.: Relaying in mobile ad hoc networks: the brownian motion mobility model. Wireless Networks 12(5), 561–571 (2006)
11. Hsu, W.J., Spyropoulos, T., Psounis, K., Helmy, A.: Modeling spatial and temporal dependencies of user mobility in wireless mobile networks. IEEE/ACM Transactions on Networking 17(5), 1564–1577 (2009)
12. Mei, A., Stefa, J.: Swim: A simple model to generate small mobile worlds. In: INFOCOM 2009, pp. 2106–2113. IEEE (2009)
13. Lee, K., Hong, S., Kim, S.J., Rhee, I., Chong, S.: Slaw: A new mobility model for human walks. In: INFOCOM 2009, pp. 855–863. IEEE (2009)
14. Newman, M.E.: The structure and function of complex networks. SIAM Review 45(2), 167–256 (2003)
15. Palla, G., Derényi, I., Farkas, I., Vicsek, T.: Uncovering the overlapping community structure of complex networks in nature and society. Nature 435(7043), 814–818 (2005)

16. Musolesi, M., Mascolo, C.: Designing mobility models based on social network theory. ACM SIGMOBILE Mobile Computing and Communications Review 11(3), 59–70 (2007)
17. Boldrini, C., Passarella, A.: Hcmm: Modelling spatial and temporal properties of human mobility driven by users social relationships. Computer Communications 33(9), 1056–1074 (2010)
18. Ekman, F., Keränen, A., Karvo, J., Ott, J.: Working day movement model. In: Proceedings of the 1st ACM SIGMOBILE Workshop on Mobility Models, pp. 33–40. ACM (2008)
19. Watts, D.J.: Small worlds: the dynamics of networks between order and randomness. Princeton university press (1999)
20. Grinstead, C.C.M., Snell, J.L.: Introduction to probability. American Mathematical Soc. (1997)
21. Keränen, A., Ott, J., Kärkkäinen, T.: The one simulator for dtn protocol evaluation. In: Proceedings of the 2nd International Conference on Simulation Tools and Techniques, ICST (Institute for Computer Sciences, Social-Informatics and Telecommunications Engineering), p. 55 (2009)
22. Pirie, W.: Spearman rank correlation coefficient. In: Encyclopedia of Statistical Sciences (1988)

FlowMaster: Early Eviction of Dead Flow on SDN Switches

Kalapriya Kannan[1] and Subhasis Banerjee[2]

[1] IBM Research, India
kalapriya@in.ibm.com
[2] IIIT-Delhi, New Delhi, India
subhasis@iiitd.ac.in

Abstract. High performance switches employ extremely low latency memory subsystems in an effort to reap the lowest feasible end-to-end flow level latencies. Their capacities are extremely valuable as the size of these memories is limited due to several architectural constraints such as power and silicon area. This necessity is further exacerbated with the emergence of Software Defined Networks (SDN) where fine-grained flow definitions lead to explosion in the number of flow entries. In this paper, we propose *FlowMaster*, a speculative mechanism to update the flow table by predicting when an entry becomes stale and evict the same early to accommodate new entries. We collage the observations from predictors into a Markov based learning predictor that predicts whether a flow is valuable any more. Our experiments confirm that *FlowMaster* enables efficient usage of flow tables thereby reducing the discard rate from flow table by orders of magnitude and in some cases, eliminating discards completely.

1 Introduction

High performance networks are becoming increasingly latency sensitive [9]. With ever escalating demands for supporting higher flow rates, particularly in emerging SDN frameworks [11], every switching device will be expected to operate within narrower latency bounds. This must translate to fast computation and high speed memory operations within the device. According to [16], in order to service a single 10Gbps link each line card of the switch must process several 100s of millions of packets every second. In order to keep up with the computational requirements of such traffic, several high performance micro-architectural components are embedded in switching devices. Flow table is one such component that serves on the critical packet forwarding path of switches and end up being extremely stressed due to a mismatch between their capacity and the sheer volume of packets traversing the switch. Flow table saturation is potentially a prime suspect for latency bottlenecks in the network.

Architects have relied on deep memory hierarchies ranging from different low latency hardware memories to software tables. Due to various design trade-off including clock speed, silicon area and power, lower level memories that are placed farther from the processing engine in the hierarchy are larger in capacity but the larger also is its lookup latency. Poor management of flow entries coupled with the small size of fast

M. Chatterjee et al. (Eds.): ICDCN 2014, LNCS 8314, pp. 484–498, 2014.

memories results in very high 'miss' rates thereby seriously impacting network performance. Core and Access networks usually employ Ternary Content Addressable Memory (TCAM) as the highest layer to achieve single clock cycle lookup. A TCAM miss is followed by a lookup to comparatively slower SRAM/DRAM. A subsequent miss in SRAM/DRAM access is then followed by the slowest software table lookup which constitutes the lowest layer.

Due to power, cost and ASIC space constraint, increase in size of higher layers of memory such as TCAM is hardly a feasible option. One approach to reduce latency in flow table lookups, is to ensure that the highest layers of memory is freed up immediately if any flow entry residing on it is no longer needed. In other words, there is merit to predict when accesses to a flow table entry is over and speculatively invalidate those entries in advance so that new flows can be accommodated. This paper attempts to build the predictive models and evaluate them thoroughly.

FlowMaster is a novel mechanism that predicts when a flow entry becomes evictable. We perform a detailed analysis on packet traces (obtained from two university data centers by the authors of [1]) arriving at a switch to dynamically predict if a flow entry should be retained for future accesses or if it should be evicted. In turn, we determine what the appropriate timeout value of a flow entry should be. The set of flows that are going to have future accesses are referred to as live/active flows, while those that will never be accessed again are referred to as stale / dead flows.

We develop a simulator that models a switch flow table of varying capacities and our key observations are the following:

1. In two real world packet traces, only 20% of the flow table entries were live, thereby providing a compelling case for the use of *FlowMaster* to improve flow table performance.
2. On an average, for 92% of the intervals between the last reference to a flow entry till the time it was evicted, the duration was long enough that 40% of the discarded flows could have been accommodated.

Subsequently, we built *FlowMaster* algorithms that adopt a spectrum of strategies to predict the likelihood of a flow entry corresponding to a stale / dead flow. Our models fall in two broad categories

1. **Flow Based Models:** These examine each flow and determine their appropriate timeout. While this provides microscopic granularity, it is computationally intensive. It is important to note though that this computation does not sit on the latency sensitive datapath.
2. **Markov based Learning Predictor:** This prediction allows identification of those flows that tend to stay longer and those flows that have shorter duration. In order to identify this, we propose a learning predictor that models bins (buckets by time units) and movement of flows across these bins. As transitions are noted, an arrival of a new flow that requires insertion into the table triggers elimination of an existing flow based on the transition probabilities.

We observe that *FlowMaster* predicts a flow's likelihood of eviction accurately about 85% of the time, while mis-predicting in the other 15% cases (varying between 11% to

19% for different configuration) compared to algorithm that uses static predefined time out period.

The rest of this paper is organized as follows: Section 2 discusses in detail, with experiments, our motivation for designing *FlowMaster*. In section 3 and 4 our flow-based and markov based learning models are discussed. Brief overview of hardware implementation of our approach is given in Section 5. Section 6 highlights some related work before the paper concludes in Section 7.

2   Motivation

Modern switching devices employ two kinds of memory systems for flow tables. These are (i) hardware based and (ii) software based tables. Often a combination of these two is employed in a hierarchical fashion. Fig. 1 shows a logical structure of the memory subsystems used in forwarding engines of switching devices. For all incoming packets, a parallel look up is performed in both SRAM and TCAM memory systems. An output arbiter mediates the outcome (miss and hit) appropriately passing the handle to the software table in case of a miss and packet editor in case of a hit to perform the associated actions. In fig. 1 we refer to TCAM memory subsystems as the highest level, followed by SRAM/DRAM as an intermediate level and finally software flow tables at the lowest level.

A miss in the highest level consisting of TCAMs leads to delays of upto several cycles (the exact delay depends on the speed of SRAM access). A fast hash based algorithm is 20 time slower than TCAM based implementation [4]. A miss in the SRAM will cost further delays, about 5x, since the lookup will then be performed on software tables. A miss in the software table subsequently will result in invoking the switch control plane and existing studies have shown that this latency is in the order of several

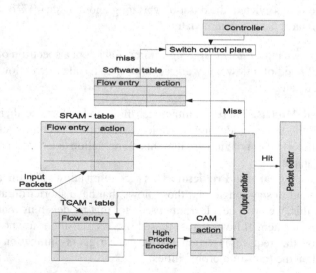

Fig. 1. Memory hierarchy for Flow Table design in Switching Devices

millisecond [2]. The question our work attempts to answer is: What is the optimal strategy for installing flow table entries so that miss latencies are kept to a minimum? In other words, we seek to develop strategies that ensure that the lowest layers of memory are available as much as possible for installing new flows.

Our hypothesis is that not all entries in the flow tables are live. A flow entry is *live* from the time it is brought into the table to the time it is referenced for the last time. During the period from its last access to the time it is evicted from the table (dead time) the entry occupies precious hardware resource which could possibly be utilized by assigning it to a flow that is referenced frequently. In this work we use the term 'discarded flows' to differentiate the flows that cannot be inserted due to flow table being full from misses that happen when the first time a packet for a flow that does not exist in the flow table arrives.

Removal of stale entries from the flow table early in time will enable insertion of new flow entries into it. Therefore, a potential discard (due to inadequate space for new entries) in the flow table that in turn leads to reference to the software flow table can be avoided. The impact of having dead entries in flow tables on overall network performance is quite significant. For example, the number of flows arriving at the switch for a rack consisting of 40 servers (with each server generating requests following a median arrival rate and mean of $35\mu s$) will result in approximately 1300/second new flow entries at the switches. A dead flow available in the table for a period of 1 second (as being the granularity of time duration for the expiry of the flows in the current OpenFlow implementations) will result in 1300 discards in case of the flow table being full. Given this large number of flows arriving at the switch and the duration of the flows being multiple-seconds, one would expect the number of misses to go higher.

Throughout this work we use OpenFlow [11] as our baseline implementation for SDN. We base our initial analysis on the real world traces used in [1] collected from university. There are two traces university 1 that we refer as univ1 and university 2 which is referred as univ2. These traces are used to drive a simulation model of varying cache sizes (512 entries, 1024 entries, 2048 entries and 4096 entries). This machine simulator, detailed in Algorithm 1, outputs the distribution of unique flows, discarded flows, live flows and dead flows based on packet arrival characteristics. For every packet encountered in the trace we extract the flow entry (line 4) and determine if the entry is present (hit) in the flow table (line 5). A hit in the flow table shows that the entry has already been visited and we determine whether that flow entry is a live flow. Recall, according to our definition a live flow is one that will have future lookup's. Therefore we mark the flow in the table as live if there appears further lookup in the future trace (line 6). For a packet that results in a miss (does not belong to an existing entry in the flow table), the flow is considered to be either 'Unique' when it appears for the first time (line 10) or 'Revisited' when it appeared earlier (line 13) but was evicted because it timed out. A 'Unique or Revisited Flow' can result in a 'discarded flow' if the flow table does not have sufficient space to accommodate the unique line. Therefore unique flows measure the new entries into the system, while 'discarded flow' measure the number of unique or revisited entries that could not be accommodated in the flow table. This leads to measuring the live lines (dead lines = flow table size - live lines) as a function of the number of flow entries accessed. A comprehensive list of terminologies used in this paper and their definitions are given in Table 1.

Table 1. List of terms used in our work

Terms	Definitions
Live entry	A flow entry which is yet to be referred for the last time.
Dropped/Discarded Flows	A flow entry that is discarded or dropped because of insufficient space in the table.
Hard timeout	A flow will be evicted when the hard time out value lapses.
Idle timeout	Time during which an observed inactivity results in eviction of the flow rule (set to 60 secs).
Unique entry	For a packet that results in a miss (does not belong to an existing entry in the flow table).
Revisited entry	Packet appeared earlier for an flow entry but was evicted because it timed out.

Each flow in the table is associated with a 'timeout' value. In SDN two types of 'timeout' have been defined, *'hard_timeout'* and *'idle_timeout'*. Hard timeout indicates that the flow will be evicted when the hard time out value lapses. Idle timeout is more flexible and is the time during which an observed inactivity results in eviction of the flow rule. The default *'idle_timeout'* used by the currently available SDN controllers is 60 secs. We consider three values for our simulator *'idle_timeout'* in our simulation studies (1, 30 and 60 secs). Evictions are performed when the simulator detects that the virtual times have passed the idle time out set for each flow.

Measurement of number of live, unique, discarded flows for varying cache sizes for a default time out value of 60 secs is presented in fig. 2. Throughout this paper we show cumulative numbers of all the performance metrics (number of unique / live / discarded / revisited flow) with respect to number of references (unless otherwise mentioned). We observe several interesting phenomena from these graphs. On an average the number of live flow entries available in the flow tables is just about 20-30% of the flow table sizes. While the occupancy of the live flows in the flow table is less, we observe high discard rate for all sizes of flow table. In fig. 2 while 80% of the flow table entries remained dead flows, the discarded flows grow at a rate of 60-70% of the unique flows (almost nearing the unique line in the case of smaller flow tables). This observation establishes the critical fact that the flow table consists of significant portion of dead flow entries which hinders effective utilization of flow table for new flow entries. Further, in fig. 2 (a) and (b) live flow entries decreases sharply briefly after the start of the appearance of discarded flows. It appears more prominent in the case of higher size flow tables. This is due to the fact that the flows are inserted at high rate at the beginning of the trace when the flow table is empty. Flows remain active and stay for a longer duration of time (60 secs) which is indicated by high live flow counts. Briefly after the flow table is full, flows are discarded and therefore no further new entry is inserted in the table. After the initial downfall, the rate of insertion in the table is just equivalent to the rate of eviction (as new flows are inserted only when there is space in the table) reflecting a steady state.

Algorithm 1. Computing Live, Unique and Discarded flows

Require: PacketTrace , UniqueFlows =0; LiveFlows =0;
Ensure: flowTable[size]
    List $< Packets >$ packetList = getAllPackets(PacketTrace);
2: **while** $packetList! = empty$ **do**
       $packet = packetList.pop()$
4:     $flowEntry = extractFlowEntry(packet)$
       if $flowEntry$ in $flowTable$ **then**
6:        **if** $!IsPacketForFlowInRemainingTrace()$ **then**
           $LiveFlows = LiveFlows - 1;$
8:        **end if**
       else $flowEntry$ NOT in $flowTable$
10:      **if** $!isNotEvictedFlow()$ **then**
           $UniqueFlows = UniqueFlows + 1;$
12:      **else**
           $EvictedFlowss = EvictedFlows + 1;$
14:      **end if**
       if $IsPacketForFlowInRemainingTrace()$ **then**
16:        $LiveFlows = LiveFlows + 1;$
       end if
18:      **if** $canFlowBeAccomodated(flowTable)$ **then**
        $insertFlowInTable()$
20:      **else**
           $discardFlows = discardFlows + 1$
22:      **end if**
     end if
24: **end while**

Low counts of live flows indicates that the majority of the flow table is holding the dead flows. On optimizing, one would expect the live flows count to be increased thereby flattening the curve.

If we set the idle timeout too low, then we notice that the number of revisited entries (ie., flows that were evicted but appeared again after evicting them from the table) start to rise. We observed that by setting the idle timeout to 1 sec the discarded flows count became zero, and in the case 30 secs the discarded flow count was reduced by about 30% (fig. 3 (c) and (d)). But this gain comes only at the cost of increased number of revisited flows. Fig. 3 shows the revisited entries graphs for time out value of 1 sec, 30 secs and 60 secs. In fig. 3(a) it can be seen that the revisited entries are nearing the unique lines. This indicates that when the time out is set at a lower value the existing flows timed out frequently while the flow was still active. Fig. 4 demonstrates the effects of the increased revisited flows. A new flow results in miss in the flow table. It invokes the control plane of the switch that results in a new flow getting inserted into the flow table. On expiry of the flow table entry, the flow is evicted from the table. Every revisited flow results in a miss and invokes the control plane again. This incurs a serious latency hit as the cost of invoking the controller is first-packet latencies of the order of few milliseconds. Additionally, the flow might even get discarded (even though it is still active) if the flow table is full upon revisit. This again will lead to dramatic latency

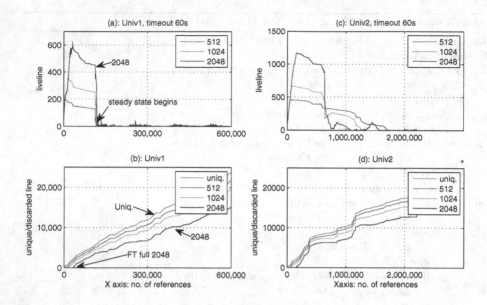

Fig. 2. Live flow, unique reference and discarded flow for a timeout of 60s. Discards appear after the available lines in Flow Table (FT) is exhausted. 26858 Unique lines for Univ1 dataset, 20244 Unique lines for Univ2 dataset. Note that all performance numbers are cumulative w.r.t number of references.

hits. Thus, this shows that mis-predictions can actually have a penalty equivalent to that of non-predictions. This would defy the entire purpose of predictive modeling of flow tables.

Our experiments lead to the following conclusions: (a) There exists significant number of stale / dead flow entries in the flow table which degrades the performance of the flow tables. (b) Wrongly predicting active flow to be dead flows will have high penalties and (c) Revisited entries might result in abortion of a flow in the middle and our observation from the traces reveal that such cases are significant. This leads us to define our goals as follows: (i) Predict dead flows with high confidence to increase the performance of flow tables. (b) While 'discarded flows' continue to remain important, prediction algorithm should prioritize minimization of revisited entries due to its effect on the existing flows and associated behavior.

3   Per Flow Predictor Algorithms

We observe that the inter arrival times of the flow follow exponential distribution and therefore the arrivals can be modeled using Poisson distributions. This allows us to predict the probability of a flow obtaining a packet in the future interval of time given the existing observations. Let Δt be some interval of time. We assume that arrivals are

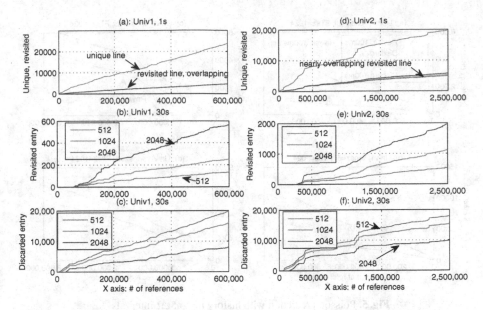

Fig. 3. Number of revisited flows in 1s and 30s timeout (a,b and d,e). Fig. (c) and (f) shows discarded entries

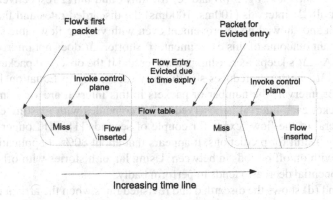

Fig. 4. Eviction and revisit penalty

likely to occur at any instant. Probability of k arrivals in Δt is given by $P(k, \Delta t) = \frac{e^{-\lambda \Delta t}(\lambda \Delta t)^k}{k!}$. Probability of at least one arrival in the interval Δt is given by Equation 1.

$$P(k \geq 1, \Delta t) = 1 - e^{-\lambda \Delta t} \tag{1}$$

We compute the probability of a flow receiving a packet in the next interval (Δt) as a function of the observed mean over all the intervals since the beginning. From the

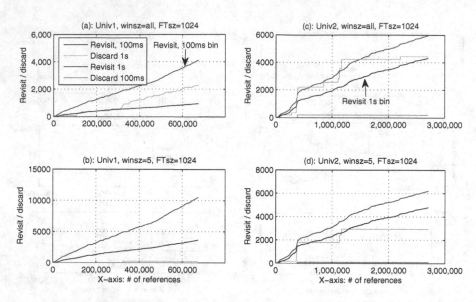

Fig. 5. Poisson prediction with history up to $5\Delta t$ intervals

results obtained (shown in fig. 5 (a) and (c) for univ1 and univ2 respectively) we observed that for all Δt intervals (100ms, 1000ms) the discarded rates and the revisited rates were high and showed no improvement even with varying flow table size. There are two important outcome of this experiment, **(i)** shorter Δt does not improve prediction accuracy. As Δt's keeps increasing in number and if the observed packets are very small in each Δt, mean rate reduces significantly (according to Equation 1). Further with shorter Δt intervals the number of packets in this interval are very small (maximum of 1 packet each interval is observed). This coincides with existing established work that several of the flows exists for couple of seconds [1]. **(ii)** Longer history is not particularly useful for predictions. It appears that about 80% of applications sends data in bursts with on/off periods in between. Using larger histories with off periods in between (exponential decrease) tends to perform badly.

Fig. 5 (b) and (d) shows the discarded and revisited rates when the arrival pattern we studied from window of Δt's (5 Δt). We notice that with lower flow table size and with 100ms duration intervals discarded flows were null, but the revisited entries were high equivalent to unique lines. On the other hand, increasing the length of the time interval reduces the revisited entries, but discarded lines start to appear. These discarded flows can be addressed by providing sufficient capacity to the flows (as with 2048 for univ 1 trace in fig. 6). This leaves us with the problem of providing efficient algorithms for addressing the revisited entries. Recall, that revisited entry happens because of evicting an active flow, therefore we need to device mechanisms to identify those flows that span multiple time intervals efficiently. Going forward, as a design strategy we consider larger intervals (of 1000 ms or higher) due to very high mis-predictions with lower intervals of time.

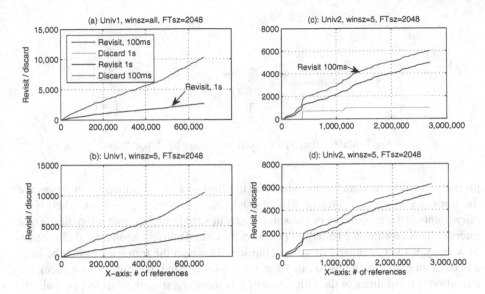

Fig. 6. Discarded and Revisited Entries for flow table of size 2048

4   Markov Based Learning Predictor

Our goal is to dynamically predict as best as possible the time at which a flow can be evicted. An arrival of an flow when the table is full requires that one of the existing flows is evicted. Further, all flow entries that are potentially dead requires to be removed periodically. To address this problem we provide a Markov Based Learning Predictor. Markov model proceed to define states and observe the transition between states as probability measures. In this work, we model the unit of time intervals as states and is expressed as follows: $\{S_i = T_i\}$, i.e., each state is a discrete time interval at the granularity of seconds. For instance, $S = T_1, T_2...T_n$ and T_0 is considered as special interval called current interval. Thus $T_0 = T_{curr}$. T_{curr} corresponds to the current interval. As flows arrive, they mark their entry in S_{curr}. They stay in S_{curr} until they have packets arriving for their entry. If there is no access to this flow for a second from their last access the flow is marked moved to S_1 to note that the flow has been idle during that interval after its last access. Similarly if a flow does not have access for consecutive 2 seconds then it is moved to S_2. Thus, the states maintain a record of those entries that are not visited from their last access and the state to which they belong. As long as they have packets arriving they are maintained in S_0 which is inherently assumed to be their current interval. Flow entries can transition from a higher state to current state. For instance, a flow entry can be accessed (due to an arrival of packets) after three idle intervals. Our model captures two kinds of informations: (a) the number of entries that are not visited in the past and (b) those flows that are periodically visited. Figure 7 shows different states and transitions.

We study the probability of transition from one state to another state. $P(i, i + 1)$ is the probability of transition observed between the ith and $(i + 1)^{th}$ state. These

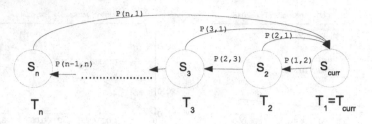

Fig. 7. Markov transitions to different states by flow entries

probability study the duration for which the the flows are idle. Further, we also observe the transition from $(i + 1), (i + 2)...(i + n)$ to $i = curr$. $P(i + k, i)$, where $i = curr$, denotes the probability of transitioning from state in higher interval to the current interval. This captures the pattern of periodically visited entries. At an arrival of the new flow entry, if the tables are full we find the state in which the transition being the least and evict an entry belonging to that state. On the other hand, periodically we check for transitions probabilities of the different states. If there is a state that has low probability of transition to a state lower than that, flows in that state are evicted. It should be notes that these states maintain only the flows that are not evicted by default expiry time set for the flow. Otherwise, the time out of the flow automatically evicts then entries by default in SDN. We observe through our experiments that the number of states as small as $i = 4$ is enough to capture 80% of the flows implying that majority of the flows if not observed to have an access for utmost 4 consecutive seconds can be marked as evictable. Therefore this approach requires only 4 states to be managed, giving us good predictions on the flows that needs to be evicted.

Fig. 8 shows the different outcome of the markov based learning predictor for varying flow table size for both the university traces. For comparisons, we have provided the results when flow timeout's were statistically defined to $1sec$ in-line as the base case (fig. 8). We have chosen the base case of $1s$ due to practical reasons. In addition to prediction being lower with fine grained sub seconds time out periods, according to [14], switches differ in the precision of time they can provide upto the $\approx$100 ms range. Therefore, the lowest range is in the order of seconds that the switches can guarantee, other granularities are estimated to be just best efforts. Further, implementing switch time outs at the granularity of milliseconds might have other protocol effects. With proactive prediction, discarded entries have been observed for lower level of flow table sizes (512 entries) as opposed to zero entries observed in the case of statically set $1sec$. This implies that our algorithm uses time conservatively higher than the static base case. While the discarded flows can be accommodated using a higher flow table size (as observed in case of 1024 and 2048), the revisits are in the order of 11 - 19% of the revisited flows for base configuration (1 s timeout setting). Thus our predictor predicts appropriate time out values for about 80-89% of the flows while mispredicting (observed as revisits) by about 10-19%. Around 10-12% of the miss predictions are flows observed to have ON and OFF periods which are difficult to trap using our algorithm. We observed the time duration for which a flow tends to stay alive and the average time when the $\Delta t = 1sec$ is around $500ms$ implying better convergence time compared to the statically assigned $1s$

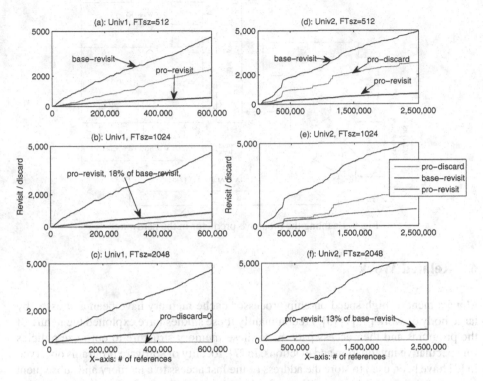

Fig. 8. *FlowMaster* Proactive predictor performance - discarded and revisited entries. Base case is taken to be 1 sec timeout for different Flow Table (FT) size, in Univ1 and Univ2.

interval for idle time out. We also observe the live lines being used by our approach. The fact that the miss rates have been zero implies that the table capacities were enough to accommodate the arrival times of the packets with this predictor. Therefore the amount of free capacity available (due to accurate predictions) is large enough to accommodate the arrival rates of the flows.

5 Hardware Implementation

We present a mechanism that can be enabled in the hardware to realize the proactive predictor. We implement our algorithm on NetFPGA [13] platform by using TCAM / SRAM combination on Xilinx Virtex-II FPGA. NetFPGA acts as an SDN (OpenFlow) switch platform that stores different counters such as number of packets, data rates, active times etc. Among several actions, one of the actions performed by the switch is setting the idle time out for individual flows and packets arrive. Only minor modification in control and data path of switching hardware is required to implement the above algorithm. Fig. 9 shows introduction of 'VALID' bit in flow table that helps identifying the status of the flow entry. The flow table controller (FT CONTROL) samples the valid bit field at regular interval and computes the idle time out.

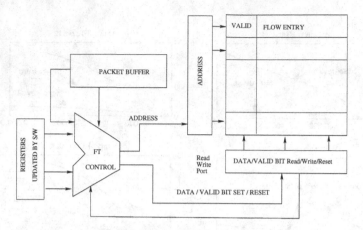

Fig. 9. Enabling the proactive predictor in the hardware

6 Related Work

Management of high speed on-chip processor cache memory have been addressed by large body of work [8] [7] [5]. Predominantly these studies have exploited the nature of the programs and their access patterns to these memory structure to optimize policies for speculative invalidation and evictions. In [7], locality of software programs observed in [3] have been used to store the address of the last access to a memory and subsequent arrival of the same address indicates the last access to that memory in that iteration. Such features are used to prefetch entries into the table and increase the utilization of these memory systems as in [8]. Three principles distinguish the nature of the problem in the domain of flow table in switching devices that makes it interesting to revisit them. They are (i) unlike locality of reference, packet arrivals do not show locality of accesses as their behavior is deterministic of the applications generating them (ii) the eviction policies are different as flow tables are guided by a time out which are some what representative of the flow characteristics (iii) the characteristics of the data i.e, the network packets and their associated flows. Naturally, we begin by studying the nature of the packet arrivals belonging to a flow in a switch.

Real world data center traces have been studied and characterized in [1] [6], with [1] focusing on especially flow level characteristics arriving at a switch. We go deeper into categorizing the nature of the packets belonging to a flow at the switches and study the nature of their arrival patterns and access patterns in the flow table. We use the traces used in [1] to study the finer aspects of flow level packets arriving at the switch. Packet sampling techniques for flows at packet level have been proposed in [15] [17] . In [15], architectural view have been taken to provide a multi-core flow level packet processing system. Work presented in [17] groups flows by developing a state machine for the different states in which a flow exists and exploiting the fact that majority of the flows flows the same states.

Yet another group of work have focused on optimal size of the flow tables in switching devices [12] [10] for various networking functionalities. Broadly these work fall into the category of optimizing lookup latencies. Split TCAM [12] provides a architectural solution for the range explosion problem by providing two TCAM's of different sizes and constraining the dimensions used to classify packets into 5 dimensions. TCAM-RAZOR [10] again addresses the range explosion problem by generating another semantically equivalent packet classifier such that least number of TCAM entries are stored in the table. Our work does not provide architectural changes to the memory subsystem but provide approaches to utilize the flow table space efficiently.

7 Conclusions

We have explored the flow characteristics from the perspective of effective methods of flow table utilization. Our observations from the real world data center traces showing that signification portion of the flow table space is occupied by non-active flows have provided us with motivation to device mechanisms to increase active lines in flow tables. Discarded flows (due to insufficient flow table capacity) and revisits (due to mis-predictions) are our primary objective functions to be optimized. Our explorations with per flow based reveals that they work stringently that capacity misses are eliminated but revisits continue to stay. We propose a conservative predictor that removes discarded flows completely and mis predicts only about 10% of the time (predicting accurately around 90%) of the time. We show that our predictor can be easily realized in the switching fabric through a hardware component. We believe that our work can be extended to output flow table sizes given a specific nature of the flow arrivals and packets belonging to a flow.

References

1. Benson, T., Akella, A., Maltz, D.A.: Network traffic characteristics of data centers in the wild. In: Proceedings of the 10th Annual Conference on Internet Measurement, IMC 2010, pp. 267–280. ACM, New York (2010)
2. Curtis, A.R., Mogul, J.C., Tourrilhes, J., Yalagandula, P., Sharma, P., Banerjee, S.: Devoflow: scaling flow management for high-performance networks. SIGCOMM Comput. Commun. Rev. 41(4), 254–265 (2011)
3. Denning, P.J., Schwartz, S.C.: Properties of the working-set model. Commun. ACM 15(3), 191–198 (1972)
4. Dharmapurikar, S., Krishnamurthy, P., Taylor, D.E.: Longest prefix matching using bloom filters. IEEE/ACM Trans. Netw. (2006)
5. Joseph, D., Grunwald, D.: Prefetching using markov predictors. In: Proceedings of the 24th Annual International Symposium on Computer Architecture, ISCA 1997, pp. 252–263. ACM (1997)
6. Kandula, S., Sengupta, S., Greenberg, A., Patel, P., Chaiken, R.: The nature of data center traffic: measurements & analysis. In: Proceedings of the 9th ACM SIGCOMM Conference on Internet Measurement Conference, IMC 2009, pp. 202–208. ACM (2009)
7. Lai, A.C., Falsafi, B.: Selective, accurate, and timely self-invalidation using last-touch prediction. In: Proc. of ISCA (2000)
8. Lai, A.C., Fide, C., Falsafi, B.: Dead-block prediction & dead-block correlating prefetchers. In: Proceedings of the 28th Annual International Symposium on Computer Architecture, ISCA 2001, pp. 144–154. ACM (2001)

9. Lee, M., Goldberg, S., Kompella, R.R., Varghese, G.: Fine-grained latency and loss measurements in the presence of reordering. SIGMETRICS Perform. Eval. Rev. 39(1), 289–300 (2011)
10. Liu, A.X., Meiners, C.R., Torng, E.: Tcam razor: a systematic approach towards minimizing packet classifiers in tcams. IEEE/ACM Trans. Netw. 18(2), 490–500 (2010)
11. McKeown, N., Anderson, T., Balakrishnan, H., Parulkar, G., Peterson, L., Rexford, J., Shenker, S., Turner, J.: Openflow: enabling innovation in campus networks. SIGCOMM Comput. Commun. Rev. 38 (March 2008)
12. Meiners, C.R., Liu, A.X., Torng, E., Patel, J.: Split: Optimizing space, power, and throughput for tcam-based classification. In: Proc. of ANCS, pp. 200–210. IEEE Computer Society (2011)
13. Naous, J., Erickson, D., Covington, G.A., Appenzeller, G., McKeown, N.: Implementing an openflow switch on the netfpga platform. In: Proceedings of the 4th ACM/IEEE Symposium on Architectures for Networking and Communications Systems, pp. 1–9 (2008)
14. OpenFlow: Openflow. In: Discussion List (2010),
https://mailman.stanford.edu/pipermail/openflow-discuss/
2012-June/003361.html
15. Qi, Y., Xu, B., He, F., Yang, B., Yu, J., Li, J.: Towards high-performance flow-level packet processing on multi-core network processors. In: Proc. of Symposium on Architecture for Networking and Communications Systems (2007)
16. Sherwood, T., Varghese, G., Calder, B.: A pipelined memory architecture for high throughput network processors. In: Proc. of ISCA, pp. 288–299. ACM (2003)
17. Whitehead, B., Lung, C.H., Rabinovitch, P.: Tracking per-flow state binned duration flow tracking. In: International Symposium on Performance Evaluation of Computer and Telecommunication Systems (SPECTS), pp. 73–80 (July 2010)

A Simple Lightweight Encryption Scheme
for Wireless Sensor Networks

Kamanashis Biswas[1], Vallipuram Muthukkumarasamy[1],
Elankayer Sithirasenan[1], and Kalvinder Singh[2]

[1] Griffith University, Gold Coast, Australia
kamanashis.biswas@griffithuni.edu.au,
{v.muthu,e.sithirasenan}@griffith.edu.au
[2] IBM, Australia Development Lab and Griffith University
Gold Coast, Australia
kalsingh@au.ibm.com

Abstract. Security is a critical issue in many sensor network applications. A number of security mechanisms are developed for wireless sensor networks based on classical cryptography. AES, RC5, SkipJack and XXTEA are some symmetric-key encryption algorithms that are deployed in sensor network environments. However, these algorithms have their own weakness, such as vulnerable to chosen-plaintext attack, brute force attack and computational complexity. We propose an energy efficient lightweight encryption scheme based on pseudorandom bit sequence generated by elliptic curve operations. We present experimental results of our proposed algorithm employed on real sensor nodes operating in TinyOS. We also discuss the security strength of our algorithm by presenting the security analysis of various tests and cryptanalytic attacks.

Keywords: Data confidentiality, Wireless Sensor Network, Elliptic Curve, Symmetric-key encryption, Cryptanalysis.

1 Introduction

Current research focuses on various properties of Wireless Sensor Networks (WSNs), for example, clustering, routing, resource usage, reliability and security [1–3]. Security is a challenging issue in WSNs, since sensor networks are usually deployed in hostile environments. Moreover, small memories, weak processors, limited energy of sensor nodes introduce a number of problems in implementing traditional cryptographic schemes in sensor networks. Hence, WSNs require efficient encryption schemes in terms of operation speed, storage and power consumption. We propose a lightweight encryption scheme for tiny sensor devices guaranteeing data confidentiality between source and destination nodes.

Our proposed scheme has a number of benefits. First, we present a simple pseudorandom bit sequence generation scheme using elliptic curve points that does not involve any floating point calculation. Thus, it avoids the problem of precision loss and also minimizes the computational costs for sensor nodes. Second, the proposed cryptosystem generates a different pseudorandom bit sequence

M. Chatterjee et al. (Eds.): ICDCN 2014, LNCS 8314, pp. 499–504, 2014.

for every new session and preserves independent behavioural characteristic of the algorithm. Third, the proposed scheme is lightweight compared to RC5 and SkipJack in terms of memory occupation, operation time and energy efficiency.

The organization of this paper is as follows: In *Section 2*, we briefly discuss the suitability of existing security mechanisms in WSN environments. *Section 3* provides details of the proposed pseudorandom sequence generation process and our proposed encryption scheme. *Section 4* and *Section 5* present the security and performance analysis of the algorithm respectively. Finally, *Section 6* concludes the paper.

2   Related Works

The Advanced Encryption System (AES) algorithm operates on a 4×4 array of bytes and has a key size of 128, 192, or 256 bits with 10, 12 or 14 number of rounds respectively. Previously, a chosen-plaintext attack can break up to seven rounds of 128-bits AES and eight rounds of 192-bits and 256-bits AES. Currently, AES running on 10, 12 and 14 rounds for 128, 192 and 256-bits size key respectively is also found vulnerable by researchers [4].

RC5 is a flexible block cipher with a variable block size (32, 64, 128 bits), number of rounds (0-255), and key size (0-2040 bits). Although, RC5 is considered more suitable for WSN applications, it requires the key schedule to be precomputed which uses 104 extra bytes of RAM per key. Moreover, RC5 is designed to take advantage of variable-bit rotation instruction (ROL) which is not supported by most embedded system, for instance, Intel architecture [5].

The SkipJack cipher uses an 80-bits key with 32-rounds to encrypt or decrypt 64-bits data blocks. But, the short key length makes SkipJack susceptible to the exhaustive key search attack [6]. An extended version, SkipJack-X is proposed to make the encryption scheme stronger against security attacks. However, the design strategy is not a proper replacement of SkipJack in WSN.

High Security and Lightweight (HIGHT) encryption algorithm is suitable for low resource devices. The algorithm suggested for 32-rounds is 64-bits block length and 128-bits key length. Although HIGHT is designed for low-cost, low power devices, it takes more memory space and operation time than RC5 [7].

Tiny Encryption Algorithm (TEA) is notable for its simplicity and small memory requirement. But it is vulnerable to related-key attack and chosen-plaintext attacks. To overcome these weaknesses, a corrected block TEA (XXTEA) has been designed with a key size of 128 bits. However, the last reported attack against full-round XXTEA presents a chosen-plaintext attack requiring 2^{59} queries and negligible work [8].

3   The Proposed Encryption Scheme

Our proposed encryption scheme is divided into three phases: i) key establishment phase, ii) pseudorandom bit sequence generation phase and iii) encryption phase. Here, we describe the protocol in detail.

3.1   The Key Establishment Process

We assume that prime field, base point and elliptic curve parameters are pre-distributed securely among all sensor nodes (SNs) in WSN. Now, each SN generates a list of elliptic curve points termed as key pool by using point addition and point doubling operation [9]. When a node requires to send data packets, it randomly selects a key from the key pool and converts it into hash code using a hash function. This code is shared with the destination node. The destination node retrieves the shared key by matching the received code with the hash codes generated for each point of its key pool. Upon successful retrieval of the secret key, the destination node acknowledges the source node with a reply message.

3.2   Generation of Pseudorandom Bit Sequence

The security level of many cryptographic systems using Linear Feedback Shift Register (LFSR) or chaotic maps depends on the properties of the random number generation schemes such as unpredictability and unlimited period. But, the security strength of LFSR is poor and cannot meet the demand of unpredictability for secure communication [10]. Again, the chaotic maps require high-precision floating point calculation which is not suitable for resource limited SNs. To avoid these problems, we use elliptic curve over prime field to generate random bit sequence. An elliptic curve (EC) over prime field is a simple algebraic expression that can be defined by the following equation:

$$y^2 \ (mod \ p) = x^3 + Ax + B \ (mod \ p) \tag{1}$$

where, A and B are the coefficients and the variables x and y take the values only from the finite field within the range of prime field p. We assume that the values of these parameters are pre-distributed and the participating nodes share a common private key using the key establishment process described in section 3.1. This shared key is used as the base point (G) to generate the random bit sequence in our proposed cryptosystem as shown in the following algorithm.

Algorithm: Pseudorandom binary sequence generation process

Input: Coefficients (A, B); Base Point G (x, y); Prime field p
Output: Binary_Sequence of length N // Initially, N equals to zero
Steps:
1. Generate a new point $\bar{G}$ $(\bar{x}, \bar{y})$ using point addition or doubling operation
2. if $\bar{x} > \bar{y}$
      Binary_Sequence$(N) \leftarrow (\bar{x} \bmod 2)$
  else
      Binary_Sequence$(N) \leftarrow (\bar{y} \bmod 2)$
3. $N \leftarrow N + 1$
4. Repeat step 1 to 3 until N $\neq$ desired length

3.3   The Encryption Procedure

The random bit sequence obtained in the previous stage works as a one time password in our proposed encryption scheme. At first step, we convert the plaintext to binary sequence by mapping the characters into their corresponding ASCII codes. Then, the sequence is xor-ed with the pseudorandom bit sequence to generate the ciphertext. We perform the XOR operation because the additive cipher is more secure when the key-stream is random and as long as the plaintext [11]. The decryption process is simply reverse of the encryption procedure.

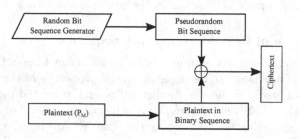

Fig. 1. The general schema of the proposed encryption algorithm

4   Security Analysis

We tested our proposed scheme against various security attacks. The security of elliptic curve cryptography (ECC) relies on the discrete logarithm problem and the best known *brute force attack* requires exponential time to solve the problem. NIST recommends to use 256-bit key for security although the ECC scheme broken to date had a 112-bit key for prime field. *Statistical analysis* is the study of the frequency of letters or common characteristics of words in ciphertext. We used an English article of more than 10,000 words as plaintext to generate the ciphertext. But the ciphertext does not have any statistical features: all of the characters are randomly distributed and do not follow any particular order. Thus, it is too hard to find a co-relation in the ciphertext. *Related-key attack* is based on decrypting ciphertext with various similar keys and analysing the difference in outputs. In our proposed scheme, the EC parameters (A and B), prime number (p), and base point $G(x, y)$ are the primary keys. Our experiment shows that it is hard to generate identical pseudorandom bit sequence if any of the above values is not same. Thus, it is too hard to decrypt the ciphertext without knowing exact value of each parameter used in the encryption process. *Timing Attack* is improbable in our cryptosystem due to data independent behavioural characteristics of the algorithm. Moreover, the binary sequence used in encryption varies each time, hence, it is not possible to derive any statistical co-relation of timing information. Due to frequent re-keying strategy, *chosen plaintext attack* is also not fruitful in our proposed encryption scheme.

5   Performance Analysis

We have implemented our encryption scheme in MICA2 sensor mote operating at 7.3728 MHz (ATmega128L), 128KB program memory and 4KB data memory. The mote supports an event-driven operating system TinyOS and a high level programming language nesC. RC5 and non-optimized SkipJack protocols are also implemented and the results are compared with our proposed scheme.

Operation Time– In this experiment, ATEMU, a high fidelity large scale sensor network emulator, is used to get the total CPU cycles required to encrypt 32 bytes data in MICA2. The results indicate that our algorithm performs better in terms of CPU elapsed time (6.207 ms) using only 45839 CPU cycles. For RC5, the number of CPU cycles and encryption time is little bit higher compared to our scheme and is about double in case of SkipJack.

Table 1. CPU use and elapsed time to encrypt 32 bytes data

Algorithms	CPU Cycles	Time
SkipJack	91224	12.353
RC5	48709	6.595
Proposed	45839	6.207

Memory and Energy Efficiency– Fig. 2(a) shows that our algorithm occupies less memory than that of RC5 and SkipJack. The flash memory (ROM) required by our proposed scheme is lower than RC5 and SkipJack but it occupies more RAM than the other two schemes. However, the total memory required by our protocol is 5868 bytes whereas the amount is 6772 bytes and 7510 bytes for RC5 and SkipJack respectively. Finally, we find the total amount of energy to encrypt 32 bytes of data in our experiments. For this purpose, we use PowerTOSSIM to

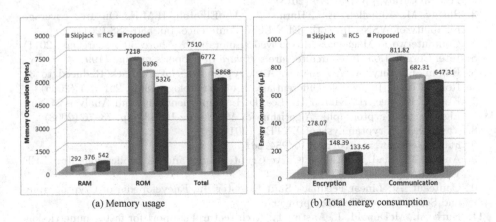

(a) Memory usage   (b) Total energy consumption

Fig. 2. Comparison on memory usage and total energy dissipation

measure the total amount of energy required to encrypt and to send the data packets by sensor node. The graph in Fig. 2(b) indicates that our encryption scheme consumes less energy than RC5 and SkipJack.

6 Conclusion

This paper presents a new idea of using different base point of an elliptic curve (i.e., shared key) to generate different pseudorandom bit sequence for two communicating nodes. Due to the ability of producing large bit sequences, our proposed scheme is suitable for large volume data encryption such as image, audio and video. The proposed algorithm uses blocks of plaintext as input and generates corresponding blocks of ciphertext. One of the limitations of block cipher is that it requires to transmit additional bits (padding) when the size of plaintext is smaller than defined block size. However, this situation can be avoided using stream cipher. Since our proposed scheme generates different random bit sequences for every new session, it can also be implemented in the form of stream cipher. The proposed scheme has a few drawbacks. First, the initial parameters need to be pre-distributed using secure channel or a key exchange mechanism. Second, we used 128-bit elliptic curve in our experiments. If we use 256-bit elliptic curve for enhanced level of security then it will result in additional computational cost and memory usage. In our future work we will implement the protocol in combination with other protocols (e.g. TinySec) in a large scale sensor network to evaluate overall message throughput, latency and key set-up costs.

References

1. Biswas, K., Muthukkumarasamy, V., Sithirasenan, E.: Maximal clique based clustering scheme for WSNs. In: 8th IEEE ISSNIP, Melbourne, pp. 237–241 (2013)
2. Biswas, K., Muthukkumarasamy, V., Sithirasenan, E., Usman, M.: An energy efficient clique based clustering and routing mechanism in WSNs. In: 9th IEEE IWCMC, Italy, pp. 171–176 (2013)
3. Shazly, M., Elmallah, E.S., Harms, J., AboElFotoh, H.M.F.: On area coverage reliability of WSNs. In: 36th IEEE LCN Conference, pp. 580–588 (2011)
4. Computerworld Magazine: AES proved vulnerable by Microsoft researchers (2011)
5. Intel Corporation: Intel architecture software developer's manual (1997)
6. Biham, E., Birykov, A., Shamir, A.: Cryptanalysis of Skipjack Reduced to 31 Rounds Using Impossible Differentials. J. of Cryptology 18(4), 291–311 (2005)
7. Koo, W.K., Lee, H., Kim, Y.H., Lee, D.H.: Implementation and Analysis of New Lightweight Cryptographic Algorithm for WSNs. In: ICISA, pp. 73–76 (2008)
8. Yarrkov, E.: Cryptanalysis of XXTEA (2010),
   http://eprint.iacr.org/2010/254.pdf
9. Amara, M., Siad, A.: Elliptic Curve Cryptography and its applications. In: IEEE WOSSPA, pp. 247–250 (2011)
10. Canteaut, A.: Linear Feedback Shift Register. In: Encyclopedia of Cryptography and Security, pp. 355–358. Springer
11. Burke, J., McDonald, J., Austin, T.: Architectural support for fast symmetric-key cryptography. In: 9th ICASPLOS, pp. 178–189 (2000)

Analyzing the Network Connectivity Probability of a Linear VANET in Nakagami Fading Channels

Ninsi Mary Mathew[1] and Neelakantan P.C.[2]

[1] M.G. University College of Engineering, Thodupuzha
[2] Adi Shankara Institute of Engineering & Technology, Ernakulam

Abstract. In this paper, we present an analytical model to determine the network connectivity probability of one dimensional linear vehicular ad hoc network (VANET) in the presence of Nakagami fading. In particular, we focus on the probability of being able to convey messages from a source vehicle to a destination vehicle, which may be multiple hops away. This analysis takes into account the variability of the channel and how it affects the network connectivity of a linear VANET. In our model, the communication range of each vehicle is modeled as a random variable due to channel fading. The analytical results are used to study the effect of parameters like path loss exponent and vehicle density on the network connectivity probability. This facility is particularly useful for distributing traffic information related to road safety, weather, and navigation without the need for expensive infrastructure.

Keywords: Network Connectivity, Nakagami fading, vehicular ad hoc network.

1 Introduction

Vehicular Ad Hoc Networks (VANETs) are highly mobile wireless networks envisioned to improve traffic safety and efficiency while providing Internet access on the move by enabling vehicle-to-vehicle (V2V) or vehicle-to-infrastructure (V2I) communications [1], [2]. The IEEE 802.11p working group is responsible for the standardization for V2V and V2I communications, while the entire communication protocol stack is being standardized by the IEEE 1609 working group under the name Wireless Access in Vehicular Environments (WAVE). The main technical challenges for communication in V2I and V2V networks are the very high mobility of the nodes, highly dynamic topology, high variability in node density, and very short duration of communication [2], [3]. This paper investigates the network connectivity probability of a VANET in the presence of Nakagami fading. Network connectivity is one of the most important issues in VANETs, since the dissemination of time critical information requires, as a preliminary condition, the network to be connected. The network connectivity

M. Chatterjee et al. (Eds.): ICDCN 2014, LNCS 8314, pp. 505–511, 2014.

problem has been extensively studied for VANETS [4-8]. The random communication range model employed in this paper is relevant for network design because it can account for variability in the communication links, and thus will be able to accurately estimate the connectivity probability after network setup. We consider a linear VANET formed by vehicles on a highway operating in the free flow state, in which the vehicle density on the highway is very low and the vehicle speed and traffic flow are independent; drivers can drive as fast as they want (subject to a limit on maximum speed known as free-way velocity) and thus overtaking is allowed [5], [6]. Presently, we do not pay attention to the MAC and assume that an ideal MAC protocol is employed. We derive analytical expression for the network connectivity probability by employing Nakagami fading model, since Nakagami fading can be used to describe small scale fading in a V2V channel [9-12]. A distance dependent power law model is used for the path loss, since recent empirical and analytical modeling studies have shown that, for highway, urban, and suburban scenarios, a classical power law model is suitable to describe the V2V path loss [13]. The proposed analytical model for network connectivity is useful to determine the impact of parameters such as transmit power, receive SNR threshold, vehicle arrival rate, vehicle density, vehicle speed, highway length and various channel dependent parameters such as path loss exponent and Nakagami fading factor on VANET connectivity. To the best of these authors' knowledge, the proposed study is the first attempt to analyze VANET connectivity in Nakagami fading channel. Remainder of this paper is organized as follows: In Sect. 2, we present the connectivity analysis. The main results are presented in Sect. 3. The paper is concluded in Sect. 4.

2   Analysis of Network Connectivity

The system model used for the connectivity analysis, which includes models for highway and vehicle mobility, is similar to that of [5], [8]. Empirical studies have shown that Poisson distribution provides an excellent model for vehicle arrival process in free flow state [14]. Hence it is assumed that the number of vehicles passing the observer per unit time is a Poisson process with rate λ veh/hr. Empirical studies have shown that the vehicle speed V in free flow state follow a Gaussian distribution [5, 14]. To avoid dealing with negative speeds or speeds close to zero, two limits are defined for the speed. For this, a truncated Gaussian PDF is used given by [5]. When the vehicle speed follows truncated Gaussian PDF, the average vehicle density ρ is computed as in [15]. Average number of vehicles on a high way segment of length L, in the steady state, is given by $N = \rho L$. Two consecutive vehicles in the network will be connected if the IVD is smaller than vehicle's communication range R. The probability that two consecutive vehicles C_n and C_{n-1} are connected is computed as $P_{link} = Pr(X_n \leq R)$. For the network to be connected, it is required that the IVDs $X_n \leq R$ for $n = 1, 2, 3, \ldots, N-1$ where N is the total average number of vehicles on the highway. Assume that the vehicle communication range R is a random variable with CDF $F_R(x)$. Since both X_n and R are random variables, P_{link} is determined as follows:

$$P_{link} = 1 - \int_0^\infty Pr[R < x | X_n = x] f_{X_n}(x) dx \; . \tag{1}$$

where $f_{X_n}(x)$ is the PDF of the IVD X_n. Let P_c be the probability that the network is connected. It follows that $P_c = Pr(X_1 \leq R, X_2 \leq R, \ldots, X_{N-1} \leq R)$. Since X_n's are i.i.d. random variables [5], P_c is determined as follows:

$$P_c = \left[1 - \int_0^\infty Pr[R < x | X_n = x] f_{X_n}(x) dx \right]^{N-1} \; . \tag{2}$$

Consider the Nakagami fading channel with the assumption that the fading is constant over the transmission of a frame and subsequent fading states are i.i.d. The PDF of the received SNR under Nakagami-m fading is given by [16]. The probability that a transmitted message is correctly received at a distance d is given by,

$$P[\gamma(d) \geq \psi] = \int_\psi^\infty f_\gamma(a) da = \frac{\Gamma(m, m\psi/\overline{\gamma})}{\Gamma(m)} \; . \tag{3}$$

Here $\Gamma(s, a)$ is the upper incomplete Gamma function [17]. To compute the connectivity probability according to (1) and (2), the CDF of the communication range is required, The CDF of the communication range can be

$$F_R(x) = P(R \leq x) = 1 - P[\gamma(x) \geq \psi] = 1 - \frac{\Gamma(m, m\psi/\overline{\gamma})}{\Gamma(m)} \; . \tag{4}$$

where $\overline{\gamma} = \beta P_T / x^\alpha P_{noise}$. Since the IVD are exponential with PDF $f_{X_i}(x) = \rho e^{-\rho x}$, the link connectivity probability, P_{link} is determined as follows (using (1) and (4)):

$$P_{link} = 1 - \int_0^\infty Pr[R < x | X_i = x] f_{X_i}(x) dx = \rho \int_0^\infty e^{-\rho x} \frac{\Gamma(m, m\psi/\overline{\gamma})}{\Gamma(m)} dx \; . \tag{5}$$

Assuming that the total average number of vehicles on the highway is equal to N, (and $N-1$ links on an average), the network connectivity probability is given by

$$P_c = \left(\rho \int_0^\infty e^{-\rho x} \frac{\Gamma(m, m\psi/\overline{\gamma})}{\Gamma(m)} dx \right)^{N-1} \; . \tag{6}$$

For integer values of s, $\Gamma(s, a)$ can be written as $\Gamma(s, a) = (s-1)! \times e^{-a} \sum_{k=0}^{s-1} \frac{a^k}{k!}$ and $\Gamma(s) = (s-1)!$ [17]. Accordingly, for integer values of m, (5) becomes:

$$P_{link} = \sum_{k=0}^{m-1} \frac{1}{k!} \left(\frac{m\psi P_{noise}}{\beta P_T} \right)^k \rho \int_0^\infty e^{-\left(\rho x + \frac{m\psi x^\alpha P_{noise}}{\beta P_T} \right)} x^{\alpha k} dx \; . \tag{7}$$

In order to evaluate the integral in (7) for a given value of α, we use the following result reported in [15]:

$$\int_0^\infty x^{p-1} e^{-(zx+\alpha x^r)} dx = (2\pi)^{\frac{1-r}{2}} r^{p-\frac{1}{2}} z^{-p} \times G_{1,r}^{r,1} \left(\frac{z^r}{\alpha r^r} \Big|_{\frac{p}{r}, \ldots, \frac{p+r-1}{r}}^{1} \right) ; \alpha, z, p > 0 \ . \quad (8)$$

Note that (8) is valid for positive integer values of r and $G_{p,q}^{m,n}$ is the Meijers G function [16, (9.301)]. Accordingly, when α is a positive integer, the integral in (7) can be written in terms of Meijers G function based on (8). Thus P_{Link} is computed as follows:

$$P_{link} = \rho(2\pi)^{\frac{1-\alpha}{2}} \sum_{k=0}^{m-1} \frac{1}{k!} \left(\frac{m\psi P_{noise}}{\beta P_T} \right)^k \alpha^{k+\frac{1}{2}} \rho^{-(\alpha k+1)} \times G_{1,\alpha}^{\alpha,1} \left(\frac{\beta P_T \rho^\alpha}{m\psi P_{noise}\alpha^\alpha} \Big|_{\frac{\alpha k+1}{\alpha}, \ldots, \frac{\alpha k+\alpha}{\alpha}}^{1} \right) \ . \quad (9)$$

Hence, for integer values of α and m, the network connectivity probability can be written as,

$$P_c = \left[\rho(2\pi)^{\frac{1-\alpha}{2}} \sum_{k=0}^{m-1} \frac{1}{k!} \left(\frac{m\psi P_{noise}}{\beta P_T} \right)^k \alpha^{k+\frac{1}{2}} \rho^{-(\alpha k+1)} \times G_{1,\alpha}^{\alpha,1} \left(\frac{\beta P_T \rho^\alpha}{m\psi P_{noise}\alpha^\alpha} \Big|_{\frac{\alpha k+1}{\alpha}, \ldots, \frac{\alpha k+\alpha}{\alpha}}^{1} \right) \right]^{N-1} \ . \quad (10)$$

For non-integer values of α, (7) has no closed-form solution and hence the connectivity probability has to be evaluated by numerical techniques.

3   Model Validation and Main Results

In this section, we present the main analytical results for network connectivity. Both the analytical and simulation results can be obtained using Matlab. We can use the Matlab environment to simulate an uninterrupted highway [5]. We consider highway of length L, and the vehicles are generated from a Poisson process with arrival rate λ veh/sec. Each vehicle is assigned a random speed chosen from a truncated Gaussian distribution. We consider one snap shot of the highway at the arrival instant of each vehicle and find the IVD values. For each link, we then calculate the average SNR ($\bar{\gamma}$) corresponding to the measured value of IVD of that link. Assuming Nakagami fading environment, we then generate a random variable representing the received SNR over that link with average value $\bar{\gamma}$. If the received SNR is greater than the threshold value ψ, the link is considered to be connected. The procedure is repeated for all the $(N-1)$ links in the network. If all the links in a snap shot are connected, the network is considered to be connected. The network connectivity probability is calculated by repeating the connectivity evaluation process 10,000 times. The parameters are fixd as given in the figures. Figure 1 shows the network connectivity probability P_c plotted against path loss exponent α for a fixed average vehicle density ρ. In Fig. 2 and Fig. 3, the connectivity probability is plotted against average vehicle density ρ for $\alpha = 1.8$ and 3.5 respectively. Results show that, as α increases, P_c decays very rapidly. The network gets almost disconnected when α becomes more than 2.5. As expected, the connectivity probability increases as average vehicle density increases. The figures also show the strong influence of Nakagami parameter m on connectivity. The connectivity gets degraded when the Nakagami parameter m is set equal to 0.5. Further, it can be observed that, the average vehicle density required to satisfy a target value for the network connectivity probability, decreases when the path loss exponent decreases. Hence our analysis results show that both the Nakagami factor and the path loss exponent have strong influence on the connectivity. The proposed analytical model is highly relevant because, it can be used to find the influence of both traffic as well as channel dependent parameters on the connectivity of a VANET.

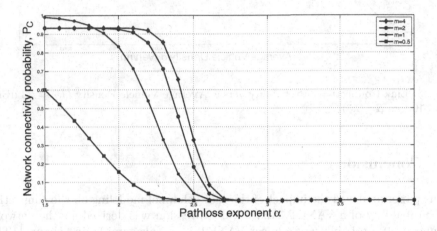

Fig. 1. Network Connectivity Probability versus Pathloss Exponent (λ= 0.1 veh/sec, $P_T = 33$ dBm, $\mu = 70$ km/hr, $\sigma = 21$ km/hr, L=10 km)

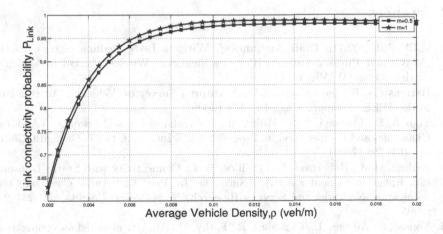

Fig. 2. Link Connectivity Probability versus Average Vehicle Density ($P_T = 33$ dBm, L = 10 km, α= 1.8)

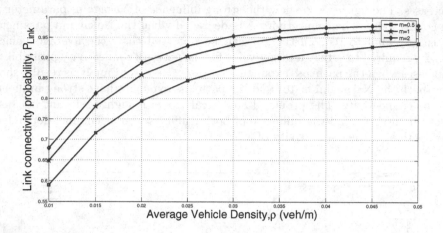

Fig. 3. Link Connectivity Probability versus Average Vehicle Density ($P_T = 33$ dBm, $L = 10$ km, $\alpha = 3.5$)

4   Conclusion

This paper analyzed the impact of the radio channel modeling on the connectivity probability of a VANET. Analytical expression was derived for the network connectivity probability of a linear VANET in a Nakagami fading channel. The results of this paper would be highly useful for a network designer dealing with the design of an intelligent transportation network for information dissemination.

References

1. IEEE Std. 802.11p Draft Amendment, Wireless LAN Medium Access Control (MAC) and Physical Layer (PHY) Specifications: Wireless Access in Vehicular Environments (WAVE) (July 2010)
2. Hartenstein, H., Laberteaux, K.P.: A Tutorial Survey on Vehicular Ad Hoc Networks. IEEE Commun. Mag., 164–171 (2008)
3. Yousefi, S., Mousavi, M.S., Fathy, M.: Vehicular Ad Hoc Networks (VANETs), Challenges and Perspectives. In: Proc. 6th IEEE Int. Conf. ITST, Chengdu, China, pp. 761–766 (2006)
4. Artimy, M.M., Robertson, W., Phillips, W.J.: Connectivity with Static Transmission Range in Vehicular Ad Hoc Networks. In: Proc. 3rd Annu. Conf. on Communication Networks and Services Research, Nova Scotia, Canada, pp. 237–242 (2005)
5. Yousefi, S., Altman, E., El-Azouzi, R., Fathy, M.: Analytical model for connectivity in vehicular ad hoc networks. IEEE Trans. Veh. Technol. 57(6), 3341–3356 (2008)
6. Wu, J.: Connectivity of Mobile Linear Networks with Dynamic Node Population and Delay Constraint. IEEE JSAC 27(7), 1215–1218 (2009)

7. Zhuang, Y., Pan, J., Cai, L.: A Probabilistic Model for Message Propagation in Two-Dimensional Vehicular Ad Hoc Networks. In: Proc. of VANET 2010, Chicago (September 2010)
8. Yousefi, S., Altman, E., El-Azouzi, R., Fathy, M.: Improving connectivity in vehicular ad hoc networks. Comput. Commun. 31(9), 1653–1659 (2008)
9. Cheng, L., et al.: Mobile Vehicle to Vehicle Narrowband Channel Measurement and Characterisation of the 5.9GHz DSRC frequency band. IEEE JSAC 25(8), 1501–1516 (2007)
10. Maurer, J., Fugen, T., Wiesbeck, W.: Narrow-band Measurements and Analysis of the Inter-vehicle Transmission Channel at 5.2 GHz. In: Maurer, J., Fugen, T., Wiesbeck, W. (eds.) Proc. of IEEE VTC Spring 2002, pp. 1274–1278 (2002)
11. Sen, I., Matolak, D.W.: Vehicle-Vehicle channel models for the 5-GHz band. IEEE Trans. Intelligent Transportation Sys. 9(2), 235–245 (2008)
12. Cheng, L.: Physical Layer Modeling and Analysis for V2V Networks. Ph.D. thesis, Carnegie Mellon University (2007)
13. Karedal, J., Czink, N., Paier, A., Tufvesson, F., Molisch, A.F.: Pathloss Modeling for Vehicle-to-Vehicle Communications. IEEE Trans. Vehicular Technology 60(1), 323–328 (2011)
14. Roess, R.P., Prassas, E.S., Mcshane, W.R.: Traffic Engineering, 3rd edn. Pearson Prentice Hall (2004)
15. Neelakantan, P.C., Babu, A.V.: Computation of minimum transmit power for network connectivity in vehicular ad hoc networks formed by vehicles with random communication range. International Journal of Communication Systems (2012)
16. Goldsmith, A.: Wireless Communication. Cambridge University Press (2005)
17. Gradshteyn, S., Ryzhik, I.M.: Table of Integrals, Series, and Products, 7th edn. Academic Press (2007)

Max-Min-Path Energy-Efficient Routing Algorithm – A Novel Approach to Enhance Network Lifetime of MANETs

Vijayalakshmi Ponnuswamy[*], Sharmila Anand John Francis,
and Abraham Dinakaran J.

Department of Computer Applications,
School of Computer Science and Technology, Karunya University, India
vijilak@karunya.edu

Abstract. Power-aware routing in wireless ad-hoc networks has to typically compensate with the utilization of energy consumed during communication. Most of the energy efficient routing algorithms try to improve the network lifetime but it lacks to guarantee the life time of individual nodes in the network. A novel and an optimal routing protocol Max-Min-Path (MMP) have been proposed that guarantee to maximize the network lifetime which is NP-hard problem. This routing strategy remains sustainable even in a non-monotonic sequence of the energy path cost and the residual energy of the individual nodes and, thereby enhancing the network lifetime with low computational complexity. A classical relationship between the total energy path and the residual energy of individual nodes has been proved. The simulation results prove that the proposed work outperforms the existing energy-efficient routing algorithms by evaluating the energy-aware performance metrics.

Keywords: Residual energy, routing algorithms, network life time, energy path cost, energy efficient communication.

1 Introduction

Energy conservation in wireless networks is of utmost importance due to the limited energy availability in the wireless devices. This paves a new path in the design of energy efficient routing algorithms for communication networks. To minimize the energy costs in communication is important by practicing energy-aware routing approaches that maximizes the network lifetime. In this paper, an energy-aware routing strategy is introduced for wireless networks where all the nodes are equipped by battery or other external power sources as solar energy. The network lifetime is quantified by the maximum number of packets that can be transferred in an wireless network before the source node and destination node gets disconnected from each other [5][7]. A suitable energy-aware routing protocol Max-Min-Path (MMP) has been designed that maximizes the network lifetime NP-hard problem [5]and, there by

---

[*] Research Scholar.

M. Chatterjee et al. (Eds.): ICDCN 2014, LNCS 8314, pp. 512–518, 2014.
© Springer-Verlag Berlin Heidelberg 2014

conserving the energy level of individual nodes by reducing the saturated nodes in the network. In developing energy efficient routing protocol, a wireless network is represented as a directed graph $G(V, E)$, where the vertices V represents the nodes and edges E represents the link between the nodes in the network. The degree of a vertex v in the graph G is the number of edges that are connected to that vertex v. The minimum energy is sustained to conserve the energy of the node is termed as threshold energy level. Let the residual energy be, $E_a(v_i)$ and it is designated as the weight w of that node. The threshold energy level is computed with the available energy $E_a(v_i)$ and the degree $\deg(v_i)$ of the ith node. The Linear Congruential Method (LCM) is used to initialize the residual energy of the nodes in the network. This paper also depicts a relationship between the total energy path and the residual energy of individual node in the network.

2   Related Work

An energy-efficient route is achieved when the transmission power is controllable [2][8] with less interference control. Their survey of energy efficiency routing protocols based on sleep/power-down node approach and local distribution approach are relatively helpful for energy imbalance problem. The relationship between routing optimality and energy-balanced data propagation [3][9] provides a maximized data flow equivalent to maximized network lifetime by using Pareto optimal routing technique. The results discussed would be better-off if they have relevant work to consider interference minimization. The Shortest Widest Residual Routing (SWRP) [4] is an energy-aware routing technique which provides a good balance between the residual energy and the energy path cost to maximize the network lifetime but for concurrent multiple data transmissions between the source and the destination node fails since the energy of the nodes reaches its energy saturation level. By reducing the energy spent in transmitting the overhead packets [9] total energy consumption is reduced with the modified DSR protocols. The mobility of nodes is considered in their modified work which can proportionally increase the energy consumption rate in MANET. The k-station network energy-efficient problem [1] is considered (1+e) - approximation algorithm where every station can receive a signal from one sender and allows a bounded hop multicast operation. A centralized on-line energy-efficient algorithm [7] based on maximizing the network lifetime that aims to minimize the transmission energy consumption without any knowledge of future disjoint path connection request arrivals and message generation rates. The usage of transmit power control [8] determines the optimal power, thereby maximizes the degree of link's satisfaction (utility), between the source and destination pair.

3   The Problem Definition and the Proposed Solution

Let $G(V, E)$ represents a wireless network comprising of V nodes, $v_i \in V$, where $i = 0,1,2, \dots, n-1$ and E represents the transmission link between nodes. Let $E_a(v)$ be the available energy at node v. Let $c(u, v)$ be the energy path cost required for transmitting a packet from node u to node v, where $c(u, v) =$

$c(v, u), for\ all\ (u, v) \in E$. Let $P(v_o, v_k)$ be the path from the node v_0 to v_k and it is denoted by: $P(v_o, v_k) = v_0, v_1, \dots v_k$. The cost of energy path is denoted by $e_c(P(v_0, v_k))$ and it is given as:

$$e_c(P(v_0, v_k)) = c(v_0, v_1) + c(v_1, v_2) + \cdots + c(v_{k-2}, v_{k-1}) + \cdots + c(v_{k-1}, v_k),$$
$$e_c(P(v_0, v_k)) = \sum_{i=0}^{k-1} c(v_{i-1}, v_i) \tag{1}$$

Let the residual energy path, $r(p(v_0, v_k))$ is defined as:

$$r(P(v_0, v_k)) = \min_i (E_a(v_i) - c(v_i, v_{i+1})), \qquad\qquad 0 \le i < k \tag{2}$$

When a data packet to be routed between the source and destination the following energy constraints has to be considered:

1. To find the *minimum energy path cost:*
$$\min (e_c(P(v_0, v_k)) = \sum_{i=0}^{k-1} c(v_{i-1}, v_i))$$
2. To select the *maximum residual energy node with minimum energy path cost:*
$$\max(r(P(v_0, v_k))) = \min_i ((E_a(v_i) - c(v_i, v_{i+1}))), 0 \le i < k$$
3. To find the *minimum residual energy of the selected node:*
$$\min(r(P(v_0, v_k))) = \min_i ((E_{threshold}) - c(v_i, v_{i+1}))), \qquad 0 \le i < k \tag{3}$$

Where $E_{threshold} = (\llbracket(E)\rrbracket_a(v_i)/(\deg(v_i))\rrbracket$ and $\deg(v_i)$ represents the degree of ith node v. If $\min(r(P(v_0, v_k))$ is equivalent to the energy path cost and the residual energy attains the threshold value the data transmission through that node is stopped. i.e.,if $(\min(r(P(v_0, v_k)) = \min (e_c(P(v_0, v_k)))$ or $\min(r(P(v_0, v_k))$ $= E_{threshold}))$, $\cdot 0 \le i < k$. With these constraints, the MMP protocol sustains the minimum residual energy at its threshold level, preventing the nodes attaining saturated level and thereby reducing the number of saturated nodes in the network. Subsequently the MMP facilitates more number of data transmissions among the nodes in the network by incurring less overhead thereby enhancing the lifetime of the network. Every time a new path is computed, the proposed MMP protocol has the computational complexity of O(n log n). Each step, the algorithm finds a minimum-energy path cost which will amount to a total time complexity of O(n log n).

3.1   Algorithm

Algorithm Max-Min-Path(***Energy, D, EG***)
//s ←Source Node, d← destination node,EG ← *Energy Graph, adj(s)* ←adjacent list represents the neighbor of the *Source,weight(u, v)* ← Capacity of edge(u, v) $width(u)$ ← weight function of the node u deg (s) ← degree of the source node s//
begin

$route \leftarrow \phi\ E\_threshold\_energy = ceil(width(u))/deg(s), cost \leftarrow 0$

for all adjacent vertices of s ,say n_A **do**

if ($width(s) \geq E\_threshold\_energy$) $i \leftarrow 1, \ldots n_A$ $\underset{nA}{e}(cost) = \underset{i}{e}(cost)$,

$e\_cost = \underset{i}{\min}(\underset{i}{e}(cost))$, $i \leftarrow 1 \cdots n_A$ $route \leftarrow route \| v$, $new\_width \leftarrow width(s) - e\_cost$,

$start\_vertex \leftarrow v$, $EG = EG - v$

if ($v \neq dest\_vertex$) do call Max-Min-Path ($new\_width, start\_vertex, EG$) ,

($route, e\_cost$), $e\_less\_cost = \underset{j}{\min}(e\_less(cost))$, $j \leftarrow 1, 2, \cdots n_A - 1$

call Max-Min-Path ($e\_cost, s, EG - e\_less\_cost$) **end if end if end for end**

3.2 Relative Comparison of Residual Energy and Total Energy Path

When the computation of the maximum residual energy path of the given energy graph $EG(V, E)$, identifies a solution path with greater number of maximum energy nodes and it leads to construct a sub graph $EG'(V, E)$ with the maximum energy node as w and the comparison with that of the total energy path is discussed as follows:

Definition: Let us assume $EG'(w)$ be the sub graph derived from the original graphEG, by running the edges whose residual energy are less than w.

Let us consider $E_{min}(w)$ represents the energy consumed along the minimum energy path from source node s to destination node t, in the sub graph $EG'(w)$. That is, as the constraint on the residual energy varies, the energy required for the minimum energy path also varies. If we continuously repeat the process by computing the minimum energy path for all possible given residual energies in the graph EG, we obtain an increasing and decreasing / decreasing and increasing non uniform graph that is discussed in the following lemmas.

Lemma 1: Let $E_{min}(w)$ be the minimum energy consumed along the energy path from the source node s to destination node t in the subgraph $EG'(w)$. When the residual energies $w1, w2, \ldots, wm$ are distributed in an non-monotonic order i.e., $w1 < w2 > w3$ then $E_{min}(w1) < E_{min}(w2) < E_{min}(w3)$, when the energy path remains in an monotonic order.

Proof: Let the graph $G_1 = EG(w1)$, graph $G_2 = EG(w2)$ and graph $G_3 = EG(w3)$, where $w1 \leq w2 \geq w3$ **and any edge in** G_2 also exist in G_1, any edge in G_3 also exist in G_1 and G_2 by definition. Hence the minimum energy path in G_1 cannot have higher energy than the minimum energy path in G_2 andG_3. We get above result by induction.

4 Experimental Evaluation

The performance of the proposed energy-aware routing protocol has been analyzed by using a simulator NS2.34. In this experimental study, proposed work is compared with the existing energy-aware routing algorithms like OML and SWRP. A topology is randomly populated as 1000 * 1000 m^2 grid with 1500 nodes. The source and destination nodes are selected at random and data packets are transmitted between them. The Linear Congruential Method (LCM) is used to set the initial energy for each node. The transmitting cost of a single packet is based on the Euclidean distance d ,i.e., $E(v_i) - (d^3 * 0.001)$ for every edge along the path between the source and destination.

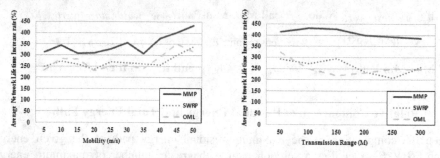

Fig. 1. Avg. network lifetime rate vs mobility   **Fig. 2.** Avg. network lifetime rate vs Trns.range

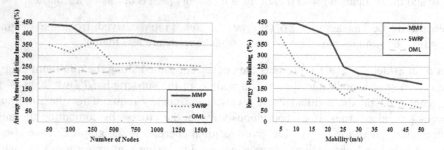

Fig. 3. Avg. network lifetime rate vs No. of nodes   **Fig. 4.** Energy remaining vs mobility

In general, the network lifetime [alive], is defined as the time taken for the first node to be drained off in the network [6]. Fig. 1-3 shows the lifetime increase rate of MMP comparing to OML and SWRP. The range of each node is assumed to be 300 m. The size of the topology area is 1000 * 1000 m² area. The numbers of nodes tested are from the range 50 – 1500. Different speeds (from 5 to 50 m/s) of level were tested. Random mobility was assumed with a pause time of 8 s and the source node initiates the data packets to be send out with enough energy. The algorithm is tested for 50 times with different topology area for each set of parameters. In most cases, the lifetime with MMP is much longer than OML and SWRP. While in some cases, they are found to be close. On an average, the lifetime is longer than that of SWRP when the number of nodes is 600 and the maximum speed is 35 m/s. This is achieved because the MMP has more choices to balance the load of the network when more nodes are in the network.

An experimental work is carried out on this MMP algorithm to evaluate the remaining energy metric in comparison with transmission range, mobility of node and varying the nodes between 100-1500. The Fig.4-6 shows the percentage of residual energy remaining by varying the mobility speed of the nodes in the network from 5-50 m/s. The percentage of energy level is higher in MMP compared to SWRP and

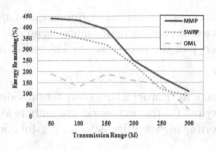 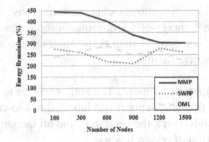

Fig. 5. Energy remaining vs trns.range   **Fig. 6.**   Energy remaining vs mobility

OML is because a threshold energy level is maintained as $E_{threshold}$ (a value where the associativity transitions are maintained between the nodes) in the MMP protocol. However, if the energy level is greater than the $E_{threshold}$ the nodes are said to be in the stale state and thus it becomes an ideal point to select the next route for transmission. This helps the MMP to sustain the energy in nodes and make the network alive.

The lifetime of the netwrok includes the time for the overhead, as this protocol requires more overhead packets than the original SWRP and OML algorithms. Fig.7-8 represents the control overhead for varying the mobility speed and the number of nodes in the network. The node mobility speed is varied from 5-50(m/s).The control overhead is calculated for 1000 and 1500 nodes. It is observed that there is no significiant changes in the control overhead as the number of nodes increases in the network. The three energy constraits discussed for the lifetime and effective data of the networks, while the effective data transfer excludes the overhead routing in networks. As the mobility speed of the node increases, the control overhead slighlty increases for low mobility speed and there is a gradual increase for high mobility.

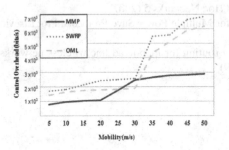 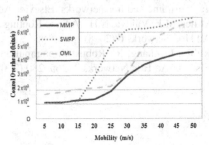

Fig. 7. Control overhead vs mobility   **Fig. 8.** Control overhead vs mobility

5   Conclusion

In this paper, a novel MMP routing protocol is designed in order to maximize the lifetime of the network. By exhibiting a simple relationship between the total energy path and the residual energy of the nodes along the path, the MMP protocol had proved to protract an increase rate in the network's lifetime. The simulation results also prove that a minimum energy level is maintained in individual nodes even after multiple concurrent data transmissions. As a future work, the performance of this MMP energy-efficient protocol motivates to use ant colony optimization technique to find an optimal path that conserves the energy of the nodes thereby enhancing the network lifetime.

Acknowledgement. The author wishes to thank the Karunya University for providing the financial support and lab facilities to carry out the research work. The authors also wish to thank the reviewers and all the supporting higher officials for successful completion of research work.

References

1. Funken, S., Laue, S., Lotker, Z., Naujoks, R.: Power assignment problems in wireless communication: covering points by disks, reaching few receivers quickly, and energy efficient travelling salesman tours. Elsevier Ad Hoc Networks 8, 1028–1035 (2011)
2. Yu, C., Lee, B., Yong Youn, H.: Energy efficient routing protocols for mobile ad hoc networks. Wireless Communications and Mobile Computing 3, 959–973 (2003)
3. Jarry, A., Leone, P., Nikoletseas, S., Rolim, J.: Optimal data gathering paths and energy-balance mechanicms in wireless networks. Elsevier Ad Hoc Networks 9, 1036–2046 (2010)
4. Mohanoor, A.B., Radhakrishnan, S., Sarangan, V.: Online energy aware routing in wireless networks. Elsevier Ad Hoc Networks 7, 918–931 (2009)
5. Li, Q., Aslam, J., Rus, D.: Online power-aware routing in wireless ad hoc networks. In: Proceedings of the 7th Annual International Conference on Mobile Computing and Networking (MobiCom), pp. 97–107 (2001)
6. Wei, X., Chen, G., Wan, Y., Mtenzi, F.: Optimized priority based energy efficient routing algorithm for mobile ad hoc networks. Elsevier Ad Hoc Networks 2 (2004)
7. Liang, W., Liu, Y.: Online disjoint path routing for network capacity maximization in energy constrained ad hoc networks. Elsevier Ad Hoc Networks 5 (2007)
8. Miller, M.J., Vaidya, N.H.: Ad hoc Routing for Multiple Power Save Protocols, Pro. Elsevier Ad Hoc Networks 6 (2008)
9. Rubin, I., Zhang, R.: Robust throughput and routing for mobile ad hoc wireless networks. Elsevier Ad Hoc Networks 7, 265–280 (2009)

Towards a New Internetworking Architecture: A New Deployment Approach for Information Centric Networks

Amine Abidi[1], Sonia Mettali Gammar[1], Farouk Kamoun[2],
Walid Dabbous[3], and Thierry Turletti[3]

[1] Cristal Laboratory, National School of Computers Sciences, Tunisia
[2] SESAME University, Tunisia
[3] INRIA Sophia Antipolis, France
amine.elabidi@cristal.rnu.tn, sonia.gammar@ensi.rnu.tn,
farouk.kamoun@sesame.com.tn, {Walid.Dabbous,Thierry.Turletti}@inria.fr

Abstract. New research efforts are trying to evolve the current Internet. With satisfying communication hardware, the intent is to switch to data oriented networks. In this new vision, data will be the heart of the architecture and protocols have to be changed to deal with this concept. Promising ideas are proposed up in order to develop clean slate design solutions. However, these propositions encounter many deployment problems. In this paper, we propose new approach based on Bloom Filter to cope with storage space problem in Data Oriented Networking Architecture DONA.

Keywords: Future Internet, Information Centric, Internetworking, Bloom Filter.

1 Introduction

Despite its tremendous success, the internet architecture is facing serious scalability and flexibility problems. In recent years, the use of the internet has changed from machine interconnection to data or service oriented communication. This new purpose has increased the number of internet users and the variety of applications supported leading to the emergence of many limitations in term of mobility, security, routing and content delivery scalability [14,3]. To overcome these problems, the research community is presenting two alternatives. One side is proposing an *evolution approach* by continuously patching the internet with overlay protocols. The other side is proposing a *revolution approach* by re-architecting the internet and giving a new design. New architecture propositions are mostly information centric. They change radically the internetworking concept from simple host to host communication to data delivery. These new approaches have revealed that many original assumptions about internetworking are no longer valid [1,3] specially the paradigm of: Naming, Forwarding and Name Resolution.

M. Chatterjee et al. (Eds.): ICDCN 2014, LNCS 8314, pp. 519–524, 2014.

The information-centric approach is explored by a number of research projects, both in Europe: PSIRP [11], 4WARD [12], PURSUIT [10] and SAIL [14] and in the US : CCN [3], DONA [4] and NDN [13]. These approaches share assumptions about reorganising the networking paradigm. But, they differ with the respect to their specific architecture [14].

Although this promising success, many problems slow down the re-architecting ambitions [3]. Splitting naming from routing and forwarding reveals new challenges. Making the *name* or the identifier related to the data drives on the researchers to use *cryptographic identifiers* to guarantee uniqueness and data security. But, these identifiers are no longer understandable by internet user and need a new search engine to find from list of key words the correspondent identifier. Also, by identifying data instead of the host, a huge storage space is needed in the network routers to save routing information about transmitted data. This kind of problem is crucial especially for DONA proposition and its deployment seems impossible due to the huge amount of storage space needed. In this paper, we propose BADONA (Bloom filter Aggregated DONA) to dial with this problem. It's an attempt to reduce used storage space by exploiting Bloom Filter structure [9]. Also, we improve DONA resolution process by adding the possibility of route selection.

The rest of this paper is organized as follows. In section 2, we present the information centric networking by discussing architectural specification. Section 3 highlights DONA deployment problems and introduces our proposition. Section 4 concludes the paper.

2   Information Centric Networking: ICN

New internetworking researches introduce information centric paradigm as the natural model for the internet architecture [3]. ICN has drawn a lot of attention from the research community, some of its challenges include: secure and persistent naming, name based routing, name resolution, network caching, replication, mobility. Any ICN approach is based especially on splitting: naming, name resolution and forwarding.

Naming: It means to attribute a unique identifier for an element. IP address was used as host name and location indicator in the same time. In data/content oriented system, the name will be attributed to some data, content or service unit. Naming mechanism can be flat, hierarchical and cryptographic.

Name Resolution Mechanism: Name resolution means trying to find any suitable location for the sought data from a given name. It's the mapping between the name and one of the data copy holder address. It's almost like name resolution in the web, when a client web browser is trying to find IP address of a known URL. Different solutions are proposed *hierarchical resolution* [4], *DHT based resolution* [14], *CHORD* [6] and *Publish/subscribe paradigm* [5,14].

Forwarding Mechanism: After name resolution is achieved, the client has located one of the hosts holding the sought data. It means that he has a valid address (locator) to contact this host. Then data delivery can be started. In data oriented mechanisms, two different ways are used: the traditional IP way [2] and content routing [14].

3   BADONA: Bloom Filter Aggregated DONA

DONA [4] is a hierarchical approach for data oriented network. It uses the route-by-name paradigm for name resolution. Its based on having *resolution handlers* (RH) hierarchically. RH is responsible for location information storing and name resolution. Each domain or administrative entity will have one logical RH but perhaps many physical incarnations. This organisation is similar to the actual DNS deployment. DONA is facing some problems disabling its deployment. One of the bothering problems is the huge storage space needed to save all location information. This giant space is making natural deployment of data oriented approaches impossible.

3.1   BADONA Presentation

We introduce BADONA to cope with the storage problem. we propose that each router will not forward any received registration. Instead, it will make a Bloom Filter from all received registrations. Then, only the Filter will be forwarded. Routers don't need to forward received filters from their children to higher level node. Each router combines these structures and forwards only the resulted filter. Such operation is possible because Bloom filter structure enables merge operation [9]. Thus, our solution will be based on a modified version of standard bloom filter [7,8]. Our approach will insert location information like hop count in the BF vector and we use counting structure [7] to enable deletion from the filter. Moreover, we rely on a clearing mechanism from [8] to reduce false positive.

3.2   BADONA Details

In our proposition, we use counting Bloom filter endowed with two vectors. The principal one is used to add data registration and to answer membership queries. The second counts the number of insertion operation for each cell. To answer membership query, it is necessary to check positions obtained by hash functions. Three cases are possible: First case: one of the cells is not used and it's set to **0**. Therefore, we can confirm that this element is not inserted in the filter. Second case: all cells are used and contain the same value. Thus, we can confirm that this element is a filter member. The found value is an approximation of the *hop count* between the router and the data provider. The real *hop count* is equal or lower than the given value. Third case: All cells are used but they contain different values. Then, we can confirm that this element is a filter member, and the lowest value is given as hop count approximation. Again, the real hop count is equal or lower than the given value.

Adding New Data Registration in the Filter: In hierarchical data oriented approach, any data provider or holder has to announce its location and the list of data units under its responsibility. This information (node address/name, data name, next hop, etc) will be sent to the nearest router. The router saves each registration in a table called registration table in addition to a Bloom Filter. To add new registration to this filter, the router hashes the new registration with every hash function. For each generated position, we check related cell. We have three possible cases: First case: If the cell is set to 0. We conclude that it's not yet used. The hop count between router and data provider will be inserted in this cell. In addition, the correspondent counter cell will be set to 1. Second case: The hop count found in the cell is equal to hop count of the new registration. Then, this cell is not modified. Only the correspondent counter cell will be increased. Third case: The found hop count is different from the new one. We will save the higher value and we increase the counter.

Processing Deletion Request: Deletion is possible in our approach because we use counting Bloom Filter. When any node announces that its no longer provider for some data units, we have to propagate this information in the network. First of all, the data provider forwards the deletion request to the nearest router. The router will delete the correspondent registration from its registration table. Then, it updates its filter and forwards the deletion request to higher level routers. Any router receiving the forwarded request will do the same actions. It checks its registration table. The entry will be deleted. Then, the filter will be checked and if the element is filter member, deletion will be processed. Finally, the request will be again forwarded. This process guarantees that the location information will be erased from all routers.

Information Forwarding: Each router will receive many data filters from its children. Every filter will be saved separately labelled by origin router. Doing so, we can later forward resolution requests to the corresponding router. To propagate registration information to higher level, the router has to merge received filters with the local one and only resulted filter will be forwarded. When the forwarded filter reaches the root, name resolution will be possible throw the whole network. Each resolution request will be handled locally as possible. In the worst case, the request reaches the root.

Processing Resolution Request: When a client is trying to contact data provider, he initiates a resolution request. This request will be processed by routers through the network. The local domain router receives the request from the client. Then, it follows these steps: First: the router checks its registration table If a valid entry for the sought data unit is found, then it responds positively to the client request. Secondly,if no entry was found, the router checks received filters. If the verification process gives a positive answer in one or many received filters, the router giving the smallest hop count will be chosen. Then, the request will be forwarded to this router. Finally, when the verification process gives a false answer in all saved filters, it means that neither the router nor its *children* has any information about the requested data unit. Then, it forwards the request to higher level router. When, the router receives forwarded requests from other routers, it processes them following the same steps. In the worst case, the request reaches the root. It's the highest router in the hierarchical organisation. Obviously, it will have location information about all manipulated data units making it able to answer any request. The positive answer will be back forwarded to the requestor. When the client gets the answer, he can initiate its communication with the data provider. It's the traditional IP layer responsibility to manage this communication. The router chooses the next hop giving the smallest hop count. This choice reduces the resolution time and gives a quick answer. This criterion can be replaced by another one to improve different network proprieties (line speed, false positive rate, activity rate, etc)

4 Conclusion

In this paper, we have proposed the use of Bloom filter to face storage problem in ICN solutions. Each data registration will be hashed and added in the Bloom vector and membership queries can be easily solved. Data registration will be represented by the correspondent hop count to improve route selection. Filter updating is also allowed spatially deletion due to the counting vector. In our solution, only filters are exchanged between routers to limit control traffic. Due to the hierarchical organisation information will be propagated up to the root and any query can be achieved. Another important advantage of BADONA is the possibility to have many copies of the same data and the ability to update deployment information without increasing data delivery latency.

In our future work, we aim to evaluate BADONA with large scale scenarios. Earlier results are promising. BADONA was effective to manage huge data amount and gives quick answers.

References

1. Calvert, K., Griffioen, J., Poutievski, L.: Separating Routing and Forwarding: A Clean Slate Network Layer Design. Broadband Communications, Network and Systems (2007)
2. Clark, D., Braden, R., Falk, A., Pingali, V.: Fara reorganizing the addressing architecture. In: ACM SIGCOMM, Workshop on Future Directions in Network Architecture (FDNA 2003), Germany (2003)
3. Jacobson, V.: If a clean slate is the solution what was the problem. Stanford clean slate seminar, USA (2006)
4. Koponen, T., Chawla, M., Chun, B.G., Ermolinskiy, A., Kim, K.H., Shenker, S.: A data-oriented (and beyond) network architecture. In: Proceedings of the 2007 Conference on Applications, Technologies, Architectures, and Protocols for Computer Communications, Japan (2007)

5. Zahemszky, A., Csaszar, A., Nikander, P., Rothenberg, C.E.: Exploring the pubsub routing/forwarding space. In: International Workshop on the Network of the Future (2009)
6. Stoica, I., Morris, R., Karger, D., Frans Kaashoek, M., Balakrishnan, H.: CHORD: A scalable peer to peer lookup protocol for internet applications. In: Proceedings of the 2001 Conference on Applications, Technologies, Architectures, and Protocols for Computer Communications, USA (2001)
7. Bonomi, F., Mitzenmacher, M., Panigraphy, R., Singh, S., Varghese, G.: Beyond bloom filters: from approximate membership checks to approximate state machines. In: Proceeding of ACM SIGCOMM, Italy (2006)
8. Donnet, B., Baynat, B., Friedman, T.: Retouched Bloom Filters: Allowing Networked applications to trade off selected false positives against false negatives. In: Proceeding of ACM CONEXT, Portugal (2006)
9. Bloom, B.: Space/time trade-offs in hash coding with allowable errors. ACM Communication (1970)
10. Fotiou, N., Nikander, P., Trossen, D., Polyzos, G.C.: Developing Information Networking Further: From PSIRP to PURSUIT. In: Tomkos, I., Bouras, C.J., Ellinas, G., Demestichas, P., Sinha, P. (eds.) Broadnets 2010. LNICST, vol. 66, pp. 1–13. Springer, Heidelberg (2012)
11. Dimitrov, V., Koptchev, V.: PSIRP project publish-subscribe internet routing paradigm: new ideas for future internet. In: The ACM International Conference Proceeding Series (ICPS), vol. 471, pp. 167–171 (2010)
12. Ahlgren, B., D'Imbrosio, M.: Second NetInf Architecture Description. Technical report, 4WARD EU FP7 Project, FP7- ICT-2007-1-216041-4WARD / D-6.2 (2010), http://www.4ward-project.eu/
13. Zhang, L., Estrin, D., Burke, J., Jacobson, V., Thornton, J.D., Smetters, D.K., Zhang, B., Tsudik, G., Claffy, K., Krioukov, D., Massey, D., Papadopoulos, C., Abdelzaher, T., Wang, L., Crowley, P., Yeh, E.: Named Data Networking (NDN) project. PARC TR-2010-3 (2010)
14. Ahlgren, B., Dannewitz, C., Imbrenda, C., Kutscher, D., Ohlman, B.: A survey of information-centric networking. IEEE Communications Magazine 50(7) (2012)

Energy-Efficient Multimedia Communication
for Cognitive Radio Networks*

Ansuman Bhattacharya[1], Koushik Sinha[2], and Bhabani P. Sinha[1]

[1] A.C.M. Unit, Indian Statistical Institute, Kolkata, India
[2] HP Labs, Bangalore, India
ansuman.bhattacharya@gmail.com, sinha_kou@yahoo.com,
bhabani@isical.ac.in

Abstract. We propose an elegant source coding technique with highly asymmetric frequencies of occurrences of different symbols. Keeping the symbol with the highest frequency of occurrence as silent during transmission, we achieve substantial savings of transmitter and receiver energies by using a hybrid *Amplitude Shift Keying (ASK) - Frequency Shift Keying (FSK)* modulation/demodulation technique. Our results show that for channels with *Additive White Gaussian Noise (AWGN)*, on an average, the transmitter side energy is reduced by about 53%, while at the receiver side there is about 17.2% savings. Due to the savings of transmitter and receiver energies and the low cost/complexity of the proposed transceiver, our proposed scheme is suitable for multi-hop communication in *Cognitive Radio Networks (CRNs)*.

Keywords: Cognitive radio network, energy-efficient communication, non-coherent detection, silent symbol communication, redundant binary number system.

1 Introduction

Cognitive Radios (CR) have been proposed in recent years to make more efficient use of the wireless spectrum on widely used frequency bands. These networks are designed to utilize the licensed spectrum when it is not used by the primary (licensed) users. Energy conservation in such a *Cognitive Radio Network (CRN)* has become an increasingly important issue due to the use of portable communication devices or remotely located sensor nodes that are energy-constrained. A lot of research work has been carried out for reducing spectrum sensing power and data transmission power in a *CRN* as given in the literature [2,4,8–10]. In *Energy based Transmissions (EbT)*, the longer the transmission duration, the more is the energy that will be consumed. However, it may be possible to reduce the energy consumption in data transmission by using some suitable source coding technique [3, 6, 12] and the concept of communication through silence [7, 11], resulting in energy savings in a *CRN*.

---

* The first author would like to thank the Council of Scientific and Industrial Research (*CSIR*) for their financial assistance.

M. Chatterjee et al. (Eds.): ICDCN 2014, LNCS 8314, pp. 525–531, 2014.
© Springer-Verlag Berlin Heidelberg 2014

1.1 Our Contribution

We propose here a new source coding technique called *Modified Redundant-radix Based Number System* ($MRBNS$), which exploits the characteristics of some forbidden bit pairs in *Redundant-radix Based Number System* ($RBNS$), introduced by Sinha et al. [3], and selectively drops out some 0's from the $RBNS$ code. Such selective removal of 0's results in a reduction of length of the encoded message compared to that in $RBNS$. Keeping the symbol 0 with the highest frequency of occurrence as silent during transmission and employing hybrid modulation scheme using FSK and ASK, we show that there is a 53% saving in energy on an average at the transmitter compared to *Binary FSK* ($BFSK$) for channels with *Additive White Gaussian Noise* ($AWGN$) using a non-coherent detection based receiver and assuming equal likelihood of all possible binary strings of a given length. Also, we save, on an average 17.2% energy at the receiver end compared to $BFSK$ as well as the $RBNS$ scheme due to the reduction of the message length. It may be noted that encoding the messages in $RBNS$ [3] did not result in any reduction in receiver energy. The savings in both transmitter and receiver energies provided by the proposed technique clearly demonstrate the usefulness of $MRBNS$ for low power CRN, particularly for multimedia signals using multi-hop communications.

2 Proposed Energy-Efficient Communication Scheme

In $MRBNS$ we use the same digit set $\{-1, 0, 1\}$ as in $RBNS$ for representing numbers using radix 2. For convenience, we denote the digit '-1' by '$\bar{1}$'. The encoding scheme of the $MRBNS$ is as follows:

1. **Reduction Rule 1 :** A run of k 1's ($k > 1$) starting from bit position i, is replaced by an equivalent representation consisting of a 1 at bit position $k + i$ and a $\bar{1}$ at bit position i, with 0's in all intermediate bit positions.
2. **Reduction Rule 2 :** Every occurrence of the bit pattern $\bar{1}1$ in a string obtained after applying reduction rule 1, is replaced by the equivalent bit pattern $0\bar{1}$.
   - **Observation 1 :** The application of the reduction rules 1 and 2 on the binary data ensures that the digit patterns $\bar{1}\bar{1}$, $1\bar{1}$ and $\bar{1}1$ do not occur in the data.
   - **Observation 2 :** After $RBNS$ coding every occurrence of $0\bar{1}$ is preceded by a 0 on its most significant bit, i.e., the bit pattern $0\bar{1}$ is found at every occurrence of $\bar{1}$.
   - **Observation 3 :** If the original data was an n-bit binary data frame, $RBNS$ encoding can result in a frame of size $n + 1$ $RBNS$ digits.
3. **Reduction Rule 3 :** Based on the observations, we thus propose to recode every occurrence of $0\bar{1}$ to only $\bar{1}$. In essence, we just drop the zero bit before every $\bar{1}$.
   - **Observation 4 :** Applying the reduction rule 3, we may encounter with the digit patterns $1\bar{1}$ and $\bar{1}\bar{1}$ in the data. But still now the digit pattern $\bar{1}1$ will not occur in the data.
   - **Observation 5 :** After reduction rule 3 the $RBNS$ data becomes less in size, i.e., if the original data was an n-bit binary data frame, after applying reduction rule 3, encoding can result in a frame of size $\leq n + 1$ $RBNS$ digits.

4. **Reduction Rule 4 :** After reduction rule 3, we recode the bit pattern $\bar{1}01$ with the bit pattern $\bar{1}1$. In other words, we just drop the '0' in between the bit pattern $\bar{1}01$, so that the bit pattern $\bar{1}01$ becomes $\bar{1}1$.

   – **Observation 6 :** The encoding and decoding processes need scanning from the least significant digit position to the most significant digit position, and these can be conveniently overlapped with a pipelined serial transmission/reception of the digits.

If we consider a binary string, say 11011101, then after applying all the above reduction rules it becomes $10\bar{1}0\bar{1}1$ ($11011101 \rightarrow 10\bar{1}100\bar{1}01 \rightarrow 100\bar{1}00\bar{1}01 \rightarrow 10\bar{1}0\bar{1}01 \rightarrow 10\bar{1}0\bar{1}1$). The following result is stated without proof.

Lemma 1. *For every binary string, there exists a unique $MRBNS$ string and vice versa.*

We now consider the following issues related to practical implementation of our proposed $MRBNS$ scheme.

Encoder and Decoder Design : We use two bits to encode each digit of the *Redundant Binary Number* (RBN). Every digit of $RBNS$ is represented by X and Y bit pair, where X is MSB and Y is LSB. Thus, the $RBNS$ digit 0 may be encoded using the bit-pair 00, while 1 and $\bar{1}$ using the bit-pairs 01 and 10 respectively as in [3]. The technique for conversion from Binary to $RBNS$ and vice-versa is already described in [3].

Encoder : For $RBNS$ to $MRBNS$ conversion, we have to drop the zero bit before every $\bar{1}$ and drop the 0 bit in between the bit pattern $\bar{1}01$. Thus, when a $\bar{1}$ is encountered at the bit position 2, i.e., ($X_2 = 1$) then digit 0 on the left of $\bar{1}$ needs to be deleted. For this, after we see that $X_2 = 1$, we take the clock pulse off from the flip-flops (FFs) at bit position 2 to n of both MSB and LSB registers. Let, C_i be the clock input to the flip-flops X_i and Y_i and C be the grand clock. We take help of another control J-K flip-flop F_1 with $J = 1$ and $K = C_2$. Initially F_1 is set to 1. When $X_2 = 0, F_1 = 1$, then C_2 should be equal to C. When $X_2 = 1, F_1 = 1$, then we need C_2 to be zero. In the next pulse, F_1 becomes 0 as J and K inputs of F_1 both are equal to 1 and so F_1 toggles to 0 and C_2 should be equal to C, so that the $\bar{1}$ digit at the second digit position will now be shifted right by one position after the clock pulse. In the next clock cycle X_2 becomes 0 (as the digit initially on left of $\bar{1}$ must not be a $\bar{1}$) and also F_1 becomes 1. Thus, the pulse C_2 to be applied to flip-flops X_2 and Y_2 is given by $C_2 = C\bar{X}_2F_1 + CX_2\bar{F}_1$. Again, $\bar{1}01$ in $RBNS$ needs to be converted to $\bar{1}1$ in $MRBNS$. When such a bit pattern is stored in the X-Y register, $X_1\bar{Y}_2Y_3 = 1$. Under this condition the X_1, Y_1 values will be shifted to right by one position (rewriting over the previous $X_2 = Y_2 = 0$ values) and there will be no movement of data from third bits of the two registers to n^{th} bits of the registers, i.e., none of the other FF outputs will be shifted right from the third bit position onwards. We effect that by taking the immediate next clock pulse off from 3rd bit position onwards to the right, but the clock pulse, will be applied to the left most two FFs of both the MSB and LSB registers. For generating the clock pulse C_i ($i \geq 3$) we similarly need another control flip-flop F_2 which is a $J-K$ flip-flop, initially set to 1, with J input always equal to 1 and K input set to C'. Thus, we get $C' = \bar{X}_1\bar{X}_2 + \bar{X}_2Y_2 + \bar{X}_2\bar{Y}_3$ and $C_i = CC'\bar{F}_2 + C\bar{C}'F_2$.

Decoder : For $MRBNS$ to $RBNS$ conversion we have to add a zero bit before every $\bar{1}$ and add a 0 in between the bit pattern $\bar{1}1$. The outputs of X_i and Y_i FFs in these shift registers will indicate the value $Q_i (i \geq 1)$ the data to the X_i and Y_i will be decoded by D_i; the D inputs of the flip-flops X_i and Y_i will be denoted by D_{X_i} and D_{y_i} respectively. Let us denote the ith digit of the number in $RBNS/MRBNS$ by Q_i, where $Q_i \in \{1, 0, \bar{1}\}$ and Q_i will be encoded by X_iY_i as (i) $Q_i = 1$ when $X_i = 0$ and $Y_i = 1$, (ii) $Q_i = 0$ when $X_i = 0$ and $Y_i = 0$ and (iii) $Q_i = \bar{1}$ when $X_i = 1$, $Y_i = 0$. The decoded data in $RBNS$ will be stored in two shift registers X and Y. Let, C_1 be a boolean variable which assumes the value 1 when $Q_1Q_2 = \bar{1}1$, i.e., $C_1 = X_1\bar{X}_2Y_2$. Thus, with $C_1 = 1$, the decoder should insert a 0 between $\bar{1}$ and 1. To achieve this, after detecting $Q_1Q_2 = \bar{1}1$, the value of Q_2 should appear at the output of fifth flip-flop FF_5 after the next clock pulse, i.e., the input line of FF_5 (i.e., D_5) should be fed from the output Q_2 when $C_1 = 1$. Also, the inputs of all FF_i $(i \geq 5)$ will receive the output values from Q_{i-3} when $C_1 = 1$, i.e., $D_i = C_1.Q_{i-3}$, $i \geq 5$. It implies that the D inputs to X_i and Y_i FFs will be given by $D_{X_i} = C_1X_{i-3}$ and $D_{Y_i} = C_1Y_{i-3}$. Further, when $C_1 = 1$, D_2 and D_4 both should be set to 0 and D_3 should get the value from Q_1, i.e., $D_3 = C_1.Q_1$. Let, C_2 be a boolean variable which assumes the value 1 when $Q_1Q_2 = \bar{1}0$, i.e., $C_2 = X_1\bar{Y}_2$. Thus, with $C_2 = 1$, the decoder will input a 0 before every $\bar{1}$. To achieve this, the value of Q_1 should appear at the output of FF_3 after the next clock pulse, i.e., D_3 should get the value of Q_1 when $C_2 = 1$. Similarly, $D_i = C_2.Q_{i-2}$, for all $i \geq 3$. Also, D_2 should be set to 0 when $C_2 = 1$. Thus, considering both these cases of $Q_1Q_2 = \bar{1}1$ and $Q_1Q_2 = \bar{1}0$, we get, $D_i = C_1Q_{i-3}+C_2Q_{i-2}+\bar{C}_1\bar{C}_2Q_{i-1} = C_1Q_{i-3} + C_2Q_{i-2} + \bar{X}_1Q_{i-1}, \forall i \geq 5$, $D_4 = C_2Q_2 + \bar{C}_1\bar{C}_2Q_3 = C_2Q_2 + \bar{X}_1Q_3$, $D_3 = C_1Q_1 + C_2Q_1 + \bar{C}_1\bar{C}_2Q_2 = C_1Q_1 + C_2Q_1 + \bar{X}_1Q_2$, $D_2 = \bar{C}_1\bar{C}_2Q_1 = \bar{X}_1Q_1$ and $D_1 =$ new input from $RBNS$ stream.

Transceiver Design: We use a hybrid modulation scheme involving FSK and ASK as in [3, 12] with a non-coherent detection based receiver.

Synchronization between the Receiver and The Transmitter : For proper synchronization between the sender and the receiver in presence of silent symbols, we can adopt one of the three possible schemes for maintaining synchronization as described for $RBNSiZeComm$ [3].

Spectrum Sensing and Collision Avoidance Issues : To avoid erroneous interpretation of the absence of any signal on air due to the silent 0's we assume that the channel sensing, allocation and deallocation algorithms provided by the protocol proposed by Bhattacharya et.al. [13] based on *Sample Division Multiplexing (SDM)* are used by the CRN, so as to enable us to retain the channel even when silent 0's are received, until a specific deallocation message is transmitted by the sender.

3   Performance Analysis

From [3] it is known that after *reduction rule* 2 for n number of bits the total number of 1's and $\bar{1}$'s in the $RBNS$ coded message is $(n+2).2^{n-2}$ and the total number of bits for all possible combinations is approximately $n.2^n$. Now in the $RBNS$ code the number of $\bar{1}$ is $n.2^{n-3}$ and the number of $\bar{1}01$ is $3.(n-3).2^{n-6}$. Using *reduction rules* 3 and

4 for every $\bar{1}$ and $\bar{1}01$, we compute the total number of bits in $MRBNS$ as $(53n + 9).2^{n-6}$. Hence, the fraction of energy savings obtained at transmitter end by applying all *reduction rules* is given by, $\eta_{te} = 1 - \left(\frac{16(n+2)}{53n+9} \cdot \frac{53n+9}{64n} \right)$. Typically, for $n = 1024$, η_{te} is nearly equal to 75% (approximately). Simultaneously, savings at the receiver end due to reduction of bits is given by, $\eta_{re} = 1 - \frac{53n+9}{64n}$. Typically, for $n = 1024$, η_{re} is nearly equal to 17.2%. Thus, it is theoretically possible to have an energy saving of 75% at the transmitter for noiseless channels, while simultaneously generating a savings of 17.2% at the receiver, when compared to EbT schemes.

Table 1. SNR for $MRBNS$ and $BFSK$

SNR for frame size 1024 bits		
$\rho = \frac{FER}{n}$	MRBNS	BFSK
0.000460224	14.0	11.4555
0.000110742	15.0	12.2609
0.000014599	16.0	13.1979
0.000001075	17.0	14.1664
0.00000004	18.0	15.1423

Table 2. Comparison of energy savings with various schemes

Communication scheme	Energy savings at transmitter (%)	Energy savings at receiver (%)
MRBNS	53%	17.2%
RBNSiZeComm	53%	0%
RZE	35.2%	12.5%
TSS	20%	36.9%

Instead of the conventional bit-error rate (BER), we consider a frame error rate (FER) as used in [3] for both the original binary frame and the $MRBNS$ frame communicated through the non-coherent hybrid $FSK - ASK$ modulation scheme. Let FCR be the probability of receiving a frame correctly (FCR may be read as *frame-correct rate*) and P_0, P_1 and $P_{\bar{1}}$ be the probabilities of occurrences of the symbols 0, 1 and $\bar{1}$ respectively in the transmitted $MRBNS$ message. Proceeding in the same manner as in [3], we get $FCR = \alpha^{n.P_0} . \beta^{n.P_1} . \delta^{n.P_{\bar{1}}}$, where n is the number of binary bits transmitted and α, β and δ are the probabilities of correctly receiving a 0, 1 and $\bar{1}$, respectively [3]. From symmetry, $\beta = \delta$. Assuming that all possible binary strings with n bits are equally likely to appear in the message, we get from above $P_0 = 0.7$ and $P_1 + P_{\bar{1}} = 0.3$. Hence, $FCR = \alpha^{0.7n} . \beta^{0.3n}$. The frame error rate (FER) for the RBNS message is, hence, given by $FER_{MRBNS} = 1 - FCR$. Let the original binary message of n bits be transmitted using non-coherent FSK with a BER of ρ. The SNR values for $BFSK$ modulation are determined from the relation, $\rho = \frac{e^{\frac{\gamma}{2}}}{2}$, where SNR in $dB \doteq 10\log_{10}\gamma$. The probability that the whole frame will be received correctly is given by $(1 - \rho)^n$. Thus, the FER for $BFSK$ will be given by $FER_{BFSK} = 1 - (1 - \rho)^n \approx n\rho$, since ρ is usually very small. Required SNR values for our proposed scheme and $BFSK$ are summarized in Table 1 where we see that for the same FER, the required SNR values with the proposed $MRBNS$ is on an average 2.76dB higher than that with $BFSK$. However, due to 30% non-zero symbols in the $MRBNS$, the average transmitter power for our scheme will be reduced from the peak power by $10\log_{10}(0.3)$dB $= 5.23$dB. All taken together, for a given $\rho = FER/n$ in the range 10^{-4} to 10^{-8}, $MRBNS$ needs approximately 2.47dB less average power than $BFSK$. Let P_b and P_M be the required average transmitter power for $BFSK$ and our proposed $MRBNS$ scheme. Noting that $10^{-\frac{2.47}{10}} = 0.57$, we have $\frac{P_M}{P_b} = 0.57$. Let T_b, T_M be the transmission times for $BFSK$ and $MRBNS$, respectively. Since message length in $MRBNS$ is reduced from that in $RBNS$ by 0.83, $\frac{T_M}{T_b} = 0.83$. Let E_b,

E_M be the transmitter energy requirements for $BFSK$ and $MRBNS$, respectively. Hence, $\frac{E_M}{E_b} = \frac{P_M}{P_b} \cdot \frac{T_M}{T_b} = 0.57 \cdot 0.83 = 0.473$, which corresponds to 53% savings in transmitter energy. Hence, we have the following results.

Theorem 1. *Assuming an AWGN channel, for equal likelihood of all possible binary strings of a given length, $MRBNS$ saves approximately 53% transmitter energy and 17.2% receiver energy as compared to $BFSK$.*

Table 2 shows the energy savings with different schemes compared to $BFSK$. We see that $MRBNS$ outperforms the TSS and RZE techniques in saving transmitter energy. Also, while the receiver energy savings by $MRBNS$ is less than that in the TSS scheme, it performs significantly better than TSS in saving transmitter energy.

4   Conclusions

We have presented an energy-efficient communication scheme based on encoding the source data in $MRBNS$, coupled with the use of silent periods during 0's in the encoded message. Our results show that for $AWGN$ channels, compared to the non-coherent transceivers using $BFSK$, the transmitter energy is reduced by about 53% on an average with equal likelihood of all possible binary strings and the receiver energy is also reduced by 17.2% on an average. This makes our proposed protocol very suitable for multimedia signals using multi-hop communication in CRNs.

References

1. Sinha, K.: An Energy Efficient Communication Scheme with Potential Application to Consumer and Personal Wireless Networks. In: 6th IEEE Consumer Communications and Networking Conference, CCNC 2009, January 10-13, pp. 1–5 (2009), doi:10.1109/CCNC.2009.4784888
2. Li, L., Zhou, X., Xu, H., Li, G.Y., Wang, D., Soong, A.: Energy-Efficient Transmission in Cognitive Radio Networks. In: 2010 7th IEEE Consumer Communications and Networking Conference (CCNC), January 9-12, pp. 1–5 (2010), doi:10.1109/CCNC.2010.5421658
3. Sinha, K., Sinha, B.P., Datta, D.: An Energy-Efficient Communication Scheme for Wireless Networks: A Redundant Radix-Based Approach. IEEE Transactions on Wireless Communications 10(2), 550–559 (2011), doi:10.1109/TWC.2010.120610.100244
4. Wu, Y., Tsang, D.H.K.: Energy-Efficient Spectrum Sensing and Transmission for Cognitive Radio System. IEEE Communications Letters 15(5), 545–547 (2011), doi:10.1109/LCOMM.2011.032811.110102
5. Miao, G., Himayat, N., Li, Y.: Energy-Efficient Transmission in Frequency-Selective Channels. In: Global Telecommunications Conference, IEEE GLOBECOM 2008, November 30-December 4, pp. 1–5. IEEE (2008), doi:10.1109/GLOCOM.2008.ECP.897
6. Sinha, K., Sinha, B.P.: An Energy Efficient Communication Scheme for Distributed Computing Applications in Wireless Sensor Networks. In: Parashar, M., Aggarwal, S.K. (eds.) ICDCIT 2008. LNCS, vol. 5375, pp. 139–144. Springer, Heidelberg (2008)
7. Zhu, Y., Sivakumar, R.: Challenges: Communication through Silence in Wireless Sensor Networks. In: MobiCom 2005, Cologne, Germany, August 28-September 2 (2005)

8. Zhou, Z., Zhou, S., Cui, S., Cui, J.-H.: Energy-Efficient Cooperative Communication in a Clustered Wireless Sensor Network. IEEE Transactions on Vehicular Technology 57(6), 3618–3628 (2008), doi:10.1109/TVT.2008.918730

9. Gao, S., Qian, L., Vaman, D.: Distributed energy efficient spectrum access in cognitive radio wireless ad hoc networks. IEEE Transactions on Wireless Communications 8(10), 5202–5213 (2009), doi:10.1109/TWC.2009.081323.

10. Ye, W., Heidemann, J., Estrin, D.: An energy-efficient MAC protocol for wireless sensor networks. Proc. IEEE Infocom, 1567–1576 (2002)

11. Chen, Y.P., Wang, D., Zhang, J.: Variable-base tacit communication: a new energy efficient communication scheme for sensor networks. In: Proc. Intl. Conf. Integrated Internet Ad Hoc Sensor Netw. (2006)

12. Ghosh, R.N., Sinha, K., Sinha, B.P., Datta, D.: TSS: An energy efficient communication scheme for low power wireless networks. In: Proceedings of 27th IEEE International Performance Computing and Communications Conference (IPCCC), USA, pp. 85–92 (December 2008)

13. Bhattacharya, A., Ghosh, R., Sinha, K., Sinha, B.P.: Multimedia communication in cognitive radio networks based on sample division multiplexing. In: 2011 Third International Conference on Communication Systems and Networks (COMSNETS), January 4-8, pp. 1–8 (2011)

Stabilizing Dining with Failure Locality 1

Hyun Chul Chung[1,*], Srikanth Sastry[2,**], and Jennifer L. Welch[1,*]

[1] Texas A&M University, Department of Computer Science & Engineering
{h0c8412,welch}@cse.tamu.edu
[2] CSAIL, MIT
sastry@csail.mit.edu

Abstract. The dining philosophers problem, or simply dining, is a fundamental distributed resource allocation problem. We propose two algorithms for solving stabilizing dining with failure locality 1 in asynchronous shared-memory systems with regular registers. Since this problem cannot be solved in pure asynchrony, we augment the shared-memory system with failure detectors. Specifically, we introduce the local anonymous eventually perfect failure detector $?\Diamond\mathcal{P}^1$, and show that this failure detector is sufficient to solve the problem at hand.

1 Introduction

The *dining philosophers problem* [1,2], or simply *dining*, is a fundamental distributed resource allocation problem, in which each process repeatedly needs simultaneous exclusive access to a set of shared resources in order to enter a special part of its code, called the *critical section*. The sharing pattern is described by an arbitrary "conflict" graph, each edge of which corresponds to a resource shared by the two processes corresponding to the endpoints of the edge.

In large scale and long-lived systems, the likelihood of some process failing at some point is high, thus sparking interest in crash fault-tolerant dining. The ideal case would be for the algorithm to isolate each crashed process such that it does not impact any other correct processes in the system. If the ideal case cannot be achieved, restricting the impact of the crash failure to a local neighborhood would still be desirable. *Failure locality* [3,4] is a metric that realizes this concept; it is the maximum distance in the conflict graph between a crashed process and any other process that is blocked from entering its critical section.

In addition to crash failures, we take into account the presence of transient failures. Transient failures correspond to unexpected corruptions to the system state; the system can be in an arbitrary state after a transient failure occurs. Algorithms tolerant of transient failures are also known as *stabilizing* algorithms.

---

* The work of Hyun Chul Chung and Jennifer L. Welch was supported in part by NSF grant 0964696.
** The work of Srikanth Sastry was supported in part by NSF Award Numbers CCF-0726514, CCF-0937274, and CNS-1035199, and AFOSR Award Number FA9550-08-1-0159. His work was also partially supported by Center for Science of Information (CSoI), an NSF Science and Technology Center, under grant agreement CCF-0939370.

M. Chatterjee et al. (Eds.): ICDCN 2014, LNCS 8314, pp. 532–537, 2014.
© Springer-Verlag Berlin Heidelberg 2014

In this paper, we consider stabilizing failure-locality-1 dining where we require that (1) eventually, no two neighbors in the conflict graph enter their corresponding critical sections simultaneously, and (2) each correct process that is trying to enter its critical section eventually does so if it is at least two hops away from any other crashed process in the conflict graph.

We consider an asynchronous shared-memory system where processes communicate through read/write operations on shared *regular* registers. Regularity states that each read operation returns the value of some overlapping write operation or of the latest preceding write operation.

Choy and Singh [4] showed that any asynchronous algorithm that solves dining must have failure locality at least 2.[1] This implies that failure-locality-1 dining cannot be solved in pure asynchrony. To circumvent this lower bound, we augment the system with failure detectors [5], system services that provide information about process crashes that need not always be correct. Specifically, we introduce the local anonymous eventually perfect failure detector $?\Diamond\mathcal{P}^1$ and show that this failure detector is sufficient to solve the problem at hand.

We propose two algorithms that solve stabilizing failure-locality-1 dining. The first algorithm is inspired by the Hierarchical Resource Allocation (HRA) algorithm [6] and the second algorithm is inspired by the Asynchronous Doorway (ADW) algorithm [3]. Both algorithms utilize stabilizing mutual exclusion subroutines which can be implemented using regular registers (e.g., Dijkstra's stabilizing token circulation algorithm using regular registers [7]). By presenting two algorithms, we observe that there exists multiple methods to solve stabilizing failure-locality-1 dining. This follows the case of solving the original dining philosophers problem: the HRA, ADW, and Hygienic algorithm presented in [2], [3], and [8], respectively, constitute the three major methodologies in solving the original dining philosophers problem.[2]

Dining algorithms that consider both crash fault tolerance and stabilization are presented in [10,11,12]. The dining algorithms in [10,11] achieve failure locality 2. A wait-free (failure-locality-0) dining algorithm is presented in [12] which utilizes the $\Diamond\mathcal{P}$ failure detector.[3] We fill in the gap between wait-freedom and failure-locality-2 by presenting two failure-locality-1 stabilizing dining algorithms that utilize $?\Diamond\mathcal{P}^1$. The $?\Diamond\mathcal{P}^1$ failure detector can be implemented using $\Diamond\mathcal{P}$ in asynchronous systems. This means that $?\Diamond\mathcal{P}^1$ is at most as powerful as $\Diamond\mathcal{P}$.

Our Contribution: We present the problem specification for stabilizing failure-locality-1 dining. This specification is the first to consider both failure locality 1 and stabilization. We present the first two stabilizing failure-locality-1 dining

---

[1] Although the failure-locality-2 lower bound in [4] is proved for asynchronous message-passing systems, it also applies to asynchronous shared-memory systems.

[2] Notice that we did not include the Hygienic approach into our stabilizing failure-locality-1 dining agenda. The Hygienic-based crash fault-tolerant dining algorithms that we are aware of (e.g., [9]) use unbounded memory which is problematic for stabilizing algorithms.

[3] $\Diamond\mathcal{P}$ satisfies the following: eventually, (1) every crashed process is suspected by every correct process, and (2) no correct process is suspected by any correct process.

algorithms in asynchronous shared-memory systems using failure detectors along with regular registers. The proposed algorithms are modular in the sense that they utilize stabilizing mutual exclusion subroutines.

2   System Model and Problem Definition

We consider a system that contains a set Π of n (dining) processes, where each process is a state machine. Each process has a unique incorruptible ID and is known to all the processes in the system. For convenience, we assume that the IDs form the set $\{0, \ldots, n-1\}$; we refer to a process and its ID interchangeably. There is an undirected graph G with vertex set Π, called the *(dining) conflict graph*. If $\{i, j\}$ is an edge of G, then we say that i and j are *neighbors*.

The *state* of a process i is modeled with a set of local variables. Each process i has a local variable $diningState_i$ through which it communicates with the user of the dining philosophers algorithm. The user sets $diningState_i$ to "hungry" to indicate that it needs exclusive access to the set of resources for i. Sometime later, the process should set $diningState_i$ to "eating", which is observed by the user. While $diningState_i$ is "eating", the user accesses its critical section. When the user is through eating, it sets $diningState_i$ to "exiting" to tell i that it can do some cleaning up, after which i should set $diningState_i$ to "thinking". This sequence of updates to $diningState_i$ can then repeat cyclically.

Process i has another local variable $?\Diamond\mathcal{P}_i^1$ through which it communicates with the failure detector $?\Diamond\mathcal{P}^1$. This variable is set to true or false at appropriate times by the failure detector and is read (but never set) by process i. The behavior of $?\Diamond\mathcal{P}^1$ is that after some time, $?\Diamond\mathcal{P}_i^1$ is always false if i has no crashed neighbors and is always true if i has at least one crashed neighbor.

The processes have access to a set of shared single-writer single-reader (SWSR) registers that satisfy the consistency condition of regularity, through which they can communicate. Reads and writes on such registers are not instantaneous. Each operation is invoked at some time and provides a response later. *Regularity* means that each read returns the value of some overlapping write or of the latest preceding write. If there is no preceding write, then any value can be returned. When a process invokes an operation on a shared register, it blocks until receiving the response. For each process, invocations and responses occur in pairs (invocation first, response second) unless the process crashes after an invocation but before receiving a response. This implies that each operation response must be preceded by an invocation for that operation.[4]

Certain subsets of processes synchronize among themselves using mutual exclusion modules (i.e., subroutines). For any mutual exclusion module X, the participants in X are all neighbors of each other in the dining conflict graph.

---

[4] For each process i, invocations/responses occurring in pairs prevent i from being in a state in which, after a transient fault occurs, i is waiting for a response without having a preceding invocation to a register. This is a common assumption for stabilizing algorithms that involve read/write operations on shared registers. (e.g., [7,13,14])

For each mutual exclusion module X in which it participates, (dining) process i has a local variable $X.mutex_i$. Process i, at an appropriate time, sets $X.mutex_i$ to "trying" when it needs access to the corresponding critical section. Subsequently, the mutual exclusion module should set $X.mutex_i$ to "critical". When i no longer needs the critical section for X, i sets $X.mutex_i$ to "exiting", and at some later point the module X should set the variable to "remainder". This sequence of updates to $X.mutex_i$ can then repeat cyclically. Note that such stabilizing mutual exclusion algorithms exist considering asynchronous shared-memory systems with regular registers (e.g. a variation of Dijkstra's stabilizing token circulation algorithm using regular registers in [7]). This implies that, by assuming that processes have access to mutual exclusion modules, we are not assuming anything more than asynchronous shared-memory systems with regular registers.

Correctness Condition: Our task is to design a distributed algorithm for the (dining) processes in Π such that every execution has a suffix in which the following four properties hold:

- Well-formedness: For all $i \in \Pi$, $diningState_i$ is set to "eating" only if the current value is "hungry", and $diningState_i$ is set to "thinking" only if the current value is "exiting".
- Finite Exiting: For each correct $i \in \Pi$, $diningState_i$ is not forever "exiting".
- Exclusion: If i and j are both correct and are neighbors, then $diningState_i$ and $diningState_j$ are not both equal to "eating" in any system state.
- FL-1 Liveness: If $i \in \Pi$ is correct and all its neighbors are correct, then if $diningState_i$ is "hungry" in some state, there is a later system state in which $diningState_i$ is "eating".

Here is an explanation for how our pseudocode maps to this model of executions. Pseudocode is presented as a set of guarded commands.[5] If a guard is continuously true, then eventually the corresponding command is executed. Each command includes at most one shared register operation. If a command includes a shared register operation, then this is actually two instantaneous steps: the first step ends with the invocation of the operation, and the second step begins with the response of the operation. If a command does not include a shared register operation, then it corresponds to a single instantaneous step.

For the complete system model and problem specification, see [15].

3   HRA-Based Stabilizing Dining

In this section, we use multiple mutual exclusion modules described in Section 2 to construct a stabilizing failure-locality-1 dining algorithm. The algorithm is inspired by the hierarchical resource allocation (HRA) algorithm from [6]. The complete algorithm description and the correctness proof can be found in [15].

---

[5] Guarded commands have the following format: $\{guard\} \rightarrow command$. For each guarded command of process i, the guard is a predicate on i's state and the command is a block of code; the command is executed only if the guard is true.

Algorithm 1. HRA-based stabilizing FL-1 dining algorithm; code for process i

⟨ **Variables** ⟩

1: local variable $diningState_i \in \{thinking, hungry, eating, exiting\}$;
2: local variable $?\Diamond \mathcal{P}_i^1 \in \{T, F\}$;
3: $\forall R_x \in C_i$: local variable $M_x.mutex_i \in \{remainder, trying, critical, exiting\}$;

⟨ **Program Actions** ⟩

4: $\{(diningState_i = thinking) \lor (diningState_i = exiting) \lor$ Action $D.1$
   $(badSuffix(\mathcal{C}_i) \lor ((diningState_i \neq eating) \land (?\Diamond \mathcal{P}_i^1)))\} \rightarrow$
5: **for all** $R_x \in C_i$ **do**
6:   **if** $M_x.mutex_i = critical$ **then**
7:     $M_x.mutex_i \leftarrow exiting$;
8: **if** $\neg ?\Diamond \mathcal{P}_i^1$ **then**
9:   $diningState_i \leftarrow thinking$;

10: $\{(diningState_i = hungry) \land (csPrefix(\mathcal{C}_i) \neq \mathcal{C}_i) \land$ Action $D.2$
    $(\neg ?\Diamond \mathcal{P}_i^1) \land (\neg badSuffix(\mathcal{C}_i))\} \rightarrow$
11: $R_x \leftarrow currentMutex(\mathcal{C}_i)$;
12: **if** $M_x.mutex_i = remainder$ **then**
13:   $M_x.mutex_i \leftarrow trying$;

14: $\{(diningState_i = hungry) \land (csPrefix(\mathcal{C}_i) = \mathcal{C}_i))\} \rightarrow$ Action $D.3$
15: $diningState_i \leftarrow eating$;

Let $G = (\Pi, E)$ be the conflict graph. Let $\mathcal{R}$ be the set of maximal cliques in G. Let $|\mathcal{R}|$ be k. For convenience, let $\mathcal{R} = \{R_x | x \in \mathbb{N}^+ \land 0 < x \leq k\}$. We assume a total order on the cliques such that R_x is ordered before R_y iff $x < y$. For each clique R_x, let Π_x denote the set of processes (diners) in R_x. Each clique $R_x \in \mathcal{R}$ represents a subset of resources to be accessed in isolation by diners in Π_x. Consequently, for each clique R_x, we associate a stabilizing mutual exclusion module M_x, and the participants in M_x constitute the set Π_x.

For each diner i, let C_i denote the set of all cliques R_x such that $i \in \Pi_x$; that is, diner i contends for exclusive access to all the resources associated with cliques in C_i. Each diner i has access to variable $M_x.mutex_i$, for each $R_x \in C_i$.

The pseudocode of the actions is given in Algorithm 1. The pseudocode is self-explanatory using the definitions of the following three functions.

Three Functions: For each diner i, for each $R_x \in C_i$, we introduce three functions $csPrefix$, $currentMutex$, and $badSuffix$ which are functions of a process's state and are used in specifying the guards for the three actions.

Sequence $\mathcal{C}_i$. Let $\mathcal{C}_i$ denote the sequence over all the cliques from C_i such that a clique R_x precedes a clique R_y in $\mathcal{C}_i$ iff $x < y$.

Functions $csPrefix$ and $currentMutex$. The function $csPrefix(\mathcal{C}_i)$ returns the longest prefix of $\mathcal{C}_i$ such that, for each clique R_x in $csPrefix(\mathcal{C}_i)$, $M_x.mutex_i = critical$ (i is in the critical section of M_x). The function $currentMutex(\mathcal{C}_i)$ returns the first clique following $csPrefix(\mathcal{C}_i)$ in $\mathcal{C}_i$, if such a resource exists; otherwise, it returns $\bot$.

Function $badSuffix$. The boolean function $badSuffix(\mathcal{C}_i)$ is T if and only if there exists some clique R_x in the suffix of $\mathcal{C}_i$ following $currentMutex(\mathcal{C}_i)$ such that $(M_x.mutex_i = trying) \lor (M_x.mutex_i = critical)$ (i is either trying or in the critical section of M_x).

4 ADW-Based Stabilizing Dining

We have also designed a stabilizing failure-locality-1 dining algorithm that is inspired by the asynchronous doorway (ADW) algorithm [3]. In the original ADW algorithm, each process shares a single token called a *fork* with each of its neighbors. For a hungry process i to eat, it must first enter the *doorway* by obtaining permission from all of its neighbors through a ping-ack protocol. Only after i enters the doorway, it requests for the missing forks. Also, while i is inside the doorway, i does not give its neighbors permissions to enter the doorway. The hungry process i can start to eat if it is both inside the doorway and holds all forks shared between itself and its neighbors. After eating, i satisfies all deferred requests and exits the doorway. In our algorithm, we simulate the ping-ack protocol using two mutual exclusion modules per neighboring processes and the fork activities using one mutual exclusion module and two SWSR regular registers per neighboring processes. The complete algorithm and its correctness proof can be found in [15].

References

1. Dijkstra, E.W.: Hierarchical ordering of sequential processes. Acta Informatica 1(2), 115–138 (1971)
2. Lynch, N.A.: Fast allocation of nearby resources in a distributed system. In: Proc. of 12th ACM Symposium on Theory of Computing, pp. 70–81 (1980)
3. Choy, M., Singh, A.K.: Efficient fault-tolerant algorithms for distributed resource allocation. ACM Toplas 17(3), 535–559 (1995)
4. Choy, M., Singh, A.K.: Localizing failures in distributed synchronization. IEEE Trans. Parall. Distrib. Syst. 7(7), 705–716 (1996)
5. Chandra, T.D., Toueg, S.: Unreliable failure detectors for reliable distributed systems. Journal of the ACM 43(2), 225–267 (1996)
6. Lynch, N.A.: Upper bounds for static resource allocation in a distributed system. Journal of Computer and System Sciences 23(2), 254–278 (1981)
7. Dolev, S., Herman, T.: Dijkstra's self-stabilizing algorithm in unsupportive environments. In: Datta, A.K., Herman, T. (eds.) WSS 2001. LNCS, vol. 2194, pp. 67–81. Springer, Heidelberg (2001)
8. Chandy, K.M., Misra, J.: The drinking philosophers problem. ACM Toplas 6(4), 632–646 (1984)
9. Pike, S.M., Song, Y., Sastry, S.: Wait-free dining under eventual weak exclusion. In: Proc. of 9th ICDCN, pp. 135–146 (2008)
10. Nesterenko, M., Arora, A.: Tolerance to unbounded byzantine faults. In: Proc. of 21st IEEE SRDS, pp. 22–29 (2002)
11. Nesterenko, M., Arora, A.: Dining philosophers that tolerate malicious crashes. In: Proc. of 22nd IEEE ICDCS, pp. 172–179 (2002)
12. Sastry, S., Welch, J.L., Widder, J.: Wait-free stabilizing dining using regular registers. In: Proc. of 16th OPODIS, pp. 284–299 (2012)
13. Hoepman, J.H., Papatriantafilou, M., Tsigas, P.: Self-stabilization of wait-free shared memory objects. J. Parall. & Distribut. Comput. 62(5), 818–842 (2002)
14. Johnen, C., Higham, L.: Fault-tolerant implementations of regular registers by safe registers with applications to networks. In: Garg, V., Wattenhofer, R., Kothapalli, K. (eds.) ICDCN 2009. LNCS, vol. 5408, pp. 337–348. Springer, Heidelberg (2008)
15. Chung, H.C., Sastry, S., Welch, J.L.: Stabilizing dining with failure locality 1. Dept. of Comput. Sci. & Eng., Texas A&M Univ. Technical Report 2013-10-1 (2013)

Machine Learning in a Policy Driven Grid Environment

Kumar Dheenadayalan, Maulik Shah, Abhishek Badjatya,
and Biswadeep Chatterjee

Qualcomm India Private Limited
Bangalore, India
{kumard,mauliks,abadjaty,bchatter}@qti.qualcomm.com

Abstract. Policy driven Grid Computing environment is widely used in professional organisation and educational institutions when complex tasks need to be performed. Policies are designed so that the performance of the system is optimal and throughput of the Grid setup is maximum and also cater to the needs of all the users who are consumers of the Grid environment. Memory is one of the key resourcing parameter and policies involving the memory usage of a job are designed so that memory starvation is prevented. Machine Learning algorithms which finds its applications in diverse fields are used to predict the memory requirements of a job which in turn leads to better utilization of the Grid infrastructure. Two different datasets are considered in this paper from diverse fields and the memory requirements were predicted. Promising results were obtained from the proposed algorithm and this can be used in any field for identifying the memory requirement of jobs at a project/user level.

Keywords: grid computing, policy driven scheduling, grid workload format, machine learning, k-nearest neighbour, neural networks.

1 Introduction

Grid computing environment can consist of hundreds of institutions and thousands of individual investigators who collectively use tens and thousands of computers. CPU time, Memory, Storage, Operating System, hardwares such as printer, DVD writer or microscopes for scientific applications, application/software and their associated licenses act as resources in Grid environment [1]. Memory being one of the key components for execution of any job has to be requested appropriately and should be utilized efficiently for improving the compute efficiency. If the memory requested are not utilized effectively, it might lead to underutilization the allocated memory slot which in turn will reduce the overall utilization. Under provisioning might lead to forceful exit of jobs which as a policy is usually in place for all large clusters to prevent huge memory excursions. Large Grid setups have a policy driven environment where policies are implemented so that each project and its users get a fair share of available resources.

M. Chatterjee et al. (Eds.): ICDCN 2014, LNCS 8314, pp. 538–543, 2014.

1.1 Fairshare Policy

Fairshare scheduling addresses the issue of sharing resources by assigning shares to users. This type of scheduling dynamically assigns priorities to users based on current and historical CPU load information. Fairshare is typically implemented at either the host level or queue level. The total available CPU time is divided by the total number of shares configured and users are given the CPU time corresponding to the number of shares they are eligible for. Queue level fairshare policies are defined on individual queues rather than at a host level that apply to all queues. Policies related to the memory are also defined at the host and the queue level. Host level memory policy relates to limiting maximum memory utilized by each job and the number of jobs that can execute on a each host [2]. Queue level policies are used to impose restriction on the memory, data and stack space that can be used by jobs.

In the next section we discuss the minimal literature available followed by Section 3 which talks about the proposed model. The discussion about the results and conclusion is presented in Section 4.

2 Literature Survey

Prediction in a distributed environment has been an area of interest for a long time [3, 4, 5]. But majority of the work focuses on load prediction in a distributed environment. It should be noted that no work has been done in predicting other critical resources like memory, specially in a Grid computing environment. Hence there is a need for a major focus on developing prediction models for various resources. Gang Simulator [6] is one of a kind simulator which has a unique ability to simulate the Grid infrastructure from a policy perspective. This is achieved by defining enforcement points at various levels which helps define and enforce policies.

Oracle Grid Engine formerly the Sun Grid Engine [7] and IBM Platform Load Sharing Facility (LSF) [8] are popular distributed resource management system that manages the workloads on available compute resources. Policies can be defined for high level policy administration which helps in meeting enterprise goals. Policy management automatically controls the use of shared resources helping to achieve high compute efficiency. Since workload manager is not the actual scheduler in the underlying Operating System, appropriate resources have to be explicitly specified along with the job that is submitted.

The importance of predicting the memory of jobs submitted to a Grid scheduler becomes more clear in Table 1. Jobs belonging to various projects in the Electronic Design and Automation (EDA) industry managed by LSF scheduler with memory requirement of jobs specified by users were analysed. It was seen that 50% jobs had wasted 90% of requested memory. If the job is terminated due to improper memory request, then apart from other compute resources, licenses associated with tools/softwares are also consumed. There is also the cost of energy associated with a failure of the job which fails the efforts of deploying green computing strategies [9] in large distributed environments.

Table 1. Memory Wastage Distribution

Percentage of Memory wasted	Percentage of Jobs		
	$x \leq 8$ GB	8 GB $< x \leq 32$ GB	$x > 32$ GB
1% - 50%	12%	10%	5%
50% - 75%	5%	2%	2%
75% - 90%	7%	2%	2%
90% - 99%	36%	12%	5%

3   Prediction Model

Two different types of datasets are considered in analysing the success of a prediction model in Grid environment. One is from the EDA industry and the other from Advanced School for Computing and Imaging whose dataset following the Grid Workload Format (GWF) [10] is available online [11]. Both datasets consists of close to 1 million jobs and have different types of jobs performing tasks which are unique to their field. The EDA dataset consists of data obtained from LSF scheduler and all the job related information is stored in a database which is used for analysis.

3.1   Feature Selection and Data Sampling

Major goal of any classification algorithm is to approximate the underlying function between the input and the output. With this as the broader task, it is important to retain only those features which will contribute to the approximator model and eliminate all the input features with little effect on the output [12]. Some of the key features [13] which distinctly identifies all the jobs and characterises it are shown in Table 2.

Table 2. Selected Features

ID	Dataset	Features
1		UserID .
2		GroupID indicating the user group
3		ExecutableID (name of the executable)
4	EDA + DAS-2	Queue similarity index
5		ReqNProcs/NProcs (processors requested/allocated)
6		OrigSiteID is the site where the job was submitted
7		JobStructure i.e. unitary or a composite job
8		JobStructureParams
9		Block of the chip which is being tested
10		EDA tool/application requested
11	EDA	Job Type
12		Operating System requested

Though more useful features are available in the DAS-2 dataset, the values are not provided which makes those features useless for the current analysis. In the results section we show the difference in the accuracy of prediction due unavailability of these extra features. When more relevant information is given about a job, it becomes easier for the prediction model to learn the data. It can also be safely presumed that if all the parameters in the DAS-2 were provided, then there can be significant improvement in the prediction accuracy.

We use Disproportionate Stratified Sampling technique with each strata chosen based on the data distribution. The four unique stratum for DAS-2 dataset are the memory categories of 0 - 1 GB, 1 - 2 GB, 2 - 3 GB and 3 - max_memory GB. For EDA dataset, 0 - 8 GB, 8 - 32 GB and 32 - max_memory GB are the three ranges of memory created which will be trained at the first stage and exponential powers of 2 in the second stage.

3.2 Training

Training phase involves processing the sampled data. The dataset provided in GWF format for DAS-2 dataset is obfuscated to ensure that sensitive Grid workload traces are not shared. Hence we have to make sense of the data which are in the form of alphanumeric string. Both datasets are transformed and scaled to a range [-1 , 1]. Two different Machine Learning algorithms are applied on the given datasets and the performance are compared. One is the neural network algorithm and the second is the k-Nearest Neighbour algorithm. We use Scaled Conjugate Gradient (SCG) algorithm [14] to minimize the objective function of the feed forward neural network with back propagation.

Training stage of neural network is divided into two stages with the first stage trying to reduce the target space and the second stage provides the memory prediction as shown in Figure 1. In the first stage, the network is trained with the entire dataset to classify the job into one of the three memory ranges and the second stage is trained with data from a specific memory range, i.e. the first neural network in the second stage is trained with the sampled data falling in the 0 - 8 GB category and similarly for the other two categories to make finer levels of prediction.

Same process is followed with kNN algorithm by splitting the data into cross validation and testing set. Cross validation in kNN is used to identify the optimal value of k which is the number of nearest neighbours to be considered to classify the job into a particular memory category. Test set is used to check the performance of the model before actually deploying it in the Grid setup.

Once the memory Prediction model is generated, the model can be deployed in Grid Scheduler which can predict memory requirement for each job. Monitoring and evaluation of the success rate is carried out to make sure that the number of false prediction is less. Also if the job is misclassified, it signifies the change in the characteristics of the job and needs to be added to the next set of training samples if the actual memory usage is more than the predicted memory.

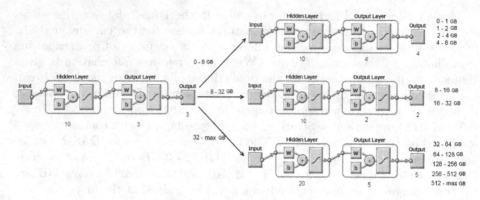

Fig. 1. Dual Stage Neural Network

4   Results and Conclusions

We analysed two sets of data from different fields. The system was developed and tested using MATLAB[15] Mean Squared Error (MSE) and percentage error for the two datasets are shown in Table 3. The correctness of the model is tested by using a new test dataset which is reported in a separate rows for both datasets in Table 3. More information about the job is available in the EDA dataset which enables sophisticated learning by Neural Networks. kNN algorithm shows very poor performance on an EDA dataset due to increase in the number of features and a lack of a good distance measure capable of handling this type of dataset. Grid computing intelligence is relatively new area and a lot can be done to provide an intelligent infrastructure to help users utilize the resource efficiently. Around 90% of the EDA jobs have been predicted optimally as compared to more than 50% of the jobs which wasted 90% of memory in our initial analysis.

Table 3. Performance Analysis

Dataset	Model	Average MSE	Average % Error
DAS-2 (25% Test set / 3153 samples)	kNN	-	1.2
	Neural Network	0.0657	15.2
DAS-2 (Test set (1,020,534 samples))	kNN	-	2.3
	Neural Network	0.103	21.1
EDA (25% Test set / 1480 samples)	kNN	-	61.6
	Neural Network	0.0357	4.2
EDA (Test set (90880 samples))	kNN	-	72.3
	Neural Network	0.703	10.1

References

1. Berstis, V.: IBM RedBook; Fundamentals of Grid Computing. Technical report (2002)
2. Sun N1 Grid Engine 6.1 Administration Guide. The grid workloadformat, http://docs.oracle.com/cd/E19957-01/820-0698/chp8-1501/index.html (accessed: May 30, 2013)
3. Liu, K., Subbarayan, S., Shoults, R.R., Manry, M.T., Kwan, C., Lewis, F.L., Naccarino, J.: Comparison of very short-term load forecasting techniques. IEEE Transactions on Power Systems 11(2), 877–882 (1996)
4. Guo, X., Zhang, W., Wang, J., Wu, G.: Resource management using dynamical load prediction and multiprocessor cooperation. In: 2011 7th International Conference on Networked Computing and Advanced Information Management (NCM), pp. 200–205 (2011)
5. Fanand, S., Hyndman, R.J.: Short-term load forecasting based on a semiparametric additive model. IEEE Transactions on Power Systems 27(1), 134–141 (2012)
6. Dumitrescu, C.L., Foster, I.: Gangsim: a simulator for grid scheduling studies. In: Proceedings of the Fifth IEEE International Symposium on Cluster Computing and the Grid (CCGrid 2005), vol. 2, pp. 1151–1158. IEEE Computer Society, Washington, DC (2005)
7. Sun Microsystems Inc. N1 Grid Engine 6 Administration Guide. Technical report (May 2005)
8. IBM. IBM Platform Computing Solutions. Technical report (December 2012)
9. Wang, D.: Meeting green computing challenges. In: International Symposium on High Density packaging and Microsystem Integration, HDP 2007, pp. 1–4 (2007)
10. Iosup, A., Li, H., Jan, M., Anoep, S., Dumitrescu, C., Wolters, L., Epema, D.H.J.: The grid workloads archive. Future Generation Computer Systems 24(7), 672–686 (2008)
11. Advanced School for Computing and Imaging, TU Delft. The grid workloads archive- DAS-2, http://gwa.ewi.tudelft.nl/pmwiki/pmwiki.php?n=Workloads.Gwa-t-1 (accessed: May 30, 2013)
12. Mitra, P., Member, S., Murthy, C.A., Pal, S.K.: Unsupervised feature selection using feature similarity. IEEE Transactions on Pattern Analysis and Machine Intelligence 24, 301–312 (2002)
13. Advanced School for Computing and Imaging, TU Delft. The grid workloadformat, http://gwa.ewi.tudelft.nl/TheGridWorkloadFormat_v001.pdf (accessed: May 30, 2013)
14. Møller, M.F.: A scaled conjugate gradient algorithm for fast supervised learning. Neural Networks 6(4), 525–533 (1993)
15. MATLAB. version 7.10.0 (R2010a). The MathWorks Inc., Natick, Massachusetts (2010)

Not So Synchronous RPC:
RPC with Silent Synchrony Switch for Avoiding Repeated Marshalling of Data

Fatema Tuz Zohora, Md. Yusuf Sarwar Uddin, and Johra Muhammad Moosa

Department of Computer Science and Engineering,
Bangladesh University of Engineering and Technology,
Dhaka-1000, Bangladesh
anne_buet@yahoo.com, {yusufsarwar,johramoosa}@cse.buet.ac.bd
http://www.buet.ac.bd

Abstract. The Remote Procedure Call (RPC) is a powerful technique for constructing distributed, client-server based applications. In traditional RPC systems, when a remote procedure call fails to return result to the client because of communication failure, client stub usually reinvokes the remote method for expected output if the method is idempotent. This results in repeated marshalling of same data multiple times which is a burden over network if the data is huge. For the first time, we prevent this repeated marshalling by introducing a behavioral pattern that we refer to as usually synchronous, but conditionally asynchronous RPC (CA-RPC). CA-RPC establishes handshaking between client stub and server stub to understand whether connection was failed after demarshalling of data at server stub. If so, the client stub runs a pulling thread to retrieve the result without remarshalling the same data. Besides that, our strategy enhances the performance by a synchrony switch at runtime under some condition. Our results show that CA-RPC has better performance than traditional RPC for cases where data marshalling has significant overhead over low rate data connections.

1 Introduction

The Remote Procedure Call (RPC) is widely used in several purpose ranging from light weighted mobile application to heavy data intensive replicated servers in distributed system. Birrell and Nelson [1] provided an extensive examination of the design possibilities for an RPC system for the first time, and proposed a full-scale implementations of RPC. Steps of RPC mechanism can be formalized as follows: client invokes a client stub procedure passing the parameters which suspends the calling environment. Client stub marshalls the parameters (conversion of the parameters to a standard format) and passes the message to the server stub. Server stub demarshalls the parameters (retrieval of the arguments and procedure signature) and calls the desired server procedure. When the server procedure completes, it returns the response to the server stub, from where the return values are further marshalled into a message and passed to the client

M. Chatterjee et al. (Eds.): ICDCN 2014, LNCS 8314, pp. 544–549, 2014.
© Springer-Verlag Berlin Heidelberg 2014

stub. Finally the client stub demarshalls the return parameters (converting the response to a user understandable format) and passes back to the calling environment where execution resumes as if returning from a simple single-machine call. RPC semantics can be categorized into three groups: exactly once, at most once, and at least once. In the last one, client keeps retransmitting the request until it gets the desired response and ensures that on return to the caller, the operation has been performed at least once, but possibly multiple times. We are concerned on the last one because this is where repeated marshalling takes place.

Whatever data is passed over RPC calls, they must deal with the unreliable nature of remote network connections and if the procedure is idempotent (have the same effect when they are invoked one or more times), then the application usually settles for at least once semantics[1]. We are concerned on preventing repeated marshalling for such case. Note here, if disconnection occurs in the time interval between two events: *completion of demarshalling at server stub* and *returning the response to client*, then after recovering, remarshalling of data by client stub is not necessary if server had received that request in the first attempt and processed it. We name this interval as *Processing Interval*. In this case, after recovery from network failure, a simple client message to the server requesting the result for the previously invoked function is enough. There is a recent work of Ivaki et al. [2] concerned on exactly once semantics. We have used its idea of checkpoints and keeping some log information (e.g, result, id) by the server stub for a predetermined amount of time so that if client sends request for result within this period of time, server will identify it and return the corresponding result.

Another issue of our concern is the silent synchrony switch in conventional RPC for performance enhancement. In case of network failure in processing interval, as the result is being processed or already have been processed, so client program can proceed for next task instead of waiting. Ananda et al. [3] provided a survey on asynchronous RPC discussing its applicability in exploiting the parallelism inherent in distributed applications. Several limitations stated in this paper are addressed later by Microsoft, in the extension 'Asynchronous Remote Procedure Call' (RPC)[2]. However, their approaches differ from ours, we mainly rely on synchronous RPC, which seldom, based on certain condition, becomes asynchronous. So calling syntax remains the same as synchronous RPC, but with an (optional) registration of callback for pushing notification back if the call ever switches to asynchronous. The user program should not care much about this synchrony switch and can mostly proceed assuming synchronous RPC. In doing this we have also taken some idea from the work of Budau et al. [4].

For the first time, we target these two issues and provide solution by introducing a behavioral pattern which is usually synchronous, but conditionally asynchronous RPC (CA-RPC). The paper is organized as follows. In Section 2

---

[1] http://publib.boulder.ibm.com/infocenter/zos/v1r12/index.jsp?topic=%2Fcom.ibm\.zos.r12.euvmn00%2Feuva5a00319.htm

[2] http://msdn.microsoft.com/en-us/library/windows/desktop/aa373550%28v=vs.85%29.aspx

we proceed with detailed description of the proposed CA-RPC approach. Then in Section 3 we compare CA-RPC with traditional RPC system to demonstrate its effectiveness. Finally, we conclude in Section 4 with discussions and future works.

2   Conditionally Asynchronous RPC

In CA-RPC we change the behavior followed by client stub and server stub if network failure is detected in the processing interval as described below[3].

2.1   Establish the Handshake with Server

We use techniques similar to 2-phase commit by allowing the server to unilaterally execute the requested call and to store the generated result (if any), even though the client may not be connected. The client may appear later and obtain the result back. For this purpose CA-RPC introduces some check-points after marshalling at the client, and demarshalling at server. Let us consider a synchronous RPC call is invoked in client script. At client stub, after data marshalling is done, it waits for acknowledgment from server. On the other hand, after server has received and demarshalled the data, it sends a unique acknowledgment say 'acknowledgment_code' to the client stub. So after getting that code client stub gets ready for the actual result. As server has the data so it starts processing. On the other hand client is waiting for the result.

2.2   Pulling Thread and Synchrony Switch

Now, while client is waiting for the actual result and server is busy with processing or has attempted to return the processed response, network connection fails. According to our designed pattern, client stub will act as below.

(i)   Instead of retransmitting the same request (repeated marshalling) to the server stub, client stub just starts a thread passing the 'acknowledgment_code' to it. This thread pulls the server stub repeatedly (for a specific amount of time) until it returns the result associated with that specific code.

(ii) Besides starting the pulling thread, client stub allows synchrony switch by sending a special exception to the client program/script as an indication that client stub is taking care of the request and after the result is retrieved, client program will be notified through the callback functions. So client program can proceed to next task. However, if client program has to perform some task based on the retrieved result then that task should be skipped temporarily and performed after arrival of the result. So RPC call is enclosed by a try-catch block and while calling the RPC, a request id is passed, so that it can perform that predetermined task inside the callback function against that request id.

---

[3] For clarification, see the sample scripts and sequence diagram uploaded at: https://drive.google.com/?pli=1#folders/0Byr9Xlo9S61BSmFldDdpX3dvZ3c

2.3   State Saving by Server Stub

After server is done with processing a request, at the time of sending the response, if it detects a connection failure with client, it keeps the result saved against its 'acknowledgment_code' at server stub storage for some minimal amount of time. If aforementioned pulling thread of client stub requests for this result within this period of time then it will return the result.

2.4   Callback Functions

Callback functions are defined by client program and registered by client stub. After receiving the result through pulling thread, the client stub calls the callback procedure assigned for this call, thus returning the result to the client program. In case of failure in retrieving result (request was not processed/deleted at server stub for some internal error), it notifies client by a message: 'Undefined Result'.

Note here, writing the additional callback function manually gives user the flexibility to decide what he wants to do after retrieval of the result. If he wants to perform something special then he needs to define that through callback, otherwise he can skip this step safely, the CA-RPC will still work perfectly by following the usual program flow. So its not preventing users from gaining the benefits. Also the overhead caused by additional processing of handshaking and server probing is negligible as these do not involve large data transmission.

3   Evaluation and Experimental Results

We implemented the CA-RPC using the xmlrpc library supplied by python. Performance of the pattern is evaluated by applying it on a face detection application. Client calls a remote procedure passing an image for face detection. Then server detects and marks the faces with rectangle and returns the image back to the client. In our experiment probability of occurring disconnection is assumed to be $\rho = .5$. Each client invokes two RPC methods one after another. For each failed RPC call (due to network disconnection), server pulling interval is 2 seconds and maximum number of attempts is 10. The term *latency* is used to denote the maximum time taken by clients in retrieving response of all RPC calls invoked. We conduct experiments to compare the latency of CA-RPC with traditional RPC system against three parameters: Disconnection probability *after* demarshalling at server stub (P), Marshalling time at client stub (m) and Number of clients (c) invoking the RPC methods concurrently.

(i) **Latency vs Disconnection probability after demarshalling (P):**
    We conduct three separate experiments for three different $m = 10, 15, 20$, with $c = 10$, and $P = 0.05\rho$ to 0.8ρ. So disconnection probability before demarshalling is $1 - P$. From Fig. 1(i), with $P \leq .2\rho$, latency in CA-RPC is almost similar with the traditional RPC as in this case network is disconnected *before* demarshalling at server stub with probability $\geq .8\rho$, so the remote procedure needs recall. But as P increases, CA-RPC prevents

recalling (repeated marshalling), thus provides much lower latency than the traditional RPC and also remains constant near 250 seconds.

(ii) **Latency vs Marshalling Time** (m): From Fig. 1(ii), we can see, with fixed $c = 10$, and $P = .6\rho$, CA-RPC outperforms the traditional RPC mechanism by keeping latency lower and almost constant (around 250 seconds) with increasing marshalling time, m.

(iii) **Latency vs Number of Clients** (c): In this experiment, m is fixed at 15 seconds and P at $.6\rho$. With the increasing number of clients c from 10 to 35, as we can see from Fig. 1(iii), latency for traditional RPC system is almost twice than CA-RPC. So again our system performs much better than the traditional RPC approach.

(iv) **Frequency of 'Undefined Result' vs Number of Clients** (c): In CA-RPC, if client stub fails in retrieving result within the predefined number of attempts, it notifies client about that 'Undefined Result' through callback function. From the Fig. 1(iv), with $c = 35$, total number of RPC requests is 70, and only 2 are returned as undefined. So frequency of 'Undefined Result' is very small as compared to the total number of RPC requests.

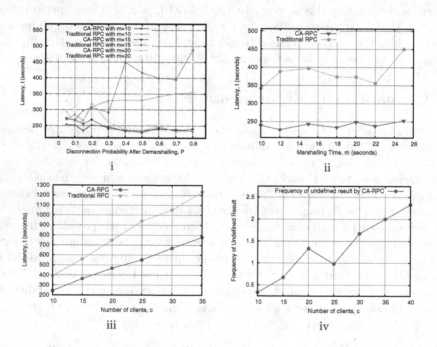

Fig. 1. In each experiment, running time of the remote procedure is considered 10 seconds. (i) Maximum Latency faced by clients at different disconnection probability (P), keeping $c = 10$; (ii) Maximum Latency faced by clients for different values of marshalling time; (iii) Maximum Latency faced by clients with the increasing number of clients; (iv) Frequency of undefined result with the increasing number of clients for $m = 15$ seconds and $P = .6\rho$.

4   Conclusion

In this paper, we propose and develop a RPC mechanism, CA-RPC, that attempts to redefine the behavior of client and server stubs of the traditional RPC system in support of preventing repeated marshalling of data under certain circumstances and thus avoiding processing of same requests unnecessarily. For better performance, it allows a synchrony switch (if applicable) by turning an otherwise synchronized call into an asynchronous one. Our implementation in Python and the associated evaluation results show that it has lower call completion time than traditional RPCs, when RPC calls are disrupted due to connection failure. And, this is achieved at a very nominal cost of some extra processing steps and state preservation.

CA-RPC has been shown to be useful where clients need to make heavy data transfers but lie inside a low bandwidth or disruption-prone edge network. For example, when some data intensive task in mobile app is offloaded onto a server and mobile goes out of range from the coverage of a network (client suffers transient disconnection with the server), then user might tempted to recall the same process. Here CA-RPC can avoid repeated marshalling and processing. Again, in replicated server environment [5], after one machine updates its data, if the change is passed to all other replicated servers through CA-RPC functions then our pattern will prevent repeated marshalling of this huge update data. Its silent synchrony switch can be beneficial also for distributed genetic algorithms [6].

Current work can lead to interesting research issues in future, such as using sever-initiated push notification instead of client stub pulling the server, handling cases involving client/server crashes, and extension of the concept for partial synchronous system, group communication etc. Evaluation with some real life data against several RPC mechanisms with a possible implementation in mobile environments, such as Android, can be another future task.

References

1. Birrell, A.D., Nelson, B.J.: Implementing remote procedure calls. ACM Transactions on Computer Systems (TOCS) 2(1), 39–59 (1984)
2. Ivaki, N., Araujo, F., Barbosa, R.: A middleware for exactly-once semantics in request-response interactions. In: 2012 IEEE 18th Pacific Rim International Symposium on Dependable Computing (PRDC), pp. 31–40. IEEE (2012)
3. Ananda, A.L., Tay, B., Koh, E.K.: A survey of asynchronous remote procedure calls. ACM SIGOPS Operating Systems Review 26(2), 92–109 (1992)
4. Budau, V., Bernard, G.: Auto-adaptation to communication environment through dynamic change of communication model. In: ICDCS Workshops, pp. 153–158. IEEE Computer Society (2003)
5. Deris, M.M., Mamat, A., Surip, M., Khalid, S.: Data replication model for remote procedure call transactions. WSEAS Transactions on Information Science and Applications 2(11), 2009–2015 (2005)
6. Rossant, C., Fontaine, B., Goodman, D.F.: Playdoh: a lightweight python library for distributed computing and optimisation. Journal of Computational Science (2011)

Author Index